12TH EDITION

KOVELS'

BOTTLES

PRICE LIST

ILLUSTRATED

RALPH & TERRY KOVEL

THREE RIVERS PRESS

NEW YORK

THE CROWN PUBLISHING GROUP

BOOKS BY RALPH AND TERRY KOVEL

American Country Furniture 1780–1875

A Directory of American Silver, Pewter, and Silver Plate

Kovels' Advertising Collectibles Price List

Kovels' American Art Pottery: The Collector's Guide to Makers,
Marks, and Factory Histories

Kovels' American Silver Marks: 1650 to the Present

Kovels' Antiques & Collectibles Fix-It Source Book

Kovels' Book of Antique Labels

Kovels' Bid, Buy, and Sell Online

Kovels' Bottles Price List

Kovels' Collector's Guide to American Art Pottery

Kovels' Collectors' Source Book

Kovels' Depression Glass & Dinnerware Price List

Kovels' Dictionary of Marks—Pottery & Porcelain

Kovels' Guide to Selling, Buying, and Fixing Your Antiques and Collectibles

Kovels' Guide to Selling Your Antiques & Collectibles

Kovels' Illustrated Price Guide to Royal Doulton

Kovels' Know Your Antiques

Kovels' Know Your Collectibles

Kovels' New Dictionary of Marks—Pottery & Porcelain

Kovels' Organizer for Collectors

Kovels' Price Guide for Collector Plates, Figurines, Paperweights,
and Other Limited Editions

Kovels' Quick Tips—799 Helpful Hints on How to Care for Your Collectibles

Kovels' Yellow Pages: A Collector's Directory

The Label Made Me Buy It: From Aunt Jemima to Zonkers—
The Best-Dressed Boxes, Bottles, and Cans from the Past

Published by Three Rivers Press. Member of the Crown Publishing Group,
a division of Random House, Inc.
www.randomhouse.com

Three Rivers Press and the Tugboat design are registered trademarks of Random House, Inc.

Printed in the United States of America

Library of Congress Catalog Card Number: 92-5192

ISBN 0-609-80623-8

10 9 8 7 6 5 4 3 2 1

Twelfth Edition

KEEP UP ON PRICES ALL YEAR LONG

Have you kept up with prices? They change! Prices change with discoveries, auction records, even historic events. Every entry and every picture in this book is new and current, thanks to modern computer technology and a staff that searches for prices all year. It includes prices from auctions, shows, price lists, and sales, as well as Internet auctions, malls, and shops. This book is a handy overall price guide, but you also need news and the very latest stories of bottle sales and discoveries.

Books on your shelf get older each month, and prices do change. Important sales produce new record prices. Rarities are discovered. Fakes appear. You will want to keep up with developments from month to month rather than from year to year. *Kovels on Antiques and Collectibles,* a nationally distributed, illustrated newsletter, includes up-to-date information on bottles and other collectibles. This monthly newsletter reports current prices, collecting trends, and landmark auction results for all types of antiques and collectibles, including bottles, and also contains tax, estate, security, and other pertinent news for collectors.

Additional information and a free sample newsletter are available from the authors at P.O. Box 22200-B, Beachwood, Ohio 44122. Read excerpts or order from our Web site: www.kovels.com.

CLUES TO THE CONTENTS OF THIS BOOK

We know that anything can be improved; and, once again with this new book, we have put in a few extra features. This is the all new, better-than-ever, twelfth edition of *Kovels' Bottles Price List.* We wrote the first bottle price guide 30 years ago. This year, the book's format has been updated to reflect the changing interests of the new century. Paragraphs have been expanded. The histories of companies and their products have been researched, and we have tried to note any important changes in ownership of modern brands. A new color-picture section explores the world of bottles plain and fancy.

All of the prices in the book are new. They are compiled from sales and offerings of the past two years. You will find that some modern bottles are no longer listed by brand, because collector interest has waned. One, Wheaton, has returned because collectors now search for them by name. We still have extensive listings of the more popular modern bottles like Jim Beam and Ezra Brooks. The pictures of old bottles are all new and were taken with special digital equipment so that they are clearer and more informative.

"Go-withs," the bottle-related items that are bought and sold at all the bottle shows, are listed in their own section at the end of the book. Jar openers, advertisements, corkscrews, bottle caps, and other items that picture or are used with bottles have been classified as bottle go-withs. There is a bibliography and a listing of publications included in this book to aid you in further research. This list was checked and is accurate as of January 2002. The national and state club lists are also accurate as of January 2002. Unfortunately, addresses do change; if you cannot find one of the listed clubs, write to us at P.O. Box 22200-B, Beachwood, Ohio 44122.

Note: Bottles which contained alcoholic beverages must be sold empty to conform with the law in most states. To sell a filled liquor bottle, you must have a liquor license from the state where you live or where you sell the bottle. It is illegal to ship full bottles across state lines. The value is the same for full or empty liquor bottles.

DEFINITIONS

Novice collectors may need a few definitions to understand the terms used in this book. A *pontil mark* is a scar on the bottom of a bottle. It was made by the punty rod that held the glass for the glassblower. If the scar is rough, it is called a *pontil*. If it is smoothed out, it is called a *ground pontil*. *Free-blown* or *blown* means that the glass was blown by the glassmaker, using a blowpipe; it was not poured into a mold. *Mold-blown* means it was blown into a mold as part of the forming process. A *kick-up* is the deep indentation on the bottom of a bottle. Kick-ups are very often found on wine bottles. Describing glass as *whittled* or having *whittle marks* means there are irregular marks that look like the rough surface of a piece of whittled wood. Such marks are found on bottles that were made before 1900 and were caused by hot glass being blown into a cold mold. *Embossed* lettering is raised lettering. *Etched* lettering was cut into the bottle with acid or a sharp instrument. *Bubbles, teardrops,* or *seeds* describe types of bubbles that form in glass. A *seam* is the line left on the bottle by the mold. A seam may go up the neck of the bottle. If it goes over the lip, the bottle was machine made. An *applied lip* is handmade and applied to the bottle after the glassmaker has formed the bottle. A *sheared lip* is found on bottles made before 1840. The top of the bottle was cut from the blowpipe with shears and the result is the sheared lip. The *2-piece,* or *BIMAL,* mold was used from about 1860 to 1900. The *3-piece mold* was used from 1820 to 1880. The automatic bottle machine was invented in 1903 and *machine-made* bottles were the norm after that date. Black glass is not really black. It is very dark olive green or olive amber and appears black unless seen in a bright light. *Milk glass* is an opaque glass made by using tin or zinc in the mixture. Although most milk glass is white, it is correct to call colored glass of this type "blue" or "green" milk glass. If glass that was made from 1880 to 1914 is left in strong sunlight, it often turns colors. This is because of the chemical content of the old glass. Bottles can turn purple, pale lavender, or shades of green or brown. These bottles are called *sun-colored.* Bottles can also be *iridized* and colored by a radiation process similar to that used for preserving vegetables. These bottles turn dark purple, green, or brown. There are a few other terms that relate to only one type of bottle, and these terms have been identified in the proper paragraphs. The word *picnic* has two meanings; it refers to a shape in the flask category and to a large size in the beer category.

Bottle clubs and bottle shows have set the rules for this edition of *Kovels' Bottles Price List.* We have used the terms preferred by collectors and have tried to organize the thousands of listings in an easy-to-use format. Many abbreviations have been included that are part of the bottle collectors' language. The abbreviations are listed below and appear throughout the book.

ABM means automatic bottle machine.

ACL means applied color label, a pyroglaze or enameled lettering.

BIMAL means blown in mold, applied lip.

DUG means literally dug from the ground.

FB means free blown.

IP means iron pontil.

ISP means inserted slug plate. Special names were sometimes embossed on a bottle, especially a milk bottle, with a special plate inserted in the mold.

OP means open pontil.

Pyro means pyroglaze or enamel lettering often found on milk bottles and soda bottles. In this book ACL means applied color label. This type of label was first used in the 1920s and became very popular in the 1930s

SC means sun-colored.

SCA means sun-colored amethyst.

To make the descriptions of the bottles as complete as possible, an identification number has been added to the description in some categories. The serious collector knows the important books about a specialty, and these books have numbered lists of styles of bottles. Included in this book are identification numbers for flasks from McKearin and Wilson, bitters from Ring and Ham, and fruit jars from *Red Book of Fruit Jars,* by Leybourne. The full titles of the books used are included in the bibliography and listed in the introductory paragraph for each category.

Medicine bottles include all medicine bottles except those under the more specific headings such as "Bitters" or "Sarsaparilla" or "Cure." Modern bottles of major interest are listed under the brand name.

If you are not a regular at bottle shows, it may take a few tries to become accustomed to the method of listing used in this book. If you cannot find a bottle, try several related headings. For instance, hair products are found under "Cosmetic" and "Cure."

Many named bottles are found under "Medicine," "Food," "Fruit Jar," etc. If your fruit jar has several names, such as "Ball Mason," look under "Fruit Jar, Ball" or "Fruit Jar, Mason." If no color is listed, the bottle is clear. We edit color descriptions to make the comparisons of bottles easier. It is impossible to explain the difference between "olive yellow," "light olive yellow," "yellow olive," "light greenish yellow," all terms used in the sales. Where possible we used the description selected by the seller.

PICTURE DICTIONARY OF BOTTLE SHAPES

Collectors and bottle makers have often given shape-inspired nicknames to their bottles.

FLASKS

The **calabash** flask is shaped like the calabash gourd, a vegetable that was often hollowed out to hold water.

The **punkinseed**, or **pumpkinseed** flask, is relatively flat and shaped like the seed of a pumpkin. In the early 1900s the bottle manufacturers called them picnic flasks.

The **coffin** flask has a hexagonal-shaped base that tapers slightly at the bottom. It resembles a coffin.

The **shoofly** flask was popular in the South. The name was used by early bottle manufacturers.

The **chestnut** flask is almost round and is named for the well-known nut from the chestnut trees that grow in Europe and the United States.

The **Pitkin-type** flask is named for the Pitkin Glassworks of East Hartford, Connecticut. The name also is used to describe similarly shaped bottles made by other factories. The blowers used the "German" method of putting a second gather of glass halfway up the post, making the glass walls of the flask thicker. The bottle was then blown into a rib mold to impress ribs. The finished bottle could have vertical or swirled ribs.

INKS

Perhaps because so many ink bottles are unmarked, ink bottle collectors have given them descriptive nicknames.

igloo

teakettle

turtle

umbrella

OTHERS

The **demijohn** is a large, narrow-necked bottle. Demijohns range in size from one to ten gallons and are often encased in wicker. A carboy is a larger, heavier-walled version of a demijohn.

The **gemel** is really two bottles joined together. It was made to hold two different liquids such as oil and vinegar. Many gemel bottles do not have a flat base and must be kept lying flat on a table or suspended in a stand.

A **jar** is a wide-mouthed cylindrical bottle made of glass or earthenware. The fruit jar or canning jar is the most common jar found today.

A **lady's leg** is a long-necked bottle that only slightly resembles the leg of a woman. It was a trademarked bottle shape first used by Boker's Stomach Bitters.

The **case gin** bottle is shaped to fit into a wooden case for shipping. The bottles were more or less rectangular, but slightly smaller at the bottom. They sat flat against each other in a case. The shape was especially favored by the Dutch, who used it for bottles of exported gin. "Dip-molded" gin bottles are the same shape but were molded in boxlike forms.

The black glass bottles used by the English in the seventeenth century were made in several shapes. One, the **mallet,** was thought to resemble a short-handled hammer. The **onion** was named for the shape of the vegetable. The **seal** bottle, used about 1630 to 1750, was named for the extra glob of glass or the seal attached to the outside of the bottle. The seal was impressed with initials and sometimes a date.

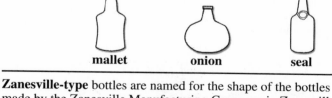

mallet   **onion**   **seal**

Zanesville-type bottles are named for the shape of the bottles made by the Zanesville Manufacturing Company in Zanesville, Ohio, from 1815 to 1838 and from 1842 to 1851. Like the Pitkin-type flask, the name is used for other companies' bottles of the same shape.

NECK FINISHES

Before the automatic bottle machine came into use, glassmakers finished the tops of bottles by hand after shaping them in molds.

sloping collar   **applied lip** or **ring**   **tooled lip**

 Early soda and mineral water bottlers used **blob-top** bottles. The sides and the top of the bottle are thicker to withstand the pressure of the carbonated drink.

CLOSURES

Soda, mineral water, and beer bottles have closures that kept the gas in the bottle until opened. Codd bottles closed with a glass ball that was held in place by the gas, so the bottles had to be filled upside down. Soda pop was nicknamed for the "pop" sound that accompanied the removal of the Hutchinson stopper.

Codd   **Hutchinson**   **lightning**   **crown**

Fruit jar closures sealed tightly with rubber rings to preserve the contents. The earliest jars sealed the rings around the shoulder. Later jars, like the lightning, sealed the ring to the lip.

shoulder seal   **lightning**

DATING CLUES

The kick-ups on wine and seal bottles vary by era and country of origin. Kick-ups are still used on wines and champagnes.

Dutch onion, late 1600s

English onion, late 1600s

Dutch onion, early 1700s

English onion, early 1700s

Dutch mallet, mid-1700s

English mallet, mid-1700s

LEGAL WORDING

Legal wording on labels or embossed on the glass can date bottles.

• The word "cure" indicates a date before 1911, when the Sherley Amendment to the Pure Food and Drug Act prohibited alcohol products from being labeled "Cure."

• Most bottles labeled with the words "For Medicinal Use Only" were used during Prohibition (1920–1933), although similar labels were used much earlier to escape liquor taxes and to appease the Temperance activists.

• "Federal Law Prohibits Sale or Re-Use of this Bottle" was used from 1933 to 1964.

• Health warnings stating, "Women should not drink alcoholic beverages during pregnancy because of the risk of birth defects" and "Drinking impairs the ability to drive a car or operate machinery," have appeared on beer, wine, and liquor labels since 1989.

• In 1999, the Bureau of Alcohol, Tobacco and Firearms allowed winemakers to add a statement to bottles about the possible health benefits of wine: "The proud people who made this wine encourage you to consult your family doctor about the health effects of wine consumption."

The prices shown for bottles are the *actual* prices asked for or bid for bottles during the past two years. We know collectors try to get discounts, so some of these bottles may have sold for a little less than the average price. Prices vary in different parts of the country. The condition of the bottle is a major factor in determining price. We do not list broken or chipped bottles, but sometimes flaws or scratches are noticed after a sale. If more than one price for a bottle has been recorded, a range is given. When selling your bottles, remember that the prices here are retail, not the wholesale price paid by a dealer. You can sell your collection to a dealer at about half the prices listed here. At auction you may get the same prices found in the book, but auctions are unpredictable. Prices may be low or high because of a snowstorm or a very determined pair of bidders. Internet auctions have the added risk of an unknown seller, so the condition may not be accurately reported. Low-priced bottles sell best at flea markets and garage sales.

Because of the idiosyncrasies of the computer, it was impossible to place a range on prices of bottles that are illustrated. The prices listed for the bottles illustrated in the book are for the bottle pictured.

Particular spellings are meant to help the collector. If the original bottle spelled "Catsup" as "Ketchup," that is the spelling that appears. The abbreviation "Dr." for doctor may appear on bottles as "Dr" (no period) or "Dr." (period). However, we have included a period each time to keep the computer alphabetizing more consistent, except in the case of bottles of Dr Pepper. The period was omitted in Dr Pepper by the company in 1950, and we use whatever appeared on the bottle. Also, if a word is written, for example, "Kennedy's," "Kennedys'," or "Kennedys," we have placed the apostrophe or omitted it as it appeared on the bottle. A few bottles are included that had errors in the original spelling in the bottle mold. In these cases the error is explained. Medicine, bitters, and other bottle types sometimes use the term "Dr." and sometimes use just the last name of the doctor. We usually have used the wording as it appears on the bottle, except for "Whiskey" which is used even if the bottle held scotch or Canadian or was spelled "Whisky."

Every bottle or go-with illustrated in black and white is indicated by the abbreviation "Illus" in the text. Bottles shown in color pictures are priced in the center section where they appear.

We have tried to be accurate, but cannot be responsible for any errors in pricing or information that may appear. Any information about clubs, prices, or content for future books will be considered for the next book. Please send it to Kovels, P.O. Box 22200, Dept. BPL, Beachwood, Ohio 44122.

Ralph M. Kovel, Life Member,
Federation of Historical Bottle Clubs

Terry H. Kovel, Life Member,
Federation of Historical Bottle Clubs

ACKNOWLEDGMENTS

The major dealers and auction houses that sell bottles are the most informed experts in the field. Special thanks for help with pictures and information to Ed & Kathy's Online Bottle Shop, Jim Hagenbuch of Glass Works Auctions, Gary Metz's Muddy River Trading Co., Monsen and Baer, Jeff Wichman of Pacific Glass Autcions, and Gary Lewis of Soda Bottle Auctions.

Information and prices were also supplied by AB!C; Truman Alexander; Americana Resources; Clarence Ashley; Autopia Advertising Auctions; BBR Auctions; Thomas Bishop; Mike Brauer; Mary Calhoun; James Chamberlain; Hector Chanez; John Cleland; Conestoga Auction Company, Inc.; Bertha Cook; Karen Cook; Joan Cottrell; Louis J. Coubal; Crowe's Bottles; Gloria Davolt; David Dias; Detwiler's Bottle List; Perry Driver; Donna Dunker; Robert W. Dyke; Dieter Eichmuller; Betty Ellis; Frank Elske; R.J. Exum; B. Forsgren; Bruce Forster; Garth's Auctions; Harry Gordon; Ed & Kathy Gray; Terry Guidroz; Timothy Haert; Marilyn Hannold; Gene Harris Antique Auction; Norman Heckler; John Henenius; Steve Hesse; Historic Glasshouse Bottles; Bob Houghton; Frances Hursey; Robert Ingle; Paul Irby; James D. Julia, Inc.; Robert Karle; Jim & Kathy Kirk; C.D. Knibbe; Larry Kolesky; Mary Krugh; Ray Lambert; Leslie's; Paul & Jeanette Lawrence; Phil Mancini; George Margraff; Diane McGrath; McMurray Antiques & Auctions; Edward Miller; Wm Morford; New England Absentee Auctions, Inc.; New Orleans Auction Galleries Inc.; Evelyn Norris; Earl Nydam; Don Pardo; Rosemary Pedrey; Dick Powell; R.J. Reid; Lorna Rogers; John Ronald; Wendell Sack; Dave Scafani; Jackie Schloe; Margaret Seweryneuk; Mike Sheridan; Wendell Short; Skinner, Inc.; Sotheby's; Patty Sparr; Lucille Stanley; Robert Swartz; Sweeneys' Emporium; Danese Thiesen; Katie Thomas; Sharon Totleben; Herb Weaver; Western Saloon Whiskey; York Town Auction. Thanks.

And to Gay Hunter and the rest of the Kovels' staff, who double check everything; to Karen Kneisley, who does magic with the pictures; to Cherrie Smrekar, who is the last word on corrections; to Grace DeFrancisco, Marcia Goldberg, Katie Karrick, Liz Lillis, Nancy Saada, Edie Smrekar, Virginia Warner, and the others who recorded prices and helped in other ways; to Dorothy Harris, our editor; Cindy Berman, senior production editor; Pam Stinson-Bell, production editorial–wonder; Karen Minster, interior designer; Merri Ann Morrell, compositor; David Tran, cover designer; Len Zimmelman, who inspired the cover; and Benjamin Margolit, who manages to get great pictures of glass bottles.

RESOURCES

MUSEUMS & ARCHIVES

COCA-COLA COMPANY ARCHIVES, Industry & Consumer Affairs, P.O. Drawer 1734, Atlanta, GA 30301, 800-438-2653, website: www.cocacola.com.

CORNING MUSEUM OF GLASS, Rakow Library, One Museum Way, Corning,

NY 14830-2253, 607-974-8649, fax: 607-974-8677, e-mail: rakow@cmog.org, website: www.cmog.org.

DR PEPPER MUSEUM, 300 S. 5th St., Waco, TX 76701, 254-757-1025, e-mail: dp-info@drpeppermuseum.com, website: www.drpeppermuseum.org.

MUSEUM OF AMERICAN GLASS, Wheaton Village, 1501 Glasstown Rd., Millville, NJ 08332-1566, 800-998-4552, e-mail: museum@wheatonvillage.org, website: wheatonvillage.org/museum

NATIONAL BOTTLE MUSEUM, 76 Milton Ave., Ballston Spa, NY 12020, 518-885-7589, e-mail: nbm@crisny.org, website: family.knick.net/nbm.

PEPSI-COLA COMPANY ARCHIVES, One Pepsi Way, Somers, NY 10589, 914-767-6000, website: www.pepsi.com.

PUBLICATIONS OF INTEREST TO BOTTLE COLLECTORS

See the club list for other publications

NEWSLETTERS

Avon Times
P.O. Box 9868
Kansas City, MO 64134
e-mail: avontimes@aol.com

Fruit Jar Newsletter
FJN Publishers, Inc.
364 Gregory Ave.
West Orange, NJ 07052-3743
e-mail: tomcaniff@aol.com

Just For Openers
P.O. Box 64
Chapel Hill, NC 27514
e-mail: jfo@mindspring.com
website: www.just-for-openers.org
(bottle openers and corkscrews)

Kovels on Antiques and Collectibles
P.O. Box 420347
Palm Coast, FL 32142-0347
website: www.kovels.com

MAGAZINES

Antique Bottle & Glass Collector
P.O. Box 180
East Greenville, PA 18041
e-mail: glswrk@enter.net
website: www.glswrkauction.com

BBR: British Bottle Review
Elsecar Heritage Center
Barnsley, South Yorkshire, U.K. S74 8HJ
e-mail: sales@bbrauctions.co.uk
website: www.bbrauctions.co.uk

Bygones
30 Brabant Rd., Cheadle Hulme
Cheadle, Cheshire, U.K. SK8 7AU
e-mail: mike@bygones.demon.co.uk
website: members.tripod.com/
~MikeSheridan/page2.htm
(for collectors of old bottles, potlids, and
old advertising)

Collectors News
P.O. Box 306
Grundy Center, IA 50638
e-mail: collectors@collectors-news.com
website: collectors-news.com

Miniature Bottle Collector
P.O. Box 2161
Palos Verdes Peninsula, CA 90274
e-mail: david@spaid.org
website: www.bottlecollecting.com

BOTTLE CLUBS

There are hundreds of bottle clubs that welcome new members. The list of local clubs is arranged by state and city so you can find the club nearest your home. If no club is listed nearby, we suggest you contact the national organizations, which follow. Any active bottle club that is not listed and wishes to be included in future editions of *Kovels' Bottles Price List* should send the necessary information to the authors, P.O. Box 22200, Beachwood, Ohio 44122. The information in this list has been compiled with the help of the National Bottle Museum, the Federation of Historical Bottle Collectors, and *The Miniature Bottle Collector.*

NATIONAL CLUBS

Many of these clubs have local chapters and shows.
Write them for more information.

American Breweriana Association, Inc.
American Breweriana Journal (magazine)
P.O. Box 11157
Pueblo, CO 81001
e-mail: breweriana1
@earthlink.net
website: www.
americanbreweriana.org

American Collectors of Infant Feeders
Keeping Abreast (newsletter)
1849 Ebony Dr.
York, PA 17402-4706
e-mail: bbottlebkdj
@juno.com
website: www.acif.org

Antique Advertising Association of America
Past Times (newsletter)
P.O. Box 5851
Elgin, IL 60123
e-mail: AAAA1121
@aol.com

Antique Poison Bottle Collectors Association
312 Summer Ln.
Huddleston, VA 24104
e-mail: joan
@poisonbottle.com.
website: antique.
poisonbottle.com

Association of Bottled Beer Collectors
What's Bottling (newsletter)
127 Victoria Park Rd.
Tunstall, Stoke-on-Trent, U.K. ST6 6D4
e-mail: JohnMann
@csi.com
website: ourworld.
compuserve.com/
homepages/John_
Mann/abbchome.htm

Beer Can Collectors of America
Beer Cans & Brewery Collectibles (magazine)
747 Merus Ct.
Fenton, MO 63026-2092
e-mail: bcca@bcca.com
website: www.bcca.com

British Beermat Collectors' Society
British Beermat Collectors' Society Newsletter (newsletter)
69 Dunnington Ave.
Kidderminster, U.K.
DY10 2YT
e-mail: cosmic
@tmmathews.freeserve.
co.uk
website: www.
britishbeermats.org.uk

Canadian Corkscrew Collectors Club
The Quarterly Worme (newsletter)
One Madison St.
East Rutherford, NJ 07073
e-mail: clarethous
@aol.com

Candy Container Collectors of America
Candy Gram (newsletter)
2711 De La Rosa St.
The Villages, FL 32162
e-mail: genedeible
@adelphia.net
website: www.
candycontainer.org

Classic Wheaton Club
Classic Wheaton Club Newsletter
(newsletter)
P.O. Box 59
Downingtown, PA
19335-0059
e-mail: cwc
@cwcusa.com
website: www.
cwcusa.com

Coca-Cola Collectors Club
Coca-Cola Collectors News (newsletter)
PMB 609, 4780
Ashford Dunwoody
Rd., Suite A
Atlanta, GA 30338
website: www.
cocacolaclub.org

Crown Collectors Society International
Crown Cappers' Exchange (newsletter)
4300 San Juan Dr.
Fairfax, VA 22030
e-mail: crownking
@erols.com
(crown caps from beer and soda bottles)

Dr Pepper 10-2-4 Collectors Club
Lion's Roar (newsletter)
3100 Monticello,
Suite 890
Dallas, TX 75205

Federation of Historical Bottle Collectors
Bottles and Extras
(magazine)
c/o Wendy Smith,
Treasurer
2230 Toub St.
Ramona, CA 92065
e-mail: antique
bottles@visto.com
website: www.
fohbc.com

Figural Bottle Opener Collectors
The Opener
(newsletter)
1774 N. 675 E.
Kewanna, IN 46939
e-mail: fbocclub
@att.net
website: www.
fbocclub.com

International Association of Jim Beam Bottle and Specialties Clubs
Beam Around the World
(newsletter)
2015 Burlington Ave.
Kewanee, IL 61443
website: www.
beam-wade.org

International Chinese Snuff Bottle Society
Journal (magazine)
2601 N. Charles St.
Baltimore, MD 21218
e-mail: icsbs
@worldnet.att.net
website: www.
snuffbottle.org

International Perfume Bottle Association
Perfume Bottle Quarterly (newsletter)
27 Foxtail Ln.
Monmouth Jct., NJ
08852
e-mail: susanarthur
@home.com
website: www.
perfumebottles.org

International Swizzle Stick Collectors Association
Swizzle Stick News
(newsletter)
P.O. Box 1117
Bellingham, WA
98227-1117
e-mail: vera.issca
@attglobal.net
website: www.swizzle
sticks-issca.com

Jelly Jammers
Jelly Jammers Journal
(newsletter)
6086 W. Boggstown
Rd.
Boggstown, IN 46110
e-mail: emshaw@in.net
(jelly container collectors)

Lilliputian Bottle Club
Gulliver's Gazette
(newsletter)
54 Village Cir.
Manhattan Beach, CA
90266-7222

Midwest Miniature Bottle Collectors
Midwest Miniature Bottle Collector
(newsletter)
6934 Brittany Ridge
Ln.
Cincinnati, OH 45233
e-mail: shooter
@fuse.net
website: www.
miniaturebottles.com

The Mini Bottle Club
The Mini Bottle Club
(newsletter)
47 Burradon Rd.
Burradon, Cramlington,
Northumberland,
U.K. NE23 7NF
e-mail: minibottleclub
@cs.com

National Association of Avon Collectors
P.O. Box 7006
Kansas City, MO 64113
(write for list of Avon clubs in your area)

National Association Breweriana Advertising
Breweriana Collector (newsletter)
P.O. Box 64
Chapel Hill, NC 27514-0064
website: www. nababrew.org

National Association of Milk Bottle Collectors
The Milk Route (newsletter)
Box 105
Blooming Grove, NY 10914
e-mail: milkroute @yahoo.com or moto2 @frontiernet.net
website: www. collectoronline.com/ club-NAMBC-wp.html

National Association of Paper and Advertising Collectors
P.A.C. (newspaper)
P.O. Box 500
Mount Joy, PA 17552
e-mail: pac @engleonline.com
website: www. engleonline.com

New England Moxie Congress
Nerve Food News (newsletter)
c/o Kurt D. Kabelac
2783 N. Triphammer Rd.
Ithaca, NY 14850-9756
website: www. moxieworld.com

Ole Time Vinegar Society
Vinegar Gazette (newsletter)
745 Beth-Rural Hall Rd.
Rural Hall, NC 27045
e-mail: speas @triad.rr.com
website: www. antiquebottles.com/ vinegarclub

Painted Soda Bottles Collectors Association
Soda Net (newsletter)
9418 Hilmer Dr.
La Mesa, CA 91942
e-mail: aclsrus @home.com
website: www. collectoronline.com/ PSBCA/PSBCA.html

Pepsi-Cola Collectors Club
Pepsi-Cola Collectors Club Newsletter (newsletter)
P.O. Box 817
Claremont, CA 91711
e-mail: spdrago @wavetech.net
website: www. dataflo.net/~jpepsi

Saratoga-Type Bottle Collectors Society
Spouter (newsletter)
1198 Main St., Box 685
Warren, MA 01083
e-mail: ctrtle @berkshire.net

Society of Inkwell Collectors
The Stained Finger (newsletter)
10 Meadow Dr.
Spencerport, NY 14559
e-mail: soic @rochester.rr.com
website: www.soic.com

Southeastern Antique Bottle Club
The Whittle Mark (newsletter)
143 Scatterfoot Dr.
Peachtree City, GA 30269
e-mail: fredtay @bellsouth.net
website: personal.atl. bellsouth.net/atl/f/r/ fredtay/whittlemark

Violin Bottle Collectors Association
Fine Tuning (newsletter)
24 Sylvan St.
Danvers, MA 01923
e-mail: fbviobot @hotmail.com

Watkins Collectors Club
Watkins Collectors Club Newsletter (newsletter)
W24024 SR 54/93
Galesville, WI 54630-8249

Whimsey Club
c/o Dale Murschell
HC 65 Box 2610
Springfield, WV 26763

ALABAMA

Mobile Bottle Collector Club
8844 Lee Circle
IRVINGTON, AL 36544

ARIZONA

Phoenix Antiques, Bottles, & Collectibles Club
c/o Charles Blake
4702 W. Lavey Rd.
GLENDALE, AZ 85306
e-mail: dig632@aol.com
website: phoenix antiquesclub.org

ARKANSAS

Indian Country Antique Bottle & Relic Society
3818 Hilltop Dr.
JONESBORO, AR 72401

Little Rock Antique Bottle Club
c/o Ed Tardy
16201 Hwy. 300
ROLAND, AR 72135

CALIFORNIA

California Miniature Bottle Club
1911 Willow St.
ALAMEDA, CA 94501

Mother Lode Antique Bottle Club
c/o Bill Ham
P.O. Box 427
DOWNIEVILLE, CA 95936

Northwestern Bottle Collectors Association
c/o Frank Sternad
P.O. Box 560
FULTON, CA 95439

Los Angeles Historical Bottle Club
2842 El Sol Drive
LANCASTER, CA 93535

San Luis Obispo Bottle Society
124-21st St.
PASO ROBLES, CA 93446

49er Historical Bottle Association
P.O. Box 561
PENRYN, CA 95663

Golden Gate H. B. S.
c/o Ken Gaeta
620 Contra Costa Blvd., #103
PLEASANT HILL, CA 94523

Superior California Bottle Club
c/o Mel Hammer
3220 Stratford Ave.
REDDING, CA 96001

Mission Trail Historical Bottle Club
1475 Teton Ave.
SALINAS, CA 93906

San Bernardino County H. C. & C.
P.O. Box 6759
SAN BERNARDINO, CA 92412

San Diego Antique Bottle Club
P.O. Drawer 5137
SAN DIEGO, CA 92165

Mission Trail Historical Bottle Club
1075 Hart St.
SEASIDE, CA 93955

Sequoia Antique Bottle & Collectable Society
P.O. Box 3695
VISALIA, CA 93278

COLORADO

Southern Colorado Antique Bottle Collectors
c/o Howard Todd
843 Ussie Ave.
CANON CITY, CO 81212

Peaks & Plains Antique Bottle & Collectors Club, Inc.
308 Maplewood Dr.
COLORADO SPRINGS, CO 80907-4326

Antique Bottle Collectors of Colorado
P.O. Box 245
LITTLETON, CO 80160
e-mail: Rick Sinnerr

Western Slope Bottle Club
P.O. Box 354
PALISADE, CO 81526

CONNECTICUT

Southern Connecticut Antique Bottle Collectors Association
34 Dartmouth Dr.
HUNTINGTON, CT 06484

Somers Antique Bottle Club
P.O. Box 253
SOUTH GASTONBURY, CT 06073-0253

DELAWARE

Tri-State Bottle Collectors & Diggers Club
26 Fremont Rd.
NEWARK, DE 19711

Delmarva Antique Bottle Collectors
c/o Ed Detwiler
50 Syracuse St.
OCEAN VIEW, DE 19970
website: www.antique bottles.com/delmarva

FLORIDA

Mid-State Antique BCA
c/o Paul Martin
P.O. Box 916
APOPKA, FL 32704-0916

Emerald Coast Bottle Collectors
c/o Scott Clary, secretary/treasurer
P.O. Box 863
DEFUNIAK SPRINGS, FL 32435
e-mail: antique bottles@starband.net
website: www.expage.com/ emeraldcoast bottlecollectors

M-T Bottle Collectors Association
P.O. Box 1581
DELAND, FL 32720

Central Florida Insulator Collector's Club
c/o Mr. & Mrs. Charles Haymond
8024 SE Carlton St.
HOBE SOUND, FL 33455

Antique Bottle Collectors of North Florida
3867 Winter Berry Rd.
JACKSONVILLE, FL 32210
e-mail: ABCNF @juno.com

Association of Florida Antique Bottle Clubs
P.O. Box 3105
SARASOTA, FL 34230

Sarasota-Manatee Antique Bottle Collectors Association
P.O. Box 3105
SARASOTA, FL 34230

Suncoast Antique Bottle Club
c/o Jay Stone
6720 Park St.
SOUTH PASADENA, FL 33707

GEORGIA

Rome Bottle Club
c/o Bob Jenkins
285 Oak Grove Rd.
CARROLTON, GA 30117

HAWAII

Hawaii Historical Bottle Collectors Club
P.O. Box 90456
HONOLULU, HI 96835

ILLINOIS

Metro-East Bottle & Jar Association
309 Bellevue Park Drive
BELLEVILLE, IL 62226

1st Chicago Bottle Club
P.O. Box A3382
CHICAGO, IL 60690

Pekin Bottle Collectors Association
c/o Ben Oertle
P.O. Box 372
PEKIN, IL 61555

Antique Bottle Club of Northern Illinois
P.O. Box 553
RICHMOND, IL 60071

INDIANA

Midwest Antique Fruit Jar & Bottle Club
P.O. Box 38
FLAT ROCK, IN 47234

Fort Wayne Historical Bottle Club
c/o Jack Potts, Secretary
P.O. Box 203
HARLAN, IN 46743

Wabash Valley Antique Glass & Pottery Club
3282 N. County Rd. 700E
POLAND, IN 47868

IOWA

Iowa Antique Bottleers
Rt. 1, Box 145
MILTON, IA 52570
e-mail: grsglass@lisco.com
website: www.antique bottles.com/iowa

KANSAS

**Southeast Kansas
 Bottle & Relic Club**
P.O. Box 471
CHANUTE, KS 66720

MAINE

**New England Antique
 Bottle Club**
c/o Herb Boothby,
Treasurer
267 Day Rd.
LYMAN, ME 04002

**Central New
 Hampshire Antique
 Bottle Club**
c/o Phyllis A. Fernald
R.R. 1, Box 6575
VASSALBORO, ME
04989-9727

MARYLAND

**Baltimore Antique
 Bottle Club**
P.O. Box 36061
TOWSON, MD
21286-6061
e-mail: scharing
 @home.com
website: www.antique
 bottles.com/baltimore

MASSACHUSETTS

**Litle Rhody Bottle
 Club**
c/o Pam Strokas, editor
27 Irving Ave.
SOUTH ATTLEBORO,
MA 02703

MICHIGAN

**Huron Valley (MI)
 Bottle & Insulator
 Club**
11843 Knob Hill
BRIGHTON, MI
48116-9220

**Flint Antique Bottle &
 Collectibles Club**
11353 W. Cook Rd.
GAINES, MI 48436

**Grand Rapids
 Antique Bottle Club**
3547 Remembrance
Rd. NW
GRAND RAPIDS, MI
49544-2284

**Metropolitan Detroit
 Antique Bottle Club**
410 Lothrop Rd.
GROSSE POINT
FARMS, MI 48236

**Kalamazoo Antique
 Bottle Club**
c/o Mark McNee
1009 Vassar Dr.
KALAMAZOO, MI
49001

**Huron Valley Bottle &
 Insulator Club**
2475 West Walton Rd.
WATERFORD, MI
48329

MINNESOTA

**Minnesota 1st Antique
 Bottle Club**
5001 Queen Ave. N.
MINNEAPOLIS, MN
55430

**North Star Historical
 Bottle Association**
3308 32nd Ave. S.
MINNEAPOLIS, MN
55406-2015

MISSOURI

**St. Louis Antique
 Bottle Collectors
 Association**
c/o Jim Potts
9925 Reavis Rd.
ST. LOUIS, MO
63123-5313

NEBRASKA

**Nebraska Antique
 Bottle & Collectible
 Club**
7913 Edgewood Blvd.
LA VISTA, NE 68128

NEVADA

**Las Vegas Antique
 Bottle & Collectibles
 Club**
c/o Dottie Daugherty
3901 E. Stewart #19
LAS VEGAS, NV
89110-3152

**Reno & Sparks
 Antique Bottle Club**
P.O. Box 1061
VERDI, NV 89439

NEW HAMPSHIRE

Yankee Bottle Club
c/o Alene Hall
382 Court St.
KEENE, NH
03431-2534

**Merrimack Valley
 Bottle Club**
c/o Jim Rogers
776 Harvey Rd., Rt. 10
MANCHESTER, NH
03103

**Central New
 Hampshire A.B.C.**
c/o Chuck & Vicki
Hussman
77 Winter St.
TILTON, NH 03276

NEW JERSEY

**South Jersey Heritage
 Bottle & Glass
 Collectors**
P.O. Box 122
GLASSBORO, NJ
08028

South Jersey Antique Bottle & Glass Collectors
548 E. Spring Rd.
HAMMONTON, NJ
08037

North Jersey Antique Bottle Collectors Association
c/o Paul Borey
251 Vista View Dr.
MAHWAH, NJ 07430

New Jersey Antique Bottle Club
c/o Joan Longo
521 Kings Hwy. E.
MIDDLETOWN, NJ
07748

Jersey Shore Bottle Club
P.O. Box 995
TOMS RIVER, NJ
08754-0649
e-mail: dtripit
@home.com
website: www.
members.home.com/
dtripet/jsbc/jsbc.html

NEW MEXICO
New Mexico Historical Bottle Society
c/o Jerry Simmons
1463A State Rd. 334
SANDIA PARK, NM
87047

NEW YORK
Greater Buffalo Bottle Club
66 Chassin Ave.
AMHERST, NY 14226
e-mail: psajablon102
@cs.com
website: www.antique
bottles.com/buffalo

Genesee Valley Bottle Collectors Association
c/o Kel Kelsey,
Membership
Chairman
17 Fifth Ave.
FAIRPORT, NY 14450-
1311
e-mail: etkelsey
@juno.com
website: www.
gvbca.org

Finger Lakes Bottle Collectors Association
P.O. Box 3894
ITHACA, NY
14852-3894

Long Island Antique Bottle Association
c/o Jack Slootweg
129 S. 4th St.
LINDENHURST, NY
11757

Capital Region Antique Bottle & Insulator Club
Robert Latham
463 Loudon Rd.
LOUDONVILLE, NY
12211
e-mail: blath@
capital.net

Empire State Bottle Collectors Association
P.O. Box 3421
SYRACUSE, NY
13220

Berkshire Antique Bottle Association
c/o Keith Van Amburgh
1 Dudley Heights
TROY, NY 12180

Hudson Valley Bottle Club
c/o David Cupina
733 Keenan Dr.
VESTAL, NY 13850

Mohawk Valley Antique Bottle Club
8646 Aitken Ave.
WHITESBORO, NY
13492

NORTH CAROLINA
Western North Carolina A.B.C.
c/o Bill Retskin, Editor
P.O. Box 18481
ASHEVILLE, NC
28814

Raleigh Bottle Club
P.O. Box 13736
DURHAM, NC 27709
e-mail: raleigh
@antiquebottles.com
website: www.antique
bottles.com/raleigh

Wilmington Antique Bottle & Artifact Club
c/o Lad Bright,
Secretary
4020 Chapra Dr.
WILMINGTON, NC
28412
e-mail: brightco
@wilmington.net
website: www.
antiquebottles.com/
wilmington/

OHIO

Ohio Bottle Club
c/o Mrs. Ann Sekerak
3937 Lake Shore Dr.
CORTLAND, OH
44410

**Findlay Antique
Bottle Club**
407 Cimarron Ct.
FINDLAY, OH 45840
e-mail:
Jack@fnet.friend-
lynet.com

The Ohio Bottle Club
c/o Dave Merker
7216 12th St.
MINERVA, OH 44657
website: www.antique
bottles.com/ohio

**Southwestern Ohio
Antique Bottle &
Jar Club**
P.O. Box 53
NORTH HAMPTON,
OH 45349

**Superior Twelve
Bottle Club**
22000 Shaker Blvd.
SHAKER HEIGHTS,
OH 44122

OKLAHOMA

**Oklahoma Territory
Bottle & Relic Club**
1300 S. Blue Haven Dr.
MUSTANG, OK 73064

**Tulsa Antiques &
Bottle Club**
P.O. Box 4278
TULSA, OK 74159

OREGON

**Northwest Miniature
Bottle Club**
P.O. Box 566
BORING, OR 97009
e-mail: grace63
@juno.com
(collectors of miniature
liquor bottles)

**Oregon Bottle
Collector's
Association**
c/o Tom Kasner
380 E. Jersey St.
GLADSTONE, OR
97027

Siskiyou A.B.C.
c/o Keith Lunt
2668 Montara Dr.
MEDFORD, OR 97504

PENNSYLVANIA

**Washington County
Antique Bottle &
Insulator Club**
c/o R.D. 2, Box 342
CARMICHAELS, PA
15320

**Laurel Valley Bottle
Club**
P.O. Box 131
LIGONIER, PA 15658

**Ligonier Historical
Bottle Collectors**
P.O. Box 188
LIGONIER, PA 15658

**Forks of the Delaware
Bottle Collectors
Association**
164 Farmview Rd.
NAZARETH, PA
18064-2500

**Pittsburgh Antique
Bottle Collectors**
235 Main Entrance Dr.
PITTSBURGH, PA
15228

**Bedford County Bot-
tle Club**
c/o Paul Long
497 Plum Creek Blvd.
ROARING SPRING,
PA 16673

**Jefferson County
Antique Bottle Club**
6 Valley View Dr.
WASHINGTON, PA
15301

**Pennsylvania Bottle
Collectors Assoc.**
251 Eastland Ave.
YORK, PA 17402

SOUTH CAROLINA

**South Carolina Bottle
Club**
c/o Eric Warren
238 Farmdale Dr.
LEXINGTON, SC
29073
e-mail: scbottles
@aol.com
website: www.
goldminers90.com/
scbottleclub

TENNESSEE

**Memphis Bottle
Collectors Club**
c/o Mr. & Mrs. William
C. Smith
6700 Palomino Dr.
ARLINGTON, TN
38002

**State of Franklin
Antique Bottle &
Collectibles
Association**
c/o Charlie Barnette
100 Coffey St.
BRISTOL,TN
37620-4229

**Middle Tennessee
Bottle Collectors
Club**
c/o Neal Ferguson
2926 Westmoreland Dr.
NASHVILLE, TN
37212

**East Tennessee
Antique Bottle Club**
220 Carter School Rd.
STRAWBERRY
PLAINS, TN 37871

VIRGINIA

**Potomac Bottle
Collectors**
c/o Jim Sears
4211 N. 2nd Rd., #1
ARLINGTON, VA
22203

**Historical Bottle
Diggers of Virginia**
c/o Casey Billhimer
2516 Hawksbill Rd.
McGAHEYSVILLE,
VA 22840

**Richmond Area Bottle
Collectors
Association**
4718 Kyloe Ln.
MOSELEY, VA 23120
e-mail: efaulk
@erols.com
website: www.antique
bottles.com/rabca/

**Apple Valley Bottle
Collectors Club**
P.O. Box 2201
WINCHESTER, VA
22604-1401
e-mail: polishbn
@shentel.net
website: www.antique
bottles.com/apple

WASHINGTON

**Washington Bottle
Collectors Associa-
tion**
c/o Michael Larson,
Treasurer
5492 Hannegan Rd.
BELLINGHAM, WA
98226

**Northwest Fruit Jar
Collectors' Club**
c/o J Spencer
12713 142nd Ave Ct. E.
PUYALLUP, WA
98374

WEST VIRGINIA

**Potomac Highlands
Antique Bottle &
Glass Collectors**
c/o DeHaven
P.O. Box 307
CAPON SPRINGS,
WV 26823

**West Virginia Bottle
Club**
39304 Bradbury Road
MIDDLEPORT, OH
45760

WISCONSIN

**Milwaukee Antique
Bottle & Advertising
Club**
c/o Michale Reiley
W 259 N 9116 Hwy. J
HARTLAND, WI
53029

**Antique Bottle Club
of Northern Illinois**
P.O. Box 571
LAKE GENEVA, WI
53147

CANADA

Bytown Bottle Seekers
P.O. Box 375
RICHMOND, ON,
CANADA K0A 2Z0

**Sleeping Giant Bottle
Club**
P.O. Box 1351
THUNDER BAY, ON,
CANADA P7C 5W2
e-mail:
pine@norlink.net

AUSTRALIA

**Australian Antique
Bottles and
Collectibles**
AABC
Box 235
GOLDEN SQUARE,
3555 AUSTRALIA

AUCTION GALLERIES

Some of the prices and pictures in this book were furnished by these auction houses and dealers and we thank them. If you are interested in buying or selling bottles or related collectibles, you may want to contact these firms.

AB!C Absentee Auctions
139 Pleasant Ave.
Dundas, ON, Canada
L9H 3T9
905-628-3433
e-mail: mdraaks
@home.com
website: www.
auctionsbyabc.com

Bothroyd & Detwiler On-line Auctions
1290 1/2 S. 8th Ave.
Yuma, AZ 85364-4509
e-mail: detwiler
@primenet.com
website:
www.primenet.com/
~detwiler/index.htm

B & B Auctions/Bottles & Bygones
30 Brabant Rd., Cheadle Hulme
Cheadle, Cheshire, U.K.
SK8 7AU
011-44-7931-812156
e-mail: bygones
@yahoo.com
website: members.
tripod.com/ ~Mike
Sheridan/index.htm

BBR Auctions
Elsecar Heritage Centre
Barnsley, S. Yorkshire,
U.K. S74 8HJ
011-44-1226-745156
fax: 011-44-1226-351561
e-mail: sales
@bbrauctions.co.uk
website: www.
bbrauctions.co.uk

Bruce & Vicki Waasdorp Auctions
P.O. Box 434
Clarence, NY 14031
716-759-2361
fax: 716-759-2397
e-mail: waasdorp
@antiques-
stoneware.com
website: www.antiques-
stoneware.com

Collectors Auction Services
R.R. 2, Box 431
Oil City, PA 16301
814-677-6070
fax: 814-677-6166
e-mail: director
@caswel.com
website: www.
caswel.com

Conestoga Auction Company, Inc.
768 Graystone Rd.
P.O. Box 1
Manheim, PA 17545
717-898-7284
fax: 717-898-6628
e-mail: ca@conestoga
auction.com
website: www.
conestogaauction.com

Early Auction Co.
123 Main St.
Milford, OH 45150
513-831-4833
fax: 513-831-1441

Fink's Off The Wall
108 E. Seventh St.
Lansdale, PA 19446-2622
215-855-9732
fax: 215-855-6325
e-mail: lansbeer
@finksauction.com
website: www.
finksauctions.com

Garth's Auctions, Inc.
2690 Stratford Rd.
P.O. Box 369
Delaware, OH 43015
740-362-4771
fax: 740-363-0164
e-mail: info@garths.com
website: www.garths.com

Gene Harris Antique Auction Center, Inc.
203 S. 18th Ave.
P.O. Box 476
Marshalltown, IA 50158
641-752-0600
fax: 641-753-0226
e-mail: ghaac
@marshallnet.com
website: www.geneharris
auctions.com

Glass-Works Auctions
P.O. Box 180
East Greenville, PA
18041
215-679-5849
fax: 215-679-3068
e-mail: glaswrk
@enter.net
website: www.
glswrk-auction.com

Howard B. Parzow
P.O. Box 3464
Gaithersburg, MD
20885-3464
301-977-6741
fax: 301-208-8947
e-mail: hparzow@aol.com
website: www.hbparzo
wauctioneer.com

John R. Pastor
Antique Bottle &
Glass Auction
7288 Thorncrest Dr. SE
Ada, MI 49301
616-285-7604

Liberty Antiques &
Auctions
The American
Pharmacy Auctioneer
934 Main St.
Newberry, SC 29108
888-321-8600
fax: 803-276-1800
e-mail: liberty
@bellsouth.com

McMurray Antiques
& Auctions
P.O. Box 393
Kirkwood, NY 13795
607-775-2321
fax: 607-775-5972

Metz's Superlatives
Auction Co.
P.O. Box 18185
Roanoke, VA 24014
540-982-3886
fax: 540-387-3233
e-mail: mudauction
@aol.com
website: muddyriver
trading.com

Monsen and Baer
P.O. Box 529
Vienna, VA 22183
703-938-2129
fax: 703-242-1357
e-mail: monsenbaer
@erolis.com
(perfume bottles)

New England
Absentee Auctions,
LLC
16 Sixth St.
Stamford, CT 06905
203-975-9055
fax: 203-323-6407
e-mail: NEAAuction
@aol.com

Norman C. Heckler &
Company
79 Bradford Corner Rd.
Woodstock Valley, CT
06282
860-974-1634
fax: 860-974-2003
e-mail: heckler
@neca.com
website: heckler
auction.com

NSA Auctions
Newton-Smith Antiques
88 Cedar St.,
Cambridge, ON,
Canada N1S 1V8
519-623-6302
e-mail: info
@nsaauctions.com
website: www.
nsaauctions.com

Pacific Glass Auctions
1507 21st St., Suite 203
Sacramento, CA 95814
800-806-7722
fax: 916-443-3199
e-mail: info@pacglass
website: pacglass.com

Phillips International
Auctioneers &
Valuers
406 E. 79th St.
New York, NY 10021
212-570-4830
fax: 212-570-2207
website: www.
phillips-auctions.com

Richard Opfer
Auctioneering, Inc.
1919 Greenspring Dr.
Timonium, MD 21093
410-252-5035
fax: 410-252-5863
e-mail: info
@opferauction.com
website: www.
opferauction.com

Richard W.
Withington, Inc.
590 Center Rd.
Hillsboro, NH 03244
603-464-3232
e-mail: withington
@conknet.com
website: www.
withingtonauction.
com

Skinner, Inc.
357 Main St.
Bolton, MA 01740
978-779-6241
fax: 978-779-5144
website: www.
skinnerinc.com

Veterinary Collectibles
Roundtable
7431 Covington Hwy.
Lithonia, GA 30058
770-482-5100
fax: 770-482-5100
e-mail: petvet
@mindspring.com
website: petvet.home.
mindspring.com/VCR

York Town Auction
Inc.
1625 Haviland Rd.
York, PA 17404
717-751-0211
fax: 717-767-7729
e-mail: info@york
townauction.com
website: www.york
townauction.com

BIBLIOGRAPHY

We've found these books to be useful. Some of them may be out of print, but your local library should be able to get them for you through interlibrary loan.

GENERAL

Barlow, Raymond E., and Joan E. Kaiser. *A Guide to Sandwich Glass: Cut Ware, A General Assortment and Bottles*. Atglen, PA: Schiffer, 1999.

Blakeman, Alan. *Antique Bottles Collectors Encyclopedia with Price Guide*, 2 vols. Elsecar, England: BBR Publishing, 1986, 1995.

Brown, William E. *The Auction Price Report*, 1998 edition. Privately printed (8251 NW 49th Ct., Coral Springs, FL 33067).

Feldhaus, Ron. *The Bottles, Breweriana and Advertising Jugs of Minnesota: 1850–1920*, 2 vols. Privately printed, 1986, 1987 (6724 Xerxes Ave. S., Edina, MN 55423).

Fletcher, Johnnie W. *Kansas Bottles: 1854 to 1915*. Privately printed, 1994 (1300 S. Blue Haven Dr., Mustang, OK 73064).

Husfloen, Kyle. *American Pressed Glass & Bottles*, 2nd edition. Iola, WI: Krause, 2000.

Ketchum, William C., Jr. *A Treasury of American Bottles*. Indianapolis: Bobbs-Merrill, 1975.

Kovel, Ralph and Terry. *Kovels' Antiques & Collectibles Price List 2002*, 34th edition. New York: Three Rivers Press/Crown, 2002.

_____. *Kovels' Know Your Antiques*. New York: Crown, 1990.

_____. *Kovels' Bottles Price List*, 12th edition. New York: Three Rivers Press/Crown, 2002.

McKearin, George L. and Helen. *Two Hundred Years of American Blown Glass*. New York: Crown, 1950.

Mario's Price Guide to Modern Bottles. Privately printed, issued quarterly (146 Sheldon Ave., Depew, NY 14043).

Megura, Jim. *Official Price Guide: Bottles*, 13th edition. New York: House of Collectibles, 2000.

Montague, H.F. *Montague's Modern Bottle Identification & Price Guide*, 3rd edition. Privately printed, 1984 (P.O. Box 4059, Overland Park, KS 66204).

Odell, John. *Indian Bottles and Brands*. Privately printed, 1997 (467B Yale Dr., Lebanon, OH 45036).

Ohio Bottle Club, Inc. *Ohio Bottles*. Privately printed, 1999. (P.O. Box 585, Barberton, OH 44203).

Polak, Michael. *Bottles Identification and Price Guide*, 3rd edition. New York: Avon Books, 2000.

AVON

Avon 8 and *Avon 8: Supplement 1*. Pleasant Hill, CA: Western World Publishing, 1985, 1987.

Hastin, Bud. *Bud Hastin's Avon Products & California Perfume Co. Collector's Encyclopedia,* 16th edition. Privately printed, 2000 (P.O. Box 11004, Ft. Lauderdale, FL 33339).

BARBER

Holiner, Richard. *Collecting Barber Bottles.* Paducah, KY: Collector Books, 1987.
Odell, John. *Digger Odell's Official Antique Bottle and Collector Magazine Price Guide: Barber Bottles,* Vol. 1. Privately printed, 1995 (1910 Shawhan Rd., Morrow, OH 45152).

BEAM

Cembura, Al, and Constance Avery. *A Guide to Jim Beam Bottles,* 12th edition. Privately printed, 1984 (139 Arlington Ave., Berkeley, CA 94707).
Higgins, Molly. *Jim Beam Figural Bottles.* Atglen, PA: Schiffer, 2000.
Honeyman, Betty, ed. *Jim Beam Bottles: A Pictorial Guide.* Privately printed, 1982 (International Association of Jim Beam Bottle & Specialties Clubs, 2015 Burlington Ave., Kewanee, IL 61443). Price guide update, 1998.
Jim Beam Bottles Price Guide. Privately printed, 1993 (International Association of Jim Beam Bottle & Specialties Clubs). Price guide update, 1998.

BEER

Bull, Donald, et al. *American Breweries.* Privately printed, 1984 (P.O. Box 106, Trumbull, CT 06611).
Friedrich, Manfred, and Donald Bull. *The Register of United States Breweries 1876–1976,* 2 vols. Privately printed, 1976 (P.O. Box 106, Trumbull, CT 06611).
Van Wieren, Dale P. *American Breweries II.* Privately printed, 1995 (Eastern Coast Breweriana Association, P.O. Box 1354, North Wales, PA 19454).
Yenne, Bill. *The Field Guide to North America's Breweries and Microbreweries.* New York: Crescent Books, 1994.

BITTERS

Odell, John. *Digger Odell's Official Antique Bottle and Glass Collector Magazine Price Guide: Bitters,* Vol. 2. Privately printed, 1995 (1910 Shawhan Rd., Morrow, OH 45152).
Ring, Carlyn, and W.C. Ham. *Bitters Bottles.* Privately printed, 1998 (P.O. Box 427, Downieville, CA 95936).
Ring, Carlyn, and Sheldon Ray Jr. *For Bitters Only Up-Date and Price Guide.* Privately printed, 1988 (P.O. Box 357, Sun Valley, AZ 83353).
Watson, Richard. *Bitters Bottles.* Fort Davis, TX: Thomas Nelson & Sons, 1965.
_____. *Supplement to Bitters Bottles.* Camden, NJ: Thomas Nelson & Sons, 1968.
Wichman, Jeff. *Antique Western Bitters Bottles.* Sacramento, CA. Pacific Glass Books, 1999.

BLACK GLASS

Fletcher, Edward. *A Bottle Collectors' Guide: European Seals, Case Gins and Bitters.* London: Anchor Press Ltd., 1976.

Odell, John. *Digger Odell's Official Antique Bottle and Glass Collector Magazine Price Guide: Black Glass,* Vol. 9. Privately printed, 1997 (1910 Shawhan Rd., Morrow, OH 45152).

CANDY CONTAINERS

Candy Containers: A Price Guide. Gas City, IN: L-W Book Sales, 1996.

Dezso, Douglas M., J. Leon Poirier, and Rose D. Poirier. *Collector's Guide to Candy Containers.* Paducah, KY: Collector Books, 1998.

Eikelberner, George, Serge Agadjanian, and Adele L. Bowden. *The Compleat American Glass Candy Containers Handbook.* Privately printed, 1986 (6252 Cedarwood Rd., Mentor, OH 44060).

Long, Jennie D. *An Album of Candy Containers,* 2 vols. Privately printed, 1978, 1983 (P.O. Box 552, Kingsburg, CA 93631).

Miller, William, and Jack Brush. *Modern Candy Containers and Novelties.* Paducah, KY: Collector Books, 2001.

COCA-COLA

Goldstein, Shelley and Helen. *Coca-Cola Collectibles with Current Prices and Photographs in Full Color,* 4 vols. and index. Privately printed, 1971–1980 (P.O. Box 301, Woodland Hills, CA 91364).

Henrich, Bob and Debra. *Coca-Cola Commemorative Bottles,* 2nd edition. Paducah, KY: Collector Books, 2001.

Hill, Deborah Goldstein. *Price Guide to Coca-Cola Collectibles.* Radnor, PA: Wallace-Homestead, 1991.

Hoy, Anne. *Coca-Cola: The First Hundred Years.* Atlanta, GA: The Coca-Cola Company, 1986.

Mix, Richard. *Commemorative Bottle Checklist and Cross-Reference Guide: Featuring Coca-Cola Bottles,* 5th edition. Privately printed, 1999 (P.O. Box 558, Marietta, GA 30061).

Munsey, Cecil. *The Illustrated Guide to the Collectibles of Coca-Cola.* New York: Hawthorn Books, 1972.

Petretti, Allan. *Petretti's Coca-Cola Collectibles Price Guide,* 11th edition. Iola, WI: Krause, 2001.

Schaeffer, Randy, and Bill Bateman. *Coca-Cola: A Collector's Guide to New and Vintage Coca-Cola Memorabilia.* London: Courage Books, 1995.

Spontak, Joyce. *Commemorative Coca-Cola Bottles: An Unauthorized Guide.* Atglen, PA: Schiffer, 1998.

COLOGNE, SEE PERFUME

CURES, SEE MEDICINE; SARSAPARILLA

DRUG, SEE MEDICINE

FIGURAL, SEE ALSO BITTERS

Christensen, Don and Doris. *Violin Bottles: Banjos, Guitars & Other Novelty Glass.* Privately printed, 1995 (21815 106th St. E., Buckley, WA 98321).

Revi, Albert Christian. *American Pressed Glass and Figure Bottles.* New York: Thomas Nelson & Sons, 1964.

FIRE GRENADES

Odell, John. *Digger Odell's Official Antique Bottle and Glass Collector Magazine Price Guide: Colognes, Pattern Mold, Label Under Glass, Fire Extinguishers and Target Balls,* Vol 6. Privately printed 1995 (1910 Shawhan Rd., Morrow, OH 45152).

FLASKS

Blakeman, Alan. *A Collectors Guide: Reform Flasks.* Elsecar, England: BBR Publishing, 1997.

Brown, William E. *The 1995 Auction Price Report: Bitters, Historical Flasks, Medicines, Whiskeys, Sodas & Mineral Waters.* Privately printed, 1995 (8251 NW 49th Ct., Coral Springs, FL 33067).

Clark, Lois. *Wheaton's: My Favorite Collectibles.* Privately printed, 1998 (Classic Wheaton Club, P.O. Box 59, Downingtown, PA 19335).

McKearin, Helen, and Kenneth M. Wilson. *American Bottles & Flasks and Their Ancestry.* New York: Crown, 1978.

Odell, John. *Digger Odell's Official Antique Bottle and Glass Collector Magazine Price Guide: Flasks,* Vol. 3. Privately printed, 1995 (1910 Shawhan Rd., Morrow, OH 45152).

Thomas, John L. *Picnics, Coffins, Shoo-Flies.* Privately printed, 1974 (P.O. Box 446, Weaverville, CA 96093).

FOOD, SEE ALSO FRUIT JARS; VINEGAR

Caniff, Tom. *The Label Space: The Book.* Privately printed, 1997 (5003 W. Berwyn Ave., Chicago, IL 60630-1501).

FRUIT JARS

Bowditch, Barbara. *American Jelly Glasses: A Collector's Notebook.* Privately printed, 1986 (400 Dorchester Rd., Rochester, NY 14610).

Caniff, Tom, ed. *The Guide to Collecting Fruit Jars: Fruit Jar Annual,* 3 vols. Privately printed, 1996-1998 (5003 W. Berwyn Ave., Chicago, IL 60630).

_____. *Fruit Jar Annual 2002,* Vol. 7. Privately printed, 2002 (Jerome J. McCann, 5003 Berwyn Ave., Chicago, IL 60630).

Creswick, Alice. *The Fruit Jar Works,* 2 vols. Privately printed, 1987 (Douglas Leybourne, P.O. Box 5417, North Muskegon, MI 49445).

Leybourne, Douglas M. Jr. *The Collector's Guide to Old Fruit Jars: Red Book 9*. Privately printed, 2001 (P.O. Box 5417, North Muskegon, MI 49445).

Roller, Dick. *Fruit Jar Patents,* Vol. 2 (1870-1884; 1885-1899), Vol. 3 (1900-1942). Privately printed, 1996 (Jerry McCann, 5003 W. Berwyn Ave., Chicago, IL 60630-0443).

_____. *The Standard Fruit Jar Reference.* Privately printed, 1983 (607 Driskell, Paris, IL 61944).

Schroeder, Bill. *1000 Fruit Jars Priced and Illustrated,* 5th edition. Paducah, KY: Collector Books, 1996.

Toulouse, Julian Harrison. *Fruit Jars: A Collector's Manual.* Jointly published by Camden, NJ: Thomas Nelson & Sons; and Hanover, PA: Everybody's Press, 1969.

INK

Blakeman, Alan. *A Collectors Guide: Inks.* Elsecar, England: BBR Publishing, 1996.

Covill, William E., Jr. *Ink Bottles and Inkwells.* Taunton, MA: William S. Sullwold, 1971.

Jaegers, Ray and Bevy. *The Write Stuff: Collector's Guide to Inkwells, Fountain Pens, and Desk Accessories.* Iola, WI: Krause, 2000.

Odell, John. *Digger Odell's Official Antique Bottle and Glass Collector Magazine Price Guide: Inks,* Vol. 4; *More Inks,* Vol. 11. Privately printed, 1995, 1998 (1910 Shawhan Rd., Morrow, OH 45152).

Rivera, Betty and Ted. *Inkstands and Inkwells.* New York: Crown, 1973.

JAR, SEE FRUIT JAR

MEDICINE

Brown, William E. *The 1995 Auction Price Report: Bitters, Historical Flasks, Medicines, Whiskeys, Sodas & Mineral Waters.* Privately printed, 1995 (8251 NW 49th Ct., Coral Springs, FL 33067).

Odell, John. *Digger Odell's Official Antique Bottle and Glass Collector Magazine Price Guide: Medicines,* Vol. 5; *Poisons: Drugstore & Apothecary Bottles* Vol. 10. Privately printed, 1995 (1910 Shawhan Rd., Morrow, OH 45152).

MILK

Edmondson, Bill. *The Milk Bottle Book of Michigan.* Privately printed, 1995 (317 Harvest Ln., Lansing, MI 48917).

Giarde, Jeffrey L. *Glass Milk Bottles: Their Makers and Marks.* Bryn Mawr, PA: The Time Travelers Press, 1980.

MILK GLASS, SEE ALSO FIGURAL

Belknap, E.M. *Milk Glass.* New York: Crown, 1959.

Ferson, Regis F. and Mary F. *Yesterday's Milk Glass Today.* Privately printed, 1981 (122 Arden Rd., Pittsburgh, PA 15216).

MINERAL WATER, SEE SODA

MINIATURES

Cembura, Al, and Constance Avery. *A Guide to Miniature Bottles.* Privately printed, 1973 (139 Arlington Ave., Berkeley, CA 94708).

Kay, Robert E. *Miniature Beer Bottles & Go-Withs.* Privately printed, 1980 (216 N. Batavia Ave., Batavia, IL 60510).

Keegan, Alan. *Scotch in Miniature: A Collector's Guide.* Privately printed, 1982 (Chiisai Bin, P.O. Box 1900, Garden Grove, CA 92642).

NURSING

Ostrander, Diane Rouse. *A Guide to American Nursing Bottles.* Privately printed, 1984; revised 1992 (Will-O-Graf, P.O. Box 24, Willoughby, OH 44094).

Pastor, John R. *Nursing Bottle Absentee Auction,* Estate of Laure Kimpton, Madison, Wisconsin, 1998 (7288 Thorncrest Dr. SE, Ada, MI 49301).

PEPSI-COLA

Ayers, James C. *Pepsi-Cola Bottles Collectors Guide.* Privately printed, 1995 (RJM Enterprises, P.O. Box 1377, Mount Airy, NC 27030)

_____. *Pepsi-Cola Bottles & More Collectors Guide,* Vol 2. Privately printed, 2001 (RJM Enterprises, 5186 Claudville Hwy, Claudville, VA 24076).

Lloyd, Everette and Mary. *Pepsi-Cola Collectibles with Price Guide.* Atglen, PA: Schiffer, 1993.

Rawlingson, Fred. *Brad's Drink: A Primer for Pepsi-Cola Collectors.* Privately printed, 1976 (FAR Publications, Box 5456, Newport News, VA 23605).

Stoddard, Bob. *Introduction to Pepsi Collecting.* Privately printed, 1991 (Double Dot Enterprises, P.O. Box 1548, Pomona, CA 91769).

Vehling, Bill, and Michael Hunt. *Pepsi-Cola Collectibles with Prices,* 3 vols. Gas City, IN: L-W Book Sales, 1988–1993.

PERFUME, COLOGNE, AND SCENT

Baccarat: The Perfume Bottles. Privately printed, 1986 (Addor Associates, P.O. Box 2128, Westport, CT 06880).

Ball, Joanne Dubbs, and Dorothy Hehl Torem. *Fragrance Bottle Masterpieces.* Atglen, PA: Schiffer, 1996.

Bowman, Glinda. *More Miniature Perfume Bottles.* Atglen, PA: Schiffer, 1996.

Diamond I Perfume Bottles Price Guide and Other Drugstore Ware. Gas City, IN: L-W Book Sales, 2000.

Forsythe, Ruth A. *Made in Czechoslovakia.* Privately printed, 1982 (Box 327, Galena, OH 43021).

Gaborit, Jean-Yves. *Perfumes: The Essences and Their Bottles.* New York: Rizzoli, 1985.

Hastin, Bud. *Bud Hastin's Avon Products & California Perfume Co. Collector's*

Encyclopedia, 16th edition. Privately printed, 2000 (P.O. Box 11004, Ft. Lauderdale, FL 33339).

Latimer, Tirza True. *The Perfume Atomizer: An Object with Atmosphere.* Atglen, PA: Schiffer, 1991.

Lefkowith, Christie Mayer. *The Art of Perfume: Discovering and Collecting Perfume Bottles.* New York: Thames and Hudson, 1994.

Magic of Perfume: Perfumes of Caron. Monsen and Baer auction catalog, 2001 (Box 529, Vienna, VA 22183).

Martin, Hazel. *A Collection of Figural Perfume & Scent Bottles.* Privately printed, 1982 (P.O. Box 110, Lancaster, CA 93535).

North, Jacquelyn Y. Jones. *Commercial Perfume Bottles.* Atglen, PA: Schiffer, 1986.

_____. *Perfume, Cologne and Scent Bottles.* Atglen, PA: Schiffer, 1986.

Odell, John. *Digger Odell's Official Antique Bottle and Glass Collector Magazine Price Guide: Colognes, Pattern Mold, Label Under Glass, Fire Extinguishers and Target Balls,* Vol. 6. Privately printed, 1995 (1910 Shawhan Rd., Morrow, OH 45152).

Prescott-Walker, Robert. *Collecting Lalique: Perfume Bottles and Glass.* London: Francis Joseph, 2001.

Ringblum, Jeri Lyn. *A Collector's Handbook of Miniature Perfume Bottles.* Atglen, PA: Schiffer, 1996.

Sloan, Jean. *Perfume and Scent Bottle Collecting with Prices.* Radnor, PA: Wallace-Homestead, 1989.

Utt, Mary Lou, Glen Utt, and Patricia Bayer. *Lalique Perfume Bottles.* New York: Crown, 1985.

PICKLE

Zumwalt, Betty. *Ketchup Pickles Sauces.* Privately printed, 1980 (P.O. Box 413, Fulton, CA 95439).

POISON

Durflinger, Roger L. *Poison Bottles Collectors Guide.* Privately printed, 1972 (132 W. Oak St., Washington Court House, OH 43160).

Kuhn, Rudy. *Poison Bottle Workbook.* Privately printed, 1988 (3954 Perie Ln., San Jose, CA 95132).

Odell, John. *Digger Odell's Official Antique Bottle and Glass Collector Magazine Price Guide: Poisons, Drugstore & Apothecary Bottles,* Vol. 10. Privately printed, 1995 (1910 Shawhan Rd., Morrow, OH 45152).

ROYAL DOULTON

Dale, Jean. *The Charlton Standard Catalog of Royal Doulton Jugs.* Toronto: Charlton Press, 1991.

Lukins, Jocelyn. *Doulton Kingsware Whisky.* Yelverton, Devon, England: M.P.E., 1981.

SARSAPARILLA

DeGrafft, Joan. *American Sarsaparilla Bottles.* Privately printed, 1980 (47 Ash St., North Attleboro, MA 92760).

Shimko, Phyllis. *Sarsaparilla Bottle Encyclopedia.* Privately printed, 1969 (Box 117, Aurora, OR 97002).

SEAL

Fletcher, Edward, *A Bottle Collectors' Guide.* London: Anchor Press Ltd., 1976.

Davis, Derek C., *English Bottles & Decanters, 1650-1900.* New York: World Publishing Company, 1972.

Dumbrell, Roger. *Understanding Antique Wine Bottles.* Woodbridge, Suffolk, England: Antique Collectors' Club, 1983.

SCENT, SEE PERFUME

SODA, SEE ALSO COCA-COLA; PEPSI-COLA

Bowers, Q. David. *The Moxie Encyclopedia.* Vestal, NY: The Vestal Press, 1984.

Brown, William E. *The 1995 Auction Price Report: Bitters, Historical Flasks, Medicines, Whiskeys, Sodas & Mineral Waters.* Privately printed, 1995 (8251 NW 49th Ct., Coral Springs, FL 33067).

Dietz, Lawrence. *Soda Pop.* New York: Simon & Schuster, 1973.

Ellis, Harry E. *Dr Pepper, King of Beverages.* Dallas, TX: Dr Pepper Company, 1979.

Ferguson, Joel. *New Orleans Soda Water Manufacturers History.* Privately printed, 1995 (106 Dixie Circle, Slidell, LA 70458).

Fowler, Ron. *Washington Sodas: The Illustrated History of Washington's Soft Drink Industry.* Privately printed, 1986 (Dolphin Point Writing Works, P.O. Box 45251, Seattle, WA 98145).

Markota, Peck and Audie. *Western Blob Top Soda and Mineral Water Bottles,* revised edition. Privately printed, 1972 (8512 Pershing Ave., Fair Oaks, CA 95628).

Marsh, Thomas E. *The Official Guide to Collecting Applied Color Label Soda Bottles,* Vol. 2. Privately printed, 1995 (914 Franklin Ave., Youngstown, OH 44502).

Mix, Richard. *Commemorative Bottle Checklist and Cross-Reference Guide: Featuring Dr Pepper, Pepsi, 7Up, NSDA and Other Soda Brands.* Privately printed, 1999 (P.O. Box 558, Marietta, GA 30061).

Odell, John. *Digger Odell's Official Antique Bottle and Glass Collector Magazine Price Guide: Soda and Mineral Waters,* Vol. 7. Privately printed, 1995 (1910 Shawhan Rd., Morrow, OH 45152).

Petretti, Allan. *Petretti's Soda Pop Collectibles Price Guide,* 2nd edition. Dubuque, IA: Antique Trader Books, 1999.

Sweeney, Rick. *Collecting Applied Color Label Soda Bottles,* 3rd edition. Privately printed, 2002 (9418 Hilmer Dr., La Mesa, CA 91942).

Tucker, Donald. *Collector's Guide to the Saratoga Type Mineral Water Bottles.* Privately printed, 1986 (North Berwick, ME 03906).

TARGET BALLS

Odell, John. *Digger Odell's Official Antique Bottle & Glass Collector Magazine Price Guide: Colognes, Pattern Mold, Label Under Glass, Fire Extinguishers and Target Balls,* Vol. 6. Privately printed, 1995 (1910 Shawhan Rd., Morrow, OH 45152).

TONIC, SEE MEDICINE

VINEGAR

Smith, Levin J. *White House Vinegar Book.* Privately printed, 1971 (P.O. Box 102, Independence, VA 24348).

WHEATON

Clark, Lois. *Wheatons: My Favorite Collectibles.* Privately printed, 1998 (Classic Wheaton Club, P.O. Box 59, Downingtown, PA 19335).

WHISKEY

Barnett, R.E. *Western Whiskey Bottles,* No. 4. Privately printed, 1997 (P.O. Box 109, Lakeview, OR 97630).

Brown, William E. *The 1995 Auction Price Report: Bitters, Historical Flasks, Medicines, Whiskeys, Sodas & Mineral Waters.* Privately printed, 1995 (8251 NW 49th Ct., Coral Springs, FL 33067).

Odell, John. *Digger Odell's Official Antique Bottle and Glass Collector Magazine Price Guide: Whiskeys,* Vol. 8. Privately printed, 1995 (1910 Shawhan Rd., Morrow, OH 45152).

Spaid, David, and Henry Ford. *The One Hundred and One Rare Whiskeys.* Privately printed, 1989 (P.O. Box 2161, Palos Verdes, CA 90274).

Thomas, John L. *Whiskey Bottles & Liquor Containers from the State of Washington.* Privately printed, 1998 (4805 Grace St., Apt. C, Capitola, CA 95010-2655).

_____.*Whiskey Bottles & Liquor Containers from the State of Oregon.* Privately printed, 1998 (4805 Grace St., Apt. C, Capitola, CA 95010-2655).

AESTHETIC SPECIALTIES

In 1979 the first bottle was released by ASI, or Aesthetic Specialties, Inc., of San Mateo, California. It was a ceramic vodka bottle that was made to honor the 1979 Crosby 38th National Pro-Am Golf Tournament. According to the company president, Charles Wittwer, 400 cases of the bottle were made. The company continued making bottles: the 1979 Kentucky Derby bottle (600 cases); 1909 Stanley Steamer (5,000 cases in three different colors made in 1979); 1903 Cadillac (2 colors made in 1979, gold version, with and without trim, made in 1980); World's Greatest Golfer (400 cases in 1979); World's Greatest Hunter (1979); 38th and 39th Crosby Golf Tournaments (1979 and 1980); 1981 Crosby 40th Golf Tournament (reworked version of World's Greatest Golfer, 100 cases); Crosby Golf Tournaments (1982, 1983, and 1984); Telephone Service Truck (1980); Ice Cream Truck (1980); 1910 Oldsmobile (1980, made in three colors); Packard (1980); 1911 Stanley Steamer (1981, 1,200 cases); 1937 Packard (1981, produced with McCormick); 1914 Chevrolet (1981); and Fire engine (1981).

Bing Crosby, 38th, 1979	38.00 to 45.00
Bing Crosby, 39th, 1980	25.00 to 38.00
Bing Crosby, 40th, 1981	36.00 to 45.00
Bing Crosby, 41st, Otter, 1982	64.00
Bing Crosby, 42nd, Seal, 1983	38.00 to 40.00
Bing Crosby, 43rd, Clam, 1984	45.00 to 51.00
Bing Crosby, 44th, 1985	48.00 to 50.00
Cadillac, 1903 Model, Blue, 1979	70.00
Cadillac, 1903 Model, Gold, 1980	120.00
Cadillac, 1903 Model, White, 1979	73.00
Chevrolet, 1914 Model, 1979	52.00 to 60.00
Chevrolet, 1980 Model, Gold	165.00 to 172.00
Golfer, World's Greatest, 1979	32.00 to 48.00
Hunter, World's Greatest, 1979	26.00 to 35.00
Kentucky Derby, 1979	47.00
Model T Ice Cream Truck, Ford, 1980	75.00
Oldsmobile, 1910 Model, Black, 1980	75.00
Oldsmobile, Gold, 1980	165.00
Oldsmobile, Platinum, 1980	307.00
Stanley Steamer, 1909 Model, Black, 1981	50.00 to 65.00
Stanley Steamer, 1909 Model, Gold, 1981	113.00
Stanley Steamer, 1909 Model, Green, 1981	42.00
Stanley Steamer, Green, 1978	52.00

ALPHA, see Lewis & Clark
AUSTIN NICHOLS, see Wild Turkey

AVON

David H. McConnell started a door-to-door selling company in 1886. He recruited women as independent sales representatives to sell his perfume. The company was named the California Perfume Company even though it was located in New York City. The first product was a set of five perfumes called Little Dot. In 1928 it was decided that CPC was too limiting a name so a new line called Avon was introduced. By 1936, the Avon name was on all of the company's products, including perfumes, toothbrushes, and baking items. Avon became a public company in 1946. Collectors want the bottles, jewelry, figurines, sales awards, early advertising, pamphlets, and other go-withs. For information on national and local clubs, books, and other publications, contact the National Association of Avon Collector Clubs, P.O. Box 7006, Kansas City, MO 64113.

After-Shave On Tap, Amber, 1974, 5 Oz.	8.00
After-Shave On Tap, Amber, 1976, 5 Oz.	8.00
Airplane, see Avon, Spirit of St. Louis	
Albee, 1978	90.00 to 125.00
Albee, 1979	75.00 to 100.00
Albee, 1980	75.00 to 125.00
Albee, 1981	40.00 to 60.00
Albee, 1981, Box	65.00
Albee, 1982	35.00 to 50.00
Albee, 1982, Box	55.00
Albee, 1983	50.00 to 60.00

Albee, 1983, Box 65.00
Albee, 1984 .... .45.00 to 60.00
Albee, 1984, Box 70.00
Albee, 1985 .... 60.00
Albee, 1985, Box 65.00
Albee, 1986 .... .60.00 to 75.00
Albee, 1986, Box 80.00
Albee, 1987 .... .50.00 to 60.00
Albee, 1987, Box 70.00
Albee, 1988 .... .60.00 to 75.00
Albee, 1988, Box 85.00
Albee, 1989 .... 85.00
Albee, 1989, Box .... 95.00 to 100.00
Albee, 1990 .... .85.00 to 100.00
Albee, 1991 .... .85.00 to 100.00
Albee, 1992 .... 75.00 to 100.00
Albee, 1993 .... .85.00 to 100.00
Albee, 1994 .... .75.00 to 100.00
Albee, 1995 .... .85.00 to 100.00
Albee, 1996, Box 100.00
Albee, 1997, Box 100.00
Albee, 1998 .... 95.00
Albee, 1998, Box, Miniature 100.00
Albee, 1999 .... 100.00
Albee, 1999, Box 125.00
Albee, Gold, 1990 .... 40.00
Albee, Silver, 1985 .... 50.00
Albee, Silver, 1988 .... 50.00
Albee, Silver, 1991 .... .25.00 to 40.00
Albee, With Dome, 1994, Miniature 35.00
Albee, With Dome, 1995, Miniature 35.00
Albee, With Dome, 1996, Miniature 35.00
Albee, With Dome, 1997, Miniature 25.00
Albee, With Dome, 1998, Miniature 35.00
Albee, With Dome, 1999, Miniature 35.00
American Eagle, Dark Amber, 1971, 5 Oz. 10.00
American Schooner, 1972, 4 1/2 Oz. .... 10.00 to 14.00
Army Jeep, 1974, 4 Oz. .... .5.00 to 10.00
Barber Bottle, see Avon, Close Harmony
Barrel, see Avon, After-Shave On Tap
Baseball Mitt, see Avon, Fielder's Choice
Bath Season, 1969, 3 Oz. .... .3.50 to 6.00
Bath Urn, Milk Glass, 1971, 5 Oz. 7.00
Bay Rum Jug, 1962, 8 Oz. 7.00
Bay Rum Keg, 1965, 6 Oz. 15.00
Be My Valentine Cologne Splash, 1995, 5 Oz. .... .1.00 to 3.00
Beautiful Awakening, 1973, 3 Oz. 8.00
Bell, Emerald, 1978, 3 3/4 Oz. .... .8.00 to 10.00
Bell, Fragrance, 1968, 1 Oz. .... 10.00 to 15.00
Bell, Hobnail, Milk Glass, 1973, 2 Oz. .... .8.00 to 12.00
Bell, Hospitality, 1976, 3 3/4 Oz. 8.00
Bell, Joyous, 1978, 1 Oz. 7.00
Bell, Liberty, 1971, 5 Oz. 10.00
Bell, Moonlightglow, 1981, 3 Oz. 10.00
Bell Jar, 1973, 5 Oz. 9.00
Benjamin Franklin, 1974, 6 Oz. 6.00
Betsy Ross, 1976, 4 Oz. .... 15.00 to 20.00
Big Game Rhino, 1972, 4 Oz. 9.00
Big Mack, 1973, 6 Oz. 9.00
Big Rig, 1975, 3 1/2 Oz. 14.00
Birdfeeder, 1967, 7 1/2 Oz. 12.00
Blacksmith's Anvil, Black, 1972, 4 Oz. 9.00
Blue Eyes, 1975, 1 1/2 Oz. 7.00

Bold Eagle, 1976, 3 Oz. 8.00
Book, First Edition, 1967, 6 Oz. 10.00
Boot, see also Avon, Fashion Boot; Avon, High-Buttoned Shoe; Avon, Western Boot
Bottled By Avon, Seltzer, 1973, 5 Oz. 8.00
Bowling Pin, see Avon, King Pin
Bridal Moments, 1976, 5 Oz. 10.00
Bucking Bronco, 1971, 6 Oz. ....5.00 to 10.00
Buffalo Nickel, 1971, 5 Oz. 11.00
Butterfly, 1972, 1 1/2 Oz. 7.00
Butterfly Fantasy Porcelain Treasure Egg, 1974 ....10.00 to 15.00
California Perfume Co., Fruit Flavors, Amethyst, 1923, 4 Oz. 40.00
California Perfume Co., Roses, 3-Sided, 1896, 1 Oz. 79.00
Cannon, see also Avon, Revolutionary Cannon
Captain's Lantern 1864, 1976, 7 Oz. 9.00
Captain's Pride, 1970, 6 Oz. 6.00
Car, Bugatti, '27 Model, 1974, 6 1/2 Oz. 14.00
Car, Country Vendor, 1973, 5 Oz. 10.00
Car, Dune Buggy, 1971, 5 Oz. ....*Illus* 10.00
Car, Dune Buggy, 1973, 5 Oz. 10.00
Car, Electric Charger, 1970, 5 Oz. 10.00
Car, Ferrari, 1953 Model, 1974, 2 Oz. 9.00
Car, Rolls Royce, 1972, 6 Oz. ....11.00 to 14.00
Car, Silver Duesenberg, 1970, 6 Oz. 14.00
Car, Stanley Steamer, 1971, 5 Oz. 5.00
Car, Stanley Steamer, Silver, 1978, 5 Oz. 14.00
Car, Station Wagon, 1971, 6 Oz. 13.00
Car, Sterling Six, 1968, 7 Oz. 11.00
Car, Stock Car Racer, 1974, 5 Oz. 9.00
Car, Straight 8, 1969, 5 Oz. ....5.00 to 10.00
Car, Studebaker, 1951 Model, 1975, 2 Oz. 9.00
Car, Stutz Bearcat, 1914 Model, 1974, 6 Oz. 10.00
Car, Thomas Flyer, 1908 Model, 1974, 6 Oz. ....10.00 to 12.00
Car, Thunderbird, 1955 Model, 1974, 2 Oz. 5.00
Car, Touring T, Silver, 1978, 6 Oz. 14.00
Car, Triumph TR-3, 1956 Model, 1975, 2 Oz. 9.00
Car, Volkswagen, Blue, 1973, 4 Oz. 9.00
Casey's Lantern, 1966, 10 Oz. 55.00
Cat, see Avon, Blue Eyes; Avon, Kitten Little; Avon, Kitten Petite; Avon, Ming Cat; Avon, Tabatha
Cement Mixer, 1979, 6 Oz., 3 Piece 14.00
Checker Cab, 1926 Model, 1977, 5 Oz. 10.00
Chief Pontiac, 1976, 4 Oz. 11.00
Christmas Ornament, Silver, 1967, 4 Oz. 14.00
Christmas Soldier, 1980, 3/4 Oz. 6.00
Christmas Surprise, 1976, 1 Oz. 3.00
Clock, see Avon, Leisure Hours
Close Harmony, Barber Bottle, 1963, 8 Oz. 15.00
Coffee Mill, see Avon, Country Store Coffee Mill
Coleman Lantern, 1977, 5 Oz. 10.00
Cologne Spray, Lahana, 1.6 Oz. 10.00
Colt Revolver 1851, 1975, 3 Oz. 10.00
Cornucopia, Milk Glass, 1971, 6 Oz. 9.00
Country Charm Butter Churn, 1973, 1 1/2 Oz. 2.00
Country Kitchen Rooster, Milk Glass, 1973, 6 Oz. 8.00
Country Store Coffee Mill, 1972, 5 Oz. 10.00
Courting Rose, 1974, 1 1/2 Oz. 6.00
Covered Wagon, 1970, 6 Oz. ....6.00 to 11.00
Daylight Shaving Time, 1968, 6 Oz. 15.00
Dear Friends, 1974, 4 Oz. 13.00
Decanter, Angel Song, 1978, 1 Oz. 7.00
Decanter, At Point, 1973, 5 Oz. 10.00
Decanter, Atlantic 4-4-2, 1973, 5 Oz. ....10.00 to 14.00
Decanter, Avon Calling 1905, 1973, 7 Oz. 14.00
Decanter, Avonshire Bath Oil, 1979, 6 Oz. 8.00

Avon, Dollars
'n' Scents,
After-Shave
Lotion, 1966,
8 Oz.

Avon, Car, Dune Buggy, 1971, 5 Oz.

Decanter, Baby Bassett, 1978, 1 1/4 Oz. 3.00
Decanter, Bird Of Paradise Cologne, 1970, 5 Oz. 13.00
Decanter, Cable Car, 1974, 4 Oz. ....10.00 to 14.00
Decanter, Cape Cod, Wine, 1977, 16 Oz. 20.00
Decanter, Capitol, 1976, 4 1/2 Oz. 9.00
Decanter, Capitol, Amber, 1970, 5 Oz. 10.00
Decanter, Country Pump, 1975, 10 Oz. 9.00
Decanter, Domino, 1978, 1 1/2 Oz. 5.00
Decanter, Electric Guitar, 1974, 6 Oz. 13.00
Decanter, Festive Facets, 1979, 1 Oz. ....3.00 to 6.00
Decanter, Gone Fishing, 1973, 5 Oz. 12.00
Decanter, Hammer On The Mark, 1978, 2 1/2 Oz. 8.00
Decanter, Hobnail, 1972, 5 Oz. 6.00
Decanter, Homestead, Brown, 1973, 4 Oz. 9.00
Decanter, Indian Tepee, 1974, 4 Oz. 7.00
Decanter, Jaguar, 1973, 5 Oz. 11.00
Decanter, Little Bo Peep, 1976, 2 Oz. 8.00
Decanter, Maxwell, 1923 Model, 1972, 6 Oz. ....5.00 to 10.00
Decanter, No Cause For Alarm, 1979, 4 Oz. 8.00
Decanter, On Tap Mug, 1979, 4 Oz. 7.00
Decanter, On The Level, Silver Coat Over Clear, 1978, 3 Oz. 6.00
Decanter, Pipe Full, Brown, 1972, 2 Oz. 9.00
Decanter, Porsche, 1968 Model, 1976, 2 Oz. ....5.00 to 9.00
Decanter, Quail, Brown, 1973, 5 1/2 Oz. 9.00
Decanter, Road Runner, 1973, 5 1/2 Oz. ....7.00 to 10.00
Decanter, Sea Legend, 1975, 6 Oz. 4.00
Decanter, Short Pony, 1968, 4 Oz. ....5.00 to 10.00
Decanter, Skin-So-Soft, 1964, 6 Oz. ....5.00 to 10.00
Decanter, Skin-So-Soft, 1965, 10 Oz. ....8.00 to 12.00
Decanter, Spark Plug, Milk Glass, 1975, 1 1/2 Oz. 6.00
Decanter, Sport Of Kings, 1975, 5 Oz. 10.00
Decanter, Strike, 1978, 4 Oz. ....4.00 to 6.00
Decanter, Sure Winner Slugger, Yellow Plastic Bat, 1973, 6 Oz. 4.00
Decanter, Tee-Off, 1973, 3 Oz. ....5.00 to 8.00
Decanter, Thermos, Plaid, 1978, 3 Oz. 5.00
Decanter, Totem Pole, 1975, 6 Oz. ....7.00 to 10.00
Decisions, 1965, 8 Oz. ....10.00 to 20.00
Derringer, 1977, 2 Oz. 10.00
Dog, see Avon, Faithful Laddie; Avon, Lady Spaniel; Avon, Noble Prince; Avon, Snoopy Surprise
Dollars 'n' Scents, After-Shave Lotion, 1966, 8 Oz. ....*Illus* 20.00
Dolphin, 1968, 8 Oz. ....8.00 to 11.00
Dovecote, 1974, 4 Oz. 4.00
Duck, see Avon, Mallard Duck
Dueling Pistoll 1760, 1973, 4 Oz. ....10.00 to 12.00
Dutch Maid, 1977, 4 Oz. 9.00
Electric Charger, see Avon, Car, Electric Charger

Elizabethan Fashion Figurine, 1972, 4 Oz. ....15.00 to 20.00
Enchanted Frog Cream Sachet, 1973, 1 1/4 Oz. 5.00
Extra Special Male, 1977, 3 Oz. ....5.00 to 9.00
Faithful Laddie, Amber, 1977, 4 Oz. 8.00
Fashion Boot, Pincushion Top, 1972, 4 Oz. 8.00
Father Christmas, Stein, 1994, 9 1/2 In. 25.00
Fielder's Choice, Brown, 1971, 5 Oz. 11.00
Firefighter 1910, 1975, 6 Oz. 9.00
First Class Male, 1970, 4 Oz. 9.00
First Down, 1973, 5 Oz. 9.00
First Edition, see Avon, Book, First Edition
First Prayer, 1981, 1 1/2 Oz. 8.00
First Volunteer, 1971, 6 Oz. 14.00
Fish, see Avon, Dolphin; Avon, Sea Spirit
Flamingo, 1971, 5 Oz. 7.00
Flower Maiden, 1973, 4 Oz. 9.00
Fly-A-Balloon, 1975, 3 Oz. 10.00
Football, see Avon, First Down
Fragrance Fling Trio, 1968, 1/2 Oz., 3 Piece 15.00
Fragrance Hours, Ivory, 1971, 6 Oz. 10.00
Fragrance Splendor, 1971, 4 1/2 In. ....4.00 to 6.00
Garden Girl, 1975, 4 Oz. 12.00
Garnet Bud Vase, 1973, 3 Oz. 4.00
Gay Nineties Set, 1974, 3 Oz. 13.00
General 4-4-0, 1971, 5 1/2 Oz. ....10.00 to 14.00
Golden Harvest, 1977, 10 Oz. ....3.00 to 6.00
Golden Rocket 022, 1974, 6 Oz. 14.00
Golden Thimble, 1972, 2 Oz. 5.00
Golf, see Avon, Swinger Golf Bag
Good Luck Elephant, 1975, 1 1/2 Oz. 6.00
Goodyear Blimp, 1978, 2 Oz. 10.00
Grecian Pitcher, Milk Glass, 1972, 5 Oz. 9.00
Hardhat, 1977, 4 Oz. 7.00
Harvester Tractor, 1973, 5 1/2 Oz. 14.00
Head, see Avon, Tribute Silver Warrior
Hearth Lamp, 1973, 8 Oz. 12.00
Heartscent Cream Sachet, 1976, .66 Oz. ....2.00 to 4.00
High-Buttoned Shoe, 1975, 2 Oz. 5.00
Hudson Locomotive 700E, 1993, 9 In. 35.00
Hummingbird, Goblet, 1994, 7 3/4 In., Pair ....25.00 to 30.00
Icicle Perfume, 1967, 1 Dram 8.00
Indian Chieftain, 1972, 4 Oz. 8.00
Indian Head Penny, 1970, 4 Oz. 11.00
Jolly Santa, 1978, 1 Oz. 3.00
Just A Twist, 1977, 2 Oz. 7.00
King Pin, 1960, 4 Oz. 10.00
Kitten Little, Milk Glass, 1972, 1 1/2 Oz. 7.00
Kitten Petite, White Plastic, Amber Ball, 1973, 1 1/2 Oz. 7.00
Kitten's Hideaway, 1974, 1 Oz. 6.00
Koffee Klatch, 1971, 5 Oz. 8.00
La Belle Telephone, 1974, 1 Oz. 9.00
Lady Spaniel, 1974, 1 1/2 Oz. 5.00
Lamp, Aladdin's, 1971, 6 Oz. 10.00
Lamp, Courting, 1970, 5 Oz. 10.00
Lamp, Library, 1976, 4 Oz. 10.00
Lamp, Mansion, 1975, 6 Oz. 10.00
Lamp, Ming Blue, 1974, 5 Oz. 8.00
Lamp, Parlor, 1971, 3 Oz. 12.00
Lamp, Tiffany, 1972, 5 Oz. ....10.00 to 13.00
Lamp Chimney, 1973, 2 Oz. 5.00
Lantern, see Casey's Lantern
Leisure Hours, Milk Glass, 1970, 5 Oz. 10.00
Leisure Hours, Milk Glass, 1974, 1 1/2 Oz. 6.00

Liberty Dollar, 1970, 6 Oz. . . . . .5.00 to 11.00
Lincoln Bottle, 1971, 4 Oz. . . . . .4.00 to 8.00
Lip Pop Colas, 1973, 13 Oz. 7.00
Little Girl Blue, 1972, 3 Oz. 9.00
Little Kate, 1973, 3 Oz. 10.00
Little Lamb, 1977, 3/4 Oz. 6.00
Little Miss Muffett, 1978, 2 Oz. 7.00
Locker Time, 1977, 6 Oz. 4.00
Love Song, 1973, Frosted, 6 Oz. 3.00
Lucy, Bubble Bath, 1970, 4 Oz. 5.00
Mallard Duck, 1967, 6 Oz. 13.00
Man's World, Globe, Plastic Stand, 1969, 6 Oz. . . . . .10.00 to 14.00
Marine Binoculars, 1973, 4 Oz. . . . . .10.00 to 12.00
Mary Mary, 1977, 2 Oz. 9.00
Ming Cat, 1971, 6 Oz. 10.00
Mini-Bike, 1972, 4 Oz. . . . . .6.00 to 9.00
NAAC, 10th Annual Club, 1981, 7 In. . . . . .15.00 to 25.00
NAAC Club Bottle, Box, 1972, 7 In. 300.00
Nile Green Bath Urn, 1975, 6 Oz. 5.00
Noble Prince, Brown, 1975, 4 Oz. 9.00
Occur! 1963, 1/2 Oz. . . . .*Illus* 6.00
One Good Turn Screwdriver, 1976, 4 Oz. 8.00
Oriental Egg Peach Orchard, 1974, 1 Oz. 7.00
Ornament, see Avon, Christmas Ornament
Owl, see Avon, Wise Choice Owl
Owl Fancy, 1974, 4 Oz. . . . . .2.00 to 4.00
Paid Stamp, Amber, 1970, 5 In. 10.00
Pass Play, 1973, 5 Oz. . . . . .9.00 to 12.00
Pepperbox Pistol 1850, 1979, 3 Oz. 8.00
Period Piece, 1972, 5 Oz. 8.00
Persian Pitcher, 1974, 6 Oz. . . . . .1.00 to 3.00
Pert Penguin, 1975, 1 Oz. . . . . .2.00 to 5.00
Petti Fleur Cologne, 1969, 1 Oz. 8.00
Pheasant, 1972, 5 Oz. 11.00
Philadelphia Derringer, 1980, 2 Oz. 11.00
Piano, Dark Amber, 1972, 4 Oz. 11.00
Pineapple, 1973, 10 Oz. . . . . .2.00 to 5.00
Pineapple Petite, 1972, 1 Oz. . . . . .1.00 to 5.00
Pipe, American Eagle, Amber, 1974, 5 Oz. 11.00
Pipe, Bulldog, Cream Milk Glass, 1972, 6 Oz. 11.00
Pipe, Collector's, 1973, 3 Oz. 8.00
Pipe, Corncob, Amber, 1974, 3 Oz. 8.00
Pipe, Dutch, 1973, 2 Oz. 9.00
Pipe, Pony Express Rider, 1975, 3 Oz. 9.00
Pipe, Uncle Sam, White Opalescent, 1975, 3 Oz. 9.00

Avon, Occur!,
1963, 1/2 Oz.

Avon, Write
Touch Mouse,
1982, 1 Oz.

Pistol, see Avon, Pepperbox Pistol
Pony Post, Bronze Paint Over Clear, 1972, 5 Oz. 9.00
Pony Post, Green, Tall, 1966, 8 Oz. ....12.00 to 18.00
Pony Post, Miniature, 1973, 1 1/2 Oz. 4.00
Pony Post, Short, 1973, 5 Oz. 6.00
Potbelly Stove, Black, 1970, 5 Oz. 10.00
Precious Doe, 1976, 1/2 Oz. 5.00
Precious Priscilla, 1982, 3 Oz. 10.00
President Washington, 1974, 6 Oz. ....5.00 to 6.00
Prima Ballerina, 1981, 1 Oz. 7.00
Proud Groom, 1978, 2 Oz. 9.00
Pump, see Avon, Town Pump
Queen Chess Piece, Oland, 1973, 3 Oz. 8.00
Radio, 1972, 5 Oz. ....7.00 to 10.00
Rainbow Trout, 1973, 5 Oz. 10.00
Remember When Gas Pump, 1976, 4 Oz. ....10.00 to 16.00
Reo Depot Wagon, 1972, 5 Oz. 13.00
Revolutionary Cannon, 1975, 2 Oz. ....6.00 to 9.00
Right Connection, Fuse, 1977, 1 1/2 Oz. ....4.00 to 6.00
Rolling Great Roller Skate, 1980, 2 Oz. 5.00
Rooster, see Avon, Country Kitchen
Royal Orb, 1965, 8 Oz. 22.00
Royal Pekinese, 1974, 1 1/2 Oz. 7.00
Royal Siamese Cat, 1978, 4 1/2 Oz. 8.00
Royal Swan, Blue, 1974, 1 Oz. 8.00
Royal Swan, White Glass, 1971, 1 Oz. 8.00
Ruby Bud Vase, 1970, 3 Oz. 5.00
Scimitar, 1968, 6 Oz. 25.00
Scottish Lass, 1975, 4 Oz. 10.00
Sea Fantasy Bud Vase, 1978, 6 Oz. 4.00
Sea Horse, 1970, 6 Oz. 9.00
Sea Horse, 1973, 1 1/2 Oz. 5.00
Sea Maiden, Skin-So-Soft, 1971, 6 Oz. 10.00
Sea Spirit, Milk Glass, 1973, 5 Oz. 5.00
Side-Wheeler, Amber, 1971, 5 Oz. 12.00
Silver Fawn, 1978, 5 Oz. 4.00
Skip-A-Rope Cologne, 1977, 4 Oz. 8.00
Smooth Going, Oil Can, 1978, 1 1/2 Oz. ....4.00 to 7.00
Snail, Perfume, 1968, 1/4 Oz. 10.00
Sniffy Skunk, 1978, 1 1/4 Oz. 6.00
Snoopy Surprise, 1969, 5 Oz. 10.00
Snow Bunny, 1975, 3 Oz. 6.00
Snow Man Petite Perfume, 1973, 1/4 Oz. 7.00
Snowmobile, 1974, 4 Oz. ....7.00 to 10.00
Song Bird, 1971, 1 1/2 Oz. 6.00
Spanish Senorita, 1975, 4 Oz. 12.00
Spirit Of St. Louis, 1970, 6 Oz. ....8.00 to 14.00
Spring Tulip Hostess Soaps, 1970, Box, 6 Piece 4.00
Stagecoach, 1970, 5 Oz. ....8.00 to 10.00
Stein, A Century Of Basketball, 1993, 9 1/2 In. 50.00
Stein, Age Of The Iron Horse, 1982, 8 1/2 In. ....35.00 to 40.00
Stein, America The Beautiful, 1998, 9 1/2 In. 45.00
Stein, American Wildlife, 1995, 9 1/2 In. 45.00
Stein, American Wildlife, 1997 .... 25.00
Stein, Armed Forces, 1990, 9 1/4 In. ....30.00 to 45.00
Stein, Babe Ruth, Legend Of The Century, 1999, 9 In. 50.00
Stein, Blacksmith, 1985, 8 1/2 In. ....30.00 to 40.00
Stein, Car Classics, 1979, 9 In. ....30.00 to 40.00
Stein, Christmas Carol, 1996, 9 1/2 In. 45.00
Stein, Christopher Columbus, 1992, 12 In. ....35.00 to 45.00
Stein, Conquest Of Space, 1991, 9 3/4 In. ....35.00 to 45.00
Stein, Country & Western Music, 1994, 8 1/4 In. ....30.00 to 40.00
Stein, Ducks Of American Wilderness, 1988, 8 3/4 In. ....35.00 to 45.00

Stein, Endangered Species, Asian Elephant, 1990, 5 1/4 In. . . . . .15.00 to 20.00
Stein, Endangered Species, Bald Eagle, 1990, 5 1/4 In. . . . . .15.00 to 20.00
Stein, Father Christmas, 1994, 9 1/2 In. . . . . .30.00 to 40.00
Stein, Fishing, 1990, 8 1/2 In. . . . . .30.00 to 45.00
Stein, Giant Panda, 1991, 5 1/2 In. 20.00
Stein, Gold Rush, 1987, 8 1/2 In. . . . . .30.00 to 40.00
Stein, Great American Baseball, 1984, 8 3/4 In. 40.00
Stein, Great American Football, 1982, 9 In. . . . . .35.00 to 40.00
Stein, Great American Wildlife, 1995, 9 1/2 In. 45.00
Stein, Great Dogs Of Outdoors, 1991, 9 In. . . . . .35.00 to 45.00
Stein, Hunters, 1972, 8 Oz. . . . . .8.00 to 15.00
Stein, Indians Of The American Frontier, 1988, 9 In. 40.00
Stein, Jaguar, 1991, 5 1/2 In. 20.00
Stein, Knight Of The Realm, 1995, 9 1/2 In. 45.00
Stein, Miniature Flying Classics, 1982, 4 1/2 In. 15.00
Stein, Mountain Zebra, 1992, 5 1/2 In. 20.00
Stein, Racing Car, 1989, 9 1/4 In. . . . . .40.00 to 50.00
Stein, Shipbuilder, 1986, 8 1/2 In. 50.00
Stein, Shipbuilder, 1986, Box, 8 1/2 In. 50.00
Stein, Silver, 1968, 6 Oz. . . . . .6.00 to 12.00
Stein, Sperm Whale, 1992, 5 1/2 In. 20.00
Stein, Sporting Stein, 1978, 9 In. 35.00
Stein, Tall Ships, 1977, 4 1/2 In. 40.00
Stein, Tribute To Firefighters, 1989, 9 In. . . . . .30.00 to 50.00
Stein, Tribute To Rescue Worker, 1997, 9 1/2 In. 45.00
Stein, Western Round Up, 1983, 5 In. 1.00
Stein, Wild West, 1993, 8 1/2 In. 50.00
Stein, Winner's Circle, 1992, 10 In. . . . . .35.00 to 40.00
Stop 'n Go, Green, 1974, 4 Oz. 7.00
Super Cycle, 1972, 4 Oz. 7.00
Super Cycle, Blue, 1974, 4 Oz. 10.00
Sure Winner Racing Car, 1972, 5 1/2 Oz. 10.00
Sure Winner Baseball, 1973, 4 Oz. 4.00
Swan Lake, Milk Glass, 1972, 3 Oz. 6.00
Sweet Shoppe Pincushion, 1972, 1 Oz. 8.00
Swinger Golf Bag, 1969, 5 Oz. 11.00
Sword, see Avon, Scimitar
Tabatha, 1975, 3 Oz. 8.00
Telephone, see Avon, La Belle Telephone
Theodore Roosevelt, 1975, 6 Oz. 8.00
Town Pump, 1968, 6 Oz. . . . . .8.00 to 13.00
Toy Soldier, 1964, 4 Oz. 12.00
Train, see Avon, General 4-4-0
Tree Mouse, 1977, .66 Oz. 4.00
Tribute Silver Warrior, 1967, 6 Oz. 23.00
Triple Crown, 1974, 4 Oz. . . . . .4.00 to 7.00
Truck, Mail, Extra Special Male, 1977, 3 Oz. 5.00
Venetian Pitcher, Blue, 1973, 3 Oz. 5.00
Victorian Washstand, 1973, 4 Oz. 8.00
Viking Discoverer, 1977, 4 Oz. . . . . .7.00 to 12.00
Viking Horn, Dark Amber, 1966, 7 Oz. 15.00
Volkswagen, Black, 1972, 4 Oz. 7.00
Volkswagen Bus, 1975, 5 Oz. 11.00
Warrior, see also Avon, Tribute
Washington Bottle, 1970, 4 Oz. . . . . .3.00 to 7.00
Wedding Flower Maiden, 1979, 1 3/4 Oz. 8.00
Western Boot, 1973, 5 Oz. 7.00
Western Choice, Steer Horns, 1967, Holds 2 Bottles, 3 Oz. 17.00
Wild Turkey, Amber, 1974, 5 Oz. 9.00
Wild West Bullet, 1977, 1 1/2 Oz. 5.00
Wilderness Classic, 1976, 6 Oz. 12.00
Winnebago Motor Home, 1978, 5 Oz. 12.00

Ballantine, Fisherman, 1969

Ballantine, Knight, 1969

Ballantine, Mallard Duck, 1969

Wise Choice Owl, 1969, 4 Oz. 10.00
Write Touch Mouse, 1982, 1 Oz. .... *Illus* 6.00

BALLANTINE

Ballantine's Scotch was sold in figural bottles in 1969. The five bottles were shaped like a golf bag, knight, mallard, zebra, or fisherman. Ballantine also made some flasks and jugs with special designs.

Charioteer, Flask, 1969 .... 5.00 to 10.00
Discus Thrower, Flask, 1969 .... 10.00
Fisherman, 1969 .... *Illus* 12.00
Gladiator, Flask, 1969 .... 5.00 to 8.00
Golf Bag, 1969 .... 10.00
Knight, 1969 .... *Illus* 15.00
Mallard Duck, 1969 .... *Illus* 15.00
Zebra, 1969 .... 15.00 to 18.00

BARBER

The nineteenth-century barber either made his own hair tonic or purchased it in large containers. Barber bottles were used at the barbershop or in the home. The barber filled the bottles each day with hair oil, bay rum, tonic, shampoo, witch hazel, rosewater, or some other cosmetic. He knew what was inside each bottle because of its distinctive shape and color. Most of the important types of art glass were used for barber bottles. Spatter glass, milk glass, cranberry, cobalt, cut, hobnail, vaseline, and opalescent glass were used alone or in attractive combinations. Some were made with enamel-painted decorations. Most of the bottles were blown. A pontil mark can be found on the bottom of many bottles. These special fancy bottles were popular during the last half of the nineteenth-century. In 1906 the Pure Food and Drug Act made it illegal to use refillable, nonlabeled bottles in a barbershop, and the bottles were no longer used.

Amber, Bulbous Base, Swirled, Stopper, Polished Pontil, 8 x 4 In. 195.00
Amber, Faceted, Porcelain Stopper, Pontil, Art Nouveau, 8 In. 330.00
Amber, Hobnail, Bulbous Base, 4-Ring Neck, 7 1/4 x 4 1/4 In. 150.00
Amberina, Silver Overlay, Sheared Lip, 8 In. 1430.00
Amberina, Spatter, Stopper, Ground Pontil, 6 1/2 In. 160.00
Amethyst, Lady's Leg Neck, Enamel Flowers, Rolled Lip, Pontil, 7 1/2 In. 110.00
Amethyst, Mallet, White Enamel Flowers, Flared Lip, Pontil, 7 3/4 In. .... *Illus* 121.00
Amethyst, Pewter Overlay, Cherries, Plums, Grapes, Flared Lip, Pontil, 8 In., Pair 1210.00
Amethyst, Pinched Waist, White, Ribs, Orange, Pontil, 1890-1925, 7 3/4 In. 110.00
Amethyst, Polished Band, Orange Enamel, Gold, White Flowers, 6 3/4 x 3 3/4 In. 200.00
Amethyst, Ribs, Cone Shape, Flowers, OP, 7 In. 69.00
Amethyst, White Enamel Daisies, Polished Pontil, 7 x 3 1/2 In. 110.00
Apple Green, White Enamel Flowers, Orange Center, Rough Pontil, 7 x 3 1/2 In. 225.00
Aqua Blue, White Swirl, c.1880, 8 x 3 1/2 In. 275.00
Aug. Kern Barber Supply Co., Cologne, Milk Glass, Enamel Flowers, 1925, 8 1/2 In. 200.00
Bay Rum, Amber, Monogram, Applied Lip, Reddington & Co., San Francisco, 10 In. 110.00
Bay Rum, Blue Milk Glass, Red Flowers, Green Leaves, Rolled Lip, Pontil, 8 3/4 In. 5880.00

Bay Rum, C.F. Hawman, Milk Glass, Multicolored Cottage, Leaves, 9 1/2 In. 660.00
Bay Rum, George Clark, Milk Glass, Label, Neck Band, Stopper, 10 7/8 In. 2070.00
Bay Rum, John W. Shaffer, Rose, Cabin Scene, Pewter Stopper, 10 1/4 In. 292.00
Bay Rum, Milk Glass, Clover, Green & Red Enamel, Rolled Lip, 9 In. 110.00
Bay Rum, Milk Glass, Dark Powder Blue, Pretty Woman, Screw Stopper, 11 In. 2352.00
Bay Rum, Milk Glass, Enamel Horseshoe, Flowers, 1920, 9 1/8 In. 210.00
Bay Rum, Milk Glass, Enamel Rose, Applied Lip, 1885-1925, 9 1/8 In. 220.00
Bay Rum, Milk Glass, Enamel Tulip, 8 5/8 In. 405.00
Bay Rum, Milk Glass, Multicolored Enamel Flowers, 1890-1925, 9 1/4 In. 280.00
Bay Rum, Milk Glass, Multicolored Scene, Gold Letters, 8 1/2 In. 110.00
Bay Rum, Milk Glass, Multicolored, Pretty Woman, Screw Stopper, 10 7/8 In. 2072.00
Bay Rum, Milk Glass, Opalescent, Clover, Pontil, 1865-1925, 9 1/2 In. 303.00
Bay Rum, Milk Glass, Opalescent, Multicolored Enamel Sparrows, Rolled Lip, 8 7/8 In. . 336.00
Bay Rum, Milk Glass, Shampoo, Toilet Water, 7 3/4 In., 3 Bottles 77.00
Bay Rum, Yellow Green, White Enamel Grist Mill, Pontil, 8 1/8 In. 1036.00
Bell Shape, Amethyst, Enamel, Sheared Lip, OP, 7 1/2 In. 132.00
Bell Shape, Amethyst, Ribs, Multicolored Enamel Stag In Oval Frame, 8 In. 715.00
Bell Shape, Blue, Enamel Flowers, Pinched Waist, OP, 7 1/2 In. 303.00
Bell Shape, Clear, Fluted, Shield, Cork Stopper, 10 3/4 In. 25.00
Bell Shape, Cobalt Blue, Enamel Flowers, Ribs, Pontil, 1925, 7 5/8 In. 360.00
Bell Shape, Cobalt Blue, White, Yellow Design, Ribs, Pontil, 1890-1925, 7 7/8 In. 231.00
Bell Shape, Grape Amethyst, Ribs, Multicolored Enamel Stag In Oval, Pontil, 8 In. 532.00
Bell Shape, Purple Amethyst, White, Orange, Gold Enamel, Ribs, 1910, 6 7/8 In. 336.00
Bell Shape, Ruby Red, Etched Clear, Red Bird, Stopper, 6 3/4 In. 468.00
Black Amethyst, White Enamel & Gilt Berries, Neck, Tooled Lip, 7 7/8 In. 392.00
Blue, Melon Ribs, Orange, Yellow, Pink & White Enamel, BR On Base, 3 In. 880.00
Blue & Cranberry, Opalescent Stripes, 7 1/2 In. 58.00
Blue Diamonds, Satin Glass, Sheared Lip, Pontil, 8 In. 110.00
Blue Green, Frosted, Berries & Leaves, Ribs, 1890-1925, 8 In. 495.00
Blue Green, White Enamel Flowers, Ribs, Pontil, 1890-1925, 7 1/4 In. 72.00
Blue Green, White, Gold Enamel Design, Ribs, Tooled Lip, 1890-1925, 6 3/4 In. 105.00
Blue Opalescent, Daisy & Fern, Rolled Lip, 7 1/2 In. 121.00
Blue Opalescent, Ferns, Melon Ribs, Rolled Lip, 7 1/2 In. 121.00
Blue Satin On White, Enamel Daisies, 7 1/2 In. 275.00
Blue Stars & Stripes, Rolled Lip, Polished Pontil, 7 In. 165.00
Brilliantine, Amethyst, Tooled Lip, 3 7/8 In. 413.00
Brilliantine, Amethyst, White Enamel, Polished Lip, 3 3/4 In. 798.00
Brilliantine, Bell Shape, Yellow Topaz, Tooled Lip, 1925, 3 7/8 In. 155.00
Brilliantine, Cobalt Blue, 2 Indented Panels, 3 1/8 In. 415.00
Brilliantine, Cobalt Blue, Red, Gold Enamel, Brass Neck, 1925, 4 In. 364.00
Brilliantine, Cut Glass, Ruby Red Overlay, 1890-1925, 5 1/8 In. 257.00
Brilliantine, Emerald Green, Yellow, Orange, White Flowers, Ribs, 1890-1925, 4 In. 448.00
Brilliantine, Frosted Cobalt Blue, Flowers, Brass Neck Band, Cap, 3 3/4 In. 660.00
Brilliantine, Light Pink Topaz, Tooled Lip, 3 7/8 In. 253.00
Brilliantine, Milk Glass, Multicolored Enamel, Light Blue Ground, 4 3/4 In. 1155.00
Brilliantine, Pink Orange, 1890-1925, 4 In. 532.00
Brilliantine, Purple Amethyst, White Design, Ribs, 3 In. 355.00
Brilliantine, Purple Amethyst, White Enamel, Crown Type Stopper, 3 3/4 In. 616.00
Brilliantine, Purple Amethyst, White Enamel, Polished Lip, 3 3/4 In. 800.00
Brilliantine, Ruby Red, Tooled Lip, Metal Stopper 121.00
Brilliantine, Turquoise Blue, White, Orange Enamel, 1890-1925, 4 In. 420.00
Brilliantine, Turquoise, Enamel Flowers, Ribs, 3 7/8 In. 690.00
Brilliantine, Turquoise, Ribs, Pink, Green Enamel Flowers, Tooled, 3 7/8 In. 688.00
Brilliantine, Yellow Green, White, Orange Enamel, Ribs, 1890-1925, 3 3/8 In. 616.00
Bristol Glass, Painted, Cherub, Sheared Lip, Pontil 165.00
Chocolate Spatter, Tortoiseshell, Pontil, 1885-1925, 8 In. 220.00
Clear, Gold & Purple Enamel, Etched, Flared Lip, Pontil, 6 3/4 In. 165.00
Clear, Raised Letters, Bottle Loaned By F.W. Finch Co., Rubber Cap, 8 In. 35.00
Clear, Removable Metal Stopper Imbedded In Cork, 6 In. 15.00
Clear, Ribs, Pale Smoky Sapphire, White, Green Flowers, Tooled Lip, Pontil, 7 7/8 In. ... 420.00
Clear, Seafoam Cut In Shoulder, Red Flashed Neck & Shoulder, 6 3/4 In. 305.00
Clear, Silver Overlay, Flowers, Polished Pontil, 7 1/2 In. 358.00
Clear Over Blue, White & Copper Spatter, Ground Pontil, 11 In. 330.00

Clear Over Milk Glass, Gold Design, Milan, Italy, 8 1/2 In. 165.00
Clear Over Ruby, Ribs, Enamel Flowers, Pontil, 1890-1925, 8 In. 198.00
Cobalt Blue, 3 Molded Thumbprint Rows, 1890-1925, 6 1/2 In. 237.00
Cobalt Blue, Enamel Tulips, Leaves & Grass, Ground Lip, Black Stopper, 7 In. 440.00
Cobalt Blue, Girl With Butterfly, Mary Gregory Type, Pontil, 1885-1925, 8 In. 260.00
Cobalt Blue, Gold & Enamel Dots, Pinched Waist, 7 1/2 In. 385.00
Cobalt Blue, Mallet, Enamel Flowers, Rolled Lip, OP, 8 In. 110.00
Cobalt Blue, Mallet, Enamel Flowers, Sheared Lip, OP, 1925, 8 In. 110.00
Cobalt Blue, Mallet, Jade & White Enamel, Sheared Lip, OP, 8 In. 110.00
Cobalt Blue, Mallet, Orange, Yellow, White Enamel, Rolled Lip, 8 In. 99.00
Cobalt Blue, Mary Gregory Type, White Enamel Boy Playing Tennis, 8 In. 165.00
Cobalt Blue, Mary Gregory Type, White Enamel Girl Playing Tennis, 8 In. 330.00
Cobalt Blue, Melon Ribs, Flowers & Butterfly, Pontil, 1885-1925, 8 1/4 In. 148.00
Cobalt Blue, Melon Ribs, Pewter Stopper, 8 1/2 In. 69.00
Cobalt Blue, Opalescent Swirl, Tooled Lip, 7 3/4 In. 963.00
Cobalt Blue, Ribs, Bell Shape, White, Yellow, Pink Enamel Flowers, 7 5/8 In. 358.00
Cobalt Blue, Ribs, Enamel Flowers, Pinched Waist, Pontil, 1890-1925, 7 5/8 In. 220.00
Cobalt Blue, Ribs, Enamel Flowers, Pinched Waist, Pontil, 7 5/8 In. 275.00
Cobalt Blue, Ribs, Enamel Flowers, Pontil, 1925, 7 1/4 In. 1020.00
Cobalt Blue, Ribs, Green, White, Orange Enamel Flowers, 1890-1925, 8 In. 140.00
Cobalt Blue, Ribs, Multicolored Enamel Flowers, Pontil, 7 1/4 In. 420.00
Cobalt Blue, Ribs, Multicolored Roses, 8 1/8 In. 550.00
Cobalt Blue, Ribs, Pinched Waist, Multicolored Enamel Flowers, Rolled Lip, 7 5/8 In. . . . 275.00
Cobalt Blue, Ribs, Pinched Waist, White & Yellow Enamel Flowers, Pontil, 7 5/8 In. 280.00
Cobalt Blue, Thumbprint, Enamel, Rolled Lip, Pontil, 1885-1925, 8 In. 154.00
Cobalt Blue, Thumbprint, Lady's Leg Neck, White Enamel, Pontil, 8 1/4 In. 110.00
Cobalt Blue, White & Orange Enamel, Rolled Lip, OP, 8 1/2 In. 132.00
Cobalt Blue, White Core, Melon Ribs, Lady's Leg Neck, Metal Stopper 88.00
Cobalt Blue, White Enamel, 1890-1925, 8 In. 2576.00
Cobalt Blue, White, Gold Enamel Flowers, Ribs, 1890-1925, 7 5/8 In. 532.00
Coin Spot, Aqua Satin, White Core, Swirls On Neck, Metal Stopper 330.00
Coin Spot, Cranberry Opalescent, Melon Ribs, Tooled Lip, 7 1/8 In. 90.00
Coin Spot, Frosted Lime Green Enamel, 1890-1925, 8 In. 364.00
Coin Spot, Teal Blue, Melon Ribs, Tooled Lip, 8 5/8 In. 90.00
Coin Spot, Turquoise Blue Flowers, 1890-1925, 9 1/4 In. 2352.00
Coin Spot, Turquoise Opalescent, Melon Ribs, Rolled Lip, 7 1/4 In. 134.00
Coin Spot, Yellow Amber, 1890-1925, 7 1/4 In. 392.00
Coral Shaded To White, White Core, Satin Glass, Pinched Waist, Stopper, 7 1/2 In. 1100.00
Cornflower Blue, Enamel Flowers, Ribbed Swirl Around Neck, Broken Pontil, 9 1/2 In. . . 225.00
Crackle, Ruby Red, 1890-1925, 7 3/4 In. 448.00
Cranberry, Gold Flowers, Enamel, Sheared Lip, Ground Pontil, 8 1/2 In. 1320.00
Cranberry, Gold Leaves & Flowers, Stopper, Pontil, 8 In. 2750.00
Cranberry, Hobnail, Rolled Lip, 4-Ring Neck, Polished Pontil, 7 x 4 In. 225.00
Cranberry, Melon Ribs, Reversed Thumbprint, Lady's Leg Neck, 8 In. 88.00
Cranberry, Porcelain Stopper, Cork, Victorian, 8 In. 318.00
Cranberry, Ribs, White, Blue Enamel Flowers, Tooled Lip, 7 1/4 In. 798.00
Cranberry, Thumbprint, Stopper, 8 1/2 In. 204.00
Cranberry, Tilting, Brass Wire Casing, Word Madeleine Under Building, 10 In. 825.00
Cranberry, White Spatter, Metal Stopper, Polished Pontil, 9 1/4 In. 275.00
Cranberry, White Spatter, Polished Pontil, 12 In. 264.00
Cranberry Flash, Cut Flowers, ABM, 1920-1930, 8 In. 77.00
Cranberry Opalescent, Daisy & Fern, Melon Ribs, Tooled Lip, 7 3/8 In. 364.00
Cranberry Opalescent, Melon Ribs, 7 In. . . . . .Illus 170.00
Cranberry Opalescent, Melon Ribs, Vertical Stripes, Porcelain Stopper, 8 1/4 In. 253.00
Cranberry Opalescent, Pink Vertical Stripes, Melon Ribs 110.00
Cranberry Opalescent, Seaweed, Rolled Lip, Original Porcelain Stopper, 10 In. 450.00
Cranberry Opalescent, Seawood, Tapered, Stopper, 8 In. 297.00
Cranberry Opalescent, Spatter, 1890-1925, 11 7/8 In. 364.00
Cranberry Opalescent, Spatter, Tooled Mouth, 9 3/8 In. .258.00 to 269.00
Cranberry Opalescent, Stars & Stripes, Rolled Lip, Improved Pontil, 7 In. 303.00
Cranberry Opalescent, White Hobnail, Metal Stopper, Polished Pontil 77.00
Cranberry Opalescent, White Hobnail, Tooled Lip, Pontil, 7 In. 134.00
Cranberry Opalescent, White Stars & Stripes, Rolled Lip, Pontil, 7 1/4 In. 176.00

Barber, Cranberry
Opalescent,
Melon Ribs, 7 In.

Barber, Emerald Green,
Gold Enamel, Flared Lip,
Pontil, Art Nouveau, 8 3/4 In.

Barber, Amethyst, Mallet,
White Enamel Flowers,
Flared Lip, Pontil, 7 3/4 In.

Cranberry Opalescent, White Stripes, Melon Ribs, Tooled Lip, 7 1/4 In. 168.00
Cranberry Opalescent, White Stripes, Polished Pontil, 1925, 7 In. 440.00
Cranberry Opalescent Splotch, Step Design, 1890-1925, 8 3/8 In. 336.00
Cream Color, Marked MA Co., 7 In. 110.00
Cut Glass, Bulbous Base, Unpolished Pontil, 7 x 4 1/4 In. 225.00
Cut Glass, Starburst, Initials C.S.W., Sterling Stopper, 7 1/2 In. 165.00
Cylindrical, Pinched Waist, Amethyst, Enamel Flowers, c.1920, 7 In. 209.00
Dark Purple Amethyst, White, Gold Enamel, 1890-1925, 8 1/8 In. 257.00
Dark Teal Green, Mary Gregory Type, White Enamel Girl Holding Flowers, 8 In. 385.00
De Vry's Exquise Tonique, Purple Amethyst, Ribs, Enamel, 1925, 7 3/4 In. 1265.00
Diamond, Light Yellow Amber, Multicolored Enamel Flowers, 1890-1925, 10 In. 1792.00
Dr. Jayne's Hair Tonic, Philada., Rolled Lip, OP, 4 1/2 In. 66.00
Emerald Green, Gold Enamel, Flared Lip, Pontil, Art Nouveau, 8 3/4 In. ....*Illus* 187.00
Emerald Green, Mary Gregory Type, White Enamel Boy With Net, Stopper 303.00
Emerald Green, Ribs, Multicolored Enamel Flowers, Tooled Lip, Pontil, 7 1/4 In. 672.00
Emerald Green, Silver Overlay Flowers, Rolled Lip, 7 5/8 In. 303.00
Emerald Green, Thumbprint, Squat, Long Neck, 7 1/4 In. 143.00
Emerald Green, White Enamel Flowers, Dotted Band Above Bulbous Base, 7 x 3 In. 200.00
Enamel Flowers, Flared Neck, 7 1/2 In. 129.00
Enamel Girl, Offering Flowers, Milk Glass Shaker Cup, 8 1/2 In. 220.00
Fenton, Jamestown Blue, 9 1/2 x 4 In. 200.00
Frosted Lime Green Enamel, Ribs, 1890-1925, 8 In. 336.00
Frosted Pink, Amethyst Glass, White, Yellow, Gold Enamel Flowers, 1925, 7 1/4 In. 1792.00
Frosted Turquoise Blue, Ribs, White, Gold Enamel, Enamel, 1890-1925, 7 5/8 In. 336.00
Grape Amethyst, Ribs, Straight Sides, Red, White Enamel Flowers, Pontil, 5 5/8 In. 157.00
Grass Green, Mallet, Enamel Design, Rolled Lip, 1895-1925, 8 In. 99.00
Green, Enamel Design, Rolled Lip, OP, 6 1/2 In. 121.00
Green, Enamel Flowers, Orange Centers, White Overlay Stopper, 1880s, 9 In. 250.00
Green, Enamel Flowers, Tooled Lip, Haze Interior, 1885-1925, 7 1/2 In. 60.00
Green, Enamel, Bubbles, 8 1/4 In. 129.00
Green, Enamel, White, Orange Crosshatch, Blue Flowers, Stopper, 9 1/4 In., Pair 165.00
Green, Enamel, White, Orange Crosshatch, White Flowers, Stopper, 9 1/4 In., Pair 187.00
Green, Gold Enamel, Satin Glass, Flared Lip, Pontil, 1885-1925, Pair 825.00
Green, Mallet, White & Orange Enamel, 1925, 7 1/2 In. 105.00
Green, Maroon, White Enamel, Flowers, 1890-1925, 8 In. 77.00
Green Aqua, Enamel Flowers, Ribs, Pontil, 1885-1925, 7 7/8 In. 412.50
Green Opalescent, 3-Sided, Pinched Style, Draped, Silver Collar, 1930, 7 1/4 In., Pair ... 413.00
Hair Oil, Milk Glass, Opalescent, Sailboats, Enamel, Rolled Lip, 9 In. 633.00
Hair Tonic, Label Under Glass, Milk Glass, Blue, Gold Letters, Stopper, 9 In. 330.00
Hair Tonic, Log Cabin, Rochester, N.Y., Root Beer Amber, Label, 9 In. 2576.00
Hair Tonic, Milk Glass, Enamel Clover, Pontil, 9 1/2 In. 300.00
Hobnail, Amber, Rolled Lip, Ground Pontil, 7 In. 99.00

Hobnail, Amethyst Opalescent, Stopper, Pontil, 8 1/2 In. 231.00
Hobnail, Blue, Rolled Lip, Improved Pontil, 7 In. 100.00
Hobnail, Cobalt Blue, Rolled Lip, Improved Pontil, 7 In. 99.00
Hobnail, Cranberry Opalescent, Tooled Lip, Pontil, 1925, 8 In. 165.00
Hobnail, Frosted Pink Design, 1890-1925, 6 3/4 In. 560.00
Hobnail, Gold, Stopper, Pontil, 7 1/4 In. 143.00
Hobnail, Gray Citron, Tooled Lip, Late 19th Century, 7 1/2 In. 125.00
Hobnail, Green, Rolled Lip, Improved Pontil, 7 In. 99.00
Hobnail, Turquoise, Rolled Lip, Polished Pontil, 1885-1925, 6 3/4 In. 77.00
Hobnail, White Opalescent, 7 In. 55.00
Hobnail, White Opalescent, Pontil, 7 In. 77.00
Hobnail, Yellow Green, Tooled Lip, Late 19th Century, 7 1/2 In. 110.00
Hobnail, Yellow, 1890-1925, 7 1/8 In. 616.00
I. Wolstencrost, Fla. Water, Milk Glass, Enamel, Cabin, Shaker Top, 1800s, 10 In. 990.00
Imperial Red, Bohemian Style, White & Blue Enamel, Gilt, Rolled Lip, Pontil, 8 3/8 In. .. 1736.00
Jade, Hand Painted House, Flowers, Sheared Lip, Polished Pontil, 7 1/2 In. 165.00
Jno. Alby, Eagle, Shield, Flags, Label, Screw Top, 9 In. 605.00
Lavender, 8-Grain, Stopper, 12 In. 143.00
Lavender, Enamel Flowers, 7 In. 119.00
Lavender Opalescent, Gold Enamel, Flared, Pontil, 7 3/4 In., Pair 413.00
Lemon Yellow, Thumbprint, Rolled Lip, Polished Pontil, 7 In. 187.00
Light Blue, Embossed Design, Inset Panel, Stopper, 10 1/2 In. 88.00
Light Blue, Enamel Flowers, 9 1/2 In. 119.00
Light Green, Daisies, Enamel, Flared Lip, 8 In. 55.00
Light Green, Mary Gregory Type, White Enamel Girl With Flower, Pontil, 9 In. 176.00
Light Green, Thumbprint, Flared Lip, 8 In. 166.00
Light Turquoise Blue, Ribs, Flowers & Vine Silver Overlay, 1890-1925, 9 In. 616.00
Lime Green, Enamel Design, Sheared Lip, OP, 7 3/4 In. 165.00
Lime Green, Enamel Flowers, OP, 7 3/4 In. 165.00
Loetz, Green Opalescent, Pontil, 1930, 7 3/4 In. 550.00
Loetz, Lavender Opalescent, Pontil, 1930, 7 3/4 In. 715.00
Loetz, Lime To Yellow, 7 1/2 In. 715.00
Lutz, Frosted Amethyst Glass, 1890-1925, 7 3/8 In. 420.00
Lutz, Light Amethyst, 1890-1925, 7 7/8 In. 448.00
Medium Amethyst, Mallet, Yellow, Orange Enamel Design, Pontil, 1885-1925, 8 In. 165.00
Melon Ribs, Flowers, Milk Glass Shaker Top, 7 1/2 In. 104.00
Melon Ribs, Satin Glass, White Interior, Enamel Flowers, 7 1/2 In. 110.00
Milk Glass, Blue, Cottage, Enamel, Multicolored, 8 5/8 In. 467.00
Milk Glass, Blue, Swirled Ribs, Label Under Glass, Woman, Seafoam, 10 3/4 In. 672.00
Milk Glass, Canary Yellow, Satin, Enamel Stipple Design, 1930, 7 1/4 In. 132.00
Milk Glass, Cherub, Blue & Yellow Ground, Pontil, 1925, 7 3/4 In. 305.00
Milk Glass, Cherub, Yellow & Blue Ground, Pontil, 7 1/2 In. 355.00
Milk Glass, Cherubs On Dog Faced Cloud, Yellow, Blue Ground, 1925, 7 In. 280.00
Milk Glass, Cherubs On Sheaf Of Grain, Light Blue, Yellow, 1890-1925, 7 3/4 In. 392.00
Milk Glass, Cherubs With Grape Cluster, Yellow, Blue Ground, 1925, 7 5/8 In. 212.00
Milk Glass, Cherubs With Pigeon Cage, Yellow, Blue Ground, 1925, 7 3/4 In. 224.00
Milk Glass, Coral Enamel, Woman's Face, Stopper, Applied Neck Ring, Pontil, 6 3/4 In. ... 209.00
Milk Glass, Cottage Design, Mint Green, Polished Lip, 1890-1925, 7 1/4 In. 281.00
Milk Glass, Enamel Flowers, Multicolored, Chrome Spout, Tooled Lip, 7 In. 121.00
Milk Glass, Frosted Amber Shaded To Yellow, White Enamel Flowers, 8 In. 140.00
Milk Glass, Gray, White Enamel Flowers, Polished Lip, 7 In. 364.00
Milk Glass, Green Opalescent, Multicolored Enamel, Boy & Girl, Rolled Lip, 8 1/2 In. 1650.00
Milk Glass, Hand Painted Cherub Scene, Stopper, 7 In. 413.00
Milk Glass, Opalescent, Multicolored Clover, Seafoam, 8 3/4 In. 242.00
Milk Glass, Opalescent, Seafoam, Clover, Pontil, 8 3/4 In. 300.00
Milk Glass, Opalescent, Seafoam, Enamel Flowers, Pontil, 1885-1925, 7 1/4 In. 72.00
Milk Glass, Painted, 3 Cherubs On Bed Of Straw, Metal Stopper, 7 In. 415.00
Milk Glass, Pink Satin Glass, Hobnail, Smooth Base, Polished Lip, 7 1/8 In. 523.00
Milk Glass, Pink, Flowers, 1930, 7 5/8 In. 240.00
Milk Glass, Powder Blue, Petals Around Shoulder, 1925, 6 1/2 In. 440.00
Milk Glass, Royal Blue, Bird With Flowers, Silver, White, Bulbous, 8 1/2 In. 79.00
Milk Glass, Swirled Ribs, Label Under Glass, Woman, Seafoam, 10 3/4 In. 672.00
Milk Glass, Yellow Diamond, 20th Century, 7 1/8 In. 207.00

Millefiori, Multicolored, Flared Lip, Pontil, 7 3/4 In. 303.00
Olive Yellow, Ribs, Enamel Flowers, Pontil, 1885-1925, 7 1/2 In. 105.00
Orange, Yellow, Red, Vertical Striping, Stopper, 6 1/4 In. 475.00
Overshot, Crystal, Original Screw-On Top, Polished Pontil, 7 1/4 In. 150.00
Pale Apple Green Glass, Enamel Art Nouveau Design, Ribs, Pontil, 8 1/4 In. 385.00
Pale Blue Satin, Gold & Enamel Art Deco Pattern, Gold Lip, Fancy Stopper, 8 In. 358.00
Parker's Hair Balsam, Amber, BIMAL, 7 1/2 In. 4.50
Peacock Blue, Enamel, Gilt, Sheared Lip, Pontil, 1885-1925, 8 In., Pair 770.00
Pink, Brown, White Spatter, Ribs, 1885-1925, 6 In. 165.00
Pink, Mocha, Hand-Painted Flower & Leaf, Ground Lip, Stopper, Polished Pontil, 9 In. ... 110.00
Pink, Yellow, Green, Spatter, 1885-1925, 11 In. 440.00
Pink & White Swirl, Variegated, Polished Pontil, 7 1/2 In. 110.00
Pink Amethyst, Ribs, Yellow & Gold Enamel Flowers, Pontil, 8 3/4 In. 305.00
Pink Lavender, Enamel Flowers, Tooled Lip, 8 In. 908.00
Pink Satin, Quilted Over White, Sheared Lip, OP, 7 1/2 In. 303.00
Pink Shaded To White, Quilt Pattern Over White Satin, Lady's Leg Neck, 9 In. 605.00
Pink Swirl, White, Geometric Design, 1880-1900, 7 3/4 In. 199.00
Porcelain, Jade Inset, Flowers, Sterling Silver Lip, 5 In. 55.00
Porcelain, White, Multicolored Enamel Flowers, 1890-1925, 6 3/4 In. 1980.00
Pressed Glass, Starburst Pattern, Swirls On Neck, Stopper, 5 1/2 In. 55.00
Purple Amethyst, Ribs, Bell Shape, Enamel Flowers, Pontil, 8 In. 465.00
Purple Amethyst, Ribs, Red, Yellow, White Enamel Flowers, Pontil, 7 3/4 In. 100.00
Purple Amethyst, Ribs, Silver Overlay Flowers, Pontil, 7 7/8 In. 605.00
Purple Amethyst, Ribs, White, Blue & Gold Flower, Pontil, 7 In. 180.00
Pyramid Shape, Clambroth Glass, Scalloped Panels, Reeded, 7 In. 45.00
Red, Clear, Blue & Green Alternating Bands, Pontil, Venice, 8 5/8 In. 385.00
Red Flash Interior, Mary Gregory Style, Ribs, 1890-1925, 10 5/8 In. 2310.00
Reddington & Co., San Francisco, Monogram, Drippy Top, 10 1/4 In. 650.00
Ruby Cut To Clear, Circles & Diamonds, Ruby Neck, 6 3/4 In. 303.00
Salmon Opalescent, Swirled Ribs, Pontil, 1930, 8 In. 440.00
Sapphire Blue, Pressed Glass, Enamel Stopper, 8 In. 358.00
Sapphire Blue, White & Orange Enamel, Bulbous, Lady's Leg Neck, Pontil, 8 1/2 In. ... 176.00
Sapphire Blue, Yellow, 1890-1925, 6 5/8 In. 672.00
Satin Glass, Multicolored Candy Stripes, White Stopper, 8 1/2 In. 660.00
Satin Glass, Pink, Painted Flowers, Chrome & Cork Stopper, 8 1/2 In. 125.00
Satin Topaz, Enamel Rose Design, Pontil, 1890-1925, 7 7/8 In. 577.00
Silver Enamel, Blue, Satin Finish, Flared Lip, OP, 7 3/4 In. 220.00
Silver Enamel, Turquoise, Leaves, Flowers, Flared Lip, OP, 7 3/4 In. 378.00
Silver Overlay, Amberina, Sheared Lip, 8 In. 1430.00
Silver Overlay, Clear, Bulbous, Initials M.L.H., Stopper, 6 3/4 In. 165.00
Silver Overlay, Clear, Stopper, 7 1/2 In. 110.00
Silver Overlay, Flowers, Polished Pontil, 7 1/2 In. 358.00
Smoky Amber, Clear Satin, Gold & Enamel Art Deco Design, Lady's Leg, Pontil, 9 In. ... 330.00
Smoky Amethyst, Straight Sides, Ribs, Yellow & Gray Flowers, Pontil, 8 5/8 In. 235.00
Spatter, Multicolored, Flared Lip, OP, 1885-1925, 7 3/4 In. 605.00
Spatter, Zigzag Ribs, 1885-1925, 11 In. 231.00
Stag Design, Dark Amethyst, White Ground, Ribs, Pontil, 1885-1925, 7 7/8 In. 413.00
Sterling Overlay, Stopper, Sterling D213, 6 3/4 In. 176.00
Teal Green, Melon Ribs, Coin Spot Pattern, Tooled Mouth, 1890-1930, 8 1/2 In. 148.00
Teal Green, Ribs, Pinched Waist, White Enamel, 7 In. 231.00
Teal Green, Ribs, White & Gold Gilt Strawberries, 7 7/8 In. 412.00
Teal Green, Ribs, White Enamel, Pinched Waist, Tooled Lip, Pontil, 7 In. .... 230.00 to 246.00
Tonique De Luxe, Clear, Yellow ACL Letters, Tooled Lip, 7 In. 179.00
Topaz, Satin, Enamel Design, Bulbous, Flared Lip, 1920, 7 7/8 In. 303.00
Topaz, Satin, Enamel White Flowers, Polished Lip, 1890-1930, 5 1/4 In. 132.00
Turquoise, Allover Crackle, Polished Lip & Pontil, 1890-1925, 6 1/2 In. 357.00
Turquoise, Quilt Over White Satin Pattern, Sheared Top, Pontil, 8 In. 121.00
Turquoise, Ribs, Orange & White Enamel Dots & Flowers, Rolled Lip, Pontil, 8 1/8 In. ... 157.00
Turquoise, Ribs, Yellow & White Enamel Flowers, Pontil, 7 3/4 In. 224.00
Turquoise, Ribs, Yellow, Orange, White Enamel, 1890-1925, 7 3/4 In. 257.00
Turquoise, Stars & Stripes, Rolled Lip, Polished Pontil, 1890-1925, 7 In. 303.00
Turquoise, White Loopings, Polished Pontil, Flared Lip, 7 3/8 In. 154.00
Turquoise, White, Onion Shape, Metal Stopper, 8 1/2 In. 110.00

Turquoise Satin, White Enamel Pussy Willow Branch, Polished Lip, 8 1/8 In. 100.00
Vegederma, Amethyst, White, 8 In. 448.00
Venetian, Red, Blue & Green Stripes, Fishnet Pattern, Tooled Lip, 8 5/8 In. 385.00
Violet Cologne, White Enamel Flowers, Bulbous, 4 3/4 In. 30.00
White, Ribs, Blue, Gold Enamel Flowers, Tooled Lip, 7 1/2 In. 179.00
White & Gold Strawberry, Ribs, c.1885, 7 7/8 In. 410.00
White Opalescent, Pink & Yellow Variegated Vertical Swirls, Lady's Leg, Tall 1650.00
White Opalescent, Spanish Lace, Tooled Lip, Pontil, 7 1/8 In. 157.00
White Opalescent, Stripes, Swirled To Right, Rolled Lip, 6 1/4 In. 176.00
White Opalescent, Swirl, Rolled Lip, Pontil, 9 In. 110.00
White Opalescent, Swirl, Tooled Lip, Pontil, 1890-1925, 7 In. 176.00
Witch Hazel, Green Crackle, White Enamel, Fred Dolle's Antiseptic, 7 1/2 In. 840.00
Witch Hazel, Milk Glass, Enamel Flowers, Sheared Lip, Mallet Shape, 8 In. 231.00
Witch Hazel, Milk Glass, Flowers, Tooled Lip, Pontil, 1885-1925, 7 In. 253.00
Witch Hazel, Milk Glass, Light Blue, Multicolored Bird, 1925, 8 3/4 In. 605.00
Witch Hazel, Milk Glass, Opalescent, Enamel Blue Flowers, Sparrow Design, 9 1/4 In. . . . 357.00
Witch Hazel, Milk Glass, Opalescent, Multicolored Poppies, Tooled Lip, 8 1/2 In. 275.00
Witch Hazel, Milk Glass, Opalescent, Tulip, 8 5/8 In. 495.00
Witch Hazel, Milk Glass, Powder Blue, Bird On Branch, Multicolored, 8 3/4 In. 605.00
Witch Hazel, Milk Glass, Roses, Flowers, 9 1/4 In. 576.00
Yellow, Milk Glass Vertical Stripes, Melon Ribs, Tooled Lip, 1920, 8 1/2 In. 220.00
Yellow, Opalescent Stripes, Melon Ribs, Metal Stopper, 7 In. 468.00
Yellow, Satin Glass, White Ferns, 7 1/2 In. 165.00
Yellow, White Swirl, c.1880, 8 x 3 1/2 In. 275.00
Yellow & Red Square Spatter, Polished Pontil, 9 1/4 In. 468.00
Yellow Amber, Allover Diamond Pattern, Enamel Flowers, Pontil, 1925, 10 1/8 In. 743.00
Yellow Amber, Thumbprint, Yellow, Orange, White Enamel Flowers, Pontil, 8 1/4 In. 179.00
Yellow Green, Lady's Leg, Yellow, Orange & White Enamel Flowers, Pontil, 8 1/8 In. . . . 140.00
Yellow Green, Ribs, Barrel, Enamel Flowers, Pontil, 1925, 7 1/2 In. 300.00
Yellow Green, Ribs, Barrel, Orange, White Enamel Flowers, 7 1/2 In. 302.00
Yellow Green, Ribs, Enamel Flowers, Tooled Lip, Pontil, 1890-1925, 6 3/4 In. 83.00
Yellow Green, Ribs, Enamel White Gold Design, Pontil, 1925, 6 3/4 In. 105.00
Yellow Green, Ribs, Orange, White Enamel Flowers, Pontil, 7 In. 100.00
Yellow Green, Ribs, Red Enamel Flowers, 1890-1925, 7 1/2 In. 100.00
Yellow Green, Ribs, White, Gold Trimmed Design, Pontil, 6 3/4 In. 100.00
Yellow Green, Ribs, Yellow, Silver Enamel, Persian Style, Tooled Mouth, Pontil, 6 3/4 In. 168.00
BATTERY JAR, see Oil

----------------------- **BEAM** -----------------------

The history of the Jim Beam company is confusing because the progeny of the founder, Jacob Beam, favored the names David and James. Jacob Beam had been a whiskey distiller in Virginia and Maryland before moving to Kentucky in 1788. He was selling Kentucky Straight Bourbon in bottles labeled *Beam* by 1795. His son David continued to market Beam bourbon. His grandson, David M. Beam, was the next to inherit the business. One of David M.'s brands was Old Tub, started in 1882 at Beam's Clear Springs Distillery No. 230. The company was called David M. Beam. The next Beam family member in the business was Col. James B. Beam, son of David M., who started working at the distillery in 1880 at the age of 16. By 1914 he owned the Early Times Distillery No. 7 in Louisville, Kentucky. J.B. Beam and B.H. Hurt were partners in the distillery from 1892 to 1899. In 1915, when the colonel died, the distillery was acquired by S.L. Guthrie and some partners. Then T. Jeremiah Beam, son of James B. Beam, inherited the James Beam Company, and with his cousin, Carl Beam, continued to make the famous bourbon. Booker Noe, Baker Beam, and David Beam, sixth-generation descendants of Jacob Beam, continued in the business. Today, Jim Beam Brands is a wholly-owned subsidiary of Fortune Brands.

Beam bottles favored by today's collectors were made as containers for Kentucky Straight Bourbon. In 1953, the company began selling some Christmas season whiskey in special decanters shaped like cocktail shakers instead of the usual whiskey bottles. The decanters were so popular that by 1955 the company was making Regal China bottles in special shapes. Executive series bottles started in 1955 and political figures in 1956. Customer specialties were first made in 1956, decanters (called *trophy series* by collectors) in 1957, and the state series in 1958. Other bottles are classed by collectors as Regal China or Glass Specialty bottles. A small number of special bottles were made by The Royal Doulton Company in England from 1983 to 1985. The rarest Beam bottle is the First National Bank of Chicago bottle; 117 were issued in 1964. The Salute to Spiro Agnew bottle made in 1970 was limited to 196. Six men making counterfeits of the very rare Beam bottles were arrested in 1970. Jim Beam stopped making decanters for the commercial trade in 1992.

The Foss Company made a limited number of decanters exclusively for the International Association of Jim Beam Bottle and Specialties Club (IJBBSC). Cinnamon Teal was issued in 1994 and Harlequin Duck in 1995 with the Ducks Unlimited label.

The Jim Beam company has also made many other advertising items or *go-withs* such as ashtrays and openers. The International Association of Jim Beam Bottle & Specialties Clubs (2015 Burlington Avenue, Kewanee, IL 61433) has regional and sectional meetings. They sell a book, *Jim Beam Bottles, A Pictorial Guide,* and a price list is also available.

Bottles are listed here alphabetically by name or as Convention, Executive, Political, or other general headings. This is because beginning collectors find it difficult to locate bottles by type. Miniature bottles are listed here also. Go-withs are in the special section at the end of the book.

101st Airborne Division, Armed Forces, 1977	15.00
ABC Florida, 1973	13.00
AC Spark Plug, 1977	20.00 to 35.00
AHEPA, 1972	6.00
Aida, Opera, 1978	95.00
Alaska Purchase, 1966	6.00
Alaska Star, 1958	45.00
Ambulance, Emergency, White, 1985	69.00
American Cowboy, 1981	20.00
AMVETS, 25th Anniversary Of American Wars, 1970	*Illus* 8.00
Antioch, 1967	7.00
Antique Trader, 1968	*Illus* 21.00
Appaloosa, 1974	10.00
Arizona, State, 1968	5.00
Armadillo, 1981	10.00 to 18.00
Armanetti, Award Winner, 1969	8.00
Armanetti, Bacchus, 1970	8.00
Armanetti, Fun Shopper, 1971	7.00
Armanetti, Vase, 1968	8.00
Army Jeep, 1986	45.00
Barney's Slot Machine, 1978	15.00 to 20.00
Barry Berish, Presidential, Bowl On Pedestal, 1986	15.00
Barry Berish, Presidential, Musical Bell, 1984	70.00
Bartender's Guild, Crystal, 1973	8.00
Baseball, 100th Anniversary, 1969	35.00
Beam Pot, 1980	12.00
Beaver Valley Club, 1977	10.00
Bell Ringer, A Fore Ye Go, 1970	9.00 to 13.00
Bell Ringer, Plaid Apron, 1970	6.00 to 9.00
Bell Scotch, Miniature, 1969	9.00 to 15.00
Big Apple, New York, 1979	11.00
Bing Crosby, 29th National Pro-AM, 1970	6.00 to 12.00
Bing Crosby, 30th, 1971	15.00
Bing Crosby, 31st, 1972	35.00
Bing Crosby, 32nd, 1973	30.00
Bing Crosby, 33rd, 1974	35.00
Bing Crosby, 34th, 1975	60.00
Bing Crosby, 35th, 1976	40.00
Bing Crosby, 36th, 1977	30.00
Bing Crosby, 37th, 1978	35.00
Black Katz, 1968	11.00
Blue Daisy, 1967	12.00
Blue Hen, 1982	14.00
Blue Jay, 1969	6.00

Beam, AMVETS, 25th
Anniversary Of American
Wars, 1970

Beam, Antique Trader, 1968

Beam, Bohemian Girl,
1974

Bluegill, 1974, 9 3/4 In. . . . . .15.00 to 25.00
Bob Hope Desert Classic, 14th, 1973 . . . . .9.00 to 17.00
Bob Hope Desert Classic, 15th, 1974 . . . . .12.00 to 19.00
Bohemian Girl, 1974 . . . .*Illus*   14.00
Bonded Gold, 1975 . . . .   6.00
Bonded Mystic, 1979 . . . .   5.00
Bonded Silver, Regal, 1975 . . . .   6.00
Boothill, 1972 . . . .   8.00
Boris Godunov, Opera, 1982 . . . .   280.00
Boy's Town, 1973 . . . .   10.00
BPO Does, 1971 . . . .   8.00
Broadmoor Hotel, 1968 . . . .*Illus*   8.00
Buccaneer, Multicolored, 1982 . . . .   28.00
Buffalo Bill, 1971 . . . .   15.00
Bulldog, 1979 . . . .   16.00
Cable Car, 1968 . . . .   4.00
Cal Neva, 1969 . . . .   6.00
California Mission, 1970 . . . .   15.00
Camellia City Club, 1979 . . . .   18.00
Cameo, Blue, 1965 . . . .   5.00
Cannon With Chain, 1970 . . . .   3.00
Canteen, 1979 . . . . .10.00 to 20.00
Captain & Mate, 1980 . . . .   8.00
Cardinal, Female, 1973 . . . .   15.00
Cardinal, Male, 1968 . . . .   22.00
Carmen, Opera, 1978 . . . .   145.00
Carolers, Holiday, 1988 . . . .   50.00
Carolers, Presidential, 1988 . . . .   65.00
Cat, Burmese, 1967 . . . .   15.00
Cat, Siamese, 1967 . . . .   20.00
Cat, Tabby, 1967 . . . .   15.00
Catfish, 1981 . . . . .22.00 to 45.00
Cathedral, Radio, 1979 . . . .   15.00
Cedars Of Lebanon, 1971 . . . .   7.00
Charisma, Decanter, 1970 . . . . .8.00 to 14.00
Charlie McCarthy, 1976 . . . .*Illus*   45.00
Chateaux, Martini, 1953 . . . .   20.00
Cherry Hills Country Club, 1973 . . . .   5.00
Chevrolet, Bel Air, 1957 Model, Black, 1987 . . . . .50.00 to 85.00
Chevrolet, Bel Air, 1957 Model, Dark Blue, 1987 . . . . .65.00 to 85.00
Chevrolet, Bel Air, 1957 Model, Gold, 1987 . . . . .95.00 to 110.00
Chevrolet, Bel Air, 1957 Model, Red, 1987 . . . . .80.00 to 90.00

Beam, Broadmoor
Hotel, 1968

Beam, Charlie
McCarthy, 1976

⌥

Remove traces of gum, adhesive tape, and other sticky tape by rubbing the glue with lemon juice.

⌥

Chevrolet, Bel Air, 1957 Model, Turquoise, 1987	55.00 to 70.00
Chevrolet, Bel Air, 1957 Model, Yellow, Decals, 1988	110.00
Chevrolet, Camaro, 1969 Model, Blue, 1989	50.00
Chevrolet, Camaro, 1969 Model, Green, 1989	125.00
Chevrolet, Camaro, 1969 Model, Pace Car, 1989	110.00
Chevrolet, Camaro, 1969 Model, Silver, 1989	110.00
Chevrolet, Camaro, 1969 Model, Yellow, 1989	70.00
Chevrolet, Convertible, 1957 Model, Cream, 1990	100.00
Chevrolet, Convertible, 1957 Model, Red, 1990	90.00
Chevrolet, Corvette Stingray, 1963 Model, Black, 1987	60.00 to 100.00
Chevrolet, Corvette Stingray, 1963 Model, Blue, 1987	70.00
Chevrolet, Corvette Stingray, 1963 Model, Red, 1987	85.00
Chevrolet, Corvette Stingray, 1963 Model, Silver, 1987	75.00
Chevrolet, Corvette, 1953 Model, White, 1989	165.00
Chevrolet, Corvette, 1954 Model, Blue, 1989	155.00
Chevrolet, Corvette, 1955 Model, Black, 1990	120.00
Chevrolet, Corvette, 1955 Model, Copper, 1989	110.00
Chevrolet, Corvette, 1955 Model, Red, 1990	110.00 to 125.00
Chevrolet, Corvette, 1957 Model, Black, 1990	50.00 to 75.00
Chevrolet, Corvette, 1957 Model, Blue, 1990	500.00
Chevrolet, Corvette, 1957 Model, Copper, 1991	125.00
Chevrolet, Corvette, 1957 Model, White, 1990	160.00
Chevrolet, Corvette, 1978 Model, Black, 1984	125.00
Chevrolet, Corvette, 1978 Model, Pace Car, 1987	250.00
Chevrolet, Corvette, 1978 Model, Red, 1988	75.00
Chevrolet, Corvette, 1978 Model, White, 1985	65.00 to 75.00
Chevrolet, Corvette, 1978 Model, Yellow, 1985	75.00
Chevrolet, Corvette, 1984 Model, Black, 1989	82.00 to 95.00
Chevrolet, Corvette, 1984 Model, Bronze, 1989	115.00
Chevrolet, Corvette, 1984 Model, Gold, 1989	95.00 to 110.00
Chevrolet, Corvette, 1984 Model, Red, 1988	59.00 to 75.00
Chevrolet, Corvette, 1984 Model, White, 1988	35.00 to 60.00
Cheyenne, 1967	6.00
Chicago Art Museum, 1972	10.00
Chicago Club Loving Cup, 1978	15.00
Chicago Cubs, 1985	76.00 to 95.00
Chicago Fire, 1971	18.00
Chicago Show, 1977	25.00
Christmas Tree, 1986	115.00
Churchill Downs, Kentucky Derby, 95th, Pink Roses, 1969	20.00 to 35.00
Churchill Downs, Kentucky Derby, 95th, Red Roses, 1969	20.00
Churchill Downs, Kentucky Derby, 96th, Double Roses, 1970	30.00
Churchill Downs, Kentucky Derby, 96th, Roses Front Side Only, 1970	18.00
Churchill Downs, Kentucky Derby, 97th, Horse & Rider, 1971	18.00
Churchill Downs, Kentucky Derby, 98th, Horse & Rider In Wreath, 1972	25.00
Churchill Downs, Kentucky Derby, 100th, 1974	19.00
Circus Wagon, 1979	26.00

Civil War, North, 1961 ....20.00 to 28.00
Civil War, South, 1961 ....20.00 to 25.00
Cleopatra, Rust, 1962 .... 4.00
Cleopatra, Yellow, 1962 .... 10.00
Clint Eastwood, 1973 .... 27.00
Clock, Antique, 1985 .... 30.00
Coach Devaney, Nebraska, 1972 .... 5.00
Cocktail Shaker, 1953 .... 4.00
Coffee Grinder, Antique, 1979 ....10.00 to 20.00
Coffee Warmer, Pyrex, Gold Metal Band, 1956 .... 6.00
Coffee Warmer, Pyrex, Gold, 1954 .... 10.00
Coho Salmon, 1976 .... 23.00
Colin Mead, 1984 .... 150.00
Collectors Edition, Vol. 1, Aristide Bruant, 1966 .... 3.00
Collectors Edition, Vol. 1, Artist, 1966 .... 4.00
Collectors Edition, Vol. 1, Blue Boy, 1966 .... 5.00
Collectors Edition, Vol. 1, Laughing Cavalier, 1966 .... 2.00
Collectors Edition, Vol. 1, Mardi Gras, 1966 .... 5.00
Collectors Edition, Vol. 1, On The Terrace, 1966 .... 4.00
Collectors Edition, Vol. 2, George Gisze, 1967 .... 4.00
Collectors Edition, Vol. 2, Night Watch, 1967 .... 5.00
Collectors Edition, Vol. 2, The Jester, 1967 .... 3.00
Collectors Edition, Vol. 3, American Gothic, 1968 .... 4.00
Collectors Edition, Vol. 3, Buffalo Hunt, 1968 .... 5.00
Collectors Edition, Vol. 3, Hauling In The Gill Net, 1968 .... 4.00
Collectors Edition, Vol. 3, Indian Maiden, 1968 .... 3.00
Collectors Edition, Vol. 3, The Kentuckian, 1968 .... 3.00
Collectors Edition, Vol. 3, The Scout, 1968 .... 4.00
Collectors Edition, Vol. 3, Whistler's Mother, 1968 .... 5.00
Collectors Edition, Vol. 4, Balcony, 1969 .... 3.00
Collectors Edition, Vol. 4, Boy With Cherries, 1969 .... 4.00
Collectors Edition, Vol. 4, Emile Zola, 1969 .... 5.00
Collectors Edition, Vol. 4, Fruit Basket, 1969 .... 3.00
Collectors Edition, Vol. 4, Sunflowers, 1969 .... 4.00
Collectors Edition, Vol. 4, The Judge, 1969 .... 5.00
Collectors Edition, Vol. 5, Au Cafe, 1970 .... 3.00
Collectors Edition, Vol. 5, Old Peasant, 1970 .... 4.00
Collectors Edition, Vol. 5, The Jewish Bride, 1970 .... 5.00
Collectors Edition, Vol. 5, Titus At Writing Desk, 1970 .... 4.00
Collectors Edition, Vol. 6, Boy Holding Flute, 1971 .... 3.00
Collectors Edition, Vol. 6, Charles I, 1971 .... 5.00
Collectors Edition, Vol. 6, The Merry Lute Player, 1971 .... 3.00
Collectors Edition, Vol. 7, Maidservant, 1971 .... 4.00
Collectors Edition, Vol. 7, Prince Baltasor, 1972 .... 5.00
Collectors Edition, Vol. 8, Frederic F. Chopin, 1973 .... 4.00
Collectors Edition, Vol. 8, Ludwig Van Beethoven, 1973 .... 5.00
Collectors Edition, Vol. 8, Wolfgang Mozart, 1973 .... 3.00
Collectors Edition, Vol. 9, Cardinal, 1974 .... 2.00
Collectors Edition, Vol. 9, Pheasant, 1974 .... 3.00
Collectors Edition, Vol. 9, Woodcock, 1974 .... 4.00
Collectors Edition, Vol. 10, Largemouth Bass, 1975 .... 5.00
Collectors Edition, Vol. 10, Sailfish, 1975 .... 4.00
Collectors Edition, Vol. 11, Bighorn Sheep, 1976 .... 5.00
Collectors Edition, Vol. 12, German Shorthaired Pointer, 1977 .... 4.00
Collectors Edition, Vol. 12, Irish Setter, 1977 .... 3.00
Collectors Edition, Vol. 12, Labrador Retriever, 1977 .... 4.00
Collectors Edition, Vol. 12, Springer Spaniel, 1977 .... 5.00
Collectors Edition, Vol. 14, Cottontail Rabbit, 1978 .... 4.00
Collectors Edition, Vol. 14, Mule Deer, 1978 .... 5.00
Collectors Edition, Vol. 14, Raccoon, 1978 .... 6.00
Collectors Edition, Vol. 14, Red Fox, 1978 .... 4.00
Collectors Edition, Vol. 15, Cowboy, 1902, 1979 .... 5.00
Collectors Edition, Vol. 15, Indian Trapper 1908, 1979 .... 6.00

Collectors Edition, Vol. 15, Lt. S.C. Robertson 1890, 1979	4.00
Collectors Edition, Vol. 16, Canvasback, 1980	5.00
Collectors Edition, Vol. 16, Mallard, 1980	6.00
Collectors Edition, Vol. 16, Red Head, 1980	5.00
Collectors Edition, Vol. 17, Great Elk, 1981	6.00
Collectors Edition, Vol. 17, Pintail Duck, 1981	5.00
Collectors Edition, Vol. 18, Cardinal, 1982	6.00
Collectors Edition, Vol. 18, Whitetail Deer, 1982	5.00
Collectors Edition, Vol. 19, Scarlet Tanager, 1983	6.00
Colorado, State, 1959	6.00
Colorado Centennial, 1976	10.00
Colorado Springs, 1972	15.00
Convention, No. 1, Denver, 1971	8.00 to 12.00
Convention, No. 2, Anaheim, June 19-25, 1972	20.00
Convention, No. 3, Detroit, 1973	12.00
Convention, No. 4, Lancaster, 1974	65.00 to 85.00
Convention, No. 5, Sacramento, 1975	6.00 to 10.00
Convention, No. 6, Hartford, 1976	7.00
Convention, No. 7, Louisville, 1977	8.00
Convention, No. 8, Chicago, 1978	10.00
Convention, No. 9, Houston, Cowboy, Antique, 1979	25.00 to 35.00
Convention, No. 9, Houston, Cowboy, Multicolored, 1979	35.00
Convention, No. 10, Norfolk, Ship & Wheel, 1980	22.00
Convention, No. 11, Las Vegas, Showgirl, Blond, 1981	20.00
Convention, No. 11, Las Vegas, Showgirl, Brunette, 1981	20.00 to 50.00
Convention, No. 12, New Orleans, 1982	27.00
Convention, No. 13, St. Louis, 1983	55.00
Convention, No. 14, Hollywood, Florida, 1984	18.00
Convention, No. 15, Las Vegas, Roulette, 1985	40.00 to 55.00
Convention, No. 16, Boston, Mass., 1986	40.00
Convention, No. 17, Louisville, Framed Picture Of Riverboat, 1987	40.00
Convention, No. 18, Portland, Bucky Beaver, 1988	35.00
Convention, No. 19, Kansas City, Horse & Wagon, 1989	45.00
Convention, No. 20, Kissimmee, Beach Hut, Barrels, 1990	35.00
Convention, No. 21, Reno, Sheriff With Guns, Dice & Money, 1991	65.00
CPO, 1974	6.00
Crappie, 1979	15.00 to 25.00
Crispus Attucks, 1976	6.00
CRLDA, 1973	*Illus* 8.00
Crystal, Amaretto, 1975	5.00
Crystal, Amber, 1973	8.00
Dancing Scot, Short, 1963	60.00
Dancing Scot, Tall, 1964	22.00
Dancing Scot, Tall, Couple, 1964	300.00
Dark Eyes Vodka Jug, 1978	6.00
Delaware, State, 1972	6.00 to 11.00
Delco Battery, 1978	25.00
Delft Blue, 1963	3.00
Delft Rose, 1963	5.00
Denver Rush To Rockies, 1970	12.00
Doe, 1963	12.00
Don Giovanni, Opera, 1980	110.00
Duck, Mallard, 1957	18.00
Ducks Unlimited, No. 1, Mallard, 1974	38.00
Ducks Unlimited, No. 2, Wood Duck, 1975	35.00
Ducks Unlimited, No. 3, Mallard Hen, 40th Anniversary, 1977	35.00
Ducks Unlimited, No. 4, Mallard, 1978	45.00
Ducks Unlimited, No. 5, Canvasback Drake, 1979	35.00 to 45.00
Ducks Unlimited, No. 6, Blue-Winged Teal, 1980	45.00
Ducks Unlimited, No. 7, Green-Winged Teal, 1981	40.00 to 55.00
Ducks Unlimited, No. 8, Wood Duck Family, 1982	50.00 to 65.00
Ducks Unlimited, No. 9, American Widgeons, 1983	40.00 to 60.00
Ducks Unlimited, No. 10, Mallard, 1984	92.00

Ducks Unlimited, No. 11, Pintail, Pair, 1985 .... 60.00
Ducks Unlimited, No. 12, Redhead, 1986 .... 50.00
Ducks Unlimited, No. 13, Bluebill, 1987 .... 35.00
Ducks Unlimited, No. 14, Gadwall Family, 1988 .... 40.00
Ducks Unlimited, No. 15, Black Duck, 1989 .... 60.00
Ducks Unlimited, No. 16, Canada Goose, 1990 .... 60.00
Ducks Unlimited, No. 17, Tundra Swan, 1991 .... 35.00
Duesenberg, 1934 Model J, Dark Blue, 1981 ....53.00 to 110.00
Duesenberg, 1935 Convertible, Coupe, Gray, 1983 .... 270.00
Duesenberg, Dark Blue, 1982 ....100.00 to 125.00
Duesenberg, Light Blue, 1982 ....100.00 to 110.00
Eagle, 1966 .... 12.00
Elks Club, 1968 .... 8.00
Emmett Kelly, Native Son Marking, 1973 .... 55.00
Emmett Kelly, Willie The Clown, 1973 ....25.00 to 35.00
Ernie's Flower Cart, 1976 .... 30.00
Evergreen State Club, 1974 .... 10.00
Executive, 1955, Royal Porcelain 195.00
Executive, 1956, Royal Gold Round 60.00
Executive, 1957, Royal Di Monte 35.00
Executive, 1958, Gray Cherub 120.00
Executive, 1959, Tavern Scene 45.00
Executive, 1960, Blue Cherub ....40.00 to 60.00
Executive, 1961, Golden Chalice 22.00
Executive, 1962, Flower Basket 25.00
Executive, 1963, Royal Rose 18.00
Executive, 1964, Royal Gold Diamond ....26.00 to 39.00
Executive, 1965, Marbled Fantasy 25.00
Executive, 1966, Majestic 15.00
Executive, 1967, Prestige 12.00
Executive, 1968, Presidential 14.00
Executive, 1969, Sovereign 10.00
Executive, 1970, Charisma 15.00
Executive, 1971, Fantasia 13.00
Executive, 1972, Regency 12.00
Executive, 1973, Phoenician 14.00
Executive, 1974, Twin Cherubs ....8.00 to 19.00
Executive, 1975, Reflections In Gold 13.00
Executive, 1976, Floro De Oro ....*Illus* 12.00
Executive, 1977, Golden Jubilee ....13.00 to 20.00
Executive, 1978, Yellow Rose Of Texas 18.00
Executive, 1979, Vase, Mother Of Pearl 18.00
Executive, 1980, Titian 16.00
Executive, 1981, Royal Filigree, Cobalt Deluxe 10.00
Executive, 1982, Americana Pitcher 22.00
Executive, 1983, Musical Bell, Embossed Partridge 35.00
Executive, 1984, Musical Bell, Noel 25.00
Executive, 1985, Vase, Italian Marble 23.00
Executive, 1986, Bowl, Italian Marble ....30.00 to 40.00
Executive, 1986, District Urn 40.00
Executive, 1987, Twin Doves 23.00
Expo '74, World's Fair, Spokane, USA, 1974 .... 7.00
Falstaff, Opera, 1979 .... 125.00
Father's Day Card, 1988 .... 18.00
Fiesta Bowl, 1973 .... 7.00
Figaro, Opera, 1977 ....110.00 to 115.00
Fighting Bull, 1981 .... 25.00
Fiji Islands, 1971 .... 5.00
Fire Chief's Car, 1981 ....66.00 to 105.00
Fire Engine, 1867 Model, Mississippi, 1978 ....125.00 to 150.00
Fire Engine, Ford, 1930 Model A, 1983 .... 150.00
Fire Pumper, Ford, 1934 Model, 1988 ....*Illus* 100.00
Fire Truck, Mack Bulldog, 1917 Model, 1982 .... 125.00

Beam, Fire
Pumper,
Ford, 1934
Model,
1988

Beam, CRLDA,
1973

Beam, Executive, 1976,
Floro De Oro

Beam, Ford,
Model T, 1913
Model, Black, 1974

First National Bank Of Chicago, 1964 .... 1500.00
Five Seasons Club, 1980 .... 10.00
Fleet Reserve, 1974 .... 7.00
Florida Shell, 1968 .... 7.00
Football, 1989 .... 55.00
Football Hall Of Fame, 1972 .... 25.00
Ford, 1903 Model, Black, 1978 .... 40.00
Ford, 1903 Model, Red, 1978 .... 40.00
Ford, Delivery Truck, Angelo's, 1900 Model, 1984 .... 200.00
Ford, Delivery Wagon, International, Woodie, 1929 Model, Black, 1984 .... 90.00
Ford, Model A, 1928 Model, 1980 .... 60.00
Ford, Model T, 1913 Model, Black, 1974 ....*Illus*   45.00
Ford, Mustang, 1964 Model, Black, 1986 .... 125.00
Ford, Mustang, 1964 Model, Red, 1986 .... 95.00
Ford, Mustang, 1964 Model, White, 1986 .... 75.00
Ford, Pickup Truck, Angelo's, 1935 Model, 1990 .... 60.00
Ford, Pickup Truck, Parkwood Supply, Model A, 1938 Model, 1984 .... 180.00
Ford, Police Car, 1929 Model, Blue, 1982 .... 95.00
Ford, Police Car, 1929 Model, Yellow, 1983 .... 445.00
Ford, Police Car, 1934 Model, Black & White, 1989 .... 120.00
Ford, Police Car, 1934 Model, Yellow, 1989 .... 120.00
Ford, Police Tow Truck, 1935 Model, 1988 .... 78.00
Ford, Roadster, 1934 Model, Cream, 1990 .... 85.00
Ford, Salesman's, 1928 Model, Black, 1981 .... 1000.00
Ford, Salesman's, 1928 Model, Yellow, 1981 .... 645.00
Ford, Thunderbird, 1956 Model, Black, 1986 .... 95.00
Ford, Thunderbird, 1956 Model, Blue, 1986 .... 125.00
Ford, Thunderbird, 1956 Model, Gray, 1986 .... 95.00
Ford, Thunderbird, 1956 Model, Green, 1986 .... 95.00
Ford, Thunderbird, 1956 Model, Yellow, 1986 .... 110.00
Ford, Woodie Delivery Wagon, 1929 Model, 1983 .... 100.00
Foremost, Black & Gold, 1956 .... 185.00
Foremost, Gray & Gold, 1956 .... 210.00
Foremost, Pink Speckled Beauty, 1956 .... 240.00
Fox, Blue, 1967 ....50.00 to 55.00
Fox, Gold, 1969 .... 25.00
Fox, Green, 1965 ....11.00 to 20.00
Fox, On Dolphin, 1980 .... 20.00
Fox, Red, 1973 .... 900.00
Fox, Renee, 1974 ....*Illus*   13.00
Fox, Rennie The Runner, 1974 .... 12.00
Fox, Rennie The Surfer, 1975 ....10.00 to 13.00
Fox, Uncle Sam, 1971 .... 20.00

Beam, Harp Seal, 1986

Beam, Fox,
Renee, 1974

Beam, Hawaiian Open,
11th, Outrigger, 1975

Beam, International
Chili Society, 1976

Fox, White, 1969	25.00
Franklin Mint, 1970	10.00
Gem City Club, 1983	30.00
General Stark, 1972	15.00
George Washington, 1976	20.00
Germany, Armed Forces, 1970	6.00
Germany, Hansel & Gretel, 1971	12.00
Germany, Pied Piper, 1974	10.00
Germany, Wiesbaden, 1973	8.00
Glen Campbell, 1976	20.00
Globe, Antique, 1980	24.00
Goose, Blue, 1979	6.00 to 15.00
Grand Canyon National Park, 50th Anniversary, 1969	10.00
Great Dane, 1976	22.00
Grecian, 1961	4.00
Green China Jug, Pussy Willow, 1965	8.00
Hannah Dustin, 1973	48.00
Harley-Davidson, 1988	200.00
Harolds Club, Covered Wagon, 1969	8.00
Harolds Club, Man In Barrel, No. 1, 1957	385.00 to 400.00
Harolds Club, Man In Barrel, No. 2, 1958	150.00
Harolds Club, Nevada, Gray, 1963	90.00
Harolds Club, Nevada, Silver, 1964	99.00
Harolds Club, Pinwheel, 1965	38.00 to 55.00
Harolds Club, Reno, 1970	40.00 to 55.00
Harolds Club, Silver Opal, 1957	18.00
Harolds Club, Slot Machine, Blue, 1967	12.00 to 25.00
Harolds Club, Slot Machine, Gray, 1968	9.00
Harolds Club, VIP, 1967	53.00
Harolds Club, VIP, 1968	58.00
Harolds Club, VIP, 1969	270.00
Harolds Club, VIP, 1970	48.00
Harolds Club, VIP, 1971	52.00
Harolds Club, VIP, 1972	21.00
Harolds Club, VIP, 1973	18.00
Harolds Club, VIP, 1974	20.00
Harolds Club, VIP, 1975	16.00
Harolds Club, VIP, 1976	20.00
Harolds Club, VIP, 1977	25.00
Harolds Club, VIP, 1978	25.00
Harolds Club, VIP, 1979	28.00
Harolds Club, VIP, 1980	20.00
Harolds Club, VIP, 1981	95.00
Harolds Club, VIP, 1982	50.00
Harp Seal, 1986 ....*Illus*	20.00

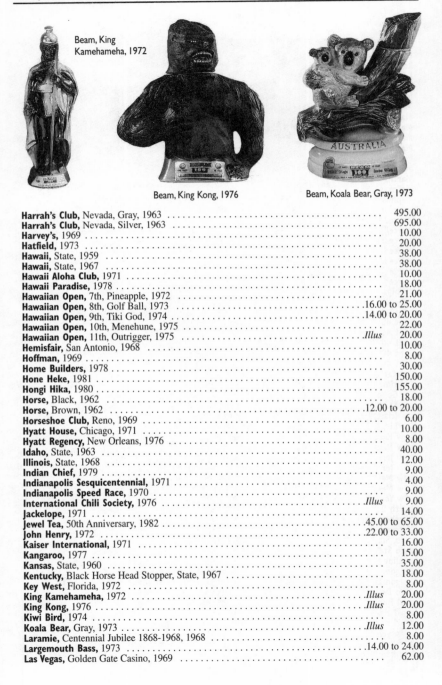

Beam, King Kamehameha, 1972

Beam, King Kong, 1976

Beam, Koala Bear, Gray, 1973

Harrah's Club, Nevada, Gray, 1963	495.00
Harrah's Club, Nevada, Silver, 1963	695.00
Harvey's, 1969	10.00
Hatfield, 1973	20.00
Hawaii, State, 1959	38.00
Hawaii, State, 1967	38.00
Hawaii Aloha Club, 1971	10.00
Hawaii Paradise, 1978	18.00
Hawaiian Open, 7th, Pineapple, 1972	21.00
Hawaiian Open, 8th, Golf Ball, 1973	16.00 to 25.00
Hawaiian Open, 9th, Tiki God, 1974	14.00 to 20.00
Hawaiian Open, 10th, Menehune, 1975	22.00
Hawaiian Open, 11th, Outrigger, 1975	*Illus* 20.00
Hemisfair, San Antonio, 1968	10.00
Hoffman, 1969	8.00
Home Builders, 1978	30.00
Hone Heke, 1981	150.00
Hongi Hika, 1980	155.00
Horse, Black, 1962	18.00
Horse, Brown, 1962	12.00 to 20.00
Horseshoe Club, Reno, 1969	6.00
Hyatt House, Chicago, 1971	10.00
Hyatt Regency, New Orleans, 1976	8.00
Idaho, State, 1963	40.00
Illinois, State, 1968	12.00
Indian Chief, 1979	9.00
Indianapolis Sesquicentennial, 1971	4.00
Indianapolis Speed Race, 1970	9.00
International Chili Society, 1976	*Illus* 9.00
Jackelope, 1971	14.00
Jewel Tea, 50th Anniversary, 1982	45.00 to 65.00
John Henry, 1972	22.00 to 33.00
Kaiser International, 1971	16.00
Kangaroo, 1977	15.00
Kansas, State, 1960	35.00
Kentucky, Black Horse Head Stopper, State, 1967	18.00
Key West, Florida, 1972	8.00
King Kamehameha, 1972	*Illus* 20.00
King Kong, 1976	*Illus* 20.00
Kiwi Bird, 1974	8.00
Koala Bear, Gray, 1973	*Illus* 12.00
Laramie, Centennial Jubilee 1868-1968, 1968	8.00
Largemouth Bass, 1973	14.00 to 24.00
Las Vegas, Golden Gate Casino, 1969	62.00

Las Vegas, Golden Nugget Casino, 1969 .... 52.00
Legion Music, Joliet Legion Band, 1978 .... 8.00
Light Bulb, 1979 .... 15.00
Lombard, Lilac, 1969 .... 6.00
London Bridge, 1971 .... 8.00
London Bridge With Medallion, 1969 .... 165.00
Louisville Downs, 1978 ....*Illus* 20.00
Madame Butterfly, Opera, 1977 .... 245.00
Magpies, 1977 .... 20.00
Maine, State, 1970 .... 6.00
Marbled Fantasy, 1965 .... 25.00
Mare & Foal, For The Love Of A Horse, 1982 .... 60.00
Marina City, 1962 .... 10.00
Marine Corps, 1975 ....35.00 to 50.00
Mark Anthony, 1962 .... 22.00
Martha Washington, 1975 ....6.00 to 15.00
McCoy, 1973 .... 18.00
Mephistopheles, Opera, 1979 .... 170.00
Mercedes Benz, 1974 Model, Blue, 1987 ....40.00 to 50.00
Mercedes Benz, 1974 Model, Gold, 1988 ....40.00 to 55.00
Mercedes Benz, 1974 Model, Green, 1987 .... 45.00
Mercedes Benz, 1974 Model, Mocha, 1987 ....45.00 to 55.00
Mercedes Benz, 1974 Model, Red, 1986 ....30.00 to 50.00
Mercedes Benz, 1974 Model, Sand Beige, 1987 .... 55.00
Mercedes Benz, 1974 Model, Silver, 1988 .... 100.00
Mercedes Benz, 1974 Model, White, 1986 ....55.00 to 65.00
Michigan, State, 1972 .... 9.00
Milwaukee, Stein, 1972 .... 26.00
Mint 400, 3rd, China Stopper, 1970 ....7.00 to 14.00
Mint 400, 4th, Metal Stopper, 1971 ....7.00 to 12.00
Mint 400, 5th, 1972 ....6.00 to 12.00
Mint 400, 6th, 1973 ....7.00 to 12.00
Mint 400, 7th, 1975 ....6.00 to 12.00
Mint 400, 8th, 1976 .... 12.00
Montana, State, 1963 .... 50.00
Mortimer Snerd, 1976 ....*Illus* 18.00
Mr. Goodwrench, 1978 .... 28.00
Mt. St. Helens, 1980 .... 22.00
Musicians On Wine Cask, 1964 .... 6.00
Muskie, 1971 ....18.00 to 25.00
New Hampshire, State, 1967 .... 8.00
New Hampshire Eagle, 1971 .... 22.00
New Jersey, State, Blue, 1963 .... 35.00
New Jersey, State, Yellow, 1963 .... 35.00
New Mexico, Bicentennial, 1976 .... 12.00
New Mexico, Wedding Vase, 1972 .... 10.00
New York World's Fair, 1964 .... 16.00
North Dakota, State, 1964 .... 39.00
Northern Pike, 1978 ....16.00 to 20.00
Nutcracker, 1978 .... 90.00
Ohio, State, 1966 ....6.00 to 10.00
Ohio State Fair, 1973 ....6.00 to 10.00
Opaline Crystal, 1969 .... 6.00
Oregon, State, 1959 ....20.00 to 28.00
Oregon Liquor Control, 1984 .... 35.00
Osco Drug, 1987 .... 16.00
Paul Bunyan, 1970 ....*Illus* 37.00
Pearl Harbor, 1972 .... 18.00
Pearl Harbor Survivors, 1976 .... 8.00
Pennsylvania, State, 1967 ....4.00 to 12.00
Pennsylvania Dutch Club, 1974 .... 9.00
Permian Basin Oil Show, 1972 ....6.00 to 10.00

Beam, Louisville Downs, 1978

Beam,
Mortimer Snerd,
1976

Beam,
Paul Bunyan,
1970

PGA, 53rd Golf Tournament, 1971 .... 18.00
Pheasant, 1960 .... 18.00
Phi Sigma Kappa, 1973 .... 15.00
Phoenician, 1973 .... 9.00
Political, Donkey, 1960, Campaigner 20.00
Political, Donkey, 1964, Boxer 20.00
Political, Donkey, 1968, Clown 10.00
Political, Donkey, 1972, Football 15.00
Political, Donkey, 1976, Drum 12.00
Political, Donkey, 1980, Superman 22.00
Political, Donkey, 1984, Computer 32.00
Political, Donkey, Democratic Convention, 1988 .... 20.00
Political, Elephant, 1960, Campaigner 20.00
Political, Elephant, 1964, Boxer 20.00
Political, Elephant, 1968, Clown 15.00
Political, Elephant, 1970, Spiro Agnew 1100.00
Political, Elephant, 1972, Miami Beach 200.00
Political, Elephant, 1972, Washington, D.C. Republican Dinner 500.00
Political, Elephant, 1976, Drum ....22.00 to 40.00
Political, Elephant, 1980, Superman 22.00
Ponderosa, 1969 .... 15.00
Ponderosa, One Millionth Visitor, 1972 .... 16.00
Pony Express, 1968 .... 10.00
Pony Express, Full Contents, 1968 .... 30.00
Poodle, Gray, 1970 .... 15.00
Poodle, White, 1970 .... 12.00
Portland Rose Festival, 1972 .... 8.00
Poulan Chain Saw, 1979 ....25.00 to 30.00
Preakness, 100th, Pimlico, 1975 .... 22.00
Pretty Perch, 1980 .... 15.00
Prima Donna, 1969 .... 6.00
Queensland, Australia, 1978 .... 20.00
Rainbow Trout, 1975 ....15.00 to 20.00
Ralph's Market, 1973 .... 12.00
Ram, 1958 .... 40.00
Ramada Inn, 1976 .... 5.00
Red Mile, 1975 ....12.00 to 18.00
Redwood Empire, 1967 .... 8.00
Reflection In Gold, 1975 .... 12.00
Reidsville, 1973 ....6.00 to 10.00
Republic Of Texas Club, 1980 .... 18.00
Richard's, New Mexico, 1967 .... 7.00
Robin, 1969 ....6.00 to 10.00
Rocky Marciano, 1973 .... 39.00
Ruidosa Downs, Pointed Ears, 1968 ....25.00 to 35.00

Sahara Invitational, 1971 .... 18.00
Sailfish, 1957 .... 22.00
Samoa, 1973 ....5.00 to 10.00
San Diego, 1968 .... 5.00
San Francisco Cable Car, 1983 ....*Illus* 50.00
Santa Claus, 1983 ....110.00 to 135.00
Santa Fe, 1960 .... 90.00
Saturday Evening Post, Benjamin Franklin, 1975 ....*Illus* 7.00
Saturday Evening Post, Elect Casey, 1975 .... 6.00
Saturday Evening Post, Game Called Because Of Rain, 1975 ....6.00 to 15.00
Saturday Evening Post, Homecoming G.I., 1975............................. 6.00
Saturday Evening Post, Pioneers, 1975.................................. 6.00
Saturday Evening Post, Ye Pipe & Bowl, 1975 .... 6.00
Screech Owl, Gray, 1979 .... 22.00
Screech Owl, Red, 1979 .... 20.00
Seafair, 1972 ....6.00 to 13.00
Seattle World's Fair, 1962 ....12.00 to 17.00
Seoul, Korea, 1988 .... 20.00
Sheraton Hotel, 1975 .... 6.00
Short Timer, Helmet & Boots, 1975 ....18.00 to 25.00
Shriners, El Kahir Pyramid, 1975 .... 12.00
Shriners, Moila, Camel, 1975 .... 20.00
Shriners, Moila, Sword, 1972 .... 20.00
Shriners, Rajah, 1977 .... 20.00
Shriners, Western Shriners Association, 1980 .... 15.00
Sigma Nu Fraternity, Kentucky, 1977...............................8.00 to 12.00
Sigma Nu Fraternity, Michigan, 1977...............................9.00 to 15.00
Smith's North Shore Club, 1972 .... 12.00
Smoked Geni, 1964 .... 50.00
Snow Goose, 1979 .... 10.00
South Carolina, State, 1970 ....5.00 to 15.00
South Dakota, Mt. Rushmore, 1969 ....6.00 to 10.00
Spenger's Fish Grotto, 1977 ....*Illus* 20.00
Sports Car Club Of America, 1976 .... 12.00
St. Bernard, 1979 ....22.00 to 35.00
St. Louis Arch, 1964 .... 9.00
St. Louis Club, 1972 .... 8.00
Stanley Steamer, 1909 .... 25.00
Statue Of Liberty, 1975 ....12.00 to 22.00
Stone Mountain, 1974 ....15.00 to 20.00
Sturgeon, 1980 ....16.00 to 20.00
Stutz Bearcat, 1914, Gray, 1977 .... 40.00
Stutz Bearcat, 1914, Yellow, 1977 .... 40.00
Submarine Redfin, 1970 .... 8.00
Sunburst Crystal, Amber, 1974 .... 4.00
Sunburst Crystal, Black, 1974 ....4.00 to 6.00

Beam, San Francisco Cable Car, 1983

Beam, Saturday
Evening Post,
Benjamin Franklin,
1975

Sunburst Crystal, Blue, 1974	4.00
Sunburst Crystal, Green, 1974	4.00
Sunburst Crystal, Red, 1974	4.00
Superdome, Louisiana, 1975	4.00
Swagman, Australian Hobo, 2nd National Convention, 1979	12.00 to 25.00
Sydney Opera House, 1977	15.00 to 23.00
Telephone, 1897 Model, 1978	30.00
Telephone, 1904 Model, 100-Digit Dial, 1983	25.00 to 50.00
Telephone, 1919 Dial, 1980	50.00
Telephone, Battery, 1982	35.00
Telephone, French Cradle, 1979	20.00
Telephone, Wall Set, 1975	20.00
Texas Rabbit, 1971	16.00
Thailand, 1969	4.00
Thomas Flyer, Blue, 1976	25.00 to 45.00
Thomas Flyer, White, 1976	20.00 to 45.00
Tiffany Poodle, 1973	19.00
Tigers, 1977	15.00
Tobacco Festival, 1973	10.00 to 15.00
Train, Box Car, 1983	60.00
Train, Casey Jones Box Car, 1990	25.00 to 45.00
Train, Casey Jones Caboose, 1989	20.00
Train, Casey Jones Tank Car, 1990	45.00
Train, Casey Jones, With Tender, 1989	40.00 to 50.00
Train, General Caboose, Gray, 1988	65.00
Train, General Caboose, Yellow, 1985	85.00
Train, General Combination Car, 1988	35.00
Train, General Flat Car, 1988	75.00 to 85.00
Train, General Locomotive, 1986	115.00 to 120.00
Train, Grant Baggage Car, 1981	45.00 to 50.00
Train, Grant Dining Car, 1982	69.00 to 90.00
Train, Grant Observation Car, 1985	50.00
Train, Grant Passenger Car, 1981	45.00 to 50.00
Train, J.B. Turner Locomotive, 1982	125.00 to 154.00
Train, Turner Log Car, 1984	75.00
Train, Turner Lumber Car, 1986	50.00
Train, Turner Tank Car, 1983	29.00 to 55.00
Train, Turner Wood Tender, 1988	79.00
Train, Water Tower, 1985	45.00
TraveLodge, Sleepy Bear, 1972	10.00 to 18.00
Treasure Chest, 1979	12.00
Trout Unlimited, 1977	20.00
Truth Or Consequences, 1974	6.00
Turtle, 1975	19.00
Twin Bridges Club, 1971	22.00

Beam, Spenger's Fish Grotto, 1977

Beam, Zimmerman Liquors, Eldorado, Gray Blue, 1978

Beam, Walleye Pike, 1977

U.S. Open, 1972 .... 25.00
Veterans Of Foreign Wars, 1971 .... 6.00
Viking, 1973 .... 12.00
Volkswagen, Blue, 1973 ....40.00 to 52.00
Volkswagen, Red, 1973 ....45.00 to 50.00
Von's 75th Anniversary, 1981 .... 25.00
Walleye Pike, 1977 ....*Illus* 55.00
Washington, State, 1975 .... 15.00
Washington State Bicentennial, 1976 .... 8.00
West Virginia, State, 1963 ....72.00 to 115.00
WGA, Western Open, 1971 .... 18.00
Wild Burro Races, Beauty, Nevada, 1970 ....14.00 to 20.00
Woodpecker, 1969 .... 8.00
Wyoming, State, 1965 ....22.00 to 40.00
Yellow Katz, 1967 .... 8.00
Yellowstone National Park, 1972 .... 10.00
Yosemite, Decal Map, 1967 .... 24.00
Yuma Rifle Club, 1968 .... 16.00
Zimmerman Liquors, 2-Handled Jug, 1965 .... 50.00
Zimmerman Liquors, 50th Anniversary, 1983 .... 30.00
Zimmerman Liquors, Art Institute, 1972 .... 8.00
Zimmerman Liquors, Bell, Dark Blue, 1976 ....5.00 to 12.00
Zimmerman Liquors, Bell, Light Blue, 1976 ....4.00 to 12.00
Zimmerman Liquors, Blue Beauty, 1969 ....7.00 to 12.00
Zimmerman Liquors, Cherubs, Lavender, 1968 ....5.00 to 10.00
Zimmerman Liquors, Cherubs, Salmon, 1968 ....6.00 to 10.00
Zimmerman Liquors, Eldorado, Gray Blue, 1978 ....*Illus* 9.00
Zimmerman Liquors, Peddler, 1971 ....6.00 to 12.00
Zimmerman Liquors, Vase, Brown, 1972 .... 9.00
Zimmerman Liquors, Vase, Green, 1972 .... 9.00
Zimmerman Liquors, Z, 1970 .... 10.00

BEER

History says that beer was first made in America in the Roanoke Colony of Virginia in 1587. It is also claimed that the Pilgrims brought some over on the already crowded Mayflower. William Penn started a brewery in 1683. By the time of the Civil War, beer was made and bottled in all parts of the United States. In the early years the beer was poured from kegs or sold in ordinary unmarked black glass bottles. English stoneware bottles were in common use in this country from about 1860 to 1890. Excavations in many inner cities still unearth these sturdy containers. A more or less standard bottle was used by about 1870. It held a quart of liquid and measured about 10 inches high. The early ones were plain and had a cork stopper. Later bottles had embossed lettering on the sides. The lightning stopper was invented in 1875 and many bottles had various types of wire and lever-type seals that were replacements for the corks. In the 1900s Crown corks were used. It wasn't long before plain bottles with paper labels appeared, but cans were soon the containers preferred by many. The standard thick-topped glass beer bottle shape of the 1870s, as well as modern beer bottles, are included in this category. The bottles can be found in clear, brown, aqua, or amber glass. A few cobalt blue, milk glass, or red examples are known. Some bottles have turned slightly amethyst in color from the sun. Picnic is the collector's name for a 64-ounce beer bottle. Collectors are often interested in local breweries and books listing the names and addresses of companies have been written. (See Bibliography.) Beer bottle collectors often search for advertising trays, signs, and other *go-withs* collected as *breweriana*. These are listed under Go-Withs at the end of this book.

A. Palmtag & Co., Eureka, Ca., Amber, Tooled Top, Pt. 55.00
A.S.B. Co., Adam Scheidt Brewing Co., Norristown, Pa., Monogram, Pt. 22.00
Adam's Ale House, Concord, N.H., Milwaukee Lager, Yellow, Pt. 275.00
American Brewing, West Berkeley, Cal., Amber, Eagle, Blob Top, 1/2 Pt. 99.00
Babb & Co., San Francisco, Cal., Medium Emerald Green, Sloping Collar, IP, 7 3/8 In. 179.00
Bass Kings Ale, Contents, Label, England, 1901 .... 71.00
Bay Bottling Co., San Francisco Cal., Amber 33.00
Bay View Brewing Co., Seattle, Washington, Green, Pt. 660.00
Bay View Brewing Co., Seattle, Washington, Green, Wire Bail, Porcelain Stopper, Qt. 3575.00

Beer Steam Bottling Co., WG & Son, Wm. Goeppert & Son, S.F., Amber, Qt. 330.00
Boca Beer, Amber, B.O.B. In Circle, Applied Top, Qt. 231.00
Boca Brewing Co., Boca, Ca., Amber, Applied Top, Qt. 121.00
Brasserie De Sochaux, Applied Top, Original Porcelain Stopper 44.00
Bru-Joy Labeled Pilsner, Reading, Pa., 12 Oz. 40.00
Buffalo Brewing Co., S.F. Agency, Amber, Monogram, Qt. 33.00
Buffalo Brewing Co., S.F. Agency, Light Amber, BBCo In Circle, 1/2 Pt. 55.00
Buffalo Brewing Co., Sacramento, Calif., Red Amber, Applied Top, Qt. 110.00
Buffalo Brewing Co., San Francisco, BBCo Monogram, Amber, Crown Stop, 11 1/4 In. .. 9.00
C. Rothfuss & Co., Boston, Mass., Aqua, Tooled Top, Pt. 44.00
C. Schnerr & Co., Sacramento, Ca., Amber, Tooled Top 55.00
C.A. Krueger, Erie, Pa., Yellow, Tooled Top, Pt. 44.00
C.H. Daniels Brewery, Manistee, Mich., Amber, Qt. 40.00
Carling's Amber Ale, London, Black Glass, Red, Black & White Label, Blob Top, 10 1/2 In. 30.00
Carlisle New Brewery Stout, Coat Of Arms, England 26.00
Carlisle Old Brewery Stout, Coat Of Arms, England 26.00
Casey & Kabanaugh, Sacramento, Ca., Amber, Tooled Top 22.00
Chicago Lager Beer, Chicago Brewing Co., S.F., Amber, Applied Top, Wire Bail 385.00
Consumers Bottling Co., Redwood Cal., Amber, Monogram, Qt. 385.00
Consumers Bottling Co., S.F., Cal., Amber, Script Letters, Porcelain Stopper, 1/2 Pt. 77.00
Corona Light, Glass, Miniature, 3 In. 12.00
D. Germanus, 228 Morrison St., Portland, Or., Light Green Aqua, Tooled Top, 1/2 Gal. ... 413.00
D. Tweedie, San Francisco, Red Hand Trademark, Amber, Tooled Top, 1/2 Pt. 110.00
D.L. Ormsby, New York, Cobalt Blue, Blob Top, IP, 7 3/8 In. 246.00
Delaney & Young, Eureka, Ca., Amber, Tooled Top, Qt. 44.00
Dr. Cronk Gibbon's & Co., Teal 468.00
Drewry & Sons, Paper Label, 7 Oz. 6.50
Duke Ale, The Prince Of Pilsners, Amber, Label, 7 Oz. .... *Illus* 8.50
Duquesne, Amber, Red, Blue, Gold, White Labels, Uniformed Man, Pittsburgh, Penn. ... 8.00
Duquesne Pilsner, Amber, Label, 12 Oz. .... *Illus* 10.00
Eagle Brewery, San Francisco, Cal., Amber, Tooled Top, 1904-1906, Qt. 77.00
Eagle Brewing Co., San Francisco, Amber, Embossed, Bubble, Wire Bail, 7 Oz. 44.00
Eagle Brewing Co., San Francisco, Amber, Wire Bail, Porcelain Stopper, 1/2 Pt. 358.00
El Dorado Brewing Co., Stockton, Ca., Amber, Tooled Top, Qt. 33.00
Elks Brewing, Raised Elk Head Emblem, Kittaning, Penn., 12 Oz. 6.00
Enterprise Brewing Co., S.F., Cal., Clear, Tooled Top, 1/2 Pt. 44.00
Enterprise Brewing Co., San Francisco, Amber, Applied Top, Pt. 160.00
Enterprise Brewing Co., San Francisco, Amber, Monogram, 3-Piece Mold, 11 7/8 In. 11.00
Enterprise Brewing Co., San Francisco, Red Amber, Applied Top, 1/2 Pt. 40.00
Etna Brewery, Etna Mills, Amber, Tooled Top 22.00
F.O. Brandt, Healdsburg, Amber, 1/2 Pt. 55.00

Beer, Duke Ale, The
Prince Of Pilsners,
Amber, Label, 7 Oz.

Beer, Duquesne
Pilsener, Amber,
Label, 12 Oz.

Beer, Frank Wright Ale,
Indianapolis, Amber,
Sloping Double Collar,
9 3/8 In.

Beer, Gambrinus Bottling
Co., Pittsburgh, Pa.,
Honey Amber, Metal
Stopper, 8 7/8 In.

Falstaff Brewing Co., Lemp, St. Louis, Crown Top, Aqua 40.00
Fancy S In Circle, Dark Green, Applied Top, 1965, Qt. 132.00
Finlay Brewing Co., Toledo, O., Aqua, Blob Top 6.00
Fort Pitt Brewing Co., Pittsburgh, Pa., Pitt Block House, Amber, Label 8.00
Frank Wright Ale, Indianapolis, Amber, Sloping Double Collar, 9 3/8 In. ....*Illus* 179.00
Frank Wright Ale, Indianapolis, Emerald Green, Sloping Collar, 9 3/8 In. 560.00
Frank Wright Ale, Indianapolis, Green, Olive Tone, Double Collar, 9 1/4 In. 588.00
Fredericksburg Bottling Co., S.F., Amber, Tooled Top, Qt. 44.00
Fredericksburg Bottling Co., S.F., Green, Applied Top, Pt. 33.00
Fredericksburg Bottling Co., S.F., Olive Green, Applied Top, Qt. 55.00
G. Schnerr & Co., Sacramento, Cal., Amber, Tooled Top, 1/2 Pt. 66.00
G.W. Hoxsie's Premium Beer, Blue Green, 1865-1875, 6 5/8 In. 308.00
G.W. McIntyre Co., Stockton, Cal., Dark Amber, Tooled Top, 1/2 Gal. 303.00
Gambrinus Bottling Co., Pittsburgh, Pa., Honey Amber, Metal Stopper, 8 7/8 In. ....*Illus* 224.00
Geo. Braun Bottler, 2219 Pine St. S.F., Amber, Monogram, Tooled Top, Qt. 55.00
Geo. J. Renner Brewing Co., Pure Beer, Akron, O., ABM 5.00
Geo. S. Lad & Co., Liquor Dealers, 19 So. Hunter St., Stockton, Amber, Tooled, 1/2 Gal. .. 143.00
Gold Medal Agency, G. Maurer, Prop., San Jose, Cal., Orange Amber, Tooled Top, Pt. ... 77.00
Golden Gate Bottling Works, Chas. Rochmann, San Francisco, Amber, 1/2 Pt. .....44.00 to 77.00
Golden Gate Bottling Works, San Francisco, Amber, Embossed Bear, Tooled Top, Qt. 88.00
Golden Gate Bottling Works, San Francisco, Bear, Amber, Porcelain Stopper, 1/2 Pt. ... 132.00
Gurney's Family Grocers, Wine Spirit Merchants, Hereford 37.50
Gustav Gnauck, Benicia Brewery, Benicia Cal., Amber, Pt. 77.00
Gustav Gnauck, Benicia, Cal., Amber, Stopper, Qt. 55.00
H. & C. Overdick, Cincinnati, Cobalt Blue, 12-Sided, IP, 1860, 8 5/8 In. 2860.00
H. Day Peterson, Watsonville Cal., Amber, Qt. 44.00
H. Day Peterson, Watsonville Cal., Green, Applied Top, Pt. 33.00
H. Ferneding, Dayton, O., Ice Blue, 3-Piece Mold, Double Collar, Qt. 700.00
H.G. Co., Amber, Blob Top, Stained, Qt. 30.00
Harrisburg Bottling Works, Harrisburg, Pa., Anheuser-Busch Eagle 45.00
Henley Ales Brakespears Brewery & Spirit Stores, Henley On Thames, White, 6 In. 16.00
Henry G. Meyer, San Francisco, Cal., Amber, Wire Bail, Porcelain Stopper, Label, 1/2 Pt. . 77.00
Herm Goring Roettgenstedt Gastwirt, Green, Germany, Qt. 33.00
Hocking Ruby, Anchor Hocking, Textured, 8 x 2 1/4 In. 80.00
Hoster Co., Columbus, O., Amber, Tooled Top, Qt. 33.00
Hoster's, Columbus, O., Wiener Beer, Amber, Blob Top 8.00
I. Roseburg Brewing, Oregon, Amber, Crown Top, Qt. 55.00
Independent Brewing & Malting Co., Davenport, Iowa, Amber, Stopper, 1/2 Gal. 125.00
Iroquois Buffalo, Indian With Headdress, Blob Top, Amber 17.00
J. Graham & Son, Queen's Brewery 57.00
J. Wise, Allentown, Pa., Cobalt Blue, Striations, Blob Top, 7 In. 336.00
J.H. Collins, Ithaca, N.Y., Blue, Stopper, Short Neck, Blob, 7 In. 39.00
James Gibb, Imported & Bottle, Amber, Tooled Top, Qt. 198.00
James Pereira, Santa Clara, Ca., Amber, Tooled Top, Qt. 44.00
Japan Brewery Company Ltd., Yokohama, Yellow, Qt. 110.00
John Strohm, Jackson, Cal., Amber, Monogram, Crown Top, Qt. 176.00
John Wieland's Export Beer, Cal. Bottling Co., S.F., Amber, Blob Top, Pt. 22.00
John Wieland's Export Beer, Cal. Bottling Co., S.F., Red, Tooled Top 33.00
Johnson Liverpool Trademark Registered With Compass, Green, Pt. 44.00
Jordan Deer, Mankato Brewing Co., Paper Label, Mankato, Minn. 15.00
Jos. Schlitz Brewing Co., Oswego, N.Y., Amber, Applied Top 143.00
Jug, Ask For Bentley's Bitter Beer, Rotherham, White, Black & Red Print, 3 In. 56.00
K & M Oakland, Amber, Tooled Top, 1/2 Pt. 55.00
M. Bixel & Sons, Lager Beer, Strathroy & Brantford, Aqua, Blob Top, 11 In. 170.00
M. Bixel & Sons, Strathroy & Brantford, Aqua, Blob Top, Canada, 10 In. 100.00
Magnus Beck Brewing Co., Buffalo, N.Y., Blob Top 8.00
Martin Bros. Angels, Amber, Tooled Top, Qt. 198.00
Mason & Co. XXX Porter, Emerald Green, Slug Plate, Blob Top, IP, 6 3/8 In. 308.00
Mettlach, Cerveza-San-Miguel, Marked 535, 55 Villeroy & Boch, Mettlach, 8 3/4 In. 69.00
Milwaukee Lager, J. Cahm, 83 State St., Boston, Mass., Lime Green, Applied Top, Pt. ... 99.00
Monongahela Brewery, H. Roth, Monongahela, Pa., Amber, Crown Top 6.00
Monongahela Valley Brewing Co., Clinton, Pa., Brown, Buck's Head, 12 Oz. ....8.00 to 29.00
N. Cervelli, 615 Francisco St., S.F., Amber, Porcelain Stopper, 1/2 Pt. 132.00

National Bottling Co., San Francisco, Amber, Eagle, Embossed, Porcelain Stopper 66.00
National Bottling Co., San Francisco, Cal., Light Amber, Tooled Top, Qt. 66.00
National Bottling Works, Embossed, Not To Be Sold, Blob Top, Wm. H. Earl, 9 1/4 In. . . 18.00
National Bottling Works, San Francisco, Cal., Amber, Wire Bail, Stopper, Qt. 99.00
National Bottling Works, San Francisco, Cal., Dark Amber, Eagle, Tooled Top, Qt. 165.00
NBWC Westminster Brewery, Emerald Green, BIMAL, Crown Top, Qt., 11 1/2 In. 30.00
Newbury Brewery, 1/2 Gal. 30.00
North Eastern Breweries Ltd., Sunderland, Embossed, Dray Cart, c.1900, 1/2 Pt., 8 In. .. 10.00
North Star Bottling Works, S.F., Cal., Dark Amber, Blob Top, Wire Bail, Stopper, 1/2 Pt. 66.00
North Star Bottling Works, S.F., Cal., Yellow Amber, Star, Blob Top, 1/2 Pt. 33.00
Oakland Bottling Co., Oakland, Cal., Amber, Blob Top, 1/2 Pt. 55.00
Old Export Premium Beer, Amber, 2 Labels, Mountain Water Makes The Difference ... 8.00
Pabst, Milwaukee, L.B. Wheat Bottler, Wheeling, W. Va., Amber, Blob Top 12.00
Pabst, Milwaukee, Raised Label, Marked WF & Sons, 12 Oz. 6.00
Pacific Bottling Co., Light Amber, Monogram, Porcelain Stopper, Qt. 132.00
Palmtag & Co., Eureka, Ca., Amber, Tooled Top, Qt. 44.00
People's Brewing Company, Hand Painted Eagle Over Logo & Shield, 11 1/2 In. 45.00
Peter Hand Brewing Co., Il., Label, 1950s, 12 Oz. 6.00
Peter Mugler Brewer, Sisson, Ca., Amber, Tooled Top, Qt. 121.00
Philadelphia XXX Porter & Ale, Honesdale, Green Aqua, Block Mouth, IP, 6 3/8 In. 209.00
Philadelphia XXX Porter & Ale, Olive Yellow Green, Sloping Collar, IP, 6 1/2 In. 588.00
Phoenix Bottling Works, Buffalo, N.Y., Amber, Crown Top 8.50
Porter, James Wadeson, Hull, Slip Glaze, England, 10 In. 21.00
Prospect Brewing Co., Phila., Amber, Crown Top, Short, 8 Oz. 5.00
Rainier Beer Brewing & Malting Co., Seattle, Wash., Green, Split Crown Top, 1/2 Pt. ... 132.00
Rainier Brewing Company, Label, Seattle, Wash., Pt. ....5.00 to 15.00
Raspiller Brewing Co., West Berkeley, Golden Amber, Eagle, Blob Top, 1/2 Pt. 121.00
Raspiller Brewing Eagle, West Berkeley, California, Amber, Crown Top, Pt. 45.00
Reinhardt & Co., Lager Beer, Toronto, Black, Blob Top, 9 1/2 In. 190.00
Richmond Bottling Works, Amber, Tooled Top, North Star Bottling Works Stopper 33.00
Robert Deuchar Limited Sandyford Road, Newcastle On Tyne, Stoneware, 8 1/2 In. 25.00
Robert Portner Brewing Co., Alexandria, Va., Aqua, Blob Top 10.00
Rochester Brew Co., Boston Branch, Aqua, Bubbles, Blob Top, Lightning Stopper 8.50
Royal Ruby Anchor Glass Beer, No Deposit No Return, 8 In. 80.00
Ruppert Knickerbocker, King Size, Neck Label, 1950s, Pt. 1.00
S. Monogram, Green, Applied Top, Monogram In Circle, Qt. 77.00
Saltzman Bros., Palace Hill Brewery, Oil City, Pa., Amber, Blob Top 12.00
Saltzman Bros. Brewery, Oil City, Pa., Amber, Blob Top 8.50
Saltzman Bros. Brewery, Oil City, Pa., Aqua, Crown Top 8.00
San Francisco Glass Works, Emerald Green, Applied Mouth, 6 7/8 In. 260.00
San Jose Bottling Co., Maurer, Amber, Wire Bail, Qt. 88.00
Schlitz, Crown Top, Aqua 35.00
Schlitz, Royal Ruby, Anniversary, Embossed, Anchor Hocking, 1950s, 10 x 3 1/2 In. 38.00
Schmulbach Brewing Co., Wheeling., W. Va., Aqua, Blob Top, Monogram 12.00
Seal Rock Bottling Co., J. Kroger, San Francisco, Ca., Amber, Tooled Top, 1/2 Pt. 99.00
Sierra Borrling Co., Wieland's Best, Jamestown, Ca., Amber, Porcelain Stopper 440.00
Spruance Stanley & Co., Wholesale Liquor Dealers, San Francisco, Ca., Amber, 1869 ... 55.00
St. Helena Bottling & Cold Storage Co., St. Helena, Ca., Amber, Tooled Top 55.00
Standard Bottling Company, Denver, Colorado 22.00
Standard Brewery, Chicago, Bottle Is Never Sold, Aqua, Blob Top 8.00
Stockton Wholesale Liquor Co., Stockton, Cal., Amber, Blob Top, Stopper, 1/2 Gal. 143.00
Swan Brewery Co., XXX Ale, Olive Yellow, Applied Top 1430.00
Swan Brewery Co., XXX Ale, This Bottle Never Sold, Swan, Olive Yellow 1430.00
Swan Brewery Co., XXX, Lime Green, Blob Top, c.1870, 1/2 Pt. 880.00
T.D. Greene's Porter Ale & Cider, New York, Blue Green, Sloping Collar, IP, 6 3/8 In. ... 336.00
T.H. Buttorf, Newport, Pa., Aqua, Stopper, Blob Top, Squat, 6 3/4 In. 39.00
Theo. Gier Co., Oakland & San Francisco, Amber, Tooled Top, 1/2 Gal. 220.00
Theodore Ludtke, San Jose, Cal., This Bottle Not To Be Sold, Amber, Applied Top, Qt. .. 132.00
Ticoulet Beshorman, Sac., Cal., Amber, Blob Top, Qt. 33.00
Tusker Beer, Elephant Shape, Jug, Brown & White Glaze, 9 1/4 In. 112.00
W.H. Burt, San Francisco, Blue Green, Blob Top, IP, 7 3/8 In. 179.00
Weiss Beer, Joseph Loder, Atlantic City, N.J., Aqua, Blob, Squat 45.00
Wreden's Lager, Oakland, Ca., Amber, Tooled Top, Original Porcelain Stopper 44.00

Wunder Bottling Co., San Francisco, Cal., Amber, Blob Top, Pt. 33.00
Wunder Bottling Works, Oakland, Ca., Red Amber 55.00
Yough Brewing Co., Connellsville, Pa., Amber, Indianhead, Feather Bonnet, Crown Top . . 6.00
Young's Botanic Brewery, West Bromwich 30.00

─────────────────────── BININGER ───────────────────────

Bininger and Company of New York City was a family-owned grocery and dry goods store. It was founded by the 1820s and remained in business into the 1880s. The store sold whiskey, wine, and other liquors. After a while they began bottling their products in their own specially designed bottles. The first bottles were ordered from England but it wasn't long before the local glass factories made the Bininger's special figural containers. Barrels, clocks, cannons, jugs, and flasks were made. Colors were usually shades of amber, green, or puce.

A.M. & Co., 19 Broad St., N.Y., Barrel, Amber, OP, Qt. 242.00
A.M. & Co., 19 Broad St., N.Y., Cannon, Amber, Tooled Lip, 1875, 12 3/8 In. 7250.00
A.M. & Co., 19 Broad St., N.Y., Cannon, Yellow Amber, 12 3/8 In. .... .700.00 to 756.00
A.M. & Co., 19 Broad St., N.Y., Jug, Gold Amber, Double Collar, 8 In. 303.00
A.M. & Co., 19 Broad St., N.Y., Jug, Yellow Amber, Double Collar, 8 In. 523.00
A.M. & Co., 19 Broad St., N.Y., Night Cap, Gold Amber, Glass Screw Stopper, 8 In. 1176.00
A.M. & Co., 19 Broad St., N.Y., Old London Dock Gin, 10 In. 130.00
A.M. & Co., 19 Broad St., N.Y., Old London Dock Gin, Amber, ISP, Applied Top . .110.00 to 160.00
A.M. & Co., 19 Broad St., N.Y., Old London Dock Gin, Forest Green, 9 1/2 In. ... .143.00 to 175.00
A.M. & Co., 19 Broad St., N.Y., Old London Dock Gin, Gold Amber, 1855-1870, 9 3/4 In. 168.00
A.M. & Co., 19 Broad St., N.Y., Old London Dock Gin, Olive Green, 1855-1870, 8 In. ... 179.00
A.M. & Co., 19 Broad St., N.Y., Peep-O-Day, Gold Amber, 1855-1870, 7 7/8 In. 924.00
A.M. & Co., 338 Broadway, N.Y., Barrel, Medium Amber, Applied Top 120.00
A.M. & Co., 338 Broadway, N.Y., Old London Dock Gin, Olive Yellow, 9 In. 420.00
A.M. & Co., 338 Broadway, N.Y., Old London Dock Gin, Yellow Green 187.00
A.M. & Co., 375 Broadway, N.Y., Smoky Topaz, 1855-1870, 9 3/4 In. 2184.00
A.M. & Co., Clock, Yellow Amber, Pontil, 6 In. 795.00
A.M. & Co., Cluster Of Grapes, Double Collar, 1855-1865, 10 5/8 In. 2184.00
A.M. & Co., Golden Apple Cordial, 19 Broad St., N.Y., Olive Green, 9 7/8 In. 3640.00
A.M. & Co., Heidelberg Branntwein, Olive Yellow Green, 1855-1870, 9 1/2 In. 672.00
A.M. & Co., Jug, Gold Amber, Sloping Collar, 1855-1870, 7 5/8 In. 17920.00
A.M. & Co., New York, Gin, Case, Blue Green, IP, 1855-1870, 9 3/8 In. 2016.00
A.M. & Co., Old Dominion Wheat Tonic, Bright Olive 193.00
A.M. & Co., Old Dominion Wheat Tonic, Olive Yellow Green, 1855-1870, 9 In. 308.00
A.M. & Co., Old Kentucky Bourbon, 1848 Reserve, Barrel, Medium Amber, OP, 8 In. 257.00
A.M. & Co., Old Kentucky Bourbon, 1849 Reserve, Barrel, Medium Amber, OP, 8 In. 330.00
A.M. & Co., Old Kentucky Bourbon, Barrel, Amber, Bubbles, OP 345.00
A.M. & Co., Old Kentucky Bourbon, Distilled In 1848, Barrel, Amber, 1855-1870, 8 In. .. 392.00
A.M. & Co., Old Kentucky Bourbon, Distilled In 1848, Barrel, Olive, 1855-1870, 9 In. ... 6160.00
A.M. & Co., Traveler's Guide, Flask, Amber, c.1880, 6 5/8 In. 358.00
A.M. & Co., Traveler's Guide, Flask, Yellow Amber, 1855-1870, 6 3/4 In. 588.00
A.M. & Co., Urn, Gold Amber, Handle, 1855-1870, 8 7/8 In. 3360.00
A.M. & Co., Urn, Yellow Amber, Flared Lip, 1855-1870, 10 In. 1624.00
Clock, Regulator, Aqua, Double Collar, 1855-1870, 5 3/4 In. 1176.00
Clock, Regulator, Gold Yellow Amber, Pontil Base, Applied Collar, 6 In. 798.00
Clock, Regulator, Yellow Amber, Double Collar, 5 In. .... .358.00 to 615.00
Great Gun Bourbon, Cannon, Amber, Wooden Carriage On Label, 12 3/8 In. 8120.00
Knickerbocker, N.Y., Gold Amber, Sloping Collar, Pontil, 6 In. 2910.00

─────────────────────── BISCHOFF ───────────────────────

Bischoff Company, founded in 1777 in Trieste, Italy, made fancy decanters. The modern collectible Bischoff bottles were imported into the United States from about 1950. Glass, porcelain, and stoneware decanters and figurals were made.

African Head, 1962 .... 14.00
Alpine Pitcher, 1969 .... 27.00
Amber Flower, 1952 .... .32.00 to 35.00
Amphora, 2 Handles, 1950 .... 25.00
Ashtray, Green Striped, 1958, Miniature .... .12.00 to 14.00
Bell Tower, 1960 .... .20.00 to 39.00
Black Cat, 1969 .... .20.00 to 23.00

Blue Gold, 1956	45.00 to 50.00
Candlestick, Antique, 1958	25.00
Candlestick, Clown, 1963	8.00 to 10.00
Candlestick, Clown, Black Hair, Low, 1963	35.00
Canteen, Floral, 1969	18.00
Canteen, Fruit, 1969	20.00
Chariot Urn, 1966, 2 Sections	25.00
Chinese Boy, 1962	35.00
Chinese Girl, 1962	35.00
Christmas Tree, 1957	55.00
Dachshund, 1966	45.00
Deer, 1969	15.00 to 23.00
Duck, 1964	45.00
Egyptian Dancers, 1961	12.00
Egyptian Musician, 1963	15.00
Emerald Rose, 1952	48.00
Festival, 1957	47.00
Mask, Columbian, Gray, 1963	25.00
Porcelain Cameo, 1962	20.00
Spanish Boy, 1961	30.00
Spanish Girl, 1961	30.00
Topaz Basket, 1958	30.00
Tower Of Fruit, 1964	15.00
Venetian Blue Green, 1953	30.00
Watchtower, 1960	10.00
White Pitcher, 1960	15.00
Wild Geese Pitcher, 1969	18.00

BITTERS

Bitters seems to have been an idea that started in Germany during the seventeenth century. A tax was levied against gin in the mid-1700s and the clever salesmen simply added some herbs to the gin and sold the mixture as medicine. Later, the medicine was made in Italy and England. Bitters is the name of this mixture. By the nineteenth century, bitters became a popular local product in America. It was usually of such a high alcoholic content that the claim that one using the product felt healthier with each sip was almost true. One brand had over 59% alcohol (about 118 proof). Although alcoholism had become a problem and social drinking was frowned upon by most proper Victorians, the soothing bitters medicine found wide acceptance. At that time there was no tax on the medicine and no laws concerning ingredients or advertising claims.

The word *bitters* must be embossed on the glass or a paper label must be affixed to the bottle for the collector to call the bottle a bitters bottle. Most date from 1862, the year of the Revenue Act tax on liquor, until 1906, the year the Food and Drug Act placed restrictions on the sale of bitters as a medicinal cure. Over 1,000 types are known. Bitters were sometimes packaged in figural bottles shaped like cabins, human figures, fish, pigs, barrels, ears of corn, drums, clocks, horses, or cannons. The bottles came in a variety of colors. They ranged from clear to milk glass, pale to deep amethyst, light aqua to cobalt blue, pale yellow to amber, and pale to dark green. A bottle found in an unusual color commands a much higher price than a clear bottle of the same shape. The numbers used in the entries in the form R-00 refer to the book *Bitters Bottles* by Carlyn Ring and W.C. Ham. Each bottle is pictured and described in detail in the book.

A.M.S.2, 1864, Constitution, Seward & Bentley, Buffalo, Amber, 9 1/4 In., R-C223	1904.00
A.M.S.2, 1864, Constitution, Seward & Bentley, Buffalo, Amber, 9 3/8 In., R-C222	1624.00
A.T. & Co., Olive Yellow, Amber Tone, Sloping Double Collar, 10 1/4 In.	868.00
Acorn, Amber, Tooled Lip, 8 3/4 In., R-A9	253.00
Acorn, Gold, Applied Lip, 9 In., R-A9	325.00
Allen's Congress, Cabin, Amber, Bubbles, IP, 10 In., R-A29	5280.00
Alpine Herb, TT & Co., Amber, Tooled Lip, 1890, 9 5/8 In., R-A37	385.00
American Life, P.E. Iler, Tiffin, Ohio, Cabin, Amber, Applied Lip, 8 In., R-A49	3920.00 to 5600.00
American Stomach, Amber, Tooled Lip, 8 1/8 In., R-A54	308.00
Angostura, Olive Yellow Amber, 5 In., R-A59	30.00
Angostura Bark, Eagle Liqueur Distiller, Amber, Tooled Lip, 7 In., R-A68	121.00

Appetine, Geo. Benz & Sons, St. Paul, Minn., Amber, Collar Mouth, 8 1/4 In., R-A78 ... 330.00
Arabian, Lawrence & Weichselbaum, Savannah, Ga., Gold Amber, 9 3/4 In., R-A80 ..... 672.00
Atwood's Jaundice, Aqua, 12-Sided, Pontil, 6 1/8 In., R-A115 ....77.00 to 198.00
Atwood's Vegetable Dyspeptic, Aqua, Pontil, R-A130F 86.00
Augauer Bitters Co., Chicago, Yellow Green, Tooled Lip, 1890, 8 In., R-A134 .... 121.00
B.G.B., Amber, Labels, Case Gin, 9 1/4 In., R-B126L 175.00
B.T. 1865, S.C. Smiths Druid, Barrel, Copper, 9 1/2 In., R-S124 .... 2800.00
B.T. 1865, S.C. Smiths Druid, Barrel, Tobacco Amber, 1870, 9 3/8 In., R-S124 .... 2576.00
Baker's Orange Grove, Amber, 9 1/2 In., R-B9 .... 220.00
Baker's Orange Grove, Green Citron, Roped Corners, Applied Top, 9 1/2 In., R-B9 ..... 8800.00
Baker's Orange Grove, Light Gold Amber, Roped Corners, R-B9 .... 495.00
Baker's Orange Grove, Medium Copper, Sloping Mouth, 9 1/4 In., R-B9 .... 2296.00
Baker's Orange Grove, Strawberry Puce, 1865-1875, 9 3/8 In., R-B9 .... 1250.00
Baker's Orange Grove, Topaz Amber, Roped Corners, 9 1/2 In., R-B9 .... 910.00
Baker's Orange Grove, Yellow Amber, Applied Collar Mouth, 9 1/2 In., R-B9 .... 755.00
Baker's Orange Grove, Yellow Amber, Sloping Collar, 9 1/2 In., R-B9 .... 385.00
Beggs Dandelion, Chicago, Ill., Orange Amber, Sloping Collar, 1875, 8 3/4 In., R-B52 ... 94.00
Beggs Dandelion, Chicago, Ill., Tooled Lip, R-B52 .... 60.00
Beggs' Dandelion, Amber, Stain, 7 In., R-B51 .... 50.00
Ben Franklin, Barrel, Amber, Applied Collar, Lip, Pontil, Partial Label, 10 In., R-F80 .... 784.00
Bennet's Wild Cherry Stomach, Chenery, Southern & Co., Orange Red, 9 In., R-B74 ... 1540.00
Berkshire, Amann & Co., Cincinnati, O., Pig, Olive Amber, 10 In., R-B81.4 .... 2912.00
Berkshire, Amann & Co., Cincinnati, O., Pig, Pottery, Brown Glaze, 8 1/4 In., R-B81 ... 853.00
Berkshire, Amann & Co., Cincinnati, O., Pig, Pottery, Brown Glaze, 9 1/2 In. 855.00
Best In America, B. Desenberg, Kalamazoo, Cabin, Amber, 9 In., R-B92 .....8000.00 to 11750.00
Big Bill Best, Amber To Red Amber, Tooled Lip, 1890, 12 In., R-B95 .... 132.00
Big Bill Best, Amber, 12 1/8 In., R-B95 .... 98.00
Big Bill Best, Gold Amber, Pyramid Shape, Labels, Closure, Contents, 12 In., R-B95 .... 330.00
Bissell's Tonic, Peoria, Ill., Red Amber, 9 1/8 In., R-B109 .... 280.00
Blue Mountain, Yellow Amber, Banded Collar, Rectangular, 1860-1880, 8 In., R-B128 .. 140.00
Bosak's Horke Vino Medicinal Bitter Wine, Amber, Lady's Leg, Bar Scene Label 77.00
Bourbon Whiskey, Barrel, Cherry Puce, Applied Lip, R-B171 .... 220.00
Bourbon Whiskey, Barrel, Light Pink Puce, 9 1/4 In., R-B171 .... 1250.00
Bourbon Whiskey, Barrel, Raspberry Puce, Applied Lip, 9 1/4 In., R-B171 .... 500.00
Bourbon Whiskey, Barrel, Strawberry Puce, 1855, 9 1/4 In., R-B171 ....644.00 to 795.00
Bourbon Whiskey, Barrel, Strawberry Puce, 9 3/8 In., RB-171 .... 1064.00
Brown's Catalina, Cannon Shape, Medium Amber, 10 7/8 In. 336.00
Brown's Celebrated Indian Herb, Gold Amber, 12 3/8 In. ....1430.00 to 1904.00
Brown's Celebrated Indian Herb, Patented 1867, Amber, 12 1/4 In., R-B223 ....650.00 to 1540.00
Brown's Celebrated Indian Herb, Patented 1867, Chocolate, 12 1/4 In., R-B223 .... 1540.00
Brown's Celebrated Indian Herb, Patented 1867, Tobacco Amber, 12 In., R-B223 ...... 868.00
Brown's Celebrated Indian Herb, Patented 1867, Yellow, 12 1/4 In., R-B223 .... 2200.00
Brown's Celebrated Indian Herb, Patented 1868, Amber, 12 1/8 In., R-B225 .....476.00 to 577.00
Brown's Celebrated Indian Herb, Patented Feb. 11, 1867, Amber, 12 1/4 In., R-B224 ... 900.00
Brown's Celebrated Indian Herb, Patented Feb. 11, 1867, Crystal, 12 1/4 In., R-B224 ... 520.00
Brown's Celebrated Indian Herb, Patented Feb. 11, 1867, Yellow, 12 1/4 In., R-B224 ... 1045.00
Brown's Celebrated Indian Herb, Patented Feb. 11, 1868, Amber, 12 1/4 In., R-B226 ... 840.00
Brown's Celebrated Indian Herb, Patented Feb. 11, 1868, Amber, 12 1/8 In., R-B226 ... 1904.00
Brown's Celebrated Indian Herb, Patented Feb. 11, 1868, Gold, 12 1/4 In., R-B226 ..... 1320.00
Brown's Celebrated Indian Herb, Patented Feb. 11, 1868, Olive, 12 1/4 In., R-B226 .... 2184.00
Brown's Celebrated Indian Herb, Patented Feb. 11, 1868, Yellow, 12 1/4 In., R-B226 ... 1120.00
Brown's Iron, Brown Chemical Co., Square, Amber, Applied Lip, 8 5/8 In., R-B231 ..... 77.00
Bryant's Stomach, Lady's Leg, Olive Green, 12 In., R-B243 .... 5880.00
Buhrer's Gentian, S. Buhrer, Proprietor, Amber, Sloping Collar, 1870, 9 In., R-B252 ... 198.00
Buhrer's Gentian, Square, Amber, Indented Panels, 8 7/8 In., R-B252 .... 112.00
Burton's Stomach, Amber, Tooled Lip, 8 5/8 In., R-B275 .... 246.00
Byrne, see Bitters, Professor Geo. J. Byrne
C&C, P.R. Delany & Co, Semi-Cabin, Aqua, 10 5/8 In., R-C1 ....495.00 to 935.00
C.H. Swains Bourbon, Amber, Applied Lip, R-S227 .... 264.00
C.H. Swains Bourbon, Amber, Applied Lip, R-S228 .... 176.00
C.H. Swains Bourbon, Yellow Amber, Sloping Double Collar, 9 1/4 In., R-S228 .... 280.00
C.W. Roback's, see Bitters, Dr. C.W. Roback's

Cabin, see Bitters, Drake's Plantation; Bitters, Golden; Bitters, Kelly's Old Cabin; Bitters, Old Homestead Wild Cherry

Caldwells Herb, Amber, IP, 12 1/2 In., R-C8	336.00
Caldwells Herb, Great Tonic, Amber, Lattice, 16 Squares, Applied Lip, 12 3/8 In., R-C8	160.00
Caldwells Wine & Iron, Medina, N.Y., Amber, 9 In., R-C10	1512.00
California Fig, California Extract Of Fig Co., Amber, 10 In., R-C15	85.00
California Herb, Pittsburgh, Pa., G.W. Frazier, Amber, 9 1/2 In., R-C20	3850.00
Canton, Star, Lady's Leg, Amber, Embossed, 12 1/8 In., R-C35	550.00
Capitol, Fredonia, N.Y., Light Turquoise, Applied Top, 9 In., R-C38	55.00
Carmeliter Stomach, Olive Yellow Green, 9 1/8 In., R-C54	695.00
Caroni, Green, Tooled Square Lip, With Ring, Cylindrical, 5 1/4 In., R-C57	25.00
Carpathian Herb, Hollander Bros. Drug Co., Amber, Square, 7 3/4 In., R-C61.3	84.00
Carpathian Herb, Hollander Bros. Drug Co., Amber, Square, 8 1/4 In., R-C61.5	134.00
Celebrated Eagle, St. Louis, Lange & Bernecker, Orange Red, 9 In., R-C94	3410.00
Chartreuse Damiana, New York, Yellow Amber, 4 Indented Panels, 9 1/4 In., R-C132	300.00
Clark's Giant, Aqua, Narrow, 7 In., R-C166	135.00
Clarke's Compound Mandrake, Aqua, Square Lip, 7 1/2 In., R-C151	60.00
Clarke's Vegetable Sherry Wine, Sharon, Mass., Aqua, Stain, 14 1/8 In., R-C155	.440.00 to 495.00
Coca, Hartwig Kantorowicz Berlin Posen, Amber, Applied Sloping Mouth, 10 1/8 In.	1018.00
Coca, Hartwig Kantorowicz, Onion, Red Amber, Deep Kick-Up, 7 3/4 In.	330.00
Columbo Peptic, L.E. Jung, New Orleans, Amber, 9 In., R-C201	44.00
Constitutional Beverage, W. Olmsted & Co, Yellow Green, 10 In., R-C224	1680.00
Covert's Modoc Stomach, Gold Amber, Label, 1860-1880, 8 7/8 In., R-C241	1100.00
Curtis & Perkins Wild Cherry, Aqua, OP, 6 7/8 In., R-C262	150.00
Curtis Cordial Calisaya, Great Stomach, Yellow Amber, 11 In., R-C261	1848.00
Damiana, Baja, Cal., Lewis Hess Manuf'r, Star, Aqua, Cylindrical, 11 1/2 In., R-D5	50.00 to 100.00
Dandelion & Wild Cherry, Aqua, 8 3/4 In., R-D14.7	61.00
David Andrews Vegetable Jaundice, Providence, R.I., Aqua, 8 In., R-A57	.2576.00 to 2860.00
De Witts Stomach, Chicago, Amber, BIMAL, Rectangular, 8 In., R-D66	65.00
De Witts Stomach, Chicago, Tooled Lip, 7 1/2 In., R-D66	.33.00 to 40.00
De Witts Stomach, Chicago, Tooled Lip, 9 1/4 In., R-D64	60.00
Dimmitt's, 50 Cts, Saint Louis, Yellow Amber, 6 1/2 In., R-D75	963.00
Doyles Hop, 1872, Semi-Cabin, Amber, 9 5/8 In., R-D93	123.00
Doyles Hop, 1872, Semi-Cabin, Amber, Sloping Double Collar, Labels, 10 In., R-D93	125.00
Doyles Hop, 1872, Semi-Cabin, Yellow Amber, Applied Double Collar, 10 In., R-D93	303.00
Doyles Hop, 1872, Semi-Cabin, Yellow Amber, Square, 9 5/8 In., R-D93	.265.00 to 330.00
Dr. A.S. Hopkins Union Stomach, Yellow Amber, 9 3/4 In., R-H179	72.00
Dr. A.W. Coleman's Anti Dyspeptic & Tonic, Blue Green, 9 1/4 In., R-C194	.3100.00 to 3484.00
Dr. Ball's Vegetable Stomachic, Northboro, Mass., Aqua, 6 7/8 In., R-B14	245.00
Dr. Beard's Alternative Tonic & Laxative, Aqua, Oval, 8 1/2 In., R-B41	185.00
Dr. Bell's Golden Tonic Bitters, IP, 1865-1875, 10 1/8 In., R-B59	8960.00
Dr. Bell's Liver & Kidney, Aqua, Embossed 2-Sided, 9 In., R-B61	94.00
Dr. Bishop's, Wa-Hoo, Wa-Hoo Bitter Co, Conn., Semi-Cabin, Amber, 10 In., R-B103	1008.00
Dr. Blakes Aromatic, New York, Blue Aqua, Pontil, 7 In., R-B120	176.00
Dr. Bohlin's Norman, Light Amber, 8 7/8 In., R-B137	155.00
Dr. Bohlin's Norman, Square, Embossed, 8 7/8 In., R-B137	242.00
Dr. C.D. Warner's German Hop, Amber, Square, 9 3/4 In., R-G25.6	110.00
Dr. C.W. Roback's Stomach, Barrel, Amber, Applied Sloping Collar, 9 3/8 In., R-R74	165.00
Dr. C.W. Roback's Stomach, Barrel, Olive Green, 9 In., R-R74	2072.00
Dr. C.W. Roback's Stomach, Barrel, Yellow Amber, 1870, 9 7/8 In., R-R73	1064.00
Dr. C.W. Roback's Stomach, Cincinnati, O, Barrel, Amber, 9 1/4 In., R-R75	106.00
Dr. C.W. Roback's Stomach, Cincinnati, O, Barrel, Amber, 9 1/2 In., R-R73	220.00
Dr. C.W. Roback's Stomach, Cincinnati, O, Barrel, Amber, 9 3/8 In., R-R74	231.00
Dr. C.W. Roback's Stomach, Cincinnati, O, Barrel, Amber, 9 3/8 In., R-R75	385.00
Dr. C.W. Roback's Stomach, Cincinnati, O, Barrel, Amber, IP, 9 7/8 In., R-R73	.523.00 to 728.00
Dr. C.W. Roback's Stomach, Cincinnati, O, Barrel, Olive Green, 10 In., R-R75	3300.00
Dr. C.W. Roback's Stomach, Cincinnati, O, Barrel, Olive Yellow, 9 1/2 In., R-R75	7840.00
Dr. C.W. Roback's Stomach, Cincinnati, O, Barrel, Smoky Moss Green, 10 In., R-R73	2576.00
Dr. C.W. Roback's Stomach, Cincinnati, O, Barrel, Yellow Amber, 9 3/8 In., R-R75	420.00
Dr. Caldwell's Herb, Amber, 3-Sided, 12 3/8 In., R-C9	185.00
Dr. Caldwell's Herb, Great Tonic, Medium Amber, Graphite Pontil, 12 3/4 In., R-C9	250.00
Dr. Campbells Scotch, Flask, Orange Amber, Strap Side, 6 1/2 In., R-C31	325.00
Dr. Campbells Scotch, Medium Orange Amber, Tooled Lip, 6 1/4 In., R-C31	224.00

Dr. Carey's Original Mandrake, Elmira, N.Y., Aqua, Paneled, 6 1/2 In., R-C48 . . . .   95.00
Dr. Corbett's Renovating Shaker, Light Green, Applied Lip, OP, 9 1/2 In., R-C234 . . . . .   1870.00
Dr. De Andries Sarsaparilla, E.M. Rusha, New Orleans, Amber, 10 In., R-D35 . . . .   1540.00
Dr. Fischs, Fish, Gold Amber, Small Collar, 11 1/2 In., R-F44 . . . .   154.00
Dr. Fischs, W.H. Ware, Fish, Patented 1866, Amber, 11 3/4 In., R-F44 . . . . .264.00 to 280.00
Dr. Flint's Quaker, Providence, R.I., Quaker On Label, Applied Lip, 9 1/2 In., R-F58 . . . .   550.00
Dr. Geo. Pierce's Indian Restorative, Lowell, Mass., Aqua, 9 In., R-P95 . . . .   75.00
Dr. Harter's Wild Cherry, St. Louis, Amber, Stain, 7 1/2 In., R-H51 . . . .   30.00
Dr. Henley's California, IXL In Oval, Blue Aqua, 12 1/4 In., R-H82 . . . .   305.00
Dr. Henley's Wild Grape Root, IXL In Oval, Aqua, Applied Lip, 12 5/8 In., R-H85 . . . . .   83.00
Dr. Henley's Wild Grape Root, IXL, Aqua, Applied Square Collar, 12 1/2 In., R-H85 . . . .   165.00
Dr. J. Hostetter's Stomach, 18 Fluid Oz., ABM, Amber, 8 3/4 In., R-H197 . . . . .9.00 to 15.00
Dr. J. Hostetter's Stomach, Amber, 9 1/2 In., R-H194 . . . .   19.00
Dr. J. Hostetter's Stomach, Dark Olive Amber, Applied Collar Lip, 9 In., R-H194 . . . . . .   330.00
Dr. J. Hostetter's Stomach, Embossed AGW On Base, 9 In., R-H195 . . . .   10.00
Dr. J. Hostetter's Stomach, Gold Yellow, 8 3/4 In., R-H197 . . . .   633.00
Dr. J. Hostetter's Stomach, L & W, Olive Yellow, Cleaned, 8 7/8 In., R-H195 . . . .   633.00
Dr. J. Hostetter's Stomach, L & W, Olive Yellow, Sloping Collar, 8 7/8 In., R-H195 . . . .   357.00
Dr. J. Hostetter's Stomach, L & W, Yellow Amber, Applied Collar, 9 In., R-H195 . . . . . .   132.00
Dr. J. Hostetter's Stomach, L & W, Yellow, Stained, Square, 9 In., R-H195 . . . .   125.00
Dr. J. Hostetter's Stomach, Olive Green, Collared Lip, 9 5/8 In., R-H194 . . . . . . .209.00 to 224.00
Dr. J. Hostetter's Stomach, Olive Yellow, Sloping Collar, 9 In., R-H195 . . . .   935.00
Dr. J. Hostetter's Stomach, S. McKee & Co., No. 2, Red Amber, 9 In., R-H195 . . . .   88.00
Dr. J. Hostetter's Stomach, W. MCG & Co., Olive Yellow Amber, 9 1/2 In., R-H195 . . . .   110.00
Dr. J. Hostetter's Stomach, W. MCG & Co., Yellow, 9 In., R-H195 . . . .   935.00
Dr. J. Hostetter's Stomach, Yellow Amber, 9 1/4 In., R-H194 . . . .   159.00
Dr. J. Sweet's Strengthening Bitters, Aqua, 8 1/4 In., R-S234 . . . .   22.00
Dr. J.G.B. Siegert & Sons, Green, ABM, 6 In., R-A65 . . . .   15.00
Dr. J.S. Wood's Elixir, Albany, N.Y., Tombstone, Emerald Green, IP, 8 7/8 In. 2128.00
Dr. John Bull's Compound Cedron, Louisville, Ky., Amber, 1865, 9 3/4 In., R-B254 . . . .   357.00
Dr. Lamot's Botanic Indian, Light Amber, Strap Sided, Flask, Label, 6 1/4 In., R-L9 . . . .   175.00
Dr. Langley's Root & Herb, 76 Union St., Boston, Blue Aqua, IP, 8 In., R-L25 . . . .   308.00
Dr. Langley's Root & Herb, 99 Union St., Boston, Aqua, Applied Lip, 8 1/2 In., R-L21 . . .   44.00
Dr. Langley's Root & Herb, 99 Union St., Boston, Golden Yellow Amber, 7 In., R-L22 . . .   235.00
Dr. Loew's Celebrated Stomach & Nerve Tonic, Green, Label, 9 3/8 In., R-L111 . . . .   1036.00
Dr. Loew's Stomach & Nerve Tonic, Cleveland, O., Green, 3 7/8 In., R-L112.5 . . . .   364.00
Dr. Lovegood's Family, XX, Cabin, Amber, 1870-1880, 10 In., R-L124 . . . .   3360.00
Dr. Lovegood's Family, XX, Cabin, Amber, 9 5/8 In., R-L125 . . . .   3696.00
Dr. Lovegood's Family, XX, Cabin, Gold Yellow Amber, 10 3/8 In., R-L124 . . . .   7560.00
Dr. Lovegood's Family, XX, Semi-Cabin, Amber, 1880, 9 In., R-L125 . . . .   3080.00
Dr. Lowe's Stomach & Nerve Tonic, Cleveland, O., Green, 3 7/8 In., R-L112.5 . . . .   303.00
Dr. Mott's Wild Cherry Tonic, Spruance Stanley & Co., Amber, Applied Top, 9 In. 303.00
Dr. Owen's European Life, Blue Aqua, 8-Sided, Pontil, 7 In., R-O98 . . . .   448.00
Dr. Petzolds Genuine German, Incpt. 1862, Amber, 10 1/8 In., R-P75 . . . .   220.00
Dr. Petzolds Genuine German, Incpt. 1862, Applied Lip, 10 3/8 In., R-P78 . . . . . .121.00 to 145.00
Dr. Place's Cunderango, Geo. W. Chesley & Co., Sacramento, Aqua, 9 3/8 In., R-P106 . .   825.00
Dr. Planett's, Aqua, Applied Sloping Collar, IP, 9 3/4 In., R-P107 . . . .   980.00
Dr. Renz's Herb, Green, Collared Mouth, 9 3/4 In., R-R37 . . . .   198.00
Dr. Renz's Herb, Olive Yellow, Sloping Collar, Cleaned, 9 5/8 In., R-R37 . . . .   660.00
Dr. Renz's Herb, Yellow Amber, Double Collar, 10 In., R-R38 . . . .   715.00
Dr. Russell Angostura, Applied Top, 8 In., R-R127.8 . . . .   30.00
Dr. Sawen's Life Invigorating, Gold Amber, Sloping Collar, 10 In., R-S41 . . . .   198.00
Dr. Skinner's Celebrated 25 Cent, Aqua, Double Collar, Pontil, 8 5/8 In., R-S115 . . . . . .   77.00
Dr. Soule Hop, 1872, Copper Topaz, 7 3/4 In., R-S147 . . . .   413.00
Dr. Soule Hop, 1872, Semi-Cabin, Yellow Topaz, 9 5/8 In., R-S145 . . . .   308.00
Dr. Soule Hop, Cabin, Gasoline Puce, 7 In., R-S147 . . . .   1075.00
Dr. Soule Hop, Cabin, Tobacco Amber, Double Collar, 1872, 9 1/2 In., R-S145 . . . .   125.00
Dr. Soule Hop, Hop Flowers & Leaf, Cabin, Root Beer Amber, 9 1/2 In., R-S145 . .165.00 to 176.00
Dr. Soule Hop, Hop Flowers & Leaf, Yellow, Applied Lip, R-S145 . . . .   187.00
Dr. Stanley's South American Indian, Pale Aqua, Label, 9 In., R-S174 . . . . .264.00 to 413.00
Dr. Stanley's South American Indian, Yellow Amber, 9 In., R-S174 . . . .   121.00
Dr. Stanley's South American Indian, Yellow Amber, Bubbles, 9 In., R-S174 . . . .   175.00
Dr. Stephen Jewett's Celebrated Health, Olive, IP, 7 1/2 In., R-J38 . . . . .2744.00 to 7280.00

Dr. Stephen Jewett's Celebrated Health, Rindge, N.H., Lime Green, 7 3/8 In., R-J37 . . .   2352.00
Dr. Von Hopf's, Curacoa, Chamberlain & Co., Des Moines, Iowa, Amber, 7 3/4 In., R-V28   85.00
Dr. Wood's Sarsaparilla & Wild Cherry, Aqua, 1845-1860, 8 3/4 In., R-W151 . . . .   140.00
Dr. Hostetter's, see Bitters, Dr. J. Hostetter's
Drake's Plantation, 4 Log, Amber, 10 1/4 In., R-D110 . . . . .95.00 to 105.00
Drake's Plantation, 4 Log, Amber, Applied Lip, 10 1/4 In., R-D110 . . . . .132.00 to 330.00
Drake's Plantation, 4 Log, Amber, Sloping Collar, 10 1/4 In., R-D110 . . . .   88.00
Drake's Plantation, 4 Log, Amber, Sloping Collar, Labels, 10 1/4 In., R-D110 . . . .   200.00
Drake's Plantation, 4 Log, Apricot Amber, 10 1/4 In., R-D110 . . . .   145.00
Drake's Plantation, 4 Log, Cabin, Medium Amber, 1862-1870, 10 In., R-D110 . . . .   112.00
Drake's Plantation, 4 Log, Cabin, Yellow Olive, 1862-1870, 10 1/8 In., R-D110 . . . .   3360.00
Drake's Plantation, 4 Log, Gold Amber, Applied Top, Smooth Base 231.00
Drake's Plantation, 4 Log, Olive Yellow, Applied Sloping Collar, 10 In., R-D110 . . . .   1870.00
Drake's Plantation, 4 Log, Yellow Amber, Olive Tone, Sloping Collar, 10 In., R-D110 . . .   1960.00
Drake's Plantation, 4 Log, Yellow Green, Applied Top, Smooth 2420.00
Drake's Plantation, 4 Log, Yellow, Sloping Collar, 9 7/8 In., R-D110 . . . .   440.00
Drake's Plantation, 5 Log, Cabin, Yellow Amber, 1862-1870, 9 7/8 In., R-D109 . . . .   420.00
Drake's Plantation, 5 Log, Light Gold, 10 In., R-D109 . . . .   550.00
Drake's Plantation, 5 Log, Yellow Amber, 9 7/8 In., R-D109 . . . .   560.00
Drake's Plantation, 6 Log, Amber, 9 5/8 In., R-D108 . . . .   88.00
Drake's Plantation, 6 Log, Amber, 9 7/8 In., R-D105 . . . .   2520.00
Drake's Plantation, 6 Log, Amber, R-D103 . . . .   90.00
Drake's Plantation, 6 Log, Apricot Puce, Sloping Collar, 10 In., R-D105 . . . .   357.00
Drake's Plantation, 6 Log, Cabin, Cherry Puce, 1862-1870, 9 7/8 In., R-D105 . . . .   2016.00
Drake's Plantation, 6 Log, Cabin, Gold Amber, 1862-1870, 9 5/8 In., R-D108 . . . .   123.00
Drake's Plantation, 6 Log, Cabin, Medium Apricot Puce, 9 7/8 In., R-D106 . . . .   924.00
Drake's Plantation, 6 Log, Cabin, Medium Copper Puce, 1862-1870, 10 In., R-D105 . . . .   246.00
Drake's Plantation, 6 Log, Cabin, Medium Copper Topaz, 1862-1870, 9 In., R-D105 . . . .   1008.00
Drake's Plantation, 6 Log, Cabin, Medium Red Puce, 1870, 10 In., R-D106 . . . .   280.00
Drake's Plantation, 6 Log, Cabin, Olive Yellow, 1862-1870, 9 7/8 In., R-D108 . . . .   2576.00
Drake's Plantation, 6 Log, Cabin, Yellow Amber, 1862-1870, 9 3/4 In., R-D108 . . . .   207.00
Drake's Plantation, 6 Log, Celery Green, 10 1/4 In., R-D125 . . . .*Illus*   2040.00
Drake's Plantation, 6 Log, Cherry Puce, 9 7/8 In., R-D105 . . . .   588.00
Drake's Plantation, 6 Log, Cherry Puce, Applied Lip, 10 In., R-D106 . . . .   358.00
Drake's Plantation, 6 Log, Cherry Puce, Applied Sloping Collar, 10 1/4 In., R-D105 . . . .   143.00
Drake's Plantation, 6 Log, Gasoline Puce, 10 In., R-D105 . . . .   2016.00
Drake's Plantation, 6 Log, Ginger Ale, 10 In., R-D103 . . . .   7560.00
Drake's Plantation, 6 Log, Gold Honey Amber, 9 3/4 In., R-D108 . . . .   176.00
Drake's Plantation, 6 Log, Light Gold Amber, Sloping Collar, 9 3/4 In., R-D105 . . . .   55.00
Drake's Plantation, 6 Log, Light Gold, Olive, Arabesque 1200.00
Drake's Plantation, 6 Log, Medium Puce, Applied Lip, 10 In., R-D106 . . . . .231.00 to 253.00
Drake's Plantation, 6 Log, Patented 1862, Cabin, Yellow Copper, 10 1/4 In., R-D105 . . .   616.00
Drake's Plantation, 6 Log, Red Amber, Red Chocolate 120.00
Drake's Plantation, 6 Log, Strawberry Puce, R-D103 . . . .   275.00
Drake's Plantation, 6 Log, Strawberry Puce, Sloping Collar, 10 In., R-D108 . . . .   165.00
Drake's Plantation, 6 Log, Tobacco Amber, 9 7/8 In., R-D108 . . . .   252.00
Drake's Plantation, 6 Log, Yellow Amber, 10 In., R-D105 . . . .   260.00
Drake's Plantation, 6 Log, Yellow Amber, Olive Tone, Sloping Collar, 9 5/8 In., R-D108 .   1736.00
Drake's Plantation, 6 Log, Yellow Amber, Sloping Collar, 10 In., R-D105 . . . . .99.00 to 220.00
Drake's Plantation, 6 Log, Yellow Copper, 10 In., R-D108 . . . .   728.00
Drake's Plantation, 6 Log, Yellow, Milky Interior, 10 In., R-D108 . . . .   1210.00
Drakes Plantation, 6 Log, Yellow Amber, 9 3/4 In., R-D102 . . . .   336.00
E. Dexter Loveridge Wahoo, DWD, Cabin, Amber, 10 In., R-L126 . . . . .880.00 to 1568.00
E.J. Rose's Magador For Stomach, Amber, Tooled Lip, 8 3/4 In., R-R98 . . . .   99.00
Eagle Angostura Aromatic, Amber, Tooled Lip, 3 5/8 In. 193.00
Ear Of Corn, see Bitters, National, Ear of Corn
Edw Wilder's Stomach, Louisville, Ky., House, 10 3/8 In., R-W116 . . . . .121.00 to 448.00
Electric Brand, H.E. Bucklen & Co., Chicago, Ill., Amber, Label, Contents, 10 In., R-E31   88.00
Estd 1834 Tellier's Herb, Gold Amber, 9 7/8 In., R-T11.5 . . . .   375.00
Excelsior Aromatic, Dr. D.S. Perry & Co., N.Y., Semi-Cabin, Red Amber, 10 In., R-E64 .   1680.00
Excelsior Aromatic, Dr. D.S. Perry & Co., New York, Amber, 10 1/2 In., R-E64 . . . .   798.00
F. Brown Sarsaparilla & Tomato, Light Aqua, Applied Lip, OP, 1856, 9 1/2 In., R-S36 . . .   198.00
Favorite, Powell & Stutenroth, Pat Applied For, Barrel, Amber, 9 In., R-F6 . . . .   2408.00

Bitters, Drake's Plantation, 6 Log, Celery Green, 10 1/4 In., R-D125

Bitters, Hertrich's Gesundheits, Olive Yellow Green, Applied Lip, 12 In., R-H104

Bitters, Fish, W.H. Ware, Patented 1866, Amber, 11 1/2 In., R-F45

Ferro Quina Stomach, Blood Maker, Tooled Lip, 1905, Qt. 50.00
Fish, W.H. Ware, Patented 1866, Amber, 11 1/2 In., R-F45 . . . . *Illus*   303.00
Fish, W.H. Ware, Patented 1866, Clear, Gray Glass, 1866-1875, 11 1/2 In., R-F46 . . . .   1344.00
Fish, W.H. Ware, Patented 1866, Fish, Amber, Applied Lip, 11 5/8 In., R-F46 . . . . .303.00 to 336.00
Fish, W.H. Ware, Patented 1866, Fish, Gold Amber, 11 3/4 In., R-F46 . . . .   357.00
Fish, W.H. Ware, Patented 1866, Olive Yellow, 11 1/2 In., R-F46 . . . .   3400.00
Fish, W.H. Ware, Patented 1866, Olive Yellow, 1866-1875, 11 In., R-F46 . . . .   3360.00
Fish, W.H. Ware, Patented 1866, Olive Yellow, Green On Back & Tail, 11 1/2 In., R-F46 .   3808.00
Fish, W.H. Ware, Patented 1866, Smoky Clear Glass, 11 5/8 In., R-F46 . . . .   2576.00
Fish, W.H. Ware, Patented 1866, Tobacco Amber, Tooled Lip, 11 3/4 In., R-F46 . . . .   110.00
Fish, W.H. Ware, Patented 1866, Yellow Amber, 11 3/4 In., R-F46 . . . .   179.00
Fish, W.H. Ware, Patented 1866, Yellow Green, 11 3/4 In., R-F46 . . . .   1036.00
Francis's, Aqua, Applied Lip, 6 5/8 In., R-F76.5 . . . .   55.00
Frisco Hop Company, Semi-Cabin, Aqua, Applied Lip, 9 1/4 In., R-F91 . . . .   231.00
G.L. Cole, Vegetable, Binghamton, N.Y., Aqua, 4 Sunken Panels, 7 1/2 In., R-C189 . . . . .   90.00
Gentiana Root & Herb, Seth E. Clapp & Co., Boston, Aqua, 9 7/8 In., R-G11 . . . .   190.00
German Hop, Reading, Mich., 1872, Semi-Cabin, Gold Amber, 9 1/2 In., R-G23 . . . .   154.00
Gilbert's Sarsaparilla, Gold Amber, 8-Sided, 1860-1890, 8 1/2 In., R-G42 . . . .   523.00
Gipps Land, Hop, Purity Trade Mark, Semi-Cabin, Green Aqua, 9 1/2 In., R-G45 . . . .   83.00
Globe, Byrne Bros & Co, New York, Amber, 11 In., R-G47 . . . .   1650.00
Golden, Geo. C. Hubbel & Co., Semi-Cabin, Aqua, 10 1/8 In., R-G63 . . . .   476.00
Greeley's Bourbon, Barrel, Cherry Puce, Square Collar, 9 1/4 In., R-G101 . . . .   560.00
Greeley's Bourbon, Barrel, Dark Puce, 9 3/8 In., R-G101 . . . .   650.00
Greeley's Bourbon, Barrel, Grape Puce, Applied Lip, 9 3/8 In., R-G101 . . . . .220.00 to 550.00
Greeley's Bourbon, Barrel, Medium Pink Puce, Square Collar, 9 1/4 In., R-G101 . . . .   2800.00
Greeley's Bourbon, Barrel, Medium Puce, Applied Square Collar, 9 3/8 In., R-G101 . . . . .   413.00
Greeley's Bourbon, Barrel, Medium Smoky Puce, Applied Lip, 9 1/8 In., R-G101 . . . . . .   420.00
Greeley's Bourbon, Barrel, Moss Green, 9 3/8 In., R-G101 . . . .   888.00
Greeley's Bourbon, Barrel, Olive Green, 9 1/4 In., R-G101 . . . .   5720.00
Greeley's Bourbon, Barrel, Olive Green, Disc Type Mouth, 9 1/2 In., R-G101 . . . .   6720.00
Greeley's Bourbon, Barrel, Pink Salmon Puce, 1855-1875, 9 3/8 In., R-G102 . . . .   2352.00
Greeley's Bourbon, Barrel, Plum Puce, Applied Lip, 9 3/8 In., R-G101 . . . . .385.00 to 413.00
Greeley's Bourbon, Barrel, Plum, 9 3/8 In., R-G102 . . . .   715.00
Greeley's Bourbon, Barrel, Ruby, 9 3/8 In., R-G101 . . . .   550.00
Greeley's Bourbon, Barrel, Smoky Copper Puce, Applied Lip, 9 3/8 In., R-G101 . . . .   2200.00
Greeley's Bourbon, Barrel, Smoky Gray Topaz, 1855-1870, 9 In., R-G101 . . . .   2500.00
Greeley's Bourbon, Barrel, Smoky Gray Topaz, 1870, 9 1/8 In., R-G101 . . . .   840.00
Greeley's Bourbon, Barrel, Smoky Gray Topaz, Square Collar, Label, 9 1/4 In., R-G101 . .   2800.00
Greeley's Bourbon, Barrel, Smoky Olive Green, 1875, 9 1/4 In., R-G101 . . . .   3360.00
Greeley's Bourbon, Barrel, Smoky Olive Green, Applied Lip, 9 1/4 In., R-G101 . . . .   5152.00
Greeley's Bourbon, Barrel, Smoky Puce, 9 1/8 In., R-G101 . . . .   812.00
Greeley's Bourbon, Barrel, Smoky Topaz Puce, 1855-1875, 9 1/4 In., R-G101 . . . .   532.00
Greeley's Bourbon, Barrel, Smoky Topaz, 9 1/4 In., R-G101 . . . .   952.00
Greeley's Bourbon, Barrel, Smoky Topaz, Applied Lip, 9 1/4 In., R-G101 . . . . . .660.00 to 756.00
Greeley's Bourbon, Barrel, Strawberry Puce, Applied Lip, 9 3/8 In., R-G101 . . . .   476.00

Greeley's Bourbon, Barrel, Topaz, 1875, 9 1/4 In., R-G101 . . . . 6160.00
Greeley's Bourbon, Mossy Green, Applied Lip, 9 3/8 In., R-G101 . . . . 850.00
Greeley's Bourbon Whiskey, Barrel, Aqua, 9 In., R-G102 . . . . 7000.00
Greeley's Bourbon Whiskey, Barrel, Copper Apricot, Square Collar, 9 1/2 In., R-G102 . . . 253.00
Greeley's Bourbon Whiskey, Barrel, Grape Amethyst, 9 3/8 In, R-G102 . . . . 4592.00
Greeley's Bourbon Whiskey, Barrel, Pink Puce, 1855-1870, 9 1/2 In., R-G102 . . . . 2500.00
Greeley's Bourbon Whiskey, Barrel, Plum, Applied Lip, 9 3/8 In., R-G102 . . . . 715.00
Greeley's Bourbon Whiskey, Barrel, Smoky Pink Puce, Applied Lip, 9 In., R-G102 . . . . . 2035.00
Greeley's Bourbon Whiskey, Barrel, Smoky Puce, 9 1/4 In., R-G102 . . . . 770.00
Greeley's Bourbon Whiskey, Barrel, Strawberry Puce, Applied Lip, 9 In., R-G102 . . . . . . 385.00
Greer's Eclipse, Light Amber, Sloping Collar Lip, Square, 8 5/8 In., R-G112 . . . . 121.00
Greer's Eclipse, Louisville, Ky., Gold Amber, Sloping Collar, Square, 9 In., R G111 . . . . . 77.00
Griffith's Opera, A.R. Griffith, Amber, Applied Collar Lip, 8 In., R-G116 . . . . 179.00
H.P. Herb Wild Cherry, Reading, Pa., Cabin, Medium Amber, 10 In., R-H93 . . . .420.00 to 952.00
H.P. Herb Wild Cherry, Reading, Pa., Cabin, Yellow Amber, Tree, 10 In., R-H93 . . . . 616.00
Hagan's, Amber, 3-Sided, Cooling Crack, 9 3/4 In., R-H5 . . . . 475.00
Hall's, Barrel, Medium Yellow Brown, Applied Lip, 9 1/2 In., R-H9 . . . . 3000.00
Hall's, Barrel, Yellow Amber, Applied Lip, 9 In., R-H9 . . . . 2184.00
Hall's, E.E. Hall, New Haven, Barrel, Amber, Applied Lip, 9 1/2 In., R-H10 . . . . 202.00
Hall's, E.E. Hall, New Haven, Barrel, Gold Amber, Label, 9 1/8 In., R-H10 . . . . . .132.00 to 364.00
Hall's, E.E. Hall, New Haven, Barrel, Medium Amber, Complete Label, 9 In., R-H10 . . . . 550.00
Hall's, E.E. Hall, New Haven, Barrel, Yellow Amber, Disc Type Lip, 9 1/8 In., R-H10 . . . 720.00
Hall's, E.E. Hall, New Haven, Barrel, Yellow, Applied Square Collar, 9 1/8 In., R-H10 . . . 440.00
Hall's, E.E. Hall, New Haven, Established 1842, Barrel, Amber, 9 1/2 In., R-H10 . . . . 231.00
Hart's Star, O.B.L.P.C., 1868, Fish Shape, Aqua, 9 1/2 In., R-H58 . . . . 1736.00
Herkules, AC Monogram, Green, Tooled Lip, 7 3/8 In., R-H98 . . . . .1600.00 to 1760.00
Hertrich's Gesundheits, Olive Green, Germany, 1880, 11 7/8 In., R-H104 . . . . 633.00
Hertrich's Gesundheits, Olive Yellow Green, Applied Lip, 12 In., R-H104 . . . .*Illus* 1265.00
Hertrichs Einzigerfabrikant, Hans Hertrich Hof, Olive, 8 3/4 In., R-H104 . . . . 550.00
Hertrichs Einzigerfabrikant, Olive Green, Applied Lip, 9 3/8 In., R-H104 . . . . 440.00
Hibernia, Braunschweiger & Bumsted., San Francisco, Cal., Amber, 10 In., R-H113 . . . . . 13200.00
Highland & Scotch Tonic, Amber, Collared Lip, 9 7/8 In., R-H117 . . . . 770.00
Highland & Scotch Tonic, Barrel, Amber, 9 3/4 In., R-H117 . . . . 868.00
Highland & Scotch Tonic, Barrel, Olive Amber, 9 1/2 In., R-H117 . . . . 4368.00
Highland Bitters & Scotch Tonic, Barrel, Amber, Graphite Pontil, 9 5/8 In., R-H117 . . . . 660.00
Holtzermann's Patent Stomach, Cabin, Amber, 9 3/4 In., R-H154 . . . . 308.00
Holtzermann's Patent Stomach, Cabin, Gold Amber, 9 1/2 In., R-H155 . . . . . .2128.00 to 2353.00
Holtzermann's Patent Stomach, Cabin, Gold Amber, Crack, 9 1/4 In., R-H155 . . . . 495.00
Holtzermann's Stomach, Cabin, Gold Amber, Tooled Lip, 4 1/8 In., R-H153 . . . . 633.00
Holtzermanns Patent Stomach, Cabin, 4-Sided, Red Amber, 9 3/4 In., R-H154 . . . . 246.00
Holtzermanns Patent Stomach, Cabin, Orange Amber, 1860-1890, 9 7/8 In., R-H154 . . . 550.00
Hop And Iron, Utica, N.Y., Amber, Smooth Base, 1875, 8 1/2 In., R-H172 . . . . 60.00
Hop Tonic, Semi-Cabin, Amber, Tooled Lip, 9 3/4 In., R-H174 . . . . 132.00
Hostetter's, see Bitters, Dr. J. Hostetter's
Hubbell Co., see Bitters, Dr. J. Hostetter's
Hutchings Dyspepsia, Rectangular, Aqua, Sloping Collar, IP, 8 3/8 In., R-H218 . . . . 220.00
Indian Queen, see Bitters, Brown's Celebrated Indian Herb
Indio Purgative, Backbar, Enameled Letters, 10-Sided, 9 1/4 In., R-I26 . . . . 242.00
Iron Bitters, Brown Chemical Co., Square, Amber, 8 3/4 In., R-I27 . . . . 55.00
Jno Moffat, Price $1, Phoenix, New York, Medium Olive Green, Pontil, 5 5/8 In., R-M110 1008.00
Jno Moffat, Price $1, Phoenix, New York, Olive Yellow Amber, 5 3/4 In., R-M110 . . . . . . 728.00
Jno Moffat, Price $1, Phoenix, New York, Tobacco Amber, 5 1/2 In., R-M110 . . . . 1925.00
John Moffat, Aqua, OP, Applied Lip, 5 1/2 In., R-M112 .125.00 to 165.00
John Moffat, Phoenix, New York, Aqua, Open Pontil, 1840-1855, 5 1/2 In., R-M112 . . . . 123.00
John Moffat, Phoenix, New York, Olive Green, Sloping Collar, Pontil, 5 3/8 In. 1010.00
John Moffat, Phoenix, New York, Yellow Olive Amber, 1840-1855, 7 In., R-M108 . . . . . . 1792.00
John Moffat, Price $1.00, New York, Olive Green, 5 In., R-M112 . . . . 1008.00
John Moffat, Price $1.00, New York, Olive Green, 6 In., R-M110 . . . . 1092.00
John Moffat, Price $2, Phoenix, New York, Olive Yellow Amber, Pontil, 6 7/8 In., R-M108 2128.00
John Root's, 1834, Buffalo, N.Y., Semi-Cabin, Blue-Green, 10 1/4 In., R-R90.4 . . . . 3024.00
John Root's, 1867, Buffalo, N.Y., Semi-Cabin, Amber, 9 3/4 In., R-R90.8 . . . . 2520.00
John Root's, Buffalo, N.Y., Blue-Green, Applied Lip, 10 1/4 In., R-R90.4 . . . . 3200.00

John W. Steele's Niagara Star, Semi-Cabin, Amber, 10 1/8 In., R-S182.5 .... 1092.00
John W. Steele's Niagara Star 1864, Semi-Cabin, Amber, 10 In., R-S182 .... 896.00
Johnson's Calisaya, Burlington, Vt., Amber, 10 In., R-J45 .... 105.00
Johnson's Calisaya, Burlington, Vt., Olive Yellow, 10 In., R-J45 .... 1650.00
Johnson's Calisaya, Burlington, Vt., Red Copper, Bubbles, 10 In., R-J45 .... 410.00
Johnson's Calisaya, Burlington, Vt., Red Copper, Sloping Collar, 10 In., R-J45 .... 450.00
Jones Universal Stomach, Amber, 9 1/4 In., R-J53 .... 413.00
Julien's Imperial Aromatic, N.Y., Lady's Leg, Olive Yellow, 12 5/8 In., R-J57 .... 4950.00
Kelly's Old Cabin, 1863, Medium Yellow Amber, 9 1/4 In., R-K21 .... 1904.00
Kelly's Old Cabin, Honey Amber, Sloping Collared Lip, 9 1/2 In., R-K21 .... 176.00
Kelly's Old Cabin, Patd March 1870, Amber, 10 In., R-K22 .... 2464.00
Kelly's Old Cabin, Patd March 1870, Dark Amber, 9 3/8 In., R-K22 .... 1848.00
Kelly's Old Cabin, Patented 1863, Amber, 9 In., R-K21 .... 2128.00
Kelly's Old Cabin, Patented 1863, Amber, Applied Top, 9 5/8 In., R-K21 .... 2200.00
Kelly's Old Cabin, Patented 1863, Amber, Sloping Collar, 9 5/8 In., R-K21 .... 2465.00
Kelly's Old Cabin, Patented 1863, Dark Amber, 9 5/8 In., R-K21 .... 888.00
Kelly's Old Cabin, Patented 1863, Yellow Amber, 9 1/4 In., R-K21 .... 1736.00
Keystone, Barrel, Chocolate Amber, 10 In., R-K36 .... 924.00
Kimball's Jaundice, Troy, N.H., Yellow Amber, Applied Collar Lip, 6 7/8 In., R-K42 .... 1288.00
Kimball's Jaundice, Troy, N.H., Yellow Amber, Iron Pontil, 1855, 7 In., R-K42 .... 1736.00
Kimball's Jaundice, Yellow Amber, Applied Mouth, Pontil, 7 In. ....1430.00 to 1650.00
L.N. Kreinbrook's, Mt. Pleasant, Pa., Amber, Indented Panels, 8 3/8 In., R-K78 .... 246.00
Lacour's Sarsapariphere, Apple Green, Applied Lip, 9 1/2 In., R-L3 .... 4950.00
Langley's Root & Herb, 99 Union St., Boston, Yellow Amber, Disc Mouth, 8 1/2 In., R-L21 ... 83.00
Lediard's Celebrated Stomach, Medium Blue Green, IP, 1860, 10 In., R-L60 .... 3750.00
Lediard's O.K. Plantation, 1840, Semi-Cabin, Medium Amber, 10 In., R-L62 .... 4200.00
Lippman's Great German, Savannah, Geo, Amber, Square, 9 3/4 In., R-L98 .... 1045.00
Lippman's Great German, Savannah, Georgia, Gold, 10 In., R-L99 .... 880.00
Litthauer Stomach, Hartwig Kantorowicz, Berlin, Medium Amber, 11 In., R-L104 ..... 123.00
Litthauer Stomach, Hartwig Kantorowicz, Milk Glass, Gin Shape, 9 In., R-L106 .... 55.00
Litthauer Stomach, Hartwig Kantorowicz, Yellow Green, 10 1/4 In., R-L106 .... 110.00
Litthauer Stomach, Milk Glass, Case Gin, Square Lip, 9 1/2 In., R-L102 .... 140.00
Louis Taussig & Co., San Francisco, Cal., Amber, Square Applied Lip, 9 1/4 In. 140.00
Marshall's, Best Laxative & Blood Purifier, Amber, Square, 8 5/8 In., R-M40 .... 80.00
McKee's, M. Shehan & Co., Troy, N.Y., Gold Amber, 1895, 6 7/8 In., R-M57 .... 123.00
McKeever's Army, Amber, Original Cork, Applied Lip, 10 1/2 In., R-M58 .... 1200.00
McKeever's Army, Drum With Cannonballs, Amber, 10 1/2 In., R-M58 .... 4144.00
McKeever's Army, Drum With Cannonballs, Medium Red Amber, 10 1/2 In., R-M58 ..... 3360.00
Mishler's Herb, Amber, Applied Lip, 9 In., R-M100 .... 77.00
Mishler's Herb, Dr. S.B. Hartman & Co., Orange Amber, Square, 9 In., R-M99 .... 48.00
Mishler's Herb, Dr. S.B. Hartman & Co., Yellow Amber, 8 3/4 In., R-M99 .... 350.00
Mishler's Herb, Tablespoon Graduation, Olive Yellow, Double Collar, 9 In., R-M100 .... 392.00
Morning Inceptum 5869, Star, Amber, 3-Sided, IP, 12 7/8 In., R-M135 ....231.00 to 350.00
Morning Inceptum 5869, Star, Yellow Amber, IP, 11 7/8 In., R-M135 .... 700.00
Moulton's Oloroso, Blue Green, Embossed Pineapple, 11 3/8 In., R-M146 .... 660.00
Moulton's Oloroso, Pineapple Trademark, Blue Aqua, 11 1/4 In., R-M146 ......275.00 to 330.00
N. Wood, Portland, Me., Blue Aqua, 8 In., R-B279 .... 280.00
Napoleon, 1866, Dingen Brothers, Semi-Cabin, 10 1/8 In., R-N2.5 .... 4592.00
Napoleon Cocktail, Dingen Brothers, Banjo Lady's Leg, Yellow Amber, 10 In., R-N3 ... 3248.00
National, Ear Of Corn, Patent 1867, Amber, Applied Lip, 12 1/2 In., R-N8 ....440.00 to 660.00
National, Ear Of Corn, Patent 1867, Amber, Label, 12 1/2 In., R-N8 .... 980.00
National, Ear Of Corn, Patent 1867, Blue Aqua, 12 5/8 In., R-N8 .... 5150.00
National, Ear Of Corn, Patent 1867, Cherry Puce, 12 1/2 In., R-N8 .... 1870.00
National, Ear Of Corn, Patent 1867, Gold Yellow Amber, 12 5/8 In., R-N8 ....Illus 756.00
National, Ear Of Corn, Patent 1867, Red Amber, 12 1/2 In., R-N8 .... 476.00
National, Ear Of Corn, Patent 1867, Straw Yellow, Applied Lip, 12 1/2 In., R-N8 .... 3248.00
National, Ear Of Corn, Patent 1867, Strawberry Puce, 1875, 12 1/2 In., R-N8 .... 1792.00
National, Ear Of Corn, Patent 1867, Yellow, 12 1/2 In., R-N8 .... 1980.00
National Stomach, Pittsburgh, Pa., Amber, Indented Panels, 9 1/4 In., R-N11 .... 2912.00
New York Hop Bitters Company, U.S. Flag, Aqua, Square, 9 3/4 In., R-N28 .....143.00 to 176.00
Oil Of Seneka, Amber, Flared Lip, OP, Label, 3 3/4 In. 88.00
Old Cabin Patented 1863, Cabin, Beer Amber, 9 1/4 In., R-O19 .... 3248.00

Old Dr. Sherman's Sherry Wine, Yellow Amber, Applied Mouth, 8 3/4 In. 853.00
Old Hickory Celebrated Stomach, Medium Amber, 1880-1900, 4 1/2 In., R-O32 . . . .   112.00
Old Home, Wheeling, W.Va., Semi-Cabin, Medium Amber, 1880, 9 In., R-O35 . . . .   2016.00
Old Homestead Wild Cherry, Cabin, Amber, 9 3/4 In., R-O37 . . . . .336.00 to 588.00
Old Homestead Wild Cherry, Cabin, Chocolate Amber, Sloping Collar, 9 5/8 In., R-O37 .   1650.00
Old Homestead Wild Cherry, Cabin, Gold Amber, 1860-1880, 9 5/8 In., R-O37 . . . .   2420.00
Old Homestead Wild Cherry, Cabin, Olive Yellow, 9 3/4 In., R-O37 . . . .   5824.00
Old Homestead Wild Cherry, Cabin, Patent, Medium Red Amber, 10 In., R-O37 . . . .   308.00
Old Sachem & Wigwam Tonic, Barrel, Amber, 1875, 9 1/2 In., R-L46 . . . .   364.00
Old Sachem & Wigwam Tonic, Barrel, Amber, 9 3/8 In., R-O46 . . . .   660.00
Old Sachem & Wigwam Tonic, Barrel, Black Olive Amber, 9 3/8 In., R-O46 . . . .   467.00
Old Sachem & Wigwam Tonic, Barrel, Blue Aqua, Applied Lip, 9 7/8 In., R-O45 . . . .   4144.00
Old Sachem & Wigwam Tonic, Barrel, Chocolate Amber, 9 3/8 In., R-O46 . . . .   495.00
Old Sachem & Wigwam Tonic, Barrel, Ginger Ale Color, 1875, 9 In., R-O46 . . . .   4760.00
Old Sachem & Wigwam Tonic, Barrel, Ginger Ale Color, 9 3/8 In., R-O46 . . . .   8530.00
Old Sachem & Wigwam Tonic, Barrel, Gold Amber, 9 3/8 In., R-O46 . . . .   550.00
Old Sachem & Wigwam Tonic, Barrel, Gold Amber, Square Collar, 9 3/8 In., R-O46 . . . .   154.00
Old Sachem & Wigwam Tonic, Barrel, Gold Yellow Amber, 9 1/2 In., R-O46 . . . . .825.00 to 853.00
Old Sachem & Wigwam Tonic, Barrel, Gold Yellow Amber, 9 1/4 In., R-O46 . . . .   728.00
Old Sachem & Wigwam Tonic, Barrel, Gold Yellow Copper, 9 3/8 In., R-O46 . . . .   687.00
Old Sachem & Wigwam Tonic, Barrel, Grape Amethyst, Applied Lip, 9 In., R-O46 . .*Illus*   3575.00
Old Sachem & Wigwam Tonic, Barrel, Light Apricot Puce, 9 1/4 In., R-O46 . . . .   2695.00
Old Sachem & Wigwam Tonic, Barrel, Light Topaz, 1875, 9 3/8 In., R-O46 . . . .   7840.00
Old Sachem & Wigwam Tonic, Barrel, Light Topaz, 9 1/2 In., R-O46 . . . .   2640.00
Old Sachem & Wigwam Tonic, Barrel, Medium Topaz Puce, 9 In., R-O46 . . . .   896.00
Old Sachem & Wigwam Tonic, Barrel, Olive Yellow, 9 1/2 In., R-O46 . . . .   2200.00
Old Sachem & Wigwam Tonic, Barrel, Orange Amber, 9 3/8 In., R-O46 . . . .   616.00
Old Sachem & Wigwam Tonic, Barrel, Pink Puce, Applied Lip, 9 3/8 In., R-O46 . . . .   5152.00
Old Sachem & Wigwam Tonic, Barrel, Red Amber, Applied Lip, 9 1/4 In., R-O46 . . . . . .   605.00
Old Sachem & Wigwam Tonic, Barrel, Red Puce, 9 1/2 In., R-O46 . . . .   1848.00
Old Sachem & Wigwam Tonic, Barrel, Topaz, 9 1/4 In., R-O46 . . . .   2520.00
Old Sachem & Wigwam Tonic, Barrel, Yellow Amber, 9 3/8 In., R-O46 . . . .   476.00
Original Pocahontas, Y. Ferguson, Barrel, Blue Aqua, 9 3/8 In., R-O86 . . . .   5488.00
Oswego 25 Cents, Amber, Applied Square Collar, 7 In., R-O93 . . . .   110.00
Oxygenated For Dyspepsia, Asthma & General Debility, Aqua, 7 1/2 In., R-O99 . . . .   148.00
Penn's Pony, H.W. Long M.D. & Co., Philadelphia, Pa., Amber, 9 In., R-P40 . . . .   605.00
Pepsin Wild Cherry, Gold Amber, Long Neck, Rectangular, 9 1/4 In., R-P53.5 . . . .   198.00
Peruvian, Chas. Noelle & Co., Amber, Double Collar, Cleaned, 9 1/2 In., R-P63.5 . . . . . .   385.00
Pig, see Bitters, Berkshire; Bitters, Suffolk
Pineapple, Gold, Applied Lip, OP, 8 7/8 In., R-P100 . . . .   413.00
Pineapple, Olive Yellow, Diamond Panels, 1860, 9 In., R-P100 . . . .   577.00
Pineapple, W & Co., N.Y., Amber, Pontil, Double Collar, 8 5/8 In., R-P100 . . . .   392.00
Pineapple, W & Co., N.Y., Medium Blue Green, 1865-1875, 8 5/8 In., R-P100 . . . .   8400.00
Pineapple, W & Co., N.Y., Olive Green, 8 5/8 In., R-P100 . . . . .3080.00 to 3360.00
Pineapple, W & Co., N.Y., Red Amber, Applied Double Collar, OP, 9 5/8 In., R-P100 . . .   605.00
Pineapple, W & Co., N.Y., Tobacco Amber, 8 1/2 In., R-P100 . . . .   157.00

Bitters, National,
Ear of Corn, Patent
1867, Gold Yellow
Amber, 12 5/8 In., R-N8

Bitters, Old Sachem &
Wigwam Tonic, Barrel,
Grape Amethyst,
Applied Lip, 9 In., R-O46

Bitters, R.S.
Gardner & Co.,
Gold Yellow Amber,
11 1/4 In., R-T4

Pineapple, W & Co., N.Y., Yellow Olive Green, Iron Pontil, 1875, 8 5/8 In., R-P100 .... 4760.00
Polo Club Trade Mark, Stomach, Amber, Tooled Lip, 9 1/4 In., R-P117 .... 110.00
Prickly Ash Bitters Co, Amber, 9 3/4 In., R-P143 .... 66.00
Professor B.E. Mann's Oriental Stomach, Semi-Cabin, Amber, 10 1/4 In., R-M29 ...... 1848.00
Professor Geo. J. Bryne, Great Universal Compound, Amber, 10 In., R-B280 .... 1450.00
Professor Geo. J. Byrne, Great Universal Compound, Amber, 10 3/4 In., R-B280 .... 1624.00
Purdy's Cottage, Amber, Pontil, 9 1/2 In., R-P156 .... 3080.00
R.S. Gardner & Co., Gold Yellow Amber, 11 1/4 In., R-T4 ....*Illus* 7150.00
Red Jacket, Bennett Pieters & Co., Amber, Square, 9 1/2 In., R-R19 .... 198.00
Red Jacket, Bennett Pieters & Co., Olive Yellow, Sloping Collar, 9 1/4 In., R-R19 ...... 1320.00
Rising Sun, John C Hurst, Philada, Amber, Sloping Collar, 9 3/8 In., R-R66 .... 154.00
Rising Sun, John C Hurst, Philada, Yellow Amber, Square, 9 3/8 In., R-R66 .... 305.00
Romaine's Crimean Patend 1863, Semi-Cabin, Amber, 10 In., R-R87 .... 672.00
Rosenheim's Great Western Remedy, Black Olive Amber, 4 Panels, 10 In., R-R96 ..... 504.00
Royal Pepsin Stomach, L & A Scharff, Sole Agents, Red Amber, 9 In., R-R113 .... 94.00
Royal Pepsin Stomach, Orange Amber, Tooled Lip, 8 3/4 In., R-R113 .... 88.00
Royce's Sherry Wine, 8 In., R-R119 .... 100.00
Russ' St. Domingo, New York, Dark Amber, Sloping Collar, 10 1/4 In., R-R125 ...135.00 to 148.00
Russian Imperial, Blue Aqua, 9 1/2 In., R-R133 .... 2072.00
S.O. Richardson's, Green Aqua, Pontil Base, 6 1/2 In., R-R57 .... 242.00
S.T. Drake's, see Bitters, Drake's Plantation
Salmon's Perfect Stomach, Red Amber, Tooled Lip, Stain, 9 1/2 In., R-S19 .... 275.00
Sanborn's Kidney & Liver Vegetable Laxative, Amber, Tooled Lip, 10 In., R-S28 ..77.00 to 145.00
Saxlehner's Hunyadi Janos, Bitterquelle, Olive Green, 9 1/4 In., R-S42B 42.00
Sazerac Aromatic, Lady's Leg, Milk Glass, Applied Lip, 10 In., R-S48 .... 728.00
Sazerac Aromatic, Phd & Co., Lady's Leg, Milk Glass, 12 In., R-S47 .... 252.00
Sazerac Aromatic, Yellow Amber, Monogram, Applied Ring, 10 In., R-S48 .... 440.00
Schroeder's, Louisville And Cincinnati, Tooled Lip, 5 1/4 In., R-S67 .... 358.00
Schroeder's, Louisville, K.Y., Amber, Applied Lip, R-S70 .... 303.00
Schroeder's, Louisville, K.Y., Yellow Tobacco Amber, 1875, 8 3/4 In., R-S70 .... 504.00
Schroeder's, Louisville, Ky., Amber, Tooled Lip, 9 In., R-S65 ....165.00 to 264.00
Schroeder's, Louisville, Ky., Red Amber, Crooked Neck, 9 In., R-S65 .... 220.00
Seaworth, Cape May, New Jersey, Lighthouse, Amber, 11 1/4 In., R-S81 .... 7560.00
Secrestat, Olive Green, Cylindrical, Kick Up Base, 12 In........................ 175.00
Simmons Liver Regulator, Macon, Philadelphia 22.00
Simon's Centennial, Bust Of Washington, Amber, 9 7/8 In., R-S110 .... 3248.00
Smyrna Stomach Prolongs Life, Dayton, Ohio, Amber, 9 In., R-S134 .... 170.00
Solomon's Strengthening & Invigorating, Cobalt Blue, 9 3/4 In., R-S139 .... 2128.00
St. Gotthard Herb, Mette & Kanne Pros, St. Louis, Mo., Amber, 8 7/8 In., R-S12 ...... 94.00
St. Nicholas Stomach, Amber, 4 Sloping Panels, Applied Collar, IP, 7 1/2 In., R-S17 .... 4400.00
Stockton's Port Wine, Amber, Monogram, 9 1/4 In., R-S198 .... 151.00
Suffolk, Philbrook & Tucker, Boston, Lemon Yellow, 10 In., R-S217 .... 7056.00
Suffolk, Philbrook & Tucker, Boston, Pig, Amber, Double Collar, 10 In., R-S217 .... 672.00
Suffolk, Philbrook & Tucker, Boston, Pig, Yellow Amber, Double Collar, 10 In., R-S17 .. 950.00
Sunny Castle Stomach, Jos. Dudenhoefer, Milwaukee, Amber, 9 In., R-S223 .... 154.00
Swan, McFarland Bro's, Penn., Applied Lip, Rounded Shoulders, 9 1/2 In., R-S229 ...... 140.00
Telinko Bitter Wine, Hollander Bros. Drug Co., Braddock, Pa., Amber, Labels, 11 In. ... 60.00
Tippecanoe, H.H. Warner & Co., Amber, 9 In., R-T30.8 ....83.00 to 140.00
Tippecanoe, H.H. Warner & Co., Gold Amber, Applied Mushroom Top, 9 In., R-T30.8 ... 145.00
Tippecanoe, H.H. Warner & Co., Rochester, Olive Yellow, Applied Lip, 9 In., R-T30.8 ... 5880.00
Tippecanoe, H.H. Warner & Co., Tobacco Amber, 9 In., R-T30.8 .... 980.00
Tyree's Chamomile, Yellow Amber, Tooled Lip, 6 1/2 In., R-T73 .... 246.00
Utica Hop, JKB & Co., Semi-Cabin, Aqua, Sloping Collar, 9 1/2 In., R-U18 .... 83.00
Van Ness Golden, Ravenna, Ohio, Clear, Amethystine Tint, 8 1/4 In., R-V9 .... 106.00
W.C. Brobst & Rentschler, Barrel, Dark To Light Amber, 10 1/2 In., R-W57 .... 605.00
W.C. Brobst & Rentschler, Reading, Pa., Barrel, Yellow Amber, 10 1/2 In., R-W57 ...... 476.00
W.M. Ward's Eureka Tonic, SCA, Square Tooled Lip, 8 3/4 In., R-W28 .... 450.00
W.R. Tyree's Chamomile, Semi-Cabin, Amber, 8 5/8 In., R-T75 .... 980.00
W.R. Tyree's Chamomile, Semi-Cabin, Orange Amber, 9 5/8 In., R-T75 .... 1680.00
Wahoo & Calisaya, Jacob Pinkerton, Semi-Cabin, Amber, 10 In., R-W3 .... 840.00
Wahoo & Calisaya, Jacob Pinkerton, Yellow Amber, Applied Lip, 9 5/8 In., R-W3 ...... 1320.00
Wallace's Tonic Stomach, Geo. Powell & Co, Chicago Ill., Applied Top, 9 In., R-W17 ... 50.00
Wampoo, New York, Applied Lip, Square, 9 5/8 In., R-W25 .... 90.00

Warner's Safe, Rochester N.Y., Amber, 7 3/8 In., R-W39 .... 924.00
Warner's Safe, Rochester, N.Y., Amber, Double Collar, 9 1/2 In., R-W34 ....364.00 to 784.00
Warner's Safe, Rochester, N.Y., Amber, Slug Plate, Applied Lip, 7 5/8 In., R-W35 ...... 924.00
Warner's Safe, Rochester, N.Y., Orange Amber, 1850-1890, 9 3/8 In., R-W34 .... 550.00
Warner's Safe, Rochester, N.Y., Red Amber, Applied Lip, 9 5/8 In., R-W34 .... 532.00
Warner's Safe Tonic, Rochester N.Y., Gold Amber, 9 5/8 In., R-W36 .... 1344.00
Wheeler's Berlin, Baltimore, Forest Green, 1855-1870, 9 3/4 In., R-W83 .... 8960.00
Wheeler's Berlin, Baltimore, Medium Yellow Olive, IP, 1870, 9 In., R-W83 .... 6160.00
Whitwell's Temperance, Boston, Aqua, OP, 7 In., R-W105 .... 110.00
William Allen's Congress, Aqua, Panel, Sloping Collar, 10 1/4 In., R-A29 .... 275.00
William Allen's Congress, Blue Green, Indented Panels, 10 3/8 In., R-A29 .....2050.00 to 2475.00
William Allen's Congress, Cabin, Yellow Amber, Sloping Collar, 10 1/8 In., R-A29 .... 1540.00
Wilson Fairbank & Co., Bourbon Whiskey, For Medicinal Purposes, Aqua, Applied Top .. 110.00
Wormser Bros, San Francisco, Barrel, Yellow Amber, Applied Lip, 9 3/4 In., R-W162.5 .. 1210.00
XXX, Dandelion, SCA, Tooled Lip, 7 3/8 In., R-D12 .... 55.00
Yerba Buena, S.F. Cal., Amber, Applied Lip, 9 1/2 In., R-Y3 .... 77.00
Yerba Buena, S.F. Cal., Flask, Red Amber, 9 1/2 In., R-Y3 .... 33.00
Yerba Buena, S.F. Cal., Green, 1870s, 9 1/2 In., R-Y3 .... 495.00
Young & Holmes, Cincinnati, O., Cabin, Dark Amber, Applied Top 171.00
Zingari, F. Rahter, Lady's Leg, Amber, Applied Lip, 12 In., R-Z4 .... 132.00

─── BLACK GLASS ───

Black glass is not really black. It is dark green or brown. In the seventeenth century, blown black glass demijohns were used to carry liquor overseas from Europe. They were usually heavy glass bottles that were made to withstand shipping. The kick-up bottom also helped deter breakage. Many types of bottles were made of very dark glass that appeared black. This was one of the most common colors for glass wine bottles of the eighteenth and early-nineteenth centuries.

Ale, Graphite Pontil, 7 1/2 In. 20.00
Ale, Olive Amber, Applied String Lip, OP 165.00
Bottle, Olive Amber, OP, Applied Ring, 11 1/4 In. 145.00
Bottle, Olive Green, Applied Double Collar, Pontil, 9 1/2 In. 85.00
Champagne, Root Beer Amber, OP, Applied Ring, 1770-1800, 11 In. 179.20
Chemist, Rolled Lip, 14 In. 112.50
Cylindrical, Double Collar, Kick-Up, OP, 11 1/4 In. 35.00
Cylindrical, Squat, OP, 8 1/4 In. 200.00
Dutch Kidney, Olive Green, Amber Tone, 6 3/4 In. ....*Illus* 770.00
Dutch Onion, Applied Band, 7 1/2 In. 100.00
Dutch Onion, Applied Band, Pontil, Early 18th Century 140.00
Dutch Onion, Applied String Collar, OP, 1725-1735, 7 In. ....100.00 to 175.00
Dutch Onion, Flat Side, Applied Top, Pontil, Early 18th Century 165.00
Dutch Onion, Olive Amber, Applied String Collar, OP, 7 3/4 In. 165.00
Dutch Onion, Olive Green, Applied Ring, Pontil, 7 1/2 In. ....140.00 to 170.00
Dutch Onion, Olive Green, Pontil, 6 1/4 In. 330.00
English Mallet, Olive Amber, Kick-Up, 1850, 8 In. 275.00
English Mallet, Olive Amber, Pontil, 8 5/8 In. ....*Illus* 175.00

Black Glass, Dutch
Kidney, Olive Green,
Amber Tone, 6 3/4 In.

Black Glass, English
Mallet, Olive Amber,
Pontil, 8 5/8 In.

English Mallet, Olive Green, 7 7/8 In. 175.00
English Mallet, Olive Green, Applied Ring, Pontil, 10 3/4 In. 110.00
English Mallet, Olive Green, Applied Ring, Pontil, 1760-1780, 8 1/2 In. 330.00
Gin, Olive Green, Flat Lip, OP, 10 1/2 In. 110.00
Globular, Olive Amber, 4 Men, Woman & 2 Children At Table, 10 In. 1900.00
Globular, Olive Amber, Man & Woman Sitting At Small Table, 11 In. 1900.00
Mallet, Bell Shape, Olive Green, Continental, Kick-Up, 1750, 8 1/8 In. 190.00
Mallet, Olive Yellow, String Lip, Kick-Up, 1740-1750, 7 3/8 In. 175.00
Onion, Blue Green, Pontil, 6 3/8 In. 1650.00
Onion, Dutch, Olive Green, Applied String Collar, OP, 10 3/8 In. 155.00
Onion, Olive Green, Pontil, 6 In. 330.00
Storage, OP, 1740-1780, 18 x 6 1/4 In. 395.00
Temple, Olive Green, Horse Scene, 1840-1860, 11 1/4 In. 210.00
BLACKING, see Household, Blacking

--- **BLOWN** ---

The American glass industry did not flourish until after the Revolution. Glass for windows and blown-glass bottles were the most rewarding products. The bottles were blown in large or small sizes to hold liquor. Many glassworks made blown and pattern-molded bottles. Midwestern factories favored twisted swirl designs. The colors ranged from green and aquamarine to dark olive green or amber. Sometimes blue or dark purple bottles were blown. Some were made of such dark glass they are known as *black glass* bottles.

Bateman's, Stopper, 10 In. 80.00
Beehive, 24 Ribs, Swirled To Right, Yellow Green, Midwest, Pontil, 7 7/8 In. 357.00
Beehive, 32 Ribs, Swirled To Left, Aqua, Midwest, Pontil, 8 1/2 In. 275.00
Bellows, Clear, Quilling, Neck Ring, Rigaree, Raspberry Prunts, Handles, 14 2/8 In. 115.00
Bellows, Cobalt Blue, White & Clear Rigaree, Prunt, Leaf, Handles, 11 1/4 In. 345.00
Bellows, Ruby, White & Ruby Quilled Neck, Rigaree, Prunt Handles, 9 3/4 In. 260.00
Cone, Olive Yellow, Long Neck, Tooled Flared Lip, Pontil, 10 5/8 In. 785.00
Dutch Onion, Dark Green, 8 In. ....*Illus* 155.00
Dutch Onion, Light Olive Green, Applied String Collar, 7 1/2 In. 55.00
Dutch Onion, Light Olive Yellow, 8 In. ....*Illus* 130.00
Fly Trap, Globular, 3 Applied Square Feet, Tooled Mouth, 1860-1890, 7 3/4 In. 155.00
Globular, 4 Flattened Sides, Cobalt Blue, 1800s, Qt. 220.00
Globular, Aqua, Zanesville Glass Works, Rolled Mouth, Pontil, 3 1/2 x 2 5/8 In. 415.00
Globular, Medium Olive Yellow, Applied String Lip, Pontil, 1780-1810, 11 In. 950.00
Globular, Olive Green, Tooled Lip, Pontil, 10 In. 475.00
Globular, Olive Yellow, Bubbles, Pontil, 10 1/4 In. 605.00
Globular, Olive, Applied Sloping Collar Mouth, Ring, Pontil, 11 In. 495.00
Olive Green, Tooled Lip, Applied Ring, Pontil, 9 In. 310.00
P.V. Gentian, Cobalt Blue, Ground Stopper, 12 In. 460.00
BROOKS, see Ezra Brooks
C.P.C., CALIFORNIA PERFUME COMPANY, see Avon
CABIN STILL, see Old Fitzgerald
CALABASH, see Flask

Blown, Dutch Onion,
Dark Green, 8 In.

Blown, Dutch Onion,
Light Olive Yellow, 8 In.

--- **CANDY CONTAINER** ---

The first figural glass candy containers date from the nineteenth century. They were made to hold candy and to be used later as toys for children. These containers were very popular after World War I. Small glass figural bottles held dime-store candy. Cars, trains, airplanes, animals, comic figures, telephones, and many other imaginative containers were made. The fad faded in the Depression years but returned in the 1940s. Today many of the same shapes hold modern candy in plastic bottles. The paper labels on the containers help a little with the dating. In the 1940s the words *Contents* or *Ingredients* were included on the labels. Earlier, this information was not necessary. Screw tops and corks were used. Some of the most popular early shapes have been reproduced in Taiwan and Hong Kong in recent years. A club with a newsletter is Candy Container Collectors of America, 2711 De La Rosa St., The Villages, FL 32162.

Airplane, Army Bomber, 15-P-7, No Propeller, J.H. Millstein	50.00
Airplane, Army Bomber, Sticker On Propeller, J.H. Millstein	24.00
Airplane, Closure	95.00
Airplane, P-38, Lightning	255.00 to 295.00
Airplane, P-51, No Closure	50.00
Airplane, P-51, Replacement Closure	75.00
Airplane, Spirit Of Goodwill	103.00 to 150.00
Airplane, Spirit Of St. Louis, Monoplane Type	578.00
Airplane, Spirit Of St. Louis, Pink	350.00 to 400.00
Airplane, T.M.A. 44	125.00
Airplane, With Left Side Rear Door	475.00
Alpine Man, With Feather Tree, Composition, 5 1/2 In.	38.00
Amos 'n' Andy Car, Replacement Closure	465.00 to 500.00
Amos 'n' Andy Car, Victory Glass Co, Jeannette, Pa., Tin Closure, 4 In.	700.00
Banty Rooster, Composition, Black, Red Head, Metal Feet, 3 3/4 x 5 1/2 In.	385.00
Barney Google, Riding Spark Plug, Sheared Lip, 1920-1935, 4 In. ....*Illus*	448.00
Barney Google & Ball	330.00 to 350.00
Barney Google & Bank	1100.00
Baseball, Milk Glass, Closure	30.00
Belsnickle, Composition, Orange Robe, 8 In.	400.00
Belsnickle, White Robe, Composition, Green Feather Tree, 11 1/4 In.	825.00
Black Cat For Luck, Glass, 4 1/4 In.	1980.00
Boat, Colorado, 1914	195.00 to 295.00
Boat, Cruiser, 1917	20.00
Boat, Remember The Maine, 7 In. ....*Illus*	45.00
Bureau, Replacement Closure	200.00 to 225.00
Bus, Greyhound, Green Paint	300.00
Bus, Greyhound, Green Paint, Replacement Closure	275.00
Bus, Jitney	525.00
Bus, Victory Lines	65.00
Bus, Victory Lines Special, Blue Paint	492.00
Bus, Victory Lines, Reproduction Closure	55.00
Camel	60.00 to 65.00
Candelabrum, Condiment Set, Vanstyle	65.00
Candlestick, With Handles, Ruby Flashed	295.00

Candy Container, Barney Google, Riding Spark Plug, Sheared Lip, 1920-1935, 4 In.

Candy Container, Boat, Remember The Maine, 7 In.

Candy Container, Car, Station Wagon

Candy Container,
Charlie Chaplin, Borgfeldt

Cannon, 2 Wheel Mount, No. 1 .... 250.00
Cannon, 2 Wheel Mount, No. 2 .... .300.00 to 350.00
Car, Air Flow, Car Of Future, Victory Glass Co. 868.00
Car, Coupe, With Long Hood 60.00
Car, Electric Coupe, Pat. Feb.18, 1913 .... .100.00 to 125.00
Car, Electric Coupe, Replacement Closure 100.00
Car, Flat Top, With Tassels 475.00
Car, Hearse, No. 1 .... 50.00
Car, Hearse, No. 1, Variant 115.00
Car, Hearse, No. 2 .... 135.00
Car, Limousine, Pat Ap'ld For 224.00
Car, Limousine, Rear Trunk & Tire, Red 150.00
Car, Limousine, Rear Trunk & Tire, Reproduction Closure 75.00
Car, Limousine, Westmoreland & Speciality Co. 75.00
Car, Little Sedan, Replacement Closure 30.00
Car, Little Sedan, Volkswagen 35.00
Car, Racer, No. 6 On Grill, 3 5/8 In. 60.00
Car, Racer, No. 12 On Side, 5 3/8 In. 225.00
Car, Sedan, Victory Glass Co., Replacement Wheels 150.00
Car, Sedan, Victory Glass Co., Reproduction Closure 125.00
Car, Sedan, Volkswagen 50.00
Car, Sedan, With 6 Vents, Victory Glass Co. .... .90.00 to 125.00
Car, Sedan, With 12 Vents, Victory Glass Co. .... .85.00 to 125.00
Car, Station Wagon .... *Illus* 40.00
Car, Streamlined, Touring 135.00
Car, Streamlined, Touring, Replacement Closure 30.00
Car, Taxi, Black & White, Reproduction Top 106.00
Car, Tin Wheeled, Streamliner, Replacement Closure 100.00
Careful Chubby Cop 560.00
Carpet Sweeper, Baby Sweeper 450.00
Charlie Chaplin, Borgfeldt .... *Illus* 125.00
Cheerful Cholly Clown 512.00
Chick, Standing .... *Illus* 125.00
Chick In Shell Car, 4 1/4 In. 532.00
Chicken, Composition, Multi-Brown Paint, Metal Feet, 7 1/4 In. 358.00
Chicken, Desk, Opaque White 145.00
Chicken, On Round Base 406.00
Chicken, Papier-Mache, Germany, 5 1/2 In., Pair 220.00
Chicken, With 3 Chicks, Papier-Mache, 2 3/4 x 4 In. 49.00
Chicken On Nest, Closure 35.00
Chicken On Nest, Green 150.00
Clock, Alarm 325.00
Clock, Mantel, Milk Glass 190.00
Condiment Set, Vanstyle 50.00
Countertop, Globe Shape, Ground Glass Stopper, 1890-1920, 11 3/4 In. 198.00
Countertop, Globe Shape, Ground Inside Tooled Lip, Glass Stopper, 15 In. 220.00

Candy Container, Iron, Flat,
Replacement Closure

Candy Container, Easter
M&M's, Cardboard Tube,
Plastic Figural Stopper,
9 1/4 In.

Candy Container,
Chick, Standing

Candy Container, Dog,
Glass Hat, Large

Dice, Bristol	.25.00 to 45.00
Dirigible, Los Angeles	275.00
Dog, Bulldog, No Closure	30.00
Dog, Circus	25.00
Dog, Glass Hat, Large	*Illus* 12.00
Dog, Hansel & Gretel, Salt & Pepper	125.00
Dog, Kiddies Breakfast Bell	85.00
Dog, Little Doggie In Window	40.00
Dog, Sitting, Smile, Damn You, Smile, 1890-1925, 4 1/4 In.	235.00
Dog, Small Glass Hat	40.00
Dog By Barrel	200.00 to 215.00
Don't Park Here	168.00 to 325.00
Drake, Composition, Glass Eyes, Painted Metal Feet, 9 x 7 1/2 In.	468.00
Duck, On Round Basket, Clear	150.00 to 165.00
Duck, On Round Basket, Green	85.00 to 165.00
Duck, With Large Bill	350.00
Easter M&M's, Cardboard Tube, Plastic Figural Stopper, 9 1/4 In.	*Illus* 5.00
Elephant, GOP, Black Paint	250.00
Fat Boy On Drum, 1915-1920, 4 3/8 In.	128.00
Fire Engine, 3 Dot, U.S.A.	125.00
Fire Engine, Little Boiler No. 2, Blue	100.00 to 125.00
Flossie Fisher's Table	810.00
Foxy Doctor, 5 Bottles	250.00
George Washington, On Horseback, Bisque Body, 8 1/2 x 10 In.	1870.00
George Washington, On Horseback, Bisque Face, 12 1/2 In.	748.00
Goblin Head, Bulging Eyes, Incised Teeth, Tin Base, 3 5/8 In.	695.00
Gun, Kolt	100.00
Gun, Orange, Red, Plastic	25.00
Gun, V.G. Co., Tiny Revolver	65.00
Hat, Military, Clear, Original Candy Pellets, Pla-Toy Co., Pa.	112.00
Hat, Military, Closure, Contents	45.00
Hat, With Tin Brim, Paper Inserts	100.00
Helicopter, 2 Blades	150.00 to 225.00
Helicopter, 2 Blades, Contents, Paper	250.00
Helicopter, No. 1029	295.00
Horn, 3 Valves	300.00
Horn, 3 Valves, Whistle Does Not Work	145.00
Horn, Millstein, 1948	35.00
Horn, Musical Clarinet, No. 515A	75.00
Horn, Red, Millstein	30.00
Horn, Trumpet, Clear, Milk Glass	175.00
Horse, Spark Plug, Orange Paint, Tin Closure, 3 In.	672.00

House, English Cottage, 1915-1930, 2 1/2 In. 157.00
Iron, Flat, Replacement Closure .... *Illus* 35.00
Jack-O-Lantern, Pop Eyed 675.00
Kiddie Pencils On Display Card 75.00
Lamp, George Washington, Reproduction Shade 255.00
Lantern, Barn Type, No. 1, Clear .... *Illus* 50.00
Lantern, Barn Type, No. 1, Ruby Flashed 75.00
Lantern, Beaded No. 2, Reproduction Closure 50.00
Lantern, Coach 100.00
Lantern, Kerosene 100.00
Lantern, Plastic, J.H. Millstein 37.00
Lantern, Ruby Flashed 125.00
Learned Fox Bottle, Replacement Closure 85.00
Liberty Bell, Redlich's, Proclaim Liberty Throughout Land, Metal Cap, 3 In. 246.00
Liberty Bell, With Hanger, Green .... *Illus* 75.00
Locomotive, Jent Glass Co., No. 888, With Coupler, Reproduction Closure 65.00
Locomotive, Lithographed Closure, No. 2 .... 375.00
Locomotive, Little No. 23 ....100.00 to 150.00
Locomotive, No. 888, Man In Window 588.00
Locomotive, PRR 666, Lithographed, Tin Slide Closure, 3 In. 280.00
Locomotive, Victory Glass Co., No. 1028, Contents 55.00
Los Angeles, V.G. Co. Jenet, Pa., U.S.A., Clear, Aluminum Screw Cap, 6 In. 308.00
Man On Motorcycle, With Side Car, No Closure, Some Paint 1025.00
Maud Muller Candies, 3 Piece 135.00
Milk Bottle, Dolly's Milk 75.00
Milk Bottle, Dolly's Milk, Reproduction Closure 50.00
Milk Carrier, Anco Candy ....100.00 to 125.00
Mother Hen, On Nest, 2 Chicks Under Wing, Composition 128.00
Mule, Pulling 2-Wheeled Barrel, Driver 125.00
Naked Child 60.00
Parrot, Papier-Mache, 9 In. 935.00
Pencil, Baby Jumbo ....75.00 to 100.00
Phonograph, With Glass Horn 475.00
Pumpkin Head Jr., Policeman 1175.00
Pumpkin Head Witch, Sun Colored Amethyst 600.00
Rabbit, Composition, White Fur, Hide Feet & Ears 121.00
Rabbit, Crouching 125.00
Rabbit, Eating Carrot 60.00
Rabbit, Eating Carrot, No Closure 60.00
Rabbit, Gold Paint, Metal Cap, 5 In. 336.00
Rabbit, Mother & Daughter ....636.00 to 710.00
Rabbit, Papier-Mache, Wood, Germany, 7 1/4 x 6 3/4 In. 88.00
Rabbit, Pushing Chick In Shell Cart, Tin Side Closure, 3 7/8 In. 235.00

Candy Container, Lantern,
Barn Type, No. 1, Clear

Candy Container, Liberty
Bell, With Hanger, Green

If it seems to good to be
true, it usually is! Trust your
instincts when buying
antiques. Experienced collectors notice many little signs
of repair or reproduction,
often without realizing it.

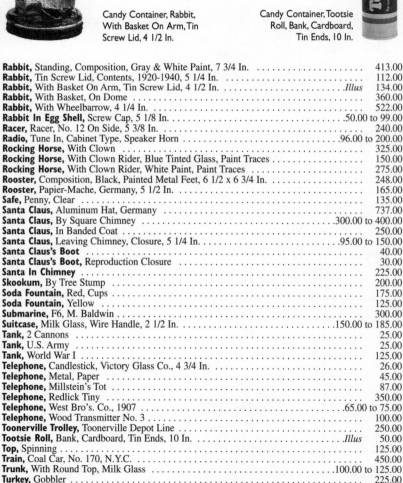

Candy Container, Rabbit,
With Basket On Arm, Tin
Screw Lid, 4 1/2 In.

Candy Container, Tootsie
Roll, Bank, Cardboard,
Tin Ends, 10 In.

Rabbit, Standing, Composition, Gray & White Paint, 7 3/4 In. 413.00
Rabbit, Tin Screw Lid, Contents, 1920-1940, 5 1/4 In. 112.00
Rabbit, With Basket On Arm, Tin Screw Lid, 4 1/2 In. ....*Illus* 134.00
Rabbit, With Basket, On Dome 360.00
Rabbit, With Wheelbarrow, 4 1/4 In. 522.00
Rabbit In Egg Shell, Screw Cap, 5 1/8 In. ....50.00 to 99.00
Racer, Racer, No. 12 On Side, 5 3/8 In. 240.00
Radio, Tune In, Cabinet Type, Speaker Horn ....96.00 to 200.00
Rocking Horse, With Clown 325.00
Rocking Horse, With Clown Rider, Blue Tinted Glass, Paint Traces 150.00
Rocking Horse, With Clown Rider, White Paint, Paint Traces 275.00
Rooster, Composition, Black, Painted Metal Feet, 6 1/2 x 6 3/4 In. 248.00
Rooster, Papier-Mache, Germany, 5 1/2 In. 165.00
Safe, Penny, Clear 135.00
Santa Claus, Aluminum Hat, Germany 737.00
Santa Claus, By Square Chimney ....300.00 to 400.00
Santa Claus, In Banded Coat 250.00
Santa Claus, Leaving Chimney, Closure, 5 1/4 In. ....95.00 to 150.00
Santa Claus's Boot 40.00
Santa Claus's Boot, Reproduction Closure 30.00
Santa In Chimney 225.00
Skookum, By Tree Stump 200.00
Soda Fountain, Red, Cups 175.00
Soda Fountain, Yellow 125.00
Submarine, F6, M. Baldwin 300.00
Suitcase, Milk Glass, Wire Handle, 2 1/2 In. ....150.00 to 185.00
Tank, 2 Cannons 25.00
Tank, U.S. Army 25.00
Tank, World War I 125.00
Telephone, Candlestick, Victory Glass Co., 4 3/4 In. 26.00
Telephone, Metal, Paper 45.00
Telephone, Millstein's Tot 87.00
Telephone, Redlick Tiny 350.00
Telephone, West Bro's. Co., 1907 ....65.00 to 75.00
Telephone, Wood Transmitter No. 3 .... 100.00
Toonerville Trolley, Toonerville Depot Line 250.00
Tootsie Roll, Bank, Cardboard, Tin Ends, 10 In. ....*Illus* 50.00
Top, Spinning 125.00
Train, Coal Car, No. 170, N.Y.C. 450.00
Trunk, With Round Top, Milk Glass ....100.00 to 125.00
Turkey, Gobbler 225.00
Uncle Sam, By Barrel ....500.00 to 600.00
Wagon, 3 3/8 In. 50.00
Watch & Chain ....450.00 to 500.00
Wheelbarrow, 6 In. 100.00

Windmill, 5 Windows ....475.00 to 500.00
Windmill, Dutch 90.00
Windmill, Dutch, Replacement Closure ....75.00 to 85.00
Windmill, Glass Tower, Pewter Top 500.00
Windmill, Stough 547.00
World Globe On Stand ....400.00 to 650.00
Ye Olde Oaken Bucket, On Lid, Milk Glass, Gold, Red Paint, Tin Lid 532.00
CANNING JAR, see Fruit Jar
CASE, see Gin

─────────────────────── **COCA-COLA** ───────────────────────

Coca-Cola was first served in 1886 in Atlanta, Georgia. John S. Pemberton, a pharmacist, originated the syrup and sold it to others. He was trying to make a patent medicine to aid those who suffered from nervousness, headaches, or stomach problems. At first the syrup was mixed with water, but in 1887, Willis E. Venable mixed it with carbonated water, and Coca-Cola was made. Pemberton sold his interest in the company to Venable and a local businessman, George S. Lowndes, in 1888. Later that year, Asa Griggs Candler, an owner of a pharmaceutical company, and some business friends became partners in Coca-Cola. A short time later they purchased the rest of the company. After some other transactions, Asa Candler became the sole owner of Coca-Cola for a grand total of $2,300. The first ad for Coca-Cola appeared in the *Atlanta Journal* on May 29, 1886. Since that time the drink has been sold in all parts of the world and in a variety of bottles and cans. The *hutchinson* bottle, sometimes called a *hutch* by collectors, was one of the earliest bottles. It has a wire loop stopper with a rubber gasket. The crown top, ten-ounce straight-sided short bottle was used from about 1900 to 1916. It was reintroduced in 1974 for special bottles like the 75th Anniversary bottle. The *root* bottle, sometimes called the *hobbleskirt* or *Maw West bottle,* first used in 1916 has a pinched "waist." In 1980 to 1992 a 10-inch tall bottle was used for commemorative bottles. The short throwaway or no return bottle was introduced in 1961. Miniature bottles have been made for many years. Over 1,000 different commemorative Coca-Cola bottle designs have been issued since 1949. The company advertised heavily, and bottles, trays, calendars, signs, toys, and lamps, as well as thousands of other items, can be found. See listings under Go-Withs at the back of the book.

Coca-Cola written in script was trademarked in 1893. *Coke* was registered in 1945. The first 16-ounce bottle was introduced in 1960. The brand name Diet Coke was first used in 1982. In 1985 the company introduced a new formula but didn't change the name. Six months later they were forced by popular opinion to bring back the old formula under the name Classic Coke. Cherry Coke was also introduced in 1985. There is a national club with a newsletter, The Coca-Cola Collectors Club, PBM 609, 4780 Ashford Dunwoody Rd., Suite A, Atlanta, GA 30338. You can learn from the national club about local meetings. Price guides and books about the history of Coca-Cola are listed in the Bibliography. The Schmidt Coca-Cola Museum in Elizabethtown, Kentucky, is associated with Coca-Cola bottlers. The Coca-Cola Company Archives (PO Drawer 1734, Atlanta, GA 30301) can answer questions about Coca-Cola memorabilia. The World of Coca-Cola museum at 55 Martin Luther King Dr. in Atlanta has exhibits of interest to collectors.

America's Cup, Australia's Defence, Fremantle, W.A., 1987, 300 Milliliter 30.00
And When You Work With Love, Kahlil Jibran, Oct.1973 .... 100.00
Atlanta, 100th Anniversary, Gold, 1986 ....20.00 to 50.00
Baltimore, Md., Blue Aqua, Crown Top, Script, BIMAL 50.00
Baltimore, Md., Orange Amber, Script, BIMAL 80.00
Barcelona Olympics, Seville, World Expo, 1992 .... 50.00
Berlin 750 Jahre, 1987, Germany ....65.00 to 75.00
Birmingham, Al., Hutchinson 3300.00
Birmingham Coca-Cola Bottling Company, Employee Open House, 1979, Short 45.00
Boy & Girl On Bench, Crown Top, ABM, 1956 .... 8.00
Brighton, Ont., Script, Straight Sides, ABM, Crown Top, c.1900 .... 725.00
Brockway, 150th Anniversary, 1936-1986, Sesquicentennial Celebration, Pa. 200.00
Calvert Rod & Gun Club, 50th Anniversary, 1936-1986 .... 300.00
Canada, Aqua, Straight Sides, Script, Crown Top, ABM, 1900 .... 75.00
Canada, Bright Lime Green, Straight Sides, ABM, c.1910 .... 110.00
Canada, Script, Blue, Straight Sides, 6 1/2 Oz. 40.00

Canada, Teal Blue, Straight Sides, ABM, 1910 .... 65.00
Carolina Panthers, NFL, 1998 .... 2.00
Chattanooga World's 1st Coca-Cola Bottling Co., 1899-1974, 75th Anniversary 5.00
Chick-Fil-A, Celebrating 50 Years Of Excellence In Food Service, 1996, 6 Pack 36.00
Christmas, Biedenharm, 1923, 3 In. 7.00
Christmas, Hobbleskirt, 1923, 3 In. 7.00
Christmas, Hutchinson, 1923, 3 In. 7.00
Cincinnati, Ohio, Amber, Tooled Crown Top, 1895-1915, 7 1/2 In. 225.00
Cincinnati, Ohio, Registered Coca-Cola, Amber, Arrow, Straight Sides, 7 1/2 In. .... *Illus* 112.00
Circleville, 75th Ohio, Pumpkin Show, October 21-24, 1981 .... 8.00
Clear, 6 Stars Around Neck, Crown Top, ABM, 7 3/4 In. 15.00
Cobb County Humane Society, C.C.H.S., 1994, 8 Oz. ....65.00 to 100.00
Coca-Cola Collectors Club Int'l, 12th Convention, Atlanta, Ga., 1986 .... 50.00
Coca-Cola Collectors Club Int'l, 13th Convention, Cincinnati, Pete Rose, 1987 .....35.00 to 68.00
Coca-Cola Collectors Club Int'l, 16th Convention, Louisville, Ky., 1990 .... 55.00
Coca-Cola Collectors Club Int'l, 17th Convention, Scottsdale, Az., Silver, 1992 .... 60.00
Coca-Cola Collectors Club Int'l, 18th Convention, Orlando, Fl., Silver, 1992 .... 65.00
Cola Clan 1979 Convention, Houston, TX, We Cordially Invite You, Short 25.00
Cola Clan 1981 National Convention, Kansas City, Short 40.00
Cola Clan 1982 National Convention, Nashville, Tennessee 20.00
Cola Clan Mid-South Annual Septemberfest, Elizabethtown, Ky., 1979 ....30.00 to 35.00
Cola Clan Of Atlanta, Second Annual Collectors Weekend 1978, Short 30.00
Columbia, 100th Anniversary, 100 Anos Coca-Cola, ACL, 1986, 195 Milliliter 125.00
Days Inn Celebrating 25 Years, 1995, 8 Oz. 62.00
Daytona Beach, Florida, 75th Anniversary, Amber, 1997 .... 10.00
Deer Lodge, Hiawassee, Ga., 1993, 8 Oz. 50.00
Diamond Throw-Aways, Blue, Savannah, Ga. 40.00
Diamond Throw-Aways, Root, Lexington, Ky. ....55.00 to 60.00
Diamond Throw-Aways, Root, Memphis, Tenn. 50.00
Diamond Throw-Aways, Root, Pittsburg, Pa. 35.00
Display Bottle, Plastic Cap, Green Glass, 1970s 38.00
Dollywood, 1994 ....5.00 to 10.00
Durham, N.C., Script, Green, Straight Sides, Stain 35.00
For Families Of Coca-Cola Bottling Co., Mid-America Inc., Nov. 14, 1976, Short 35.00
Fred Meyer Days, Supermarket, 75 Years, 1981 .... 20.00
Gainesville College, 25th Anniversary, 1988 .... 33.00
Georgia Bulldogs, 1980 National Football Champions 4.00
Get Together '84, Atlanta, June 18, Coca-Cola Enterprise, 1984, 16.9 Oz. 45.00
Grand Opening Coca-Cola Bottling Co, Mich.-Ohio Corp. Offices, 1979, 32 Oz. ...40.00 to 100.00
Great Get Together, Coca-Cola Collectors Club, February 11-13, 1994, 8 Oz. 60.00
Great Get Together, Houston Coca-Cola Bottling Company, 1920, Short 35.00
Hamilton, Ont., H, Aqua, Script, ABM, Crown Top, c.1900 .... 65.00
Hawaii, Outline Of Hawaiian Islands, Destination Series 6.00
Holly Hill, S.C. 1887-1987, Proud Past, Progressive Future, 10 Oz. ....200.00 to 300.00
Inauguracion Planta Mexicali, 1993 .... 10.00
Indiana Sesquicentennial, 1836-1986 .... 300.00

Coca-Cola, Cincinnati,
Ohio, Registered Coca-
Cola, Amber, Arrow,
Straight Sides, 7 1/2 In.

Coca-Cola, Kentucky
Derby, May 4, 1996,
ACL, 8 Oz.

Coca-Cola, Super
Bowl XXVIII,
Georgia Dome,
Atlanta, ACL,
1994, 8 Oz.

Industria Italiana Della Coca-Cola, 50th Anniversary, 1927-1977, 10 Oz. . . . . .50.00 to 55.00
Jefferson City, Green, Embossed Base, Crown Top, 1945, 7 3/4 In. 4.00
Jim Thomas & Family, Coca-Cola Bottling Works, Cincinnati, Oh., 1977, 6 1/2 Oz. 150.00
Jimmy Carter, 39th President Of The United States, 1985, 10 Oz. 200.00
Jug, Stoneware, Paper Label, Cork, c.1910 . . . . 4730.00
Kentucky Derby, 110th Run For The Roses, 1984, 10 Oz. 5.00
Kentucky Derby, May 4, 1996, ACL, 8 Oz. . . . .*Illus* 6.00
Kiwanis Club Of Jonesboro, Ga., Home Of Gone With The Wind, 1993, 8 Oz. 50.00
Knott's Berry Farm, Gold, 1994 . . . . 200.00
Kroger, 100th Anniversary, 1883-1983 . . . . 10.00
La Celebracion Del Milenio Carnaval Mazatlan 2000 . . . . 25.00
Light Green, ABM, 9 1/2 In. 1.00
Lime, Light Green, ABM, Crown Top, 8 In. 8.00
Long John Silver's, Always Working Together, 1995, 8 Oz. 75.00
Louisville, Kentucky, 75th Anniversary, 1976, 10 Oz. 5.00
Macon, Mo., Green, Hobbleskirt, Crown Top, ABM, 7 3/4 In. 4.50
Manteca, California 4th Annual July 4 Celebration, 1988 . . . . 35.00
McDonald's, Ronald McDonald House, Charities, Oct. 12, 1996 . . . . 100.00
McDonald's 6th Ronald McDonald House Show, Nov. 13th & 14th, 1993, 8 Oz. 65.00
Mexico Coca-Cola 50th Anniversary, 1926-1976, 296 Milliliter 60.00
Milford, Sesquicentennial, 1836-1986, Indiana, 10 Oz. 300.00
Mr. & Mrs. Chuck McCurdy, Coca-Cola Bottling Co. Of Louisville, 1977, 6 1/2 Oz. 125.00
Mundial, World Cup Soccer, Spain, 1982, 33 Centiliter 50.00
Muskingum County Fair, 152nd, August 16-22, 1988, 8 Oz. 2.00
Nashville, 75th Anniversary, 1975, 10 Oz. 5.00
New Liskeared, Flint, Script, ABM, Crown Top, Canada, 1900 . . . . 100.00
Norfolk, Va., Script, Light Green, Straight Sides 35.00
Old Dominion Chapter TCCCC Fall Fest, 1996, Gold, 8 Oz. 30.00
Orangeburg, S.C., Aqua, BIMAL . . . . .50.00 to 60.00
Parkview Panthers, AAAA State Champs, 1997 . . . . 20.00
Patricia Q. Fitzgerald From Friends At Dorsey Corporation, 1978, 6 1/2 Oz. 15000.00
Pittsburgh, Pa., Amber, BIMAL . . . . .55.00 to 69.00
Portland, Me., Light Green, Hobbleskirt, ABM, Crown Top, 1953, 7 3/4 In. 2.00
Portland Trail Blazers, 25th Anniversary, 6 Bottles, 1995 . . . . 24.00
Presented To Dr. Ahmed Esmat Abdel Meguid, From Dorsey Corp., 1979, 6 1/2 Oz. 125.00
Presented To Harry A. Tulley Int'l Prs., GBBA, Chattanooga Glass, 1974, 6 1/2 Oz. 125.00
Presented To Hubert H. Trip Rand, North Carolina Soft Drink Assn., 1977, 6 1/2 Oz. . . . 150.00
Property Of Coca-Cola Co., Canada, Light Olive Green 6.00
Property Of Coca-Cola Co., Canada, Medium Teal Blue, 7 5/8 In. 12.00
Publix, Atlanta Division Stores, April 30, 1998 . . . . 12.00
Royal Wedding, July 29, 1981, HRH Prince Of Wales, Diana Spencer, ACL, 250 Milliliter 60.00
Salute Glamour Women Of The Year, At Their Best, Nov. 11, 1997, Diet Coke, 10 Oz. . . 50.00
Santa Claus, Christmas, 1994 . . . . 7.00
Santa Claus, Christmas, 1997 . . . . 7.00
Santa Claus, Evolution Of Santa, 6 Piece 35.00
Schmidt's Marvelous Museum, Cola Clan 2nd Annual Convention, 1976, 10 Oz. 30.00
Seltzer, Acid Etching, Superior, Wisconsin, Original Top 1045.00
Sign, Sold Here, Coca-Cola, Ice Cold, 29 7/8 x 7 11/16 In. 950.00
Since Dec. 18,1950 Marion Cook, Coca-Cola Bottling Works, Dallas, Tex., 1980 . . . . 150.00
Smokeyfest, Nascar Set, 1998 . . . . 4.00
Soft Drink Of Europe, Foil Label, 1992, 0.2 Liter 75.00
Somersworth, N.H., Christmas, 1923 . . . . 80.00
South Bend, In., Coca-Cola Bottling Co. 80th Anniversary 400.00
Southwest Airlines, 20 Years Of Loving You, 1981, 8 Oz. 75.00
Springtime In Atlanta, Unforgettable Forties, 1984, 10 Oz. 45.00
Springtime In Tennessee, Gatlinburg, March 27-29, 1986 . . . . 24.00
St. Joseph, Mo., Light Green, Crown Top, ABM, 1947 . . . . 4.00
St. Louis, Mo., Green, Crown Top, ABM, 1953 . . . . 2.00
Super Bowl XXVIII, Georgia Dome, Atlanta, ACL, 1994, 8 Oz. . . . .*Illus* 4.00
Super Bowl XXVIII, Georgia Dome, Atlanta, Jan. 1994, Gold, 8 Oz. 30.00
Swainsboro, c.1910 . . . . 45.00
Syrup, Drink Coca-Cola, White ACL, Tooled Mouth, Tin Cap, c.1915, 11 1/2 In. 530.00
Tampa, 80 Years Of Bottling, New Plant Grand Opening, 1983, 10 Oz. 40.00

Tarpon Springs, 75th Anniversary, 1913-1988, 10 Oz. 13.00
Texaco Grand Prix, Houston Inaugural Race, 1998, 8 Oz. 2.00
Texas Tech University 75th Anniversary, 1923-1998 .... 2.00
Toronto, This Bottle Is Not Sold & Must Be Returned, BIMAL, c.1900 .... 95.00
Treaty Of Greene Ville, Fort Greene Ville, Ohio, 1992, 8 Oz. 40.00
Tullahoma, Destination Series, Miniature 5.00
Ty Cobb, The Georgia Peach, 1994, 8 Oz. 125.00
Welcome John & Irene Cushion From Charlotte & Tom Hooker, 1978, 6 1/2 Oz. 150.00
Wendy's Old Fashioned Hamburgers, 25 Years, Dallas, Texas, October 1994 .... 40.00
Westminster, Md., Cylindrical, ABM, 11 1/2 In. 60.00
White Castle, Celebrating 75 Years, 1996, 8 Oz. 62.00
Wilkes-Barre, Blue Aqua, Crown Top, Stars On Shoulder, 6 Oz. 25.00
World Cup Soccer, 8 Oz., 9-City Set ....25.00 to 50.00
World Cup USA, 1994, Washington D.C., Gold, 8 Oz. 25.00
World Cup USA, Soccer, 1994, Gold, 12 Oz. 25.00
World Of Coca-Cola, Atlanta, Grand Opening, August 3, 1990 .... 80.00

────────────────── **COLLECTORS ART** ──────────────────

Collectors Art bottles are made of hand-painted porcelain. The bird series was made in the 1970s. The first issued was the bluebird, then the meadowlark, canary, hummingbird, parakeet, and cardinal. Only 12 birds were issued each year and each was limited to 1,200 pieces. The later editions included bulls (1975), dogs, other animals, and a 1971 Corvette Stingray.

Afghan Hound, 1975, Miniature ....15.00 to 20.00
Angus Bull, 1975, Miniature ....20.00 to 25.00
Basset Hound, 1977, Miniature 20.00
Blue Bird, 1971, Miniature 24.00
Blue Jay, 1972, Miniature 25.00
Brahma Bull, 1975, Miniature 32.00
Bunting, 1973, Miniature 18.00
Canary, 1971, Miniature 22.00
Cardinal, 1971, Miniature 20.00
Charolais Bull, 1975, Miniature 26.00
Chipmunks, 1972, Miniature ....18.00 to 25.00
Collie, 1976, Miniature 22.00
Corvette, Goodyear Tires, 1971 .... 30.00
Corvette Stingray, Blue, 1971 .... 60.00
Corvette Stingray, Red, 1971 .... 30.00
Dachshund, 1977, Miniature 21.00
Dalmatian, 1976, Miniature 25.00
Doberman, Black, 1976, Miniature 24.00
Doberman, Red, 1976, Miniature 22.00
German Shepherd, Black, 1976, Miniature ....25.00 to 30.00
German Shepherd, Brown, 1976, Miniature 18.00
Goldfinch, 1972, Miniature 22.00
Hereford, 1972 .... 36.00
Hummingbird, 1971, Miniature 24.00
Irish Setter, 1976, Miniature 18.00
Koala, 1972, Miniature 30.00
Longhorn Bull 27.00
Meadowlark, 1971, Miniature 20.00
Mexican Fighting Bull, 1975, Miniature 30.00
Oriole, 1972, Miniature 24.00
Parakeet, 1971, Miniature ....20.00 to 25.00
Pointer, Brown, White, 1976, Miniature 15.00
Poodle, Black, 1976, Miniature ....15.00 to 20.00
Poodle, Brown, 1976, Miniature ....15.00 to 20.00
Rabbits, 1972, Miniature 34.00
Raccoons, 1973, Miniature 24.00
Robin, 1972, Miniature 18.00
Schnauzer, 1976, Miniature 20.00
Skunks, 1972, Miniature 27.00
St. Bernard, 1977, Miniature ....20.00 to 28.00

Texas Longhorn, 1974 .... 33.00
Texas Longhorn, 1975, Miniature 23.00

COLOGNE

Our ancestors did not bathe very often and probably did not smell very good. It is no wonder that the perfume and cologne business thrived in earlier centuries. Perfume is a liquid mixture with alcohol. Cologne is a similar mixture but with more alcohol, so the odor is not as strong or as lasting. Scent was also popular. It was a perfume with some ammonia in the mixture so it could be used to revive someone who felt faint. The mixture dictated the type and size of bottle. Scent bottles usually had screw tops to keep the ammonia smell from escaping. Because its odor did not last as long as that of perfume, cologne was used more often and was sold in larger bottles. Cologne became popular in the United States about 1830; the Boston and Sandwich Glass Company of Sandwich, Massachusetts, was making cologne bottles at that time. Since cologne bottles were usually put on display, they were made with fancy shapes, brightly colored glass, or elaborate labels. Blown figural and scroll bottles were favored. The best-known cologne bottle is the 1880 Charlie Ross bottle. It has the embossed face of Charlie, a famous kidnap victim—a strange shape to choose for a cologne bottle! Today the name *perfume* is sometimes used incorrectly as a generic term meaning both cologne and perfume. Old and new bottles for cologne, perfume, and scents are collected. Related bottles may be found in the Perfume and Scent categories.

3-Sided, Ann Haviland, Lily Of The Valley Toilet Water, 1940s 22.00
4-Sided, Indian, Clear, Open Pontil, 1840-1850 .... 110.00
6-Sided, Metal Collar & Top, Pontil, German, Late 18th Century, 4 1/2 In. 22.00
8-Sided, Apple Green, Gilt Design, Stopper, Pontil, 1850-1870, 8 In. 275.00
8-Sided, Emerald Green, Gilt Design, Stopper, Pontil, 1850-1870, 6 5/8 In. 242.00
8-Sided, Ice Blue, Applied Ring Top, 7 1/2 In. 165.00
8-Sided, Madame Rochas, White Plastic Screw Cap, 2 5/8 In. 14.00
8-Sided, Peacock Blue, Corset Waist, 4 3/4 In. ....*Illus* 745.00
8-Sided, Purple Amethyst, Corset Waist, 1850-1870, 4 1/2 In. 413.00
8-Sided, Spring Delights, Milk Glass, 1865-1885, 7 1/4 In. 60.00
12-Sided, Amethyst, Boston & Sandwich Glass Works, 4 3/4 In. 110.00
12-Sided, Amethyst, Boston & Sandwich Glass Works, 5 1/2 In. 66.00
12-Sided, Amethyst, Boston & Sandwich Glass Works, 4 7/8 In. 176.00
12-Sided, Amethyst, Flowers, Bird & Cherub Label, Superior, 1860-1888, 8 3/4 In. 770.00
12-Sided, Amethyst, Sloped Shoulders, Pontil, 1880, 4 In. 260.00
12-Sided, Amethyst, Tooled Lip, Boston & Sandwich Glass Works, 7 3/8 In. 77.00
12-Sided, Blue Green, Sloped Shoulders, Rolled Lip, 6 1/8 In. 168.00
12-Sided, Blue, Boston & Sandwich Glass Works, 4 1/2 In. 253.00
12-Sided, Cobalt Blue, Rolled Lip, 6 1/2 In. 120.00
12-Sided, Peacock Blue, Sloped Shoulders, Rolled Lip, 4 7/8 In. 200.00
12-Sided, Pink Amethyst, Rolled Lip, 6 1/4 In. 100.00
12-Sided, Pink Amethyst, Sloped Shoulders, 6 1/8 In. 155.00
12-Sided, Powder Blue Opalescent, Tooled Lip, 8 1/2 In. 467.00
12-Sided, Purple Amethyst, Pontil, Rolled Lip, 1855-1875, 4 3/4 In. 176.00

Cologne, 8-Sided,
Peacock Blue, Corset
Waist, 4 3/4 In.

Cologne, 12-Sided,
Purple Amethyst,
Rolled Lip, 1860-
1870, 5 5/8 In.

Cologne, Barrel,
Anchors, Ship,
Aqua, 4 3/8 In.

12-Sided, Purple Amethyst, Rolled Lip, 1860-1870, 5 5/8 In. . . . .*Illus* 179.00
12-Sided, Purple Amethyst, Rolled Lip, 1860-1870, 7 3/8 In. 200.00
12-Sided, Sapphire Blue, Boston & Sandwich Glass Works, 4 5/8 In. 231.00
12-Sided, Sapphire Blue, Boston & Sandwich Glass Works, 6 1/2 In. 198.00
12-Sided, Sapphire Blue, Tooled Mouth, Boston & Sandwich Glass Works, 4 7/8 In. 230.00
12-Sided, Teal Blue, Rolled Lip, 1865-1875, 9 In. 154.00
12-Sided, Teal Green, Tooled Lip, 6 3/8 In. 110.00
12-Sided, Teal Green, Tooled Lip, Boston & Sandwich Glass Works, 4 3/4 In. 187.00
16 Ribs, Amethyst, Swirled Left, Bulbous, Tooled Lip, Pontil, 5 1/2 In. 2576.00
20 Vertical Ribs, Sapphire Blue, Tapered, Long Neck, Tooled Rolled Lip, Pontil, 6 In. . . . 504.00
36 Ribs, Cobalt Blue, Toilet Water, Pontil, 1815-1830, 5 5/8 In. 330.00
Amethyst, Diamond Daisy Design, Ground Lip, 2 3/4 In. 55.00
Artichoke Form, Robin's-Egg Blue, Tooled Flared Lip, Pontil, Sandwich, 4 3/8 In. 308.00
Barrel, Anchors, Ship, Aqua, 4 3/8 In. . . . .*Illus* 300.00
Basket Design, Green, Gold Trim, Flared Lip, OP, Stopper, 5 1/2 In. 143.00
Basketweave, Rolled Lip, OP, 3 In. 66.00
Benjamin's Jamaica, Khus Khus, Bell Hop Sculpture, Painted, 1940s 45.00
Bohemian, Clear, Allover Meandering Gold Trailings, Ball Stopper, 7 1/2 In. 88.00
Breathless For Women, Box 10.00
Bride's, Enameled Colors, Stiegel Type, 6 1/2 In. 375.00
Bride's, Stiegel Style, Enameled, Mustard, Green, Blue, Red, 6 1/2 In. 375.00
Cake Walk, Blue, Yellow, Fuchsia, Purple, Green, Black Man Dancing, Stopper, 12 In. . . . 280.00
Capitol Building, Aux Grand Gommes La Patrie Rec, Naissante, France, 3 5/8 In. 440.00
Chantilly, Enameled, Pigory, 1803, 5 1/8 x 2 1/2 In. 375.00
Ciro, Le Chevalier De La Nuit Eau De Toilette, Knight, Head Stopper, 7 3/8 In. 495.00
Classic Churon, Gold For Women 5.00
Cobalt Blue, 3-Piece Mold, Rolled Lip, Pontil, Toilet Water, 1835, 5 5/8 In. 176.00
Cobalt Blue, Flared Lip, OP, Tam-O-Shanter Stopper, Toilet Water, 7 In. 209.00
Cobalt Blue, Knight Standing In Gothic Pillars, Rectangular, 1830-1860, 4 In. 935.00
Coin Dot, Blue, Stopper, Fenton, 4 1/2 In. 170.00
Cone, Amethyst, Inward Rolled Lip, Pontil, Sandwich, 6 7/8 In. 2128.00
Corset Shape, Plum Over Fern Design, Open Pontil, 1840-1870, 5 1/2 In. 440.00
Corset Shape, Sapphire Blue, Palmette, Lattice, OP, 5 1/2 In. 1300.00
Corset Shape, Sapphire Blue, Scrolled Acanthus, 1845-1855, 5 5/8 In. 1705.00
Corset Shape, Sapphire Blue, Scrolled Acanthus, Rolled Lip, Pontil, 5 5/8 In. 1092.00
Cote D'Azur For Women, Box 10.00
Cranberry, Clear Pedestal & Stopper, Etched Flower, 8 In. 160.00
Cranberry, Clear Pedestal Base, Etched Flower, Clear Stopper, Victorian, 8 In. 160.00
Cranberry, Daisy Flowers, Gold Leaves & Trim, 7 1/4 In. 175.00
Cranberry, Faceted, Crown Shape Stopper, c.1880, 10 In. 105.00
Cranberry, Flower Pattern, Fluted Top, Clear Stopper, Victorian, 7 1/2 In. 185.00
Cut Glass, Cobalt Blue, Cut To Clear, Corseted, Long Neck, 6 Petals, Flared Lip, 6 3/4 In. 336.00
Cut Glass, Emerald Green, Enamel, Roses, Gilding, Faceted Stopper, 5 1/8 In., Pair 500.00
Cut Glass, Milk Glass To Robin's-Egg Blue, Flared Lip, Stopper, Sandwich, 7 3/4 In. 146.00
Darnay, My Folly Eau De Toilette, Clear, Black Frosted Floral Panels, Stopper, 4 In. 154.00
Dorothy Gray, Floral Fantasy, Ribs, Turquoise Plastic Cap, 1940s 22.00
Embossed Ship, Flared Lip, Pontil, 4 7/8 In. 275.00
Everafter For Women, Box 10.00
Flowerlace, Gold For Woman 9.00
Girl, Label Under Glass, Bark Encased, 7 3/4 In. 413.00
Guerlain, Eau De Cologne Imperial, Glass Stopper, Signed, 2 In. 357.50
H.E. Swan & Co., Rolled Lip, 1875-1885, 11 1/8 In. 83.00
Herringbone, Ice Blue, 1820, 6 1/4 In. 550.00
Hobnail, Milk Glass, Stopper, Impressed L Mark, 6 In. 14.00
Imperial, Sticker, Ground Stopper, 8 1/4 x 2 1/4 In. 30.00
Lander, Apple Blossom, Toilet Water, Red Metal Cap, 3 Oz., 4 1/2 In. 14.00
Lavender Blue, 3-Piece Mold, Tooled Lip, Hollow Stopper, Pontil, Sandwich, 6 1/8 In. . . 448.00
Leaf & Pineapple, Bulbous, Canary Yellow, Flared Lip, Stopper, 8 3/4 In. 336.00
Loop Pattern, 6 Petals At Base, Canary Yellow, Flared Lip, Stopper, 6 5/8 In. 235.00
Marquise Shape, Aqua, Indian 2 Sides, Panels, Flared Lip, Pontil, 4 3/4 In. 250.00
Memorial Hall, Philadelphia, Pa., 1876, Flowers, Geometric Designs, 6 1/8 In. 280.00
Milk Glass, Blue, Enamel Cottage, Pontil, 8 5/8 In. 465.00
Milk Glass, Eau De Cologne, 8-Sided, 4 1/4 In. 165.00

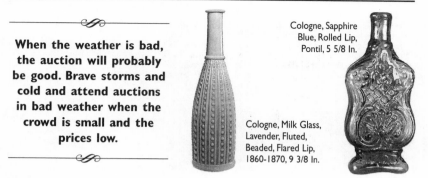

When the weather is bad, the auction will probably be good. Brave storms and cold and attend auctions in bad weather when the crowd is small and the prices low.

Cologne, Sapphire Blue, Rolled Lip, Pontil, 5 5/8 In.

Cologne, Milk Glass, Lavender, Fluted, Beaded, Flared Lip, 1860-1870, 9 3/8 In.

Milk Glass, Hobnail, Impressed L On Bottom, Stopper, 6 In.	14.00
Milk Glass, Lavender, Fluted, Beaded, Flared Lip, 1860-1870, 9 3/8 In. ....*Illus*	504.00
Milk Glass, Opalescent, Flower & Leaf Pattern, Over Painted, Stopper, 9 In.	285.00
Milk Glass, Opaque, Flared Rolled Lip, 1855-1875, 12 1/2 In.	523.00
Molyneux, Le Numero Cinq, Art Deco, Label, Stopper, 6 3/8 In.	440.00
Monument, 6-Sided, Flared Lip, Pontil, 5 In.	220.00
Monument, Q.T. Embossed On Side Base, Pontil, 5 1/8 In.	198.00
Monument, Rolled Lip, Stopper, Pontil, 5 1/8 In. ....132.00 to	413.00
Monument, Tooled Lip, Pontil, 1845-1860, 5 In.	275.00
Muhlens, No. 4711, Embossed, Paper Label, Red Cap, 4 3/4 In.	10.00
Murano, 3-Sided, Rainbow Swirl, Dome Stopper, 7 x 4 1/8 In.	35.00
Napoleon, 2 Panels, Embossed Hat, Sword, Eagle, Embossed N, 3 5/8 In.	231.00
Opaline, Apple Green, Allover Gilt Stars, Gilt Stopper, France, 5 x 3 In.	460.00
Overshot, Mold Blown, Screw Top, 7 1/4 In.	150.00
Paneled Body, Topaz, Scalloped Base, Flared Lip, Stopper, 5 3/4 In.	179.00
Petit Fleur, Flower Shape, Gold Cap, 1969-1970, 1 Oz.	6.00
Pinched Waist, Green, Gilt, Flared Lip, Stopper, Pontil, 6 In.	364.00
Pinched Waist, Yellow Green, Loop Design, Flared Lip, Glass Stopper, Pontil, 5 5/8 In. . .	146.00
Pocahontas Indian, Aqua	132.00
Porcelain, Couples Reserve, Jacob Petit Type, Knopped Stopper, 3 1/2 x 8 In., Pair	6325.00
Porcelain, Figural, Child, Tall Hat, Gold Crown Shape Screw Top, Stopper, 3 1/4 In.	82.00
Powder Blue, White Casing, Fry Glass Works	145.00
Ribs, Pinched Waist, Sapphire Blue, Plum Over Fern, Tooled Lip, Pontil, 5 5/8 In.	504.00
Ribs, Purple Cobalt Blue, Flared Lip, OP, Tam-O-Shanter Stopper, Toilet Water, 6 3/4 In. .	187.00
Ribs Swirled Right, Applied Top, Pontil, Mid 19th Century, 5 1/2 In.	44.00
Ricksecker's, Jug, Pottery, White, Multicolored Flowers, Letters, Handle, 4 1/4 In.	100.00
Ricksecker's, Sweet Clover, Milk Glass, Multicolored, Gold Letters, Handles, 8 1/2 In. . . .	157.00
Ricksecker's New York, Etched Fleur-De-Lis, Gold Bands, Label, 12 In.	112.00
Sapphire Blue, Knight, Between Pillars, Open Pontil, 4 In.	1100.00
Sapphire Blue, Rolled Lip, Pontil, 5 5/8 In. ....*Illus*	1595.00
Scalloped Facets, Molded Band Of Flowers, Stopper, 7 In.	33.00
Schiaparelli, Shocking You, Dress Dummy Shape, Metal Cap, Gold Overlay, 1 In.	77.00
Schiaparelli, Shocking, Glass Flowers, Pink, Gold Box, Glass Stopper, 3 In.	385.00
Schiaparelli, Shocking, Gold Cap, Pink Box, 4 In.	88.00
Schiaparelli, Shocking, Pink Plastic Stopper, 5 x 2 In.	77.00
Schiaparelli, Shocking, Pink Stone Lattice, Pink Box, 5 In.	220.00
Schiaparelli, Si, Red Cap, Musical Note Design, 4 In.	220.00
Spiral Optic, Opalescent, France, 6 x 4 In.	36.00
Square, Tapered, Herringbone Corners, Amethyst, Tooled Lip, Sandwich, 5 3/4 In.	364.00
Square, Tapered, Herringbone Corners, Sapphire Blue, Tooled Lip, Label, 5 1/2 In.	504.00
Square, Turquoise, Stopper, Fostoria, 6 x 2 1/4 In.	550.00
Star & Punty, Canary, Apple Green, Boston & Sandwich, 6 1/2 In.	440.00
Swan, DB Embossed Side Base, Rolled Lip, Pontil, 5 7/8 In.	198.00
Thumbprint, Herringbone Corners, 1860-1880	66.00
Toilet Water, Cobalt Blue, Ribs, White Enamel Windmill, Pontil, 8 In.	1232.00
Toilet Water, Milk Glass, Multicolored Flowers, Rolled Lip, 7 In.	440.00

Vaseline, Opalescent, Hobnail, Imperial Glass, Gold Green, c.1930, 6 1/2 In. 55.00
Vertical Ribs, Flared Lip, OP, Stopper, 6 1/4 In. 88.00
Vertical Ribs, Green, Stopper, Toilet Water, Sandwich, 4 1/2 In. 275.00
Vertical Ribs, Purple Cobalt Blue, Tam-O-Shanter Stopper, OP, Toilet Water, 6 3/4 In. ... 242.00
Vertical Ribs, Yellow Tint, OP, Tam-O-Shanter Stopper, 5 1/4 In. 165.00
W.N. Walton, Pat. Sept. 23, 1862, Yellow, Amber Tint, Cylindrical, 8 1/4 In. 60.00
Wrisley, Hobnail, French Opalescent, Fenton, Chicago, c.1938 .... 40.00

━━━━━━━━━━━━━━━━━━━━━━━━ **CORDIAL** ━━━━━━━━━━━━━━━━━━━━━━━━

Cordials are liqueurs that are usually drunk at the end of the meal. They consist of pure alcohol or cognac, plus flavors from fruits, herbs, flowers, or roots. A cordial may also be a medicinal drink. Curacao is a cordial containing orange peel, Creme de Menthe contains mint, Triple Sec has orange and cognac, and Kummel has coriander and caraway seeds.

American Family Bitter Cordial, Pittsburgh, Pa., Paul Conday, Amber, 1870, 9 In. 605.00
Balm Of Gilead, Liverpool, Light To Medium Olive, Pontil, 7 In. 3024.00
Balm Of Gilead, Liverpool, Medium Olive Green, 1835-1850, 7 In. 2700.00
Balm Of Gilead, Liverpool, Olive Green, 1835-1850, 7 1/4 In. 3600.00
Balm Of Gilead, Liverpool, Olive, Beveled Corners, England, 7 1/4 In. 4032.00
Booth & Sedgwick's, London, Blue Green, Applied Collar, Ring, Square, IP, 9 3/4 In. ... 330.00
Booth & Sedgwick's, London, Cordial Gin, Emerald Green, 1845, 9 1/2 In. 395.00
Booth & Sedgwick's, London, Emerald Green, IP, 1855, 9 7/8 In. 495.00
Booth & Sedgwick's, London, Medium Green, Case, Applied Top, IP, 7 3/4 In. 264.00
Charles London, Sea Green, Square, Wrapped Lip, 3 Embossed Sides 9.00
Chas. Backman's Holland Genever, Olive Yellow, Square, 1870, 9 7/8 In. 248.00
Dr. Raspail's Specific, Blue, Applied Band Top, 9 In. 175.00
Dr. Solomon, Cordial Balm, Gilead House, Near Liverpool, Pontil, 4 1/4 In. 336.00
Jacob's Cholera & Dysentery, Aqua, Open Pontil, 6 3/4 In. 242.00
Lucina, Elixir Of Love, Blue Aqua, Pontil, Applied Sloping Collar Mouth, 1855, 6 In. ... 672.00
Lucina, Elixir Of Love, Flared Lip, OP, 6 In. 650.00
Peychaud's American Aromatic Cocktail, L.E. Jung, New Orleans, 11 In. 139.00
Quaker Caster, St. Paul, Minn., Sealed, Image Of Quaker At Top, 7 x 2 1/4 In. 83.00
Swayne's Bowel Cordial, Philada, Blue Aqua, Square Collar, Pontil, 5 1/4 In. 504.00
Wishart's Pine Tree Tar, Blue Green, Pine Tree, 10 1/2 In. 224.00
Wishart's Pine Tree Tar, Emerald Green, Sloping Collar, 7 1/2 In. 260.00
Wishart's Pine Tree Tar, Light Blue Green, 7 7/8 In. 132.00
Wishart's Pine Tree Tar, Phila., Amber, Tooled Mouth, 1880-1890, 9 7/8 In. 176.00
Wishart's Pine Tree Tar, Phila., Blue, Green, 1860-1870, 7 7/8 In. 257.00
Wishart's Pine Tree Tar, Phila., Embossed Tree, Emerald Green, 7 1/2 In. 258.00
Wishart's Pine Tree Tar, Phila., Embossed Tree, Olive Yellow, 7 7/8 In. 143.00
Wishart's Pine Tree Tar, Phila., Embossed Tree, Teal Blue, 7 1/2 In. 204.00
Wishart's Pine Tree Tar, Phila., Orange Amber, Label, Square, 9 3/4 In. 120.00
Wishart's Pine Tree Tar, Phila., Patent 1859, Blue Green, 8 In. ....88.00 to 143.00
Wishart's Pine Tree Tar, Phila., Patent 1859, Emerald Green, 7 In. 268.00
Wishart's Pine Tree Tar, Phila., Patent 1859, Emerald Green, 1870, 8 In. ....156.00 to 198.00
Wishart's Pine Tree Tar, Phila., Patent 1859, Green, Bubbles, 9 In. 360.00
Wishart's Pine Tree Tar, Phila., Patent 1859, Teal Green, 9 5/8 In. 895.00
Wishart's Pine Tree Tar, Phila., Yellow Tobacco Amber, 1875-1895, 10 In. 743.00

━━━━━━━━━━━━━━━━━━━━━━━━ **COSMETIC** ━━━━━━━━━━━━━━━━━━━━━━━━

Cosmetics of all kinds have been packaged in bottles. Hair restorer, hair dye, creams, rosewater, and many other product bottles can be found. Paper labels on early bottles add to their value.

Ayer's Hair Vigor, Cobalt Blue, ABM, Stopper, 6 3/8 In. ....*Illus* 100.00
Ayer's Hair Vigor, J.G.A. Co., Sapphire Blue, Tooled Mouth, 1890-1910, 6 3/8 In. 105.00
Ayer's Hair Vigor, Peacock Blue, Tooled Lip, Stopper, 1880-1890, 7 1/4 In. 175.00
Bear Oil, Embossed Standing Bear, Flared, Rolled Lip, Label, Pontil, 2 7/8 In. 616.00
Bogle's Hyperion Fluid For The Hair, Aqua 17.00
Buckingham Whisker Dye, Yellow, 5 In. 55.00
C.S. Emerson, Indian Hair Tonic, Cleveland, Ohio, 25 Cents, 1865, 5 In. 225.00
C.S. Emerson's American Hair Restorative, Clear 193.00
Cook's Hair Invigorator, Aqua 50.00
Cremex, Vase, Shampoo, Notched Handles, Tooled Lip, 7 1/2 In. ....*Illus* 165.00

Cosmetic, Ayer's Hair Vigor, Cobalt Blue, ABM, Stopper, 6 3/8 In.

Cosmetic, Cremex, Vase, Shampoo, Notched Handles, Tooled Lip, 7 1/2 In.

Cosmetic, Lavender Bath Salts, Yardley's Old English, Label, Contents, 7 In.

Cosmetic, Mary T. Goldman Co., Gray Hair Color Restorer, Box, 7 1/2 In.

Dermetics Complexion Cleanser, Pink Plastic Cap, Paper Labels, 1 Oz., 4 In. 8.00
Dr. E.L. Graves Tooth Powder, Best Made, Chicago, Il., Embossed, 3 1/2 In. 143.00
Dr. Kelemen's Grecian Hair Balsam, N.Y., Light Blue Aqua, OP, 1860, 7 In. 1100.00
Dr. Tebbetts' Physiological Hair Regenerator, Plum Amethyst, Rectangular, 7 1/4 In. . . .   264.00
Dr. Tebbetts' Physiological Hair Regenerator, Puce . . . . .99.00 to 165.00
DuBarry Day Cream, Green Satin, Molded Petal Stopper, Foil Label, 3 1/2 In. 209.00
Empire Hair Tonic, Quinine, Screw Cap, Marked, Minn., Gal., 12 x 6 1/2 In. 25.00
Face Lotion, Green Aqua, Enameled Woman With Laundry, Dutch, 5 1/2 In. 55.00
Fish's Infallible Hair Restorative, Dark Cobalt Blue, 1863, 7 1/4 In. 3080.00
Fitch's Dandruff Remover, F.W. Fitch Mfg. Co., 2 5/8 Oz., 5 In.   8.00
Fitch's Ideal Hair Tonic, Des Moines, Iowa, 2 Labels, 3 1/2 In. 15.00
Fountain Of Youth Hair Restorer, Blue, Applied Top, 7 1/2 In. . . . . .880.00 to 1430.00
Fountain Of Youth Hair Restorer, Cobalt Blue, 7 1/2 In. 1045.00
Hair Dye, Mayor Walnut Oil Co., Kansas City, Mo., Amber, ABM, Cork, 3 3/4 In. 8.00
Hair Removal Of Superfluous Hair, Embossed, 3 1/8 x 1 1/4 In.   61.00
Hall's Hair Renewer, Peacock Blue, 6 3/4 In. 90.00
Haywood's, Balm Of Savannah, Exterminator Of Dandruff, Aqua, 1860, 7 1/4 In. 154.00
Hill's Hair Dye No. I, OP, 3 1/8 In. 10.00
Kathairon For The Hair, New York, Lyons, USA, Aqua, Rectangular, c.1860, 6 In. 21.00
Kickapoo Sage Hair Tonic, Cobalt Blue 165.00
Lady Luxury, Label, Lady In Pink Hoop Skirt, Swan, Screw-On Cap, 4 3/4 x 2 1/4 In. . . .   5.00
Lavender Bath Salts, Yardley's Old English, Label, Contents, 7 In. . . . .*Illus*   7.50
Lavender Salt, Ribbed Top, Ground Stopper, 6 3/4 In. 115.00
Luby's For The Hair, Amber, Crooked Neck, 7 1/2 In. 33.00
Lyman, Montreal, Arctusine For Promoting Growth Of The Hair, BIMAL, Label, 4 In. . . .   50.00
Lyon's Kathairon For The Hair, Aqua 55.00
Mary T. Goldman Co., Gray Hair Color Restorer, Box, 7 1/2 In. . . . .*Illus*   10.00
McCracken & Urich's Hair Restorative, Mechanicsburg, Pa., Blue Aqua, OP, 6 3/4 In. . . .   532.00
Mrs. Allen's World's Hair Color Restorer, Amber . . . . .50.00 to 80.00
Mrs. H.E. Wilson's Hair Dressing, Manchester, N.H., Blue Aqua, OP, 1855, 6 In. 231.00
Mrs. S.A. Allen's World's Hair Restorer, Amber, 7 1/8 In. 187.00
Mrs. S.A. Allen's World's Hair Restorer, Amber, BIMAL, Label, Box, 7 1/4 In. 35.00
Mrs. S.A. Allen's World's Hair Restorer, N.Y., Deep To Light Purple Amethyst, 7 In. 812.00
Mrs. S.A. Allen's World's Hair Restorer, N.Y., Yellow Amber 30.00
Murray & Lanman New York, Florida Water, Body & Neck Labels, ABM, 9 In. 40.00
Oldridge's Balm Of Columbia For Restoring Hair, Philadelphia, Aqua, OP, 5 In. 220.00
Orris Tooth Powder, Ball Knob, 12 In. 58.00
Owl Drug Co., Florida Water, Aqua, 8 1/2 In. 125.00
P. & R. King Hair Restorer, S. Parent & Co., Millville, N.J., Yellow Green, 7 5/8 In. 660.00
Parisian Sage Hair Tonic, Giroux Mfg. Co., Buffalo, Aqua 4.50
Prof. Mott's Magic Hair Invigorator, Aqua 165.00
Professor Wood's Hair Restorative, St. Louis, New York, Blue Aqua, Pontil, 7 In. .90.00 to 100.00

Professor Wood's Hair Restorative, St. Louis, New York, Aqua, 7 In. 125.00
Pulv. Dentifric Zahnpulver, Amber, Eisenglas White Label, Stopper, 7 In. 22.00
Rathgeber's Bijou Empyreal For The Hair, New Haven, Ct., Milk Glass, 6 5/8 In. 868.00
Royal Hair Restorer, Cobalt Blue 50.00
Sharp Brothers Anglo American, Hair Restorer, Amber 18.00
St. Clair's Hair Lotion, Blue, Applied Top, Side Panel Archways, Bubbles, 8 In. 220.00
St. Clair's Hair Lotion, Blue, Tooled Top, 7 In. 44.00
Swayne's London Hair Color Restorer, Philada., Aqua, 7 1/2 In. 45.00
Unrivaled Hair Tonic, L.S. Bliss Hatfield Mass., Aqua, Pontil, 7 In. 350.00
Voltchock's Russian Hair Restorer, Amber, Rectangular, BIMAL, Australia, c.1890 ..... 70.00
W.C. Montgomery's Hair Restorer, Philada, Dark Purple Amethyst, 7 5/8 In. 275.00
Watkins Shampoo Jelly, Medical Complaint, Winona, Minn., 3 x 2 In. 35.00
West's Vegetable Fluid For The Hair, Aqua, OP, 5 7/8 In. 157.00
White's Hair Restorative, Aqua 94.00
Zenobia, Gardenia Talc, Flowering Plant Shape, Plastic Base, Enameled, Box, 2 3/4 In. .. 385.00

─────────────────────────── **CURE** ───────────────────────────

Collectors have their own interests and a large group of bottle collectors seek medicine
bottles with the word *cure* embossed on the glass or printed on the label. A cure bottle
is not a *remedy bottle*. The word cure was originally used for a medicine that treated
many diseases. A *specific* was made for only one disease. The Pure Food and Drug Act
of 1906 made label changes mandatory and the use of the word *cure* was no longer
permitted. Related bottles may be found in the Medicine and Bitters categories.

Alicsalutice Regd For All Rheumatic Pains, Aqua, 1900, 4 3/4 In. 8.50
Arnot's Arnica Anodyne, Pain Reliever, G.S. Hobart, Kingston, Canada, Label, 5 In. 30.00
Baker's Vegetable Blood & Liver, Lookout Mountain Co., Amber, 9 3/4 In. 308.00
Bishop's Granular Citrate Of Caffeine, Headaches Cured 15.00
Bromo Bracer Cures Headache, Stopper, 8 3/4 In. 1090.00
Cactus Blood, By Alva's Brazilian Specific Co., Cactus Shape, 9 1/4 In. 2860.00
Craig's Kidney & Liver Cure Company, Amber, Double Collar, 1890, 9 3/4 In. 137.00
Craig's Kidney & Liver Cure Company, Medium To Light Amber, 1880-1890, 9 3/4 In. .. 132.00
De Witt's Colic & Cholera Cure, Chicago, Blue, Tooled Top 11.00
Dr. Craig's Kidney Cure, Amber, Applied Double Collar Mouth, 1890, 9 3/4 In. 560.00
Dr. Devincent Magic Cough, San Francisco, Applied Top, 7 In. 330.00
Dr. L.E. Keeley's Double Chloride Of Gold Cure, Drunkenness, Dwight, Ill. 65.00
Dr. Miles' Pain Pill, Dr. Miles' Anti Pain Pills Cure Headache, 16 1/2 In. 748.00
Dr. Pierce's Pleasant Pellets, Rectangular, 6 1/2 In. 400.00
Dr. Simmon's Aspirin, Lid, Beveled Corners, 12 In. 518.00
Ex. Pleurisy, Stopper, 8 1/2 In. 115.00
Foley's Kidney's Pill, Black Lettering, Orange Ground, 12 In. 690.00
Frank's Kidney & Liver Cure, Amber, Marked Wheaton, N.J., Wheaton, 3 In. 5.00
French's Trade, Kidney & Liver & Dropsy Cure Co., Amber, 9 5/8 In. 6440.00

Cure, Munyon's Heart
Cure, Homeopathic Home
Remedy, Box, 3 3/4 In.

Cure, Standard Medicine Co.,
Pain Cure, Aqua, Embossed,
Box, 5 1/2 In.

Cure, Warner's Safe Cure,
Olive Green, Applied
Mouth, 1890-1900, 9 1/2 In.

Germ Bacteria, Fungus Destroyer, Gold Yellow Amber, Tooled Mouth, 10 1/2 In. 140.00
Gono Pills, Man's Friend For Gonorrhea, Glass Lid, Johnson City, Tenn., 11 In. 1150.00
H.H. Warner & Co. Ltd., Melbourne, Amber, Applied Top, ABM 33.00
Harding's Toothache, Aqua, Rectangular, 6 7/8 In. 150.00
Hart's Swedish Asthma Cure Co., Buffalo, N.Y., Aqua 10.00
Healy & Bigelow's Kickapoo Indian, Aqua, Embossed Panel, Cylindrical 25.00
Here's Health To Contemptible Little Army, 1914-1918 .... 98.00
Hills Horehound & Irish Moss, Lid, Green Paint 127.50
Hood's Pills, Cure Liver, Aqua, 1 3/4 In. 55.00
J.B. Reeves Co., Anderson, Ind., Rosewood Dandruff, Amethyst, 6 1/4 In. 15.00
Kloroil Dandruff Cure, Glass Label, 7 1/2 In. 187.00
L.F. Ganter's Magic Chicken Cholera, Glasco, Ky., Gold Amber, 1880-1900, 6 In. 121.00
L.P. Dodge, Rheumatic Liniment, Newburg, Dark Olive Amber, 1855, 5 7/8 In. 2600.00
L.P. Dodge, Rheumatic Liniment, Newburg, Olive Yellow Green, 1855, 6 In. 1400.00
L.P. Dodge, Rheumatic Liniment, Newburg, Yellow Amber, OP, 1855, 6 In. 5995.00
Miner's Damiana & Celery Compound, H.C. Miner, New York, Amber, 8 1/2 In. 5936.00
Munyon's Heart Cure, Homeopathic Home Remedy, Box, 3 3/4 In. ....*Illus* 20.00
O.L. Jasmin, Cylindrical, Ground Stopper, 8 In. 58.00
Otto's Cure For Throat & Lungs, Aqua 6.00
Park's Liver & Kidney, Frank O. Reddish & Co., Le Roy, N.Y., Amber, 1895, 9 3/4 In. ... 504.00
Red Star Cough Cure, Aqua, Charles A. Vogeler Co., Baltimore, Aqua, 6 In. 40.00
Rheumatic Cure, Alicsalutice For All Rheumatic Pains, Regd, Aqua, 4 3/4 In. 8.50
Sallade Co., Magic Mosquito Bite Cure & Insect Exterminator, Green Aqua, 7 5/8 In. 40.00
Sanford's Radical Cure, Blue, Striations, Applied Top, 7 1/2 In. 50.00
Sanford's Radical Cure, Cobalt Blue, Applied Mouth, 1880, 7 1/2 In. 85.00
Seaver's Joint & Nerve Liniment, Olive 1430.00
Shiloh's Consumption Cure, Aqua, 7 3/4 In. 28.00
Shiloh's Consumption Cure, Leroy, N.Y., Blue, Tooled Top 33.00
Spelcher Dandruff Cure Co., Philadelphia, Monogram, Label, Dispensing Top, 8 In 75.00
Squibb's Brown Mixt. Lozenges, Ground Stopper, Pat'd Apr. 2, 1889, 8 In. 230.00
Standard Medicine Co., Pain Cure, Aqua, Embossed, Box, 5 1/2 In. ....*Illus* 25.00
Tonisan, Tones The Nerves, Cobalt Blue, Tooled Lip, Cylindrical, 1885-1895, 9 3/4 In. .. 231.00
Valentine's Vanilla, Pat'd Apr. 2, 1889, Stopper, 10 In. 115.00
Vaughn's Vegetable Lithontriptic Mixture, Aqua, Applied Collar, 1870, 6 1/2 In. 125.00
Vaughn's Vegetable Lithontriptic Mixture, Buffalo, Aqua, Smooth Base, 8 In. 175.00
Warner's Safe Cure, Amber, Applied Top, Embossed, c.1900, 7 1/2 In. 40.00
Warner's Safe Cure, Frankfurt, A/M, Green, 4 1/4 In. 4400.00
Warner's Safe Cure, Frankfurt, Amber, Applied Mouth, Whittled, 1900, 9 1/8 In. 209.00
Warner's Safe Cure, Frankfurt, Green, Applied Mouth, 1890-1900, 9 1/2 In. 330.00
Warner's Safe Cure, Frankfurt, Olive Green, Applied Top, 9 In. 605.00
Warner's Safe Cure, Frankfurt, Yellow Green, Oval, Applied Mouth, 9 1/8 In. 330.00
Warner's Safe Cure, London, Amber, Pt. ....30.00 to 50.00
Warner's Safe Cure, London, Apricot Amber Puce, 9 1/2 In. 80.00
Warner's Safe Cure, London, Olive Green, Oval, 1900, 7 3/8 In. ....44.00 to 80.00
Warner's Safe Cure, London, Olive Yellow Green, Applied Mouth, Whittled, 9 3/8 In. ... 154.00
Warner's Safe Cure, London, Orange Amber, Tooled Mouth, 1896, 11 In. 896.00
Warner's Safe Cure, Olive Green, Applied Mouth, 1890-1900, 9 1/2 In. ....*Illus* 495.00
Warner's Safe Cure, Olive Green, Tooled Mouth, 1880-1900, 9 1/4 In. 550.00
Warner's Safe Cure, Red Amber, Applied Mouth, 1895, 9 1/2 In. 157.00
Warner's Safe Cure, Rochester, N.Y., Amber, Tooled Mouth, 1910, 4 1/4 In. 90.00
Warner's Safe Cure, Rochester, N.Y., Amber, Tooled Mouth, Label, Contents, 7 1/2 In. .. 275.00
Warner's Safe Cure, Root Beer Amber, Applied Mouth, 1880-1900, 9 5/8 In. 303.00
Warner's Safe Cure, Toronto, Canada, London, England, Amber, Safe, BIMAL, 9 1/2 In. . 46.00
Warner's Safe Diabetes Cure, Rochester, N.Y., Amber, Tooled Lip, 1895, 9 5/8 In. .80.00 to 130.00
Warner's Safe Kidney & Liver Cure, Amber, Applied Double Collar Mouth, 1890, 9 In. .. 231.00
Warner's Safe Kidney & Liver Cure, Honey Amber, 9 1/2 In. 55.00
Warner's Safe Kidney & Liver Cure, Rochester, N.Y., Amber, 9 5/8 In. 20.00
Warner's Safe Kidney & Liver Cure, Rochester, N.Y., Amber, BIMAL, 9 3/4 In. 27.00
Warner's Safe Kidney & Liver Cure, Rochester, N.Y., Clear, Tooled Mouth, 9 In. 308.00
Warner's Safe Kidney & Liver Cure, Rochester, N.Y., Yellow Amber, 9 5/8 In. 155.00
Warner's Safe Kidney & Liver Cure, Yellow Amber, Tooled Lip, 9 1/4 In. 157.00
Warner's Safe Rheumatic Cure, London, Yellow Amber, Tooled Lip, 9 1/4 In. 198.00
Warner's Safe Rheumatic Cure, Rochester, N.Y., Amber, 9 1/4 In. 100.00

Warner's Safe Rheumatic Cure, Rochester, N.Y., Amber, Part Label, 9 3/8 In. 77.00
Warner's Tinct. Kino, Pat'd Sept 18, 1875, 9 In. 288.00
White Rose Extract, Embossed, Pat'd Sept. 18, 1875, 10 1/2 In. 690.00

─────────────────────────── **CYRUS NOBLE** ───────────────────────────

This complicated story requires a cast of characters and names: Cyrus Noble, a master distiller; Ernest R. Lilienthal, owner of Bernheim Distillery; Crown Distillers, trade name of Lilienthal & Company; Haas Brothers, successor to Lilienthal & Co.; and another Ernest R. Lilienthal and grandson of the original Ernest Lilienthal, president of Haas Brothers Distributing. Cyrus Noble was in charge of the quality of the whiskey made at the Bernheim Distillery in Kentucky. He was said to be a large man, over 300 pounds, and liked to taste his own product. According to the stories, he tasted to excess one day, fell into a whiskey vat, and drowned. The company, as a tribute, named the brand for him in 1871 and so Cyrus Noble Bourbon came into being.

Ernest R. Lilienthal, the original owner of Bernheim Distillery, moved to San Francisco and opened Lilienthal & Company with the trade name of Crown Distillers. Their best-selling brand was Cyrus Noble. It was made in three grades and sold by the barrel. The company later became Haas Brothers Distributing Company.

In 1901 John Coleman, a miner in Searchlight, Nevada, was so discouraged with the results of his digging that he offered to trade his mine to Tobe Weaver, a bartender, for a quart of Cyrus Noble whiskey. The mine was named Cyrus Noble and eventually produced over $250,000 worth of gold.

One of the early bottles used for Cyrus Noble whiskey was amber with an inside screw top; it was made from the 1860s to 1921. Haas Brothers of San Francisco marketed special Cyrus Noble bottles from 1971 to 1980. The first, made to commemorate the company's 100th anniversary, pictured the miner, the unfortunate John Coleman. Six thousand bottles were made and sold, filled, for $16.95 each. Tobe Weaver, the fortunate bartender, was pictured in the next bottle. A mine series was made from 1971 to 1978, the full size about 14 inches high and the miniatures about 6 inches; a wild animal series from 1977 to 1978; and a carousel series in 1979 and 1980. Other series are birds of the forest, Olympic bottles, horned animals, and sea animals. W.A. Lacey, a brand of 86 proof blended whiskey distributed by Haas Brothers, was also packed in a variety of figural bottles. They are listed separately under Lacey. Production of decanters for both brands ended in 1981.

Assayer, 1972 .... 100.00
Bartender, 1971 .... 100.00
Bear & Cubs, 1978, 1st Edition 110.00
Bear & Cubs, 1978, 2nd Edition 75.00
Beaver & Kit, 1978, 1st Edition 65.00
Blacksmith, 1976 .... 44.00
Blacksmith, 1976, Miniature 15.00
Buffalo Cow & Calf, 1977, 1st Edition 108.00

Cyrus Noble, Carousel,
Lion, 1979

Cyrus Noble, Seal Family,
1978

Cyrus Noble, South Of The
Border, Dancers, 1978

Buffalo Cow & Calf, 1977, 2nd Edition 60.00
Burro, 1973 .... 50.00
Carousel, Horse, Black Flyer, 1979 .... 55.00
Carousel, Horse, White Charger, 1979 ....50.00 to 55.00
Carousel, Lion, 1979 ....*Illus* 44.00
Carousel, Pipe Organ, 1980 .... 36.00
Carousel, Tiger, 1979 .... 50.00
Deer, Mule, 1980 .... 80.00
Deer, White Tall Buck, 1979 .... 135.00
Delta Saloon, 1971, Miniature 270.00
Dolphin, 1979 .... 46.00
Elk, Bull, 1980 .... 124.00
Gambler, 1974 ....40.00 to 50.00
Gambler's Lady, 1977, Miniature 44.00
Gold Miner, 1970 .... 170.00
Gold Miner, 1974, Miniature 20.00
Harp Seal, 1979 .... 50.00
Landlady, 1977 .... 30.00
Middle Of Piano, Trumpeter, 1979 .... 40.00
Mine Shaft, 1978 .... 40.00
Miner's Daughter, 1975 .... 40.00
Moose, 1976, 1st Edition 90.00
Mountain Lion & Cubs, 1977, 1st Edition 82.00
Mountain Sheep, 1978, 1st Edition 85.00
Music Man, 1978, Miniature 34.00
Oklahoma Dancers, 1978 .... 32.00
Olympic Skater, 1980 .... 45.00
Owl In Tree, 1980 .... 37.00
Penguins, 1978 .... 50.00
Sea Turtle, 1979 .... 42.00
Seal Family, 1978 ....*Illus* 45.00
Snowshoe Thompson, 1972 .... 130.00
South Of The Border, Dancers, 1978 ....*Illus* 35.00
Tonopah, Octagonal, Milk Glass, 1972 .... 125.00
USC Trojan, 1980 .... 75.00
Violinist, 1978, Miniature 35.00
Walrus Family, 1978 .... 40.00
Walrus Family, 1980, Miniature 42.00
Whiskey Drummer, 1975 ....32.00 to 40.00
Whiskey Drummer, 1977, Miniature 32.00
Wood Duck 40.00

---------------------------------- DANT ----------------------------------

Dant figural bottles were first released in 1968 to hold J.W. Dant alcoholic products. The figurals were discontinued after a few years. The company made an Americana series, field birds, special bottlings, and ceramic bottles. Several bottles were made with *errors*. Collectors seem to have discounted this in determining value.

Alamo, 1969 .... 4.00
American Legion, 1969 .... 10.00
Atlantic City, 1969 .... 6.00
Boeing 747, 1970 .... 8.00
Boston Tea Party, Eagle Right, 1968 .... 5.00
Boston Tea Party, Reverse Eagle, 1968 ....*Illus* 10.00
Burr-Hamilton Duel, 1969 .... 6.00
Constitution & Guerriere, 1969 .... 6.00
Field Bird Series, No. 1, Ring-Necked Pheasant, 1969 .... 10.00
Field Bird Series, No. 2, Chukar Partridge, 1969 ....7.00 to 10.00
Field Bird Series, No. 3, Prairie Chicken, 1969 ....7.00 to 10.00
Field Bird Series, No. 4, Mountain Quail, 1969 ....7.00 to 10.00
Field Bird Series, No. 5, Ruffled Grouse, 1969 ....7.00 to 10.00
Field Bird Series, No. 6, California Quail, 1969 ....7.00 to 10.00
Field Bird Series, No. 7, Bob White, 1969 .... 8.00
Field Bird Series, No. 8, Woodcock, 1969 ....*Illus* 10.00

Dant, Boston Tea Party,
Reverse Eagle, 1968

Dant, Field Bird Series, No. 8,
Woodcock, 1969

Dant, Fort Sill, Canteen,
1969

Fort Sill, Canteen, 1969	*Illus*	8.00
Indy 500, 1969		10.00
Mt. Rushmore, 1969		8.00
Patrick Henry, 1969		6.00 to 8.00
Paul Bunyan, 1969		8.00
San Diego Harbor, 1969		5.00
Washington At Delaware, 1969		5.00 to 10.00

DAVIESS COUNTY

Daviess County ceramic bottles were made from 1978 to 1981. The best-known were the American Legion Convention bottles. About 14 figural bottles were made, including a series of large tractor trailers and Greensboro Golf Tournament souvenirs.

American Legion, Boston, 1980	18.00
American Legion, Hawaii, 1981	25.00
American Legion, Houston, 1979	15.00 to 24.00
American Legion, New Orleans, 1978	20.00
Greensboro Open, Golf Ball & Tee, 1981	45.00
Iowa Hog, 1978	20.00
Jeep CJ-7, Yellow, 1979	55.00
Kentucky Long Rifle, 1978	55.00
Mallard Decoy, 1989	35.00
Oil Tanker, Gulf, 1979	50.00
Pontiac Trans Am, 1980	35.00

DECANTER

Decanters were first used to hold the alcoholic beverages that had been stored in kegs. The undesirable sediment that formed at the bottom of old wine kegs was removed by carefully pouring off the top liquid, or decanting it. At first a necessity, the decanter later became merely an attractive serving vessel. A decanter usually has a bulbous bottom, a long neck, and a small mouth for easy pouring. Most have a cork or glass stopper. They were popular in England from the beginning of the eighteenth century. By about 1775 the decanter was elaborate, with cut, applied, or enameled decorations. Various early American glassworks made decanters. Mold-blown decanters were the most popular style and many were made in the East and the Midwest from 1820 to the 1860s. Pressed glass was a less expensive process introduced in about 1850, and many decanters were made by this method. Colored Bohemian glass consisting of two or three cased layers became popular in the late-nineteenth century. Many decanters are now made for home or restaurant use or with special logos to promote products. Bar bottles, decanter-like bottles with brand names in the glass, were used from about 1890 to 1920 in saloons. The law no longer permits the use of bar bottles because no bottle may be refilled from another container. Other decanters may be found in the Beam, Bischoff, Kord, and other modern bottle categories.

16 Ribs, Swirled To Left, Applied Rings, Hollow Stopper, 10 In.	*Illus*	350.00
Amber, Parcel Gilt, Whiskey & Brandy, Spigot, Edwardian, 30 In., Pair		2300.00

Decanter, 16 Ribs, Swirled To Left, Applied Rings, Hollow Stopper, 10 In.

Decanter, Backbar, Label Under Glass, Brandy, Pretty Woman, Glass Stopper, 9 In.

Decanter, Diamond Diaper Band, Sunburst, Olive Yellow, Pontil, Pt.

Arch Pattern, Applied Lip, Pontil, 12 In.	44.00
Arch Pattern, Embossed Rum, Ferns, Stopper, Qt.	413.00
Backbar, Fluted Neck, Enameled Word Hannisville, Stopper, 8 1/2 In.	70.00
Backbar, Green, Gold Cut Words, Old Green Bottle, Qt., 11 1/2 In.	200.00
Backbar, Label Under Glass, Brandy, Pretty Woman, Glass Stopper, 9 In. *Illus*	210.00
Barrel, Brown, Applied Rings, Pontil, Germany, 1840, 8 1/4 In.	193.00
Barrel, Green Aqua, 18 Ribs, Sled Footed, Continental, 1850, 4 3/8 x 7 1/4 In.	357.00
Barrel, Whiskey, Ground Cover, Metal Spigot, 10 In.	145.00
Cascade, White Enameled Script, Zipper, Cut Neck, 9 1/4 In.	80.00
Co-Operative Club, Backbar, Pinched Waist, Gold Leaf, Stopper, 6 1/4 In.	70.00
Cobalt Blue, 2 Double Rigaree Bands, Pontil, South Jersey, 9 1/4 In.	468.00
Cobalt Blue, Enameled White Flowers, Gold Trim, Sticker, Bohemian, 10 In.	85.00
Cobalt Blue, Rum, Mother Of Pearl & Brass Stopper, Pontil, 7 3/4 In.	121.00
Coin Spot, Milk Glass Cut To Red, Flowers, Tooled Lip, Pontil, 7 7/8 In.	231.00
Cranberry Cased, Gold Enamel, Square, Clear Stopper, 11 1/2 In.	165.00
Cut Glass, Amber To Clear, Grapevine, Stopper, 1890	1200.00
Cut Glass, Blue To Clear, Grapes & Vine, Stopper, Mid 19th Century, 12 In.	275.00
Cut Glass, Fluted, Backbar, Enamel Word Wildwood, Oval Base, 9 1/4 In.	80.00
Cut Glass, Paneled, Knopped Faceted Stopper, Anglo-Irish, 10 1/2 x 4 In., Pair	748.00
Cut Glass, Ribbed Waist, 19th Century, 6 3/4 x 5 In., Pair	345.00
Cut Glass, Ruby To Clear, Allover Diamond, Stopper, Pontil, 8 3/4 In.	165.00
Cut Glass, Ruby To Clear, Grape Cluster, Backbar, Pontil, 7 1/2 In.	88.00
Cut Glass, Ruby To Clear, Rings, Panels, Diamonds, Stopper, Anglo-Irish, 9 x 5 In., Pair	1840.00
Cut Glass, Ruby To Clear, Scotch, Heart Shape, Stopper, 1910, Qt.	70.00
Cut Glass, Ruby To Clear, Stags, Doe & Fawn, Stopper, Tag, 8 1/4 In.	190.00
Cut Glass, Swirled Flutes, Neck Rings, Flared Mouth, Stopper, 12 In.	358.00
Cut Glass, Word Rye In Gold Leaf, Bowling Pin Shape, Stopper, 9 1/4 In.	85.00
D.F.C. Whiskey, Frankfort, Ky., Cut Neck Flutes, Stopper, 8 1/2 In.	75.00
Diamond Diaper, Flared Lip, Pontil, Sunburst, 2 1/2 In.	500.00
Diamond Diaper, Horizontal Ribs, Applied Lip, Pontil, Stopper, Qt.	77.00
Diamond Diaper, Rib Band, Stopper, Pontil, Pt.	88.00
Diamond Diaper, Ribs, Medium Green, Flared Lip, Pontil, 8 In.	6720.00
Diamond Diaper, Sunburst, Olive Green, 7 In.	330.00
Diamond Diaper Band, Alternating Ribs, Tooled Lip, Stopper, Pontil, 1/2 Pt.	100.00
Diamond Diaper Band, Rounded Ribs, 3 Triple Neck Rings, Stopper, 9 In.	82.00
Diamond Diaper Band, Rounded Ribs, Base Mark, Stopper	220.00
Diamond Diaper Band, Rounded Ribs, Stopper, OP, Qt., 9 In.	132.00
Diamond Diaper Band, Rounded Ribs, Stopper, Pontil, Pt.	77.00
Diamond Diaper Band, Sunburst, Double Rigaree, Flat Stopper, 7 1/8 In.	165.00
Diamond Diaper Band, Sunburst, Flared Mouth, Pontil, Ground Stopper, Pontil, 4 In.	633.00
Diamond Diaper Band, Sunburst, Olive Green, Sheared Mouth, OP, Qt.	935.00
Diamond Diaper Band, Sunburst, Olive Yellow Amber, Flared Mouth, Pt.	3025.00
Diamond Diaper Band, Sunburst, Olive Yellow, Pontil, Pt. *Illus*	784.00
Diamond Diaper Band, Sunburst, Olive Yellow, Tooled Lip, Pontil, Pt.	952.00
Diamond Diaper Band, Sunburst, Olive, Pt.	650.00
Diamond Diaper Band, Sunburst, Stopper, OP, Qt.	154.00

Diamond Diaper Band, Sunburst, Stopper, Pontil, 9 1/2 In. 209.00
Diamond Diaper Band, Swirled Ribs, Olive Green, Pontil, 1/2 Pt. 2352.00
Drape Pattern, Applied Square Collar, 11 1/2 In. 90.00
Enameled, Castle Hunting Scene, Engraved, 13 In., Pair 120.00
Enameled, Coat Of Arms, Engraved Fleur-De-Lis, Gold Trim, 12 3/4 In. 165.00
Etched, 1796, Bear, Flowers & Sunbursts, Applied Foot, Pontil, 12 1/4 In. 213.00
Etched, Grapes & Grape Leaves On Shoulder, Stopper, Pair 121.00
Greek Key Band, Stopper, 14 In. 49.00
Green, Leather Covered, Florence, Italy, 13 In. 50.00
Horn-O-Plenty Pattern, Stopper, Qt., 11 1/4 In. 44.00
J.H. Wolf, Whiskey, Swirled Ribs, Stopper, Qt. 358.00
Keene, Medium Olive Green, Sheared Top, OP, 7 1/2 In. 440.00
Kentucky Tavern, Treasure Island, Pirate Scene, Stopper, 1948 .... 75.00
Lattice Pattern, Embossed Word Brandy Flared Mouth, Stopper, Pontil, Qt. 413.00
Lattice Pattern, Embossed Word Cherry Flared Mouth, Pontil, Pt. 605.00
Lattice Pattern, Embossed Word Cherry Flared Mouth, Pontil, Qt. 187.00
Midwestern, 18 Vertical Ribs, Yellow Olive, 1820-1835, 7 5/8 In. 1232.00
Old I.W., B.B. Harper, Gold, Cut Neck Flutes, 1920, 8 In. 75.00
Olive Amber, Funnel Mouth, Applied Ring, c.1840, 10 3/4 x 3 In. 360.00
Paul Jones, Enameled, Backbar, Pinched Back, 6 3/4 In. 245.00
Pineapple Shape, Clear, 8 1/2 In., Pair 88.00
Rigaree Band, Engraved Bird & Grape Band, 2 Handles, Pontil, 8 7/8 In. 155.00
Rigaree Band, Sunburst Stopper, Flared Lip, Pontil, 10 1/2 In. 154.00
Rounded Ribs, Flared Lip, Pontil, Teardrop Stopper, 7 1/2 In. .... .88.00 to 132.00
Rounded Ribs, Wider Ribs At Neck, Pontil, Qt. 77.00
Rum, Cobalt Blue, Brass Neck Ring, Applied Handle, Pontil, 7 3/4 In. 120.00
Sapphire Blue, Fluted Base & Shoulders, Applied Band, Stopper, 12 1/2 In. 230.00
Sapphire Blue, Paneled, Applied Rings, Pewter & Quartz Stopper, Pontil, 12 In. 1792.00
Scrolled Leaf, Graduated Rounded Ribs, Stopper, 9 In. 110.00
Scrolls, Cable Band, Leaves, Stopper, Qt. 359.00
Sherwood Rye, Burrichter Bros., Gold Leaf, Fluted Neck, Wooden Stopper, 9 In. 90.00
Silver Deposit, Ruby, Pinched Waist, Stopper, Qt. 79.00
Sunburst Band, Embosssed Rum, Swirled Ribs, Stopper, Qt. 303.00
Sunburst Band, Swirled Ribs, Flared Mouth, Stopper, Pontil, Qt. 448.00
Sunburst Band, Swirled Ribs, Olive, 1840, Pt. 1100.00
Thumbprint Block Pattern, Stopper, Pontil 44.00
Tom Hudson, Gold Trim, Cut Flutes & Base Ovals, 8 1/2 In. 70.00
W.H. McBrayers, Cedar Brook, Engraved, Gold Trim, Stopper, 9 1/4 In. 90.00
Wine, Cone, Cut Glass, Flutes At Neck & Base, Stopper, 1740-1780, 11 1/2 In. 80.00
Wine, Onion Swirl Marble, Pink, White, Metal Stopper, Pontil, 11 In. 110.00

DEMIJOHN

A demijohn is a very large bottle that is usually blown. Many held alcoholic beverages, molasses, or other liquids. It was usually bulbous with a long neck and a high kick-up. Early examples have open pontils. A carboy is a bottle that was covered with wicker to avoid breakage when the bottles were shipped. A demijohn could hold from one to ten gallons. Most early demijohns were made of dark green, amber, or black glass. By the 1850s the glass colors were often aqua, light green, or clear.

Amber, Applied Lip, Gal., 13 3/4 In. 77.00
Amber, Applied Top, 16 In. 11.00
Amber, Bubbles, Applied Lip, OP, 14 In. 110.00
Amber, Bubbles, Applied Lip, Pontil, 16 In. 121.00
Amber, Bulbous, OP, 5 In. 70.00
Amber, Embossed VK 1859, Domed Kick-Up, 18 1/4 x 13 1/2 In. 172.00
Aqua, Applied Top, Pontil, Carboy, 19 In. 88.00
Aqua, IP, 1/2 Gal. 20.00
Aqua, IP, 1850-1860, 1/2 Gal., 12 In. 25.00
Aqua, Squat Cylindrical, IP, 1/2 Gal., 12 1/2 In. 30.00
B.F.C., Black Glass, Stoddard, Cylindrical, Bubbles, Mid 1800s, 15 1/4 In. 60.00
Black Glass, Applied Mouth, Pontil, 9 3/4 In. 176.00
Black Glass, Bulbous, 3-Piece Mold, OP, 1840-1860, 18 In. 90.00
Black Glass, IP, Gal. 70.00
Blue Green, Applied Lip, Bubbles, Gal., 13 In. 66.00

Demijohn, Yellow Amber, Sloping Collar, Pontil, 11 3/4 In.

Demijohn, Bread Loaf Shape, Medium Blue Green, Applied Sloping Collar, Pontil, 8 1/2 In.

For a pollution-free glass cleaner, use a mixture of white vinegar and water.

Blue Green, Pontil Kick-Up, Applied Collar Mouth, 1845-1865, 16 1/4 In.	176.00
Blue Green, Sloping Collar, Stain, 1855-1865, IP, 15 1/8 In.	176.00
Bread Loaf Shape, Blue Green, ABM, 1890-1910, Gal.	45.00
Bread Loaf Shape, Blue Green, Sloping Collar, Pontil, 1860-1880, 8 1/2 In.	112.00
Bread Loaf Shape, Gold Amber, Applied Sloping Collar, Bubbles, 9 In.	880.00
Bread Loaf Shape, Medium Blue Green, Applied Sloping Collar, Pontil, 8 1/2 In. . . .*Illus*	448.00
Bread Loaf Shape, Sea Green, Pontil, 9 x 9 1/2 x 6 In.	413.00
Dark Amber, Bubbles, 16 In.	120.00
Dark Amethyst, Center Dot, 3-Piece Mold, Pontil, 12 In.	176.00
Dark Chocolate Amber, Coggle Wheel, String Lip, Continental, 1865, 17 1/2 In.	275.00
Dark Green, Wicker, 1860-1880, Gal.	31.00
Dark Olive Green, Applied Sloping Mouth, Pontil, 17 In.	176.00
Golden Amber, Tooled Mouth, 12 1/2 In.	33.00
Green, Applied Rigaree Mouth, Pontil, 13 In.	99.00
Green, Applied Top, Pontil, 4-Piece Mold, Carboy	165.00
Green, Crooked Neck, Applied Lip, Pontil, 14 In.	88.00
Green Aqua, Pebbly, Applied Lip, Gal., 12 1/2 In.	22.00
Light Green, Applied Top, 1/2 Gal., 12 1/2 In.	40.00
Light Green Aqua, Applied Lip, Gal., 12 1/2 In.	20.00
Medium Apple Green, Applied Sloping Collar, 1860-1880, 12 In.	202.00
Medium Blue Aqua, Applied Top, 17 1/2 In.	40.00
Medium Blue Green, Applied Sloping Collar, IP, 1845-1860, 9 1/4 In.	134.00
Medium Cobalt Blue, Tooled Mouth, 1880-1910, 14 1/2 In.	364.00
Medium Orange Amber, Tooled Mouth, 1880-1890, 14 1/2 In.	100.00
Medium Yellow Amber, Whittled, 1860-1880, 17 1/4 In.	89.00
Olive, 4-Piece Mold, 13 In.	11.00
Olive, Applied Top, Pontil, Carboy, 20 In.	130.00
Olive, Applied Top, Pottery Stopper, Pontil, Carboy, 5 Gal., 20 In., 1860s	240.00
Olive Amber, Applied Top, 14 1/2 In.	55.00
Olive Green, 1875-1895, 18 In.	95.00
Olive Green, Applied Sloping Collar, Pontil, 16 1/2 In.	22.00
Olive Green, Aqua, 19 1/4 In., Pair	165.00
Olive Green, Domed Kick-Up, 14 1/4 In.	143.00
Olive Green, Enamel Flowers, Applied Mouth, Bubbles, 1860-1880, 17 1/4 In.	198.00
Olive Green, Sapphire Blue, Applied Sloping Collar, 1880, 12 In.	1400.00
Olive Yellow, Applied Sloping Collar, 2-Piece Mold, Pontil, 10 3/4 In.	364.00
Olive Yellow, Olive Streaks, Bubbles, Applied Lip, 13 1/4 In.	99.00
Olive Yellow, OP, Gal.	90.00
Olive Yellow Amber, Sloping Collar, Bubbles, Swirls, 1840, 11 1/2 In.	143.00
Orange Amber, Applied Mouth, 1870-1890, 13 1/4 In.	77.00
Orange Amber, Cylindrical, 1/2 Gal., 12 1/2 In.	20.00
Painted, Landscape, Coat Of Arms, Lion, Applied Collar, Holland, Early 18th Century	750.00
Red Amber, 1875-1895, 19 1/2 In.	532.00
Red Amber, Applied Mouth, Pontil, 15 In.	55.00
Sapphire Blue, Applied Sloping Collar, 1860-1880, 12 1/4 In.	1568.00
Storage, Stoddard, Olive Amber, IP, Qt.	48.00
Tobacco, Amber, Pebbled, Applied Lip, 13 1/2 In.	66.00

Tobacco, Applied Lip, Gal., 13 1/2 In. 66.00
Wright & Lutz, Old Sherwood, Aqua, Sloping Double Collar, Original Crate, 17 In. 448.00
Yellow, Olive Tint, Applied Mouth, 1870-1885, 17 5/8 In. 165.00
Yellow Amber, Applied Mouth, 1870-1885, 17 In. 83.00
Yellow Amber, Applied Sloping Collar, Pontil, 1840-1865, 13 In. 112.00
Yellow Amber, Olive Tone, Applied Sloping Collar Mouth, 1835-1855, 11 In. 145.00
Yellow Amber, Olive Tone, Sloping Collar, Pontil, Bubbles, 1855, 10 7/8 In. 145.00
Yellow Amber, Sloping Collar, Pontil, 11 3/4 In. . . . .*Illus*   84.00
Yellow Amber, Tapered Collar, Pontil, 11 1/2 In. 77.00
Yellow Emerald, Applied Lip, 15 In. 110.00
Yellow Green, Applied Lip, Swirls, Gal., 13 In. 66.00

DICKEL

George Dickel Tennessee sour mash whiskey was sold in figural bottles in about 1967. The golf club, powder horn, and ceramic jug were widely advertised then but are of limited interest to today's collectors.

Golf Club, 1967 . . . .   14.00
Golf Club, 1979, Miniature 7.00
Jug, Ceramic 8.00
Powder Horn, 1/2 Gal. . . . . .70.00 to 80.00
Powder Horn, Gal. 180.00
Powder Horn, Miniature 8.00
Powder Horn, Qt. 12.00

DOUBLE SPRINGS

Double Springs of Louisville, Kentucky, made ceramic figural bottles from 1968 to 1978. They had a classic car series made by the Century Porcelain Company, a Bicentennial series, and other figural bottles.

Bentley, 1927 Model, 1972 . . . .   44.00
Bicentennial, Colorado, 1976 . . . .   14.00
Bicentennial, South Dakota, 1976 . . . .   14.00
Cadillac, 1913 Model, 1971 . . . .   36.00
Cord, 1937 Model, 1978 . . . .   33.00
Coyote, Gold, 1971 . . . .   10.00
Ford, Model T, 1910 Model, 1970 . . . .   40.00
Georgia Bulldog, 1971 . . . .   28.00
Kentucky Derby, With Glass, 1964 . . . .   10.00
Matador, 1969 . . . .   12.00
Mercedes Benz, 1936 Model, 1975 . . . .   40.00
Milwaukee Buck, 1971 . . . .   12.00
Owl, Brown, 1968 . . . .   15.00
Owl, Red, 1968 . . . .   12.00
Peasant Boy, 1968 . . . .   5.00
Peasant Girl, 1968 . . . .   5.00
Rolls-Royce, 1912 Model, 1971 . . . .   46.00
Stanley Steamer, 1909 Model, 1971 . . . .   37.00
Stutz Bearcat, 1919 Model, 1970 . . . .   40.00
DRUG, see Bitters; Cure; Medicine

EZRA BROOKS

Ezra Brooks fancy bottles were first made in 1964. The Ezra Brooks brand was purchased by Glenmore Distilleries Company of Louisville, Kentucky, in 1988, three years after Ezra Brooks had discontinued making decanters. About 300 different ceramic figurals were made between 1964 and 1985. The dates listed here are within a year of the time they appeared on the market. Bottles were often announced and then not produced for many months. Glenmore sold the Ezra Brooks label to Heaven Hill Distillery in Bardstown, Kentucky, who sold it to David Sherman Corporation of St. Louis, Missouri, in 1994.

100th Bottle Award, 1972 . . . .   25.00
American Legion, Champaign, Urbana, 1983 . . . .   25.00
American Legion, Chicago, Salute, 1972 . . . .   50.00
American Legion, Denver, 1977 . . . .   15.00
American Legion, Hawaii, 1973 . . . . .12.00 to 15.00

American Legion, Houston, 1971 ....30.00 to 35.00
American Legion, Miami Beach, 1974 ....9.00 to 12.00
American Legion, New Orleans, 1978 .... 25.00
American Legion, Salt Lake City, 1984 ....45.00 to 50.00
American Legion, Seattle, 1983 ....30.00 to 35.00
American Legion, Water Tower, 1982 .... 15.00
AMVET, Dolphin, 1974 ....10.00 to 30.00
AMVET, Polish Legion, 1978 .... 10.00
Antique Cannon, Gold, 1969 .... 8.00
Arizona, Desert Scene, 1969 .... 27.00
Auburn, Boat Tail, 1932 Model, 1978 .... 30.00
Auburn, U-War Eagle, 1982 .... 30.00
Badger, Boxer No. 1, 1973 .... 32.00
Badger, Football, No. 2, 1975 .... 24.00
Badger, Hockey, No. 3, 1975 .... 20.00
Baltimore Oriole, 1979 .... 34.00
Bareknuckle Boxer, 1971 ....25.00 to 30.00
Basketball Player, 1974 .... 21.00
Beaver, 1973 .... 12.00
Betsy Ross, 1975 .... 10.00
Bicycle, Penny Farthington, 1973 .... 14.00
Big Daddy Lounge, 1969 .... 12.00
Bordertown Nevada, 1970 .... 10.00
Bowler, 1973 .... 12.00
Brahma Bull, 1972 ....18.00 to 21.00
Bronco Buster, 1974 .... 15.00
Bucket Of Blood, 1970 .... 14.00
Buffalo Hunt, 1971 ....10.00 to 12.00
C.B. Convoy Radio, 1976 ....8.00 to 15.00
Canadian Honker, 1975 ....13.00 to 15.00
Cannon, 1969 ....8.00 to 10.00
Card, Jack Of Diamonds, 1969 ....9.00 to 25.00
Card, King Of Clubs, 1969 ....14.00 to 25.00
Card, Queen Of Hearts, 1969 ....14.00 to 25.00
Cardinal, Virginia, 1972 .... 18.00
Casey At Bat, 1973 .... 60.00
Charolais Bull, 1972 .... 15.00
Cheyenne Shootout, 1970 ....10.00 to 12.00
Chicago Fire Team, 1974 .... 25.00
Chicago Water Tower, 1969 .... 8.00
Christmas Tree, 1979 .... 22.00
Cigar Store Indian, 1968 .... 8.00
Clown, No. 1, Smiley, 1979 .... 32.00
Clown, No. 2, Cowboy, 1979 ....26.00 to 30.00
Clown, No. 3, Pagliacci, 1979 ....22.00 to 32.00
Clown, No. 4, Keystone Cop, 1980 .... 30.00
Clown, No. 5, Cuddles, 1980 .... 30.00
Clown, No. 6, Tramp, 1980 .... 30.00
Clown, With Accordion, 1971 .... 25.00
Clown, With Balloons, 1973 .... 25.00
Club, No. 1, Distillery, 1970 .... 7.00
Club, No. 2, Birthday Cake, 1971 .... 7.00
Club, No. 3, U.S.A. Map, 1972 .... 7.00
Clydesdale, 1974 .... 22.00
Corvette, 1957 Model, Blue, 1976 .... 125.00
Corvette, 1957 Model, Yellow, 1976 .... 125.00
Corvette, 1962 Model, Mako Shark, 1979 .... 30.00
Court Jester, 1971 .... 9.00
Creighton Blue Jay, 1975 .... 25.00
Dakota Cowboy, 1975 ....30.00 to 44.00
Dakota Cowgirl, 1976 .... 30.00
Dakota Grain Elevator, 1978 .... 25.00
Dakota Shotgun Express, 1977 ....15.00 to 18.00

Deadwagon, Nevada, 1970 .... 10.00
Decanter, Glass, 1964 ....10.00 to 12.00
Decanter, Glass, 1965 .... 15.00
Decanter, Glass, 1966 .... 7.00
Decanter, Glass, 1967 .... 6.00
Decanter, Glass, 1968 .... 7.00
Decanter, Glass, 1969 .... 7.00
Deer, Whitetail, 1974 .... 15.00
Delta Belle, Riverboat, 1969 .... 10.00
Dog, Setter, 1974 .... 10.00
Drum & Bugle, Conquistador, 1971 .... 10.00
Duesenberg, 1971 .... 35.00
Eagle, Gold, 1971 .... 15.00
Elephant, Asian, 1973 .... 20.00
Elephant, Big Bertha, 1970 .... 20.00
Elk, 1972 .... 25.00
English Setter With Bird In Mouth, 1971 .... 65.00
Equestrian, 1974 .... 10.00
F.O.E. Eagle, 1978 .... 15.00
F.O.E. Eagle, 1979 ....18.00 to 20.00
F.O.E. Eagle, 1980 .... 35.00
F.O.E. Eagle, 1981 .... 35.00
Fire Engine, 1971 ....25.00 to 40.00
Fireman, 1975 .... 32.00
Fisherman, 1974 .... *Illus* 12.00
Football Player, 1974 .... 18.00
Ford Thunderbird, 1956 Model, Blue, 1976 .... 80.00
Ford Thunderbird, 1956 Model, Yellow, 1976 .... 60.00
Foremost Astronaut, 1970 .... 20.00
Foremost Dancing Man, 1969 .... 20.00
Fox, Redtail, 1979 .... 45.00
Fresno Grape, 1970 .... 10.00
Fresno Grape, With No Gold, 1970 .... 60.00
Gamecock, 1970 ....10.00 to 15.00
Gator, Florida, No. 1, Passing, 1972 .... 45.00
Gator, Florida, No. 2, Running, 1973 .... 45.00
Gator, Florida, No. 3, Blocker, 1975 .... 45.00
Gavel, President, 1982 ....50.00 to 55.00
Gavel & Block, V.I.P., 1982 .... 15.00
Georgia Bulldog, 1971 .... 30.00
Go Big Red, No. 1, Football, 1970 ....28.00 to 32.00
Go Big Red, No. 2, With Hat, 1971 .... 28.00
Go Big Red, No. 3, Football, 1972 .... 23.00
Golden Grizzly Bear, California, 1968 .... 8.00
Goldpanner, 1969 ....8.00 to 9.00
Golfer, Seal, 1973 .... 15.00
Goose, Happy, 1974 .... 15.00
Gopher, Minnesota Hockey Player, 1975 .... 18.00
Grandfather Clock, 1970 ....7.00 to 10.00
Greater Greensboro Open, No. 1, 1972 .... 25.00
Greater Greensboro Open, No. 2, 1973, Golfer 25.00
Greater Greensboro Open, No. 3, 1974, Map 40.00
Greater Greensboro Open, No. 4, 1975, Cup 25.00
Greater Greensboro Open, No. 5, 1976 .... 25.00
Greater Greensboro Open, No. 6, 1977, Club & Ball 23.00
Groucho Marx, 1977 .... 75.00
Hambletonian, Gold, 1970 .... 25.00
Hambletonian, Race Track, 1970 .... 15.00
Hardy, Oliver, 1976 .... 37.00
Harold's Club Dice, Red, Reno, Nevada, 1968 ....14.00 to 15.00
Hereford, 1971 .... 19.00
Historical Flask, 1970 ....4.00 to 6.00
Horseshoe Casino, 1970 .... 14.00

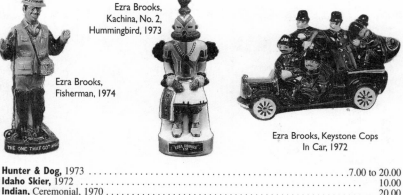

Ezra Brooks,
Kachina, No. 2,
Hummingbird, 1973

Ezra Brooks,
Fisherman, 1974

Ezra Brooks, Keystone Cops
In Car, 1972

Hunter & Dog, 1973	.7.00 to 20.00
Idaho Skier, 1972	10.00
Indian, Ceremonial, 1970	20.00
Indy Pace Car, Corvette, 1978	45.00
Indy Pace Car, Ford Mustang, 1979	40.00
Indy Pace Car, Penske Pacemaker, No. 1, 1982	95.00
Indy Pace Car, Pontiac, 1980	33.00 to 50.00
Indy Race Car, No. 21, 1970	.45.00 to 60.00
Indy Race Car, Sprint, No. 21, 1971	80.00
Indy STP No. 20, 1983	75.00
Indy STP No. 40, 1983	85.00
Iowa Farmer, 1977	30.00
Iowa Farmer's Elevator, 1978	30.00
Jayhawk, Kansas, 1969	16.00
Jug, Old Time, 1977	20.00
Jug, Owl, 1980, 1.75 Liter, 1980	18.00
Kachina, No. 1, Morning Singer, 1971	.80.00 to 95.00
Kachina, No. 2, Hummingbird, 1973	*Illus* 75.00
Kachina, No. 3, Antelope, 1975	.68.00 to 70.00
Kachina, No. 4, Maiden, 1975	35.00
Kachina, No. 5, Longhair, 1976	45.00
Kachina, No. 6, Buffalo Dancer, 1977	47.00
Kachina, No. 7, Mudhead, 1978	.50.00 to 55.00
Kachina, No. 8, Drummer, 1979	.75.00 to 80.00
Kachina, No. 9, Watermelon, 1980	25.00
Katz Cats, Gray, Tan, 1969	11.00
Katz Cats, Philharmonic, 1970	10.00
Keystone Cops In Car, 1972	*Illus* 70.00
Kitten On Pillow, 1975	.10.00 to 12.00
Laurel, Stan, 1976	.37.00 to 45.00
Laurel & Hardy, 1976, 7 3/4 & 6 3/4 In., Pair	*Illus* 90.00
Leopard, Snow, 1980	40.00
Liberty Bell, 1969	6.00
Lighthouse, Maine, 1971	25.00
Lincoln Continental, 1979	34.00
Lion, African, 1980	35.00
Lion On Rock, 1971	14.00
Liquor Square, 1972	.8.00 to 10.00
Lobster, 1970	.22.00 to 50.00
Loon, 1979	27.00
M & M, Brown Jug, 1974	18.00
Macaw, 1980	.18.00 to 52.00
Maine Potato, 1973	14.00
Man O'War, Horse, 1969	.25.00 to 45.00
Max The Hat Zimmerman, 1976	28.00
Minuteman, 1975	15.00

Moose, 1972 .... .25.00 to 34.00
Motorcycle, 1971 .... 25.00
Mr. Foremost Dancing Man, 1969 .... 22.00
Mr. Merchant, 1970 .... 8.00
Mule, Missouri, Gold, 1971 .... 35.00
New Hampshire, Old Man On Mountain, 1970 ....9.00 to 12.00
New Hampshire, State House, 1969 .... 8.00
North Carolina Bicentennial, 1975 .... 12.00
Nugget Classic, 1970 .... 15.00
Nugget Classic, Gold, 1970 .... 25.00
Nugget Gold Rooster, No. 1, 1969 .... 30.00
Oil Gusher, 1969 .... 10.00
Old Capital, Iowa, 1971 ....35.00 to 40.00
Old Ez Owl, No. 1, Barn Owl, 1977 .... 25.00
Old Ez Owl, No. 2, Eagle, 1978 .... 55.00
Old Ez Owl, No. 3, Snowy, 1979 .... 34.00
Old Ez Owl, No. 4, Scops, 1980 ....16.00 to 22.00
Old Ez Owl, No. 5, Great Gray, 1982 .... 30.00
Ontario Racer No. 10, 1970 .... 30.00
Panda, 1972 ....15.00 to 19.00
Penguin, 1973 ....*Illus* 12.00
Phoenix Bird, 1971 ....24.00 to 27.00
Phonograph, 1970 .... 25.00
Pirate, 1971 ....5.00 to 14.00
Pistol, Dueling, Flintlock, 1968 ....11.00 to 17.00
Pistol, Dueling, Flintlock, Made In Japan, 1968 .... 40.00
Political, Democratic & Republican Conventions, 1976, Pair 15.00
Potbelly Stove, 1968 ....8.00 to 10.00
Quail, California, 1970 .... 10.00
Raccoon, 1978 .... 45.00
Ram, 1973 .... 18.00
Razorback Hog, Arizona, 1969 ....20.00 to 30.00
Razorback Hog, Arizona, No. 2, 1979 .... 35.00
Reno Arch, 1968 ....10.00 to 25.00
Saddle, Silver, 1972 .... 25.00
Sailfish, 1970 ....8.00 to 12.00
Salmon, Washington, 1971 ....22.00 to 25.00
San Francisco Cable Car, Gray, Green, Brown, 1968 .... 18.00
Sea Captain, 1971 .... 15.00
Seal, Gold, 1972 ....10.00 to 12.00
Senator, 1972 ....8.00 to 12.00
Senator, Gold, 1972 .... 25.00

Ezra Brooks, Laurel &
Hardy, 1976,
7 3/4 & 6 3/4 In., Pair

Ezra Brooks, Ski Boot, 1972

Ezra Brooks,
Penguin, 1973

Ezra Brooks, Spirit Of
'76, Drummer, 1974

Ezra Brooks,
Strongman, 1974

Ezra Brooks, Tennis
Player, 1973

To make a quick "photo" of
your old bottle, try using a
photocopying machine. Put the
bottle on the machine, then
cover it with white paper or
cloth to block out any extra
light. Lower the cover gently
and take the picture.

Shark, White, 1972	20.00
Shriner, Clown, 1978	9.50 to 28.00
Shriner, Fez, 1976	7.00 to 9.00
Shriner, Golden Pharaoh, 1981	42.00
Shriner, Jester, 1972	10.00
Shriner, King Tut Tomb Guard, 1979	20.00
Shriner, Sphinx, 1980	12.00
Silver Dollar 1804, 1969	10.00
Silver Spur Boot, 1971	16.00
Ski Boot, 1972	*Illus* 10.00
Slot Machine, Liberty Bell, 1971	18.00 to 24.00
Snow Egret, 1980	28.00
Snowmobile, 1972	15.00
South Dakota Air National Guard, 1976	20.00
Spirit Of '76, Drummer, 1974	*Illus* 10.00
Spirit Of St. Louis, 1977	10.00 to 12.00
Stagecoach, 1969	13.00 to 20.00
Stonewall Jackson, 1974	25.00
Strongman, 1974	*Illus* 20.00
Sturgeon, 1975	25.00
Tank, Military, 1972	35.00
Tecumseh, 1969	10.00
Telephone, 1971	15.00
Tennis Player, 1973	*Illus* 20.00
Terrapin, Maryland, 1974	14.00
Texas Longhorn Steer, 1971	25.00
Ticker Tape, 1970	8.00
Tiger, Bengal, 1979	*Illus* 35.00
Tiger, On Stadium, 1973	16.00
Tonapah, 1972	15.00
Totem Pole, No. 1, 1972	20.00
Totem Pole, No. 2, 1973	17.00
Tractor, Fordson, 1971	20.00
Train, Casey Jones Locomotive, 1980	20.00
Train, Iron Horse Engine, 1969	9.00
Trojan, USC, 1973	22.00
Trojan Horse, 1974	20.00
Trout & Fly, 1970	14.00
Truckin' An' Vannin', 1976	11.00
Turkey, White, 1971	26.00 to 70.00
Vermont Skier, 1972	*Illus* 12.00
VFW, Blue, 75th Anniversary, 1973	12.00
VFW, Illinois, 1982	25.00

Ezra Brooks, Tiger, Bengal, 1979   Ezra Brooks, Vermont Skier, 1972

VFW, No. 2, White, 1975	6.00
Walgreen Mortar & Pestle, 1974	34.00
Weirton Steel, 1974	18.00
West Virginia Mountain Lady, 1972	23.00
West Virginia Mountain Man, 1970	60.00
Whale, 1973	20.00
Wheat Shocker, Kansas, 1971	15.00 to 20.00
Whooping Crane, 1982	17.50 to 25.00
Wichita Centennial, 1970	12.00
William Penn, 1981	65.00
Winston Churchill, 1969	6.00
Zimmerman's Hat, 1968	5.00 to 9.00

FAMOUS FIRSTS

Famous Firsts Ltd. of Port Chester, New York, was owned by Richard E. Magid. The first figural bottles, issued in 1968, were a series of race cars. The last figurals were made in 1985.

Animals, Mother & Baby, 1981, Miniature, 6 Piece	220.00
Balloon, 1971	34.00
Bell, Alpine, 1970	18.00
Bell, Liberty, 1976	8.00
Bell, St. Pol, 1970	22.00
Bennie Bow Wow, 1973	*Illus* 16.00
Bersaglieri, 1969	34.00
Bugatti Royale, 1930 Model, 1973	310.00
Butterfly, 1971	24.00
Cable Car, 1973	50.00
Centurian, 1969	40.00
China Clipper, 1979	130.00
Circus Lion, 1979	25.00

Famous Firsts, Dino Ferarri, White, 1975

Famous Firsts, Bennie Bow Wow, 1973

Famous Firsts, Yacht America, 1978

Circus Tiger, 1979	25.00
Coffee Mill, 1971	35.00
Corvette Stingray, 1963 Model, 1975	90.00
Corvette Stingray, 1963 Model, 1977	95.00
Dino Ferarri, Green, 1975	65.00
Dino Ferarri, Red, 1983	75.00
Dino Ferarri, White, 1975 ....*Illus*	35.00
Don Sympatico, 1973	18.00
Duesenberg, 1980	85.00
Duesenberg, 50th Anniversary, Red, 1982	250.00
Egg House, 1975	16.00
Fireman, 1980	85.00
Garibaldi, 1969	37.00
Golfer, He, 1973	32.00
Golfer, She, 1973	32.00
Hen, Filamena, 1973	22.00
Hippo, Baby, 1980	60.00
Honda Motorcycle, 1975	71.00
Hurdy Gurdy, 1971	20.00
Indy Racer, No. 11, 1971	78.00
Lockheed Transport, Jungle, 1982	63.00
Lockheed Transport, Marine Gray, 1982	81.00
Lockheed Transport, USAF Rescue, 1982	80.00
Locomotive, DeWitt, Clinton, 1969	30.00
Lotus, Racer, No. 2, 1971	120.00
Macaw	60.00
Marmon Wasp No. 32, Gold, 1/2 Pt., 1971	30.00
Minnie Meow, 1973	18.00
Mustang, P-51-D, Fighter Plane, 1974	110.00
Napoleon, 1969	22.00
National Racer, No. 8, 1972	55.00
Panda, Baby, 1981	86.00
Pepper Mill, 1978	20.00
Phonograph, 1969	48.00
Phonograph, 1969, Miniature	18.00
Porsche Targa, 1979	75.00
Renault Racer, No. 3, 1969	65.00
Riverboat, Natchez, Mail Packet, 1975	45.00
Riverboat, Robert E. Lee, 1971	60.00
Rooster, Ricardo, 1973	18.00
Roulette Wheel, 1972	40.00
Scale, Lombardy, 1970	30.00
Sewing Machine, 1979, 200 Milliliter	45.00
Ship, Sea Witch, 1976	70.00
Ship, Sea Witch, 1980, 200 Milliliter	25.00
Skier, He, 1973	18.00
Skier, Jack & Jill, 1975, Pair	20.00
Skier, She, 1973	18.00
Spirit Of St. Louis, 1969, Pt.	120.00
Spirit Of St. Louis, 1972, Miniature	62.00
Spirit Of St. Louis, Golden, 1977	90.00
Stamps, 1847, 1980	26.00
Swiss Chalet, 1974	32.00
Telephone, Floral, 1973	25.00
Telephone, French, 1973	63.00
Telephone, French, Blue, 1969	40.00
Telephone, French, White, 1973, Miniature	22.00
Telephone, Johnny Reb, 1973	30.00
Telephone, Yankee Doodle, 1973	30.00
Tennis, He, 1973	27.00
Tennis, She, 1973	27.00
Warriors, 1979, Miniature	23.00
Winnie Mae, Airplane, 1972	95.00

Winnie Mae, Airplane, 1972, Miniature	70.00
Yacht America, 1970, 24 In.	170.00
Yacht America, 1978 ....*Illus*	70.00

FIGURAL

Figural bottles are specially named by the collectors of bottles. Any bottle that is of a recognizable shape, such as a human head, a pretzel, or a clock, is considered to be a figural. There are no restrictions as to date or material. A *Soaky* is a special plastic bottle that holds shampoo, bubble bath, or another type of bath product. They were first made by Colgate-Palmolive in the late 1950s. Figurals are also listed by brand name or type in other sections of this book, such as the Bitters, Cologne, Perfume, Pottery, and Whiskey categories.

Angry Bulldog, Boer War Propaganda, Bisque, 6 In.	195.00
Atterbury Duck, Milk Glass, Sheared Ground Mouth, 1871-1885, 11 5/8 In.	560.00
Baby, Flapper Headband, Feather, Ceramic, Metal Crown Stopper, Brown Co., 3 1/3 In. . .	132.00
Baby Crying, P.S. & Co., N.Y., 6 In.	61.00
Banjo, Amethyst, 9 1/2 In. ....40.00 to 76.00	
Banjo, Emerald Green, 9 1/2 In.	78.00
Banjo, Emerald Green, Hanger, 9 1/2 In.	51.00
Banjo, Green, 9 1/2 In. ....27.00 to 71.00	
Barrel, Milk Glass, Tooled Lip, 1890-1910, 11 In.	303.00
Bear, Amber, Oil, C.F. Knapp, Philada., Contents, Label, 3 3/4 In.	95.00
Bear, Aqua, Applied Face, 1880-1915, 8 1/4 In.	392.00
Bear, Black Amber, Applied Face, 1880-1915, 10 7/8 In.	336.00
Bear, Black Amethyst, Applied Face, 1890, 11 1/4 In.	415.00
Bear, Black Glass, Applied Face, Tooled Lip, 11 1/8 In.	784.00
Bear, Blue Aqua, Applied Face, 1895, 10 1/2 In.	880.00
Bear, Blue Aqua, Applied Face, A.N.T. On Base, 1890, 8 1/8 In.	825.00
Bear, Blue Aqua, Applied Face, Tooled Lip, 1880-1895, 10 3/8 In.	358.00
Bear, Ice Blue, Applied Face, 1880-1915, 10 3/8 In.	343.00
Bear, Kummel, Dark Grape Amethyst, Tooled Lip, 1885-1895, 11 1/8 In.	110.00
Bear, Kummel, Dark Green, 11 In.	80.00
Bear, Kummel, Milk Glass, Applied Lip, 10 7/8 In.	123.00
Bear, Moss Green, Applied Face, Tooled Lip, 10 3/8 In.	532.00
Bear, Ointment Jar, Black, 1860, 3 3/4 In.	275.00
Bear, Olive Green, Applied Face, 1880-1915, 8 1/4 In.	1680.00
Bear, Olive Green, Applied Face, Tooled Lip, A.T. 1892 On Base, 9 7/8 In. ....*Illus*	812.00
Bear, Olive Green, Partial Label, Russia	100.00
Bear, Seated, Black Glass, Applied Face, Pontil, 1880-1900, 10 3/4 In.	440.00
Bear, Seated, Blue Aqua, Applied Face, 1880-1900, 10 1/4 In.	468.00
Bear, Seated, Chocolate Amber, Applied Face, Tooled Lip, 1900, 10 3/4 In.	440.00
Bear, Seated, Milk Glass, Applied Face, 1900, 10 1/4 In.	1210.00

Figural, Bear, Olive Green, Applied Face, Tooled Lip, A.T. 1892 On Base, 9 7/8 In.

Figural, Book, Coming Thru The Rye, Stoneware, Cobalt Blue Glaze, 1910, 5 In.

Figural, Frog, Olive Yellow, Gold Painted Warts, Depornirt, Germany, 1925, 4 5/8 In.

Bear, Seated, Moss Green, Applied Face, 1900, 10 3/8 In. . . . .　275.00
Bear, Seated, Olive Green, Applied Face, Tooled Mouth, 1890, 8 1/2 In. . . . .　165.00
Beehive, Clear, Embossed Bees Around Hive, 1890-1915, 6 1/2 In. . . . .　123.00
Bellboy, Baby, Holding Letter, Porcelain, Metal Crown Stopper, Goebel, 4 7/8 In. . . . .　440.00
Billiken, God Of Things As They Ought To Be, Milk Glass, 4 In. . . . . .123.00 to 200.00
Bird, With Wings & Tail Outstretched, Stopper, 8 In. . . . .　22.00
Book, Battle Of Bennington, Bennington Pottery, Brown, Mottled Glaze, 1880, 6 In. . . . .　130.00
Book, Battle Of Bennington, Pottery, Brown, Tan & Green Glaze, 1840-1880, 6 In. . . . . . .　132.00
Book, Brown & Green Glaze, Bennington, 7 3/4 x 5 3/4 In. . . . .　1668.00
Book, Coming Thru The Rye, Pottery, Cobalt Blue Glaze, 1870-1890, 5 In. . . . .　190.00
Book, Coming Thru The Rye, Stoneware, Cobalt Blue Glaze, 1910, 5 In. . . . .*Illus*　450.00
Book, Dark Brown Glaze, Bennington, 10 1/2 x 8 In. . . . .　2013.00
Book, Patersons De Luxe Scotch Whisky, Black & White Glaze, 8 1/4 In. . . . .　31.00
Boy, Naughty, Victorian, Wearing Blue Nightcap, Bisque, 7 In. . . . .　132.00
Broom, Light Blue, Tooled Lip, Pottery, 8 In. . . . .　88.00
Bulldog, Sitting, Frosted, Head Stopper, 1890-1910, 7 In. . . . .　165.00
Bunch Of Asparagus, Frosted, Tooled Lip, 1890-1915, 12 3/8 In. . . . .　99.00
Bust, Daniel Webster, Frosted, Pontil, 1880-1895, 9 3/8 In. . . . .　633.00
Bust, Gambeth, France, Pontil, 1890-1915, 11 1/8 In. . . . .　165.00
Bust, Garibaldi, Military Uniform, Clear, BIMAL, c.1890, 12 1/2 In. . . . .　60.00
Bust, George Washington, Green, OP, 10 In. . . . .　50.00
Bust, Joan Of Arc, Milk Glass, John Tavernier, France, 1910, 16 1/2 In. . . . .　275.00
Bust, La Tsar, Milk Glass, John Tavernier, France, 1914, 12 1/2 In. . . . .　330.00
Bust, La Tsarine, Milk Glass, John Tavernier, France, 1914, 13 In. . . . . .242.00 to 330.00
Bust, Man, Poincare, Milk Glass, Ground Lip, Tin Cap, 1900, 13 1/2 In. . . . .　825.00
Bust, Nude Woman, Generous Bosom, Ceramic, Painted, 3 3/8 In. . . . .　176.00
Bust, Washington, Amber, Kick-Up Base, 8 In. . . . .　30.00
Bust, Washington, Green, Ground Lip, Clevenger, Pt. . . . .　29.00
Cannon, Amber, Tooled Lip, Bubbles, 1870-1880, 9 5/8 In. . . . .　413.00
Cannon, J.T. Gayen Altona, Amber, Applied Lip, 1860-1870 . . . .　1650.00
Cannon, RS Inside Shield & Crossed Flags, No Stopper, France, 1915, 12 1/2 In. . . . .　357.00
Canteen, R.F. Wright, Silver Eagle Saloon, Terrell, Tex., Stoneware, Handle, 9 In. . . . . . .　1430.00
Cat, Sitting, Frosted, Depose, France, 1900-1920, 1 3/4 In. . . . .　253.00
Cherub Holding Clock, Topaz, Milk Glass, Flared Ruffle Mouth, 1900, 13 3/4 In. . . . .　231.00
Cherub Holding Post, Label, Puce, Pontil, 11 1/2 In. . . . .　100.00
Child, Tall Hat, Porcelain, Crown Screw Cap, Cork Stopper, 3 1/4 In. . . . .　82.00
Child In Rocker, Clear, Painted, Ground Lip, 1890-1910, 5 In. . . . .　99.00
Christmas Tree, Clear, Tooled Lip, Glass Star Stopper, 1890-1920, 13 3/4 In. . . . . .110.00 to 209.00
Cigar, Amber, Tooled Mouth, 5 1/2 In. . . . .　90.00
Cigar, Cuban, Amber, 5 1/4 In. . . . .　55.00
Cigars, Humidor, Light Gold Amber, Copper Body, 8 3/4 In. . . . .　72.00
Clam, Amber, Ground Lip, Original Metal Screw Cap, 5 1/4 In. . . . . .100.00 to 135.00
Clam, Blue Aqua, Ground Lip, Metal Screw Cap, 1890-1910, 4 3/4 In. . . . .　90.00
Clock, Clear, Stopper, D & D, Pontil, 1900, 16 1/4 In. . . . .　80.00
Clown, Brockway, Red Lid, 1940s, 3 Oz. . . . .　12.00
Clown, Pierrot, Pink Roses, Ceramic, Metal Crown Stopper, Germany, 3 7/8 In. . . . .　319.00
Coachman, Dark Brown & Cream Glaze, Bennington, 10 1/2 In. . . . .　863.00
Coachman, Figure Wrapped In Cloak, Holding Cup, Bennington, 1849, 10 1/2 In. . . . . . .　880.00
Coachman, Lyman Fenton & Co., Bennington Pottery, 1849, 10 In. . . . .　385.00
Coachman, Van Dunck's Genever, Ware & Schmitz, Amber, 8 5/8 In. . . . .　200.00
Coachman, Van Dunck's Genever, Ware & Schmitz, Orange Amber, 8 3/4 In. . . . .　83.00
Coal, Ground Lip, Metal Screw Cap, 3 In. . . . .　134.00
Cockatoo, Amethyst, 1890-1915, 13 3/8 In. . . . .　523.00
Columbus Monument, Milk Glass Base, Gold Paint, 18 1/4 In. . . . .　644.00
Domino, Frosted, Black Painted Dots, Continental, 1890-1915, 12 5/8 In. . . . .　253.00
Duck, Leather Covered, Red Glass Eyes, Italy, 12 x 6 1/2 In. . . . .　125.00
Dutch Girl, Singing, Blue Dress, Metal Crown Stopper, 3 In. . . . .　143.00
Ear Of Corn, Amber, Applied Collar, 9 1/2 In. . . . . .145.60 to 187.00
Ear Of Corn, Clear, Tooled Lip, 1880-1890, 10 5/8 In. . . . .　61.00
Ear Of Corn, Dark Amber, Applied Collar, 9 1/2 In. . . . .　88.00
Ear Of Corn, Green Carnival Glass, Ground & Polished Lip, 1900-1920, 5 In. . . . .　645.00
Ear Of Corn, Marigold Carnival Glass, 4 3/4 In. . . . .　336.00
Ear Of Corn, Purple Carnival Glass, 4 3/4 In. . . . . .448.00 to 644.00

Egyptian Woman, Clear, Flared Lip, 6 In. 420.00
Eiffel Tower, Clear, Early 20th Century, 13 1/2 In. 110.00
Elephant, Amber, 10 1/2 In. 29.00
Elephant, Trunk Up, Federal Law Forbids Sale Or Reuse Of This Bottle, 1935, 8 1/4 In. . 83.00
Father's Baby Bottle, French Armagnac Brandy, Milk Glass, 11 1/2 In. 99.00
French Sailor, Standing On Dock, Dana Canoe, Ceramic, 17 Oz., 15 In. 77.00
Frog, Olive Yellow, Gold Painted Warts, Depornirt, Germany, 1925, 4 5/8 In. ....*Illus* 175.00
Girl Riding Bicycle, Tooled Lip, 1890-1915, 4 1/4 In. 550.00
Golfer, Jolly, Deep Cobalt Blue, Frosted, Pat. Appld For, 11 1/2 In. 504.00
Grant's Tomb, Milk Glass Base, Ground Lip, 10 In. 980.00
Ham, Amber, Ground Lip, Metal Screw Cap, 6 In. 67.00
Hand Holding Bottle, Peacock Blue, Stopper, BIMAL, Pontil, 7 1/2 In. 60.00
Hand Holding Dagger, Turquoise, Depose, Pontil, 1910, 11 1/2 In. 3410.00
Heart, John Hart & Co., Amber, Applied Double Collar Mouth, 1880, 6 7/8 In. 812.00
Helmet, Helmet Rye, Brown Glaze, Spike On Top, Pottery, Nip, 2 5/8 In. 34.00
Helmet With Plume, Haselhorst Dresden, Embossed Star Inside, Germany, 3 3/8 In. 198.00
Hessian Soldier, 7 1/4 In. 20.00
Hot Air Balloon, Ballon Captif 1878, Depose, Tooled Mouth, France, 9 In. 505.00
Indian Queen, see Bitters, Brown's Celebrated
Japanese Mikado, Primicerio & Co., Baltimore, Md., Medium Amber, 6 1/2 In. .....*Illus* 235.00
Jester, Clear, Tooled Lip, 1890-1910, 6 7/8 In. 75.00
Joan Of Arc, Crusader Uniform, Pontil, 13 5/8 In. 70.00
Johnnie Walker, Clear, Painted, 11 In. 45.00
Kewpie, Sitting, Hands On Legs, Ceramic, Metal Crown Stopper, Germany, 3 In. 231.00
Liberty Bell, Proclaim Liberty, Chocolate Amber, 20th Century, 3 3/4 In. 66.00
Loaf Of Bread, Amber, Sheared Mouth, 7 In. 209.00
Locomotive, Machined Mouth, 1900-1920, 11 1/2 In. 231.00
Mail Box, U.S. Eagle, Mail Patented Dec. 15, 1891, Partial Label, 7 In. 50.00
Man In Robe, Here's The Poison That I've Taken For Years, Germany, 8 7/8 In. 357.00
Man Sitting On Stump, With Cane & Dog, Emerald Green, Tooled Top, 6 In. 187.00
Monk, Clear, Original Aluminum Cap Closure, 1900-1930, 3 In. 123.00
Monkey, Sitting On A Barrel, Pulling Hat Down Over Ears, Milk Glass, 9 In. 1568.00
Moses, Poland Water, Painted, Green, Black, Brown, Pink, White, 1890, 11 3/8 In. 121.00
Moses In Bulrushes, Tooled Lip, 1890-1910, 4 3/4 In. 95.00
Napoleon, Clear Hat Stopper, France, 1911, 10 3/4 In. 2530.00
Negro Waiter, Clear, Painted, Ground Lip, 1885-1915, 14 3/8 In. ....*Illus* 196.00
Old Quaker Wheat Man, Embossed, Screw Cap, 7 1/2 In. 30.00
Owl, Standing, Metal Crown Lip, Germany, 3 In. 330.00
Penis, Amber, Applied Ring, Testicles, Ceramic Stopper, Josef Jung, 12 3/4 In. 880.00
Pig, Beiser & Fisher, N.Y., Gold Amber, 9 5/8 In. 1092.00
Pig, Corn Cob In Mouth, Tooled Lip, 1890-1910, 6 1/4 In. 522.00
Pig, Drink While It Lasts, From This Hog's, Tooled Lip, 6 5/8 In. 128.80
Pig, Duffy Crescent Saloon, 204 Jefferson, Louisville, Ky., Amber, 7 In. 1176.00
Pig, Duffy Crescent, Rooster On Crescent Moon, Aqua, Sheared Mouth, 7 5/8 In. 2240.00
Pig, Good Old Bourbon In A Hog's..., Amber, Tooled Mouth, 6 7/8 In. ....150.00 to 308.00
Pig, Kiss Me For My Mother, Dark Brown Glaze, Stoneware, 1900-1920, 5 5/8 In. 896.00

Figural, Japanese Mikado,
Primicerio & Co.,
Baltimore, Md., Medium
Amber, 6 1/2 In.

Figural, Negro Waiter,
Clear, Painted,
Ground Lip,
1885-1915, 14 3/8 In.

Figural, Statue Of
Liberty, Milk Glass,
Cast Metal, Sheared
Ground Lip, 15 1/2 In.

Pig, Sitting, Depose, Embossed, Ground Lip, Original Tin Lid, 7 In. 145.00
Pig, Something Good In A Hog's..., He Won't Squeal, Clear, 4 1/2 In. . . . . .123.00 to 129.00
Pineapple, J.F.L. Capitol, Amber Red Iron Pontil, 1865-1875, 9 1/4 In. 2016.00
Pointing Hand, W. Zeige & Sohn Berlin, Olive Yellow, Germany, 10 3/4 In. 94.00
Policeman, Amber To Yellow Arms, Continental, 1915, 9 1/8 In. 185.00
Policeman, Cobalt Blue, Contents, Labels, France, 15 In. 295.00
Policeman, Milk Glass, Gold Paint Traces, Pontil, 1910, 9 1/2 In. 155.00
Poodle, Hind Legs In Begging Position Sitting On Drum, 20th Century, 13 In. 110.00
Portly Man, Applied Mirror On Stomach, 1890-1915, 7 1/8 In. 72.00
Pretzel, Embossed, Salt Flecks, Patent 1908, 5 1/2 In. 380.00
Pretzel, Pat. Appl'd For 1908, N.Y., Pottery, 5 5/8 In. 75.00
Rabbit, Standing, Basket Of Eggs, Milk Glass, 1880-1910, Ground Lip, 8 1/8 In. 4144.00
Radio Bank, Cobalt Blue, Embossed Dials & Numbers, 1940-1960, 3 In. 175.00
Revolver, C.P.P. Co. Pat-D App For, Amber, Ground Lip, 8 1/4 In. 56.00
Revolver, Screw Cap, 8 In. 132.00
Revolver, Yellow Amber, Ground Lip, Metal Screw Cap, 9 5/8 In. 80.00
Roast Turkey, Amber, Ground Lip, Metal Screw Cap, 4 3/4 In. 95.00
Sailor & Chinese Man, On Tower, Ground Stopper, Depose, 12 1/2 In. 196.00
Sandeman, Prince Of Wales, July 1969, Ceramic, Wedgwood, 10 1/2 In. 28.00
Santa Claus, Clear, Painted, Plastic Base, 1940s, 4 1/2 In. 11.00
Santa Claus, Clear, Painted, Tooled Mouth, 1910, 7 1/2 In. . . . . .145.00 to 305.00
Santa Claus, Santa Picture Label, 1915, 12 1/4 In. 65.00
Santa Claus, Tooled Lip, 5 1/2 In. 130.00
Shoe, Wales Goodyear, Ground Lip, 1900-1915, 2 1/8 In. 121.00
Skeleton, Sitting On Barrel, Ceramic, Germany, 1920, 13 In. 231.00
Soaky, Creature From The Black Lagoon 135.00
Soaky, Dopey, From Snow White 18.00
Soaky, Felix The Cat 80.00
Soaky, Frankenstein 98.00
Soaky, Huckleberry Hound, 1960s 25.00
Soaky, Magilla Gorilla, 1960s 75.00
Soaky, Morocco Mole, 1966 . . . . 75.00
Soaky, Mummy, 1960s 90.00
Soaky, Secret Squirrel, 1960s 50.00
Soaky, Wolfman, Blue Pants, 1960s . . . . .40.00 to 95.00
Soaky, Yogi Bear, 1960s 25.00
Southern Belle, Manhattan Cal. Muscatel Wine, Licor Angelical, 1930s, 4 In., Pair 45.00
Statue Of Liberty, Milk Glass, Cast Metal, Sheared Ground Lip, 15 1/2 In. . . . .*Illus* 560.00
Strawberry, Frosted Ruby, Ground Lip, 20th Century, 6 In. 504.00
Tower, Mark Duffy's, Amber, Tapered Shape, Embossed Tower On 2 Sides, 9 In. 812.00
Uncle Sam, Blue, 15 In. 95.00
Victorian Bust, Clear, Tooled Lip, 1900, 11 1/2 In. 75.00
Violin, Amber, Clevenger, 9 1/2 In. . . . . .77.00 to 80.00
Violin, Amber, George West, 1892, 6 3/8 In. . . . . .113.00 to 160.00
Violin, Amberina, Clevenger, 9 1/2 In. 605.00
Violin, Amethyst, Hanger, Music Notes, 9 1/2 In. . . . . .30.00 to 45.00
Violin, Aqua, Pontil, 9 1/2 In. . . . . .26.00 to 45.00
Violin, Blue, Hanger, Clevenger, 9 1/2 In. 71.00
Violin, Blue, Musical Notes, Made In Japan, 9 1/2 In. 89.00
Violin, Clear, Garnier, 14 In. 60.00
Violin, Cobalt, Clevenger, 9 1/2 In. . . . . .90.00 to 100.00
Violin, Emerald Green, Clevenger, 9 1/2 In. . . . . .37.00 to 50.00
Violin, Green, Dark Green Striations, Clevenger, 9 1/2 In. 81.00
Violin, Green, Leaf Hanger, 7 1/2 In. 67.00
Violin, Light Blue, 7 1/2 In. 51.00
Violin, Light Blue, 9 1/2 In. . . . . .31.00 to 51.00
Violin, Light Blue, Leaf Hanger, 9 1/2 In. 97.00
Violin, Olive Green, 9 1/2 In. 270.00
Violin, Teal Green, Blue Swirls, Clevenger, 9 1/2 In. 236.00
Water Bird, Clear, 1890-1920, 12 3/4 In. 112.00
Whisk Broom, 6 In. 65.00
Whisk Broom, Bisque, Original Red, Silver, Yellow Paint, 1890-1915, 7 In. 145.00
Woman, 18th Century-Style Dress, Fan, Ceramic, Metal Crown Stopper, Goebel, 5 In. . . . 198.00

Woman, Standing, Praying, Green Aqua, Tooled Mouth, Pontil, 1920, 6 1/2 In. 50.00
Woman Holding Dog, Suffragette, Clear, Ground Lip, Metal Screw Cap, 6 In. 784.00
Woman With Muff, Tooled Mouth, 1890-1910, 6 3/8 In. 80.00
Woman's Leg, Gilt Glass, Mercury Glass Stopper, Germany, 3 1/8 In. 253.00
Woman's Torso, Clear, Original Metal Screw Cap, 6 1/2 In. 44.80

FIRE GRENADE

Fire grenades were popular from about 1870 to 1910. They were glass containers filled with a fire extinguisher such as carbon tetrachloride. The bottle of liquid was thrown at the base of a fire to shatter and extinguish the flames. A particularly ingenious *automatic* type was hung in a wire rack; theoretically, the heat of the fire would melt the solder of the rack and the glass grenade would drop into the fire. Because they were designed to be broken, not too many have survived for the collector. Some are found today that still have the original contents sealed by cork and wax closures. Handle these with care. Fumes from the contents are dangerous to your health.

1001, Cobalt Blue, Diamond Center Pattern, England, 1880-1900, 7 1/4 In. 360.00
Autofyrstop, Camphor Glass, Paper Labels, Philadelphia, Ball Mount, 11 In. 132.00
California Fire Extinguisher, Amber, Walking Bear, Drippy Top, 6 1/4 In. 4100.00
Cobalt Blue, Middle Ridge, Original Contents, 6 1/2 In. 358.00
Diamond, Pale Aqua, Sunken Diamond Panels, 1880-1900, 7 1/4 In. 1568.00
Grenade Extinctrice, Clear, Ground Lip, 1880-1900, Pt., 5/12 In. 560.00
Hanging, Medium Honey Amber, 2 3/8 x 11 In. 12.00
Harden's Hand, Aqua Blue, Footed, Contents 138.00
Harden's Hand, Blue, Fire Extinguisher, Pat No. 1, Aug 8 1871, Footed, 6 1/8 In. 56.00
Harden's Hand, Fire Extinguisher, Turquoise Blue, Ground Lip, 8 In. 151.00
Harden's Hand, Fire Extinguisher, Turquoise Blue, Ground Lip, Pt., 6 3/4 In. 112.00
Harden's Hand, Star, Fire Extinguisher, Turquoise Blue, Ribs, 6 5/8 In. . . . . 105.00 to 121.00
Harden's Improved Hand Grenade, Cobalt Blue, Tooled Mouth, Pt., 6 1/2 In. 1792.00
Hayward's, Cobalt Blue 220.00
Hayward's Hand, Amber, Pat Aug 8 1871, Tooled Mouth, 1895, 6 1/4 In. 231.00
Hayward's Hand, Blue, Pat Aug 8 1871, Embossed 4, Paneled, 6 1/4 In. 258.00
Hayward's Hand, Cobalt Blue, Tooled Lip, No. 407 Broadway, N.Y., Contents, 6 In. 269.00
Hayward's Hand, Gold Yellow Amber, Pat Aug 8 1871, Pt. 253.00
Hayward's Hand, Orange Amber, Red Foil Seal, Contents, 6 In. 952.00
Hayward's Hand, Pat Aug 8 1871, Aqua, Lip Ring, Embossed 3, 5 1/4 In. 168.00
Hayward's Hand, Pat Aug 8 1871, Clear, Diamond Panels, Tooled Mouth, 6 1/4 In. 179.00
Hayward's Hand, Pat Aug 8 1871, Orange Amber, Foil Seal, Contents, 6 1/8 In. 364.00
Hayward's Hand, Pat Aug 8 1871, Yellow Amber, Diamond Form, Contents, 6 In. 392.00
Hayward's Hand, Smoky Sapphire Blue, Diamond Panels, Pt., 6 In. 392.00
Hazelton's High Pressure Chemical Fire-Keg, Amber . . . . *Illus*   350.00
Healy's Hand Fire Extinguisher, Olive Yellow, Tooled Mouth, Qt., 11 In. 1176.00
HNS, Yellow Amber, Sheared & Ground Lip, 1880-1900, 7 1/4 In. 179.00
Horizontal Rib, Cobalt Blue, Embossed, Oval Panel, Label, 1870-1890, 6 In. 616.00
Little Giant Fire Extinguisher, Aqua, Tooled Mouth, Pt., 6 1/2 In. 2184.00
Magic Fire Extinguisher, Gold Yellow Amber, Sheared Lip, Pt., 6 1/4 In. 700.00
Star, Blue 99.00

Fire Grenade, Systeme Labbe,
Paris, Yellow Orange Amber,
1885-1895, 5 3/4 In.

Fire Grenade, Hazelton's
High Pressure Chemical
Fire-Keg, Amber

Systeme Labbe, Diamond Pattern, Yellow Amber, Contents, 1900, 5 3/4 In. 385.00
Systeme Labbe, Extincteur L'Incombustibilite, Paris, Yellow Amber, 5 7/8 In. 467.00
Systeme Labbe, L'Incombustibilite, Paris, Straw Yellow, Orange, 1900, 5 3/4 In. 224.00
Systeme Labbe, L'Incombustibilite, Paris, Topaz, 1880-1890, Pt., 5 3/4 In. 358.00
Systeme Labbe, Paris, Yellow Orange Amber, 1885-1895, 5 3/4 In. . . . .*Illus*   364.00
Unix Extinctrice, Orange Amber, 3 Circular Panels, Contents, 5 1/2 In. 235.00
Unix Extinctrice, Yellow, 1880-1900, France, 5 5/8 In. 359.00
V. Fournier & Cie, 8 Rue Des Prairies, Paris, Ice Blue, 1880-1900, Pt. 1680.00
Vertical Rib Pattern, Orange Amber, Ground Lip, France, 1880-1900, 5 1/4 In. 633.00
FITZGERALD, see Old Fitzgerald

────────────────── **FLASK** ──────────────────

Flasks have been made in America since the eighteenth century. Hundreds of styles and variations were made. Free-blown, mold-blown, and decorated flasks are all popular with collectors. Prices are determined by rarity, condition, and color. In general, bright colors bring higher prices. The numbers used in the entries in the form McK G I-000 refer to the book *American Bottles and Flasks* by Helen McKearin and Kenneth M. Wilson. Each flask listed in that book is sketched and described and it is important to compare your flask with the book picture to determine value, since many similar flasks were made.

Many reproductions of flasks have been made, most in the last 25 years, but some as early as the nineteenth century. The reproduction flasks that seem to cause the most confusion for the beginner are the Lestoil flasks made in the 1960s. These bottles, sold in grocery stores, were filled with Lestoil, a liquid cleaner, and sold for about 65 cents. Three designs were made: a Washington Eagle, a Columbia Eagle, and a ship Franklin Eagle. Four colors were used—purple, dark blue, dark green, and amber—and mixes were also produced. Over one million of the flasks were made and they now are seen at the collectible shows. The only mark on the bottles was the name Lestoil on the stopper. Other reproductions that are often found are marked *Nuline* or *Taiwan*. A picture dictionary of flask shapes can be found in the front of this book.

10 Diamond, Medium Amber, Midwest, Pontil, 1920-1830, 5 1/4 In. 798.00
10 Diamond, Olive Yellow, Tooled Lip, Pontil, 1820-1835, 5 1/8 In. 413.00
12 Ribs, Yellow Green, Globular, Midwest, 1835, 9 In. 365.00
15 Diamond, Blue Aqua, Inward Rolled Mouth, Midwest, Pontil, 4 3/4 In. 187.00
16 Broken Ribs, Swirled To Right, Blue Aqua, Midwest, 1825-1835, 8 1/4 In. 125.00
16 Diamond, Emerald Green, Midwest, 1820-1835, 7 5/8 In. 616.00
16 Ribs, Medium Pink Amethyst, 1810-1860, 6 3/4 In. 308.00
16 Ribs, Swirled To Right, Teardrop Shape, Cobalt Blue, Pontil, 1815-1835, 6 1/2 In. 358.00
16 Ribs, Vertical, Aqua, Mantua, Ohio, 5 1/8 In. 138.00
16 Ribs, Vertical, Pale To Medium Citron, Pontil, 1820-1840, 6 In. 467.00
16 Ribs, Vertical, Teardrop, Gold Amber, Rolled Mouth, Pontil, 6 7/8 In. 784.00
18 Ribs, Teardrop, Swirled To Right, Amethyst, Tooled Lip, Pontil, 7 1/8 In. 168.00
20 Ribs, Yellow Green, Midwest, Pontil, 1800-1830, 6 1/4 In. 385.00
21 Ribs, Vertical, Blown, Amber, Flattened Oval, Bubbles, OP, 7 In. . . . . .375.00 to 975.00
24 Broken Ribs, Swirled To Right, Blue Aqua, 1820-1835, Pontil, 8 1/2 In. 121.00
24 Ribs, Blue Aqua, Midwest, 1820-1835, 7 5/8 In. 210.00
24 Ribs, Swirled To Left, Globular, Blue Aqua, Pontil, 1820-1835, 7 7/8 In. 190.00
24 Ribs, Swirled To Left, Globular, Medium Orange Amber, 1820-1835, 8 1/2 In. 525.00
24 Ribs, Swirled To Left, Globular, Orange Amber, Rolled Lip, Pontil, 8 1/4 In. 896.00
24 Ribs, Swirled To Left, Globular, Yellow Amber, Pontil, Rolled Lip, 1820-1835, 8 In. . .   525.00
24 Ribs, Swirled To Left, Gold Amber, Midwest, 1820-1840, 4 7/8 In. 330.00
24 Ribs, Swirled To Right, Cobalt Blue, Pontil, 1780-1830, 7 1/4 In. 303.00
24 Ribs, Swirled To Right, Globular, Gold Amber, Midwest, Pontil, 7 1/2 In. 715.00
24 Ribs, Vertical, Aqua, Handles, c.1830, Pocket, 5 5/8 In. 523.00
24 Ribs, Vertical, Globular, Aqua, Midwest, Pontil, 7 1/2 In. 165.00
24 Ribs, Vertical, Globular, Olive Yellow, Pontil, Rolled Lip, 1820-1835, 8 In. 3410.00
24 Ribs, Vertical, Gold Amber, Midwest, Pontil, 1820-1840, 4 3/4 In. 275.00
24 Ribs, Vertical, Orange Amber, Sheared Mouth, Midwest, Pontil, 1820-1840, 4 3/4 In. .   264.00
24 Ribs, Yellow Amber, Globular, Midwest, 1820-1835, 7 In. 3080.00
25 Ribs, Swirled To Right, Yellow Olive, Globular, Midwest, 1820-1835, 8 5/8 In. 1570.00
32 Broken Ribs, Vertical, Swirled Left, Blown, Green, Horseshoe Shape, 7 In. 900.00
A Wee Bit Of Scotch, Pottery, Pocket 39.00

Adolph Harris & Co., Amber, ISP, Pewter Cap, 1/2 Pt. 30.00
Amethyst, Flattened Globular, Pontil, 1763-1774, 6 In. 1045.00
Andy Balich, Pumpkinseed, 170 Pacific Ave., Santa Cruz, Cal., 1/2 Pt. 30.00
Arlington, Barkersfield, Cal., Pumpkinseed, Amber, Seeds, 1/2 Pt. 1210.00
Bell Of Lexington, Woodford Distilling Co., Gold Amber, Glass Stopper, 1/2 Pt. 9.00
Blown, Pewter Screw Top, Shot Cup, Wicker Cover, England, 1880, 3 x 6 In. 155.00
Brown-Forman Co., Diamond Shape, Sandy Brown, 1/2 Pt. 6.00
C.A. Richards & Co., Blue Aqua, Applied Collar, Pt. 77.00
C.E. Crowley Wine Merchant, St. Butte, Mont., Ribbed Base, Bubbles, Pt. 660.00
Chestnut, 16 Broken Ribs, Medium Pink Amethyst, Early 20th Century, 5 5/8 In. 420.00
Chestnut, 16 Broken Ribs, Swirled To Left, Cobalt Blue, OP, 6 1/4 In. 825.00
Chestnut, 16 Ribs, Aqua, Mantua, Ohio, 5 1/8 In. 3578.00
Chestnut, 16 Ribs, Vertical, Light Green, 5 3/4 In. 275.00
Chestnut, 16 Ribs, Violet Blue, 4 1/2 In. 495.00
Chestnut, 18 Ribs, Swirled To Left, Cobalt Blue, 3 In. 412.00
Chestnut, 20 Broken Ribs, Swirled To Left, Olive Yellow, Midwest, Pontil, 7 In. 5500.00
Chestnut, 20 Ribs, Midwest, 1820-1835, 6 3/8 In. 420.00
Chestnut, 20 Ribs, Swirled To Left, Midwest, 1820-1835, 7 1/4 In. 1344.00
Chestnut, 23 Ribs, Amber, Sheared Mouth, OP, 4 3/4 In. 303.00
Chestnut, 24 Broken Ribs, Medium Amber, 1820-1835, 4 5/8 In. 728.00
Chestnut, 24 Broken Ribs, Medium Amber, 1820-1835, 8 In. 2688.00
Chestnut, 24 Ribs, Cobalt Blue, 1825-1845, 7 1/4 In. 476.00
Chestnut, 24 Ribs, Gold Yellow, Pontil, 5 3/8 In. 633.00
Chestnut, 24 Ribs, Lime Green, Tooled Lip, Pontil, 5 In. 308.00
Chestnut, 24 Ribs, Medium Gold Amber, 1820-1835, 5 3/4 In. 420.00
Chestnut, 24 Ribs, Medium Orange Amber, Pontil, 1820-1835, 5 In. 303.00
Chestnut, 24 Ribs, Red Amber, 1820-1835, 5 1/4 In. 212.00
Chestnut, 24 Ribs, Red Amber, 1820-1835, 8 In. 1400.00
Chestnut, 24 Ribs, Red Amber, Midwest, Pontil, 1820-1830, 6 1/2 In. 264.00
Chestnut, 24 Ribs, Swirled To Left, Amber, Midwest, Pocket 209.00
Chestnut, Amber, Applied Handle & Lip, OP, 8 1/2 In. 77.00
Chestnut, Amber, Applied Handle, Band, Bubbles, OP, 7 3/4 In.   77.00
Chestnut, Amber, Applied Handle, OP, 8 In. 210.00
Chestnut, Amber, Sheared Mouth, OP, 1/2 Pt. 143.00
Chestnut, Blue Green, Flattened, Continental, Pontil, 1740-1770, 4 In. 523.00
Chestnut, Chocolate Amber, Outward Rolled Mouth, Pontil, 1780-1810, 10 1/2 In. 357.00
Chestnut, Emerald Green, Flattened, Applied Lip, Pontil, 1780-1810, 7 3/4 In. 413.00
Chestnut, Emerald Green, Flattened, Applied Lip, Pontil, Bubbles, 8 1/4 In. 420.00
Chestnut, Forest Green, Applied Lip, Pontil, 8 1/2 In. . . . . .336.00 to 532.00
Chestnut, Forest Green, Pontil, 1780-1830, 5 7/8 In. 495.00
Chestnut, Gold Amber, Applied Handle, Collar, OP, 7 1/2 In. 154.00
Chestnut, Grape Amethyst, Applied Lip, Handle, IP, 8 1/2 In. 269.00
Chestnut, Green Aqua, Ring Pontil Base, 19th Century, 3 1/4 In. 150.00
Chestnut, Light Olive Yellow, Applied Lip, Pontil, 1830, 5 In. 468.00
Chestnut, Light To Medium Olive Green, Applied Lip, Bubbles, Pontil, 1780-1810, 7 In. . .   357.00
Chestnut, Light To Medium Olive Yellow Green, Applied Lip, Pontil, 1810, 8 1/8 In. 231.00
Chestnut, Medium Emerald Green, Tooled Lip, Pontil, 5 1/8 In.   112.00
Chestnut, Medium Green, Applied Lip, Pontil, 5 1/2 In. 392.00
Chestnut, Medium Olive Yellow, Applied Lip, Pontil, 1780-1820, 10 3/4 In. . . . . .413.00 to 500.00
Chestnut, Moss Green, Applied Lip, Pontil, 1780-1810, 5 1/4 In. 963.00
Chestnut, Olive Amber, 8 1/4 In. 220.00
Chestnut, Olive Amber, Applied Lip, Pontil, 6 5/8 In. 420.00
Chestnut, Olive Green, Applied Lip, Pontil, 1780-1810, 5 1/2 In. 1276.00
Chestnut, Olive Green, Applied Lip, Pontil, 1780-1810, 7 In. 357.00
Chestnut, Olive Green, Applied Lip, Pontil, 7 7/8 In. 168.00
Chestnut, Olive Green, Applied Lip, Swirled Bubbles, 1810, 5 1/2 In. 231.00
Chestnut, Olive Green, Applied Mouth, Pontil Scar, 1780-1830, 6 7/8 In. 330.00
Chestnut, Olive Green, Bubbles, Swirls, Pontil, 1780-1810, 10 In. 357.00
Chestnut, Olive Green, Rolled Lip, Pontil, 1780-1810, 5 3/8 In.   264.00
Chestnut, Olive Yellow, Applied Collar, Pontil, Partial Label, 11 1/2 In. 952.00
Chestnut, Olive Yellow, Applied Lip, 1780-1810, Pontil, 7 In. 357.00
Chestnut, Olive Yellow, Applied Lip, Pontil, 1780-1810, 6 3/8 In. 143.00
Chestnut, Olive Yellow, Applied Lip, Pontil, 1780-1810, 8 3/4 In. 330.00

Chestnut, Olive Yellow, Applied Lip, Pontil, 6 3/4 In. 336.00
Chestnut, Olive Yellow, Enamel Tree, Applied Mouth, Pontil, 1780-1830, 5 1/4 In. 303.00
Chestnut, Olive Yellow, Pontil, 1780-1830, 6 5/8 In. 275.00
Chestnut, Olive Yellow, Pontil, 1780-1830, 9 1/2 In. 413.00
Chestnut, Olive Yellow, Pontil, Rolled Mouth, 5 1/8 In. 303.00
Chestnut, Olive Yellow, Sheared Mouth, Tooled Lip, Pontil, 1780-1810, 5 3/4 In. 231.00
Chestnut, Orange Amber, Collared Mouth, Pontil, 1800-1830, 11 In. 330.00
Chestnut, Orange Amber, Midwest, Pontil, 11 In. 330.00
Chestnut, Yellow Amber, Applied Lip, Handle, 1855-1870, 9 In. 89.00
Clear, Painted, Yellow, Red, White, Green, Blue, Turkish Man Drinking, Pontil, 5 1/4 In. . 143.00
Cleveland & Stevenson, Our Choice, Rooster, Half Barrel, Amber, 1/2 Pt. 785.00
Coffin, Orange Amber, Inward Rolled Mouth, Applied Lip, Qt. 60.00
Coffin, Sheared Mouth, Pontil, Pt. 55.00
Commemorative, Military, Clear, Silvered, Screw Cap, Eagle Finial, Germany, 8 1/4 In. . 235.00
Dancing Lion, Bunch Of Grapes, Cobalt Blue, Sheared Mouth, Pontil, 1/2 Pt. 193.00
Dismounted Horseman, On Each Side, Scalloped Neck, Rockingham Glaze, 7 1/4 In. . . . 385.00
Eagle, Morning Glory, Pottery, Tan, Brown Mottled Glaze, Rockingham, 7 1/8 In. .192.00 to 440.00
Embossed Cigars, Amber, Waist Band, Metal Lid, 1/2 Pt. 150.00
F.J. Corbett, San Mateo, Pumpkinseed, 1/2 Pt. 60.00
F.W. Elder, Blairstown, N.J., Medium Golden Amber, Tooled Lip, Pt. 146.00
Fleckenstein & Mayer, Portland, Ore., Amber, Applied Top, Qt. 715.00
G.W. Cheslsey Importer, Sacramento, Cal., Pumpkinseed, Pt. 88.00
Hallahan & MacCallum, Anaconda, Mont., Tooled Lip, 1/2 Pt. 600.00
Henry Chapman & Co., Montreal, Bright Straw Yellow, 5 3/4 In. 1018.00
Henry Chapman & Co., Montreal, Teardrop, Amber, BIMAL, 6 In. 230.00
Henry Chapman & Co., Montreal, Teardrop, Straw Yellow, 6 In. 1020.00
Henry Chapman & Co., Sole Agents, Montreal, Dark Amber, Tooled Lip, 6 In. 121.00
Henry Chapman & Co., Sole Agents, Montreal, Yellow Amber, 1875-1885, 5 7/8 In. 168.00
Honeycomb, Ribs, Aqua, Pontil, 1770-1830, 5 1/8 In. 275.00
Honeycomb, Vertical Ribs, Pink Puce, Flattened, Pontil, 6 1/4 In. 715.00
Honeycomb Diaper, 14 Cells, Light Yellow Green, Oval, 7 7/8 In. 475.00
Horse Pulling Cart & Eagle, Olive Yellow Amber, Sheared Mouth, Pt. 310.00
Hunter & Hound, Cobalt Blue, Continental, Pontil, 1850-1875, Pt. 176.00
I Got My Fill At Jakes, But Where Did I Eat That Dog, Pumpkinseed, Pt. 440.00
J. DeBruin Kimberley, Hand Shape, Pottery, Germany 120.00
J.H. Cutter, Old Bourbon, Hotaling & Co., Shoofly, Amber, Tooled Lip 750.00
J.J. McCaffrey & Son, 634 State St., Santa Barbara, Amber, Screw Top, 1/2 Pt. 66.00
James Dixon & Sons, Sapphire Blue, Unembossed, Pewter Neck Band & Cap, 1/2 Pt. . . . 495.00
Jas. Tharp's Sons, Washington, D.C., Amber, Strap Side, 1/2 Pt. 50.00
Jim Crow, Salt Glaze 134.40
John Coyne, Fayette & Seneca Sts., Utica, N.Y., Lime Green, Strap Sides, 7 1/2 In. 375.00
John De Kuyper & Co., Rotterdam, Coffin, Medium Olive Green, 1890-1900, 1/2 Pt. 95.00
Johnson & Burke Turf Exchange, Anaconda, Mont., 1/2 Pt. 467.00
La Grange Dispensery, La Grange, Ga., Honest Measure, Amethyst, Qt. 60.00
Label Under Glass, Clear, Woman, Multicolored Picture, Pink Ground, 7 In. 605.00
Lilienthal & Co Distillers, Amber, Applied Lip, Pt. 275.00
Lilienthal & Co Distillers, Amber, Tooled Lip, Banded, 1/2 Pt. 220.00
Lion & Grapes, Purple Blue, Germany, 1850-1870, 1/2 Pt. 308.00
McK G I-1, Washington & Eagle, Blue Green, Pontil, 1820-1840, Pt. 770.00
McK G I-1, Washington & Eagle, Light Blue Green, OP, Pt. 570.00
McK G I-2, Washington & Eagle, Aqua, Sheared Mouth, Pontil, Pt. . . . . .123.00 to 220.00
McK G I-2, Washington & Eagle, Tooled Mouth, Green Aqua, Pt. 145.60
McK G I-2, Washington & Eagle, Yellow Green, Sheared Mouth, Pontil, Pt. 413.00
McK G I-3, Washington & Eagle, Aqua, Sheared Mouth, Pontil, 1820-1840, Pt. 154.00
McK G I-3, Washington & Eagle, Green Aqua, Sheared Mouth, Pontil 650.00
McK G I-4, Washington & Eagle, Aqua, Sheared Mouth, Pontil, 1820-1840, Pt. 825.00
McK G I-5, Washington & Eagle, Green Aqua, Pontil, 1820-1840, Pt. 4630.00
McK G I-6, Washington & Eagle, Aqua, Sheared Mouth, Pontil, 1820-1840, Pt. 154.00
McK G I-7, Washington & Eagle, Aqua, Pontil, Pt. 660.00
McK G I-7, Washington & Eagle, Green Aqua, Pontil, 1820-1840, Pt. 121.00
McK G I-9, Washington & Eagle, Yellow Green, Pontil, 1820-1840, Pt. 275.00
McK G I-10, Washington & Eagle, Green Aqua, Pontil, 1820-1840, Pt. . . . . .176.00 to 303.00
McK G I-11, Washington & Eagle, Aqua, Pontil, 1820-1840, Pt. . . . . .440.00 to 650.00

McK G I-11, Washington & Eagle, Blue Aqua, Pontil, Pt. 495.00
McK G I-12, Washington & Eagle, Aqua, Sheared Lip, OP, Pt. 187.00
McK G I-12, Washington & Eagle, Gray Blue Green, Pontil, 1820-1840, Pt. 770.00
McK G I-13, Washington & Eagle, Deep Green Aqua, Crack, Pontil, 1820-1840, Pt. 770.00
McK G I-14, Washington & Eagle, Aqua, Pontil, Pt. 303.00
McK G I-14, Washington & Eagle, Blue Aqua, Pontil, 1820-1840, Pt. 385.00
McK G I-14, Washington & Eagle, Emerald Green, Pontil, Pt. 5180.00
McK G I-16, Washington & Eagle, Aqua, Sheared Mouth, Pontil, 1820-1840, Pt. 231.00
McK G I-17, Washington & Taylor, Green, Pontil, Pt. 358.00
McK G I-17, Washington & Taylor, Plum Puce, Pontil, Crack, 1830-1850, Pt. 605.00
McK G I-21, Washington & Monument, Aqua, Long Neck, Pontil, Qt. 121.00
McK G I-21, Washington & Monument, Clear, OP, Qt. 500.00
McK G I-21, Washington & Monument, Light Green, Qt. 247.00
McK G I-22, Washington & Clay, Taylor, Light To Medium Green, Sheared Mouth, Qt. .. 3575.00
McK G I-24, Washington & Taylor, Aqua, Pontil, Pt. 246.00
McK G I-24, Washington & Taylor, Aqua, Sheared Mouth, Pontil, Pt. 330.00
McK G I-25, Washington, Classical Bust, Aqua, Sheared Mouth, Pontil, Qt. 165.00
McK G I-26, Washington & Eagle, Light Green Aqua, Sheared Mouth, Pontil, Qt. 220.00
McK G I-28, Washington & Sailing Ship, Aqua, Double Collar, IP, Pt. 728.00
McK G I-28, Washington & Sailing Ship, Green, IP, Pt. 6720.00
McK G I-28, Washington & Sailing Ship, Yellow Amber, IP, Pt. 2016.00
McK G I-30, Washington & Albany, Aqua, OP, 1/2 Pt. 325.00
McK G I-31, Washington & Jackson, Olive Green, Sheared Mouth, Pontil, Pt. 200.00
McK G I-31, Washington & Jackson, Olive Yellow, Pontil, Pt. ....220.00 to 532.00
McK G I-31, Washington & Jackson, Yellow Amber, Pontil, 1825-1835, Pt. 358.00
McK G I-31, Washington & Jackson, Yellow Green, Pontil, 1825-1835, Pt. 412.00
McK G I-32, Washington & Jackson, Gold Olive, Pt. 220.00
McK G I-32, Washington & Jackson, Olive Amber, Pontil, Pt. 242.00
McK G I-32, Washington & Jackson, Olive, Pontil, Pt. 413.00
McK G I-32, Washington & Jackson, Yellow Amber, Pontil, Pt. ....143.00 to 246.00
McK G I-34, Washington & Jackson, Olive Green, Pontil, 1825-1835, 1/2 Pt. 825.00
McK G I-34, Washington & Jackson, Olive Yellow Amber, 1/2 Pt. ....364.00 to 504.00
McK G I-35, Washington & Tree, Calabash, Aqua, Applied Collar, OP, Qt. 121.00
McK G I-37, Washington & Taylor Never Surrenders, Aqua, OP, Qt. 330.00
McK G I-37, Washington & Taylor Never Surrenders, Grass Green, Pontil, Qt. 357.00
McK G I-37, Washington & Taylor Never Surrenders, Sapphire Blue, Pontil, Qt. 3250.00
McK G I-38, Washington & Taylor Never Surrenders, Olive Green, OP, Qt. 440.00
McK G I-38, Washington & Taylor Never Surrenders, Pale Aqua, Pontil, Qt. 110.00
McK G I-38, Washington & Taylor Never Surrenders, Smoky Pink Puce, 1850, Pt. 5320.00
McK G I-38, Washington & Taylor Never Surrenders, Yellow To Copper, Pontil, Pt. 1540.00
McK G I-38, Washington & Taylor Never Surrenders, Emerald Green, Pontil, Pt. 1320.00
McK G I-38, Washington & Taylor Never Surrenders, Grape Amethyst, Pt. .....3900.00 to 4370.00
McK G I-38, Washington & Taylor Never Surrenders, Olive Yellow Amber, Pt. 2016.00
McK G I-39, Washington & Taylor, Green, Applied Double Collar, Pontil, Qt. 173.00
McK G I-39, Washington & Taylor, Medium Blue Green, OP, Qt. 468.00
McK G I-39, Washington & Taylor, Smoky Topaz, Olive, 1850-1860, Pt. 1375.00
McK G I-39, Washington & Taylor, Teal Green, Pontil, Qt. 1456.00
McK G I-40, Washington & Taylor, Aqua, Sheared Mouth, Pontil, Pt. 600.00
McK G I-40a, Washington & Taylor, Cobalt Blue, Pontil, Pt. 3250.00
McK G I-40a, Washington & Taylor, Sapphire Blue, Sheared Mouth, Pontil, Pt. 4887.00
McK G I-40b, Washington & Taylor, Cobalt Blue, OP, Pt. ....1100.00 to 5040.00
McK G I-40c, Washington & Taylor, Aqua, Bubbles, Sheared Lip, Pontil, Pt. 121.00
McK G I-41, Washington & Taylor, Blue Aqua, 1860, 1/2 Pt. 95.00
McK G I-41, Washington & Taylor, Light Yellow Green, Inward Rolled Mouth, 1/2 Pt. ... 2310.00
McK G I-42, Washington & Taylor, Applied Lip, Pontil, Qt. 80.00
McK G I-42, Washington & Taylor, Aqua, Yellow Amber Striation, Pontil, Qt. 110.00
McK G I-42, Washington & Taylor, Emerald Green, Applied Lip, Pontil, Qt. 375.00
McK G I-43, Washington & Taylor, Deep Yellow, Sheared Mouth, Pontil, Qt. 3250.00
McK G I-43, Washington & Taylor, Deep Yellow Green, Pontil, Qt. 3250.00
McK G I-44, Washington & Taylor, Light Blue Green, Pontil, 1840-1860, Qt. 302.00
McK G I-45, Washington & Taylor, Aqua, Qt. 220.00
McK G I-45, Washington & Taylor, Blue Aqua, Qt. 90.00
McK G I-46, Washington & Taylor, Aqua, Sheared Mouth, Pontil, Qt. 121.00

McK G I-48, Washington, Father Of His Country, Olive Yellow, 1860, Pt. 5040.00
McK G I-48, Washington, Father Of His Country, Yellow Green, Pontil, Pt. 1568.00
McK G I-48, Washington, Father Of His Country, Teal Blue, OP, Qt. 924.00
McK G I-50, Washington & Taylor, Forest Green, Applied Collar, Pontil, Pt. 715.00
McK G I-51, Washington & Taylor, Blue Green, Sheared Mouth, Pontil, Qt. 253.00
McK G I-51, Washington & Taylor, Cobalt Blue, Sheared Lip, Qt. 10000.00
McK G I-51, Washington & Taylor, Lime Green, Applied Double Collar, IP, Qt. 1430.00
McK G I-52, Washington & Taylor, Gold Amber, Sheared Mouth, Pontil, Pt. 990.00
McK G I-54, Washington & Taylor, Blue Green, OP, Qt. 300.00
McK G I-54, Washington & Taylor, Turquoise, Pontil, Qt. 825.00
McK G I-55, Washington & Taylor, Copper Amber, Pontil, Pt. 840.00
McK G I-56, Washington & Taylor, Gold Amber, OP, 1/2 Pt. 2750.00
McK G I-56, Washington & Taylor, Gold Yellow Amber, Tooled Mouth, 1/2 Pt. 3024.00
McK G I-57, Washington & Sheaf, Yellow Green, Qt. 3000.00
McK G I-59, Washington & Sheaf, Aqua, OP, 1/2 Pt. ....77.00 to 120.00
McK G I-60, Washington & Lockport, Green, Applied Double Collar, IP, Qt. 4025.00
McK G I-60, Washington & Lockport, Ice Blue, IP, Qt. 2632.00
McK G I-64, Jackson & Eagle, Green Aqua, Pontil, 1820-1840, Pt. 330.00
McK G I-67, Jackson & Eagle, Sheared Mouth, Pontil, 1820-1840, Pt. 7700.00
McK G I-68, Jackson & Flowers, Aqua, OP, Pt. 2200.00
McK G I-71, Taylor & Ringgold, Aqua, Pontil, Pt. 154.00
McK G I-71, Taylor & Ringgold, Clear, Gray Tint, Sheared Mouth, Pt. 209.00
McK G I-72, Taylor & Ringgold, Rough & Ready, Aqua, Pt. 187.00
McK G I-73, Taylor & Monument, Grape Amethyst, Pt. 1232.00
McK G I-73, Taylor & Monument, Gray Aqua, c.1850, Pt. 265.00
McK G I-73, Taylor & Monument, Smoky Amethyst, Pontil, Pt. ....784.00 to 1760.00
McK G I-74, Taylor & Corn, Strawberry Puce, Sheared Mouth, Pontil, Pt. 825.00
McK G I-75, Taylor & Corn, Aqua, Pt. 588.00
McK G I-77, Taylor & Masterson, Light Pale Green, Qt. 1430.00
McK G I-79, Grant & Eagle, Aqua, Applied Lip, c.1880, Pt. 110.00
McK G I-79, Grant & Eagle, Aqua, Pt. 247.00
McK G I-80, Lafayette & Clinton, Olive Amber, Pontil, Pt. 1018.00
McK G I-80, Lafayette & Clinton, Olive Yellow, Pontil, Pt. ....1176.00 to 1456.00
McK G I-81, Lafayette & Clinton, Light Olive Yellow, 1/2 Pt. 1035.00
McK G I-81, Lafayette & Clinton, Olive Yellow, 1/2 Pt. ...._Illus_ 1232.00
McK G I-82, Lafayette & Clinton, Olive Green, 1/2 Pt. 5600.00
McK G I-83, Lafayette & Masonic, Green, Sheared Mouth, Pontil, Pt. 5500.00
McK G I-83, Lafayette & Masonic, Olive Green, Pt. 3248.00
McK G I-83, Lafayette & Masonic, Olive Yellow, Pontil, Pt. 3920.00
McK G I-84, Lafayette & Masonic, Olive Green, 1/2 Pt. 5152.00
McK G I-85, Lafayette & Liberty, Olive Yellow Amber, Pontil, Pt. ...._Illus_ 963.00
McK G I-85, Lafayette & Liberty, Yellow Blue, OP, Pt. 1100.00

Flask, McK G I-81,
Lafayette & Clinton,
Olive Yellow,
1/2 Pt.

Flask, McK G I-85,
Lafayette & Liberty,
Olive Yellow Amber,
Pontil, Pt.

Flask, McK G I-99, Jenny
Lind & Glasshouse,
Calabash, Teal Blue
Green, OP, Qt.

Flask, McK G II-12, Eagle
W.C. & Cornucopia,
Blue Aqua, Tooled
Mouth, 1/2 Pt.

McK G I-86, Lafayette & Liberty, Olive Yellow, Pontil, Pt. 672.00
McK G I-87, Lafayette & Liberty, Yellow, Sheared Mouth, Pontil, 1/2 Pt. 3025.00
McK G I-88, Lafayette & Masonic, Olive Green, Pt. 3472.00
McK G I-89, Lafayette & Masonic, Olive Green, 1835, 1/2 Pt. 1680.00
McK G I-89, Lafayette & Masonic, Olive Green, 1/2 Pt. 1120.00
McK G I-90, Lafayette & Eagle, Aqua, Sheared Mouth, Pontil, Pt. 143.00
McK G I-91, Lafayette & Eagle, Aqua, Sheared Mouth, Pontil, 1820-1840, Pt. 303.00
McK G I-94, Franklin & Dyott, Gold Amber, Pontil, Pt. 2530.00
McK G I-94, Franklin & Dyott, Olive Amber, Pt. 4144.00
McK G I-96, Franklin & Dyott, Aqua, Sheared Mouth, Pontil, Qt. 231.00
McK G I-97, Franklin & Franklin, Aqua, Qt. 137.00
McK G I-97, Franklin & Franklin, Gray Aqua, Sheared Mouth, Pontil, Qt. 303.00
McK G I-98, Franklin & Franklin, Aqua, Pt. 742.00
McK G I-99, Jenny Lind & Glasshouse, Calabash, Olive Yellow, Qt. 3080.00
McK G I-99, Jenny Lind & Glasshouse, Calabash, Teal Blue Green, OP, Qt. .... *Illus* 495.00
McK G I-100, Jenny Lind & Kossuth, Calabash, Aqua, OP, Qt. 170.00
McK G I-102, Jenny Lind & Glasshouse, Calabash, Blue Aqua, Pontil, Qt. 213.00
McK G I-103, Jenny Lind & Glasshouse, Calabash, Blue Aqua, Pontil, Qt. 83.00
McK G I-104, Jenny Lind & Glasshouse, Calabash, Blue Aqua, Double Collar, IP, Qt. 165.00
McK G I-104, Jenny Lind & Glasshouse, Calabash, Ice Blue, Double Collar, IP, Qt. 420.00
McK G I-104, Jenny Lind & Glasshouse, Sapphire Blue Calabash, IP, Qt. 7840.00
McK G I-109, Jenny Lind & Lyre, Blue Aqua, Tooled Mouth, Qt. 1008.00
McK G I-110, Jenny Lind & Lyre, Aqua, Qt. 412.00
McK G I-110, Jenny Lind & Lyre, Blue Aqua, Pontil, Qt. 687.00
McK G I-111, Kossuth & Frigate, Aqua, Pontil, Pt. 258.00
McK G I-112, Kossuth & Frigate, Calabash, Aqua, Qt. 303.00
McK G I-113, Kossuth & Tree, Calabash, Light Yellow Green, Pontil, Qt. 165.00
McK G I-113, Kossuth & Tree, Calabash, Olive Yellow, Ring Collar, Pontil, Qt. 440.00
McK G I-113, Kossuth & Tree, Calabash, Olive, OP, Qt. 935.00
McK G I-114, Byron & Scott, Light To Medium Amber, 1/2 Pt. 198.00
McK G I-114, Byron & Scott, Olive Amber, Pontil, 1/2 Pt. 242.00
McK G I-114, Byron & Scott, Olive Yellow Amber, Tooled Mouth, OP, 1/2 Pt. 252.00
McK G I-114, Byron & Scott, Olive Yellow, Pontil, 1/2 Pt. 176.00
McK G I-114, Byron & Scott, Yellow Amber, Sheared Mouth, Pontil, 1/2 Pt. 209.00
McK G I-117, Columbia & Eagle, Aqua, Pontil, Pt. 900.00
McK G I-121, Columbia & Eagle, Aqua, Pontil, Pt. .... .392.00 to 440.00
McK G I-121, Columbia & Eagle, Blue Aqua, Pontil, Pt. 275.00
McK G I-123a, Cleveland & Stevenson, Rooster, Barrel, Yellow Amber, 1/2 Pt. 1568.00
McK G I-124, Cleveland & Stevenson, Rooster, Barrel, Golden Amber, 1/2 Pt. 644.00
McK G I-124, Cleveland & Stevenson, Rooster, Barrel, Yellow Amber, 1/2 Pt. 784.00
McK G I-126, Bryan & Eagle, Yellow Amber, 1/2 Pt. 2072.00
McK G I-127, Columbus & Globe, Ground Mouth, Metal Screw Cap, Pt. 176.00
McK G I-129, Roosevelt & TVA, Calabash, Aqua, Qt. 123.00
McK G II-1, Double Eagle, Blue Aqua, Ground Mouth, Pontil, 1820-1840, Pt. 385.00
McK G II-4, Double Eagle, Green Aqua, Sheared Mouth, Pontil, 1820-1840, Pt. 413.00
McK G II-6, Eagle & Cornucopia, Aqua, OP, Pt. 300.00
McK G II-6, Eagle & Cornucopia, Green Aqua, OP, Pt. 575.00
McK G II-11, Eagle & Cornucopia, Blue Aqua, Tooled Mouth, 1/2 Pt. 448.00
McK G II-11, Eagle & Cornucopia, Green Aqua, Sheared Lip, Pontil, 1/2 Pt. 176.00
McK G II-11, Eagle & Cornucopia, Green Aqua, OP, 1/2 Pt. 575.00
McK G II-11, Eagle & Cornucopia, Yellow Amber, Tooled Mouth, 1/2 Pt. 2856.00
McK G II-12, Eagle W.C. & Cornucopia, Blue Aqua, Tooled Mouth, 1/2 Pt. .... *Illus* 1092.00
McK G II-13, Eagle & Cornucopia, Green Aqua, OP, 1/2 Pt. 1600.00
McK G II-14, Eagle & Cornucopia, Aqua, OP, 1/2 Pt. 550.00
McK G II-14, Eagle & Cornucopia, Yellow Green, OP, 1/2 Pt. 450.00
McK G II-15, Eagle & Cornucopia, Blue Aqua, OP, 1/2 Pt. 190.00
McK G II-17, Eagle & Cornucopia, Aqua, OP, 1/2 Pt. 550.00
McK G II-19, Eagle & Morning Glory, Aqua, Applied Lip, OP, Pt. 500.00
McK G II-19, Eagle & Morning Glory, Aqua, Sheared Mouth, Pontil, Pt. 358.00
McK G II-21, Eagle & Prospector, Blue Aqua, Pt. 258.00
McK G II-24, Double Eagle, Aqua, Pt. .... .82.00 to 180.00
McK G II-24, Double Eagle, Blue Aqua, Pontil, Pt. 165.00
McK G II-24, Double Eagle, Cobalt Blue, OP, Tooled Lip, 1835, Pt. 4480.00

McK G II-24, Double Eagle, Gray Clambroth, Rolled Lip, Pontil, Pt. 1210.00
McK G II-24, Double Eagle, Green, Pt. 1980.00
McK G II-24, Double Eagle, Olive Yellow, OP, Pt. 2860.00
McK G II-24, Double Eagle, Sapphire Blue, OP, Pt. . . . . .4620.00 to 5940.00
McK G II-26, Double Eagle, Aqua, Sheared Mouth, IP, 1850-1855, Qt. 143.00
McK G II-26, Double Eagle, Blue Green, Applied Ring, IP, Qt. 1456.00
McK G II-26, Double Eagle, Emerald Green, IP, Qt. 2860.00
McK G II-26, Double Eagle, Green, Sheared Mouth, IP, Qt. 2744.00
McK G II-26, Double Eagle, Lime Green, Pontil, Qt. 1344.00
McK G II-26, Double Eagle, Medium Blue Green, Pontil, Qt. 2475.00
McK G II-26, Double Eagle, Olive Yellow, Sheared Mouth, IP, Qt. 5880.00
McK G II-26, Double Eagle, Steel Blue, Sheared Mouth, OP, Qt. 660.00
McK G II-26, Double Eagle, Tobacco Olive, Sheared Mouth, OP, Qt. 3584.00
McK G II-29, Double Eagle, Aqua, Pontil, Pt. 476.00
McK G II-30, Double Eagle, Aqua, 1/2 Pt. 138.00
McK G II-30, Double Eagle, Aqua, Pontil, 1/2 Pt. 560.00
McK G II-30, Double Eagle, Dark Amethyst, Pontil, 1/2 Pt. 1120.00
McK G II-31, Double Eagle, Aqua, Double Collar Mouth, Pontil, Qt. 134.00
McK G II-33, Eagle & Louisville, Vertical Ribs, Aqua, 1/2 Pt. 179.00
McK G II-33, Eagle & Louisville, Vertical Ribs, Dark Amber, Applied Lip, 1/2 Pt. 2576.00
McK G II-33, Eagle & Louisville, Vertical Ribs, Olive Yellow Amber, 1/2 Pt. 3284.00
McK G II-33, Eagle & Louisville, Vertical Ribs, Root Beer Amber, 1/2 Pt. 413.00
McK G II-34, Eagle & Louisville, Vertical Ribs, Aqua, Applied Lip, IP, Pt. 560.00
McK G II-37, Eagle & Ravenna, Aqua, Sheared Mouth, IP, 1857-1860, Pt. 330.00
McK G II-37, Eagle & Ravenna, Olive Yellow Green, IP, Pt. 2128.00
McK G II-37, Eagle & Ravenna, Shaded Amber, IP, Pt. 357.00
McK G II-37, Eagle & Ravenna, Yellow Amber, Applied Lip, 1860-1870, Pt. 605.00
McK G II-37, Eagle & Ravenna, Yellow Amber, Pt. 1155.00
McK G II-40, Double Eagle, Aqua, Pt. . . . . .88.00 to 190.00
McK G II-40, Double Eagle, Teal Green, Pontil, Pt. 3080.00
McK G II-40, Double Eagle, Yellow Green, Amber Splotch, Pontil, 1830-1838, Pt. 385.00
McK G II-41, Eagle & Tree, Aqua, Sheared Mouth, OP, Pt. 335.00
McK G II-42, Eagle & Sailing Ship, Aqua, Pontil, 1825-1835, Pt. 330.00
McK G II-43, Eagle & Cornucopia, Aqua, 1/2 Pt. 700.00
McK G II-43, Eagle & Cornucopia, Aqua, Pontil, 1/2 Pt. 400.00
McK G II-43, Eagle & Cornucopia, Aqua, Sheared Mouth, Pontil, 1/2 Pt. 440.00
McK G II-48, Eagle & Coffin, Aqua, Sheared Mouth, Pontil, Qt. 176.00
McK G II-48, Eagle & Coffin, Blue Aqua, OP, Qt. 265.00
McK G II-48, Eagle & Coffin, Emerald Green, Sheared Mouth, Pontil, Qt. 1210.00
McK G II-48, Eagle & Coffin, Light Green, Sheared Mouth, OP, Qt. 143.00
McK G II-48, Eagle & Coffin, Pale Green, Sheared Mouth, Pontil, Qt. 358.00
McK G II-49, Eagle & Coffin, Aqua, Sheared Mouth, Pontil, Pt. 468.00
McK G II-52, Eagle & Flag, Aqua, Sheared Mouth, OP, Pt. 130.00
McK G II-53, Eagle & Flag, Aqua, Sheared Mouth, Pontil, 1836-1847, Pt. . . . . .146.00 to 231.00
McK G II-53, Eagle & Flag, Light Green Aqua, Sheared Lip, OP, Pt. 220.00
McK G II-54, Eagle & Flag, Olive Yellow Amber, Pt. 2800.00
McK G II-55, Eagle & Grapes, Aqua, Sheared Mouth, Pontil, 1836-1847, Qt. . . . . .143.00 to 210.00
McK G II-56, Eagle & Grapes, Aqua, Sheared Lip, OP, 1/2 Pt. . . . . .224.00 to 365.00
McK G II-56, Eagle & Grapes, Pale Aqua, Pontil, 1/2 Pt. 146.00
McK G II-60, Eagle & Oak Tree, Blue Aqua, Pontil, 1/2 Pt. . . . .*Illus* 550.00
McK G II-60, Eagle & Oak Tree, Chocolate Amber, OP, 1/2 Pt. 1600.00
McK G II-60, Eagle & Oak Tree, Root Beer Amber, Pontil, 1/2 Pt. 3080.00
McK G II-60, Eagle & Oak Tree, Yellow Amber, Tooled Lip, 1835, 1/2 Pt. 2464.00
McK G II-61, Eagle & Willington, Olive Yellow, Qt. 448.00
McK G II-61, Eagle & Willington, Red Amber, Qt. 825.00
McK G II-62, Eagle & Willington, Emerald Green, Pt. 425.00
McK G II-62, Eagle & Willington, Olive Green, Pt. . . . . .308.00 to 605.00
McK G II-63, Eagle & Willington, Forest Green, Double Collar, 1860-1872, 1/2 Pt. 413.00
McK G II-63, Eagle & Willington, Olive Green, 1/2 Pt. . . . . .220.00 to 420.00
McK G II-63, Eagle & Willington, Olive Yellow, 1/2 Pt. .132.00 to 253.00
McK G II-63, Eagle & Willington, Red Amber, Double Collar, 1860-1872, 1/2 Pt. 440.00
McK G II-63, Eagle & Willington, Yellow Amber, 1860-1870, Pt. 633.00
McK G II-64, Eagle & Willington, Forest Green, Applied Collar, Pt. 303.00

McK G II-65, Eagle & Westford, Dark Amber, 1/2 Pt. . . . . .275.00 to 300.00
McK G II-65, Eagle & Westford, Olive Amber, 1/2 Pt. 198.00
McK G II-65, Eagle & Westford, Olive Amber, Double Collar, 1860-1872, 1/2 Pt. 330.00
McK G II-65, Eagle & Westford, Olive Green, 1/2 Pt. 192.00
McK G II-66, Eagle & Anchor, Olive Yellow Amber, Applied, Double Collar, IP, Qt. 6440.00
McK G II-66, Eagle & Anchor, Olive Yellow Amber, Qt. 6440.00
McK G II-67, Eagle & Anchor, Blue Green, 1/2 Pt. 504.00
McK G II-67, Eagle & Anchor, Blue Green, Pontil, 1/2 Pt. 605.00
McK G II-68, Eagle & Anchor, Blue Green, Pt. 1344.00
McK G II-69, Eagle & Cornucopia, Light Olive Yellow, Sheared Mouth, Pontil, 1/2 Pt. . . . 7150.00
McK G II-69, Eagle & Cornucopia, Yellow Green, Pontil, 1/2 Pt. 6500.00
McK G II-70, Double Eagle, Tobacco Amber, Pontil, Sheared, Pt. 412.00
McK G II-71, Eagle & Cornucopia, Gold Yellow Amber, Pontil, 1825-1835, Pt. 385.00
McK G II-71, Eagle & Cornucopia, Olive, Amber, Pontil, Tooled Lip, 1825-1835, 1/2 Pt. . 303.00
McK G II-72, Eagle & Cornucopia, Amber, Pt. 110.00
McK G II-72, Eagle & Cornucopia, Olive Amber, OP, Pt. .77.00 to 146.00
McK G II-72, Eagle & Cornucopia, Olive Green, Pt. 187.00
McK G II-72, Eagle & Cornucopia, Olive Green, Pontil, Pt. 132.00
McK G II-72, Eagle & Cornucopia, Olive Yellow, Pontil, 1830-1850, Pt. 121.00
McK G II-72, Eagle & Cornucopia, Yellow Amber, Pontil, Pt. 110.00
McK G II-73, Eagle & Cornucopia, Amber, OP, Pt. 250.00
McK G II-73, Eagle & Cornucopia, Blue Aqua, OP, Pt. 70.00
McK G II-73, Eagle & Cornucopia, Green, Sheared Mouth, Pontil, Pt. 140.00
McK G II-73, Eagle & Cornucopia, Olive Amber, 1/2 Pt. 71.00
McK G II-73, Eagle & Cornucopia, Olive Yellow, Sheared Mouth, Pontil, Pt. 195.00
McK G II-73, Eagle & Cornucopia, Olive, Amber Tint, Pontil, Pt. 121.00
McK G II-73a, Eagle & Cornucopia, Forest Green, Pontil, Pt. 1008.00
McK G II-74, Eagle & Cornucopia, Aqua, Sheared Mouth, Pontil, Pt. 523.00
McK G II-76a, Concentric Ring Eagle, Apple Green, Pontil, Qt. . . . . .5250.00 to 6440.00
McK G II-78, Double Eagle, Olive Yellow Amber, Pontil, Qt. 495.00
McK G II-80, Double Eagle, Olive Amber, Pontil, Qt. 1120.00
McK G II-81, Double Eagle, Olive Amber, Pontil, Tooled Lip, Pt. 358.00
McK G II-81, Double Eagle, Olive Yellow, Pontil, Pt. 179.00
McK G II-84, Double Eagle, Olive Yellow Amber, Pontil, 1835-1845, Pt. 176.00
McK G II-86, Double Eagle, Amber, OP, 1/2 Pt. . . . . .88.00 to 132.00
McK G II-86, Double Eagle, Gold Amber, Pontil, 1/2 Pt. 154.00
McK G II-86, Double Eagle, Olive Yellow Amber, Pontil, 1835-1845, 1/2 Pt. 143.00
McK G II-86, Double Eagle, Yellow Amber, Sheared Mouth, Pontil, 1/2 Pt. 132.00
McK G II-88, Double Eagle, Amber, 1/2 Pt. 121.00
McK G II-93, Double Eagle, Light Green Aqua, Pt. 44.00
McK G II-96, Double Eagle, Olive Yellow Amber, Pontil, Pt. 303.00
McK G II-101, Double Eagle, Olive Yellow Green, Amber Tint, Qt. 504.00
McK G II-101, Double Eagle, Olive Yellow Green, Applied Ring, Qt. 440.00

Flask, McK G II-60, Eagle
& Oak Tree, Blue Aqua,
Pontil, 1/2 Pt.

Flask, McK G III-1, Cornucopia
& Medallion, Aqua, Pontil,
1820-1840, 1/2 Pt.

McK G II-106, Double Eagle, Forest Green, Applied Ring, Pt. 253.00
McK G II-111, Double Eagle, Aqua, Pt. 44.00
McK G II-140, Eagle & Banner, Blue Aqua, Pt. 2464.00
McK G II-142, Eagle & Indian Shooting Bird, Aqua, Qt. .165.00 to 415.00
McK G II-143, Eagle, Calabash, 7-Up Green, Sloping Collar, IP, Pt. . . . . .176.00 to 550.00
McK G III-1, Cornucopia & Medallion, Aqua, Pontil, 1820-1840, 1/2 Pt. . . . .*Illus*   2200.00
McK G III-2, Cornucopia & Medallion, Aqua, Sheared Mouth, Pontil, 1/2 Pt. 121.00
McK G III-4, Cornucopia & Urn, Light To Medium Olive Green, OP, Pt. 88.00
McK G III-4, Cornucopia & Urn, Olive Amber, Sheared Lip, OP, Pt. 77.00
McK G III-4, Cornucopia & Urn, Olive Green, Pontil, Tooled Lip, 1825-1835, Pt. 143.00
McK G III-4, Cornucopia & Urn, Olive Yellow, Coventry Glass Works, c.1848, Pt. 385.00
McK G III-7, Cornucopia & Urn, Amber, 1/2 Pt. 55.00
McK G III-7, Cornucopia & Urn, Gold Amber, Sheared Mouth, OP, 1/2 Pt. 143.00
McK G III-7, Cornucopia & Urn, Gray Olive Green, OP, 1/2 Pt. . . . .   88.00 ·
McK G III-7, Cornucopia & Urn, Green, 1/2 Pt. . . . . .99.00 to 135.00
McK G III-7, Cornucopia & Urn, Green, Tooled Lip, 1/2 Pt. 448.00
McK G III-7, Cornucopia & Urn, Olive Green, Pontil, Tooled Lip, 1/2 Pt. . . . . .66.00 to 105.00
McK G III-10, Cornucopia & Urn, Olive Yellow Amber, Pontil, 1825-1835, 1/2 Pt. 137.00
McK G III-11, Cornucopia & Urn, Light Gold Amber, OP, 1/2 Pt. 77.00
McK G III-14, Cornucopia & Urn, Blue Aqua, Pontil, 1/2 Pt. 550.00
McK G III-15, Cornucopia & Urn, Aqua, OP, 1/2 Pt. . . . . .110.00 to 132.00
McK G III-16, Cornucopia & Urn, Blue Aqua, IP, Sheared Lip, Pt. 448.00
McK G III-16, Cornucopia & Urn, Emerald Green, IP, Sheared Lip, Pt. 2296.00
McK G III-16, Cornucopia & Urn, Green, Sheared Mouth, Pontil, Pt. 715.00
McK G III-16, Cornucopia & Urn, Sapphire Blue, IP, Sheared Lip, Pt. 2632.00
McK G III-16, Cornucopia & Urn, Yellow Amber, IP, Sheared Lip, Pt. 2464.00
McK G III-17, Cornucopia & Urn, Aqua, Pontil, 1840-1860, Pt. . . . . .165.00 to 240.00
McK G III-17, Cornucopia & Urn, Blue Green, Applied Collar, OP, Pt. 770.00
McK G III-17, Cornucopia & Urn, Emerald Green, Sheared Mouth, Pontil, Pt. 770.00
McK G III-17, Cornucopia & Urn, Olive Yellow, Sheared Mouth, Pontil, Pt. 1120.00
McK G III-18, Cornucopia & Urn, Blue Green, Pontil, Pt. 1160.00
McK G IV-1, Masonic & Eagle, Blue Green, Sheared Lip, Pontil, Pt. 330.00
McK G IV-1, Masonic & Eagle, Green Aqua, Pontil, Pt. 400.00
McK G IV-1, Masonic & Eagle, Green Blue, Rolled Lip, Pt. 605.00
McK G IV-1, Masonic & Eagle, Ice Blue, Green Tint, Pontil, Pt. 364.00
McK G IV-1, Masonic & Eagle, Light Blue Green, Sheared Mouth, OP, Pt. 187.00
McK G IV-1, Masonic & Eagle, Olive, Pontil, Pt. 2750.00
McK G IV-1a, Masonic & Eagle, Blue Green, Rolled Lip, Pontil, 1820-1840, Pt. 303.00
McK G IV-3, Masonic & Eagle, Copper Topaz To Yellow Green, 1/2 Pt. 6325.00
McK G IV-3, Masonic & Eagle, Green Blue, Pt. 412.00
McK G IV-3, Masonic & Eagle, Teal Blue, Tooled Mouth, Pt. 1092.00
McK G IV-4, Masonic & Eagle, Green Aqua, Pontil, Pt. 800.00
McK G IV-5, Masonic & Eagle, Yellow Green, Pontil, Pt. .660.00 to 1100.00
McK G IV-7, Masonic & Eagle, Green Aqua, Tooled Lip, Pt. 980.00
McK G IV-7, Masonic & Eagle, Yellow Green, Pontil, 1815-1830, Pt. 330.00
McK G IV-8, Masonic & Eagle, Green, Pontil, 1815-1830, Pt. 770.00
McK G IV-10, Masonic & Eagle, Blue Green, Tooled Lip, Pontil, Pt. 935.00
McK G IV-14, Masonic & Eagle, Olive Green, Long Neck, Collar, Ring, Pontil, 1/2 Pt. . . . 15680.00
McK G IV-17, Masonic & Eagle, Medium Olive Green, Sheared Mouth, Pontil, Pt. 134.00
McK G IV-17, Masonic & Eagle, Olive Yellow Amber, Pontil, Tooled Lip, Pt. 275.00
McK G IV-17, Masonic & Eagle, Olive Yellow, Pontil, Pt. .218.00 to 420.00
McK G IV-18, Masonic & Eagle, Olive Yellow, Sheared Mouth, Pontil, Pt. 330.00
McK G IV-18, Masonic & Eagle, Tobacco Amber, Pontil, Pt. 260.00
McK G IV-20, Masonic & Eagle, Olive Yellow Amber, Tooled Mouth, Pt. 280.00
McK G IV-20, Masonic & Eagle, Olive Yellow, Pontil, 1820-1830, Pt. 303.00
McK G IV-24, Masonic & Eagle, Olive Yellow Amber, Tooled Mouth, 1/2 Pt. . . . . .308.00 to 355.00
McK G IV-24, Masonic & Eagle, Olive, Pontil, 1/2 Pt. 440.00
McK G IV-26, Masonic & Eagle, Aqua, Inward Rolled Lip, Pontil, 1/2 Pt. 1064.00
McK G IV-27, Masonic & Eagle, Blue Aqua, Pontil, 1820-1840, Pt. . . . . .143.00 to 303.00
McK G IV-27, Masonic & Eagle, Green Aqua, Pontil, Pt. 775.00
McK G IV-27, Masonic & Eagle, Ice Blue Aqua, Tooled Mouth, Pt. 364.00
McK G IV-28, Double Masonic, Light Blue Green, Pontil, 1/2 Pt.   242.00
McK G IV-28, Double Masonic, Olive Green, Pontil, 1/2 Pt. 350.00

McK G IV-32, Masonic & Eagle, Aqua, Sheared Mouth, OP, Pt. . . . . .231.00 to 385.00
McK G IV-32, Masonic & Eagle, Gold Amber, Pt., 6 1/2 In. 2970.00
McK G IV-32, Masonic & Eagle, Green, Sheared Mouth, Pontil, Pt. 413.00
McK G IV-32, Masonic & Eagle, Ohio, Shepards, Aqua, Pt. 385.00
McK G IV-32, Masonic & Eagle, Olive Yellow, Amber Tint, Pontil, Pt. . . . . .3000.00 to 3360.00
McK G IV-32, Masonic & Eagle, Red Amber, Sheared Mouth, OP, Pt. . . . . .770.00 to 1175.00
McK G IV-33, Masonic & Eagle, Blue Green, Pontil, 1820-1830, Pt. 990.00
McK G IV-34, Masonic Arch & Frigate, Aqua, Pontil, 1820-1830, Pt. . . . . .198.00 to 420.00
McK G IV-37, Masonic & Eagle, Amethyst, Pt. 2090.00
McK G IV-37, Masonic & Eagle, Aqua, Pontil, Pt. 253.00
McK G IV-43, Masonic & Seeing Eye, Gold Amber, Applied Mouth, 1850-1860, Pt. 440.00
McK G IV-43, Masonic & Seeing Eye, Olive Green, Sheared Mouth, Pontil, Pt. 220.00
McK G IV-43, Masonic & Seeing Eye, Olive Yellow, Pontil, Pt. . . . . .385.00 to 504.00
McK G V-1, Success To The Railroad, Aqua, Pt. . . . . .192.00 to 560.00
McK G V-1, Success To The Railroad, Cobalt Blue, Tooled Lip, Pt. 4144.00
McK G V-1, Success To The Railroad, Emerald Green, Tooled Lip, Pt. 8120.00
McK G V-1, Success To The Railroad, Gold Amber, Pontil, Pt. . . . . .4312.00 to 6440.00
McK G V-1, Success To The Railroad, Olive Green, Tooled Lip, Pt. 2072.00
McK G V-1a, Success To The Railroad, Blue Green, Pontil, 1849-1860, Pt. 825.00
McK G V-3, Success To The Railroad, Gray Olive Green, Sheared Mouth, OP, Pt. 176.00
McK G V-3, Success To The Railroad, Olive Yellow Green, Pontil, Pt. . . . . .220.00 to 616.00
McK G V-3, Success To The Railroad, Olive Amber, Pt. 137.50
McK G V-3, Success To The Railroad, Yellow Amber, Pontil, Pt. 504.00
McK G V-4, Success To The Railroad, Olive Yellow, Pontil, 1830-1850, Pt. 264.00
McK G V-5, Success To The Railroad, Emerald Green, Pontil, Pt. . . . . .1232.00 to 1512.00
McK G V-5, Success To The Railroad, Olive Amber, Pontil, Pt. 336.00
McK G V-5, Success To The Railroad, Olive Yellow, Pontil, Pt. 258.00
McK G V-5, Success To The Railroad, Olive Green, Pontil, Pt. 209.00
McK G V-5, Success To The Railroad, Yellow Amber, 1835, Pt. 476.00
McK G V-6, Success To The Railroad, Olive Green, Pontil, 1830-1848, Pt. 357.00
McK G V-8, Success To The Railroad, Light Olive Yellow, Pontil, Pt. 303.00
McK G V-8, Success To The Railroad, Olive Green, Pt. 209.00
McK G V-8, Success To The Railroad, Olive Yellow Amber, Sheared Mouth, Pt. 616.00
McK G V-9, Horse Pulling Cart & Eagle, Olive Yellow, Pontil, Pt. 364.00
McK G V-9, Horse Pulling Cart & Eagle, Olive Amber, OP, Pt. . . . . .235.00 to 308.00
McK G V-10, Lowell Railroad & Eagle, Citron, OP, 1/2 Pt. 187.00
McK G V-10, Lowell Railroad & Eagle, Medium Amber, OP, 1/2 Pt. 154.00
McK G V-10, Lowell Railroad & Eagle, Olive Green, Pontil, 1/2 Pt. 605.00
McK G V-10, Lowell Railroad & Eagle, Olive Amber, Sheared Lip, OP, Pt. 253.00
McK G V-10, Lowell Railroad & Eagle, Olive Green, Tooled Lip, 1/2 Pt. 1036.00
McK G VI-1, Monument, A Little More Grape, Copper Amber, OP, 1/2 Pt. 3000.00
McK G VI-2, Monument & Fell's Point, Amethyst, Pink Tint, Pontil, 1/2 Pt. 1925.00
McK G VI-2, Monument & Fell's Point, Copper Puce, 1/2 Pt. . . . . .3360.00 to 4760.00
McK G VI-2, Monument & Fell's Point, Olive Green, Pontil, 1/2 Pt. 4730.00
McK G VI-3, Monument, Liberty & Union, Aqua, Sheared Mouth, Pontil, Pt. . . . .*Illus* 385.00
McK G VI-4, Corn For The World, Blue Green, Qt. 7840.00
McK G VI-4, Corn For The World, Gold Amber, 1865-1875, Qt. . . . . .908.00 to 1760.00
McK G VI-5, Corn For The World, Light Aqua, Sheared Mouth, Pontil, Qt. 440.00
McK G VI-6, Corn For The World, Aqua, Pontil, Pt. . . . . .212.00 to 336.00
McK G VI-7, Corn For The World, Copper Puce, 1/2 Pt. 4144.00
McK G VII 4, see Whiskey, E.G. Booz's Old Cabin
McK G VIII-1, Sunburst, Amethyst, Tooled Lip, Pt. 896.00
McK G VIII-1, Sunburst, Green, Tooled Lip, Pt. 1064.00
McK G VIII-1, Sunburst, Yellow Olive Green, Striations, 1825, Pt. 14000.00
McK G VIII-2, Sunburst, Clear Green, Pontil, Pt. . . . .*Illus* 1540.00
McK G VIII-2, Sunburst, Light To Medium Green, Pontil, 1815-1830, Pt. . . . . .413.00 to 700.00
McK G VIII-2, Sunburst, Medium Olive Yellow, Sheared Lip, 1810-1825, Pt. 840.00
McK G VIII-3, Sunburst, Olive Yellow Green, Tooled Lip, Pt. . . . . .980.00 to 1176.00
McK G VIII-3, Sunburst, Olive Yellow, Sheared Lip, Pontil, Pt. 1232.00
McK G VIII-8, Sunburst, Medium Olive Green Amber, Pontil, 1815-1835, 1/2 Pt. 715.00
McK G VIII-8, Sunburst, Olive Yellow, Pontil, 1815-1830, Pt. . . . . .413.00 to 715.00
McK G VIII-9, Sunburst, Olive Green, Tooled Lip, 1/2 Pt. . . . . .560.00 to 924.00
McK G VIII-10, Sunburst, Olive Green, Sheared Mouth, Pontil, 1/2 Pt. 330.00

McK G VIII-15a, Sunburst, Olive Green, 1/2 Pt. 660.00
McK G VIII-16, Sunburst, Olive Green, 1/2 Pt. ....357.00 to 605.00
McK G VIII-16, Sunburst, Smoky Blue Green, 1815-1825, 1/2 Pt. 1064.00
McK G VIII-17, Sunburst, Light Aqua, OP, 1/2 Pt. 1980.00
McK G VIII-18, Sunburst, Yellow Amber, Tooled Lip, 1/2 Pt. ....209.00 to 840.00
McK G VIII-22, Sunburst, Red Puce, 1825-1835, Pt. 6500.00
McK G VIII-25, Sunburst, Medium Copper Puce, 1825-1835, 1/2 Pt. ....6250.00 to 7000.00
McK G VIII-25, Sunburst, Pink Amethyst, Sheared Mouth, Pontil, 1/2 Pt. 3750.00
McK G VIII-26, Sunburst, Citron, Pontil, Pt. 687.00
McK G VIII-27, Sunburst, Aqua, Sheared Mouth, Pontil, 1/2 Pt. ....300.00 to 633.00
McK G VIII-29, Sunburst, Blue Aqua, Pontil, Tooled Mouth, 1815-1825, 3/4 Pt. ....55.00 to 385.00
McK G IX-2, Scroll, Blue Green, Lip, OP, Qt. 100.00
McK G IX-2, Scroll, Chocolate Amber, Qt. 660.00
McK G IX-2, Scroll, Lime Green, IP, Qt. ....504.00 to 688.00
McK G IX-2, Scroll, Moonstone, Amethyst Tint, Pontil, Qt. 908.00
McK G IX-2, Scroll, Olive Green, OP, Qt. 880.00
McK G IX-3, Scroll, Yellow Green, Pontil, 1845-1860, Qt. 1100.00
McK G IX-5, Scroll, Yellow Green, IP, 1845-1855, Qt. 1064.00
McK G IX-9, Scroll & Louisville, Aqua, IP, 1855-1860, Pt. 253.00
McK G IX-10, Scroll, Amber, OP, Pt. ....*Illus* 425.00
McK G IX-10, Scroll, Aqua, Sheared Lip, Pontil, Pt. ....784.00 to 840.00
McK G IX-10, Scroll, Blue Green, Teal, OP, 1845-1855, Pt. 840.00
McK G IX-10, Scroll, Bright Sapphire Blue, Pontil, Pt. 2640.00
McK G IX-10, Scroll, Gold Amber, Pontil, Pt. 440.00
McK G IX-10, Scroll, Light Apple Green, Sheared Mouth, 1845-1855, Pt. 140.00
McK G IX-10, Scroll, Milky Jade Green, Pontil, Pt. 688.00
McK G IX-10a, Scroll, Dark Olive Green, Yellow Tint, IP, Pt. 1100.00
McK G IX-10b, Scroll, Blue Green, Sheared Lip, OP, Pt. 2588.00
McK G IX-11, Scroll, Apple Green, Pontil, Pt. 577.00
McK G IX-11, Scroll, Aqua, Pontil, Pt. 733.00
McK G IX-11, Scroll, Gold Amber, OP, Pt. 303.00
McK G IX-11, Scroll, Moonstone, Pontil, Pt. 688.00
McK G IX-11, Scroll, Red Amber, IP, Pt 853.00
McK G IX-11, Scroll, Yellow Amber, Applied Mouth, IP, 1845-1855, Pt. 962.00
McK G IX-11, Scroll, Yellow Green, OP, Pt. ....336.00 to 644.00
McK G IX-11a, Scroll, Aqua, Pontil, Pt. 798.00
McK G IX-14, Scroll, Gold Amber, OP, Pt. ....605.00 to 660.00
McK G IX-14, Scroll, Olive Green, Sheared Mouth, Pontil, Pt. 121.00
McK G IX-14, Scroll, Yellow Green, OP, Pt. 825.00
McK G IX-15, Scroll, Emerald Green, Pontil, Pt. 578.00
McK G IX-16a, Scroll, Red Amber, Tooled Mouth, Pt. 952.00
McK G IX-16a, Scroll, Sapphire Blue, IP, Pt. 3640.00

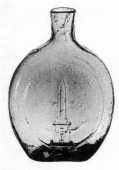

Flask, McK G VI-3, Monument,
Liberty & Union, Aqua,
Sheared Mouth, Pontil, Pt.

Flask, McK G VIII-2,
Sunburst, Clear Green,
Pontil, Pt.

Flask, McK G IX-10,
Scroll,
Amber, OP, Pt.

Flask, McK G IX-34, Scroll,
Gold Amber, Pontil,
1845-1860, 1/2 Pt.

Flask, McK G X-4, Cannon, A
Little More Grape, Apricot,
Sheared Mouth, Pontil, Pt.

Flask, McK G X-15,
Summer & Winter, Dark Puce,
Applied Collar, Pt.

McK G IX-17, Scroll, Citron, OP, Pt. 770.00
McK G IX-18, Scroll, Sapphire Blue, Pontil, Pt. 2145.00
McK G IX-19, Scroll, Green Aqua, OP, Pt. 210.00
McK G IX-23, Scroll, Green Aqua, OP, Pt. 350.00
McK G IX-25, Scroll, Aqua, IP, Pt. 200.00
McK G IX-29, Scroll, Blue Aqua, Pontil, 1/2 Gal. 476.00
McK G IX-30, Scroll, Green Aqua, Pontil, Gal. .... 2050.00 to 2296.00
McK G IX-31, Scroll, Yellow Green, Sheared Lip, Pontil, 1845-1855, Pt. 990.00
McK G IX-34, Scroll, Gold Amber, Pontil, 1845-1860, 1/2 Pt. ....*Illus* 1760.00
McK G IX-34, Scroll, Red Amber, Sheared, Pontil, 1/2 Pt. 660.00
McK G IX-34, Scroll, Yellow Green, Sheared Mouth, OP, 1845-1855, 1/2 Pt. 990.00
McK G IX-34a, Scroll, Aqua, Sheared, Pontil, 1/2 Pt. 110.00
McK G IX-37, Scroll, Aqua, 1/2 Pt. 95.00
McK G IX-38a, Scroll & BP & B, Aqua, Sheared Mouth, Pontil, 1/2 Pt. 330.00
McK G IX-41, Scroll, Green Aqua, Inward Rolled Lip, Pontil, 1/2 Pt. 650.00
McK G IX-42, Scroll, J.R. & Son, Green Aqua, Sheared Mouth, OP, 1/2 Pt. 1400.00
McK G IX-43, Scroll, J.R. & Son, Aqua, Sheared Mouth, Pontil, Pt. 605.00
McK G IX-44, Scroll, Green Aqua, Pontil, 1830-1834, Pt. 303.00
McK G IX-51, Scroll, Aqua, Pontil, 1845-1860, Qt. 2090.00
McK G X-1, Stag & Willow Tree, Aqua, Pontil, Pt. ....187.00 to 264.00
McK G X-4, Cannon, A Little More Grape, Apricot, Sheared Mouth, Pontil, Pt. ......*Illus* 6005.00
McK G X-4, Cannon, A Little More Grape, Aqua, Sheared Mouth, Pontil, Pt. .....660.00 to 770.00
McK G X-6, Cannon, A Little More Grape, Copper Puce, 1/2 Pt. 4368.00
McK G X-7, Sloop & Bridgeton, Aqua, OP, 1/2 Pt. 600.00
McK G X-8, Sloop & Star, Aqua, 1/2 Pt. ....72.00 to 132.00
McK G X-9, Sloop & Star, Pale Apple Green, Tooled Lip, Pontil, 1/2 Pt. 1010.00
McK G X-12, 2 Men Arguing, Green Aqua, Pontil, 1/2 Pt. 303.00
McK G X-12, 2 Men Arguing, Yellow, Pontil, 1/2 Pt. 990.00
McK G X-15, Summer & Winter, Applied Lip, Pt. 80.00
McK G X-15, Summer & Winter, Dark Puce, Applied Collar, Pt. ....*Illus* 3696.00
McK G X-15, Summer & Winter, Gold Amber, Applied Collar, Pt. ....1176.00 to 2128.00
McK G X-16, Summer & Winter, Aqua, 1870, 1/2 Pt. 225.00
McK G X-16, Summer & Winter, Pale Aqua, 1860-1880, 1/2 Pt. 187.00
McK G X-17, Summer & Summer, Aqua, OP, Applied Lip, Pt. 170.00
McK G X-18, Summer & Winter, Olive Yellow, Double Collar, Pontil, Qt. 2576.00
McK G X-19, Summer & Winter, Aqua, Qt. ....195.00 to 305.00
McK G X-21, Steamboat & Sheaf Of Rye, Aqua, OP, Pt. 17500.00
McK G X-21, Steamboat & Sheaf Of Rye, Green Aqua, Pt. 7150.00
McK G X-22, Log Cabin & Flag, Blue Aqua, Pt. 6160.00
McK G X-27, Flag & Stoddard, Gold Amber, OP, Pt. 8000.00
McK G X-30, Hunter & Stag, Aqua, Pt. 1288.00
McK G XI-1, For Pike's Peak, Prospector, Green Aqua, Qt. 198.00

McK G XI-8, For Pike's Peak, Prospector, Aqua, Qt. 85.00
McK G XI-9, For Pike's Peak, Prospector, Eagle, Blue Aqua, Pt. 202.00
McK G XI-14, For Pike's Peak, Prospector, Eagle, Blue Green, Applied Ring, Pt. 7150.00
McK G XI-17, For Pike's Peak, Prospector, Eagle, Citron, Applied Lip, Pt. 908.00
McK G XI-22, For Pike's Peak, Prospector, Eagle, Aqua, Pt. ....60.00 to 82.00
McK G XI-24, For Pike's Peak, Prospector, Eagle, Yellow Green, Qt. 908.00
McK G XI-36, For Pike's Peak, Prospector, Eagle, Light Apple Green, 1/2 Pt. 420.00
McK G XI-41, For Pike's Peak, Prospector, Eagle, Aqua, Pt. 55.00
McK G XI-46, For Pike's Peak, Prospector, Hunter, Blue Aqua, IP, Pt. 532.00
McK G XI-50, For Pike's Peak, Prospector, Hunter, Yellow Amber, Pt. ....1500.00 to 2184.00
McK G XI-50, For Pike's Peak, Prospector, Hunter, Yellow Green, 1860-1870, Pt. 605.00
McK G XI-52, For Pike's Peak, Prospector, Hunter, Blue Aqua, 1/2 Pt. ....162.00 to 202.00
McK G XII-1, Union, Clasped Hands & Eagle, Aqua, Applied Collar, Qt. ....77.00 to 120.00
McK G XII-9, Union, Clasped Hands & Eagle, Citron, Qt. ....900.00 to 1430.00
McK G XII-13, Union, Clasped Hands & Eagle, Amber, Applied Mouth, Qt. ......550.00 to 825.00
McK G XII-13, Union, Clasped Hands & Eagle, Aqua, Applied Band, Qt. 132.00
McK G XII-18, Union, Clasped Hands & Eagle, Amber, Pt. 275.00
McK G XII-19, Union, Clasped Hands & Eagle, Amber, Applied Lip, Pt. 176.00
McK G XII-19, Union, Clasped Hands & Eagle, Aqua, Pt. 220.00
McK G XII-29, Union, Clasped Hands & Eagle, Red Amber, Applied Mouth, 1/2 Pt. 121.00
McK G XII-31, Union, Clasped Hands & Eagle, Amber, Applied Ring, 1/2 Pt. 330.00
McK G XII-31, Union, Clasped Hands & Eagle, Lime Green, 1/2 Pt. 605.00
McK G XII-34, Union, Clasped Hands & Eagle, Aqua, 1870, 1/2 Pt. 95.00
McK G XII-37, Union, Clasped Hands & Eagle, Aqua, Applied Ring, 1860-1870, Qt. 193.00
McK G XII-38, Union, Clasped Hands & Cannon, Blue Aqua, Qt. ....165.00 to 220.00
McK G XII-39, Union, Clasped Hands & Cannon, Ice Blue, Applied Mouth, Pt. 269.00
McK G XII-40, Union, Clasped Hands & Cannon, Amber, Pt. 173.00
McK G XII-40, Union, Clasped Hands & Cannon, Gold Red Amber, Applied Ring, Pt. ... 275.00
McK G XII-41, Union, Clasped Hands & Cannon, Aqua, Applied Lip, Pt. 66.00
McK G XII-41, Union, Clasped Hands & Cannon, Orange Amber, Applied Lip, Pt. 253.00
McK G XII-41a, Union, Clasped Hands & Cannon, Amber, Pt. 385.00
McK G XII-41a, Union, Clasped Hands & Cannon, Aqua, Pt. 198.00
McK G XII-42, Union, Clasped Hands & Cannon, Aqua, 1/2 Pt. 104.50
McK G XII-43, Union, Clasped Hands & Cannon, Calabash, Deep Gold Amber, IP, Qt. ... 275.00
McK G XII-44, Sheaf Of Grain & Star, Calabash, Blue Aqua, OP, Qt. 110.00
McK G XIII-4, Hunter & Fisherman, Calabash, Amber, Applied Collar, Qt. ....264.00 to 300.00
McK G XIII-4, Hunter & Fisherman, Calabash, Blue Green, OP 330.00
McK G XIII-4, Hunter & Fisherman, Calabash, Blue Aqua, IP, Qt. 80.00
McK G XIII-4, Hunter & Fisherman, Calabash, Copper Puce, IP, Qt. 896.00
McK G XIII-4, Hunter & Fisherman, Calabash, Gold Amber, IP, Qt. ....176.00 to 248.00
McK G XIII-4, Hunter & Fisherman, Calabash, Strawberry Puce, IP, 1855-1865, Qt. 825.00
McK G XIII-4, Hunter & Fisherman, Calabash, Teal, Qt. ....330.00 to 385.00
McK G XIII-5, Hunter & Fisherman, Calabash, Aqua, Qt. 52.00
McK G XIII-7, Hunter & Hounds, Olive Yellow Green, Double Collar, Pontil, Pt. 3584.00
McK G XIII-7, Hunter & Hounds, Olive Yellow, Double Collar, Pt. ....2420.00 to 4480.00
McK G XIII-8, Sailor & Banjo Player, Gold Amber, 1860-1880, 1/2 Pt. 550.00
McK G XIII-8, Sailor & Banjo Player, Medium Amber, 1880, 1/2 Pt. 468.50
McK G XIII-9, Sailor & Banjo Player, Aqua, c.1860, 1/2 Pt. 198.00
McK G XIII-9, Sailor & Banjo Player, Pale Gray Blue, Double Collar, 1/2 Pt. 495.00
McK G XIII-12, Soldier & Dancer, Yellow Green, Applied Ring, Pt. 1232.00
McK G XIII-13, Soldier & Dancer, Olive Yellow Green, Pt. ....*Illus* 1568.00
McK G XIII-14, Soldier & Dancer, Aqua, Sheared Mouth, Pontil, Pt. 132.00
McK G XIII-16, Soldier & Hound, Olive Yellow, Double Collar, Qt. 715.00
McK G XIII-17, Horseman & Hound, Amber, Handle, Tooled Lip, Pt. 10640.00
McK G XIII-17, Horseman & Hound, Olive Green, Pt. 495.00
McK G XIII-17, Horseman & Hound, Strawberry Puce, Tooled Lip, Pt. 2464.00
McK G XIII-19, Flora Temple, Red Puce, Handle, Qt. 616.00
McK G XIII-21, Flora Temple, Copper, Handle, Pt. 336.00
McK G XIII-21, Flora Temple, Medium To Deep Copper, Applied Lip, Pt. 179.00
McK G XIII-23, Flora Temple, Light Apple Green, Pt. 756.00
McK G XIII-29a, Will You Take A Drink, Duck, Aqua, Applied Ring, 1860-1880, 1/2 Pt. ... 550.00
McK G XIII-30, Will You Take A Drink, Duck, Aqua, Strap Side, 1/2 Pt. ....220.00 to 523.00
McK G XIII-34, Sheaf Of Grain, Mechanic Glass Works, Aqua, Sheared, Pontil, Qt. 242.00 to 975.00

McK G XIII-35, Sheaf Of Grain, Westford Glass Co., Olive Amber, Pt. 242.00
McK G XIII-35, Sheaf Of Grain, Westford Glass Co., Olive Yellow, Pt. . . . . .110.00 to 231.00
McK G XIII-35, Sheaf Of Grain, Westford Glass Co., Tobacco Amber, Pt. 143.00
McK G XIII-37, Sheaf Of Grain, Westford Glass Co., Olive Amber, Applied Collar, 1/2 Pt.   330.00
McK G XIII-39, Sheaf Of Grain & Star, Blue Green, Pontil, Pt. . . . . .1050.00 to 1176.00
McK G XIII-44, Sheaf Of Grain & Star, Calabash, Light Green, Qt. 413.00
McK G XIII-45, Sheaf Of Grain & Star, Calabash, Brown Amber, Applied Lip, IP, Qt. 275.00
McK G XIII-45, Sheaf Of Grain & Star, Calabash, Amber, Handle, IP, Qt. . . . .*Illus* 1344.00
McK G XIII-46, Sheaf Of Grain & Tree, Calabash, Burgundy Puce, Qt. 770.00
McK G XIII-47, Sheaf Of Grain, Calabash, Aqua, Double Collar, Pontil, Qt. 176.00
McK G XIII-48, Anchor & Sheaf Of Grain, Olive Green, IP, Qt. 125.00
McK G XIII-49, Anchor & Sheaf Of Grain, Olive Yellow, 1/2 Pt.   2912.00
McK G XIII-53, Eagle & Anchor, Resurgam, Olive Green, Pt. 3920.00
McK G XIII-53, Eagle & Anchor, Resurgam, Yellow Amber, c.1870, Pt. 220.00
McK G XIII-55, Isabella & Anchor, Ice Blue, Pontil, Qt. 1018.00
McK G XIII-58, Spring Garden & Anchor, Apricot, Red Tint, 1860-1870, Pt. 264.00
McK G XIII-58, Spring Garden & Anchor, Olive Yellow, OP, Pt.   1456.00
McK G XIII-58, Spring Garden & Anchor, Prussian Blue, Pt. . . . . .15000.00 to 16800.00
McK G XIII-59, Spring Garden & Anchor, Strawberry Puce, Applied Lip, Pt. 672.00
McK G XIII-61, Spring Garden & Anchor, Burgundy, Double Collar, 1/2 Pt. 5320.00
McK G XIII-61, Spring Garden & Anchor, Yellow Amber, 1860-1880, 1/2 Pt. 660.00
McK G XIII-90, C.C. Goodale, Deer, Amber, Tooled Lip, 1/2 Pt.   420.00
McK G XIV-1, Traveler's Companion & Star, Olive Amber, Applied Lip, Qt. 550.00
McK G XIV-1, Traveler's Companion & Star, Red Amber, Qt. 209.00
McK G XIV-2, Traveler's Companion, Ravenna, Amber, IP, Pt. 364.00
McK G XIV-2, Traveler's Companion, Ravenna, Olive Green, c.1860, Pt. 1430.00
McK G XIV-2, Traveler's Companion, Ravenna, Yellow Amber, IP, Pt. 616.00
McK G XIV-3, Traveler's Companion, Ravenna, Aqua, Pt. .193.00 to 265.00
McK G XIV-4, Traveler's Companion, Lancaster, Aqua, Applied, Ring, Pt. 242.00
McK G XIV-5, Traveler's Companion, Lancaster, Teal Blue, Pt. 1288.00
McK G XIV-6, Traveler's Companion, Lockport, Blue Green, Pt.   2800.00
McK G XIV-7, Traveler's Companion & Star, Amber, Applied Collar, Pt. 523.00
McK G XIV-7, Traveler's Companion & Star, Aqua, Sheared Mouth, Pontil, 1/2 Pt. 264.00
McK G XIV-7, Traveler's Companion & Star, Aqua, 1845-1860, IP, 1/2 Pt. . . . . . . .165.00 to 264.00
McK G XIV-7, Traveler's Companion & Star, Smoky Sapphire Blue, 1/2 Pt. 3360.00
McK G XIV-9, Traveler's Companion & Railroad Guide, Apple Green, 1/2 Pt. 532.00
McK G XV-6, Granite Glass Co., Stoddard, N.H., Olive Amber, Pt. . . . . .756.00 to 1232.00
McK G XV-7, Granite Glass Co., Stoddard, N.H., Olive Yellow, Applied Collar, Pt. 728.00
McK G XV-7, Granite Glass Co., Stoddard, N.H., Amber, Double Rolled Collar, Pt. 275.00
McK G XV-8, Granite Glass Co., Stoddard, N.H., Olive Amber, Pontil, c.1860, Pt. 495.00
McK G XV-15, Newburgh Glass Co., Olive Amber, Applied Lip, Pt. . . . . .1120.00 to 2408.00
McK G XV-28, Zanesville City Glass Works, Amber, Strap Side, Pt. 935.00

Flask, McK G XIII-13,
Soldier & Dancer, Olive
Yellow Green, Pt.

Flask, McK G XIII-45, Sheaf Of
Grain & Star, Calabash, Amber,
Handle, IP, Qt.

Flask,
Warranted,
Clear, Pt.

McK G XV-32, Henry Luther Wines & Liquors, Amsterdam, N.Y., Aqua, Pt. 475.00
Merry Christmas, Happy New Century, Milk Glass, Pocket Watch, Cap, 4 In. 150.00
Merry Christmas, Happy New Year, Clear, Label Under Glass, 7 3/8 In. 440.00
Merry Christmas, Happy New Year, Clear, Ribs, Screw Cap, 1890, 7 3/8 In. 440.00
Merry Christmas, Pumpkinseed, Plum Tree, Clear, Tooled Lip, 1890-1910, 4 5/8 In. 275.00
Metropolitan AAA, Philadelphia, White Label, ABM, Rectangular, 1/2 Pt. 8.00
Mount Stewart Hotel, Cardiff, Cream, Brown Glaze, Handle, England 132.00
Murdock & Cassel, Zanesville, Blue Green, Pontil, c.1837, Pt. 523.00
Newman's Richelieu Kearny, Pumpkinseed, Market & Geary Sts., 1/2 Pt. 275.00
Olive Yellow, Painted, Yellow, Red, Portrait, Squat, Holland, 1730, 5 3/4 x 3 3/8 In. 523.00
Phoenix Old Bourbon, Shoofly, Tooled Lip 50.00
Picnic, Pumpkinseed, Amber To Yellow Amber, Tooled Lip, 5 1/4 In. 200.00
Picnic, Pumpkinseed, Pap's, Amber, Tooled Mouth, 4 In. 145.00
Pitkin Type, 16 Ribs, Swirled To Right, Forest Green, OP, Pocket, Pt. 990.00
Pitkin Type, 16 Ribs, Swirled To Right, Green, Midwest, Pontil, 6 3/8 In. 357.00
Pitkin Type, 16 Ribs, Swirled To Right, Olive Green, Midwest, Pontil, 5 In. 467.00
Pitkin Type, 16 Ribs, Swirled To Right, Olive Yellow, Pontil, 5 3/4 In. 616.00
Pitkin Type, 18 Broken Ribs, Swirled To Right, Emerald Green, Pontil, 7 In. 687.00
Pitkin Type, 20 Broken Ribs, Swirled To Right, Medium Green, Pontil, 4 1/2 In. 644.00
Pitkin Type, 20 Ribs, Amber, Pontil, 1780-1830, 5 1/4 In. 303.00
Pitkin Type, 20 Ribs, Yellow Green, Oval, Sheared Mouth, 5 1/4 In. 165.00
Pitkin Type, 24 Broken Ribs, Swirled To Left, Medium Yellow Green, 1810-1820, 7 In. .. 616.00
Pitkin Type, 24 Ribs, Swirled To Left, Yellow Green, Midwest, Sheared Mouth, 6 5/8 In. . 523.00
Pitkin Type, 24 Ribs, Swirled To Right, Medium Yellow Green, Sheared Mouth, Pt. 770.00
Pitkin Type, 30 Ribs, Swirled To Left, Gold Amber, Midwest, Pontil, 5 1/2 In. 605.00
Pitkin Type, 30 Ribs, Swirled To Right, Aqua, Midwest, Pontil, 5 In. 330.00
Pitkin Type, 30 Ribs, Swirled To Right, Yellow Amber, Midwest, Pontil, 6 1/2 In. 770.00
Pitkin Type, 30 Ribs, Swirled To Right, Yellow Amber, Sheared Mouth, Pontil, 6 1/2 In. . 952.00
Pitkin Type, 32 Broken Ribs, Swirled To Left, Forest Green, Pontil, 1790-1820, 7 In. 523.00
Pitkin Type, 32 Ribs, Swirled To Left, Light Olive Yellow, Sheared Mouth, 4 1/2 In. 1650.00
Pitkin Type, 32 Ribs, Swirled To Left, Olive, Sheared Mouth, Pontil, 1/2 Pt. 715.00
Pitkin Type, 32 Ribs, Swirled To Left, Sea Green, Midwest, Pontil, 7 In. 605.00
Pitkin Type, 36 Broken Ribs, Swirled To Left, Medium Olive Green, Pontil, 5 In. .385.00 to 440.00
Pitkin Type, 36 Broken Ribs, Swirled To Left, Tobacco Amber, Pontil, 1820-1830, 6 In. .. 743.00
Pitkin Type, 36 Ribs, Swirled To Left, Medium Olive Green, Pontil, 1780-1820, 5 1/2 In. . 963.00
Pitkin Type, 36 Ribs, Swirled To Left, Olive Yellow, OP, 5 In. 495.00
Pitkin Type, 36 Ribs, Swirled To Left, Olive Yellow, Pontil, 1783-1830, 5 In. 715.00
Pitkin Type, 36 Ribs, Swirled To Left, Olive Yellow, Pontil, 5 3/8 In. 440.00
Pitkin Type, 36 Ribs, Swirled To Left, Olive, Sheared Mouth, Pontil, Pt. 770.00
Pitkin Type, 36 Ribs, Swirled To Right, Sea Green, Midwest, Pontil, 5 1/4 In. 440.00
Pitkin Type, 38 Broken Ribs, Aqua, Pontil, 1/2 Pt. 110.00
Pitkin Type, 38 Broken Ribs, Aqua, Sheared Lip, OP, Pt. 523.00
Pumpkinseed, Sunburst & Spider Web, Amber, Pt. 45.00
Roth & Co, 214 & 215 Pine St., San Francisco, Amber, Tooled Lip, 1/2 Pt. 440.00
S.F. Rose Straight Goods, Wood Vallejo, Pumpkinseed, 5 Oz. 357.00
S.S.P.B., Green, Strap Side, Applied Band, 9 1/2 In., Qt. 66.00
S.S.P.B., Lime Green, Tooled Lip, Pt. 66.00
Scroll, Light, Medium Yellow Green, Open Pontil, 1845-1855, Pt. 224.00
Smoky Sapphire Blue, Purple Amethyst Swirl, Pontil, 1800-1840, 6 In. 908.00
Sterling Silver, 2 Etched Scotty Dogs, We're Both Scotch, Cork, 7/8 Pt., 7 1/2 In. 325.00
Sterling Silver, Incised Dragon, Monogram, Chinese, 5 1/2 In. 60.00
Sterling Silver, Inlaid Gold, Monogram, International Silver, 3/4 Pt. 113.00
Stiegel Type, Amethyst, 12 Diamond Pattern, Tooled Lip, Pontil, 5 In. 2688.00
Stoddard Type, Red Amber, Pt. 17.00
Strap Side, Aqua, Embossed Safe Inside Circle, Pt. 45.00
Strap Side, Black Amber, 5-Point Star Base, Bubbles, 1/2 Pt. 120.00
Superior Warranted, Clear, Leather Case, England 55.00
Swirled, Light Green Aqua, Midwest, Pontil, 6 1/2 In. 77.00
Teardrop, 21 Ribs, Swirled To Right, Cobalt Blue, Pontil, Continental, 1840-1870, 7 In. ... 121.00
Teardrop, Cobalt Blue, Tooled Lip, Pontil, c.1840, 4 3/4 In. 127.00
Tom Chesterfield, Reform, Clear 225.00
Travel, Cut Shoulders & Sides, Leather Case, 1920s 90.00
Travel, Faux Snake Skin Cover, Plated Cap, 3 In. 49.00

Travel, Pewter Cup, Leather Wrapped Shoulder, Rings, 6 In. 55.00
Try It, Pumpkinseed, Medium Amber, 4 3/4 In. 100.00
Warranted, Clear, Pt. ....*Illus* 9.00
Wharton's Whiskey, Deep Amber, Applied Lip 250.00
Wheat Price & Co., Bust, Fairview Works, Blue Green, c.1840 .... 8800.00
Wicker Cover, Aqua, Civil War, 7 1/2 In. 68.00
World's Fair Flag, St. Louis, U.S.A. 1904, Clear, Ground Lip, 1/2 Pt. ....190.00 to 235.00
Wormser Bros., San Francisco, Dark Amber, Rolled Mouth, 8 1/2 In. 231.00
Yellow Green, Blown, Honeycomb Diaper Horizontal Rows, Oval, Kick-Up, 7 7/8 In. ... 475.00

─────────────────────── **FOOD** ───────────────────────

Food bottles include all of the many grocery store containers, such as those for catsup, horseradish, jelly, and other foodstuffs. Vinegar bottles and a few other special bottles are listed under their own headings.

American Oyster Co., Providence, R.I., Milk Shape, Round 36.00
Atlantic Prepared Mustard, R.T. French Company, Label, 4 3/4 In. ....*Illus* 30.00
Beehive & Bees, Aqua, Indented Panel, Rolled Lip, 7 1/8 In. 355.00
Berry, Light Aqua, Applied Mouth, IP, 11 In. 44.00
Berry, San Francisco, Light Turquoise, OP 33.00
Berry, Tobacco Amber, 10 Petals Around Neck, Double Collar, 11 In. 1230.00
Biedenharn Candy Company, Green, Embossed, Hutchinson 110.00
California Perfume Co., see Avon, California Perfume Co.
Candy Jar, Countertop, 4-Sided, Clear, ABM Lip, Original Glass Stopper, 12 1/8 In. 78.00
Chas. Benard, San Francisco, Spice, Aqua, Applied Top, 6 1/2 In. 66.00
Condiment, 3-Piece Mold, Folded & Flared Lip, Pontil, 4 1/2 In. 72.00
Crown Celery Salt, Yellow Amber, Twisted Ribs, Screw Lid, Label, 8 1/4 In. ....*Illus* 364.00
Dorlan & Shaffer Pickled Oysters, Fulton Market, Aqua, Glass Lid, Wire Clamp, Pt. 700.00
F.A. Howard Pure Honey, Oakland, Coles Pure Honey, Qt. 50.00
First Weideman Brand, Cleveland, Bo Peep Stuffed Olives, Clamp Type 6.50
G. Bernard, San Francisco, Spice, Aqua, 6 3/4 In. 33.00
Ghiradelli & Co., San Francisco, Spice, Aqua 99.00
Golden Tree Mustard, Aqua, No Lid, 4 1/4 In. 20.00
Green & Clark Missouri Cider, Regd Aug. 27, 1878, Amber, Blob Top, 9 7/8 In. 165.00
H.J. Heinz Catsup, Pittsburg, Pa., 1891 .... 85.00
Happy Time, Dutch Lunch Sauce, Nash-Underwood, Chicago, Label, 4 1/2 In. ......*Illus* 34.00
Harry Hornes Mello Cremo, Toronto, Canada, Paper Label, ABM, 1920-1930, 64 Oz. ... 31.00
Heinz Apple Butter, Jar, 7 1/2 In. 201.00
Home Made Peanut Butter, No Lid, 4 1/4 In. 20.00
Honey Amber, 1860s, 9 1/4 In. 10.00
Huckleberry, Amber, Willington Glass Works, Collar, Ring Lip, 11 1/8 In. 840.00
J.T. Morton, Leade & Hall Street, London, Blue, Table Salt 253.00
Jackson Piccadilly, Caviar, Lid 38.00
Jar, Canning, Black Splotches, Redware, 10 5/8 In. 38.00

Food, Atlantic Prepared
Mustard, R.T. French Company,
Label, 4 3/4 In.

Food, Crown Celery Salt,
Yellow Amber, Twisted Ribs,
Screw Lid, Label, 8 1/4 In.

Food, Happy Time, Dutch Lunch
Sauce, Nash-Underwood,
Chicago, Label, 4 1/2 In.

BOTTLES
PLAIN & FANCY

BOTTLES HAVE BEEN MADE SINCE ANCIENT TIMES.
The earliest bottles were core-formed or blown. Molten glass was
put on the end of a punty rod and the glass was blown, then shaped
with a hand-held tool. A free-blown bottle has a neck, shaped body,
flattened base, and a pontil mark showing where the punty rod was
removed. It may or may not have painted or engraved decoration or
added pieces of glass that decorate the body. A free-blown bottle
has no mold seams. Each bottle has a slightly different size and
shape. Standard sizes were not possible until the development of the
mold-blown bottle in the early 1800s. Many types of metal molds
were used during the nineteenth century and each left telltale seam
lines. The automatic bottle machine was invented in 1903, and since
that time most bottles have been made entirely by machine.

It is easy to put a pattern into a mold-blown glass bottle or one
made by machine. The mold, usually brass or iron, is formed like the
bottle in reverse. The glass is poured into the mold, removed, then
cooled slowly. A raised design is seen on the exterior of the bottle.
Some bottles, like milk bottles or soda bottles, are made in a mold
with a slug plate. This is a part of the mold that can be changed for
each customer so the bottle has a unique company design.

Plain and fancy bottles help to sell products. The "waisted" bottle used by Coca-Cola is one of the most recognizable objects in the world. The cathedral pickle, the poison bottle with raised hobs, and the wide-mouthed fruit jar are all easily identified by shape alone. Twentieth-century manufacturers of perfume, whiskey, maple syrup, or even liquid cleaning products often used bottles in attractive shapes to encourage sales. They were influenced by the figural bottles of the nineteenth century which also held whiskey, perfume, food, or medicine.

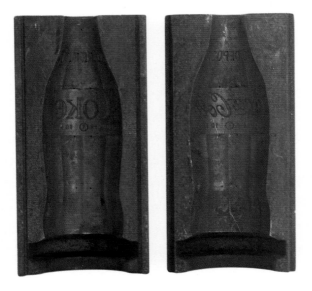

This "shapely" collectible isn't a bottle at all
but would still interest some collectors.
It's a mold from an automatic bottle
machine used to make Coca-Cola bottles.
Value, $500.

Some of the earliest bottles sought by collectors are free-blown, meaning the glass on the pontil rod was shaped by hand. Collectors refer to these bottles with descriptive names like onion and mallet. This light olive green wine bottle is called a Dutch onion because of the squatty, bulb-shaped body. It was made in the early eighteenth century and has a high, conical kick-up. The 7 1/2-inch bottle has an applied string collar. The bottle auctioned for $155.

Storage jars are simple in shape but come in a variety of colors (from left to right): olive yellow, 6 inches, $120; teal, embossed "2" on base, 4 3/4 inches, $120; medium amber, 4 7/8 inches, $120; cobalt blue, 6 1/4 inches, $165; orange amber, 3 3/4 inches, $65. All of the jars have pontil scars and were made in the mid- to late-1800s.

Ink bottles were used in the United States as early as 1819. Small ones, like these cone inks, were made to be opened and used with dip pens. They sold at a recent auction (left to right): turquoise, $110; bright green, $88; teal blue, $77; Carter's No. 95, apricot amber, $55; Carter's citron, $165.

PLAIN WITH WORDS

Before the automatic bottle machine was invented in 1903, bottles were expensive to make. Soda and mineral water distributors wanted to make sure their bottles were returned, so they sold their drinks in bottles with embossed names.

The bottles here are called "blob tops" because of the rounded applied collar (left to right): L & B (Lippincott & Belding) soda, green, Stockton, after 1868, 7³/₄ in., $121 ☛ Boley & Co. soda, Sac City, Cal., cobalt blue, graphite pontil, 1850s, 7¹/₄ in., $24 ☛ Chase & Co. mineral water, San Francisco, Stockton & Marysville, green, $413 ☛ Soda with embossed eagle, green teal, white graphite pontil, $231 ☛ Taylor & Co. soda, Valparaiso, teal, graphite, iron pontil, $275 ☛ Bay City Soda Water Co., S.F., sapphire blue, embossed star, $12.

Dairies also wanted their bottles returned. Many milk and cream bottles are one basic round shape. The molds had a slot to insert metal plates with different dairies' names. These half-pint bottles have the telltale circular ISP (inserted slug plate) section around the embossed names.

The Crescent bottle (left) sold for $44 at auction. Liberty Dairy Products sold for $33.

Beer and ginger beer were sold in plain stoneware bottles that were often stamped or incised with the brewery name. This bottle was made for the Union Brewery and is stamped with the owner's name, Ch. [Charles] Gipfel. The brewery operated in Milwaukee, Wisconsin, from 1849 to 1872.

Food jars were embossed with either the maker of the contents or the maker of the jar.

This aqua quart fruit jar bears the patent holder's name, Bloeser. The glass lid is embossed "Pat. Sept 27, 1887." Value online, $325.

N.W. Opermann's factory prepared the mustard that was sold in this aqua jar. It has a pontil and is 4^3/4 inches high. Because of its condition and scarcity, it sells for $220.

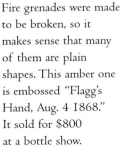

Fire grenades were made to be broken, so it makes sense that many of them are plain shapes. This amber one is embossed "Flagg's Hand, Aug. 4 1868." It sold for $800 at a bottle show.

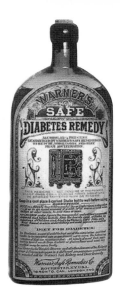

This medium-amber medicine bottle has a plain shape, but it's embossed "16 Fl. Oz. Warner's Safe Diabetes Remedy [picture of safe], Rochester, N.Y." The paper label has more information about the medicine. The 9⅝-inch bottle was made around 1890 and still has its original contents. Value at auction, $364.

FANCY AND FIGURAL

Decorative historic flasks are among the earliest bottles with fancy embossed designs. Early flasks were probably not sold to the manufacturers of beverages. They distributed their products in demijohns or carboys and did not package them in small quantities until the 1850s. Druggists and grocers were the primary retailers of wines and liquor, and it is likely that the flasks were purchased and filled by the store owner. In the 1930s, George McKearin categorized the known figural flasks into groups and assigned them numbers that are still used by collectors. Numbers and sketches appear in the revised book *American Bottles & Flasks and Their Ancestry* (see Bibliography).

Many of the embossed flasks made in the 1820s to 1850s had political or historic designs on them. "The American System" flask (McKearin number GX-21) features a large paddlewheel steamboat flying two flags. It says "Use me but do not abuse me," referring to Henry Clay's fight for a protective tariff law in the 1820s. The green aqua flask is a rare and important example of one of McKearin's original list of the most desirable bottles. It sells for $8,500.

There are more eagle-decorated flasks than any other kind. This McKearin number GII-72 flask has an eagle on one side and a fruit-filled cornucopia on the other. The light to medium olive green pint flask has a pontil and sheared lip. It is a common flask worth $270.

The half-pint cornucopia and urn flask (McKearin number GIII-7), shown here in deep forest green, is embossed with popular design elements of the 1820s and 1830s. The fruit-laden cornucopia and urn symbolize the land of plenty. Value, $200.

George McKearin also categorized glass items blown in three-piece molds. This 5⅝-inch medium-purple toilet water bottle is McKearin number GI-7, type 2. It sold for $400.

This aqua scent bottle was made
around 1815 to 1830.
Only about 2 inches high,
it's rare and sells for $375.

Even the most utilitarian jar can be
beautiful. This milk glass Flaccus
Brothers steer's-head fruit jar is
embossed with floral decorations
and has a matching glass screw-on
lid. At $450, you'd probably want
to save it for your best preserves.

Teakettle inkwells are more
decorative than their cone-
shaped counterparts. This deep cobalt
blue example has a five-lobed body embossed with floral designs.
Even with no brass cap, it's worth $650.

Many colorful figural bottles were made during the patent medicine era of the nineteenth century.

John Hart & Co. sold medicine in this medium-amber figural heart bottle around 1870 to 1880. It is 6⁷⁄₈ inches high and sold for $812 at auction.

This deep teal green L.Q.C. Wishart's Pine Tree Tar Cordial bottle is aptly embossed with the motif of a tree. The 9⁵⁄₈-inch bottle says "Patent" and "1859," and was made between 1860 and 1870 in Philadelphia. It auctioned for $896.

William Radam used an image of a skeleton being clubbed by a man to represent the dreaded microbes that his product was supposed to kill. His bottle is embossed "Germ Bacteria or Fungus Destroyer" and "Wm. Radam's Microbe Killer." The 10¹⁄₂-inch golden amber bottle was made between 1890 and 1910. Value at auction, $190.

When the American temperance movement picked up steam after the Civil War, alcoholic beverages were packaged as medicinal spirits or bitters. The bottles were often fancy figural shapes.

One of the most famous bitters is the Indian Queen. This 12 1/8-inch example is embossed "Brown's Celebrated Indian Herb Bitters, Patented Feb 11 1868." The medium yellow amber color and partial original yellow paint helped bring $1,008 at auction.

W.H. Ware's Fish Bitters was appropriately packaged in a fish. This clear example is embossed "W.H. Ware, Patent 1866" on its base and is 11 1/2 inches high. It auctioned for $1,344.

Here's a strange choice of bottle shapes: the National Bitters ear-of-corn-shaped bottle. The original contents were made of grain alcohol, but not corn. This golden yellow amber bottle shades upward to yellow. It is 12 5/8 inches high and embossed "Patent 1867" on the base. Value at auction, $756.

The Owl Drug Co. wanted to make sure the customer was careful with the contents of this bottle, so the word "Poison" is embossed along the side. The 3¼-inch bottle is cobalt blue and sold for $125 at auction.

Nineteenth-century food packers used attractive bottles to sell their wares. One of the most common food bottle shapes is the cathedral pickle. This 11½-inch green example is probably from a western state. It auctioned for $198.

The bottom of this pepper sauce bottle is embossed "S & P." The initials are those of Stickney & Poor, a Massachusetts food and spice company that was founded in 1815 and still exists. The 8½-inch bottle was made around 1870. Value, $80.

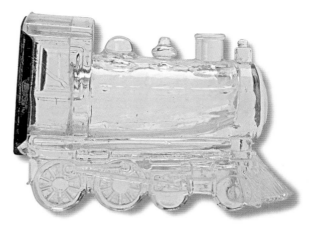

Children love candy and toys. Candy containers give them
the best of both worlds. This 4-inch locomotive was made around
1914 to 1924. The tin closure on the end is lithographed with a scene
showing the fire box, gauges, the fireman, and the engineer.
This unmarked version is worth $100.

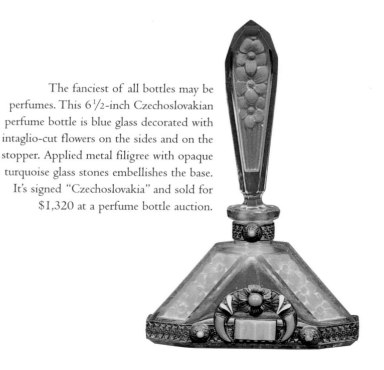

The fanciest of all bottles may be
perfumes. This 6½-inch Czechoslovakian
perfume bottle is blue glass decorated with
intaglio-cut flowers on the sides and on the
stopper. Applied metal filigree with opaque
turquoise glass stones embellishes the base.
It's signed "Czechoslovakia" and sold for
$1,320 at a perfume bottle auction.

Bottles in the twentieth century may not be as pricey as older bottles, but they appeal to collectors nonetheless.

This whiskey bottle is rather plain, but its label tells an interesting story. The contents were distilled before Prohibition and hadn't finished aging before the Eighteenth Amendment banned the sale of beverages with more than $1/2$ percent alcohol. The whiskey was bottled after the repeal of Prohibition in 1933 and labeled "Special Old Reserve" by the American Medicinal Spirits Company, owned by Richard Wathen. A similar bottle sold in an online auction for $75.

In the mid-1930s, bottlers developed a new way to label their products. This Sweetie soda has a pyroglazed decoration, called ACL (applied color label) by collectors. The 8-inch bottle is marked "Philadelphia, PA" and sold for $55 at a bottle show.

Reproductions of bottles have been widely made since the 1930s, when collectors developed a keener interest in old flasks. The sapphire blue log cabin bottle, 7¹/₂ inches, and golden amber Jefferson Davis bottle, 8 inches, were sold filled with maple syrup in the 1970s. The cobalt blue Jenny Lind bottle says "American Glass Works" and is a copy of an early calabash flask. These machine-made bottles can be picked up at flea markets and antiques malls. Don't pay more than $25 to $30 for them.

In the 1940s, bar owners gave customers humorous miniature pottery bottles like this 3¹/₂-inch golfer. The bottle says "The Nineteenth Hole." This example is worth $50. Other subjects include babies, pretty ladies, and drunks. Most were made in Germany or Japan and some can be worth more than $150.

Collecting new figural bottles became a craze in the 1970s when such companies as Avon Products packaged their lines in unusual and attractive bottles.

There is renewed interest in Avon bottles.
This "Side Wheeler" held Wild Country After Shave in 1971.
Collectors have clubs and trade among themselves, but you
can also pick up Avon bottles at garage sales, thrift shops,
and flea markets, as well as antiques malls.

Distillers also issued
collectible ceramic
bottles. These 5$^{1}/_{2}$-inch
leprechauns, called
Mr. Lucky and
Mrs. Lucky, were
sold by Hoffman
in 1975. He sells
for $30 and
she sells for $25.

Food, N.W. Opermann
Mustard Factory, Aqua,
Pontil, 4 7/8 In.

Food, Nash's Prepared Mustard,
Lucky Joe Bank, Lip Label,
4 1/4 In.

Food, Reyam Brand Glace
Cherries, Cincinnati, Oh.,
Label, 4 3/4 In.

Jar, Ice Blue, Wide Mouth, Applied Lip, Red IP, 9 1/4 In.	125.00
Jar, Wampoles Milk Food	22.00
Jelly Jar, Blue Aqua, Flared & Folded Lip, Pontil, 3 3/4 In.	110.00
Lily White Corn Syrup, Jar, White Calla Lilies, Paper Label, 3 1/2 Lb.	12.50
Lime Juice, 3-Piece Mold, Black Glass, British Admiralty Anchor, Mid 1800s, 10 1/2 In.	130.00
M. Michaelis & Sons Red Cross Fruit Extracts, Crooked Long Neck, 5 1/2 In.	10.00
Mellin's Infants Food, London, Kick-Up, 6 1/2 In.	3.50
Mustard, Barrel, Dark Olive Amber, Applied Mouth, 1850-1870, 3 3/4 In.	176.00
Mustard, Barrel, Dark Olive Green, Applied Mouth, 1850-1870, 3 3/4 In.	99.00
Mustard, Barrel, Grape Puce, Applied Mouth, 1850-1870, 4 3/8 In.	550.00
Mustard, Barrel, Olive Green, Rolled Lip, 1850-1870, 3 3/4 In.	209.00
Mustard, Milk Glass, Eagle Glass Lid, Metal Screw Band, Pt.	110.00
N.W. Opermann Mustard Factory, Aqua, Pontil, 4 7/8 In. *Illus*	120.00
Nash's Prepared Mustard, Lucky Joe Bank, Lip Label, 4 1/4 In. *Illus*	24.00
Palmer Green, Barrel Shape, Ribs, Wide Mouth, Tooled Top, Mickey's Big Mouth	55.00
Pepper Sauce, see Pepper Sauce category	
Pickle, see Pickle category	
Planters Peanuts, Embossed On 4 Sides, ABM, Lid, Peanut Finial, 13 3/4 In.	385.00 to 392.00
Planters Peanuts, Pennant, 5¢ Salted Peanuts, Embossed Mr. Peanut, ABM, 12 1/2 In.	330.00
Planters Peanuts Jumbo Block Bar, Countertop, Labels, 1930s, 9 1/2 x 7 3/4 In.	2035.00
Putnam's Grocery, Citron, Rectangular, Wide Mouth, Applied Top, 4 1/4 In.	358.00
R. & F. Atmore, Blue Aqua, Pontil, 11 1/2 In.	605.00
Red Amber, Outward Tooled Lip, Stoddard, N.H., 8 In.	420.00
Reyam Brand Glace Cherries, Cincinnati, Oh., Label, 4 3/4 In. *Illus*	22.00
Sarmour's Salad Oil, Light Aqua, Bubbles, Rectangular, 9 1/2 In.	5.00
Shriver's Oyster Ketchup, Baltimore, Emerald Green, 1865, 7 5/8 In. *Illus*	1265.00
Shriver's Oyster Ketchup, Baltimore, Light Green, Applied Top	1980.00
Spice, Aqua, Bernard San Francisco, Applied Top, Smooth Base	30.00
Spice, Blue, Applied Top, Smooth Base	30.00
Square, Green, Outward Rolled Lip, Pontil, 7 1/2 In.	280.00
Storage, 2-Piece Mold, Olive Green, 1860-1880, 5 7/8 In.	99.00
Storage, 2-Piece Mold, Olive Green, Tooled Expanded Lip, Pontil, 4 1/4 In.	784.00
Storage, Apricot Puce, Applied String Lip, Pontil, 4 1/8 In.	143.00
Storage, Emerald Green, Square, Outward Rolled Mouth, Pontil, 1830-1860, 7 3/4 In.	413.00
Storage, Lime Green, Goofus, Wide Mouth, Embossed Roses, Sheared Lip, 15 In.	308.00
Storage, Olive Yellow Green, Wide Neck, Pontil, 1800-1840, 10 In.	132.00
Storage, Pale To Medium Yellow Green, Snuff Type, Pontil, 1860, 4 5/8 In.	99.00
Storage, Stoddard, Gold Amber, 3-Piece Mold, Cylindrical, OP, 10 1/2 In.	80.00
Storage, Torpedo, Olive Yellow, Ring Collar, Pontil, 1830-1860, 6 1/4 In.	660.00
T.A. Bryan & Co.'s Perfection Tomato Sauce, Amber, 8 1/4 In. *Illus*	265.00
T.A. Bryan & Co.'s Perfection Tomato Sauce, Gold Yellow, 1895, 8 5/8 In.	231.00
T.A. Lytle & Co., Tomato Catsup, Toronto, Aqua, Label, BIMAL, Canada, 1885, 12 In.	40.00
Terry Bradshaw's Crunchy Peanut Butter, Jar, Terry Picture, With Hair, 18 Oz.	9.50

Food, Shriver's Oyster Ketchup, Baltimore, Emerald Green, 1865, 7 5/8 In.

Food, T.A. Bryan & Co.'s Perfection Tomato Sauce, Amber, 8 1/4 In.

Food, Tropicana Orange Juice, Girl With Fruit On Head, ACL, Qt.

Food, Yacht Club Salad Dressing, Embossed, 5 1/4 In.

Tropicana Orange Juice, Girl With Fruit On Head, ACL, Qt. ....*Illus*	25.00
Utility, 8-Sided, Olive Amber, Applied Mouth, Pontil, 1830-1840, 6 5/8 In.	220.00
Utility, Dark Tobacco Amber, Partial Flared Lip, Bubbles, Pontil, 1835-1850, 6 1/4 In. ...	110.00
Utility, Olive Green, Applied Mouth, Pontil, 1780-1810, 8 1/2 In.	231.00
Utility, Olive Green, Applied String Lip, 1830-1860, 11 3/4 x 3 3/8 In.	88.00
Utility, Olive Green, Sheared, Tooled Lip, Pontil, 1800-1830, 4 In.	231.00
Utility, Pale Olive Green, Wide Mouth, Pontil, 1800-1830, 8 3/4 x 3 3/4 In.	275.00
Vermont Maple Syrup, Cream Shape, 1/2 Pt.	18.00
Vinegar & Oil, Blown, Green, Divided Middle, Pear Shape, OP, 5 1/2 In.	39.00
W.P., Spice, Aqua, Applied Top, Western, 6 1/2 In.	22.00
Wm. Underwood & Co., Boston, Light Green, Rolled Collar, 1860-1880, 32 Oz.	110.00
Yacht Club Salad Dressing, Embossed, 5 1/4 In. ....*Illus*	20.00

─────────── **FRUIT JAR** ───────────

Fruit jars made of glass have been used in the United States since the 1850s. More than 1,000 different jars have been found with varieties of closures, embossing, and colors. The date 1858 on many jars refers to a patent and not the age of the bottle. Be sure to look in this listing under any name or initial that appears on your jar. If not otherwise indicated, the jar listed is of clear glass and quart size. The numbers used in the entries in the form RB-0 refer to the book *Red Book of Fruit Jars Number 8* by Douglas M. Leybourne Jr. A publication for collectors is *Fruit Jar Newsletter,* 364 Gregory Avenue, West Orange, NJ 07052-3743.

A. & D.H. Chambers Union, Pittsburgh, Pa., Amber, Tin Lid, Qt., RB-582	715.00
A. & D.H. Chambers Union, Pittsburgh, Pa., Aqua, Bubbles, No Lid, Qt., RB-582	32.00
A. & D.H. Chambers Union, Pittsburgh, Pa., Cornflower Blue, Qt., RB-582	70.00
A. & D.H. Chambers Union, Pittsburgh, Pa., Yellow, Wax Sealer, Qt., RB-582	715.00
A. Dufour & Co., Bordeaux, Barrel, Aqua, Bubbles, France, Liter, RB-860	120.00
A. Stone & Co., Phila, Aqua, Stopper, Pt., RB-2750-2	1045.00
A. Stone & Co., Philada, Aqua, Lug Stopper, Glass Lid, 1/2 Gal., RB-2750-3	1760.00
A. Stone & Co., Philada, Aqua, Stopper, 1/2 Gal., RB-2752	1540.00
A. Stone & Co., Philada, Clear, Stopper, Ground Pontil, 1/2 Gal., RB-2752 ......467.00 to 550.00
A.B.C., Aqua, Glass Lid, Iron Yoke Clamp, Pt., RB-4	467.00
A.E. Bray, 4-Leaf Clover, Pat. Pend'g, Amber, Glass Lid, Screw Band, 1/2 Gal., RB-509-1	3025.00
A.E. Bray, 4-Leaf Clover, Pat. Pend'g, Amber, Milk Glass Lid, c.1910, Qt., RB-509	550.00
A.E. Bray, 4-Leaf Clover, Pat. Pend'g, Clear, Glass Lid, Metal Screw Band, Qt., RB-509 ..	925.00
A.G. Smalley & Co., Boston & New York, Amber, No Lid, Qt., RB-2644	75.00
A.G. Smalley & Co., Boston, Mass., Amber, Milk Glass Lid, Square, Qt., RB-2645	50.00
Acme L.G. Co., Trademark 1893, Clear, Pt., RB-15	400.00
Acme L.G. Co., Trademark 1893, Clear, Qt., RB-14	215.00
Acme Seal, Clear, Flint, ABM, Canada, Qt., RB-16	20.00
Air-Tight, Barrel, Aqua, IP, Qt., RB-51 ....756.00 to 867.00

Air-Tight, Barrel, Dark Aqua, Wax Sealer, Qt., RB-51-2 ....385.00 to 880.00
Air-Tight, Barrel, SCA, Qt., RB-50 .... 50.00
All Right, Patd Jan 28, 1868, Aqua, Tin Lid, Wire Bail, Qt., RB-61 .... 88.00
Almy, Aqua, Screw Lid, 1/2 Gal., RB-63 .... 157.00
Alston Bail Here, Tin Lid, Wire Bail, Qt., RB-65 .... 253.00
American, Eagle & Flag, Aqua, Lightning Seal, Wire Bail, Qt., RB-73 .... 88.00
American Condensed Milk Co., Amber, Metal Screw Lid, Pt., RB-72 .... 66.00
American Condensed Milk Co., Clear, Metal Screw Lid, Pt., RB-72 .... 55.00
American Porcelain Lined, NAGCo., Aqua, Zinc Lid, 1/2 Gal., RB-75 .... 33.00
American Porcelain Lined, NAGCo., Aqua, Zinc Lid, Midget Pt., RB-75 ....60.00 to 258.00
Atherholt, Fisher & Co., Philada., Aqua, Applied Collar, Kline Stopple, 1/2 Gal., RB-103 495.00
Atlas E-Z Seal, 4-Leaf Clover, Clear, Lightning Seal, Qt., RB-128 .... 16.00
Atlas E-Z Seal, Amber, Lightning Seal, ABM, Qt., RB-114 .... 28.00
Atlas E-Z Seal, Aqua, Lightning Seal, 48 Oz., RB-124.......................... 20.00
Atlas E-Z Seal, Aqua, Lightning Seal, 58 Oz., RB-126.......................... 45.00
Atlas E-Z Seal, Aqua, Lightning Seal, Qt., RB-111 ....*Illus*   7.00
Atlas E-Z Seal, Clear, Lightning Seal, 1/2 Pt., RB-111 .... 4.00
Atlas E-Z Seal, Clear, Lightning Seal, 1/2 Pt., RB-112 .... 6.00
Atlas E-Z Seal, Clear, Lightning Seal, Qt., RB-116 .... 1.00
Atlas E-Z Seal, Clear, Lightning Seal, Squat, Pt., RB-109-4 .... 30.00
Atlas E-Z Seal, Olive Green, Lightning Seal, Pt., RB-109 .... 20.00
Atlas Good Luck, Clear, Lightning Seal, 1/2 Pt., RB-131........................ 23.00
Atlas Good Luck, Clear, Lightning Seal, Pt., RB-128 .... 10.00
Atlas Good Luck, Clear, Lightning Seal, Qt., RB-128 .... 5.00
Atlas Mason, Clear, Qt., RB-134 .... 1.00
Atlas Mason Improved Pat'd, Aqua, Screw Lid, Qt., RB-145 .... 10.00
Atlas Mason Improved Pat'd, Clear, Screw Lid, Pt., RB-145..................... 40.00
Atlas Special Mason, Aqua, Zinc Lid, Qt., RB-158 .... 8.00
Atlas Special Mason, Clear, Square, Pt., RB-160 .... 1.00
Atlas Strong Shoulder Mason, Clear, Lid, Miniature, RB-162 .... 15.00
Atlas Strong Shoulder Mason, Clear, Pt., RB-162 .... 1.00
Atlas Strong Shoulder Mason, Cornflower Blue, 1/2 Gal., RB-161 .... 8.00
Atlas Strong Shoulder Mason, Cornflower Blue, Pt., RB-161 .... 25.00
Atlas Strong Shoulder Mason, Olive Green, Pt., RB-161 .... 50.00
Atlas Wholefruit, Clear, Bail & Lid, Pt., RB-170............................. 5.00
Automatic Sealer, Sample 5832.00
Ball, 3-L Loop, Blue, Zinc Lid, Qt., RB-193 .... 3.00
Ball, Clear, Wide Mouth, 2-Piece Metal Lid, 1/2 Pt., RB-190 .... 15.00
Ball Eclipse, Pat. 7-14-08, Clear, Lightning Seal, Pt., RB-196-5 .... 8.00
Ball Eclipse, Pat. 7-14-08, Clear, Lightning Seal, Qt., RB-196-5 .... 4.00
Ball Ideal, Blue, Lightning Seal, Qt., RB-202 .... 2.00
Ball Ideal, Blue, Pat'd July 14, 1908, 1/2 Gal., RB-206 .... 2.00
Ball Ideal, Blue, Pat'd July 14, 1908, Pt., RB-207-5 .... 6.00
Ball Ideal, Blue, Pt., RB-203-5 .... 50.00
Ball Ideal, Clear, Inverted Dimple, Qt., RB-210 .... 25.00
Ball Ideal, Clear, Lightning Seal, 1/2 Pt., RB-204 .... 10.00
Ball Ideal, Clear, Lightning Seal, 1/3 Pt., RB-204-1 .... 10.00
Ball Ideal, Clear, Lightning Seal, Qt., RB-213-6 .... 4.00
Ball Ideal, Made In U.S.A., Clear, Lightning Seal, 1/2 Pt., RB-215-5 .... 6.00
Ball Ideal, Made In U.S.A., Clear, Qt., RB-215 .... 3.00
Ball Ideal, Pat'd July 14, 1908, Blue, Square, Qt., RB-212-5 .... 10.00
Ball Improved, Aqua, Erased Mason, Pt., RB-222-5 .... 15.00
Ball Improved, Ball Blue, Pt., RB-220....................................... 2.00
Ball Improved, Blue, Pt., RB-220-5 .... 6.00
Ball Improved Mason's Patent 1858, Aqua, Erased Improved, Qt., RB-230-6 .... 8.00
Ball Mason, Aqua, 1/2 Gal., RB-239 .... 15.00
Ball Mason, Aqua, Qt., RB-234-4 .... 2.00
Ball Mason, Blue, Pt., RB-238 .... 10.00
Ball Mason, Blue, Qt., RB-234 .... 1.00
Ball Mason, Olive Green, Amber Swirls, Screw Lid, Qt., RB-234 .... 465.00
Ball Mason Improved, Aqua, 1/2 Gal., RB-249 .... 30.00
Ball Mason's Patent, Clear, Qt., RB-252-5 .... 6.00
Ball Mason's Patent Nov 30th 1858, Aqua, Qt., RB-263-5 .... 40.00

Fruit Jar, Atlas E-Z Seal, Aqua, Lightning Seal, Qt., RB-111

Fruit Jar, Baltimore Glass Works, Aqua, Wide Mouth, Rolled Lip, Qt., RB-399

Fruit Jar, Clarke Fruit Jar Co. Cleveland, O., Aqua, Glass Lid, Wire Bail, Qt., RB-603

Ball Pat. Apl'd For, Aqua, Tin Lid, Wire Bail, RB-267 .... 440.00
Ball Perfect Mason, A Minus Bar, Blue, Pt., RB-348 .... 10.00
Ball Perfect Mason, Amber, 6 Gripper Ribs, 1/2 Gal., RB-293-5 ....35.00 to 45.00
Ball Perfect Mason, Aqua Green, Qt., RB-274 .... 50.00
Ball Perfect Mason, Aqua, Pt., RB-280 .... 2.00
Ball Perfect Mason, Aqua, Qt., RB-271-7 .... 25.00
Ball Perfect Mason, Blue, 1/2 Gal., RB-274 .... 1.00
Ball Perfect Mason, Blue, Pt., RB-274..................................... 1.00
Ball Perfect Mason, Blue, Pt., RB-277-5 .... 4.00
Ball Perfect Mason, Blue, Zinc Lid, 1/2 Pt., RB-274 .... 125.00
Ball Perfect Mason, Clear, 1/2 Gal., RB-277 .... 5.00
Ball Perfect Mason, Clear, 1/2 Gal., RB-290-6 .... 3.00
Ball Perfect Mason, Clear, Qt., RB-293.................................... 4.00
Ball Perfect Mason, Clear, Side Measures, Qt., RB-293-5 .... 1.00
Ball Perfect Mason, Clear, Square, 1/2 Gal., RB-277-5 .... 6.00
Ball Perfect Mason, Made In U.S.A., 8 Ribs, Aqua, Qt., RB-283-5 .... 15.00
Ball Perfect Mason, Made In U.S.A., Clear, 1/2 Pt., RB-292-5 .... 1.00
Ball Perfect Mason, Olive Amber, Zinc Lid, 1/2 Gal., RB-274 .... 504.00
Ball Refrigerator & Freezer Jar, Clear, Pt., RB-297........................ 10.00
Ball Sanitary Sure Seal, Aqua, Qt., RB-298 .... 11.00
Ball Sanitary Sure Seal, Blue, Qt., RB-299 .... 15.00
Ball Special, Aqua, Made On Ball Bingham Machine, Qt., RB-301-6 .... 20.00
Ball Special, Blue, Made On Owens Machine, Qt., RB-301-5 .... 8.00
Ball Special, Clear, 9 Ribs, Pt., RB-309 .... 15.00
Ball Special Made In U.S.A., Clear, 8 Ribs, Qt., RB-305-5 .... 5.00
Ball Special Wide Mouth Made In U.S.A., Clear, 6 Ribs, Qt., RB-311-5 .... 2.00
Ball Square Mason, Carpenter's Square, Qt., RB-313-5 .... 20.00
Ball Standard, 3-L Loop, Aqua, Qt., RB-314 ....4.00 to 12.00
Ball Standard, 3-L Loop, Aqua, Qt., RB-314-1 ....13.00 to 15.00
Ball Standard, 3-L Loop, Olive Green, Amber Swirls, Qt., RB-314 .... 275.00
Ball Sure Seal, Aqua, Erased Sanitary, Pt., RB-317-2........................ 30.00
Ball Sure Seal, Blue, Pt., RB-317.. 8.00
Ball Sure Seal, Pat'd July 14, 1908, Blue, ABM, Glass Lid, Wire Bail, 22 Oz., RB-320-5 . 106.00
Baltimore Glass Works, Aqua, Wide Mouth, Rolled Lip, Qt., RB-399 ....*Illus* 420.00
Banner, Pat. Feby 9th 1864, Aqua, Press Down Glass Lid, 1/2 Gal., RB-403 .... 145.00
Battleship Maine & Morro Castle, Milk Glass, Lid, Metal Screw, Pt., RB-3086 .... 330.00
BBGMCo., Monogram, Amber, Qt., RB-194-5 .... 25.00
Beaver, Amber, Ground Lip, Glass Lid, Zinc Band, Qt., RB-424 .... 660.00
Beaver, Blue, Aqua Lid, Zinc Screw Band, Midget Pt., RB-424 .... 660.00
Beaver, Clear, Ground Lip, Glass Lid, Screw Band, c.1890, Midget Pt., RB-424 ....55.00 to 120.00
Beaver, Gold Amber, Ground Lip, Zinc Screw Lid, 1875, Qt., RB-424 .... 578.00
Beaver, Light Green, Lid, c.1890, 1/2 Gal., RB-424 .... 85.00

Beaver, Olive Amber, Zinc Screw Band, No Glass Insert, 1/2 Gal., RB-424 . . . . 2352.00
Beaver, Pale Aqua, Glass Insert, Zinc Band, Midget Pt., RB-425 . . . . 100.00
Bee, Aqua, Ground Lip, 2-Piece Metal Screw Lid, 1/2 Gal., RB-429 . . . . 440.00
Belle, Pat. Dec 14th, 1869, Aqua, Glass Lid, Wire Bail, Qt., RB-438 . . . . .1210.00 to 4144.00
Bennett's No. 2, Aqua, Glass Stopper, Footed Base, Qt., RB-446 . . . . .500.00 to 1100.00
Best, Clear, Glass Lid, Qt., RB-458 . . . . 1650.00
Bloeser Jar, Aqua, Glass Lid, Metal Clamp, Qt., RB-468 . . . . .230.00 to 336.00
Bosco Double Seal, Clear, Pt., RB-485 . . . . 45.00
Boyd Perfect Mason, Blue, 1/2 Gal., RB-501 . . . . 15.00
Boyd Perfect Mason, Light Green, Qt., RB-499-10 . . . . 20.00
Boyd Perfect Mason, Light Green, Qt., RB-500 . . . . 15.00
Brighton, SCA, Glass Lid, Wire Clamp, Qt., RB-512 . . . . .55.00 to 80.00
Brookfield, 55 Fulton St., N.Y., Aqua, Glass Lid, Iron Yoke Clamp, Qt., RB-519 . . . . 2640.00
Buckeye I, Apple Green, Glass Lid, Metal Yoke Clamp, Pt., RB-528 . . . . 770.00
Buckeye I, Clear, Ground Lip, Glass Lid, Metal Yoke Clamp, Qt., RB-528 . . . . 303.00
Burlington B.C.GO, R'd 1876, Error, SCA, Qt., RB-539 . . . . 60.00
C. Burnham & Co. Manufacturers, Philada., Aqua, Iron Lid, Qt., RB-544 . . . . 1200.00
C.C. Calidad Coronado, Original Lid, Qt., RB-550-1 . . . . 30.00
C.D. Brooks, Boston, Amber, Metal Lid, Side Clamps, 1/2 Gal., RB-520 . . . . 77.00
C.F. Spencer's Patent Rochester, N.Y., Aqua, Stopper, Qt., RB-2682 . . . . 25.00
Canton Domestic, Clear, 1/2 Gal., RB-566 . . . . 125.00
Canton Domestic, Cobalt Blue, Glass Lid, Wire Bail, Qt., RB-565 . . . . 13200.00
Canton Domestic, SCA, Glass Lid, Wire Bail, Pt., RB-565 . . . . 112.00
CFJCo, see Fruit Jar, Mason's CFJCo
Champion, Pat. Aug. 31 1869, Aqua, Glass Lid, Iron Yoke Clamp, 1/2 Gal., RB-583 . . . . . 165.00
Champion, Pat. Aug. 31, 1869, Aqua, Glass Lid, Iron Yoke Clamp, Pt., RB-583 . . . . 1430.00
Chef Trademark The Berdan Co., Pat'd July 14, 1908, Clear, Pt., RB-591 . . . . 8.00
Chicago Trade CFPJ Mark, Aqua, Glass Immerser, 1/2 Gal., RB-592 . . . . 215.00
Chief, Aqua, Ground Lip, Tin Lid, Locking Wire, 1/2 Gal., RB-594 . . . . .154.00 to 468.00
Clarke Fruit Jar Co. Cleveland, O., Aqua, Glass Lid, Wire Bail, 24 Oz., RB-603 . . . . 175.00
Clarke Fruit Jar Co. Cleveland, O., Aqua, Glass Lid, Wire Bail, Qt., RB-603 . . . .*Illus* 95.00
Cohansey, Aqua, Glass Lid, Wire Clamp, 1/2 Pt., RB-628 . . . . 231.00
Cohansey, Aqua, Glass Lid, Wire Clamp, 3/4 Pt., RB-628 . . . . 231.00
Cohansey, Aqua, Glass Lid, Wire Clamp, Qt., RB-628 . . . . .25.00 to 38.00
Cohansey, Cornflower Blue, Glass Lid, Wire Clamp, 1/2 Gal., RB-628 . . . . 9900.00
Cohansey Glass Mf'g Co., Barrel, Pale Blue, Wax Sealer, Qt., RB-633-1 . . . . 132.00
Cohansey Glass Mf'g Co., Pat. Mch 20, 77, Barrel, Aqua, Ring, Wax Sealer, Qt., RB-631 . 138.00
Cohansey Glass Mf'g. Co., Pat. Feb. 12 1867, Aqua, Soldered Clamp, 48 Oz., RB-630 . . . 176.00
Columbia, Amber, Glass Lid, Wire Clamp, Pt., RB-641 . . . . 1870.00
Columbia, Clear, Glass Lid, Wire Clamp, Pt., RB-641 . . . . 30.00
Columbia, Light Green, Glass Lid, Wire Clamp, Pt., RB-641 . . . . 25.00
Columbia, Made In Canada, SCA, Tin Lid, Spring Metal Clamp, Qt., RB-643 . . . . 170.00
Common Sense, Aqua, Clear Lid, Wire Bail, Iron Lock, Qt., RB-649 . . . . 3640.00
Common Sense, Gregory's Patent Aug. 17th 1869, Aqua, Iron Yoke, Qt., RB-648 .605.00 to 825.00
Commonwealth Fruit, Aqua, Glass Lid, Wire Bail, Qt., RB-650-1 . . . . 99.00
Crown, Crown Emblem, Amber, Smooth Lip, c.1910, Qt., RB-686 . . . . 65.00
Crown, Crown Emblem, Aqua, Smooth Lip, Midget Pt., RB-686-1 . . . . 15.00
Crown, Crown Emblem, Aqua, Smooth Lip, Pt., RB-686-8 . . . . 5.00
Crown, T. Eaton Co. Limited, Toronto, Yellow Green, Qt., RB-691 . . . . 48.00
Crown Imperial Pt., Aqua, Midget Pt., RB-693-4 . . . . 12.00
Crown Imperial Pt., Light Steel Blue, Qt., RB-694 . . . . 9.00
Crown Mason, Clear, Pt., RB-704 . . . . .6.00 to 12.00
Crystal, Aqua, Ground Lip, Glass Screw Lid, Qt., RB-705 . . . . 88.00
Crystal, Aqua, Ground Lip, Zinc Screw Lid, Qt., RB-1847 . . . . 50.00
Crystal Food Holder Trademark, Clear, Metal Screw Lid, 1/2 Gal., RB-705-2 . . . . 140.00
Crystal Jar, SCA, Glass Lid, Midget Pt., RB-706 . . . . 55.00
Crystal Jar C G, SCA, Glass Lid, Qt., RB-708 . . . . 40.00
Cunningham & Co., Pittsburgh, Pa., Blue Aqua, 1/2 Gal., RB-722 . . . . 83.00
Cunningham & Co., Pittsburgh, Pa., Light Kelly Green, Qt., RB-722 . . . . 440.00
Cunningham & Co. Lim., Pittsburgh, Pa., Light Cobalt Blue, Qt., RB-730 . . . . .2200.00 to 3025.00
Cunningham's & Co., Pittsburgh, Pa., Aqua, c.1880, Qt., RB-724 . . . . 83.00
Cutting & Co., San Francisco, Aqua, Wax Seal, 1/2 Gal., RB-735 . . . . 660.00
D.A. Knowlton, Saratoga N.Y., Green Black, Flared Lip, Qt., RB-1431 . . . . . . .3575.00 to 6050.00

Daisy Jar, Clear, Glass Lid, Metal Clamp, Ground Lip, Pt., RB-745 . . . . 1650.00
Dakin & Company Tea & Coffee Merchants, Olive Amber, 1/2 Gal., RB-746-8 . . . . 364.00
Dayton, Prentiss & Borden, New York, Aqua, Rolled Lip, OP, Qt., RB-756 . . . . 286.00
Deutsches Reichs-Gebrauchmuster, Flat Metal Strap, Aqua 75.00
Dexter Improved, Aqua, Glass Lid, Zinc Band, Qt., RB-775 . . . . 88.00
DGCo, Aqua, Glass Insert, Screw Band, 1/2 Gal., RB-776 . . . . 80.00
Dictator, D.I. Holcomb, Dec. 14th, 1869, Aqua, Wax Sealer, 1/2 Gal., RB-783-1 . . . . 88.00
Doctor Ramsay's, Aqua, 12 Panels, Glass Stopper, Ground Lip, Qt., RB-2464 . . . . 6600.00
Doctor Ramsay's, Light Green, 12 Panels, 2 Liter, RB-2465 . . . . 4550.00
Dome, Clear, Glass Lid, Wire Bail, Neck Band, 1890, Qt., RB-797 . . . . 880.00
Double Safety, Clear, Old Style Lightning Seal, Pt., RB-818 . . . . 2.00
Double Safety, Clear, Pt., RB-815 . . . . 30.00
Drey Improved Ever Seal, Erased Pat'd 1920, Clear, Pt., RB-834-2 . . . . 5.00
Drey Perfect Mason, Clear, Pt., RB-848 . . . . .2.00 to 7.00
Drey Perfect Mason, Clear, Qt., RB-843 . . . . 4.00
Drey Perfect Mason, Clear, Zinc Lid, 1/2 Pt., RB-846 . . . . .15.00 to 20.00
Dyson's Pure Food Products, Aqua, ABM, Canada, c.1910, Qt., RB-865 . . . . 17.00
E. Wagner, Manchester, N.H., Yellow Green Citron, Lightning Stopper, Blob Top 60.00
E.C. Flaccus Co., Stag Head, Milk Glass, Lid, Screw Band, Pt., RB-1016 . . . . .193.00 to 303.00
Eagle, Aqua, Glass Lid, 1880, Qt., RB-871 . . . . 264.00
Eagle, Aqua, Glass Lid, Qt., RB-872 . . . . 145.00
Eagle, Aqua, Willoughby Stopple, Qt., RB-871-1 . . . . 935.00
Eagle, Patd Dec 28th 1858, Aqua, Glass Lid, Iron Yoke Clamp, RB-873 . . . . 123.00
Eclipse, Amber, Applied Lip, Tin Lid, 1880, 1/2 Gal., RB-884 . . . . 2090.00
Economy, Kerr Lid & Clamp, SCA, Pt., RB-888 . . . . 12.00
Economy Trademark, SCA, Qt., RB-893 . . . . 8.00
Edwardsburg Crown Pure Corn Syrup, SCA, Square, Qt., RB-910 . . . . 9.00
Electric, Around World Globe, Aqua, Glass Lid, Wire Bail, 1/2 Gal., RB-922 . . . . . .77.00 to 125.00
Electric, Around World Globe, Aqua, Glass Lid, Wire Bail, 1885, Pt., RB-921 . . . . 275.00
Electric, Around World Globe, Aqua, Glass Lid, Wire Bail, Pt., RB-922 . . . . .231.00 to 880.00
Electric, Around World Globe, Aqua, Glass Lid, Wire Bail, Qt., RB-922-1 . . . . 176.00
Electric, In Circle, Aqua, Old Style Lightning Seal, Wide Mouth, Pt., RB-915 . . . . 8.00
Empire, Blue Aqua, Metal Stopple, Qt., RB-924 . . . . 1485.00
Erased Patd Aug 5th 1862 W.W. Lyman, Aqua, Ground Lip, Tin Lid, Gal., RB-1568 . . . 3025.00
Erased Patd Aug 5th 1862 W.W. Lyman, Aqua, Ground Lip, Tin Lid, Pt., RB-1567 . . . . . 121.00
Erie Lightning, Clear, Wire Bail Closure, Qt., RB-942 . . . . 45.00
Eureka No. I Pat'd Dec 27th 1864, Aqua, Metal Lid, 1/2 Gal., RB-948 . . . . 66.00
Eureka No. I Pat'd Dec 27th 1864, Aqua, Metal Lid, c.1880, Pt., RB-948 . . . . 165.00
F. & J. Bodine, Philadelphia, Pa., Aqua, Tin Lid, Wire Clamp, Qt., RB-473 . . . . 132.00
F.B. Co. No. I, Amber, Groove Ring Wax Sealer, Qt., RB-987 . . . .*Illus* 198.00
F.B. Co. No. I, Gold Amber, Groove Ring Wax Sealer, Qt., RB-987 . . . . 61.00
F.B. Co. No. I, Gray Blue, Groove Ring Wax Sealer, Qt., RB-987 . . . . 21.00
F.H. Franke & Co., North Side Fair, Aqua, 1/2 Gal., RB-1032 . . . . 880.00
Fahnstock Albree & Co., Aqua, Pontil, Qt., RB-970 . . . . 89.00
Fahnstock Albree & Co., Blue Aqua, Qt., RB-972 . . . . 550.00
Family Fruit Jar, Clear, Ground Lip, Glass Lid, Wire Bail, 1900, Pt., RB-975 . . . . 1540.00
Federal Fruit Jar, Light Green, Aqua, Ground Lip, Qt., RB-996 . . . . 60.00
Fink & Nasse, St. Louis, Aqua, Ground Lip, Cohansey Lid, Wire Clamp, Qt., RB-1002 . . . 134.00
Flaccus Bros., Steers Head, Amber, Glass Screw Lid, Pt., RB-1015 . . . . 523.00
Flaccus Bros., Steers Head, Clear Glass Screw Lid, Pt., RB-1015 . . . . 80.00
Flaccus Bros., Steers Head, Green, Glass Screw Lid, Pt., RB-1014 . . . . 2750.00
Flaccus Bros., Steers Head, Milk Glass, Metal Screw Lid, Pt., RB-1013 . . . . .385.00 to 550.00
Foster Sealfast, Clear, Old Style Lightning Seal, Qt., RB-2580 . . . . 4.00
Fridley & Cornman's, Patent Oct. 25th 1859, Ladies Choice, Aqua, Qt., RB-1038 . . . . 1210.00
Fruit Keeper, GCCo., Aqua, Glass Lid, Metal Clamp, Pt., RB-1068 . . . . 75.00
Fruit Keeper, GCCo., Clear, Glass Lid, Wire Clamp, Qt., RB-1042 . . . . 60.00
Garden Walk All Purpose Jar, Clear, Pt., RB-296 . . . . 35.00
Gem, Aqua, Glass Insert, Screw Band, 1/2 Gal., RB-1069 . . . . 15.00
Gem, Aqua, Glass Lid, Metal Band, Qt., RB-1078 . . . . 33.00
Gem, Aqua, Ground Lip, Glass Insert, Zinc Screw Band, Gal., RB-1071 . . . . 1512.00
Gem, Hero Glass Works, Aqua, Glass Lid, Zinc Screw Band, 3 Gal., RB-1058 . . . . 2200.00
Genuine Mason, Aqua, Pt., RB-1103 . . . . .8.00 to 10.00
Geo. W. Helme Co., N.J., Patented July 16, 1872, Amber, 1 1/2 Pt., RB-1236 . . . . 20.00

Gilberds, Star, Aqua, Glass Lid, Wire Clamp, 1/2 Gal., RB-1107 . . . . 440.00
Gilberds, Star, Aqua, Glass Lid, Wire Clamp, Qt., RB-1107 . . . . .250.00 to 303.00
Gilberds Improved Jar, Aqua, Glass Lid, Wire Clamp, 1/2 Gal., RB-1108 . . . . 264.00
Gilberds Improved Jar, Aqua, Glass Lid, Wire Clamp, Pt., RB-1108 . . . . 784.00
Gilberds Improved Jar, Aqua, Glass Lid, Wire Clamp, Qt., RB-1108 . . . . .242.00 to 660.00
Gilchrist, see Fruit Jar, GJ Co.
GJCo, Gilchrist, Aqua, Milk Glass Liner, Qt., RB-1109 . . . . 50.00
Globe, Amber, Glass Lid, Iron Clamp, Seed Bubbles, Qt., RB-1123 . . . . 85.00
Globe, Aqua, Glass Lid, Iron Clamp, Qt., RB-1123 . . . . 30.00
Globe, Aqua, Wide Mouth, Glass Lid, Iron Clamp, Qt., RB-1124 . . . . 150.00
Globe, Olive Yellow, Glass Lid, Iron Clamp, Qt., RB-1123 . . . . 1760.00
Globe, Red Amber, Glass Lid, Iron Clamp, Qt., RB-1123 . . . . .180.00 to 495.00
Globe, Yellow Amber, Glass Lid, Iron Clamp, 1/2 Gal., RB-1123 . . . . 77.00
Globe, Yellow Amber, Glass Lid, Iron Clamp, Qt., RB-1123 . . . . .179.00 to 605.00
Golden State Trade, Pat'd. Dec 20th 1910, Clear, Pt., RB-1133 . . . . 30.00
Golden State Trade, Pat'd. Dec 20th 1910, Clear, Qt., RB-1133 . . . . 30.00
Good House Keepers, R In Circle, Clear, Smooth Lip, 1/3 Pt., RB-1145 . . . . 40.00
Good House Keepers Mason, Clear, Pt., RB-1142 . . . . 5.00
Good Housekeeping, Clear, Embossed Aluminum Lid, Qt. . . . .*Illus*   7.00
Granger, Aqua, Ground Lip, Qt., RB-1149-1 . . . . 1650.00
Griffen's Patent Oct. 7 1862, Aqua, Glass Lid, Cage-Like Clamp, 1/2 Gal., RB-1154 . . . 179.00
Griffen's Patent Oct. 7 1862, Aqua, Glass Lid, Cage-Like Clamp, Qt., RB-1154 . . . . 440.00
H & S, Aqua, Ground Lip, Metal Stopper, Qt., RB-1185 . . . . 5225.00
H & S, SCA, Reproduction Metal Stopper, Pt., RB-1184 . . . . 715.00
H & S Phila, Aqua, Ground Lip, Metal Stopper, Lid, Pt., RB-1187 . . . . 1980.00
H.W. Pettit, Westville, N.J., Aqua, Safety Valve Clamp, Qt., RB-2362 . . . . 12.00
H.W.P., Aqua, Ground Lip, Old Style Lightning Seal, Pt., RB-1496 . . . . 40.00
Hahne & Co., Mason's Patent Nov 30th 1858, Aqua, Zinc Lid, Qt., RB-1166 . . . . 121.00
Haines Combination, Aqua, Glass Lid, c.1880, Qt., RB-1168 . . . . 230.00
Haines' I Improved March 1st 1870, Aqua, Glass Lid, Wire Clamp, Qt., RB-1171 . . . . . 72.00
Haines' 3 Improved March 1st 1870, Aqua, Glass Lid, Wire Clamp, Qt., RB-1171-1 . . . . 100.00
Haines' Patent March 1st 1870, Aqua, Glass Lid, Wire Clamp1/2 Gal., RB-1169 . . . . . . 110.00
Haines's 3 Patent March 1st 1870, Aqua, Glass Lid, Wire Bail, Qt., RB-1170 . . . . 110.00
Haines's Improved March 1st 1870, Blue Aqua, Wire Closure, Qt., RB-1172 . . . . 187.00
Hamilton, Clear, Ground Lip, Glass Lid, Metal Clamp, 1886, Pt., RB-1188 . . . . 213.00
Hansee's Palace Home Jar, PH Monogram, Clear, Glass Lid, Wire Clamp, Qt., RB-1206 . 90.00
Hansee's Palace Home Jar, PH Monogram, SCA, Glass Lid, Wire Clamp, Qt., RB-1206 . 100.00
Hartell & Letchworth, Patent May 22 1866, Aqua, Zinc Screw Threads, Pt., RB-1213 . . . 525.00
Hartell's Glass Air-Tight Cover, Aqua, Ground Lip, Glass Lid, 1/2 Gal., RB-1211-1 . . . . . 110.00
Hartell's Glass Air-Tight Cover, Patented Oct. 12 1858, Green, Glass Lid, Pt., RB-1211 . . 896.00
Harvest Mason, Clear, 2-Piece Lid, Qt., RB-1215 . . . . 15.00
Haserot Company, Cleveland, Mason Patent, Aqua, Qt., RB-1216 . . . . 14.00
Helme's Railroad Mills, Amber, Glass Insert, Screw Band, 1 1/2 Pt., RB-1235 . . . . 50.00
Hero, Above Cross, Aqua, Ground Lip, Tin Lid, 1/2 Gal., RB-1241 . . . . 80.00
Hero, Above Cross, Clear, Glass Lid, Wire Bail, 1/2 Gal., RB-1240 . . . . 75.00
Hero Cross, see Fruit Jar, Mason's Cross
Hero Ine, Aqua, Ground Lip, Tin Lid, Screw Band, Pt., RB-1249 . . . . 83.00
Hero Ine, Aqua, Tin Lid, Screw Band, Qt., RB-1248 . . . . 90.00
Hilton's Pat. Mar. 10th 1868, Aqua, Glass Lid, Metal Yoke Clamp, 1/2 Gal., RB-1256 . . 1595.00
Hilton's Pat. Mar. 10th 1868, Aqua, Glass Lid, Metal Yoke Clamp, Qt., RB-1256 . . . . . . 523.00
Hilton's Pat. Mar. 10th 1868, Aqua, Yellow Striation, Glass Lid, 1/2 Gal., RB-1256 . . . . 1870.00
Hoosier, Green Aqua, Ground Lip, Glass Lid, 1/2 Gal., RB-1266 . . . . 2016.00
Hoosier, Green Aqua, Ground Lip, Glass Lid, Qt., RB-1265-9 . . . . 440.00
Household, W.T. Co., Clear, Glass Lid, Flat Metal Clamp, Qt., RB-1272 . . . . 1430.00
Howe, Scranton, Pa., Aqua, Dome Glass Lid, Wire Bail, Pt., RB-1274 . . . . 303.00
Imperial Trademark, Aqua, Glass Lid, 3-Piece Metal Clamp, Pt., RB-1291 . . . . 1980.00
Imperial Trademark, Clear, Glass Lid, 3-Piece Metal Clamp, 1/2 Gal., RB-1291 . . . . 470.00
Improved Corona Jar, Clear, Qt., RB-656 . . . . 6.00
Improved Crown, Aqua, Pt., RB-697 . . . . 3.00
Improved Gem Trademark Reg'd, Aqua, Glass Insert, Screw Band, Qt., RB-1096 . . . . . . 12.00
Improved Jam, L G Co., Gem, Aqua, Ground Lip, Screw Band, Qt., RB-1302 . . . . 40.00
Independent Jar, Clear, Ground Lip, Glass Screw Lid, Midget Pt., RB-1308 . . . . 100.00
Indicator, Aqua, 2-Piece Metal Lid, 1875, Qt., RB-1313 . . . . .440.00 to 2860.00

| Fruit Jar, F.B. Co. No. 1, Amber, Groove Ring Wax Sealer, Qt., RB-987 | Fruit Jar, Good Housekeeping, Clear, Embossed Aluminum Lid, Qt. | Fruit Jar, Johnson & Johnson, New York, Cobalt Blue, Glass Lid, Screw Band, Qt., RB-1344 | Fruit Jar, Joshua Wright, Philad, Barrel, Aqua, 1/2 Gal., RB-3035 |

J & B, Aqua, Pat'd June 14th 1898, Ground Lip, Screw Zinc Lid, Qt., RB-1321 . . . . 94.00
J.C. Baker's Patent Aug 14 1860, Aqua, Glass Lid, Iron Yoke Clamp, Qt., RB-188 . . . . . 303.00
J.C. Baker's Patent Aug 14 1860, Aqua, Tin Lid, Iron Yoke Clamp, Qt., RB-188 . . . . 275.00
J.D. Willoughby & Co. New York, Aqua, c.1880, Qt., RB-1183 . . . . 880.00
J.D. Willoughby Patented Jan 4 1859, Aqua, Metal Stopper, Qt., RB-3016-1 . . . . 330.00
J.M. Clark & Co., Louisville, Ky., Amber, Square Mouth, Qt., RB-601 . . . . 165.00
J.O. Schimmel, Pres'g. Co., Philada, Aqua, Glass Lid, Wire Clamp, Pt., RB-2563 . . . . 385.00
J.P. Barstow, Sun, Aqua, Ground Lip, Glass Lid, Metal Yoke, Qt. 100.00
J.P. Smith & Son & Co., Pittsburgh, Aqua, Wax Sealer, Qt., RB-2670 . . . . 55.00
Jersey, Aqua, Threaded Glass Lid, Zinc Screw Band, Pt., RB-1325 . . . . 1064.00
Jewel Jar, Clear, Smooth Lip, Glass Insert, Screw Band, Canada, 1/2 Gal. 125.00
John M. Moore & Co Manufacturers, Fislerville, N.J., Aqua, 1/2 Gal., RB-2205-1 . . . . . . 2310.00
John M. Moore & Co Manufacturers, Fislerville, N.J., Aqua, Glass Lid, Qt., RB-2205 . . . 385.00
John M. Moore & Co. Manufacturers, Fislerville, N.J., Aqua, Glass Lid, Pt., RB-2205 . . . 495.00
Johnson & Johnson, New York, Amber, Lid, Buckle Clamp, Square, 1/2 Pt., RB-1342 . . . 75.00
Johnson & Johnson, New York, Cobalt Blue, Glass Lid, Screw Band, Qt., RB-1344 . .*Illus* 364.00
Jones Yerkes, Philada, Aqua, Willoughby Stopple, Qt., RB-1346 . . . . 303.00
Joshua Wright, Philad, Barrel, Aqua, 1/2 Gal., RB-3035 . . . .*Illus* 392.00
K C Finest Quality Mason Square Space Saver, Clear, Zinc Lid, Pt., RB-1354 . . . . 12.00
K.Y.G.W., Yellow Green, Wax Sealer, Reproduction Tin Lid, Qt., RB-1446 . . . . 355.00
Kerr Glass Top Mason, Clear, 2-Piece Lid, Glass Insert, Pt., RB-1368 . . . . 4.00
Kerr Self Sealing Mason, Clear, 2-Piece Metal Lid, 1/2 Pt., RB-1380 . . . . 3.00
Kerr Self Sealing Trademark Reg. Mason, Clear, 2-Piece Metal Lid, Pt., RB-1379 . . . . . . 1.00
King, Banner, Clear, Glass Lid, Wire Bail, Pt., RB-1415 . . . . 75.00
Kinsella 1874 True Mason, Clear, Metal Lid, Qt., RB-1421 . . . . 9.00
Kline's Patent Oct. 27 63, Blue Aqua, Rolled Lip, Stopper, Qt., RB-1422 . . . . 77.00
Knowlton Vacuum, Star, Aqua, Glass Insert, Qt., RB-1432 . . . . 11.00
Knox K Mason, Clear, 2-Piece Lid, 1/2 Pt., RB-1436 . . . . 30.00
Knox K Mason, Clear, 2-Piece Lid, Pt., RB-1435 . . . . .4.00 to 5.00
L & W, Aqua, Applied Collar, Tin Lid, Wire Bail, Qt., RB-1523 . . . . 77.00
L & W, Manufactured For Rice & Burnett, Aqua, Stopper, Qt., RB-1529 . . . . 358.00
Lafayette, Aqua, 3-Piece Glass & Metal Stopper, Pt., RB-1450 . . . . .3410.00 to 4675.00
Lafayette, Aqua, 3-Piece Glass & Metal Stopper, Pt., RB-1452 . . . . 198.00
Lafayette, Aqua, 3-Piece Glass & Metal Stopper, Qt., RB-1450 . . . . .1320.00 to 2520.00
Lafayette, Aqua, 3-Piece Glass & Metal Stopper, Qt., RB-1452 . . . . 132.00
Lafayette, SCA, 3-Piece Glass & Metal Stopper, Qt., RB-1452 . . . . .175.00 to 375.00
Leader, Amber, Ground Lip, Glass Lid, 2-Piece Wire Clamp, Pt., RB-1465 . . . . 330.00
Leader, Amber, Ground Lip, Glass Lid, 2-Piece Wire Clamp, Qt., RB-1466 . . . . 75.00
Leader, Gold Amber, Glass Lid, Wire Clamp, Qt., RB-1465 . . . . 415.00
Leader, Gold Amber, Ground Lip, Glass Lid, Wire Clamp, 1/2 Gal., RB-1466 . . . . 448.00
Leader, Gold Amber, Ground Lip, Glass Lid, Wire Clamp, Qt., RB-1466 . . . . .209.00 to 252.00

Leotric, Aqua, Erased E, Old Style Lightning Seal, Qt., RB-1478 .... 20.00
Leotric, Aqua, Erased H.W. Pettit, Old Style Lightning Seal, Qt., RB-1479-1 .... 8.00
Leotric, Aqua, Old Style Lightning Seal, Qt., RB-1473 .... 15.00
Leotric, In Circle, Aqua, Old Style Lightning Seal, Qt., RB-1476 .... 10.00
Lindell Glass Co., Gold Amber, Groove Ring Wax Sealer, Qt., RB-1509 .... 120.00
Liquid Carbonic Company, Clear, Old Style Lightning Seal, 1/2 Gal., RB-1510-2 .... 2.00
Ludlow's Patent June 28 1859, Aqua, Glass Lid, Iron Cage Clamp, Pt., RB-1546 ...... 605.00
Ludlow's Patent June 28 1859, Aqua, Glass Lid, Iron Cage Clamp, Qt., RB-1547 165.00 to 176.00
Lustre R.E. Tongue & Bros. Co. Inc., Phila., Blue, Smooth Lip, Pt., RB-1557 .... 10.00
Lustre R.E. Tongue & Bros. Co. Inc., Phila., Blue, Smooth Lip, Qt., RB-1557 .... 125.00
Lynchburg Standard Mason, Aqua, Qt., RB-1594 .... 20.00
M. Seller & Co., Portland, O., Aqua, Groove Ring Wax Sealer, 1/2 Gal., RB-2615 .... 605.00
M. Seller & Co., Portland, O., Aqua, Groove Ring Wax Sealer, Tin Lid, Qt., RB-2615 .... 110.00
M.G. Co., Amber, Groove Ring Wax Sealer, Qt., RB-2169 .... 253.00
M.G. Co., Citron, Groove Ring Wax Sealer, Qt., RB-2170 .... 330.00
Macomb Pottery Co. Pat. Jan. 24, 1899, Stoneware, Zinc Lid, 1/2 Gal., RB-1603 ...... 50.00
Made In Canada, Perfect Seal Wide Mouth Adjustable, Aqua, Square, Qt., RB-2347 ..... 10.00
Made In Canada, Perfect Seal Wide Mouth Adjustable, Clear, Pt., RB-2344 .... 10.00
Made In Canada, Perfect Seal Wide Mouth, Aqua, Glass Lid, Qt., RB-2342 .... 10.00
Made In Canada Crown, Clear, Glass Insert, Screw Band, Imp. Qt., RB-696 ....4.00 to 5.00
Made In Canada Crown, Clear, Glass Insert, Screw Band, Pt., RB-695 .... 4.00
Magic Fruit Jar, Star, Aqua, Glass Lid, Wire Clamp, Qt., RB-1606 .... 275.00
Magic Fruit Jar, Star, Yellow Amber, Glass Lid, Wire Clamp, 1/2 Gal., RB-1606 1300.00 to 1456.00
Mansfield Glass Works Sole Mfr's, Clear, Glass Lid, Screw Cap, Qt., RB-1618 .... 504.00
Manufactured By Arthur, Burnham & Gilroy Philadelphia, Clear, Qt., RB-95 .... 1870.00
Marion Jar Mason's Patent Nov. 30th 1858, Aqua, Ground Lip, 1/2 Gal., RB-1624 ..... 15.00
Marion Jar Mason's Patent Nov. 30th 1858, Aqua, Ground Lip, Qt., RB-1624 .... 12.00
Mason, Amber, Ground Lip, 1/2 Gal., RB-1665 .... 210.00
Mason, Amber, Smooth Lip, 1/2 Gal., RB-1644 .... 210.00
Mason, Aqua, Ground Lip, Qt., RB-1639 .... 30.00
Mason, Keystone In Circle, Dark Olive Green, Smooth Lip, ABM, 1/2 Gal., RB-1682 ... 190.00
Mason, Star, Clear, 2-Piece Closure, Qt., RB-1746 .... 1.00
Mason, Straight Line, Amber, Pt., RB-1640 .... 85.00
Mason, Yellow, Zinc Lid, Qt., RB-1644 .... 190.00
Mason's, Bicentennial, Embossed Liberty Bell Logo, Screw Top, Anchor Hocking 7.00
Mason's, Patent Nov. 30th 1858, Apple Green, I On Base, Qt., RB-1787 .... 90.00
Mason's, Patent Nov. 30th 1858, Keystone In Circle, Amber, Zinc Lid, Qt., RB-1964 .... 1210.00
Mason's, Patent Nov. 30th 1858, Keystone, Aqua, Zinc Lid, Qt., RB-1965 .... 10.00
Mason's, Patent Nov. 30th 1858, Keystone In Circle, Aqua, Zinc Lid, Qt., RB-1964-1 .... 143.00
Mason's 1 Patent Nov. 30th 1858, Apple Green, ABM, Qt., RB-2027 .... 60.00
Mason's 2 Patent Nov. 30th 1858, Aqua, Smooth Lip, Qt., RB-2029 .... 12.00
Mason's 2 Patent Nov. 30th 1858, Aqua, Zinc Screw Lid, Midget Pt., RB-2029 .... 22.00
Mason's 5 Patent Nov 30th 1858, Aqua, 1/2 Gal., RB-2050-5 .... 20.00
Mason's 8 Patent Nov. 30th 1858, SCA, Qt., RB-2061 .... 110.00
Mason's CFJCo Improved, Amber, Zinc Screw Band, 1/2 Gal., RB-1711 ....179.00 to 255.00
Mason's CFJCo Improved, Clyde, N.Y., Clear, Screw Band, Qt., RB-1712 .... 15.00
Mason's CFJCo Patent Nov 30th 1858, Amber, Zinc Lid, Qt., RB-1920 .... 280.00
Mason's CFJCo Patent Nov 30th 1858, Amber, Zinc Screw Lid, Midget Pt., RB-1920 ... 4125.00
Mason's CFJCo Patent Nov 30th 1858, Apple Green, Zinc Lid, Qt., RB-1920 .... 75.00
Mason's CFJCo Patent Nov 30th 1858, Aqua, Zinc Lid, 1890, Gal., RB-1920 .... 3300.00
Mason's CFJCo Patent Nov 30th 1858, Aqua, Zinc Lid, Midget Pt., RB-1920 .... 30.00
Mason's CFJCo Patent Nov 30th 1858, Citron, Zinc Lid, Qt., RB-1920 .... 100.00
Mason's CFJCo Patent Nov 30th 1858, Cornflower Blue, Qt., RB-1920 ....*Illus* 179.00
Mason's CFJCo Patent Nov 30th 1858, Green, Zinc Lid, 1/2 Gal., RB-1920 .... 110.00
Mason's CFJCo Patent Nov 30th 1858, Light Olive Green, Zinc Lid, Qt., RB-1920 ..... 80.00
Mason's CFJCo Patent Nov 30th 1858, Light Yellow Green, Zinc Lid, Qt., RB-1920 .... 27.00
Mason's CFJCo Patent Nov 30th 1858, Olive Amber, Zinc Lid, 1/2 Gal., RB-1920 ..... 1232.00
Mason's CFJCo Patent Nov 30th 1858, Yellow Amber, Zinc Lid, Qt., RB-1920 .532.00 to 1870.00
Mason's CFJCo Patent Nov 30th 1858, Yellow Green, Zinc Lid, 1/2 Gal., RB-1920 ..... 825.00
Mason's CFJCo Patent Nov 30th 1858, Yellow Green, Zinc Lid, Qt., RB-1920 .... 40.00
Mason's Cross Patent Nov. 30th, 1858, Yellow Amber, 1/2 Gal., RB-1939 .... 305.00
Mason's Cross Patent Nov. 30th 1858, Yellow Amber, Zinc Screw Lid, Qt., RB-1940 ... 202.00
Mason's latent Nov. 30th 1858, N.C.L. Co., SCA, Error Bottle, 1/2 Gal., RB-1862 ..... 45.00

Mason's IGCo Patent Nov 30th 1858, Aqua, Screw Lid, Midget Pt., RB-1955 . . . .   193.00
Mason's Improved, Amber, Zinc Screw Lid, 1/2 Gal., RB-1939 . . . . .303.00 to 330.00
Mason's Improved, Aqua, Glass Lid, Screw Band, Gal., RB-1703 . . . . .1100.00 to 2750.00
Mason's Improved, Aqua, Zinc Screw Lid, Qt., RB-1939 . . . .   6.00
Mason's Improved, CFJCo, Aqua, Screw Band, Qt., RB-1709 . . . .   15.00
Mason's Improved, Cross, Aqua, Screw Band, Midget Pt., RB-1724 . . . .   38.00
Mason's Improved, Cross, Aqua, Screw Band, Pt., RB-1728 . . . .   8.00
Mason's Improved, Cross, Aqua, Screw Band, Qt., RB-1728 . . . .   10.00
Mason's Improved, Cross, Erased Glassboro, Trade Mark, Aqua, Qt., RB-1733 . . . .   18.00
Mason's Improved, Cross, Yellow, Amber Lid, Screw Band, Qt., RB-1733 . . . . 1064.00
Mason's Improved, Reverse CFJCo, Aqua, Screw Band, Gal., RB-1710 . . . . 2530.00
Mason's Improved, Yellow Amber, Glass Insert, 1/2 Gal., RB-1694-1 . . . .   156.00
Mason's Jar Of 1872, Aqua, Glass Lid, Zinc Screw Band, Gal., RB-1753-1 . . . . 2530.00
Mason's Keystone, Aqua, Zinc Screw Band, 1/2 Gal., RB-1737 . . . .   275.00
Mason's Keystone, Aqua, Zinc Screw Band, Midget Pt., RB-1737 . . . . 1456.00
Mason's Keystone, Aqua, Zinc Screw Band, Qt., RB-1737 . . . .   250.00
Mason's LGW Improved, Amber, Zinc Screw Lid, 1/2 Gal., RB-1938 . . . .   155.00
Mason's LGW Improved, Aqua, Qt., RB-1938 . . . .   6.00
Mason's N Patent Nov. 30th 1858, Aqua, Pt., RB-2007 . . . .   10.00
Mason's P Patent Nov 30th 1858, Aqua, 1/2 Gal., RB-2012 . . . .   150.00
Mason's Patent 1858, Ball, Aqua, Pt., RB-1769 . . . .   12.00
Mason's Patent 1858, Ball, Aqua, Qt., RB-1769 . . . .   8.00
Mason's Patent 1858, Port, Aqua, Qt., RB-1767 . . . . .5.00 to 14.00
Mason's Patent Nov 30th 1858, Amber, Zinc Screw Lid, Qt., RB-1787 . . . .   190.00
Mason's Patent Nov 30th 1858, Amber, Zinc Screw Lid, Qt., RB-1787-6 . . . .   400.00
Mason's Patent Nov 30th 1858, Apple Green, Zinc Screw Lid, 1/2 Gal., RB-1787-5 . . . .   231.00
Mason's Patent Nov 30th 1858, Apple Green, Zinc Screw Lid, Midget Pt., RB-1875 . . .   840.00
Mason's Patent Nov 30th 1858, Aqua, Milk Glass Swirls, Opalescent, Qt., RB-1787 . . . 1280.00
Mason's Patent Nov 30th 1858, Christmas Mason, Blue, Pt., RB-1780 . . . .   100.00
Mason's Patent Nov 30th 1858, Dupont, Aqua, Zinc Screw Lid, 1/2 Gal., RB-1848 . . . .   392.00
Mason's Patent Nov 30th 1858, HC&T, Aqua, Qt., RB-2050-4 . . . .   35.00
Mason's Patent Nov 30th 1858, Hourglass, Aqua, Midget Pt., RB-1869 . . . .   100.00
Mason's Patent Nov 30th 1858, Olive, Amber, Zinc Screw Lid, Pt., RB-1787 . . . .   90.00
Mason's Patent Nov 30th 1858, Olive Green, Zinc Screw Lid, ABM, Qt., RB-1787 . . . . .   532.00
Mason's Patent Nov 30th 1858, SCA, Screw Lid, Porcelain Cap, Midget Pt., RB-1875 . .   672.00
Mason's Patent Nov 30th 1858, Yellow Amber, Zinc Screw Lid, Qt., RB-1787 . .728.00 to 1092.00
Mason's Patent Nov 30th 1858, Yellow Green, Screw Lid, Porcelain Cap, Qt., RB-1875 . 1456.00
Mason's Patent Nov 30th 1858, Yellow, Zinc Screw Lid, Qt., RB-1787 . . . .   784.00
Mason's Patent Nov. 30th 1858, Amber, Ground Lip, 1/2 Gal., RB-1787 . . . .   231.00
Mason's Patent Nov. 30th 1858, Amber, Zinc Lid, Midget Pt., RB-1787 . . . . . .1980.00 to 4125.00
Mason's Patent Nov. 30th 1858, Apple Green, Zinc Screw Lid, Qt., RB-1811 . . . .   90.00
Mason's Patent Nov. 30th 1858, Aqua, Midget Pt., RB-1787-3 . . . . .8.00 to 30.00
Mason's Patent Nov. 30th 1858, Aqua, Zinc Lid, Midget Pt., RB-1787 . . . .   55.00
Mason's Patent Nov. 30th 1858, Aqua, Zinc Lid, Pt., RB-1787 . . . .   22.00
Mason's Patent Nov. 30th 1858, Aqua, Zinc Screw Lid, Midget Pt., RB-1772 . . . . 5040.00
Mason's Patent Nov. 30th 1858, Ball Blue, Zinc Lid, Pt., RB-1787 . . . .   15.00
Mason's Patent Nov. 30th 1858, Blue, Zinc Lid, Midget Pt., RB-1787 . . . .   187.00
Mason's Patent Nov. 30th 1858, CFJCo, Black, Zinc Lid, Qt., RB-1930 . . . . 10450.00
Mason's Patent Nov. 30th 1858, Christmas Mason, Blue, Pt., RB-1780 . . . .   250.00
Mason's Patent Nov. 30th 1858, Citron, Ground Lip, Qt., RB-1787 . . . .   209.00
Mason's Patent Nov. 30th 1858, Citron, Ground Lip, Zinc Screw Lid, Pt., RB-1836 . . . .   420.00
Mason's Patent Nov. 30th 1858, Citron, Screw Band, Midget Pt., RB-1784 . . . .   413.00
Mason's Patent Nov. 30th 1858, Dark Green, Zinc Lid, Pt., RB-1787 . . . . 1980.00
Mason's Patent Nov. 30th 1858, Dupont, Aqua, Zinc Screw Lid, 1/2 Gal., RB-1848 . . . .   330.00
Mason's Patent Nov. 30th 1858, Gold Amber, Zinc Lid, 1/2 Gal., RB-1964 . . . .   330.00
Mason's Patent Nov. 30th 1858, HGCo, Aqua, Zinc Lid, Midget Pt., RB-1851 . . . .   825.00
Mason's Patent Nov. 30th 1858, N.C.L. Co., Amber, 1/2 Gal., RB-1862 . . . . 4400.00
Mason's Patent Nov. 30th 1858, N.C.L. Co., Amber, Zinc Lid, Qt., RB-1861 . . . . 1430.00
Mason's Patent Nov. 30th 1858, Olive Yellow, Smooth Lip, 1/2 Gal., RB-1787 . . . . 2090.00
Mason's Patent Nov. 30th 1858, Reversed N's, Aqua, Qt., RB-1805 . . . .   40.00
Mason's Patent Nov. 30th 1858, SCA, Ground Lip, 1/2 Gal., RB-1787 . . . .   30.00
Mason's Patent Nov. 30th 1858, Teal, Ground Lip, Zinc Lid, Qt., RB-1787 . . . . 3030.00
Mason's Patent Nov. 30th 1858, U.G. Co., Aqua, Ground Lip, Qt., RB-1866 . . . .   25.00

Mason's Patent Nov. 30th 1858, Vaseline, Zinc Lid, Qt., RB-1787 . . . . 275.00
Mason's Patent Nov. 30th 1858, Yellow Amber, Glass Lid, 1/2 Gal., RB-1784 . . . . 230.00
Mason's Patent Nov. 30th 1858, Yellow Green, Zinc Lid, Qt., RB-1787 . . . . 1430.00
Mason's S Patent 1858, Cross, Aqua, Ground Lip, Qt., RB-1949 . . . . 15.00
Mason's SGCo Patent Nov. 30th 1858, Apple Green, Ground Lip, Pt., RB-1974 . . . . 105.00
Mason's SGCo Patent Nov. 30th 1858, Aqua, Ground Lip, 1/2 Gal., RB-1974 . . . . 20.00
Mason's SGCo Patent Nov. 30th 1858, Aqua, Ground Lip, Pt., RB-1974 . . . . 15.00
Mason's SGCo Patent Nov. 30th 1858, Aqua, Ground Lip, Qt., RB-1974 . . . . .8.00 to 16.00
Mason's SGCo Patent Nov. 30th 1858, Lime Aqua, Ground Lip, 1/2 Gal., RB-1974 . . . . . 198.00
Mason's Shield Union, Aqua, Zinc Lid, 1/2 Gal., RB-2133 . . . . 2750.00
Mason's Shield Union, Aqua, Zinc Lid, Qt., RB-2133 .550.00 to 1650.00
Mastodon, Aqua, Wax Sealer, Crack On Base, Qt., RB-2135 . . . . 83.00
McCarty, Pat Mar 7 1899, Clear, Glass Stopper, Pt., RB-2142 . . . . 210.00
McDonald New Perfect Seal, In Circle, Blue, Qt., RB-2148-3 . . . . 6.00
MFA, In Shield, Clear, Smooth Lip, Beaded Neck Seal, 40 Oz., RB-2166 . . . . 10.00
Michigan Mason, Aqua, Pt., RB-2172 . . . . 23.00
Mid West Canadian Made, Clear, Glass Insert, Screw Band, 1/2 Gal., RB-2177 . . . . 12.00
Mid West Canadian Made, Clear, Glass Insert, Screw Band, Pt., RB-2177 . . . . 15.00
Millville, Aqua, Glass Lid, Iron Yoke Clamp, Pt., RB-2179 . . . . 880.00
Millville, Aqua, Ground Lip, Glass Lid, Screw Band, 1/2 Pt., RB-2188 . . . . 1540.00
Millville, Hitall's Paten, Aqua, Glass Lid, Iron Yoke Clamp, 1/2 Pt., RB-2185 . . . . 231.00
Millville Atmospheric, Aqua, Glass Lid, Iron Yoke Clamp, 1/2 Gal., RB-2181 . . . . 80.00
Millville Atmospheric, Aqua, Glass Lid, Iron Yoke Clamp, Pt., RB-2180 . . . . 560.00
Millville Atmospheric, Aqua, Glass Lid, Iron Yoke Clamp, Pt., RB-2181-4 . . . . 220.00
Millville Atmospheric, Aqua, Glass Lid, Iron Yoke Clamp, Pt., RB-2183 . . . . .385.00 to 605.00
Millville Atmospheric, Aqua, Glass Lid, Iron Yoke Clamp, Qt., RB-2181 . . . . .60.00 to 198.00
Millville Atmospheric, Aqua, Glass Lid, Iron Yoke Clamp, Qt., RB-2181-5 . . . . 60.00
Millville Atmospheric, Aqua, Glass Lid, Iron Yoke Clamp, Qt., RB-2183 . . . . 88.00
Millville Atmospheric, Clear, Glass Lid, Iron Yoke Clamp, Pt., RB-2182 . . . . 467.00
Millville WTCo Improved, Aqua, Ground Lip, Glass Lid, Pt., RB-2187 . . . . 130.00
Millville WTCo Improved, Aqua, Ground Lip, Glass Lid, Qt., RB-2187 . . . . 100.00
Mission, Trade Bell Mark, Made In California, Clear, Cardboard Lid, Qt., RB-2190 . . . . . 17.00
Model Jar, Patd Aug. 27 1867, Rochester, N.Y., Aqua, Cardboard Lid, Qt., RB-2195 . . . . . 264.00
Mold Preventer, Patent Nov. 30th 1858, Aqua, Zinc Lid, Qt., RB-2197 . . . . 1760.00
Monarch Finer Foods, Around Lion's Head, Zinc Lid, Qt., RB-2200 . . . . 8.00
Moore Brothers & Co., Fislerville, N.J., Aqua, Willoughby Stopple, Qt., RB-2203 . . . . . . 660.00
Moore's Patent Dec 3d 1861, Aqua, Glass Lid, Iron Yoke Clamp, Pt., RB-2204 . . . . 357.00
Moore's Patent Dec 3d 1861, Aqua, Glass Lid, Iron Yoke Clamp, Qt., RB-2204 . . . . 95.00
Moore's Patent Dec 3d 1861, Clear, Glass Lid, Iron Yoke Clamp, Qt., RB-2204 . . . . 75.00
Mrs. Chapin's Mayonnaise, Boston, Mass., Clear, Lightning Seal, Pt., RB-585 . . . . . . .7.00 to 20.00
My Choice, Amber, Ground Lip, Glass Lid, Wire Clamp, Qt., RB-2217-1 . . . . 6005.00
Myers Test Jar, Aqua, Glass Lid, Brass Strap Clamp, 1880, Qt., RB-2218 . . . . 110.00
Myers Test Jar, Aqua, Metal Lid, Brass Strap Clamp, 1/2 Gal., RB-2218 . . . . 550.00
N E Plus Ultra Airtight, Bodine & Bros., Aqua, Glass Lid, 1/2 Gal., RB-475 . . . . 1456.00
N E Plus Ultra Airtight, Bodine & Bros., Aqua, Glass Lid, Pt., RB-475 . . . . . . .1540.00 to 5225.00
N E Plus Ultra Airtight, Bodine & Bros., Aqua, Glass Lid, Qt., RB-476 . . . . 990.00
N. Osborn, Rochester, N.Y., Aqua, Stopper Neck, Waxed Cork, Qt., RB-2276 . . . . 660.00
N. Osburn, Rochester, N.Y., Blue Green, Stopper Neck, Waxed Cork, Qt., RB-2277 . . . . . 1045.00
N. Osburn, Rochester, N.Y., Ice Blue, Stopper Neck, Waxed Cork, Qt., RB-2277 . . . . 700.00
National I, Aqua, Metal Willoughby Stopple, 1860-1880, Qt., RB-2234 . . . . 305.00
New Paragon, Aqua, Ground Lip, Glass Lid, Metal Band, Qt., RB-2289 . . . . .77.00 to 132.00
New Paragon 3, Aqua, Ground Lip, Glass Lid, Metal Band, 1/2 Gal., RB-2290 . . . . 179.00
New Paragon 5, Aqua, Ground Lip, Glass Lid, Metal Band, Qt., RB-2291 . . . . 200.00
Newmans Patent Dec. 20 1859, Blue Green, Metal Reproduction Lid, Qt., RB-2240 . . . . 672.00
OC Monogram, Aqua, Glass Lid, Wire Bail, Pt., RB-2255-9 . . . . 242.00
Ohio Fruit Jar Co., A.W. Brinkerhoff's, Aqua, 1/2 Gal., RB-2259-1 . . . . 784.00
Ohio Quality Mason, Clear, Smooth Lip, Beaded Neck Seal, 1/2 Gal., RB-2263 . . . . 18.00
Ohio Quality Mason, Clear, Smooth Lip, Beaded Neck Seal, Qt., RB-2263 . . . . .10.00 to 15.00
OK, Pat'd Feby 9th 1864, Reisd June 22d 1867, Aqua, 1/2 Gal., RB-2268 . . . . 1045.00
OK, Pat'd Feby 9th 1864, Reisd June 22d 1867, Aqua, Qt., RB-2268 . . . . 550.00
Old Judge Coffee, Owl, Clear, Smooth Lip, Wide Mouth, Gal., RB-2271-1 . . . . 25.00
Osotite, In Diamond, Clear, Metal Spring Clamp, Qt., RB-2279 . . . . 150.00
Owl, Figural, Milk Glass, Embossed Eagle Insert, Metal Screw Band, Pt., RB-3085 . . . . . 83.00

P. Lorillard Co., Amber, Cohansey Lid & Wire Clamp, Qt., RB-1542 .... 28.00
Packed By Collins Wheaton & Luhrs S.F., Aqua, 1/2 Gal., RB-637-1 .... 2860.00
Pansy, Yellow Amber, 20 Vertical Panels, Glass Lid, Zinc Band, Qt., RB-2287 .... 413.00
Paragon Valve Jar, Patd April 19th, 1870, Aqua, Glass Lid, Metal Band, Qt., RB-2292 ... 550.00
Patd March 26th 1867, 7, B.B. Wilcox, Aqua, Glass Lid, Wire Bail, 1/2 Gal., RB-3006 . 67.00
Patd March 26th 1867, B.B. Wilcox, Aqua, Embossed, Qt., RB-3003 .... 125.00
Patd March 26th 1867, B.B. Wilcox, Aqua, Glass Fin Lid, Wire Bail, Qt., RB-3000 .... 78.00
Patd March 26th 1867, B.B. Wilcox, Aqua, Glass Lid, c.1880, Qt., RB-3002 .... 110.00
Patd March 26th 1867, B.B. Wilcox, Aqua, Wire Bail, Glass Lid, Qt., RB-3001 .... 110.00
Patd. Octr. 18th 1864, J.J. Squire 4, Aqua, Glass Lid, Cross Bar, Qt., RB-2693-1 ...... 2310.00
Patd. Octr. 18th 1864, J.J. Squire, Pale Blue Green, Glass Lid, Qt., RB-2694 .... 1100.00
Patent Pending M. P. Co., Macomb, Ill., Stoneware, Zinc Lid, Pt., RB-1603-2 .... 90.00
Patent Sept. 18, 1860, Aqua, Ground Lip, Groove Ring Wax Sealer, Qt., RB-2295 .95.00 to 165.00
Pearl, Aqua, Ground Lip, Glass Lid, Metal Screw Band, c.1890, Pt. 305.00
Peerless, Aqua, Glass Lid, Iron Yoke Clamp, 1/2 Gal., RB-2322 .... 120.00
Peerless, Aqua, Glass Lid, Iron Yoke Clamp, Qt., RB-2322 .... .148.00 to 200.00
Perfect Seal Wide Mouth Adjustable, Clear, Square, Qt., RB-2348 .... 12.00
Perfection, Clear, Ground Lip, Glass Lid, Wire Clamp, Qt., RB-2330 .... 50.00
Perfection, SCA, Ground Lip, Glass Lid, Wire Clamp, Qt., RB-2330 .... .45.00 to 50.00
Pet, Aqua, Glass Lid, Spring Wire Clamp, Coil, 1/2 Gal., RB-2359 .... 198.00
Pet, Aqua, Glass Lid, Spring Wire Clamp, Coil, Qt., RB-2359 .... 143.00
Petal, Aqua, Applied Lip, IP, 1/2 Gal., RB-3067 .... .280.00 to 330.00
Petal, Aqua, Applied Lip, IP, Qt., RB-3067 .... 160.00
Petal, Blue Aqua, Applied Lip, IP, Qt., RB-3067 .... .90.00 to 140.00
Petal, Cobalt Blue, Applied Lip, IP, Qt., RB-3067 .... 7150.00
Petal, Dark Olive Green, Applied Lip, IP, Qt., RB-3067 .... 1430.00
Petal, Olive Green, Applied Lip, IP, 1/2 Gal., RB-3067 .... 2585.00
Pine Deluxe Jar, Clear, Smooth Lip, Lightning Seal, Pt., RB-2366 .... 12.00
Pine P Mason, P In Square, Smooth Lip, Lightning Seal, Qt., RB-2367 .... 35.00
Pomona Patented Mar 10th 1868, Aqua, Glass Lid, Metal Yoke Clamp, Qt., RB-2372 .. 1344.00
Porcelain Lined, Aqua, 1/2 Gal., RB-2374 .... 18.00
Porcelain Lined, Aqua, Qt., RB-2374 .... 18.00
Potter & Bodine Philadelphia, F. & J., Aqua, Ground Lip, Wire Closure, Qt., RB-2381 .. 94.00
Potter & Bodine's Air-Tight, Philada, Aqua, Wax Sealer, 1/2 Gal., RB-2382 .... 177.00
Potter & Bodine's Air-Tight, Philada, Aqua, Wax Sealer, Pt., RB-2383-1 .... 1064.00
Potter & Bodine's Air-Tight, Philada, Barrel, Aqua, IP, Qt., RB-2390 .... 1624.00
Potter & Bodine's Air-Tight, Philada, Barrel, Aqua, Pontil, Pt., RB-2387 .... 1700.00
Potter & Bodine's Air-Tight, Philada, Barrel, Aqua, Pontil, Qt., RB-2387 .... 1092.00
Potter & Bodine's Air-Tight, Philada, Barrel, Aqua, Pontil, Qt., RB-2387-1 .... 990.00
Potter & Bodine's Air-Tight, Philada, Barrel, Aqua, Pt., RB-2386 .... 770.00
Potter & Bodine's Air-Tight, Philada, Barrel, Aqua, Qt., RB-2385 .... 1625.00
Potter & Bodine's Air-Tight, Philada, Barrel, Blue Aqua, Qt., RB-2385 .... 963.00
Presto, Clear, Square, Smooth Lip, Lightning Dimple Neck Seal, 1/2 Pt., RB-2399 ...... 25.00
Presto Glass Top W88X, Clear, Lightning Dimple Neck Seal, 1/2 Pt., RB-2406 .....18.00 to 20.00
Presto Supreme Mason, Clear, Smooth Lip, Beaded Neck Seal, Qt., RB-2407 .... 2.00
Presto Supreme Mason Duraglas, Clear, Smooth Lip, Beaded Neck Seal, Pt., RB-2412 .. 1.00
Protector, Aqua, 6-Sided, Ground Lip, Metal Lid, Pt., RB-2421 .... 264.00
Protector, Aqua, Ground Lip, Metal Lid, Wire Clamp, 1/2 Gal., RB-2420 .... .55.00 to 90.00
Protector, Aqua, Ground Lip, Metal Lid, Wire Clamp, Pt., RB-2420 .... 467.00
Puritan, L.S. Co., Aqua, Glass Citron Lid, Iron Ring & Wire Clamp, Pt., RB-2425 ...... 165.00
Puritan Trade Mark, Aqua, Glass Lid, Iron Ring, Wire Clamp, Qt., RB-2426 .... 660.00
Put On Rubber Before Filling, Mrs. S. T. Rorer's, Star & Crescent, Aqua, Qt., RB-2728 . 660.00
Putnam, Amber, Ground Lip, Old Style Lightning Seal, Qt., RB-1492 .... 40.00
Queen, Aqua, Glass Insert, Screw Band, 1/2 Gal., RB-2433 .... 50.00
Queen, Patd Dec 28th 1858, Patd June 16th 1868, Aqua, Qt., RB-2432 .... 50.00
Quick Seal, In Circle, Blue, Smooth Lip, Pt., RB-2452 .... 5.00
Quick Seal, In Circle, Blue, Smooth Lip, Qt., RB-2451 .... 5.00
Quick Seal, In Circle, Pat'd July 14, 1908, Aqua, Qt., RB-2455 .... 7.00
Quick Seal, In Circle, Pat'd July 14, 1908, Clear, Qt., RB-2454 .... 5.00
Railroad, see Fruit Jar, Helme's
Ravenna Glass Works, Air-Tight, Barrel, Aqua, Wax Seal, Lid, Pt., RB-2471 .... 6440.00
Ravenna Glass Works Ohio, Air-Tight, Barrel, Aqua, Wax Seal Lid, Qt., RB-2472 ...... 2750.00

Fruit Jar, Mason's CFJCo Patent
Nov 30th 1858, Cornflower
Blue, Qt., RB-1920

Fruit Jar, Sun Trademark,
Circle, Aqua, Glass Lid, Metal
Yoke Clamp, Pt., RB-2761

Fruit Jar, Weideman Boy
Brand Cleveland, Clear,
Glass Lid, Qt., RB-2931

Reliance Brand Wide Mouth Mason, Clear, 40 Oz., RB-2491 .... 15.00
Retentive, Aqua, Ground Lip, Glass Lid, Wire Clamp, Pt., RB-2498 .... 880.00
Root Mason, Aqua, Zinc Lid, 1/2 Gal., RB-2510 .... 8.00
Root Mason, Aqua, Zinc Lid, Qt., RB-2510 .... 6.00
Root Mason, Olive Green, Zinc Lid, Pt., RB-2510 .... 100.00
Rose, Clear, Smooth Lip, Glass Lid, Screw Band, Qt., RB-2511 .... 20.00
Royal, Aqua, Glass Insert, Zinc Collar, Qt., RB-2514 .... 200.00
Royal, Aqua, Ground Lip, Glass Insert, Zinc Collar, Qt., RB-2513 .... 209.00
Royal Of 1876, Apple Green, Glass Lid, Screw Band, 1/2 Gal., RB-2515 .... 231.00
Royal Of 1876, Aqua, Glass Lip, Screw Band, Qt., RB-2515 .... 125.00
Royal Trademark Full Measure Registered Pint, Clear, Pt., RB-2519 .... 10.00
Royal Trademark Full Measure Registered Quart, SCA, Qt., RB-2518 .... 10.00
S Mason's Patent 1858, Aqua, 1/2 Gal., RB-1770 .... 10.00
S.G.W. Lou Ky, Aqua, Groove Ring Wax Sealer, Qt., RB-2617 .... 20.00
Safe Seal, Aqua, Lightning Beaded Neck Seal, Pt., RB-2530 .... 9.00
Safety, Aqua, Ground Lip, Glass Lid, Wire Clamp, Qt., RB-2534 .... 70.00
Safety, Yellow Amber, Ground Lip, Glass Lid, Wire Clamp, Pt., RB-2534 .... 385.00
Salem Jar, Holz Clark & Taylor Salem N.J., Aqua, Threaded Glass Stopper, Qt., RB-2544 280.00
Samco Genuine Mason, Clear, Beaded Neck Seal, Qt., RB-2545 .... 4.00
San Francisco Glass Works, Aqua, Groove Ring Wax Seal, Qt., RB-2553 .... 715.00
Schaffer Jar Rochester, N.Y., JCS, Aqua, Glass Lid, Wire Bail, Pt., RB-2562 .... 1232.00
Schram, Clear, Metal Lid, 1/2 Gal., RB-2572 .... 12.00
Schram Automatic Sealer, Clear, Metal Lid, Wire Clamp, Pt., RB-2566 .... 12.00
Schram Automatic Sealer B, Clear, Metal Lid, Wire Clamp, Pt., RB-2569 .... 18.00
Schram Automatic Sealer B, Clear, Metal Lid, Wire Clamp, Qt., RB-2569 ....10.00 to 12.00
Scranton Jar, Aqua, Glass Lid, Spring Wire Clamp, Qt., RB-2576 .... 935.00
Seal Tite, Clear, Lightning Beaded Neck Seal, Pt., RB-2605 .... 20.00
Security Seal FGCo, Clear, Old Style Lightning Seal, Qt., RB-2608 .... 16.00
Security Seal FGCo, SCA, Old Style Lightning Seal, Qt., RB-2608 .... 10.00
Simplex, In Diamond, Clear, Glass Screw Lid, 1/3 Pt., RB-2632 ....20.00 to 22.00
SKO Queen Trademark Wide Mouth Adjustable, Aqua, Pt., RB-2444 .... 5.00
SKO Queen Trademark Wide Mouth Adjustable, Clear, Pt., RB-2447 .... 5.00
SKO Queen Trademark Wide Mouth Adjustable, SCA, Twin Wire Clamps, Pt., RB-2444 . 13.00
Smalley, Aqua, Ground Lip, Dome Lid, Wire Bail, Pt., RB-2668 .... 522.00
Smalley Full Measure AGS Quart, Amber, Aluminum Lid, Square, Qt., RB-2648 .... 75.00
Smalley Full Measure AGS Quart, Amber, Aluminum Lid, Square, Qt., RB-2650-1 ...... 75.00
Smalley Full Measure AGS Quart, Clear, Aluminum Lid, Square, Qt., RB-2648 .... 10.00
Smalley Self Sealer Wide Mouth, Clear, Old Style Lightning Seal, Qt., RB-2667 .... 10.00
Smalley's Nu-Seal Trademark, In Diamond, Clear, Pt., RB-2658 .... 12.00
Standard, W. Mc C & Co., Aqua, Groove Ring Wax Sealer, Qt., RB-2705 .... 33.00

Star, A. Liebenstein & Co., Aqua, Glass Lid, Qt., RB-2723 .... 2420.00
Star Emblem, Circle Of Fruit, Aqua, Ground Lip, Tin Lid, Qt., RB-2724 .... 255.00
Star Glass Co. New Albany, Ind., Amber, Groove Ring Wax Sealer, 1/2 Gal., RB-2729 ... 2800.00
Steer's Head, see Fruit Jar, Flaccus Bros.
Stevens Tin Top, Patd July 27, 1875, Aqua, Metal Lid, Qt., RB-2738 .... 85.00
Stevens Tin Top, Patd July 27, 1875, Lewis & Neblett, Aqua, Qt., RB-2741 .... 275.00
Sun Trademark, Circle, Apple Green, Glass Lid, Metal Yoke Clamp, Qt., RB-2761 ...... 121.00
Sun Trademark, Circle, Aqua, Glass Lid, Metal Yoke Clamp, Qt., RB-2761 .... 125.00
Sun Trademark, Circle, Aqua, Glass Lid, Metal Yoke Clamp, Pt., RB-2761 .... *Illus* 157.00
Sunshine Brand Coffee, Clear, Beaded Neck Seal, 40 Oz., RB-2766 .... 15.00
Sure, Pat'd June 21st, 1870, Aqua, Glass Lid, Wire Bail, Qt., RB-2771 .... 825.00
Sure Seal, In Circle, Blue, Lightning Beaded Neck Seal, Pt., RB-2773 .... 8.00
Swayzee's Improved Mason, Apple Green, Smooth Lip, Qt., RB-2780-1 .... 230.00
Swayzee's Improved Mason, Aqua, Smooth Lip, 1/2 Gal., RB-2782 ....10.00 to 15.00
Swayzee's Improved Mason, Aqua, Smooth Lip, Pt., RB-2780 .... 15.00
Swayzee's Improved Mason, Aqua, Smooth Lip, Qt., RB-2780 ....10.00 to 16.00
Swayzee's Improved Mason, Light Green, Smooth Lip, Qt., RB-2780 .... 12.00
T. Hopkins Jr., Skipton, Md., Aqua, Pontil, Qt., RB-1267 .... 2200.00
Texas Mason, Map Of Texas, Clear, Metal Lid, Pt., RB-2796 .... 25.00
Thompson & Hills Ltd. Auckland, SCA, Lid, Smooth Lip, Qt., RB-2799 .... 255.00
Thompson's Flavors New York, Aqua, Glass Lid, Wire Bail, 1/2 Gal., RB-2798 .... 330.00
Thorne & Wilcox Co., Wellsville, N.Y., Pat May 10, '90, Clear, Metal Lid, Gal. 305.00
Tight Seal, Pat'd July 14, 1908, Blue, 1/2 Gal., RB-2808 .... 22.00
Tight Seal, Pat'd July 14, 1908, Blue, Qt., RB-2808 .... 6.00
Trade Mark Bee Hive, Aqua, Glass Lid, Screw Band, Qt., RB-433 ....180.00 to 357.00
Trademark Climax Registered, Blue, Smooth Lip, 1/2 Pt., RB-612-1 .... 125.00
Trademark Lightning, Aqua, Old Style Lightning Seal, Qt., RB-1499 .... 50.00
Trademark Lightning, H.W.P. Monogram, Amber, Qt., RB-1500 ....500.00 to 1175.00
Trademark Lightning, H.W.P. Monogram, Aqua, Qt., RB-1500 .... 325.00
Trademark Lightning, H.W.P. Monogram, Yellow Amber, Qt., RB-1500 .... 3025.00
Trademark Lightning, H.W.P. On Base, Amber, 1/2 Gal., RB-1498 .... 33.00
Trademark Lightning, H.W.P. On Base, Aqua, 1/2 Gal., RB-1498 .... 40.00
Trademark Lightning, Putnam On Base, Amber, 1/2 Pt., RB-1491 .... 1980.00
Trademark Lightning, Putnam On Base, Amber, Lightning Seal Type 2, Qt., RB-1489 ... 110.00
Trademark Lightning, Putnam On Base, Amber, Qt., RB-1489 ....38.00 to 55.00
Trademark Lightning, Putnam On Base, Aqua, Qt., RB-1489 .... 5.00
Trademark Lightning, Putnam On Base, Aqua, Qt., RB-1491 .... 231.00
Trademark Lightning, Putnam On Base, Citron, Pt., RB-1489 .... 385.00
Trademark Lightning, Putnam On Base, Citron, Qt., RB-1489 .... 385.00
Trademark Lightning, Putnam On Base, Clear, 1/2 Pt., RB-1495 .... 20.00
Trademark Lightning, Putnam On Base, Cornflower Blue, Aqua Glass Lid, Qt., RB-1489 770.00
Trademark Lightning, Putnam On Base, Emerald Green, Aqua Glass Lid, Qt., RB-1489 .. 4675.00
Trademark Lightning, Putnam On Base, Olive Yellow, Qt., RB-1489 ....209.00 to 330.00
Trademark Lightning, Putnam On Base, Red Amber, Qt., RB-1489 .... 75.00
Trademark Lightning, Putnam On Base, Yellow Amber, 1/2 Gal., RB-1489 ....40.00 to 110.00
Trademark Lightning, Putnam On Base, Yellow Amber, Qt., RB-1489 ....130.00 to 210.00
Trademark Lightning Registered U.S. Patent Office, Aqua, 1/2 Gal., RB-1502 .... 413.00
Trademark Lightning Registered U.S. Patent Office, Aqua, Pt., RB-1502 .... 20.00
Trademark Lightning Registered U.S. Patent Office, Aqua, Qt., RB-1501 .... 15.00
Trademark Lightning Registered U.S. Patent Office, Clear, 1/2 Gal., RB-1501 .... 8.00
Trademark Lightning Registered U.S. Patent Office, Cornflower Blue, Pt., RB-1501 .... 88.00
Trademark Lightning Registered U.S. Patent Office, Cornflower Blue, Qt., RB-1501 ... 100.00
Trademark The Dandy, Amber, Glass Lid, Wire Bail, 1/2 Gal., RB-751 .... 198.00
Trademark The Dandy, Olive Amber, Glass Lid, Wire Bail, Pt., RB-751 ....255.00 to 935.00
Trademark The Dandy, SCA, Glass Lid, Wire Bail, 1/2 Gal., RB-751 .... 60.00
Triumph No. 1, Aqua, Wax Seal Groove, 1/2 Gal., RB-2814 .... 908.00
Triumph No. 1, Aqua, Wax Seal Groove, Qt., RB-2814 ....355.00 to 357.00
Triumph No. 2, Aqua, Wax Seal Groove, Qt., RB-2815 .... 330.00
Union No. 2, Aqua, Wax Seal Groove, Qt., RB-2840 .... 467.00
Union No. 4, Beaver Falls, Aqua, Groove Ring, Wax Sealer, 1/2 Gal., RB-2851 .... 450.00
Union No. 4, Beaver Falls, Aqua, Groove Ring, Wax Sealer, Qt., RB-2851 .... 99.00
United Drug Co., Boston, Mass., Clear, Old Style Lightning Seal, Qt., RB-2853 .... 20.00
Unmarked, 3-Piece Mold, Teal, Tin Lid, Qt., RB-3063 .... 784.00

Unmarked, Aqua, Applied Lip, IP, 1/2 Gal., RB-3060 .... 88.00
Unmarked, Aqua, Bell Shape, Groove Ring, Wax Sealer, Qt., RB-3061 .... 77.00
Unmarked, Aqua, Embossed, 1/2 Gal. 35.00
Unmarked, Aqua, Rolled Lip, IP, RB-3059 .... 110.00
Unmarked, Freeblown, Applied Lip, Pontil, 6 In. 190.00
Unmarked, Lime Green, Tooled Lip, Rolled Lip, IP, 1855-1865, Qt. 550.00
Unmarked, Yellow Amber, Groove Ring, Wax Sealer, Qt., RB-3062 .... 100.00
Vacuum Tite Jar, Clear, Metal Lid, Qt., RB-2871 .... 18.00
Valve Jar Co. Philadelphia, Aqua, Wire Coil Clamp, Qt., RB-2873 .... 412.00
Valve Jar Co. Philadelphia, Patent March 10th 1868, Aqua, Lid, Coil Clamp, Qt., RB-2875   357.00
Van Vliet Improved, Patd May 3-81, Amber, Glass Lid, Qt., RB-2881 .... 19800.00
Van Vliet Jar Of 1881, Aqua, Glass Lid, Metal Yoke Clamp, Pt., RB-2878 .... 1760.00
Van Vliet Jar Of 1881, Aqua, Glass Lid, Metal Yoke Clamp, Qt., RB-2879 .... 880.00
Van Vliet Jar Of 1881, Aqua, Glass Lid, Metal Yoke Clamp, Qt., RB-2880 ......925.00 to 952.00
Victory, Patd Feby 9th 1864, Aqua, Glass Cap, Zinc Screw Band, Qt., RB-2894-1 .412.00 to 880.00
Victory I, In Shield On Lid, Clear, Glass Lip, Twin Wire Clamps, 1/2 Pt., RB-2897 ..... 20.00
Victory I, Patd Feby 9th 1864, Apple Green, Glass Cap, Zinc Screw Band, Qt., RB-2895 . 1045.00
Victory I, Patd Feby 9th 1864, Aqua, Glass Cap, Zinc Screw Band, 1/2 Gal., RB-2891 .. 99.00
Victory I, Patd Feby 9th 1864, Aqua, Glass Cap, Zinc Screw Band, Pt., RB-2892 .... 99.00
Victory I, Patd Feby 9th 1864, Aqua, Glass Cap, Zinc Screw Band, Qt., RB-2891 ...... 65.00
Victory I, Patd Feby 9th 1864, Blue, Glass Cap, Screw Band, 1/2 Gal., RB-2895 .... 1320.00
Victory I, Patd Feby 9th 1864, Blue, Glass Cap, Zinc Screw Band, Qt., RB-2896 .... 1210.00
Victory I, Patd Feby 9th 1864, Yellow Green, Aqua Glass Lid, 1/2 Gal., RB-2895 ...... 990.00
Victory Jar, Clear, Glass Lid, Twin Metal Clips, 1/4 Pt., RB-2900 .... 50.00
Victory Jar, Clear, Glass Lid, Twin Metal Clips, Pt., RB-2900 .... 10.00
Violin, Aqua, 1920s, 6 In. 35.00
Wampoles, Milk Food, Aqua, Ground Lip, Metal Lid, Square, 1/2 Gal., RB-2908-1 ..... 40.00
Wan-Eta Cocoa Boston, Amber, Smooth Lip, Qt., RB-2909 .... 35.00
Weideman Boy Brand Cleveland, Clear, Glass Lid, Qt., RB-2931 .... *Illus*   12.00
Weir, Pat Mar 1st 92 April 16th 1901 No. 2, Stoneware, Metal Clamp, Qt., RB-2935-1 .. 30.00
Western Pride, Patented June 22, 1875, Aqua, Glass Lid, Metal Clamp, 1/2 Gal., RB-2945   77.00
Western Pride, Patented June 22, 1875, Aqua, Glass Lid, Metal Clamp, Qt., RB-2945 ... 303.00
Wheeler, Aqua, Ground Lip, 6-Piece Hinged Wire Clamp, Qt., RB-2953 .... 468.00
Whitall Tatum & Co. Philadelphia New York, Clear, Glass Lid, RB-2958 .... 80.00
White Crown Mason, Aqua, Milk Glass Insert, Zinc Lid, Pt., RB-2961 .... 8.00
Whitney, Aqua, Threaded Glass Lid, Zinc Screw Band, Qt., RB-2967 .... 825.00
Whitney Mason Pat'd 1858, Gold Amber, Zinc Lid, Qt., RB-2968 .... 4130.00
Winslow Improved Valve Jar, Aqua, Glass Lid, Iron Yoke Clamp, 1/2 Gal., RB-3021 .... 770.00
Winslow Improved Valve Jar, Aqua, Glass Lid, Iron Yoke Clamp, Qt., RB-3021 .... 264.00
Winslow Jar, Aqua, Glass Lid, Brass Wire Clamp, 1/2 Gal., RB-3023 .... 143.00
Winslow Jar, Aqua, Glass Lid, Brass Wire Clamp, 20 Oz., RB-3023 ....99.00 to 220.00
Wm L. Haller, Carlisle Pa., Ladies Favorite, Aqua, Willoughby Stopple, Pt., RB-1180 .... 15400.00
Wm L. Haller, Carlisle Pa, Aqua, Willoughby Stopple, 1/2 Gal., RB-1179 .... 231.00
Woodbury, Aqua, Ground Lip, Glass Lid With Vent Hole, Qt., RB-3027 .... 50.00
Woodbury Improved WGW, Aqua, Glass Lid, Zinc Screw Cover, 1/2 Gal., RB-3029 .40.00 to 60.00
Woodbury Improved WGW, Aqua, Glass Lid, Zinc Screw Cover, Qt., RB-3029 .....35.00 to 40.00
Yeoman's Fruit Bottle, Patent Applied For, Aqua, Wax Cork, 1/2 Gal., RB-3040 .... 50.00

─────────────────────── GARNIER ───────────────────────

The house of Garnier Liqueurs was founded in 1859 in Enghien, France. Figurals have
been made through the nineteenth and twentieth centuries, except for the years of Prohibition and World War II. Julius Wile and Brothers, a New York City firm established
in 1877, became the exclusive U.S. agents for Garnier in 1885. Many of the bottles
were not sold in the United States but were purchased in France or the Caribbean and
brought back home. Only miniature bottles were sold in the United States from 1970 to
1973. From 1974 to 1978, Garnier was distributed in the United States by Fleischmann
Distilling Company. In 1978 the Garnier trademark was acquired by Standard Brands,
Inc., the parent company of Julius Wile Sons and Company and Fleischmann Distilling
Co., and a few of the full-sized bottles were again sold in the United States. Standard
Brands later merged with Nabisco Brands, Inc. In 1987 Nabisco sold the Garnier
Liqueurs trademark to McGuiness Distillers, Ltd., of Canada, which was sold to Corby
Distillers. The liquor is no longer made.

Acorn, 1910 .... 43.00

Aladdin's Lamp, 1963 . . . . .40.00 to 50.00
Alfa Romeo, 1913 Model, 1969 . . . . .27.00 to 29.00
Alfa Romeo, 1924 Model, 1969 . . . . 30.00
Alfa Romeo, 1929 Model, 1969 . . . . 25.00
Apollo, 1969 . . . . 20.00
Aztec, 1965 . . . . 18.00
Baby Foot, 1963 . . . . .14.00 to 16.00
Bacchus, 1967 . . . . 25.00
Baseball Player, 1970 . . . . .18.00 to 20.00
Bellows, 1969 . . . . .17.00 to 19.00
Blue Bird, 1970 . . . . 17.00
Bouquet, 1966 . . . . 20.00
Bulldog 20.00
Bullfighter, 1963 . . . . 27.00
Burmese Man, 1965 . . . . .18.00 to 20.00
Butterfly, 1970, Miniature 10.00
Candlestick, Bedroom, 1967 . . . . 24.00
Candlestick, Glass, 1965 . . . . 20.00
Cannon, 1964 . . . . 55.00
Cardinal, 1969 . . . . 16.00
Cards, Miniature, 1970 . . . . 14.00
Carrossee Coach, 1970 . . . . 28.00
Cat, 1930 . . . . 76.00
Cat, Black, Gray, 1962 . . . . 20.00
Chalet, 1955 . . . . .40.00 to 45.00
Chimney, 1956 . . . . 58.00
Chinese Man, 1970 . . . . 20.00
Chinese Woman, 1970 . . . . 20.00
Christmas Tree, 1956 . . . . 65.00
Citroen, 1922 Model, 1970 . . . . 25.00
Clock, 1958 . . . . .20.00 to 30.00
Clown, No. 20, 1910 . . . . 42.00
Clown, With Tuba, 1955 . . . . 15.00
Clown's Head, 1931 . . . . 75.00
Coffee Mill, 1966 . . . . 25.00
Coffeepot, 1962 . . . . 35.00
Collie, 1970 . . . . 20.00
Country Jug, 1937 . . . . 30.00
Deer, 1964 . . . . 28.00
Diamond Bottle, 1969 . . . . 13.00
Drunkard, Millord, 1956 . . . . 22.00
Duck, No. 21, 1910 . . . . 16.00
Duckling, 1956 . . . . 35.00
Duo Firefly, 1959 . . . . 15.00
Egg House, 1956 . . . . 73.00
Eiffel Tower, 1950 . . . . 21.00
Elephant, No. 66, 1932 . . . . 7.00
Empire Vase, 1962 . . . . 15.00
Fiat, 1913 Model, Nuevo, 1969 . . . . 28.00
Fiat, 1924 Model, 1969 . . . . 25.00
Football Player, 1970 . . . . 16.00
Ford, 1913 Model, 1969 . . . . 25.00
German Shepherd, 1970 . . . . 18.00
Goldfinch, No. 11, 1970 . . . . 17.00
Goose, 1955 . . . . 17.00
Greyhound, 1930 . . . . 75.00
Guitar & Mandolin 18.00
Harlequin, No. 166, 1958 . . . . 35.00
Hockey Player, 1970 . . . . 20.00
Hula Hoop, 1959 . . . . 30.00
Humoristiques, 1934, Miniature 30.00
Hunting Vase, 1964 . . . . 28.00

```
Inca, 1969 .........................................................  17.00
Indian, 1958 .......................................................  17.00
Indian Princess ....................................................  14.00
Indy 500, No. 1, 1970 ........................................35.00 to 40.00
Jockey, 1961 .......................................................  28.00
LaDona, 1963 ......................................................  35.00
Lafayette, 1949 ....................................................  20.00
Laurel Crown, 1963 ................................................  22.00
Locomotive, 1969 ..................................................  20.00
Log, Quarter, 1958 ................................................  30.00
Log, Round, 1958 ..................................................  25.00
Loon, 1970 ........................................................  14.00
Maharajah, 1958 ...................................................  74.00
Marquis, 1931 .....................................................  74.00
Marseilles, 1970 ...................................................  20.00
Meadowlark, 1969 ............................................15.00 to 20.00
MG, 1913 Model, 1970 .............................................  27.00
Mocking Bird, 1970 ...........................................20.00 to 25.00
Montmartre, 1960 ..................................................  15.00
Napoleon, 1969 ....................................................  27.00
Oasis, 1959 .......................................................  20.00
Oriole, 1970 ......................................................  20.00
Packard, 1930 Model, 1970 .........................................  20.00
Painting, 1961 .....................................................  28.00
Paris Monuments, 1966 ............................................  35.00
Parrot, 1910 ......................................................  34.00
Pelican, 1935 .....................................................  50.00
Penguin, 1930 .....................................................  50.00
Pheasant, 1969 ....................................................  25.00
Pistol, Horse, 1964 ...............................................  20.00
Policeman, 1970 ...................................................  23.00
Policeman, Bahamas, 1970 ..........................................  20.00
Policeman, New York, 1970 .........................................  20.00
Policeman, Paris, 1970 .............................................  20.00
Pony, 1961 ........................................................  30.00
Poodle, Black, 1954 ...............................................  15.00
Poodle, White, 1954 ...............................................  15.00
Quail Valley, 1969 ................................................  20.00
Rainbow, No. 143, 1955 ............................................  28.00
Renault, 1911 Model, 1969 .........................................  29.00
Roadrunner, 1969 ............................................20.00 to 25.00
Robin, 1970 .......................................................  20.00
Rolls-Royce, 1908 Model, 1970 .....................................  25.00
Rooster, Black, 1952 ..............................................  16.00
Rooster, Maroon, 1952 .............................................  20.00
Soccer Shoe, 1962 .................................................  35.00
Soldier, Faceless, 1949 ............................................  61.00
Soldier, With Drum, 1949 ..........................................  53.00
SS France, 1962 ...................................................  100.00
SS Queen Mary, 1970 ...............................................  28.00
Stanley, 1907 Model, 1970 .........................................  27.00
Tam Tam, 1961 ....................................................  50.00
Taxi, Paris, 1960 ............................................54.00 to 60.00
Tierce, Musical, 1965 ..............................................  45.00
Trout, 1967 .......................................................  20.00
Vase, Miniature, 1935 .............................................  10.00
Violin, 1966 ......................................................  35.00
Watch, Blue, 1966 .................................................  26.00
Watch, Tan, 1966 .................................................  25.00
Watering Can, 1958 ..........................................15.00 to 17.00
Woman, With Jug, 1930 ............................................  50.00
```

Gemel, Nailsea
Type, White Loops
On Clear, Cobalt
Rings On Mouth,
Pontil, 9 3/8 In.

Want to remove a bottle stopper that is stuck? Mix a teaspoon of rubbing alcohol with a half-teaspoon of glycerin and a half-teaspoon of salt. Pour the liquid around the stopper, let it seep in. Try removing the stopper after 24 hours.

GEMEL

Gemel bottles are made in pairs. Two bottles are blown separately then joined together, usually with the two necks pointing in different directions. Gemels are popular for serving oil and vinegar or two different types of liqueurs.

Gourd Shape, Pedestal, 10 In. 375.00
J.P.S., Etched, Flowers & Ferns, Pontil, 7 1/2 In. 220.00
Nailsea Type, White Loops On Clear, Cobalt Rings On Mouth, Pontil, 9 3/8 In. . . . . .*Illus* 336.00

GIN

The word gin comes from the Dutch word genever, meaning juniper. It is said that gin was invented in the seventeenth century in Holland to be used as a medicine. One of the earliest types of gin was what today is called *Geneva* or *Hollands* gin. It is made from a barley malt grain mash and juniper berries. The alcohol content is low and it is usually not used for cocktails. In some countries it is considered medicine. In England and America, the preferred drink is dry gin, which is made with juniper berries, coriander seeds, angelica root, and other flavors. The best dry gin is distilled, not mixed by the process used during Prohibition to make bathtub gin. Another drink is Tom gin, much like dry gin but with sugar added. Gin bottles have been made since the 1600s. Most of them have straight sides. Gin has always been an inexpensive drink, which is why so many of these bottles were made. Many were of a type called *case bottles* today. The case bottle was made with straight sides so that 4 to 12 bottles would fit tightly into a wooden packing case.

A. Houtman & Co., Case, Dark Amber, Applied Top, 9 3/4 In. 35.00
A. Van Hoboken & Co., Case, Olive Green, AVH Seal, Bubbles, Rolled Lip, 10 1/2 In. . . . 69.00
A. Van Hoboken & Co., Rotterdam On 2 Sides, Olive Green, AVH Seal, 9 3/4 In. 49.00
A. Van Hoboken & Co., Rotterdam, Case, Olive Green, Applied Seal & Lip, AVH Seal . . . 55.00
A. Van Hoboken & Co., Rotterdam, Seal, Applied Top . . . .*Illus* 50.00
A. Van Hoboken & Co., Rotterdam, Seal, Mushroom Top 50.00
A.C.A. Nolet, Schiedam, Case, Amber, Applied Top, 10 In. 45.00
A.C.A. Nolet, Schiedam, Case, Olive Green, Milky Swirls, Applied Top, 9 In. 35.00
Beefeater, Doulton, Miniature 52.00
Bininger, see the Bininger category
Black Glass, Applied Lip, Pontil Base, 9 1/2 In. 225.00
Black Glass, OP, Applied Lip, Early 19th Century, 9 3/4 In. 125.00
Blankenheym & Nolet, Case, Dark Olive Green, 10 1/2 In. 31.00
Blankenheym & Nolet, Olive Green, Applied Tapered Top, 9 1/2 In. 36.00
Boll & Dunlop, Rotterdam, Holland, Case, Olive Green, Applied Top, 10 In. 30.00
Booth's Superior, Old Tom, Aqua, Labels, 1884-1885, Qt. 9.00
Carbon's Medicated Gin, Clear, Tooled Mouth, 1890-1910, 10 3/4 In. 616.00
Case, Amber, Green Tint, Applied Flanged Top, Pontil, 8 1/4 In. 143.00
Case, Light Olive Green, Applied Top, Smooth Base, 1870s, 10 In. 110.00
Case, Light Olive Green, Pontil, Applied Top, 9 3/4 In. 99.00
Case, Medium Olive Amber, Dip Mold, Applied Mouth, 1770-1810, 13 1/4 x 4 1/4 In. . . . 220.00
Case, Medium Olive Amber, Dip Mold, Applied Mouth, Pontil, 1780-1810, 9 1/2 In. .*Illus* 121.00
Case, Olive Amber, Dip Mold, Applied Mouth, OP, 10 1/2 In. 235.00

Gin, A. Van
Hoboken & Co.,
Rotterdam, Seal,
Applied Top

Gin, Case, Medium
Olive Amber, Dip
Mold, Applied
Mouth, Pontil, 1780-
1810, 9 1/2 In.

Gin, Vanderveer's
Medicated Gin,
Schiedam,
Schnapps, Olive
Green, 7 In.

Case, Olive Green, Applied Flared Lip, Bubbles, 9 1/2 In. 55.00
Case, Olive Yellow Amber, Dip Mold, Applied Mouth, Pontil, 1770-1800, 10 In. 110.00
Case, Olive Yellow, 1780-1810 . . . . 150.00
Case, Tapered, Olive Amber, OP, Bubbles, 10 1/2 In. 235.00
Cosmopoliet, J.J. Melchers, WZ, Schiedam, Case, Amber, Embossed Man, 9 1/4 In. 165.00
Cosmopoliet, J.J. Melchers, WZ, Schiedam, Case, Olive Green, 9 1/2 In. . . . . 130.00 to 132.00
Daniel Visser & Zonen, Scheidam, Case, Cobalt Blue, Seal, 11 In. 415.00
Daniel Visser & Zonen, Schiedam, Case, Amber, Embossed & Label 120.00
Daniel Visser & Zonen, Schiedam, Case, Cobalt Blue, Shoulder Seal, 11 1/4 In. 250.00
Daniel Visser & Zonen, Schiedam, Case, Light Amethyst, Seal, 11 In. 413.00
Daniel Visser & Zonen, Schiedam, Case, Turquoise, Shoulder Seal, 11 1/4 In. 300.00
E. Kiderlen, Olive Green, Applied Top, Fishnet Base, 9 In. 20.00
Emerald Green, Applied 3-Tier Top, Case, 10 In. 154.00
Field, Son & Co., London, Sloe Gin, Amber, Neck Label, Cup Mold, 1880s 9.00
H. Cosmopoliet, Olive Green, Beveled Base Corners, Man, Holding Bottle, 11 In. 325.00
Highest Medal Vienna, Medium Olive Green, Applied Lip, 1873, 8 5/8 In. 85.00
Holland, 3-Piece Mold, Label, Tooled Lip 5.00
Hynes Van Horn, Olive Amber, 3-Piece Mold, Applied Double Rounded Lip, Qt. 9.00
Hynes Van Horn, Olive Amber, 3-Piece Mold, Sand Pontil, Qt. 15.00
I.A.I. Nolet, Schiedam, Case, Olive Green, Tapered, 9 In. 30.00
J.H. Henkes, Case, Olive Green, 7 In. 77.00
Juniper Leaf, Red Amber, Tooled Top, Embossed, 10 3/4 In. 154.00
Kinderlens Pure Hollands Geneva, Rotterdam, Shield, Etched, Gentleman, Round, 9 In. . 30.00
Lange & Bernecker, St. Louis, Mo., Amber, Applied Top, 1864, 9 1/2 In. 770.00
Light Olive, Footed, Large 138.00
London Jockey Club House, Emerald Green, Horse & Rider, 9 5/8 In. 1015.00
London Jockey Club House, Green, Horse & Rider, Applied Tapered Top, IP 1650.00
London Jockey Club House, Olive, Horse & Rider, 1865-1875, 9 3/8 In. 385.00
Meder & Zoon, Clear Shoulder Seal, Applied Top, 9 1/2 In. 143.00
Milk Glass, Opalescent, Enamel Flowers, Pewter Neck Ring, Pontil, 1770-1790, 4 1/2 In. . 633.00
Old Holland & Dutch Maid, Pair 50.00
Olive Green, Applied Square Collar, 1873, 8 5/8 In. 85.00
P. Hoppe Night Cap, Schiedam, Case, Green, Open Bubble On Panel, 12 In. 65.00
Sapphire Blue, Multicolored Enamel Design, Tooled Lip, Pontil, 5 1/2 In. 715.00
Serrao Liquor Co., Ltd, Hilo, Hawaii, Aqua 99.00
Stoddard's, Case, Amber 50.00
V. Hoytema & C., Case, Amber, Drippy Top, 9 In. 45.00
Van Den Burgh & Co., Case, Olive Green, Bell, Shoulder Seal, Applied Top, 11 In. 66.00
Vanderveer's Medicated Gin, Schiedam, Schnapps, Olive Green, 7 In. . . . . *Illus* 60.00
Windsor Castle Brand, Old Tom, London, Aqua, 3-Piece Mold, Label, Qt. 9.00

———————————————— **GINGER BEER** ————————————————

Ginger beer was originally made from fermented ginger root, cream of tartar, sugar,
yeast, and water. It was a popular drink from the 1850s to the 1920s. Beer made from
grains became more popular and very little alcoholic ginger beer was made. Today it is
an alcohol-free carbonated drink like soda. Pottery bottles have been made since the
1650s. A few products are still bottled in stoneware containers today. Ginger beer, vine-

gar, and cider were usually put in stoneware holders until the 1930s. The ginger beer bottle usually held 10 ounces. Blob tops, tapered collars, and crown tops were used. Some used a cork, others a Lightning stopper or inside screw stopper. The bottles were of shades of brown and white. Some were salt glazed for a slightly rough, glassy finish. Bottles were stamped or printed with names and usually the words *ginger beer.*

A Edge Ye Olde Brewed Ginger Beer, Longsight, Champagne Shape, 1919 . . . . 40.00
Anchor Scene, Amber 20.00
Aston Grounds Gold Medal, Birmingham 45.00
Beufoy & Co., Lambeth, Stopper 23.00
Brantingham & Raingill Altrincham 27.00
C.C. Dornate, Barnstaple, Deep Honey Glaze, Oak Tree 20.00
C.C. Haley & Co., California Beer, Stoneware, Gray, 10 1/2 In. 30.00
Country Club Beverage Company, Vancouver, B.C., Tan, Cream, Crown Top, 8 In. 45.00
Crockery, 1860s, 8 x 2 3/4 In. 38.00
Cross & Co., Vancouver, B.C., Tan, Cream, Banners, Maltese Cross, Blob Top, 7 In. 41.00
Cummer & Son, Hamilton, Cream, Black Transfer, Eagle Holding Arrows, Blob Top 45.00
Dolan Bros., Cream, Cobalt Shoulders & Blob Top, Blue Transfer, 1911, 10 1/2 In. 85.00
Double Eagle Bottling Co., Cleveland, O., 2-Headed Eagle, Black Stencil, 7 In. 60.00
Dove Phillips & Pett Ltd., Brewed Ginger Beer, Busty Lady On Front 75.00
Duncan Flockhart & Co., Edinburgh, Black Transfer, Early 1900s, 8 1/2 In. 18.00
E.R. Shaw & Co., Ld., Old English Ginger Beer, Wakefield, 7 1/8 In. 28.00
Emmerson Jnr, Newcastle On Tyne, Amber, Cyclist Riding Old-Fashioned Bike 75.00
Fisher Perrie, Galtee Moor, Tan 22.00
G. Kickley, Tan Over Cream, Black Transfer, Blob Top, 7 1/2 In. 40.00
Glass Bros. & Co., London, Ont., Cream, Black Transfer, Blob Top, 8 1/4 In. 180.00
Groves & Whitnall, Globe Works, Salford, White, 6-Pointed Star 20.00
H. Harris & Co., Rockspring Works, Hythe Kent, Champagne 22.50
Hansards, Abergavenny, Tan 30.00
Hay & Sons, Stoneware, 2-Tone, Blue Print Diamond Transfer, Aberdeen, 9 In. 40.00
Howard Bros., B'ham 22.50
John Mackay & Co., Glasgow, Green Top, Green Transfer, Scotland 164.00
John Thompson, Kickley Brewed Ginger Beer, Hamilton, Ont., Cream, Tan, 8 In. 40.00
Joseph Gidman, Canute Scene 56.00
L. Perin Jr., Stoneware, Gray, Brown Flecks, Cobalt Blue Blob Top, 9 1/2 In. 160.00
L.A. Kirkland, Toronto, Cream, Brown, Gray Print, Crown Top, 6 In. 50.00
Lee & Green Co., Buffalo, U.S.A., Stoneware 30.00
Leigh & Co., Globe Works, Salford, White, 6-Pointed Star 15.00
Leitch Edinburgh, Regd Trade Mark, 2-Tone, 8 1/2 In. 15.00
Lemon & Co.'s Dingwall, Buchan Copyright Portobello, 7 1/2 In. 50.00
London Ginger Beer Co., Stone Ginger Beer, Cream, Brown, Blob Top, 6 1/2 In. 150.00
Lowerdale & Son, Kirby Moorside, Horse On Barrel, England 36.00
M.P. Harrison, Gray, Cobalt Blue Letters, Canada, 1865-1885, Qt. 65.00
MacKintosh Bros. Brewed, Flagon Plumstead, Gal. 22.50
Milnes & Sons, Bradford, Boy On Donkey 45.00
Moerleins Old Jug Lager Spring Bier, Cincinnati, 8 3/4 x 2 3/4 In. 165.00
O'Keefe's Beverages Ltd., Toronto, Cream, Tan, Label, Crown Top, c.1910 . . . . 85.00
Old English Brewed, A.E. Burke, Brantford, Stoneware, Blob Top 80.00
Old Homestead, International Drug Co., Cream, Black Transfer, House, Crown Top 60.00
Pilgrim Bros. & Co., Hamilton, Cream, Black Transfer, Eagle In Circle, 7 In. 65.00
R. Gordineer & Co., Dark Brown, Blob Top, 7 In. 150.00
S. Fulford, Manchester, Honey Glaze 35.00
S.S. Albion Rd., Edinburgh 22.00
Saxons Flagon, Birmingham 30.00
Smith & Clody, Buffalo, N.Y., Cream, Black Screen Print, Blob Top, 7 In. 26.00
Stocker St. Ives, Superior Effervescing Gingerade 375.00
T.F. Adams & Sons, Halstead, Rose, Thistle, Clover 18.00
T.W. Lawson, XX Stone Ginger Beer, Manchester, Honey Blaze, Star & Water 20.00
Toronto Pure Ginger Beer Co., English Stone Ginger, Cream, Brown, 6 1/2 In. 85.00
Toronto Stone Ginger Beer Co., Clear, Ribs, 1920s, 7 Oz. 25.00
Tudor Mineral Water Co., Brewed, Flagon 22.00
Walter G. Woolls, Honey . . . . .7.00 to 22.00
Watts & Bower, Honey 37.00

Wentworth Mineral Water Co. Ltd., Hamilton, Ont., Cream, Tan, Crown Top, 7 1/2 In. . .   45.00
Wm. Innes, Home Brewed Ginger Beer, West Lothian, c.1900, 8 1/2 In. 33.00
Wm. Innes West Lothian Aerated Water Works, Boness, 2-Tone, 1900, 8 1/2 In. 33.00
Wm. Kegan, Stoneware, Gray, Cobalt Blue Letters, Blob Top, 10 In. 80.00
Ye Olde Country Stone Ginger Beer, Vancouver, B.C., Stoneware, 7 In. 15.00

—————————————————— **GLUE** ——————————————————

Glue and paste have been packaged in bottles since the nineteenth century. Most of these bottles have identifying paper labels. A few have the name embossed in the glass.

Carter's Mucilage, The Great Stickist, 2 3/4 In. 85.00
Edwards Pure Gum Mucilage, Toronto, Erie On Base, Brush, Canada, 1890 . . . .   360.00
Sanford's Inks & Library Paste, Embossed, Pt., 7 1/2 In. 12.00
Spaulding's, OP 28.00

—————————————————— **GRENADIER** ——————————————————

The Grenadier Spirits Company of San Francisco, California, started making figural porcelain bottles in 1970. Twelve soldier-shaped fifths were in Series No. 1. These were followed by Series 2 late in 1970. Only 400 cases were made of each soldier. The company continued to make bottles in series, including the 1976 American Revolutionary Army regiments in fifths and tenths, and many groups of minibottles. They also had series of club bottles, missions, foreign generals, horses, and more. The brothel series was started in 1978 for a special customer, Mr. Dug Picking of Carson City, Nevada. These are usually sold as *Dug's Nevada Brothels* and are listed in this book under Miniature. The Grenadier Spirits Company sold out to Fleishmann Distilling Company and stopped making the bottles about 1980. Jon-Sol purchased the remaining inventory of bottles.

Alabama Roughs, 1975, Miniature 10.00
Eugene, 1970 . . . .   25.00
Father's Gift, 1979 . . . .   30.00
Father's Gift, 1979, Miniature 10.00
Fire Chief, 1973 . . . .   120.00
Fireman Statue, 1974 . . . .   600.00
Ford T-Bird, No. 15, Bud Moore, 1979 . . . . *Illus*   50.00
Fray Junipero Serra, 1974 . . . .   20.00
Fray Junipero Serra, 1979, Miniature 12.00
Frosty The Snowman, 1978 . . . .   25.00
Frosty The Snowman, 1980, Miniature 14.00
Horse, American Saddle Bred, 1978 . . . .   40.00
Horse, American Thoroughbred, 1978 . . . .   60.00
Horse, Appaloosa, 1978 . . . .   50.00
Horse, Arabian, 1978 . . . . *Illus*   50.00
Horse, Tennessee Walker, 1978 . . . .   50.00
Horse, Thoroughbred, 1978 . . . .   60.00
Joan Of Arc, 1972 . . . .   60.00
Mission San Carlos, 1977 . . . .   20.00

Grenadier, Ford T-Bird, No. 15, Bud Moore, 1979

Grenadier, Horse, Arabian, 1978

Grenadier, Soldier, John Paul Jones,

Mission San Francisco De Asis, 1978		29.00
Mission San Gabriel Archangel, 1978		15.00
Mission Santa Clara De Asis, 1978		15.00
Moose Lodge, 1970		15.00
Mr. Spock, Bust, 1979		70.00
Pancho Villa, Standing, 1977		10.00
Pontiac Trans Am, 1979		50.00
San Fernando Mfg. Co., 1976		66.00
Santa Claus, Blue Sack, 1978		33.00
Santa Claus, Green Sack, 1978		30.00
Soldier, 1st Officers Guard, 1970		20.00
Soldier, 1st Officers Guard, 1971, Miniature		12.00
Soldier, 1st Pennsylvania, 1970		30.00
Soldier, 1st Regiment, Virginia Volunteers, 1974, Miniature		20.00
Soldier, 2nd Maryland, 1969		30.00
Soldier, 2nd Regiment, U.S. Sharpshooters, 1975, Miniature		18.00
Soldier, 6th Regiment, Wisconsin, 1975, Miniature		14.00
Soldier, 11th Regiment, Indiana, 1975		14.00
Soldier, 14th Virginia Cavalry, 1975, Miniature		17.00
Soldier, Baron Johann DeKalb, 1978		35.00
Soldier, Baron Von Steuben, 1978		40.00
Soldier, Baylor's 3rd Continental, 1969		23.00
Soldier, Billy Mitchell, 1975		50.00
Soldier, Captain Confederate, 1970		35.00
Soldier, Captain, Union Army, 1975, Miniature		30.00
Soldier, Comte DeRochambeau, 1978	30.00 to 40.00
Soldier, Connecticut Governor's Foot Guard, 1972		23.00
Soldier, Continental Marines, 1969		26.00
Soldier, Corporal, French, 1970		25.00
Soldier, Corporal, French, 1970, Miniature		15.00
Soldier, Count Pulaski, 1978		64.00
Soldier, Dragoon 17th, 1970		25.00
Soldier, General Custer, 1970		27.00
Soldier, General MacArthur, 1975		70.00
Soldier, General Robert E. Lee, 1974		30.00
Soldier, General Ulysses S. Grant, 1975		20.00
Soldier, Indiana Zouave, 1975, Miniature		15.00
Soldier, Jeb Stuart, 1970		30.00
Soldier, Jeb Stuart, 1970, Miniature		15.00
Soldier, John Paul Jones, 1976	*Illus*	23.00
Soldier, Kings African Rifle Corps., 1970		35.00
Soldier, Kings African Rifle Corps., 1970, Miniature		15.00
Soldier, Kings African Rifle Corps., 1970, Qt.		28.00
Soldier, Lannes, 1970		20.00
Soldier, Lassal, 1969		35.00
Soldier, Marquis De Lafayette, 1978		34.00
Soldier, Marquis De Lafayette, 1979, Miniature		16.00
Soldier, Mosby's Ranger, 1975, Miniature		20.00
Soldier, Murat, 1970		20.00
Soldier, Napoleon, 1969		34.00
Soldier, New York Highlander, 1975, Miniature		12.00
Soldier, Ney, 1969		21.00
Soldier, Officer, 1st Guard Regiment, 1971		25.00
Soldier, Officer, 3rd Guard Regiment, 1971		23.00
Soldier, Officer, British, 1970		27.00
Soldier, Robert E. Lee, 1976	36.00 to 40.00
Soldier, Scots Fusilier, 1971	21.00 to 25.00
Soldier, Scots Fusilier, 1975		25.00
Soldier, Sergeant Major, Coldstream Guard, 1971		27.00
Soldier, Teddy Roosevelt, 1976	30.00 to 40.00
Soldier, Teddy Roosevelt, 1977	30.00 to 40.00
Soldier, Texas Ranger, 1977		38.00
Soldier, Texas Ranger, 1979		33.00

Soldier, Thaddeus Kosciuszko, 1978 .... 35.00
Soldier, Wisconsin, 6th, 1975 .... 13.00
Washington Blue Rifles, Miniature 13.00
Washington On Horse, 1974 ....24.00 to 30.00
HAIR PRODUCTS, see Cosmetic; Cure
HAND LOTION, see Cosmetic; Medicine

————————————— **HOFFMAN** —————————————

J. Wertheimer had a distillery in Kentucky before the Civil War. Edward Wertheimer
and his brother Lee joined the business as young men. When Edward Sr. died at age 92,
his son Ed Wertheimer Jr., became president. Edward Jr.'s sons, Ed Wertheimer III and
Thomas Wertheimer, also worked in the family company. L. & E. Wertheimer Inc. made
the products of the Hoffman Distilling Company and the Old Spring Distilling Company, including Old Spring Bourbon, until 1983 when the company was sold to Commonwealth Distillery, a company still in existence. Hoffman Originals, later called the
Hoffman Club, was founded by the Wertheimers in 1971 to make a series of figural bottles. The first was the Mr. Lucky series, started in 1973. These were leprechaun-shaped
decanters. Five series of leprechauns were made. Other series include wildlife, decoy
ducks (1977-1978), Aesop's fables, C.M. Russell (1978), rodeo (1978), pool-playing
dogs (1978), belt buckles (1979), horses (1979), Jack Richardson animals, Bill
Ohrmann animals (1980-1981), cheerleaders (1980), framed pistols (1978), political
(1980), and college football (1981-1982). The miniature Hoffman bottles include series
such as leprechauns (1981), birds (1978), dogs and cats (1978-1981), decoys (1978-
1979), pistols on stands (1975), Street Swingers (musicians, 1978-1979), pistols (1975),
wildlife (1978), and horses (1978). Hoffman decanters are no longer made.

A.J. Foyte, No. 2, 1972 .... 104.00
Aesop's Fables, Androcles & The Lion, 1978 .... 25.00
Aesop's Fables, Fox & Grapes, 1978 .... 30.00
Aesop's Fables, Goose With The Golden Egg, 1978 .... 25.00
Aesop's Fables, Hare & The Tortoise, 1978 .... 17.00
Alaska Pipeline, 1975 .... 24.00
Animal, Bear & Cub, Fishing, 1978 .... 90.00
Animal, Bear & Cub, In Tree, 1978 .... 50.00
Animal, Big Trouble On The Trail, 1979 .... 325.00
Animal, Big Trouble On The Trail, 1979, Miniature 350.00
Animal, Bobcat & Pheasant, 1978 .... 50.00
Animal, Doe & Fawn, 1975 .... 45.00
Animal, Falcon & Rabbit, 1978 .... 65.00
Animal, Fox & Eagle, 1978 .... 50.00
Animal, Fox & Rabbit, 1981 .... 44.00
Animal, Jaguar & Armadillo, 1978 .... 35.00
Animal, Kangaroo & Koala Bear, 1978 .... 36.00
Animal, Lion & Crane, 1979 .... 20.00
Animal, Lion & Dall Sheep, 1977, 3 Piece 190.00
Animal, Lynx & Rabbit, 1981 .... 100.00
Animal, Mountain Goat & Puma, 1981 .... 120.00
Animal, Musk Ox, 1979, Pair ....*Illus* 49.00
Animal, Owl & Chipmunk, 1978 .... 32.00
Animal, Panda, 1976 .... 55.00
Animal, Panda, 1976, Miniature 12.00
Animal, Penguins, 1979 .... 48.00
Animal, Pup Seals, 1979, Miniature 20.00
Animal, Rams, Fighting, 1977, 4 Piece 255.00
Animal, Stranger This Is My Land, 1978 .... 295.00
Animal, Wolf & Raccoon, 1978 .... 60.00
Animal, Wolf & Raccoon, 1978, Miniature 14.00
Betsy Ross, Music Box, 1974 .... 48.00
Big Red Machine, 1973 .... 44.00
Bird, Blue Jay, 1979 ....36.00 to 40.00
Bird, Canada Geese, 1980 .... 20.00
Bird, Dove, Open Wing, 1979 .... 25.00
Bird, Egret, Baby, 1979 .... 17.00
Bird, Love, 1979 .... 16.00

Bird, Swan, Closed Wing, 1980 .... 20.00
Bird, Titmice, 1979 ....27.00 to 35.00
Bird, Turkeys, 1980, 200 Milliliter 50.00
Bird, Wood Ducks, 1980 .... 20.00
Cat, Miniature, Set Of 6 .... 65.00
Cat, Perry Persian, 1981, 50 Milliliter 10.00
Cat, Sammy Siamese, 1981, Miniature 12.00
Cheerleader, Dallas, 1979 .... 50.00
Cheerleader, Dallas, Topless 150.00
Children Of The World, France, 1978 .... 24.00
Children Of The World, Jamaica, 1979 .... 24.00
Children Of The World, Mexico, 1979 .... 24.00
Children Of The World, Panama, 1979 ....*Illus* 24.00
Children Of The World, Spain, 1979 .... 24.00
Children Of The World, Yugoslavia, 1979 .... 24.00
College, Auburn Tigers, Helmet, 1981 .... 24.00
College, Clemson Tigers, Helmet, 1981 .... 35.00
College, Georgia Bulldogs, Helmet, 1981 .... 37.00
College, Kentucky Wildcats, Helmet, 1981 .... 25.00
College, Kentucky, Basketball, Mascot, 1979 .... 35.00
College, Kentucky, Football, Mascot, 1979 .... 40.00
College, LSU Tiger, Mascot, No. 1, 1978 .... 38.00
College, LSU Tiger, Mascot, No. 2, 1981 .... 28.00
College, Mississippi Southern, Mascot, 1982 .... 43.00
College, Mississippi State, Bulldog, Mascot, 1977 .... 42.00
College, Mississippi University, Rebel, Mascot, 1977 .... 55.00
College, Missouri Tiger, Helmet, 1981 .... 22.00
College, Nebraska Cornhusker, Helmet, 1981 .... 39.00
College, Nevada, Wolfpack, Mascot, 1979 .... 50.00
College, Ohio State, Fan, 1982 .... 40.00
College, Oklahoma Sooners, Helmet, 1981 .... 40.00
College, Tennessee Volunteers, Helmet, 1981 .... 31.00
Convention, Leprechaun On Barrel, 1982 .... 42.00
Cowboy & Puma, 1978 .... 360.00
Dog, Alfy Afghan, 1981 .... 27.00
Dog, Beagle, 1978 .... 27.00
Dog, Boston Terrier, 1978, Miniature 34.00
Dog, Boxer, 1978, Miniature 27.00
Dog, Cocker Spaniel, 1978, Miniature 50.00
Dog, Coon Dog, 1979 .... 49.00
Dog, Dachshund, 1978, Miniature 27.00
Dog, Dalmatian, Miniature 27.00
Dog, Dog & Squirrel, 1981 .... 45.00
Dog, Percy Poodle, 1981, Miniature 20.00
Dog, Pointer, 1979 .... 41.00
Dog, Pool Hustler, 1979 .... 150.00
Dog, Scotch Terrier, 1978, Miniature 27.00
Dog, Scotch Terrier, 1981, Miniature 19.00
Dog, Setter, 1979 .... 45.00
Dog, Springer Spaniel, 1979 .... 60.00
Dog, Terry Terrier, 1981, Miniature 12.00
Donahue Commemorative, 1972 .... 25.00
Donahue Sunoco, No. 66, 1972 .... 85.00
Duck, Decoy, Blue Bill, 1978, Miniature, Pair 12.00
Duck, Decoy, Blue-Winged Teal, 1978, Pair 17.00
Duck, Decoy, Canada Goose, 1977 .... 25.00
Duck, Decoy, Canvasback, 1978, Miniature, Pair 14.00
Duck, Decoy, Golden Eye, 1978, Miniature, Pair 14.00
Duck, Decoy, Green-Winged Teal, 1977, Miniature, Pair 17.00
Duck, Decoy, Loon, 1978 .... 29.00
Duck, Decoy, Mallard, 1977, Miniature, Pair 14.00
Duck, Decoy, Merganser, 1978 .... 25.00
Duck, Decoy, Merganser, Hooded, 1978, Miniature, Pair 13.00

Hoffman, Animal, Musk Ox, 1979, Pair

Hoffman, Children Of The World, Panama, 1979

Hoffman, Mr. Lucky, Harpist, 1975

Hoffman, Mr. Lucky, With Bag Of Gold, 1975, 5 1/2 In.

Duck, Decoy, Merganser, Red Breast, 1978, Miniature, Pair	17.00
Duck, Decoy, Pintail, 1977, Miniature, Pair	13.00
Duck, Decoy, Redhead, 1977, Miniature, Pair	13.00
Duck, Decoy, Ruddy Duck, 1978, Miniature, Pair	13.00
Duck, Decoy, Swan, White, 1978	22.00
Duck, Decoy, Widgeon, 1978	28.00
Duck, Decoy, Wood Duck, 1977	36.00
Duck, Mallard, Open Wing, 1980	15.00
Jack The Ripper, Pool Hustler, 1979	150.00
Lady Godiva, 1974	40.00
Mr. & Mrs. Retired, Set	60.00
Mr. Baker, 1978	36.00
Mr. Barber, 1980	25.00
Mr. Bartender, 1975	40.00
Mr. Blacksmith, 1976	40.00
Mr. Butcher, 1979	30.00
Mr. Carpenter, 1979	31.00
Mr. Charmer, 1974	25.00
Mr. Cobbler, 1973	30.00
Mr. Dancer, 1974	35.00
Mr. Dentist, 1980	35.00
Mr. Doctor, 1974	45.00
Mr. Electrician, 1978	40.00
Mr. Farmer, 1980	30.00
Mr. Fiddler, 1974	25.00
Mr. Fireman, 1976	70.00
Mr. Fireman, 1976, Miniature	25.00
Mr. Guitarist, 1975	30.00
Mr. Lucky, 1973	40.00
Mr. Lucky, 1974, Miniature	10.00
Mr. Lucky, Carolers, 1979	35.00
Mr. Lucky, Carolers, 1979, Miniature	15.00
Mr. Lucky, Harpist, 1975	*Illus* 25.00
Mr. Lucky, Mini Set, No. 1, 1980	75.00
Mr. Lucky, Mini Set, No. 2	75.00
Mr. Lucky, Mini Set, No. 3	100.00
Mr. Lucky, Mini Set, No. 4	75.00
Mr. Lucky, Mini Set, No. 5	80.00
Mr. Lucky, Organ Player, 1979	30.00
Mr. Lucky, Organ Player, 1979, Miniature	15.00
Mr. Lucky, Retired, 1978, Miniature	20.00
Mr. Lucky, Retired, With Wooden Chair, 1981	35.00
Mr. Lucky, White & Gold, 1981	185.00

Mr. **Lucky,** With Bag Of Gold, 1975, 5 1/2 In. . . . .*Illus* 30.00
Mr. **Lucky,** With Wooden Chair, 1981, Miniature 35.00
Mr. **Lucky & Rockwell,** 1980, Miniature . . . . .47.00 to 75.00
Mr. **Mailman,** 1976 . . . . 45.00
Mr. **Mechanic,** 1979 . . . . 32.00
Mr. **Organ Player,** 1979 . . . . 29.00
Mr. **Photographer,** 1980 . . . . 34.00
Mr. **Pilot,** 1989, Miniature 20.00
Mr. **Plumber,** 1978 . . . . 34.00
Mr. **Policeman,** 1975 . . . . 48.00
Mr. **Policeman,** Retired, 1986, Miniature 28.00
Mr. **Railroad Engineer,** 1980 . . . . 34.00
Mr. **Salesman,** 1982, Miniature 30.00
Mr. **Sandman,** 1974 . . . . 27.00
Mr. **Saxophonist,** 1975 . . . . 35.00
Mr. **Stockbroker,** 1976 . . . . 45.00
Mr. **Tailor,** 1979 . . . . 32.00
Mr. **Teacher,** 1976 . . . . 29.00
Mr. **Tourist,** 1980 . . . . 40.00
Mrs. **Lucky,** Dancer. 1974 . . . . 20.00
Penguins, 1979 . . . . 50.00
Pistol, Civil War Colt, Framed, 1978 . . . . 28.00
Pistol, Civil War Colt, With Stand, 1975, Miniature 16.00
Pistol, Colt 45 Automatic, Framed, 1978 . . . . 28.00
Pistol, Colt 45 Automatic, With Stand, 1975, Miniature 17.00
Pistol, Derringer, Silver, Framed, 1979 . . . . 25.00
Pistol, Dodge City Frontier, Framed, 1978 . . . . 29.00
Pistol, Dodge City Frontier, With Stand, 1976, Miniature 17.00
Pistol, German Luger, Framed, 1978 . . . . 18.00
Pistol, German Luger, With Stand, 1975, Miniature 14.00
Pistol, Kentucky Flintlock, With Stand, 1975 . . . . 27.00
Pistol, Lawman, With Stand, 1978, Miniature 27.00
Pistol, Tower Flintlock, 1975 . . . . 25.00
Pistol, Tower Flintlock, With Stand, 1975 . . . . 27.00
Political Donkey, 1980 . . . . 25.00
Political Elephant, 1980 . . . . 25.00
Rodeo, All Around Clown, 1978 . . . . 45.00
Rodeo, Bareback Rider, 1978 . . . . 43.00
Rodeo, Belt Buckle, Saddle Bronc, 1979 . . . . 30.00
Rodeo, Bull Rider, 1978 . . . . 70.00
Rodeo, Calf Roping, 1978 . . . . 60.00
Rodeo, Clown, 1971 . . . . 44.00
Rodeo, Saddle, 1978 . . . . 60.00
Rodeo, Steer Wrestler, 1978 . . . . 60.00
Russell, Buffalo Man, 1976 . . . . 45.00
Russell, Bust, 1978 . . . . 30.00
Russell, Cowboy, 1978 . . . . 34.00
Russell, Flathead Squaw, 1976 . . . . 45.00
Russell, Half Breed Trader, 1978 . . . . 45.00
Russell, I Rode Him, 1978 . . . . 40.00
Russell, Indian Buffalo Hunter, 1978 . . . . 44.00
Russell, Last Of 5000, 1975 . . . . 20.00
Russell, Northern Cree, 1978 . . . . 40.00
Russell, Prospector, 1976 . . . . 27.00
Russell, Red River Breed, 1976 . . . . 42.00
Russell, Scout, 1978 . . . . 43.00
Russell, Stage Coach Driver, 1976 . . . . 35.00
Russell, Stage Robber, 1978 . . . . 50.00
Russell, Trapper, 1976 . . . . 38.00
Rutherford, No. 3, 1974 . . . . 90.00
Soldier, Concord, 1973 . . . . 25.00
Soldier, Queen's Ranger, 1978, Miniature, 4 Piece 55.00
Soldier, Tennessee Volunteers, Helmet, 1981 . . . . 25.00

Street Swingers, Accordion Player, 1978, Miniature 15.00
Street Swingers, Bass Player, 1979, Miniature 15.00
Street Swingers, Clarinet Player, 1978, Miniature 15.00
Street Swingers, Cymbal Player, 1978, Miniature 15.00
Street Swingers, Drummer, 1979, Miniature 15.00
Street Swingers, Fiddler, 1978, Miniature 15.00
Street Swingers, Mandolin Player, 1979, Miniature 15.00
Street Swingers, Saxophone Player, 1978, Miniature 15.00
Street Swingers, Train, I Think I Can, 1981 .... 65.00
Street Swingers, Tuba Player, 1978, Miniature 15.00
Street Swingers, Violin Player, 1979, Miniature 15.00
Tom Cat, 1981, Miniature, 50 Mllliliter 12.00
Truck Distillery, 1981 .... 60.00
Women's Lib, 1976, Miniature, Pair 14.00

───────────────── HOUSEHOLD ─────────────────

Many household cleaning products have been packaged in glass bottles since the nineteenth century. Shoe polish, ammonia, stove blacking, bluing, and other nonfood products are listed in this section. Most of these bottles have attractive paper labels that
interest the collector.

Ammonia, California Ammonia Works, San Francisco Washing Ammonia, Qt. 90.00
Ammonia, Clarkes Clear Fluid Ammonia, Aqua, Vertical Lines, Large 40.00
Ammonia, Co-Op, Stoneware 63.00
Ammonia, F.D., SF Gas Light Co., Aqua, Bubbles, Tooled Top 44.00
Ammonia, MNFD, S.F. Gaslight Co., Apple Green, Tooled Top, Slug Plate 130.00
Ammonia, MNFD, S.F. Gaslight Co., Green, Bubbles, Qt. 800.00
Ammonia, MNFD, S.F. Gaslight Co., Tooled Top, Slug Plate, Whittled, Qt. 300.00
Ammonia, Plynine Company Limited Of Edinburgh, Transfer, Stopper, 1905, 11 In. 15.00
Ammonia, Poison, Caution, Not To Be Taken, Light Aqua, Knobs, Beehive, 6 In. 25.00
Ammonia, Poisonous Not To Be Taken, Aqua, Oval, Embossed, Large 20.00
Ammonia, Poisonous Not To Be Taken, Cobalt Blue, Oval, Embossed, Large 45.00
Ammonia Ginormour, Plynine Limited, Dark Green, Embossed, Large 40.00
Anthony's Diamond Varnish For Single Ambrotypes, Blue, Label, 5 7/8 In. 810.00
Beau Peep Baby Shoe Cleaner, Figural, Paper Label, 1920s-1930s, 6 1/4 In. 50.00
Black Cat Shoe Dressing, Aqua, 3-Sided, Multicolored Label, Cat, 1920, 5 In. 35.00
Blacking, Aqua, Oval, Inward Rolled Mouth, Scar, Albany, c.1860, 4 1/2 In. 210.00
Blacking, Olive Yellow Amber, Sheared Mouth, Pontil, 1820-1845, 4 1/2 In. 155.00
Blacking, Purple, Sheared Lip, Pontil, 4 1/2 In. 66.00
Blacking, Stoddard Blacking Bottle, Medium Olive Green 88.00
Boston Varnish Co., Old English Walnut, Tin, Label, 4 3/4 In. ....*Illus* 18.00
C.W. Cole Co., Three In One, Aqua, Applied Top, 4 1/2 In. 1.50
Frank Tea & Spice, Turpentine, 1 1/2 Oz. 35.00
French Dressing, For Ladies' & Children's Boots & Shoes, Label, 5 In. ....*Illus* 45.00
Gypsy Dy-Kleen, Chicago, Ill., Paper Labels, Screw Cap, 3 x 1 1/2 x 5/8 In. 32.00
I.M. Singer & Co., Extra Machine Oil, New York, Blue Aqua, Pontil, 5 7/8 In. 202.00
Inmans Household Ammonia, Stoneware, 2-Tone, Brown Glaze Stopper, 11 In. 25.00

Household,
Boston Varnish
Co., Old English
Walnut, Tin, Label,
4 3/4 In.

Household, French
Dressing, For Ladies'
& Children's Boots &
Shoes, Label, 5 In.

Household,
Kinning's Bluing,
Sapphire,
Rochester, N.Y.,
Embossed,
5 1/4 In.

Household, Osborn's Liquid Polish, Olive Yellow, Rolled Lip, Pontil, 3 7/8 In.

Household, Utility, Aqua, Tin Lid

Killgerm Disinfectant, Poisonous, Not To Be Taken, Aqua, Oval, Embossed, Large	20.00
Kinning's Bluing, Sapphire, Rochester, N.Y., Embossed, 5 1/4 In. . . . . *Illus*	8.00
Lysol, Light Olive Green, Applied Lip, 3 3/4 x 2 1/4 In.	9.00
Mobro Household Bleach, Derby & Leicester, England	21.00
Monster, Dark Olive Green, Not To Be Taken, Large	45.00
Monster, Plynine & Co., Dark Green, BIMAL, Internal Screw Stopper, Large	45.00
Osborn's Liquid Polish, Olive Yellow, Rolled Lip, Pontil, 3 7/8 In. . . . . *Illus*	504.00
Price's Patent Candle Company Limited, Cobalt Blue, Pyramid, Stopper, 8 In.	88.00
Shoe Polish, Figural, Mikado, Amber	310.00
Stove, Nonsuch Mfg. Co., Stuart & Panton, London, Amber, Honey Amber	6.00
Stove Dressing, Nonsuch Mfg. Co., Toronto, Aqua, Square, Tooled Lip	3.00
Three In One, Aqua, Applied Top, 3 1/2 In.	1.00
Three In One, Emerald Green, Contents, Triangular, Sample, 1 3/4 In.	6.00
Utility, Aqua, Tin Lid . . . . *Illus*	8.00

INK

Ink was first used about 2500 B.C. in ancient Egypt and China. It was made of carbon mixed with oils. By the fifteenth century, ink was usually made at home by the housewife who bottled it for later use. In the late eighteenth century, ink was sold by apothecary shops and bookstores. The first patented ink was made in England in 1792. Ink bottles were first used in the United States about 1819. Early ink bottles were of ceramic and were often imported. Small ink bottles were made to be opened and used with a dip pen. Large ink bottles, like the cathedral-shaped Carter's inks, held a quart of ink to be poured into small bottles with dips. Inks can be identified by their shapes. Collectors have nicknamed many and the auctions often refer to *teakettles, cones, igloos,* or *umbrellas.*

Ink bottles were made to be hard to tip over. Some inks, especially English examples, were made with *bust-off* tops. The glass was cracked to open the bottle and the rough edge remained. In general the shape tells the age. Cones and umbrellas were used from the early 1800s to the introduction of the automatic bottle machine in the early 1900s. Hexagonal and octagonal bottles were preferred from about 1835 to 1865. Igloos, or turtles, were introduced in 1865 and were very popular for schools until about 1895. Barrels were made from 1840 to 1900. Square bottles became popular after 1860. Rectangular was the shape chosen in the 1900s. Figural bottles, especially ceramic types, were also made.

For further research, consult the book *Ink Bottles and Inkwells* by William E. Covill Jr. There is a national club, The Society of Inkwell Collectors, 10 Meadow Dr., Spencerport, NY 14559.

3-Sided, Red Amber, Embossed Base, Tooled Lip, 2 1/4 In.	55.00
8-Sided, Aqua, Rolled Lip, Pontil	77.00
8-Sided, Cobalt Blue, Burst Top, 2 1/2 In.	55.00
8-Sided, Cobalt Blue, Shoulder Rings, Long Neck, Burst Top, 2 1/2 In.	77.00
8-Sided, Lime Green, Burst Top, Australia, c.1885	23.00
8-Sided, Sapphire Blue, Burst Top, 2 1/8 In.	44.00
12-Sided, Emerald Green, Inward Rolled Lip, Pontil, 1840-1860, 1 3/4 In. . . . . 165.00 to 246.00

12-Sided, Gold Amber, Outward Rolled Lip, Pontil, 1840-1860, 2 In. 784.00
12-Sided, Olive Green, Spout, IP, 1/2 Gal., 10 In. 6440.00
12-Sided, Puce, Inward Rolled Lip, Pontil, 1840-1860, 2 1/8 In. 672.00
18 Ribs, Cobalt Blue, Pontil, 1820-1840, 2 In. 420.00
32 Ribs, Aqua, Funnel Lip, Pontil, 1820-1840, 1 9/16 In. 1232.00
A.B. Tallman, Pat. Apl. For, Aqua, Tooled Lip, Domed Base, 2 5/8 In. 615.00
A.D.R., Albany, Igloo, Green Aqua, 2 1/8 In. 525.00
Amethyst, Bell Shape, Scalloped, Flower Design On Base, Ground Lip, 2 3/4 In. 77.00
Arthur's Pure Carmine, Burlington, Vt., Cylindrical, Label, Flared Lip, Pontil, 6 1/4 In. . . . 209.00
Barrel, Flared Lip, Pontil, 2 x 2 In. 121.00
Barrel, Pat March 1st 1870, Rolled Lip, 2 In. 44.00
Barrel, Sapphire Blue, Pat Oct 17 1865, 3 1/4 In. 170.00
Bertinguiot, Dome, Olive Amber, Tooled Lip, Pontil, 1845-1860, 2 1/4 In. ...... .330.00 to 365.00
Bertinguiot, Dome, Olive Yellow, Sheared Mouth, Pontil, 1830-1860, 2 In. 253.00
Bertinguiot, Dome, Olive Yellow, Tooled Mouth, Pontil, 1845-1860, 2 1/8 In. 743.00
Blue Green, Applied Double Collar Mouth, IP, 1845-1855, Master, 9 3/4 In. 165.00
Boot's Cash Chemists & Perfumer, Round, Emerald Green, 3 In. 120.00
Boss Patent, Dome, 6-Sided, Aqua Green, Rolled Lip, OP, 2 3/8 In. 468.00
Boss Patent, Umbrella, Aqua, Inward Rolled Lip, Pontil, 1840-1860, 2 1/2 In. 448.00
Brickett & Thayer, New Ipswich, N.H., Olive Amber, Pour Spout, 1860, 9 In. 156.00
C. Crolius, Stoneware, Brown Glaze, Dark Blue Rim, Cylindrical, 1800-1815, 1 1/2 In. . . . 784.00
Cabin, Blue Aqua, Tooled Mouth, 2 5/8 In. 280.00
Cabin, Clear, Gray Tint, Tooled, Collared Lip, Mid 1800s, 2 1/2 In. 770.00
Cabin, Tooled Mouth, 1865-1875, 2 3/8 In. .... *Illus* 852.00
Caldwell's Ink, Round, Aqua, BIMAL, 2 1/2 In. 18.00
Carter, 6-Sided, Cobalt Blue, ABM, 2 7/8 In. .... .94.00 to 120.00
Carter, Cathedral, Sapphire Blue, Labels, Machined Mouth, 1900-1920, 9 3/4 In. . . .176.00 to 200.00
Carter's, Blue Green, Applied Mouth, Tooled Pour Spout, 1875-1885, 8 In. 121.00
Carter's, Cathedral, 6-Sided, Cobalt Blue, ABM, Pt., 7 7/8 In. .... .95.00 to 175.00
Carter's, Cathedral, Cobalt Blue, ABM Lip, Qt., 9 3/4 In. .... .95.00 to 145.00
Carter's, Cathedral, Cobalt Blue, ABM, 1920-1930, 1/2 Pt., 6 1/4 In. .... .225.00 to 270.00
Carter's, Cathedral, Cobalt Blue, Machined Lip, Pour Spout, Label, 1900-1920, 10 1/2 In. 280.00
Carter's, Cone, Cobalt Blue, 2 1/2 In. 121.00
Carter's, Cone, Olive Green, Rolled Lip, 2 1/4 In. 66.00
Carter's, Cone, Rose, Rolled Lip, 2 1/4 In. 358.00
Carter's, Cylindrical, Teal Blue, 5 1/2 In. 80.00
Carter's, Dome, Aqua, Tooled Lip, 1 3/4 In. 467.00
Carter's, Emerald Green, Tooled Pour Spout, 1875-1885, 7 7/8 In. 100.00
Carter's, Igloo, Aqua, Tooled Lip, 1875-1895, 1 3/4 In. ....660.00 to 743.00
Carter's, Ma & Pa Carter, Porcelain, Multicolor, Head Stoppers, Germany, 3 1/2 In., Pair . 165.00
Carter's, Ma & Pa Carter, Porcelain, White, Germany, 1900-1915, 3 5/8 In., Pair . .165.00 to 187.00
Carter's, Schoolhouse, Dome, Offset Neck, Aqua, Burst Top, 2 In. 220.00
Carter's, Square, Aqua, 4 Pen Rests, Label, 1890-1910, 2 5/8 In. 121.00
Carter's Automatic, Daisy Sinsmore & Co., Boston, ABM, Screw Lid, 1890, 3 In. . . *Illus* 213.00

Ink, Cabin, Tooled Mouth,
1865-1875, 2 3/8 In.

Ink, Carter's Automatic, Daisy
Sinsmore & Co., Boston, ABM,
Metal Screw Lid, 1890, 3 In.

Ink, Davids', Igloo, Gold
Amber, 1 3/4 In.

Carter's No. 95, Cone, Apricot Amber, 2 1/2 In. 55.00
Caw's Black Fluid, Blue Green, Applied Lip, Pour Spout, 9 In. 230.00
Chas. Hardt., Philada, Blue Green, 3-Piece Mold, Pt. 70.00
Clark's Mfg. Co., Boston, Umbrella, 8-Sided, Tobacco Amber, Label, 2 3/8 In. 660.00
Cone, Amber, Rolled Lip, 2 1/2 In. 33.00
Cone, Aqua, Ribs, Rolled Lip, Label Panel, OP, 1820-1840, 2 1/8 In. 60.00
Cone, Blue Green, 2 1/2 In. 121.00
Cone, Blue Green, Square Shoulders, Inward Rolled Lip, Pontil, 1840-1860, 2 3/8 In. 224.00
Cone, Cobalt Blue, Rolled Lip, 2 1/2 In. 55.00
Cone, Green, Rolled Lip, Pontil, 1890-1910, 2 1/2 In. 242.00
Cone, Light Turquoise, Rolled Lip, OP, 2 1/2 In. 88.00
Cone, Medium Blue Green, Open Pontil, Rolled Lip, 1845-1855, 1 7/8 In. 364.00
Cone, Medium Green, Outward Rolled Lip, Pontil, 1840-1860, 2 5/8 In. 269.00
Cone, Medium To Deep Steel Blue, Rolled Lip, 2 1/2 In. 121.00
Cone, Olive Amber, Tooled Lip, Pontil, 1860, 2 3/8 In. 253.00
Cone, Olive Yellow Amber, Tooled Lip, X, Reversed 200, Pontil, 2 1/8 In. 810.00
Corset, 16 Ribs, Swirled To Right, Orange Amber, Pontil, 1820-1840, 1 5/8 In. 213.00
Corset, Aqua, Tooled Lip, Pontil, 2 1/4 In. 258.00
Cut Glass, Honey Amber, Square, Brass Collar, Faceted Lid, 1840-1880, 2 1/2 In. 157.00
Cut Glass, Vaseline, Tooled Lip, Brass Collar, Glass Lid, 1850-1870, 2 1/8 In. 213.00
Cylindrical, Apricot Puce, Heavy Puce Swirls, Collar, Pour Spout, 1865-1875, 9 5/8 In. .. 896.00
Cylindrical, Aqua, Disc Lip, Pontil, 1820-1840, 2 In. 392.00
Cylindrical, Aqua, Rings Around Shoulder & Base, Applied Lip, Pontil, 5 3/4 In. 44.00
Cylindrical, Clear, Disc Lip, Pontil, 1820-1840, 1 3/4 In. 3640.00
Cylindrical, Clear, Tooled Flared Lip, Pontil, 1820-1840, 2 5/8 In. 2128.00
Cylindrical, Cobalt Blue, Fluted, Tooled Lip, Pen Shelf, England, 1840-1860, 2 1/8 In. ... 504.00
Cylindrical, Dark Amber, Applied Lip, Pour Spout, 7 1/2 In. 33.00
Cylindrical, Emerald Green, Applied Lip, 7 3/4 In. 33.00
Cylindrical, Emerald Green, Applied Lip, Pour Spout, 6 1/2 In. 88.00
Cylindrical, Emerald Green, Burst Top, 2 3/4 In. 44.00
Cylindrical, Green, Applied Top, Pontil, 6 1/4 In. 44.00
Cylindrical, Ice Blue, Sheared Mouth, Pontil, 1830-1845, 1 1/4 In. 252.00
Cylindrical, Medium Teal, Applied Pour Spout, OP, 7 1/2 In. 99.00
Cylindrical, Olive Amber, Disc Lip, Pour Spout, 7 5/8 In. 77.00
Cylindrical, Olive Green, 4 Narrow & 3 Wide Bands, Disc Lip, Pontil, 1810-1830, 1 3/8 In. 952.00
Cylindrical, Olive Green, Pour Spout, 8 In. 44.00
Cylindrical, Olive Green, Round, C On Base, Wide Mouth, Tooled Lip, 2 3/8 In. 33.00
Cylindrical, Olive Yellow, Disc Lip, Pontil, 1820-1840, 1 3/4 In. .... .308.00 to 505.00
Cylindrical, Purple Blue, Ring Around Shoulder & Base, Ground Lip, 2 1/4 In. 33.00
Cylindrical, Robin's-Egg Blue, Leaf & Flowers, Tooled Lip, France, 1840-1860, 2 In. 112.00
Cylindrical, Root Beer Amber, Pontil, Master, 1845-1855, 9 3/4 In. 242.00
Cylindrical, Sapphire Blue, Disc Lip, Pontil, 1820-1840, 1 7/8 In. 6720.00
Cylindrical, Teal Blue, Applied Lip, Pour Spout, Master 70.00
Cylindrical, Violet Blue, 22 Flutes, 1 9/16 In. 1344.00
Cylindrical, Yellow Green, Applied Lip, Spout, 8 In. 55.00
Cylindrical, Yellow Green, Disc Lip, Pontil, 1820-1830, 1 3/4 In. 10800.00
Cylindrical, Yellow Green, Disc Lip, Pontil, 1820-1840, 1 3/4 In. 6720.00
Davids & Black, New York, Blue Green, Flared Lip, OP, 5 In. 357.00
Davids', Igloo, Gold Amber, 1 3/4 In. ....*Illus* 575.00
Davids', Igloo, Teal Blue, 1 3/4 In. 605.00
Dawley's, Umbrella, Aqua 83.00
De Halsey, Dome, Olive Yellow, Pontil, France, 1830-1860, 2 1/4 In. 392.00
Diamond & Onyx, House, Tooled Lip, 2 1/2 In. 66.00
Dome, 10-Sided, Aqua, Sheared Mouth, 2 3/8 In. 44.00
Dome, Blue & White Swirls, Pewter Collar & Cap, Pontil, 1840-1860, 2 1/4 In. 3640.00
Dome, Blue Green, Rolled Lip, 2 In. 336.00
Dome, Bull's Eye & Drape, Smoky, Clear, 2 3/4 In. 45.00
Dome, Forest Green, Disc Lip, Pontil, 1820-1840, 1 3/4 In. 2240.00
Dome, Rose & White Swirls, Pewter Collar & Cap, Pontil, 1830-1860, 2 1/2 In. 3920.00
Dome, Teal Green, Inward Rolled Lip, Pontil, 1840-1860, 2 1/4 In. 616.00
Doulton Lambeth, Round, Stoneware, Tan Glaze, Squared Lip, Spout, 6 In. 17.00
Dovell's Patent, Cone, Aqua, 2 3/4 In. 77.00

E. Waters, Troy, N.Y., Aqua, Applied, OP, 2 1/2 In. 523.00
E. Waters, Troy, N.Y., Aqua, Large Applied Lip, OP, 3 In. . . . . .330.00 to 440.00
E.B. Estes' Metropolitan, Stoneware, Brown Glaze, Applied Handle, 8 1/2 In. 198.00
E.S. Curtis Ink Warranted, Yellow Amber, Pontil, Label, 9 1/2 In. 357.00
F.D.A., Dome, Blue Green, Rolled Lip, 2 In. 335.00
Farley's, 8-Sided, Gold Amber, Sheared Mouth, Pontil, 1845-1860, 1 7/8 In. 467.00
Farley's, 8-Sided, Olive Amber, Tooled Flared Lip, Pontil, 1846-1860, 3 1/2 In. 504.00
Farley's, 8-Sided, Olive Green, Pontil, 1846-1860, 1 3/4 In. 1064.00
Farley's, 8-Sided, Yellow Amber, c.1860, 1 3/4 x 1 7/8 In. 1210.00
Franklin Black Ink, Umbrella, 8-Sided, Olive Amber, Pontil, 1840-1860, 2 1/2 In. 1064.00
Funnel, Sapphire Blue, 30 Ribs, Cylindrical, Pontil, 1830-1860, 2 1/4 In. 504.00
G.A. Moss, Igloo, Blue Aqua, 1 5/8 In. 275.00
G.E. Ohr, Pottery, Olive Green, Tan, Log Cabin, 1880-1890, 2 1/8 In. 3640.00
G.M.W. & A.A.S., Aqua, Ground Lip, 1875-1890, 1 3/8 In. 121.00
G.W.M., Aqua, Tooled Lip, 1875-1890, 1 3/4 In. 132.00
Geometric, Dark Olive Amber, Tooled Disc Lip, Pontil, 1810-1835, 1 5/8 In. . . . . .135.00 to 196.00
Geometric, Diamond & Square Band, Yellow Amber, Disc Lip, Pontil, 1 1/2 In. . . .134.00 to 269.00
Geometric, Diamond Point, Forest Green, Pontil, 1 3/4 x 2 3/8 In. 176.00
Geometric, Diamond Point, Ribbed Top, Emerald Green, Disc Lip, Pontil, 1 3/4 In. 1904.00
Geometric, Diamond Point, Ribs, Olive Amber, Disc Lip, Pontil, 1815-1835, 1 5/8 In. . . . 134.00
Geometric, Diamond Point, Ribs, Olive Green, Pontil, 1820-1840, 1 1/2 In. 242.00
Geometric, Diamond Point, Ribs, Yellow Amber, Tooled Disc Lip, Pontil, 1 3/4 In. 252.00
Geometric, Olive Amber, Tooled Disc Lip, Pontil, 1800-1830, 2 In. 132.00
Geometric, Olive Amber, Tooled Disc Lip, Pontil, 1815-1835, 2 In. 187.00
Geometric, Olive Green, Tooled Disc Lip, Pontil, 1 7/8 In. 190.00
Geometric, Olive Green, Tooled Disc Lip, Pontil, 1800-1830, 1 1/2 In. 198.00
Geometric, Olive Green, Tooled Disc Lip, Pontil, 1810-1835, 1 1/2 In. 209.00
Geometric, Ribs, Emerald Green, 1820-1840, 1 5/8 In. 672.00
Geometric, Waffle Band, Olive Amber, Disc Mouth, Pontil, 1 1/2 x 2 1/4 In. 132.00
Geometric, Waffle Band, Olive Yellow Green, Disc Mouth, Pontil, 1 1/2 In. 275.00
Gross & Robinson's American Writing Fluid, Aqua, Flared Lip, IP, 1845-1860, 5 3/4 In. . . 896.00
GWR, Stoneware, Embossed, 4 1/2 In. 120.00
Harrison's Columbian, 8-Sided, Aqua, Applied Mouth, Pontil, 2 1/2 In. 168.00
Harrison's Columbian, 8-Sided, Aqua, Disc Lip, OP, 3 3/4 In. 146.00
Harrison's Columbian, 8-Sided, Aqua, Inward Rolled Lip, Pontil, 1 1/2 In. 137.00
Harrison's Columbian, 8-Sided, Aqua, Label, Disc Lip, Pontil, 3 5/8 In. 687.00
Harrison's Columbian, 8-Sided, Aqua, Tooled Lip, 1845-1860, 1 7/8 In. . . . . .121.00 to 170.00
Harrison's Columbian, 8-Sided, Blue Green, Inward Rolled Lip, Pontil, 1 1/2 In. 1008.00
Harrison's Columbian, 8-Sided, Green, Inward Rolled Lip, Pontil, 1840-1860, 1 3/4 In. . . 616.00
Harrison's Columbian, 12-Sided, Aqua, Applied Mouth, OP, 5 5/8 In. . . . . .100.00 to 123.00
Harrison's Columbian, 12-Sided, Aqua, Patent On Shoulder, Pontil, 1860, 7 1/8 In. 385.00
Harrison's Columbian, 12-Sided, Aqua, Pontil, 7 In. 165.00
Harrison's Columbian, Cobalt Blue, Disc Lip, Applied Ring, Pontil, 5 3/4 In. 1705.00
Harrison's Columbian, Cobalt Blue, Inward Rolled Lip, OP, 2 1/8 In. 645.00
Harrison's Columbian, Cobalt Blue, Rolled Lip, OP, 2 1/8 In. 644.00
Harrison's Columbian, Cylindrical, Sapphire Blue, Inward Rolled Lip, Pontil, 2 In. 896.00
Harrison's Columbian, Igloo, 8-Sided, Aqua, 1860-1870, 1 1/2 In. 420.00
Harrison's Columbian, Igloo, 8-Sided, Blue Aqua, Sheared Mouth, 1 7/8 In. . . . . .330.00 to 385.00
Harrison's Columbian, Sapphire Blue, Disc Lip, Applied Ring, OP, 7 1/4 In. 1375.00
Harrison's Columbian, Turtle, 8-Sided, Blue Aqua, 1865-1875, 1 7/8 In. 485.00
Hibbert, Pittsburgh, Cone, Blue Aqua, Rolled Lip, OP, 1845-1860, 3 1/4 In. 616.00
House, Aqua, Applied Top 198.00
House, Aqua, Embossed Roof Tiles, Burst Top, 2 3/4 In. .330.00 to 358.00
House, Blue Aqua, Sheared Lip, 1880-1890, 2 5/8 In. . . . .*Illus* 358.00
House, Green, Olive Striations, Burst Top, 2 3/8 x 1 1/8 In. 495.00
House, Pale Aqua, Tooled Mouth, 1880-1895, 2 5/8 In. 303.00
House, Sky Blue, Burst Top, 2 3/8 x 1 1/8 In. 495.00
Igloo, Amethyst, Ground Lip, 1875-1890, 2 In. 633.00
Igloo, Blue Green, Ground Lip, 1875-1890, 1 3/4 In. 242.00
Igloo, Cobalt Blue, Ground Lip, 1875-1890, 1 7/8 In. 1540.00
Igloo, Light Blue Green, Ground Lip, 1875-1890, 1 7/8 In. . . . . .143.00 to 170.00
Igloo, Purple Amethyst, Ground Lip, 1875-1890, 2 In. 1375.00

Ink, J. Sargant's, Allegheny, 6-Sided,
Blue Aqua, Tooled Lip, OP, 4 3/4 In.

Ink, House, Blue Aqua, Sheared
Lip, 1880-1890, 2 5/8 In.

Ink, J. & I.E.M., Igloo, Olive
Yellow, 1 7/8 In.

Igloo, Root Beer Amber, Ground Lip, 1875-1890, 1 7/8 In.	825.00
J. & I.E.M., Igloo, Amber, Ground Lip, 1875-1895, 1 3/4 In.	121.00
J. & I.E.M., Igloo, Amber, Moore's Excelsior School Writing Label, 1 3/4 In.	413.00
J. & I.E.M., Igloo, Amber, Tooled Lip, 1875-1890, 1 3/4 In.	308.00
J. & I.E.M., Igloo, Aqua, 1 7/8 In.	40.00
J. & I.E.M., Igloo, Blue Green, Sheared Mouth, 1 7/8 In.	130.00
J. & I.E.M., Igloo, Chocolate Amber, Tooled Lip, 1 3/4 In.	500.00 to 800.00
J. & I.E.M., Igloo, Light To Medium Blue Green, Tooled Lip, 1 3/4 In.	880.00
J. & I.E.M., Igloo, Olive Yellow, 1 7/8 In. *Illus*	1100.00
J. & I.E.M., Igloo, Straw Yellow, Tooled Lip, 1875-1895, 1 7/8 In.	1155.00
J. & I.E.M., Igloo, Yellow Amber, Ground Lip, 1875-1890, 1 1/2 In.	275.00 to 365.00
J. & I.E.M., Turtle, Blue Green, Tooled Lip, 1860-1880, 1 5/8 In.	635.00 to 1568.00
J. & I.E.M., Turtle, Citron, Tooled Lip, 1860-1880, 1 5/8 In.	770.00 to 1200.00
J. & I.E.M., Turtle, Cobalt Blue, Tooled Lip, 1875-1890, 1 7/8 In.	1100.00 to 3850.00
J. & I.E.M., Turtle, Smoky Clear, Ground Lip, 1875-1890, 1 5/8 In.	440.00
J. & I.E.M., Turtle, Yellow Amber, Ground Lip, 1875-1890, 1 5/8 In.	242.00
J. & I.E.M., Turtle, Yellow, Tooled Lip, Offset Neck, 1860-1880, 1 5/8 In.	2352.00
J. Sargant's, Allegheny, 6-Sided, Blue Aqua, Tooled Lip, OP, 4 3/4 In. *Illus*	305.00
J.B. Davids & Co., Aqua, Tooled Mouth, 1875-1890, 1 7/8 In.	357.00
J.F. Smith, Stockton-On-Tees, Teakettle, Aqua, Square Burst Top, England	142.00
J.M. & S., Dome, Aqua, Ground Lip, 1875-1890, 2 In.	94.00
J.P.F., Forest Green, Square, Scene On Each Side, Disc Lip, Pontil, 1815-1825, 1 3/8 In.	3920.00
John Bond's Crystal Palace, Square, Cobalt Blue, Flared Lip, Label, 1865-1875, 1 1/2 In.	130.00
Jones' Empire Ink, N.Y., 12-Sided, Emerald Green, Applied Lip, IP, 5 7/8 In.	4730.00
Josiah Jonson Japan Writing Fluid, London, Teakettle, 6-Sided, Pottery, 2 1/8 In.	110.00
L.H. Thomas, Aqua, Star On Base, Applied Lip, 7 In.	33.00
L.H. Thomas, Cone, Lime Green, Tooled Lip, 2 3/4 In.	198.00
Lake's Superior Black Writing, Umbrella, 8-Sided, Aqua, OP, 2 1/2 In.	413.00
Little Banner, Light Amber, 6 Stars, 1 1/2 In.	33.00
Locomotive, Pat. Oct. 1874, Aqua, Ground Lip, 2 In. *Illus*	1790.00
Maynard & Noyes, Boston, Yellow Olive Amber, 1840-1855, 5 5/8 In.	235.00
Monroe's Patent School, Igloo, 8-Sided, 1865-1885, 2 1/2 In.	633.00
Moody's Inks, Alpha Chemical Co., Berlin, Aqua, Multicolored Label, BIMAL, 3 In.	530.00
Ne Plus Ultra Fluid, Schoolhouse, Blue Aqua, Square, Burst Top, 2 In.	275.00
North & Warrins, Gray & Green, Slag, Sloped Collar, Pontil, 1820-1850, 4 3/4 In.	728.00
Opdyke Bros., Barrel, Aqua, Embossed	220.00
Pancake, Black, Tooled Mouth, 1890-1915, 1 1/2 In.	88.00
Paul's Safety Ink, Full 10 Ounces, Stoneware, Tan & Brown Glaze, 7 In.	85.00
Pitkin Type, 36 Ribs, Swirled Left, Cone, Medium Olive Yellow, 2 In.	522.00
Pitkin Type, 36 Ribs, Swirled Left, Forest Green, Disc Lip, Pontil, 1783-1830, 1 1/2 In.	392.00
Pitkin Type, 36 Ribs, Swirled Left, Forest Green, Funnel Lip, Pontil, 1783-1830, 2 In.	728.00
Pitkin Type, 36 Ribs, Swirled Left, Olive Yellow, Disc Lip, Pontil, 1 1/2 In.	633.00
Pitkin Type, 36 Ribs, Swirled Left, Olive Yellow, Disc Lip, Pontil, 2 15/16 In.	4200.00
Pitkin Type, 36 Ribs, Swirled Left, Olive Yellow, Tooled Lip, Pontil, 1783-1830, 1 5/8 In.	336.00

Ink, Locomotive, Pat. Oct. 1874, Aqua, Ground Lip, 2 In.

Ink, Pitkin Type, 36 Ribs, Swirled Right, Olive Green, Tooled Lip, Pontil, 1 3/8 In.

Pitkin Type, 36 Ribs, Swirled Left, Olive, Tooled Lip, Pontil, 2 3/8 In. 550.00
Pitkin Type, 36 Ribs, Swirled Left, Square, Dark Olive Green, Disc Lip, Pontil, 1 3/8 In. . 1624.00
Pitkin Type, 36 Ribs, Swirled Left, Square, Olive, Disc Lip, Pontil, 1 1/2 In. . . . .728.00 to 2128.00
Pitkin Type, 36 Ribs, Swirled Right, Forest Green, Funnel Lip, Pontil, 1 7/8 In. 672.00
Pitkin Type, 36 Ribs, Swirled Right, Medium Olive Yellow, Tooled Lip, 1 7/8 In. 770.00
Pitkin Type, 36 Ribs, Swirled Right, Olive Green, Tooled Lip, Pontil, 1 3/8 In. . . . . .*Illus* 308.00
Pressed Glass, Square, Cobalt Blue, Faceted Diamond, Metal Ring, Cover, 1 3/4 In. 253.00
R.F., Black, Round, Inward Rolled Lip, Pontil, France, 1800-1840, 2 In. 269.00
Rectangular, Blue Green, 2 Pen Shelves, Burst Top, 2 1/4 In. 33.00
Rectangular, Gray Green, 2 Pen Shelves, Burst Top, 2 1/4 In. 55.00
Ross's Excelsior Ink, 12-Sided, Emerald Green, Pour Spout, OP, 7 3/8 In. 4620.00
S.M. Bixby & Co., N.Y., Dome, 9-Sided, Aqua, 2 3/8 In. 88.00
S.M.F.G. Co., Aqua, Ground Lip, 1875-1890, 1 7/8 In. 330.00
S.O. Dunbar, Taunton, Mass., 12-Sided, Aqua, Inward Rolled Lip, Pontil, 2 1/8 In. 476.00
S.S. Stafford's Inks, Made In USA, Cobalt Blue, Pour Spout, BIMAL, 4 1/2 In. 75.00
Schoolhouse, Aqua, Door & Windows On Sides, 2 3/8 In. 231.00
Schoolhouse, Aqua, Square, Windows On Sides, Tooled Top 165.00
Schoolhouse, Blue Aqua, Door & Windows, Tooled Lip, 2 In. 303.00
Schoolhouse, Patd. Mar 14 1871, Aqua, Door & Windows, Applied Lip, 2 1/2 In. 468.00
Ship, Utica, N.Y., Aqua, Tooled Lip, 1875-1890, 1 5/8 In. 744.00
Skull, Ceramic, White, Tan, Black, Red, Metal Collar, 1880-1890, 2 In. 190.00
Square, Cobalt Blue, Beveled Panels Shoulder, Burst Top, Australia, c.1885, 2 In. 23.00
Square, Turquoise, Ornate Metal Cap, 2 5/8 In. 99.00
Stafford's, Blue Green, Tooled Lip, Pour Spout, 1875-1885, 9 5/8 In. 123.00
Stafford's, Cobalt Blue, Pour Spout, 3 5/8 In. 125.00
Stafford's, Cylindrical, Blue Aqua, Pour Spout, Qt., 9 3/4 In. 66.00
Stafford's, Teal Blue, Pt., 6 1/4 In. 45.00
Stafford's Green Ink, Unchangeable, S.S. Stafford, Inc., New York 2966.00
Steel & Co., Philada., Pa., Blue Green, Embossed Shoulders, Pt. 70.00
Stoddard, Amber, Sheared Mouth, OP, 4 In. 154.00
Stoddard, Cone, Olive Yellow, 1846-1860, 2 1/4 In. 269.00
Stoddard, Umbrella, 16-Sided, Amber, Pontil, 2 1/4 x 2 3/8 In. 660.00
T. Davids, N.Y., Stoneware, Pt., 7 In. 95.00
Teakettle, 5-Sided, Gasoline, Raised Flowers, No Cap, France, 1830-1860, 2 1/8 In. 728.00
Teakettle, 6-Sided, Emerald Green, Panel Ellipses, 2 1/4 In. 336.00
Teakettle, 6-Sided, Fiery Opalescent, Brass Collar & Cap, 2 3/8 In. 413.00
Teakettle, 6-Sided, Milk Glass, Blue, Round Panels, Brass Collar, France, 1830-1860, 3 In. 336.00
Teakettle, 6-Sided, Porcelain, Kutani, Red, Black, Gold, Bird, Flowers, Japan, 3 In. 392.00
Teakettle, 6-Sided, Yellow, Brass Collar, Lid, England, 1830-1860, 2 In. 101.00
Teakettle, 8-Sided, Amethyst, Brass Collar, Lid, England, 1830-1860, 2 In. . . . . . .190.00 to 336.00
Teakettle, 8-Sided, Black Amethyst, Ground Lip, Brass Collar, 1895, 2 In. 235.00
Teakettle, 8-Sided, Blue, Gilt, Brass Collar, Lid, England, 1830-1860, 3 1/2 In. 190.00
Teakettle, 8-Sided, Blue, Gilt, Floral Enamel, Brass Collar, Lid, 1830-1860, 2 1/4 In. 258.00
Teakettle, 8-Sided, Ceramic, White Glaze, Blue, Green, Lavender, Rose, 2 1/4 In. 213.00
Teakettle, 8-Sided, Cobalt Blue, Ground Lip, Brass Collar, Hinged Lid, 2 1/4 In. 448.00
Teakettle, 8-Sided, Cobalt Blue, Hinged Lid, 1875-1895, 2 In. 687.00
Teakettle, 8-Sided, Cobalt Blue, Tooled Lip, Brass Collar, Lid, England, 1830-1860, 2 In. 392.00

Teakettle, 8-Sided, Dark Amethyst, Brass Collar, Hinged Lid, 2 1/8 In. 588.00
Teakettle, 8-Sided, Emerald Green, 1875-1895, 2 In. 392.00
Teakettle, 8-Sided, Emerald Green, Flowers, Brass Collar, Lid, France, 2 1/4 In. 269.00
Teakettle, 8-Sided, Green, Ground Lip, Brass Collar, 2 1/8 In. 688.00
Teakettle, 8-Sided, Medium Green, Olive Tint, Ground Lip, 2 1/8 In. 448.00
Teakettle, 8-Sided, Milk Glass, Green Flowers, England, 1830-1860, 2 In. 179.00
Teakettle, 8-Sided, Milk Glass, Green, France, 1830-1860, 2 In. 308.00
Teakettle, 8-Sided, Milk Glass, Multicolored Flowers, Brass Collar, France, 2 In. 280.00
Teakettle, 8-Sided, Milk Glass, Robin's Egg Blue, Gilt, Brass Collar, 2 In. 264.00
Teakettle, 8-Sided, Smoky Peacock Blue, Brass Collar, 2 1/8 In. 448.00
Teakettle, 8-Sided, Yellow Amber, Gilt, Lip, Brass Collar, 1830-1860, 1 3/4 In. 308.00
Teakettle, 9-Sided, Yellow, Hinged Lid, Brass Ring, Pontil, 1875-1895, 1 7/8 In. 770.00
Teakettle, 10-Sided, Amethyst, Pontil, Brass Collar, Lid, 1830-1860, 1 5/8 In. 364.00
Teakettle, 10-Sided, Cobalt Blue, Cut & Polished Panels, 1875-1895, 2 In. 303.00
Teakettle, 10-Sided, Yellow Green, Flowers, 1870, 2 1/2 In. 595.00
Teakettle, 12-Sided, Sapphire Blue, 2 1/8 In. 616.00
Teakettle, Amethyst, Ground Lip, 1885-1895, 2 In. 385.00
Teakettle, Amethyst, Sheared Mouth, Metal Collar, 1875-1895, 2 In. 440.00
Teakettle, Aqua, Olive Striations, 1 3/4 In. 110.00
Teakettle, Barrel, Blue Green, Ground Lip, Brass Collar, Lid, 1860, 2 1/8 In. 825.00
Teakettle, Barrel, Ceramic, Gray, Blue, Green, Gilt, Ball Feet, England, 2 3/4 In. 308.00
Teakettle, Barrel, Cobalt Blue, 1875-1895, 2 1/4 In. 924.00
Teakettle, Barrel, Ice Blue, Ground Lip, Brass Collar, Hinged Lid, 2 1/8 In. 672.00
Teakettle, Barrel, Plum Amethyst, Brass Collar, Lid, 1830-1860, 2 1/8 In. 1008.00
Teakettle, Barrel, Sapphire Blue, Brass Collar, Lid, 1830-1860, 2 3/16 In. 532.00
Teakettle, Beehive, 8-Sided, Yellow Green, Gilt, Brass Collar, 1830-1860, 2 3/8 In. 1120.00
Teakettle, Cranberry, Gilt, Brass Collar, France, 1830-1860, 1 1/2 In. 280.00
Teakettle, Dog, Clear, Ground Lip, 1880-1900, 1 7/8 In. 504.00
Teakettle, Dome, Yellow Green, Tooled Lip, Pontil, Finial Cap, 2 1/2 In. 246.00
Teakettle, Double Font, Cobalt Blue, Sheared & Polished Lip, 3 1/2 In. 1760.00
Teakettle, Double Font, Green, 1830-1860, 3 3/8 In. 896.00
Teakettle, Fiery Opalescent, Gold & Green Stripes, Brass Collar, Cap, 1830-1840, 2 In. . . . 336.00
Teakettle, Fiery Opalescent, Multicolored Flowers, Enamel, 1830, 2 In. . . . . .500.00 to 578.00
Teakettle, Light Pink Amethyst, Striations, Ground Lip, 2 In. 1092.00
Teakettle, Light Sapphire Blue, Curved Spout, Ground Lip 330.00
Teakettle, Milk Glass, Lime Green, Embossed Flowers, Polished Lip, 1895, 2 In. 550.00
Teakettle, Milk Glass, Powder Blue, Brass Neck Ring, Hinged Lid, 1895, 2 3/8 In. 660.00
Teakettle, Pyramid, Black, France, 1830-1860, 2 1/8 In. 476.00
Teakettle, Sapphire Blue, Ridged Panels, Ground Lip, Brass Collar, 2 In. . . . .*Illus* 392.00
Teakettle, Turtle, Amethyst, Brass Collar, Cap, France, 1830-1860, 1 1/2 In. 1232.00
Temple London, Diamond, Embossed, 4 Pen Rests 90.00
Tippecanoe Extract, Hard Cider, Barrel, Rolled Lip, Pontil, 1 7/8 In. 532.00
Trapezoidal, Ruby To Clear, Tooled, Smooth Base, 1840-1880, 2 In. 308.00
Turtle, Aqua, X's Around Base, 2 In. 44.00
Turtle, Citron, Burst Top, 2 In. 330.00
Turtle, Dome, Light To Medium Blue Green, 1880, 2 1/4 In. 121.00
Umbrella, 6-Sided, Black Amethyst, Tooled Lip, 2 1/2 In. 330.00
Umbrella, 6-Sided, Olive Green, Squat, Rolled Lip, OP, 2 1/4 In. 358.00
Umbrella, 8-Sided, Amber, Rolled Lip, OP, 2 5/8 In. 413.00
Umbrella, 8-Sided, Amethyst, Tooled Lip, 2 3/4 In. 1045.00
Umbrella, 8-Sided, Aqua, Burst Top 66.00
Umbrella, 8-Sided, Black Olive Amber, Traveler's, Copper Neck, 2 1/8 In. 196.00
Umbrella, 8-Sided, Blood Red Amber, Tooled Lip, Pontil, 1860, 1 1/2 In. 908.00
Umbrella, 8-Sided, Blue Aqua, IP, 1845-1860, 3 1/8 In. 220.00
Umbrella, 8-Sided, Blue Green, Rolled Lip, OP, 1845-1860, 2 5/8 In. . . . . .88.00 to 110.00
Umbrella, 8-Sided, Burgundy Puce, Rolled Lip, OP, 2 3/4 In. 1210.00
Umbrella, 8-Sided, Cobalt Blue, Inward Rolled Lip, 1820-1840, 2 1/2 In. . . . . . .2015.00 to 2576.00
Umbrella, 8-Sided, Cobalt Blue, Inward Rolled Lip, 1860-1870, 2 1/2 In. . . . . .336.00 to 660.00
Umbrella, 8-Sided, Cobalt Blue, Tooled Mouth, 1870-1880, 2 5/8 In. . . . .*Illus* 305.00
Umbrella, 8-Sided, Cornflower Blue, Tooled Lip, 2 5/8 In. 165.00
Umbrella, 8-Sided, Emerald Green, Inward Rolled Mouth, Pontil, 2 1/2 In. 413.00
Umbrella, 8-Sided, Gold Amber, Inward Rolled Lip, 1860-1870, 2 1/2 In. 146.00

Ink, Teakettle, Sapphire Blue,
Ridged Panels, Ground Lip, Brass
Collar, 2 In.

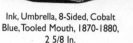

Ink, Umbrella, 8-Sided, Cobalt
Blue, Tooled Mouth, 1870-1880,
2 5/8 In.

Ink, Wood's Black Ink, Aqua,
Rolled Lip, OP, 2 1/2 In.

Umbrella, 8-Sided, Gold Amber, Sheared Mouth, Pontil, 2 3/8 In. 231.00
Umbrella, 8-Sided, Golden Amber, Inward Rolled Lip, Pontil, 1840-1860, 2 1/8 In. 202.00
Umbrella, 8-Sided, Grape Puce, Rolled Lip, 2 5/8 In. 715.00
Umbrella, 8-Sided, Grass Green, Rolled Lip, 2 1/2 In. 242.00
Umbrella, 8-Sided, Honey Amber, Rolled Lip, 2 1/2 In. 468.00
Umbrella, 8-Sided, Light Blue Green, Rolled Lip, OP, 1860, 2 3/8 In. . . . . .105.00 to 385.00
Umbrella, 8-Sided, Light Green, Inward Rolled Lip, Pontil, 1840-1860, 2 1/2 In. 90.00
Umbrella, 8-Sided, Medium Amber, 3 Dots On Base, Rolled Lip, 2 1/2 In. 110.00
Umbrella, 8-Sided, Moss Green, Inward Rolled Lip, Pontil, 1840-1860, 2 1/4 In. 1456.00
Umbrella, 8-Sided, Olive Amber, Rolled Lip, 2 3/8 In. 280.00
Umbrella, 8-Sided, Olive Amber, Tooled Lip, Pontil, 1840-1860, 2 1/2 In. . . . . . .260.00 to 280.00
Umbrella, 8-Sided, Olive Green, Inward Rolled Lip, Pontil, 1840-1860, 2 1/2 In. . .504.00 to 672.00
Umbrella, 8-Sided, Olive Green, Pontil, Tooled Lip, 1845-1855, 2 1/2 In. 275.00
Umbrella, 8-Sided, Olive Green, Tooled Lip, OP, 2 1/2 In. . . . . .165.00 to 303.00
Umbrella, 8-Sided, Olive Yellow, Inward Rolled Lip, Pontil, 1840-1860, 2 1/2 In. .260.00 to 392.00
Umbrella, 8-Sided, Olive Yellow, Rolled Lip, Pontil, 1845-1860, 2 1/2 In. 990.00
Umbrella, 8-Sided, Olive Yellow, Square Collar, 2 5/8 In. 440.00
Umbrella, 8-Sided, Orange Amber, Pontil, 1840-1860, 2 5/8 In. 336.00
Umbrella, 8-Sided, Peacock Blue, Square Collar, 1860-1880, 2 5/8 In. 728.00
Umbrella, 8-Sided, Purple Cobalt, Applied Lip, 2 3/4 In. 605.00
Umbrella, 8-Sided, Red Amber, Tooled Lip, Pontil, 2 1/2 In. 168.00
Umbrella, 8-Sided, Salmon Puce, Rolled Lip, OP, 2 5/8 In. 2640.00
Umbrella, 8-Sided, Sapphire Blue, Tooled Lip, 2 5/8 In. 385.00
Umbrella, 8-Sided, Teal Green, Rolled Lip, OP, 2 5/8 In. . . . . .130.00 to 358.00
Umbrella, 8-Sided, Yellow Amber, Inward Rolled Lip, Pontil, 1840-1860, 2 3/8 In. 179.00
Umbrella, 8-Sided, Yellow Amber, Open Pontil, 1845-1860, 2 1/2 In. 145.00
Umbrella, 12-Sided, Green, Inward Rolled Lip, Pontil, 1840-1860, 2 3/16 In. 270.00
Umbrella, 12-Sided, Medium Emerald Green, OP, 2 1/4 In. 220.00
Umbrella, 16-Sided, Gold Amber, Tooled Mouth, Pontil, 1846-1860, 2 1/4 In. 660.00
Umbrella, 16-Sided, Olive Green, Pontil, 1840-1860, 2 5/16 In. 728.00
Umbrella, Light Green, Bird Swing, Rolled Lip, OP 160.00
Umbrella, Teal Green, Rolled Lip, OP, Label, 2 1/2 In. 143.00
Underwood's, Cobalt Blue, Embossed, 9 In. 140.00
Universal Bristol, Amber, ABM, 2 1/2 In. 33.00
W.E. Bonney, Aqua, Label, Tooled Mouth, 1860-1875, 2 3/8 In. 83.00
W.E. Bonney, Barrel, Aqua, Applied Lip, Pour Spout, 1880s . . . . .66.00 to 90.00
W.E. Bonney, Hanover, Mass., National Writing, Barrel, Aqua, Label, Pontil, 2 3/4 In. 330.00
W.E. Bonney, W.A. Wilde & Co., Boston, Barrel, Aqua, Label, 2 5/8 In. 357.00
Ward's Black Record, Umbrella, 8-Sided, Teal Green, Label, Cork, Rolled Lip, 2 1/2 In. . . 110.00
Waters Ink, Umbrella, 6-Sided, Aqua, Inward Tooled Mouth, Pontil, 2 3/4 In. 935.00
Waters Ink, Umbrella, 6-Sided, Light Green, Inward Rolled Lip, Pontil, 2 5/8 In. 3360.00
Wood's Black Ink, Aqua, Rolled Lip, OP, 2 1/2 In. . . . .*Illus* 364.00
Wood's Black Ink, Cone, Yellow Amber, Pontil, 1840-1860, 2 1/4 In. 5040.00

JAR

Jar is the name for a container of a special shape. It has a wide mouth and almost no neck. Today we see jars of cold cream, but in earlier days jars made of glass or ceramic were used for storage of home-canned produce and for many commercial products. Jars are also listed in the Stoneware category in this book.

Acetato Plomo, Blue, Applied Top, 3-Piece Mold, Label, 13 In.	110.00
American Eagle Tobacco Works, Cobalt Blue, Barrel Form, Zinc Lid, Wire Bail, 7 5/8 In.	3640.00
Amethyst, 2 Embossed Rings, Greek Key Pattern, Ground Lip, Canada, 1/2 Gal., 8 In.	30.00
Battery, Aqua, Ground Mouth, Swirl Design, Late 19th Century, 6 In.	65.00
Battleship Maine, Morro Castle, Milk Glass, Ground Lip, Metal Screw Band	336.00
Butter, Gilberts, Airtight, Ground Mouth, Smooth Base, 1880-1900, 8 1/2 x 7 In.	330.00
Canning, Orange Spots, Dark Green, Olive Glaze, Lid, Redware, 5 3/4 In.	138.00
Canning, Red Glaze, Lid, Redware, 9 3/4 In.	412.00
Columbia Exposition, Teardrop, 3-Piece Mold, Swirled Stopper, 16 In.	286.00
Countertop, Columbia, Clear, Swirls On Neck, Glass Stopper, Smooth Lip, 19 3/4 In.	308.00
Countertop, Columbia, Clear, Teardrop Shape, Swirls On Neck, Glass Stopper, 15 1/4 In.	213.00
Countertop, Franklin Caro Co., Clear, Square, Ground Lip, Glass Stopper, 12 3/8 In.	62.00
Countertop, Globe, Clear, Diamond Pattern Rim, Thumbprint Stopper, Foot, 12 3/4 In.	140.00
Countertop, Globe, Diamond Pattern Rim, Thumbprint Stopper, Foot, 11 1/2 In.	168.00 to 196.00
Countertop, Globe, Diamond Pattern Rim, Thumbprint Stopper, Foot, 13 1/2 In.	157.00 to 258.00
Countertop, Kis-Me Gum Co., Louisville, Ky., Clear, Glass Stopper, 1915-1930, 9 In.	50.00
Figural, Owl, Milk Glass, Ground Lip, Metal Screw Band, Pt.	113.00
Flowers, Raised Enamel, Ribs, Porcelain, Lid	165.00
Hine Bros., Southampton, Gal.	30.00
Johnson & Johnson, New York, Cobalt Blue, Square, Glass Lid, 1880-1900, Qt.	550.00
Lilly, 5 Lbs. Chloroform Throat Lozenges, 3-Piece Mold, Stopper, Counter, 12 In.	176.00
Mader Brothers Colour Works, Wolver Hampton, England	52.00
Milk, Countertop, Blue Aqua, 5 Gal.	1400.00
Milk Glass, Blue, Ground Lip, 5 In.	12.00
Newbury Brewery, 1/2 Gal.	30.00
Ramon's Display, Metal Cover, Green Ground, 7 3/4 x 7 1/4 In.	60.00
Stacking, Haller's P. Hood, Cylindrical, 2 Tiers, 11 1/2 In., 2 Piece	115.00
Storage, Amber, Flared Rim, 1820-1850, Pontil, 2 3/4 In.	523.00
Storage, Amber, Wide Mouth, Folded Rim, Pontil, 1860s, 8 1/4 In.	132.00
Storage, Amber, Wide Mouth, Folded Rim, Pontil, 1860s, 12 In.	143.00
Storage, Applied Blue Bands, Cylindrical, Lid, 1840-1860, 10 1/2 In.	55.00
Storage, Aqua, Blown, Flared Mouth, Pontil, 1840-1860, 4 1/4 In.	385.00
Storage, Aqua, Dip Mold, OP, 1770-1820, 5 In.	29.00
Storage, Copper Puce, Wide Outward Rolled Lip, Pontil, 1840-1869, 7 1/2 In.	413.00
Storage, Dark Amber, Folded Lip, Pontil, 6 1/4 In.	55.00
Storage, Dutch, Olive Amber, Tooled Flared Mouth, Pontil, 1780-1800, 6 In.	358.00
Storage, Green Aqua, Dip Mold, Seed Bubbles, OP, 1790-1830, Qt., 8 1/2 In.	160.00
Storage, Green, Folded Lip, 17 1/2 In.	144.00
Storage, Green, Wide Mouth, Original Ball Closure, 13 In.	330.00
Storage, Light Aqua, Wide Mouth, Folded Lip, Pontil, 12 In.	77.00
Storage, Light Green Aqua, Wide Mouth, Folded Lip, Pontil, 8 In.	55.00
Storage, Light Olive, Applied Top, 7 In.	155.00
Storage, Medium Amber, Folded Lip, Pontil, 4 7/8 In.	55.00
Storage, Medium Olive Green, Olive Tone, Wide Mouth, Flared Rim, Pontil, 10 1/4 In.	246.00
Storage, Medium Olive Green, Wide Mouth, Flared Rim, Pontil, 9 3/4 In.	364.00
Storage, Olive Amber, Wide Mouth, Tooled Flared Lip, Pontil, 1790-1830, 12 3/4 In.	253.00
Storage, Olive Green, Wide Mouth, Tooled Flared Lip, Pontil, 1770-1810, 10 1/2 In.	209.00
Storage, Olive Green, Wide Tooled Rim, 1780-1830, Pontil, 11 1/4 In.	209.00
Storage, Olive Yellow, Blown, Flared Mouth, 1830-1860, 10 3/8 In.	264.00
Storage, Olive Yellow, Blown, Tooled Lip, Pontil, 8 5/8 In.	420.00
Storage, Olive Yellow, Blown, Tooled Wide Flared Lip, Pontil, 4 1/8 In.	2800.00
Storage, Olive Yellow, Tooled Lip, Pontil, 1860-1880, 13 7/8 In.	264.00
Storage, Olive Yellow, Torpedo Shape, Collared Mouth, Pontil, 1830-1860, 6 In.	660.00
Storage, Rolled Lip, OP, 4 1/2 In.	55.00
Storage, Stoddard, Gold Amber, Folded Rim, Bubbles, OP, 8 1/2 In.	358.00
Storage, Stoddard, Rolled Out Lip, Cylindrical, 7 1/8 In.	700.00
Storage, Strawberry Puce, Sloping Collar, OP, Bubbles, c.1810, 17 In.	980.00

Storage, Teal, Folded Lip, Pontil, 4 3/4 In. 77.00
Storage, Yellow, Folded Lip, 1840-1870, 6 In. 122.00
Tobacco, Man In Barrel Cover, Ceramic, Impressed JM Base, 1890-1930, 7 1/2 In. 110.00
Tobacco, Pink Amethyst, Applied Knob Lid, Pontil, 5 1/8 In. 198.00
Walla Walla Pepsin Gum, Embossed Indian Head, Lid 358.00
Warn & Sons, Brewers Tetbury, Newbury Brewery, 1/2 Gal. 38.00
Wells Miller, Provost, Pontil, 1850, 6 In. 55.00
JIM BEAM, see Beam

─────────────────────────── JUG ───────────────────────────

A jug is a deep container with a narrow mouth and a handle. It is usually made of pottery. Jugs were often used as containers for liquor. Messages, mottoes, and the name of the distillery or bar are often printed on the jug. Jugs are also listed in the Stoneware category in this book.

Brampton Puzzle, Salt Glaze, Windmills, Musical Instruments, Flowers, England, 1830 . .   483.00
British Airways, Blue 78.00
C. Barry & Co., Boston, Gal. 65.00
Cherry Smash, Embossed Label, c.1930, Gal. 55.00
Cider, Aqua, 5 Gal. 165.00
Coors, Pure Malted Milk, 6 3/4 x 6 3/4 In. 75.00
Crown Devon John Peel, Leek & Moorlands Bldg. Society, 1936 .... 263.00
Golden Hill, Toledo, Ohio, Pottery, White, 4 3/4 In. 77.00
Handled Chestnut, Ambrosial, B.M. & E.A.W. & Co., Amber, Handle, 8 1/4 In. 190.00
Indian Chief, 2 Handles, Doulton, 1908, 6 7/8 In. 330.00
King George IV, Blue Glaze, Doulton, 1900, 6 In. 154.00
Little Polveir, The Seagram 1989 Grand National Winner, Dark Blue Glaze, 5 1/2 In. 124.00
Paul Cushman, Gray Brown Glaze, Oval, Applied Handle, 19th Century, 8 3/8 In. 253.00
Pickwick Delux, Doulton 67.00
Purple Amethyst, Handle, IP, 6 1/4 In. 476.00
Rum Carioca, San Juan, Puerto Rico, Blue, Tan, 1950s, Gal. 120.00
Shepherd Neame Abbey, Draught Wade Pub 52.00

─────────────────────────── LACEY ───────────────────────────

Haas Brothers of San Francisco, California, was established in 1851. They made W.A. Lacey and Cyrus Noble bottles in the 1970s. The firm discontinued its ceramic business about 1981 and destroyed all of the molds. Lacey bottles include the log animal series (1978-1980) and the tavern series (1975). Also see the Cyrus Noble category.

Bank Exchange, Exterior, 1976 ....22.00 to 25.00
Bank Exchange, Interior, 1976 ....22.00 to 23.00
Continental Navy, 1976 ....15.00 to 18.00
Fargo Bank, 1975 ....20.00 to 22.00
Harold's Club, 1970, Miniature ....25.00 to 28.00
Rabbit, Log, 1978 ....   29.00
Rabbit, Log, 1980 ....   29.00
Raccoon, Log, 1978 ....   35.00
Raccoon, Log, 1980 ....   35.00
Squirrel, Log, 1979 ....   29.00
Tennis Player, 1976, Pair ....33.00 to 35.00
Tonapah Saloon, 1975, Miniature ....11.00 to 25.00
Tun Tavern, No. 1, 1975 ....10.00 to 14.00
Tun Tavern, No. 2, U.S. Marines, 1975 ....   25.00
Willits Frontier, 1976 .... 116.00

─────────────────────────── LAST CHANCE ───────────────────────────

Last Chance Whiskey was presented in ceramic figural bottles in 1971 and 1972. One series of 8-ounce bottles called Professionals pictured a doctor, dentist, banker, entertainer, politician, and salesman. Another series was a group of six bottles that joined together to form a long bar scene. Two versions of this bar scene were made, one with and one without a frame.

Bar Scene, With Frame, 1971, Miniature, 6 Piece ....120.00 to 148.00
Dentist, 1971, Miniature 8.00
Doctor, 1971, Miniature 8.00
Entertainer, 1971, Miniature 8.00

Politician, 1971, Miniature 8.00
Salesman, 1971, Miniature 8.00
Wyoming Stockgrowers .... 55.00 to 85.00

---------- LEWIS & CLARK ----------

Lewis & Clark bottles were created by Alpha Industries of Helena, Montana. The first bottles, full-length representations of historical figures, were made from 1971 to 1976. The pioneer series of 1977-1978 was released in two-bottle sets. Each bottle was 13 inches high and two placed together created a scene. For example, one was an Indian (bottle) offering to sell some furs to a white man (bottle). A set of six troll bottles was made in 1978-1979.

Arizona, 1981, Miniature 8.00
Barnyard Clown, 1981 .... 38.00 to 44.00
Bighorn, 5 Piece 110.00
Blinking Owl, 1981 .... 44.00
California, 1981, Miniature 8.00
Charbonneau, 1973 .... 60.00
Cook, 1977 .... 50.00
Cousin, 1979 .... 20.00
Cowboy, 1977 .... 50.00
Curlee Indian Scout, 1974 .... 50.00
Daughter, Troll, 1978 .... 24.00
Family, 1978, Pair 113.00
General Custer, 1974 .... 30.00 to 35.00
Grandfather, Troll, 1978 .... 20.00
Grandmother, Troll, 1979 .... 20.00
Hobo, 1981 .... 44.00
Idaho, 1981, Miniature 8.00
Indian, 1978 .... 67.00
John Lennon .... 190.00 to 193.00
Lewis & Clark, Miniature, 5 Piece 103.00
Major Reno, 1976 .... 27.00
Maryland, 1981, Miniature 8.00
Meriwether Lewis, 1971 .... 50.00
Minnesota, 1981, Miniature 10.00
Montana, 1976 .... 50.00
Mr. & Mrs. Troll, 1978 .... 20.00
New Mexico, 1981, Miniature 8.00
North Dakota, 1981, Miniature 8.00
Oregon, 1981, Miniature 8.00
Plaque Peace Pipe, 1978 .... 45.00
Prowling Panther, 1982 .... 42.00
Sacajawea, 1972 .... 74.00
Sheepherder 70.00
Sitting Bull, 1976 .... 95.00 to 105.00
South Carolina, 1981, Miniature 8.00
South Dakota, 1981, Miniature 8.00
States, 1981, Miniature .... 8.00 to 10.00
States, 1984, Miniature .... 8.00 to 10.00
Trader, 1978 .... 72.00
Trooper, 1976 .... 32.00
Utah, 1981, Miniature 10.00
William Clark, 1971 .... 50.00
Wisconsin, 1981, Miniature 8.00
Wyoming, 1981, Miniature 8.00
York, 1972 .... 44.00

---------- LIONSTONE ----------

Lionstone Distilleries Inc. of Lawrenceburg, Kentucky, started making porcelain figural bottles to hold their whiskey for national sale in 1969. The first bottles were Western figures, each with a black label that told the historical facts about the figure. About 15,000 bottles were made for each of the first six subjects, the cowboy, proud Indian, casual Indian, sheriff, gentleman gambler, and cavalry scout. About half of the bottles were never filled with liquor because they leaked. These *leakers* were used by bars as display items on shelves and were clearly labeled with decals stating that they were for display only. More bottles were made for the series, about 4,000 of each. The set had 16 bottles. Lionstone then made a series of race cars (1970-1984), more Western figures (1970-1976), a Western bar scene (1971), birds (1970-1977), circus figures (1973), dogs (1975-1977), European workers (1974), oriental workers (1974), Bicentennial series (1976), clowns (1978-1979), sports series (1974-1983), and others. They also made many miniature bottles. Lionstone was sold to Barton Brands in December 1979. It was sold back to Mark Slepak, the original owner, in December 1983. The whiskey was distilled in Bardstown, Kentucky, but the bottles were made in Chicago. Over 800 styles were made. No decanters were made after 1995.

AMVET Riverboat, 1983	18.00
Baseball Players, 1974	89.00
Bass, No. 1, 1983	70.00 to 85.00
Betsy Ross, 1975	25.00
Bird, Blue Jay, 1971	23.00
Bird, Blue-Crowned Chlorophonia, 1974, Miniature	42.00
Bird, Bluebird, Eastern, 1972	24.00
Bird, Bluebird, Western, 1972	20.00 to 24.00
Bird, Canada Goose, 1980	49.00
Bird, Canary, 1973, Miniature	40.00
Bird, Capistrano Swallow, Gold Bell, 1972	21.00
Bird, Capistrano Swallow, Gold Bell, 1972, Miniature	8.00
Bird, Capistrano Swallow, Silver Bell, 1972	35.00
Bird, Cardinal, 1973	27.00
Bird, Doves Of Peace, 1977, Miniature	30.00
Bird, Emerald Toucanet, 1974	16.00
Bird, Falcon, 1973	27.00
Bird, Hummingbird, 1973, Miniature	35.00
Bird, Mourning Dove, 1981	49.00
Bird, Northern Royal Flycatcher, 1974, Miniature	40.00
Bird, Ostriches, 1977, Miniature	15.00
Bird, Owls, 1973	25.00
Bird, Painted Bunting, 1974, Miniature	17.00
Bird, Pheasant, 1977	49.00
Bird, Pheasant, No. 6, 1981	39.00
Bird, Quail, 1969	26.00
Bird, Roadrunner, 1969	24.00
Bird, Roadrunner, 1969, Miniature	9.00
Bird, Robin, 1975, Miniature	12.00
Bird, Scarlet Macaw, 1974, Miniature	36.00
Bird, Snow, Goose, 1981	45.00
Bird, Wood Duck, 1981	40.00 to 45.00
Bird, Woodhawk, 1969, Miniature	25.00 to 27.00
Bird, Woodpecker, 1975	26.00
Bird, Woodpecker, 1975, Miniature	11.00
Bird, Yellow Head, 1974, Miniature	42.00
Blacksmith, 1973	26.00 to 29.00
Buccaneer, 1973	26.00
Car, Corvette, 1984 Model, 1984	65.00
Car, Corvette, 1984 Model, Black, 1984	110.00
Car, Duesenberg, 1978, Miniature	16.00
Car, Jaguar, 1936 Model, 1978	18.00
Car, Johnnie Lightning, No. 1, Gold, 1972	116.00
Car, Johnnie Lightning, No. 2, Silver, 1973	100.00
Car, Mercedes, 1978, Miniature	16.00
Car, Olsonite Eagle, No. 6, 1970	106.00
Car, Stutz Bearcat, 1978, Miniature	16.00
Car, Turbo Car STP, Gold, 1972	152.00
Car, Turbo Car STP, Platinum, 1972	152.00
Car, Turbo Car STP, Red, 1972	57.00
Cherry Valley, 1971, Gold	25.00

Cherry Valley, 1971, Silver 35.00
Circus, Burmese Girl, 1973, Miniature 25.00
Circus, Fire Eater, 1973, Miniature 25.00
Circus, Snake Charmer, 1973, Miniature 25.00
Circus, Strongman, 1973, Miniature 25.00
Circus, Sword Swallower, 1973, Miniature 25.00
Circus, Tattooed Lady, 1973, Miniature 25.00
Clown, No. 1, Monkey Business, 1978 .... 44.00
Clown, No. 1, Monkey Business, 1978, Miniature 21.00
Clown, No. 2, Sad Sam, 1978 .... 38.00
Clown, No. 2, Sad Sam, 1978, Miniature 21.00
Clown, No. 3, Say It With Music, 1978 .... 38.00
Clown, No. 3, Say It With Music, 1978, Miniature 21.00
Clown, No. 4, Salty Tails, 1978 .... 38.00
Clown, No. 4, Salty Tails, 1978, Miniature 20.00
Clown, No. 5, Pie Face, 1979 .... 31.00
Clown, No. 5, Pie Face, 1979, Miniature 20.00
Clown, No. 6, Lampy, 1979 .... 38.00
Clown, No. 6, Lampy, 1979, Miniature 20.00
Dog, Afghan, 1977, Miniature 25.00
Dog, Alaskan Malamute, 1977, Miniature 18.00
Dog, Beagle, 1977, Miniature 18.00
Dog, British Pointer, 1975, Miniature ....*Illus* 25.00
Dog, British Rough Collie, 1975, Miniature ....14.00 to 15.00
Dog, Cocker Spaniel, 1975, Miniature ....15.00 to 35.00
Dog, Doberman, 1977, Miniature ....15.00 to 25.00
Dog, French Poodle, 1975, Miniature 18.00
Dog, German Boxer, 1975, Miniature 18.00
Dog, German Dachshund, 1977, Miniature 18.00
Dog, German Shepherd, 1975, Miniature 18.00
Dog, Golden Retriever, 1977, Miniature 18.00
Dog, Great Dane, 1977, Miniature 18.00
Dog, Irish Setter, 1977, Miniature 18.00
Dog, Labrador Retriever, 1977, Miniature 18.00
Dog, Schnauzer, 1977, Miniature 16.00
Dog, Scottish Terrier, 1977, Miniature 16.00
Dog, St. Bernard, 1977, Miniature 25.00
Duck, Canvasback, 1981 .... 37.00
Duck, Mallard, 1981 .... 34.00
Duck, Pintail, 1981 ....45.00 to 47.00
European Worker, Cobbler, 1974 .... 35.00
European Worker, Horseshoer, 1974 .... 35.00
European Worker, Potter, 1974 .... 35.00
European Worker, Silversmith, 1974 .... 35.00
European Worker, Watchmaker, 1974 .... 35.00
European Worker, Woodworker, 1974 .... 35.00
F.O.E. Eagle, Las Vegas, 1982 .... 32.00
F.O.E. Eagle, Nashville, 1983 .... 33.00
F.O.E. Eagle, White, 1983 .... 20.00
Firefighter, Fire Alarm Box, Red, 1983 .... 120.00
Firefighter, Fire Equipment, 1976, Miniature, 3 Piece ....70.00 to 73.00
Firefighter, Fire Extinguisher, No. 9, 1983 ....80.00 to 81.00
Firefighter, Fire Hydrant, No. 6, 1981 ....92.00 to 95.00
Firefighter, Fireman No. 1, Red Hat, 1972 ....93.00 to 95.00
Firefighter, Fireman No. 1, Yellow Hat, 1972 ....133.00 to 135.00
Firefighter, Fireman No. 2, With Child, 1974 ....85.00 to 90.00
Firefighter, Fireman No. 3, Down Pole, 1975 ....95.00 to 100.00
Firefighter, Fireman No. 4, Emblem, 1978 .... 30.00
Firefighter, Fireman No. 5, Emblem, 1979 .... 35.00
God Of Love, 1978 .... 22.00
God Of War, 1978 .... 22.00
Goldfinch, 1975 .... 24.00
Horse, Cannonade, 1976 .... 142.00

Lionstone, Dog, British Pointer,
1975, Miniature

Lionstone, Old West,
Madame, 1969

Lionstone, Oriental Worker,
Sculptor, 1974

Horse, Secretariat, 1977	185.00
Horse, Secretariat, 1977, Miniature	18.00
Indian, Bust, No. 2, With Pipe, 1980	45.00
Lantern, Brass, 1983	125.00
Mailman, 1974	45.00
Oil Filter, Delco	65.00
Old West, Annie Christmas, 1969	30.00
Old West, Annie Oakley, 1969	30.00
Old West, Backpacker, 1980	29.00
Old West, Bar Scene & Nude, With Frame, 1970	520.00 to 640.00
Old West, Barber, 1976	37.00
Old West, Barber, 1976, Miniature	15.00
Old West, Bartender, 1969	30.00
Old West, Bartender, 1969, Miniature	15.00
Old West, Bath, 1976	70.00
Old West, Bath, 1976, Miniature	16.00
Old West, Belly Robber, 1969	27.00
Old West, Buffalo Hunter, 1973	35.00
Old West, Calamity Jane, 1973	22.00
Old West, Camp Cook, 1969	35.00
Old West, Camp Follower, 1969	35.00
Old West, Cavalry Scout, 1969	20.00
Old West, Cavalry Scout, 1970, Miniature	15.00
Old West, Chinese Laundry Man, 1969	25.00
Old West, Country Doctor, 1969	20.00
Old West, Cowboy, 1969	27.00
Old West, Cowboy, 1970, Miniature	12.00
Old West, Cowgirl, 1973	33.00
Old West, Custer's Last Stand, 1979	520.00
Old West, Dancehall Girl, 1973	50.00
Old West, Frontiersman, 1969	23.00
Old West, Gambler, 1969	20.00
Old West, Gambler, 1969, Miniature	12.00
Old West, Gold Panner, 1969	46.00
Old West, Highway Robber, 1969	15.00
Old West, Indian, Bust With Pipe, No. 2, 1980	45.00
Old West, Indian, Bust With Spear, No. 1, 1980	45.00
Old West, Indian, Casual, 1969	18.00
Old West, Indian, Casual, 1970, Miniature	18.00
Old West, Indian, Proud, 1969	21.00
Old West, Indian, Proud, 1970, Miniature	15.00
Old West, Indian, Squaw, 1973	27.00
Old West, Indian, Squawman, 1969	27.00

Old West, Indian, Tribal Chief, 1973 .... 27.00
Old West, Jesse James, 1969 .... 22.00
Old West, Judge Roy Bean, 1973 .... 25.00
Old West, Judge, Circuit Riding, 1969 .... 20.00
Old West, Lonely Luke, 1974 .... 30.00
Old West, Lonely Luke, 1975, Miniature 10.00
Old West, Lucky Buck, 1974 .... 30.00
Old West, Lucky Buck, 1975, Miniature 10.00
Old West, Madame, 1969 ....*Illus* 45.00
Old West, Molly Brown, 1973 .... 17.00
Old West, Mountain Man, 1969 .... 25.00
Old West, Photographer, 1976 .... 58.00
Old West, Photographer, 1976, Miniature 15.00
Old West, Professor, 1973 .... 45.00
Old West, Railroad Engineer, 1969 .... 25.00
Old West, Rainmaker, 1976 .... 35.00
Old West, Rainmaker, 1976, Miniature 15.00
Old West, Renegade Trader, 1969 .... 25.00
Old West, Riverboat Captain, 1969 .... 25.00
Old West, Sheepherder, 1969 .... 45.00
Old West, Sheepherder, 1975, Miniature 16.00
Old West, Sheriff, 1969 .... 25.00
Old West, Sheriff, 1970, Miniature 14.00
Old West, Shootout At OK Corral, 1971, 3 Piece 425.00
Old West, Shootout At OK Corral, 1971, Miniature, 3 Piece 230.00
Old West, Sodbuster, 1969 .... 23.00
Old West, Stage Driver, 1969 .... 27.00
Old West, Telegrapher, 1969 .... 25.00
Old West, Tinker, 1974 .... 25.00
Old West, Trapper, 1976 .... 30.00
Old West, Vigilante, 1969 .... 22.00
Old West, Wells Fargo Man, 1969 .... 25.00
Oriental Worker, Basket Weaver, 1974 .... 30.00
Oriental Worker, Egg Merchant, 1974 .... 30.00
Oriental Worker, Gardener, 1974 .... 30.00
Oriental Worker, Sculptor, 1974 ....*Illus* 30.00
Oriental Worker, Tea Vendor, 1974 .... 30.00
Oriental Worker, Timekeeper, 1974 .... 30.00
Police Association Convention, 1980 .... 30.00
Prima Donna Club, 1978, 5 Piece 475.00
Rose Parade, 1973 .... 18.00
Safari, Buffalo, 1977, Miniature 25.00
Safari, Elephants, 1977, Miniature 25.00
Safari, Gazelles, 1977, Miniature 25.00
Safari, Giraffes, 1977, Miniature 25.00
Safari, Hippos, 1977, Miniature 25.00
Safari, Kangaroos, 1977, Miniature 25.00
Safari, Koala Bears, 1977, Miniature 25.00
Safari, Leopards, 1977, Miniature 25.00
Safari, Lion & Cub, 1977 .... 25.00
Safari, Lion & Cub, 1977, Miniature 25.00
Safari, Mona Monkeys, 1977, Miniature 25.00
Safari, Rhinos, 1977, Miniature 25.00
Safari, Zebras, 1977, Miniature 25.00
Shamrock, 1983 .... 35.00
Sport, Backpacker, 1980 .... 29.00
Sport, Baseball Players, 1974 .... 90.00
Sport, Basketball Players, 1974 ....50.00 to 55.00
Sport, Boxers, 1974 ....60.00 to 65.00
Sport, Brooks Robinson, 1983 ....160.00 to 170.00
Sport, Fisherman, 1983 .... 40.00
Sport, Football Players, 1974 .... 55.00
Sport, Golfer, 1974 ....43.00 to 62.00

Sport, Hockey Players, 1974 ....63.00 to 65.00
Sport, Johnny Unitas, 1983 .... 175.00
Sport, Tennis Player, Female, 1980 .... 27.00
Sport, Tennis Player, Male, 1980 .... 27.00

---------- LORD CALVERT ----------

Lord Calvert Canadian whiskey has been sold in several types of special decanters. A series of glass flasks with ball stoppers was offered in 1961, and a series of duck decanters was made from 1978 to 1980.

Canada Goose, 1977 .... 35.00
Canvasback Duck, 1979 .... 19.00
Common Eider Duck, 1980 .... 17.00
Wood Duck, 1978 .... 25.00

---------- LUXARDO ----------

In 1821 Girolamo Luxardo began making a liqueur from the marasca cherry. The company literature calls this famous drink *the original maraschino*. The business has remained in the family through five generations. Decorative Luxardo bottles were first used in the 1930s at Torreglia near Padua, Italy. Most of the Luxardo bottles found today date after 1943. The date listed here is the first year each bottle was made. The bottles are still being made and some are sold at stores in the United States and Canada. Bottles are of glass or ceramic and come in many sizes, including miniatures. Many of the bottles were pictured in the now-out-of-print book *Luxardo Bottles* by Constance Avery and Al Cembura (1968).

African Head 20.00
Amphora, 1956, Miniature 11.00
Ampulla, 1959 .... 26.00
Apothecary Jar, 1960 ....20.00 to 25.00
Apothecary Jar, 1960, Miniature 16.00
Autumn Wine Pitcher, 1958 .... 34.00
Babylon, 1960 .... 23.00
Bacchus, 1969 .... 25.00
Bantu, 1969 .... 15.00
Bizantina, 1959 .... 32.00
Blue & Gold Amphora, 1968 .... 25.00
Buddha, Joogan, Gray, 1962 .... 18.00
Burma Ashtray, 1960 ....22.00 to 23.00
Burma Ashtray, 1960, Miniature 18.00
Burma Pitcher, 1960 .... 15.00
Calypso, 1962 ....22.00 to 24.00
Candlestick, Alabaster, 1961 .... 33.00
Cannon, Brass Wheels, 1969 ....25.00 to 29.00
Cat, Black, Miniature 12.00
Cellini, 1952 .... 40.00
Cellini, 1968 .... 15.00
Ceramic Barrel, 1968 .... 26.00
Chess Horse, Quartz, 1969 .... 38.00
Clock, 1960 .... 22.00
Clown, Miniature 17.00
Coffeepot, 1962 .... 12.00
Congo, 1960 .... 20.00
Deruto Cameo, 1959 .... 28.00
Dog, Bulldog, Miniature 22.00
Dog, English Bulldog, Miniature 6.00
Dolphin, 1959 .... 48.00
Duck, Green, 1960 .... 48.00
Eagle, Onyx, 1970 .... 68.00
Faenza, 1972 .... 8.00
Fakir, 1960 .... 31.00
Fish, Alabaster, 1960 .... 36.00
Fish, Green & Gold, 1960 .... 35.00
Fish, Quartz, 1969 .... 43.00
Fish, Ruby, 1961 .... 37.00

Frog, Miniature	7.00
Fruit, 1960, Miniature	28.00
Gambia, 1961	10.00
Gambia, 1961, Miniature	6.00
Gazelle, 1957	35.00
Gondola & Gondolier, 1959	25.00
Goose, Alabaster, 1960	30.00
Maraboo, 1957	35.00
Mayan, 1960	20.00
Mazzo, Amphora, 1954	25.00
Medieval Palace, 1952	34.00
Medieval Palace, 1970	9.00
Miss Luxardo, 1970	16.00
Mosaic Ashtray, 1959	18.00
Mosiac Ashtray, 1959, Miniature	12.00
Mud Bucket, Miniature	14.00
Nubian, 1959	17.00
Nubian, 1959, Miniature	8.00
Owl, Miniature	13.00
Owl, Onyx, 1970	55.00
Paestum, 1959	21.00
Paestum, 1959, Miniature	5.00
Pagliacci, 1959	18.00
Penguin, 1968	37.00
Pheasant, 1968	175.00
Pheasant, Modern, 1960	53.00
Pheasant, Quartz, 1969	51.00
Pheasant, Red & Gold, 1960	53.00
Pierrot, 1959	53.00
Pre-Historic, 1974, Miniature	11.00
Puppy, Cicciola, 1961	28.00
Puppy, Cicciola, On Base, 1960	34.00
Safari Animals, 1972, Miniature	8.00
Santa Maria Ship, 1969	19.00
Sphinx, 1961	13.00
Squirrel, 1968	45.00 to 48.00
Tamburello, 1959	26.00
Torra Bianca, 1962	20.00
Torre Tinta, 1962	21.00
Tower Of Flowers, 1968	23.00
Tower Of Fruit, 1968	23.00
Turkey, 1961	24.00 to 25.00
Twist, Miniature	9.00
Venetian, Gold Rosy, 1952	23.00
Venetian, Merletto, 1957	26.00
Venus, 1969	19.00 to 22.00
Wobble Bottle, 1957	11.00
Zodiac, 1970	31.00

MCCORMICK

It is claimed that the first white men to find the limestone spring near Weston, Missouri, were Lewis and Clark on their famous expedition. Over 20,000 gallons of fresh water gush from the spring each day. An Indian trading post was started near the spring by a man named McPhearson about 1830. His friend Joseph Moore decided to establish a town and paid a barrel of whiskey for the land. Bela Hughes and his cousin Ben Holladay came to the new town in 1837. They soon had a dry goods store, a drugstore, a tavern, and a hotel. They even built a Pony Express station. In 1856, Ben Holladay and his brother David started a distillery to make bourbon using the spring water. David's daughter later married a man named Barton and the distillery was renamed Barton and Holladay. It was sold in 1895 to George Shawhan but closed from 1920 to 1936. The property became a cattle and tobacco farm.

In 1936, after the repeal of Prohibition, Isadore Singer and his two brothers purchased the plant and began making Old Weston and Old Holladay bourbon. About 1939 they bought the name *McCormick* from a nearby distillery founded years before by E.R. McCormick. Legend says that Mrs. McCormick would not allow her husband to reopen the distillery because she had "gotten religion." The Singer brothers' new distillery used part of the grain for the mash, and their cattle feed lot used the leftover parts.

During World War II, alcohol was needed by the government and Cloud L. Cray bought the distillery to make industrial alcohol at a company he called Midwest Solvents. After the war, Bud and Dick Cray, sons of Cloud Cray, started making bourbon at the old plant by old-fashioned methods, producing about 25 barrels a day. The bourbon was sold in Missouri, Kansas, Iowa, and Oklahoma. The old plant, listed in the National Register of Historic Sites, is open for tours. In about 1980 the company, under the direction of the new president, Marty Adams, started marketing on a national instead of a local scale, and it is now selling in all of the states. They have a full line, including wine, beer, and many alcoholic beverages such as rum, tequila, vodka, dry gin, blended whiskey, and brandy that are now sold under the McCormick name.

McCormick Distilling Company was bought by Midwest Grain Products in 1950. They created many types of figural bottles for their bourbon, ranging from a bust of Elvis Presley (made in 1979) to a musical apple (1982). The company discontinued making decanters in 1987.

Abe Lincoln, 1976	40.00
Air Race, Pylon, 1970	19.00
Alabama	150.00
Arizona Wildcat	54.00 to 65.00
Bat Masterson, 1972	32.00 to 40.00
Baylor Bears, 1972	41.00 to 50.00
Betsy Ross, 1975	25.00
Betsy Ross, 1976, Miniature	20.00
Billy The Kid, 1973	33.00 to 38.00
Billy The Kid, 1973, Box	48.00
Bing Crosby Golf	52.00
Blue Bird, Creighton, 1971	18.00
Buffalo Bill, 1979	55.00
Calamity Jane, 1974	38.00
California Bears	125.00 to 158.00
Capt. John Smith, 1977	19.00
Captain's Lamp, No. 2, 1983	21.00
Chair, Queen Anne, 1979	33.00
Charles Lindbergh, 1977, Miniature	12.00
Christmas House, 1984	42.00
Cowboy Hall Of Fame, 1983	95.00
Daniel Boone, 1975	28.00
Deer Trophy Plaque, 1983	90.00
Doc Holiday, 1972	36.00
Doc Holiday, 1972, Box	41.00
Dune Buggy, 1976	35.00
Eleanor Roosevelt, 1977	28.00
Elvis, 25th Anniversary, 1980	135.00
Elvis, 50th Anniversary, 1986	450.00
Elvis, Aloha, 1981	80.00 to 155.00
Elvis, Christmas Tree	200.00
Elvis, Graceland Gate	240.00 to 255.00
Elvis, Hound Dog	550.00
Elvis, Karate, 1982	260.00 to 335.00
Elvis, Memories, 1987	630.00 to 650.00
Elvis, On Rising Sun, 1984	650.00
Elvis, Sergeant, 1983	320.00
Elvis, With Teddy Bear	645.00 to 695.00
Fire Extinguisher, 1983	45.00
FOE, 1984	74.00
FOE, 1985	52.00
FOE, 1986	25.00
Frontiersman Davy Crockett, 1975	25.00

George Washington, 1975 ....24.00 to 25.00
Georgia Tech, 1974 .... 50.00
Hank Williams Jr., Bocephus, 1980 .... 105.00
Hank Williams Sr., 1980 ....125.00 to 140.00
Henry Ford, 1977 .... 30.00
Ice Box, 1983 .... 35.00
Imperial Council, 1984 .... 30.00
Iowa Hawkeye, 1974 .... 100.00
Iowa Northern Panther, 1974 ....50.00 to 59.00
Jesse James, 1973, Box 35.00
Jimmy Durante 55.00
Johnny Rogers, No. 1, 1972 .... 185.00
Joplin Miner, 1972 .... 23.00
Jug, Bourbon, 1967 .... 12.00
Jug, Gin, 1967 .... 10.00
Jug, Vodka, 1967 .... 10.00
Julia Bullette, 1974 .... 105.00
Kansas City Chiefs, 1969 .... 26.00
Kansas City Club, 1982 .... 25.00
Kansas City Royals, 1971 .... 12.00
King Arthur, 1979 ....42.00 to 55.00
Kit Carson, 1975 .... 25.00
Meriwether Lewis, 1978 .... 25.00
Merlin, 1979 .... 46.00
Michigan Wolverine, 1974 .... 43.00
Minnesota Gopher, 1974 .... 50.00
Mississippi Rebel, 1974 .... 50.00
Missouri, China, 1970 .... 10.00
Missouri, Glass, 1971 .... 6.00
Muhammad Ali, 1980 .... 180.00
Nebraska Football Player, 1972 ....68.00 to 73.00
New Mexico Lobo, 1973 .... 42.00
Oregon Duck, 1974 .... 45.00
Oregon State Beaver, 1974 .... 50.00
Ozark Ike, 1979 .... 33.00
Packard, Hood Ornament, 1985 .... 29.00
Packard, Model 1937, Black, 1980 .... 47.00
Packard, Model 1937, Cream, 1980 .... 47.00
Packard, Model 1937, Gold ....77.00 to 79.00
Packard, Model 1937, Silver ....77.00 to 79.00
Paul Bunyan, 1979 ....32.00 to 35.00
Paul Revere, 1975 ....25.00 to 30.00
Pendleton Roundup ....52.00 to 54.00
Pirate, No. 1, 1972, 1/2 Pt. 16.00
Pirate, No. 2, 1972, 1/2 Pt. 16.00
Pirate, No. 5, 1972, 1/2 Pt. 12.00
Pirate, No. 6, 1972, 1/2 Pt. 12.00
Pirate, No. 7, 1972, 1/2 Pt. 12.00
Pirate, No. 9, 1972, 1/2 Pt. 12.00
Pony Express, 1978 .... 50.00
Pony Express, 1980 .... 50.00
Quail Gamal, 1982 .... 49.00
Quail Gamal, 1984 .... 50.00
Queen Guinevere, 1979 .... 24.00
Robert E. Lee, 1976 .... 60.00
Robert Peary, 1977 ....30.00 to 35.00
Rose Garden, 1980, Miniature 20.00
Samuel Houston, 1977 .... 35.00
Seal, With Ball ....52.00 to 54.00
Shriner, Noble, 1976 .... 35.00
Sir Lancelot, 1979 ....25.00 to 27.00
Skibob, 1971 .... 13.00
Skier Club Of Kansas City 77.00

Spirit Of 76, 1976 .... 47.00
TCU Horned Frogs, 1972 ....46.00 to 55.00
Telephone Operator, 1982 .... 57.00
Texas 150th Anniversary 24.00
Texas Long Horns, 1972 .... 40.00
Texas Tech Raider, 1972 .... 42.00
Thelma Lu ....30.00 to 33.00
Tom Sawyer, 1980 .... 31.00
Tom T. Hall, 1980 ....90.00 to 96.00
Train, Locomotive, 1969 ....25.00 to 29.00
Train, Mail Car, 1969 .... 35.00
U.S. Marshall, 1979 ....36.00 to 42.00
Ulysses S. Grant, 1976 .... 55.00
Victorian, 1984 .... 20.00
Weston, 1856, Miniature, 6 Piece 275.00
Wild Bill Hickok, 1973 .... 36.00
Willie Weary, 1981 .... 100.00
Woman, Feeding Chickens, 8 Piece 35.00
Woman, Washing Clothes, 1980 .... 35.00
Wood Duck, 1980 ....35.00 to 37.00
Wood Duck, 1984 ....35.00 to 37.00
World's Greatest Fan ....31.00 to 38.00
Wyatt Earp, 1972 .... 40.00
Wyatt Earp, 1972, Box 45.00

---------------------------- MEDICINE ----------------------------

If you have friends with scrofula or catarrh, they probably can find a medicine from the
nineteenth century. The extravagant claims for cures and the strange names for diseases
add to the fun of collecting early medicine bottles. Bottles held all of the many types of
medications used in past centuries. Most of those collected today date from the 1850-
1930 period. An early bottle often had a pontil. Some of the names, like Kickapoo
Indian Oil, Lydia Pinkham's Female Compound, or Wahoo Bitters, have become part
of the slang of America. Bitters, cures, sarsaparilla, and a few other types of medicine
are listed under their own headings in this book. Apothecary and other drugstore bottles are listed here. Collectors prefer early bottles with raised lettering. Labeled bottles
in original boxes are also sought. For more information, look for *The Bottle Book, A
Comprehensive Guide to Historic, Embossed Medicine Bottles* by Richard E. Fike.
Related bottles may be found in the Bitters, Cure, Sarsaparilla, and Tonic categories.

A. Grandjean's Composition For The Hair, Jar, Wide Flared Mouth, Pontil, 3 In. 448.00
A. McEckron's Ring Bone Liniment, N.Y., 6 3/4 In. 240.00
A.B. Stewart & Co., Druggist, Gold Hill, Nev., 3 1/2 In. 176.00
A.B.L. Myers, A.M. Rock Rose, New Haven, Blue Green, OP, 1855, 9 In. 3700.00
A.B.L. Myers, A.M. Rock Rose, New Haven, Medium Blue Green, Blob Top, OP, 9 1/2 In. 4144.00
A.E. Smith's Electric Oil, Phila., Aqua, Rolled Lip, Pontil, 3 3/4 In. 73.00
A.M. Cole, Virginia, Nev., Embossed, Square, 5 In. 60.00
Acacetic, Gold, White, Black, Red, Umbrella Shaped Stopper, 13 In. 145.00
Al. S. Lamb, Druggist, Aspen, Colorado, Lamb Picture, 4 3/4 In. 75.00
Albert's Eckert's, Edelraute, Yellow Amber, Rectangular, Indented Bands, 9 1/2 In. 392.00
Alex Leitch, Apothecary, Saint Louis, Blue Aqua, Oval, Pontil, 8 1/4 In. 123.00
Alexander's Silameau, Violin Shape, Sapphire Blue, Pontil, 1845-1855, 6 1/4 In. 550.00
Alexander's Sure Cure For Malaria, Akron, O., Amber, Label, 7 3/4 In. 50.00
Allan's Anti-Fat Botanic Medicine Co., Buffalo, N.Y., Sapphire Blue, 7 1/2 In. 220.00
Ambrosial Oil, Clark & Fuller, Nashville, Tenn., Blue Aqua, Pontil, 4 5/8 In. 688.00
American Liniment, Auburn, N.Y., Blue Aqua, OP, 1855, 5 In. 812.00
American Oil, Burkesville, Ky., Aqua, Rectangular, Arched Panels, Pontil, 6 1/4 In. 550.00
American Oil, Cumberland River, Ky., Blue Aqua, OP, 6 7/8 In. 868.00
Andrew Daigger Pharmacist, Lincoln Ave., Slug Plate, BIMAL, 4 3/8 In. 8.00
Apothecary, Acide Citriq, Porcelain, White, Enamel Label, Lid, 1880, 10 1/4 In. 143.00
Apothecary, Aeth. Butyr., Glass Label, Stopper, 6 3/4 In. ....*Illus* 16.00
Apothecary, Agent. Nit., Cobalt Blue, Glass Label, Round, 7 In. 110.00
Apothecary, Amethyst, Cylindrical, Flat Feet, Ball Stopper, 1800s, 12 1/4 In., Pair 715.00
Apothecary, Ant. Pot. Tart., W.T.Co., Amber, Recessed Label, Square, 4 1/2 In. 38.00
Apothecary, Antim. Sulph., Cobalt Blue, Round, 1880s, 7 1/4 In. 220.00

Apothecary, Applied Cobalt Blue Rings, Lid, Applied Handle, Pontil, 12 In. 440.00
Apothecary, Aq. Menth. V., Oval Colored Label, Round, 1860s, 8 3/4 In. 55.00
Apothecary, Arsenic, White China, Multicolored Flowers, 1880-1910, 3 5/8 In. 385.00
Apothecary, Asafoetid Tincture, Glass Label, 7 1/2 In. 55.00
Apothecary, Belladonna Tincture, Blue & Gold Paper Label, 7 1/2 In. 16.50
Apothecary, Cera Flav., 7 1/2 In. 132.00
Apothecary, Cimicifug Tincture, 7 1/2 In. 8.25
Apothecary, Clear, 6-Sided, Tooled Mouth, Original Glass Stopper, 1890-1910, 14 In. ... 963.00
Apothecary, Clear, ABM Lip, Original Glass Stopper, 1910-1920, 11 In. 138.00
Apothecary, Clear, ABM Lip, Original Glass Stopper, 1910-1920, 15 In. 176.00
Apothecary, Clear, Tooled Lip, Original Glass Stopper, 1915-1925, 15 3/4 In. 83.00
Apothecary, Clear, Tooled Mouth, Original Glass Stopper, 1890-1910, 20 3/4 In. 413.00
Apothecary, Clear, Tooled Mouth, Original Glass Stopper, 1900-1910, 13 1/2 In. 330.00
Apothecary, Cobalt Blue, Round, Tall, BIMAL, Australia, c.1890 .... 31.00
Apothecary, Cocaina Clorh', Cobalt Blue, Gold Lettering, Owl, 3 1/4 In. 385.00
Apothecary, Cold Cream, Porcelain, White, Enameled Label, Lid, 10 1/4 In. 132.00
Apothecary, Deep Cobalt Blue, Cylindrical, Applied Mouth, 15 5/8 In. 146.00
Apothecary, Egg Shape, Ball Knop Stopper, 19th Century, 27 In. 1955.00
Apothecary, El. Bism. Pepsin, W.T.Co., Round, Ground Stopper, 9 In. 77.00
Apothecary, Erythroxylon Coca, Light Blue Glaze, Multicolored Enamel, 10 In. 358.00
Apothecary, Fe. Humuli, Cobalt Blue, Glass Label, Stopper, 1860s, 7 1/2 In. 83.00
Apothecary, Fe. Simaruba, Flat Top, Ground Stopper, 9 In. 230.00
Apothecary, Ferri Hypophos, Reverse Painted Label, 9 In. 16.50
Apothecary, Fruct. Capsic. Pub., Amber, Eisenglas White Label, Stopper, 7 In. 20.00
Apothecary, Grape Amethyst, Rolled Lip, Blown Stopper, Pontil, 1875, 13 7/8 In. 193.00
Apothecary, Green, Squat, Coat Of Arms, Applied Ring Top, Pontil, 1750, 10 3/4 In. 715.00
Apothecary, Green, Stopper, 6 3/4 In., Pair 66.00
Apothecary, Heroin, White China, Multicolored Flowers, 1880-1910, 3 5/8 In. 385.00
Apothecary, Humulus Lup, Tin Lid, Cylindrical, 13 In. 115.00
Apothecary, I. Tr. Calumba, Ribbed Top, Ground Stopper, 9 In. 92.00
Apothecary, Iodine, Blue & Gold Paper Label, 8 In. 8.00
Apothecary, Isis, Porcelain, Medieval Style Pattern, Italy, 10 In. 220.00
Apothecary, Label Under Glass, Clear, Tooled Lip, Square, No Stopper, 6 1/2 In. 45.00
Apothecary, Label Under Glass, Gold Amber, Late 19th Century, 8 In. 85.00
Apothecary, Label Under Glass, W.T. & Co., Gold Amber, 8 In. 85.00
Apothecary, Milk Glass, OP, 8 1/2 In. 55.00
Apothecary, Multicolored, White China, 1880-1900, 10 1/2 In. 303.00
Apothecary, Myrrha, Round, Glass Label, Contents, 8 1/2 In. 60.00
Apothecary, Ol. Gaulth, Ribbed Top, Ground Stopper, 9 In. 58.00
Apothecary, Ol. Menth.P., Ribbed Top, Ground Stopper, 9 In. 92.00
Apothecary, P. Capsici, Lid, 7 1/2 In. 86.00
Apothecary, P. Cinnam, 7 1/2 In. 173.00
Apothecary, Pil. Cacao., Porcelain, Pattern, Signed AH, Stopper, Germany, 9 In. 77.00
Apothecary, Powd. Kino Et Opii, Morgan, Amber, Label, 3 In. 58.00
Apothecary, Quinine Sulphate, Recessed Blue & Gold Paper Label, 7 1/2 In. 26.00
Apothecary, Red Amber, Tooled Lip, Pontil, 1860-1880, 12 In. 99.00
Apothecary, Rotulsacch, Grape Amethyst, Pontil, 1850-1875, 13 In. 176.00
Apothecary, Sp. Lavan Co., Ribbed Top, Ground Stopper, 10 1/2 In. 58.00
Apothecary, T.R. Capsici, Ground Stopper, 10 1/2 In. 288.00
Apothecary, Teardrop Shape, Milk Glass, Applied Foot, Stem, Flared Lip, 14 In. . .364.00 to 448.00
Apothecary, Tr. Aloes, Ribbed Top, Ground Stopper, 9 In. 81.00
Apothecary, Tr. Strophant., Cobalt Blue, Round, 1880s, 9 1/4 In. 104.00
Apothecary, Ung. Aq. Rosae, Milk Glass, Label Under Glass, Glass Lid, 4 1/4 In. 157.00
Ascato Laboratory, Gnu Logo, Ascato, Cork, Wrapper, Adult Dose 7 Drops, 3 In. 28.00
Ayer's Cherry Pectoral, Lowell, Mass., Applied Top, OP, 7 In. 33.00
Ayer's Cherry Pectoral, Lowell, Mass., U.S.A., Aqua, 5 1/3 In. 7.00
Azmola Tablets, For Hay Fever & Asthma, Clear, Oval, BIMAL, 3 1/2 In. 16.00
B.O. & G.C. Wilson, Botanic Druggist, Boston, Turquoise, OP, 4 1/4 In. 33.00
Bach's American Compound, Auburn, N.Y., Aqua, Embossed, OP 150.00
Barnard & Co., Druggists, St. Louis, Aqua, Sloping Collar, IP, 6 1/4 In. 123.00
Barry's Tricopherous, New York, Straw Yellow, Pontil, 6 1/8 In. 672.00
Bartine's Lotion, Blue Aqua, 1845-1855, 6 1/2 In. 112.00
Bayer, Aspirin, Tin Cap, Paper Label, 2 1/2 In. 3.00

Apothecary, ABM, Clear 2.00
Benner Wells Pharmacists, Weston, Mo., Clear, 5 In. 20.00
Benzin Fuergefahrlich, Amber, Eisenglas White Label, Stopper, 7 In. 20.00
Bim Wright's Lung Balsam, Label, Contents 25.00
Blood Life, Puts Life Into Your Blood, Amber, Embossed, 7 3/4 In. 209.00
Blose Drug Co., In Banner, 5 In. 30.00
Bonpland's Fever & Ague Remedy, Label 175.00
Boots The Chemist & Perfumer, Medallion Shape, Dark Green 35.00
Bosserman & Williamson Druggists, Clinton, Il., Dose Glass, 2 In. 17.00
Boswell & Warner's Colorific, Amethyst, Square, Flared Lip, 1860-1880, 5 3/8 In. 672.00
Boswell & Warner's Colorific, Cobalt Blue, 5 1/2 In. 65.00
Bowker Boston, BIMAL, 5 In. 8.00
Bowman's Drug Store, Alton, Ill., Clear, BIMAL, 5 In. 7.00
Brant's Indian Purifying Extract, Aqua 165.00
Brant's Purifying Extract, M.T. Wallace & Co., Aqua, Pontil, 6 1/8 In. 532.00
Brecklein & Williams Prescriptionists, Kansas City, Mo., BIMAL, Oval, 5 1/2 In. 16.00
Brewster, Dentist, Clear, Ground Glass Stopper, 1850-1865, 3 3/4 In. 235.00
Bromo Caffeine, Light Cobalt, BIMAL, 3 1/4 In. 20.00
Bromo-Seltzer, Emerson Drug Co., Baltimore, Md., Cobalt, ABM, 2 1/2 In. 5.00
Bromo-Seltzer, Emerson Drug Co., Cobalt, Embossed, 4 In. .... *Illus* 7.00
Brown's Blood Treatment, Philadelphia, Deep Green, Tooled Mouth, 1895, 6 In. ..106.00 to 198.00
Bucklen's Arnica Salve, Salve For All The World, 10 1/2 In. 173.00
Burton's Family Remedies, Burton's Medicines, Blue Aqua, 9 1/2 In. 28.00
C. Brinckerhoff's Health Restorative, Olive Yellow Amber, Pontil, 7 5/8 In. ...1430.00 to 2090.00
C. Brinckerhoff's Health Restorative, Olive Yellow Green, Pontil, 7 3/8 In. 413.00
C. Brinckerhoff's Health Restorative, Price $1.00, Olive Yellow, Pontil, 7 3/8 In. 448.00
C. Heimstreet & Co., Troy, N.Y., Cobalt Blue, 8-Sided, Pontil, 1845-1855, 7 1/8 In. 330.00
C. Manly, Patent, London, Flared Lip, Pontil, England, 4 In. 179.00
C. Rimmel, Aqua, BIMAL, 4 1/2 In. 3.00
C.A. Melcher, South Omaha, Neb., 4 In. 15.00
C.A. Morris & Co., York, Pa., Aqua, Open Pontil, 1845-1855, 5 In. 89.00
C.W. Marsh's Pain Reliever, Aqua, Rectangular 195.00
C.W. Snow & Co., Druggists, Syracuse, N.Y., W.T. & Co., Cobalt Blue, 8 1/8 In. 523.00
California Fig Syrup Co., San Francisco, Purple, 7 In. 50.00
Canfield's One Horse Drug Store, Leadville, Colo., 4 In. 225.00
Canfield's One Horse Drug Store, Leadville, Colo., 6 1/2 In. 253.00
Carlo Erba Milano, Dark Aqua, BIMAL, 6 In. 15.00
Carnrick's Soluble Food For Infants & Invalids, Amber, Flared Lip, 5 In. 44.00
Carter & Brio, Erie, Pa., Ice Blue Aqua, Sloping Double Collar, IP, 8 5/8 In. 476.00
Carter's Spanish Mixture, Gold Amber, Ring Collar, IP, 8 1/8 In. 715.00
Carter's Spanish Mixture, Green, Applied Top, IP, 1850s, 8 1/4 In. 935.00
Carter's Spanish Mixture, Olive Green, Cleaned, OP, 8 1/4 In. ....523.00 to 577.00
Carter's Spanish Mixture, Olive Green, IP, 7 7/8 In. 1456.00
Carter's Spanish Mixture, Olive Green, OP, 8 In. 525.00
Carter's Spanish Mixture, Olive Green, Sloping Double Collar, Label, 8 In. 1455.00
Carter's Spanish Mixture, Olive Yellow Green, Sloping Double Collar, IP, 8 In. 578.00
Carter's Spanish Mixture, Olive Yellow, Pebbly, IP, 7 3/4 In. 413.00
Carter's Spanish Mixture, Olive, Applied Collar Mouth, Ring, Pontil, 8 3/8 In. 715.00
Carter's Spanish Mixture, Yellow Amber, IP, 1855, 8 3/8 In. ....1050.00 to 1176.00
Castor Oil, Flask Type, 2 Oz. 35.00
Caswell Hazard & Co., N.Y., Medium Yellow Amber, 1875-1885, 7 3/8 In. 106.00
Caswell Hazard & Co., Omnia Vincit Labor, Gold Yellow Amber, 7 1/2 In. 357.00
Celery Compound, Embossed Celery, Olive Yellow, 1880-1890, 10 In. 176.00
Chamberlain's Cough Remedy, Des Moines, Ia., U.S.A., Aqua, 5 3/4 In. 5.00
Chamberlain's Immediate Relief, Elkhart, Ind., Blue Aqua, OP, 5 In. 202.00
Chamberlain's Pain Balm, Des Moines, Iowa, Aqua, BIMAL, 5 1/2 In. 7.50
Champlin's Liquid Pearl, Milk Glass, Graphic Wrap Around Label, 4 3/4 In. 66.00
Chang Fhu Or Chinese Liniment, Deep Aqua Blue, Rolled Lip, OP, 5 In. 644.00
Chapman's Genuine, No. 4, Salem St., Boston, Olive Amber, Square, Collar, Pontil, 8 In. . 952.00
Charles A. Keucher, 64 Main Str., Bar Harbor, Me., 5 In. 40.00
Chas. D. Barnes, Rexall Store, Glenwood Springs, Colo., 5 1/4 In. 25.00
Chas. H. Ziegler, Physician & Pharmacist, Vesta, Neb., 5 In. 50.00
Chas. N. Clarke, Hood River, Oregon, The Glacier Pharmacy, 6 5/16 In. 55.00

Medicine, Apothecary,
Aeth. Butyr., Glass
Label, Stopper, 6 3/4 In.

Medicine, Bromo-Seltzer,
Emerson Drug Co.,
Cobalt, Embossed, 4 In.

Medicine, DeWitt's Headache Tablets,
Instruction, Box, Contents, 2 3/4 In.

Cheeseboro Vaseline, Amber, 2 1/2 In. 15.00
Chester A. Baker, Boston, C.L.G. Co., Cobalt Blue, 1890-1910, 6 3/8 In. 523.00
Citrate Of Magnesia, Eastern Drug Co., Boston, Mass., BIMAL, Blob Top, 8 In. 4.00
Citrate Of Magnesia, Light Amethyst, BIMAL, Original Bail, Stopper, 8 In. 10.00
Clark Stanley's Snake Oil Liniment, Clear, 6 1/4 In. 35.00
Climax Syrup, Owego, N.Y., Pale Aqua, Pontil, 1845-1855, 4 3/4 In. 198.00
Clinton E. Warden, San Francisco, Ca., Amber, BIMAL, Tooled Top, 3 1/2 In. 14.00
Club Coltsfoot Rock Lozenges, Lid, 12 In. 115.00
Cold Pressed Castor Oil, Dr. Sheet's, Dayton, O., Aqua, Double Collar, OP, 6 1/4 In. 364.00
Collins Bros. Drug Co., St. Louis, Aqua, 5 1/2 In. 3.00
Columbian Pharmacy Inc., Perth Amboy, N.J., Green, 1890-1910, 5 In. 1210.00
Compound Fluid Extract, Sacramento City, Ca., Light Green, OP 200.00
Conkey's Canker Special, ABM, 4 1/2 In. 132.00
Couley's Fountain Of Health, Baltimore, Aqua, Fountain, Pontil, 9 5/8 In. 448.00
Craft's Distemper & Cough Remedy, Dark Amber, Embossed, 6 3/4 In. 198.00
Crane & Brigham, San Francisco, Golden Honey Amber, Applied Mouth, 10 1/4 In. 868.00
D.F. Cantrall, Druggist, Greenville, Tex., Wreath & Mortar & Pestle Design, 6 1/4 In. . . . 45.00
Daffy's Elixir, Aqua, Graphite Pontil, Collar Lip, 1850 . . . . 218.00
Dalby's Carminative, Rolled Lip, OP, 3 3/4 In. 88.00
Davis & Miller, Druggists, Baltimore, Blue Aqua, OP, 9 1/4 In. 213.00
Davis & Miller, Druggists, Baltimore, Light Blue Green, Flared Lip, OP, 4 1/2 In. 260.00
Davis Drug Co., Rexall Store, Leadville, Colo., Amber, 12-Sided, 4 3/4 In. 80.00
Davis Drug Co., Rexall Store, Leadville, Colo., 14-Sided, Gold Amber, 4 3/4 In. 165.00
Davis Drug Co., Rexall Store, Leadville, Colo., Amber, 5 1/8 In. 45.00
Davis' Vegetable Pain Killer, Aqua, ABM, Complete Label, 6 In. 77.00
Davis' Vegetable Pain Killer, Aqua, BIMAL, 5 1/2 In. 12.00
Davis' Vegetable Pain Killer, Aqua, BIMAL, OP, 4 3/4 In. 30.00
Days Pharmacy, San Rafael, Ca., 6 1/4 In. 35.00
Delavau's Remedy Whooping Cough Croup, Phila., Aqua, BIMAL, 6 1/4 In. 8.00
Dent's Toothache Gum, Ribbed Glass Lid, 12 In. 633.00
Derwent Cough Balsam, Aqua, 5 In. 8.00
Deveny & Orin Pharmacists, Chico, Ca., 5 3/4 In. 35.00
DeWitt's Headache Tablets, Instruction, Box, Contents, 2 3/4 In. . . . . *Illus* 10.00
Dioxogen Oakland Chemical Co., Light Amber, BIMAL, 5 1/4 In. 3.00
Doct. Curtis' Cherry Syrup, New York, Clear, OP, 1845-1855, 7 3/8 In. 94.00
Doct. Marshall's Aromatic Catarrh & Head-Ache Snuff, Aqua, Flared Lip, 3 3/8 In. 260.00
Doctor BF Cornell, Edgewood, Mo., Cornell's Electric Liniment, c.1890, 6 7/8 In. 20.00
Doctor Hall's Bronchialine Coughs & Colds, Dark Amber, 5 3/4 In. 121.00
Doctor Henry's Botanic Preparation, Light Green, Applied Top, 6 1/4 In. 176.00
Doctor McLane's American Worm Specific, Aqua, OP 50.00
Doherty Apothecary, Atlantic City, N.J., C.L.G. Co., Cobalt Blue, 1910, 5 In. 110.00
Doremus Pharmacy, The Rexall Store, Union Springs, N.Y., 6 1/4 In. 20.00

Dr. A. Atkinson, New York, Blue Aqua, Rectangular, 7 3/4 In. . . . . .84.00 to 129.00
Dr. A. Rogers, Liverwort, Tar & Canchalagua, Blue Aqua, Pontil, 7 1/4 In. 110.00
Dr. A.P. Sawyer's Family Cure, Family Sitting Around Table, 4 1/4 In. 94.00
Dr. Beach's Vegetable Composition, Aqua, Label, Pontil, 7/8 x 4 In. . . . . .45.00 to 80.00
Dr. Browder's Compound Syrup Of Indian Turnip, Aqua, Contents, 7 In. 525.00
Dr. Browder's Compound Syrup Of Indian Turnip, Aqua, OP, 6 7/8 In. . . . . .187.00 to 364.00
Dr. C. Bouvier's Buchu Gin, For Kidney & Bladder, Embossed, Label, 12 In. 100.00
Dr. C.J. Weatherby, Kansas City, Mo., Cobalt Blue, Tooled Mouth, 6 5/8 In. 179.00
Dr. Campbell's Hair Invigorator, Aurora, N.Y., Blue, Aqua, 1845-1855, 6 1/2 In. 134.00
Dr. Clarke's Herb Syrup, Aqua, Open Pontil, 5 In. 633.00
Dr. D. Jaynes Alternative, 242 Chest. St., Phila., Aqua, Applied Top 33.00
Dr. D. Jaynes Carminative Balsam, Philada, Aqua, BIMAL, 6 In. 25.00
Dr. D.C. Kellinger's Remedies, N.Y., Aqua, Recessed Panels, Whittled, 7 In. 275.00
Dr. Davis's Depurative, Phila., Teal, Sloping Collar, IP, 9 1/2 In. 5040.00
Dr. Dow's Pure Sturgeon Oil, Liniment, Aqua Blue, Rectangular, Canada, 1870-1880 . . . . 36.00
Dr. E.C. Balm, Blue Aqua, Sloping Collar, OP, 5 1/8 In. 202.00
Dr. Elmore's Rheumatine Goutaline, Bayonne, N.J., Amber, Label, 7 1/2 In. 235.00
Dr. Ford's Pectoral Syrup, New York, Blue Aqua, Pontil, 5 3/8 In. 168.00
Dr. Forsha's Alterative Balm, Green Aqua, Olive Tint, Double Collar, OP, 5 1/2 In. 476.00
Dr. G.H. Dow's Cough & Catarrh Remedy, Troy, N.Y., Aqua, BIMAL, 5 1/2 In. 6.00
Dr. Geo. W. Blocksom, Druggist, Zanesville, Ice Blue, 12-Sided, Square Collar, IP, 8 In. . . 280.00
Dr. H. Van Vleck's Family Medicines, Pittsburgh, Pa., Aqua Blue, IP, 6 3/4 In. 532.00
Dr. H.S. Thacher's Worm Syrup, Chattanooga, Tenn., Aqua, 4 1/2 In. 20.00
Dr. Hart's Rheumatic Remedy, Buffalo, N.Y., Aqua 10.00
Dr. Hawk's Universal Stimulant, Aqua, OP, 1845-1855, 3 7/8 In. 209.00
Dr. Haynes' Arabian Balsam, For Poisoning, Burns, Bruises, Pain, 4 1/8 In. 33.00
Dr. J. McClintock's Family, Flared, 5 1/2 In. 55.00
Dr. J. Watson's Cancer & Scrofula Syrup, Fulton, N.Y., Blue Aqua, 1880, 9 3/8 In. 73.00
Dr. J. Woodward's Horse Liniment, Cookshire, Quebec, Round, ABM, 5 In. 10.00
Dr. J.A. Burgoon's System Renovater, Aqua Blue, Tooled Mouth, 8 3/8 In. 504.00
Dr. J.D. Covell, Druggist, Forreston, Ill., 5 1/2 In. 15.00
Dr. J.F. Churchill's Specific Remedy For Consumption, Blue Aqua, 9 In. 39.00
Dr. J.H. McLean's Volcanic Oil Liniment, Aqua, ABM, Box, 4 In. 44.00
Dr. J.L. Saugherty, Eclips Liniment, Blue Aqua, Oval Panel, Rolled Lip, Pontil, 4 3/8 In. . . 1036.00
Dr. J.M. Lindsay's World Renowned Panacea, Aqua, Sloping Collar, 9 5/8 In. 179.00
Dr. J.S. Wood's Elixir, Albany, N.Y., Tombstone, Blue Green, IP, 8 7/8 In. 5390.00
Dr. Jones' Beaver Liniment, Aqua, BIMAL, 5 In. 3.00
Dr. Jones' Beaver Liniment, M. Spiegal Medicine Co., Albany, N.Y., Aqua, 7 In. 41.00
Dr. Jones' Red Co., Ottawa, Il., Amber, Applied Top 100.00
Dr. Jones' Sangvin For Blood & Nerves, Albany, N.Y., Yellow Green, 7 In. 45.00
Dr. Kelemen's Grecian Hair Balsam, N.Y., Blue Aqua, Roped Corners, OP, 7 1/4 In. 1232.00
Dr. Kennedy's Medical Discovery, Aqua, BIMAL, 8 1/2 In. 9.00
Dr. Kennedy's Salt Rheum Ointment, Jar, Blue Aqua, OP, 3 1/2 In. 130.00
Dr. Kennedy's Salt Rheum Ointment, Salt Jar, Blue Aqua, OP, 3 5/8 In. . . . . .132.00 to 185.00
Dr. Keyser's Blood Searcher, Pittsburgh, Pa., Ice Blue, Double Collar, 9 1/8 In. 532.00
Dr. Kilmer's Ocean Weed Heart Remedy, Binghamton, N.Y., Blue Aqua, 8 3/8 In. 235.00
Dr. Kilmer's Swamp Root Kidney Remedy, Binghamton, N.Y., Aqua, Round, 4 In. 61.00
Dr. King's Liver & Kidney Alterative, Goshen, Ind., Aqua, Large 8.50
Dr. King's New Discovery, Labeled Wrapper, Contents, Sample 22.00
Dr. L.D. LeGear Medicine Co., Antiseptic Oil, Box, 7 1/2 In. . . . .*Illus* 18.00
Dr. Larbor's Extract Of Lungwort, Pale Aqua, OP, 1855, 6 3/4 In. 420.00
Dr. Lesure's Family Liniment, For Nerve, Muscle, Bone, 6 In. 33.00
Dr. M.L. Byrn's Extract Of Buchu, Hoagland & Stiger, N.Y., Aqua, 6 3/4 In. 253.00
Dr. Mile's New Heart Cure, Aqua, Label, 8 In. 413.00
Dr. Mile's Restorative Blood Purifier, Aqua, ABM, 8 1/4 In. 297.00
Dr. N.G. White's Pulmonary Elixir, Aqua, BIMAL, 4 In. 6.00
Dr. Perry's Last Chance Liniment, Blue, Applied Top, 5 3/4 In. 77.00
Dr. Queen's Balsam, For Coughs, Howell, Mich., Box, 5 3/4 In. . . . .*Illus* 40.00
Dr. R.L. Bernard's Cholera Medicine, Norfolk, Va., Aqua, Rolled Lip, Pontil, 5 5/8 In. . . . 448.00
Dr. Reynolds Nerve & Rheumatic Liniment, Aqua, Rolled Lip, OP, 2 1/4 In. 420.00
Dr. Robertson's Family Medicine, T.W. Dyott, Green Aqua, OP, 5 3/8 In. 2700.00
Dr. Robt. B. Folger's, Olosaonian, N.Y., Aqua, Open Pontil, 1835-1845, 7 1/2 In. 123.00
Dr. Rooke's Rheumatic Lixile, Cobalt Blue, Tooled Top 33.00

Medicine, Dr. L.D. LeGear
Medicine Co., Antiseptic Oil,
Box, 7 1/2 In.

Medicine, Dr. Queen's Balsam,
For Coughs, Howell, Mich.,
Box, 5 3/4 In.

Medicine, Dr. Thacher's
Worm Syrup, Chattanooga,
Tenn., Label, 4 1/4 In.

Dr. S.A. Weaver's Canker & Salt Rheum Syrup, Aqua, IP, 9 3/8 In.	202.00
Dr. Sage's Catarrh Remedy, Buffalo, Aqua, BIMAL, 2 1/4 In.	10.00
Dr. Sanford's Liver Invigorator, New York, Aqua	10.00
Dr. Shiloh's System Vitalizer, Sample, Leroy, N.Y., Aqua, Wrap Around Label, 4 In.	61.00
Dr. Shoop's Family Medicines, Racine, Wi., Aqua, 6 1/2 In.	44.00
Dr. Slack's Mexican Catarrh Remedy, Clayton, N. Mex., Tooled Top, 6 In.	77.00
Dr. Stafford's Vegetable Composition, Aqua Blue, Open Pontil, 1850, 1 7/8 x 5 In.	45.00
Dr. Stafford's Vegetable Composition, Blue Label	52.00 to 91.00
Dr. Thacher's Liver & Blood Syrup, Chattanooga, Tenn., Aqua	3.50
Dr. Thacher's Worm Syrup, Chattanooga, Tenn., Label, 4 1/4 In. *Illus*	12.00
Dr. Thomas' Ultimatum, For Liver & Kidney, Bladder, Label, Aqua, 8 1/4 In.	176.00
Dr. Thompson's Eye Water, New London, Conn., Shaded Yellow Green, OP, 3 7/8 In.	364.00
Dr. Van Vleck's Red Liniment, Pittsburgh, Pa., Aqua Blue, Rolled Lip, OP, 4 3/8 In.	269.00
Dr. W.B. Farrell's Arabian Liniment, Chicago Ill., Green, Pontil, 7 5/8 In.	303.00
Dr. W.W. Watkins & Co Liniment, Aqua, 6 1/4 In.	5.00
Dr. Wistar's Balsam Of Wild Cherry, BIMAL, 3 In.	10.00
Dr. Wistar's Balsam Of Wild Cherry, Philada., OP, Green, 6 1/4 In.	77.00
Duff's Colic & Diarrhoea Remedy, Stopper, 10 1/2 In.	288.00
Duff's Remedy, Stopper, Label Under Glass, 10 In.	358.00
Dyer's Healing Embrocation Prov., R.I., 12-Sided, Aqua, OP	150.00
E. Horton, Avon Springs, Olive Yellow Green, Pontil, 1840-1860, 6 3/8 In.	5230.00
E. Sprondli Pharmacist, Hayward Drug Store, Hayward, Cal., 7 In.	8.00
E.B. Norton, Druggist, Birmingham, Ala., BIMAL, 3 1/2 In.	5.00
E.H. Flagg's Instantaneous Relief, Phila., Blue Aqua, Pontil, 1845-1855, 3 7/8 In.	357.00
E.L. Buchanan City Drug Store, Lacon, Ill., 5 In.	15.00
E.R. Squibb, Teal Blue, Applied Square Collar, 6 1/2 In.	67.00
E.S. Reed's Sons Apothecary, Atlantic City, N.J., Milk Glass, Glass Stopper, 5 In.	112.00
Edw. Western Tea & Spice Co., St. Louis, Mo., Aqua, 5 In.	5.00
Eilert's Extract Of Wild Cherry, Deep Aqua, BIMAL, 8 1/4 In.	2.50
Eli Lilly & Company Pharmaceutical Chemist, Amber, Round, 8 1/2 In.	198.00
Emerald Green, Rectangular, 1845-1860, IP, 9 1/2 In.	77.00
Epsom Salt, Apothecary, Jar, Cylindrical, Wide Mouth, Tin Lid, Label, Pontil, 7 1/2 In.	110.00
Esbachs Reagens, Amber, Eisenglas Red & White Label, Stopper, 7 In.	20.00
Essence Of Peppermint, Hackleford & Crichton Druggist, Portsmouth, Aqua, 4 In.	60.00
Eugene Arnstein, Chicago., Ill., Clear, BIMAL, Rectangular, 3 1/2 In.	5.00
Eugene Meyer City Drug Store, Helena, Mt., Amethyst, Slug Plate, 4 In.	10.00
Extr. Ratann, Ceramic, 5 3/4 In.	58.00
F.A. Richter & Co., Old Pain Expeller For Rheumatism, Aqua, Cloudy	4.50
F.J. Steinmeta, Carson City, Nevada, 6 In.	135.00
F.P. Duconce, New Orleans, Blue Aqua, Double Collar, IP, 6 3/4 In.	190.00
Farmer's Horse Medicine, S.F., Cal., Aqua, 6 1/2 In.	33.00
Father John's, Lowell, Mass., Amber, Screw Threads, 10 1/2 In.	.75

Febrifuge Wine, N.Y., Aqua, Applied Mouth, Residue Interior, Labels, Pontil, 13 In. 385.00
Ferris-Maghee Drug Co., Rawlins, Wyo., Clear, Tooled Top, 6 In. 44.00
Finfrock & Thobro, Laramie, Wyo., Eagle On Mortar & Pestle, Clear, 4 1/4 In. 55.00
Force's Asthmania, S.B. Force Mfg, Chemist, Amber, 8 7/8 In. 160.00
Forest Lawn, Jv.H., Medium Olive Green, 1855-1870 .... 308.00
Frank E. Morgan, Warburton Laxative Pills, Label, Display Type, Contents, 20 In. 66.00
Frank E. Morgan & Sons, Bay Water, Cobalt Blue, Label, 7 1/2 In. 77.00
Frank E. Morgan & Sons, Headache Cologne, Cobalt Blue, 7 1/2 In. 77.00
Frazier's Distemper Remedy, Nappanee, Ind., Embossed, 7 1/4 In. 154.00
Fred D. Rogers, Druggist, Chicago, Slug Plate, BIMAL, 4 1/4 In. 10.00
Fred L. Heath Druggist, Hastings, Mich., 4 1/4 In. ....*Illus* 15.00
Frost's Liniment, Gratis, Aqua, Indented Panels, Double Collar, Pontil, 5 In. 179.00
G.R. Lewis & Co., Opposite National Hotel, Cripple Creek, Colo, 3 Oz. 30.00
G.W. Gardner's American Liniment, Pittsburgh, Blue Aqua, OP, 5 1/2 In. 812.00
G.W. Merchant, Chemist, Lockport, N.Y., Green, Applied Top, 5 1/2 In. 231.00
G.W. Merchant, Chemist, Lockport, N.Y., Blue Green, 1855-1870, 5 5/8 In. 224.00
G.W. Merchant, Chemist, Lockport, N.Y., Blue Green, IP, 1845-1855, 7 In. 330.00
G.W. Merchant, Chemist, Lockport, N.Y., Emerald Green, Pontil, 5 1/2 In. ....176.00 to 198.00
G.W. Merchant, Chemist, Lockport, N.Y., Green, Applied Lip, 7 In. 220.00
G.W. Merchant, Chemist, Lockport, N.Y., Teal Blue, IP, 1855, 5 5/8 In. 924.00
G.W. Merchant, Lockport, N.Y., Green, Label, Gargling Oil, Man & Beast, 5 In. 110.00
G.W. Merchant, Lockport, N.Y., Green, Sloping Collar, Pontil, 5 1/8 In. 134.00
G.W. Merchant, Lockport, N.Y., Yellow Green, 1865-1880, 5 1/8 In. 308.00
Gargling Oil, Lockport, N.Y., Blue, Green, 1855-1865, 7 1/2 In. 89.00
Gargling Oil, Lockport, N.Y., Bright Green, Label, Tooled Top 44.00
Gargling Oil, Lockport, N.Y., Cobalt Blue, Rectangular, Sunken Panels, Tooled Top 44.00
Gargling Oil, Lockport, N.Y., Dark Green, Tooled Top, 7 1/2 In. 121.00
Gargling Oil, Lockport, N.Y., Turquoise, Rectangular, Sunken Panels, Tooled Top 44.00
Gargling Oil, Lockport, N.Y., Yellow Green, 5 1/2 In. 30.00
Gargling Oil, Teal Green, 7 1/2 In. 72.00
Genuine Essence, Turquoise, Rolled Lip, OP, 5 In. 55.00
Geo M. Good & Co. Pharmacists, St. Joseph, Mo., SCA, Mortar & Pestle, 5 In. 5.00
Geo. Fairbanks, Druggists, Worcester, Golden Yellow Amber, Long Neck, 12 3/8 In. 364.00
Geo. Leis & Bro. Druggists, Lawrence, Kansas, Amber, 1878, 4 In. 185.00
Geo. P. Morrill, Apothecary, Virginia City, Nev., Light Green, 1863-1874 .... 3400.00
George M. Moore, Druggist, Granite City, Ill., 6 In. 25.00
Gibb's Bone Liniment, 6-Sided, Olive Amber, OP, 6 3/8 In. 2128.00
Glover's Imperial Distemper Remedy, Citron Yellow, 5 In. 58.00
Gonder & Co., Druggist, Yuma, Arizona, 4 1/4 In. 65.00
Good Samaritan's Immediate Relief, S.B. Folsom & Co., Aqua, Label, 1890, 5 1/4 In. .. 385.00
Granular Citrate Of Magnesium, Cobalt Blue, Paneled, 6 In. 20.00
Great Home Luxury, Blodgettes Persian Balm, Aqua, Rectangular, Panels, OP, 5 In. 55.00
Greisamer's New Tubercular, Quakertown, Pa., Amber, Beveled Corners, 11 In. 179.00
Gun Wa's Chinese Remedy, Amber, 7 3/4 In. 300.00
Gun Wa's Chinese Remedy, Dark Amber, 8 1/4 In. 523.00
Gun Wa's Chinese Remedy, Gold Yellow Amber, 1875-1885, 8 In. 532.00
H. Kuhlmeier, Cleveland, O., Embossed, 6 3/8 In. ....*Illus* 18.00
H. Lake's Indian Specific, Aqua, OP, 8 1/2 In. 1320.00
H. Lake's Indian Specific, Blue Aqua, Tooled Lip, Pontil, 8 1/4 In. 3135.00
H. Pharazyn Phila., Indian Queen, Gold Yellow Amber, 1865-1870, 12 3/8 In. 1700.00
H. Smyser Genuine Preparations, Pittsburgh, Aqua, Rolled Lip, Pontil, 5 3/4 In. 868.00
H.B. Slaven Chemist, The Baldwin Pharmacy, S.F., 4 1/4 In. 33.00
H.C. Hudson, Light Green, Applied Top 40.00
H.C. Kirk & Co., Druggist, Sacramento, S.F., Embossed, Clear, Tooled Top, 4 In. 33.00
H.D. Scully, Pittsburgh, Blue Aqua, Double Collar, IP, 7 1/2 In. 190.00
H.F. Maccarthy, Druggist, Ottawa, Red Amber, Square, Embossed, BIMAL, 5 In. 120.00
H.H. Warner & Co., Ltd., Melbourne, Amber, 1/2 Pt., 7 In. 150.00
H.H. Warner & Co., Rochester, N.Y., Log, Amber, Applied Mouth, Label, 9 In. 231.00
H.H. Warner & Co., Tippecanoe, Gold Amber, Applied Mushroom Top 143.00
H.H. Warner & Co., Tippecanoe, Pat. Nov. 20, 1888, Olive Yellow, 9 In. 5880.00
H.H. Warner & Co., Tippecanoe, Rochester, N.Y., Log, Gold Amber, 9 1/4 In. 121.00
H.H. Warner & Co., Tippecanoe, Rochester, N.Y., Root Beer Amber, 9 In. 105.00
H.H. Warner & Co., Tippecanoe, Rochester, N.Y., Yellow Amber, Olive Tint, 9 In. 308.00

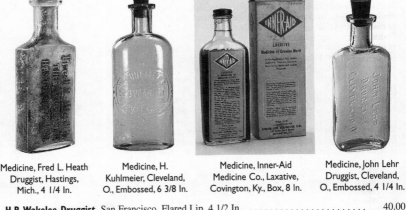

Medicine, Fred L. Heath Druggist, Hastings, Mich., 4 1/4 In.

Medicine, H. Kuhlmeier, Cleveland, O., Embossed, 6 3/8 In.

Medicine, Inner-Aid Medicine Co., Laxative, Covington, Ky., Box, 8 In.

Medicine, John Lehr Druggist, Cleveland, O., Embossed, 4 1/4 In.

H.P. Wakelee Druggist, San Francisco, Flared Lip, 4 1/2 In. 40.00
H.R. Schumann, Prescription Druggist, New Braunfels, Texas, Green, 5 3/4 In. 175.00
H.T. Helmbold, Genuine Preparations, N.Y., Milk Glass, 1855-1865, 6 1/4 In. 588.00
H.T. Hembold Genuine Fluid Extracts, Phila., Aqua, BIMAL, 6 In. 10.00
H.W. Meinzen Druggist, Fort Wayne, Clear, BIMAL, 4 3/8 In. 5.00
Hagan's Magnolia Balm, White Opaque, Label, Embossed Reverse, 5 In. 50.00
Haller & Beck & Co., Bromine, Allegheny City, Pa., Teal Blue, 9 1/2 In. 448.00
Hampton's V Tincture, Mortimer & Mowbray, Balto., Cherry Puce, OP, 6 1/4 In. 1232.00
Hampton's V Tincture, Mortimer & Mowbray, Balto., Gold Amber, 6 1/2 In. 235.00
Hampton's V Tincture, Mortimer & Mowbray, Balto., Puce, OP, 6 3/8 In. ....476.00 to 1036.00
Hampton's V Tincture, Mortimer & Mowbray, Balto., Yellow Amber, Pontil, 6 3/8 In. ... 588.00
Handyside's Blood Food, Bubbles, Aqua, 10 1/4 In. 225.00
Handyside's Blood Purifier, Black Glass, 11 In. ....135.00 to 150.00
Harper's Headache Medicine, Washington, D.C., Label, Rectangular, 5 In. 22.00
Harrison & Roth Wholesale & Retail Druggist, Evanston, Wyo., 4 1/2 In. 75.00
Hartwell & Shephard's, Soter Capilli, Pittsburgh, Pa., Blue Aqua, IP, 6 1/4 In. 476.00
Hazard & Caswell Chemists, New Port, Rhode Island, Aqua 22.00
Hazard & Co., New York, Prussian Blue, Tooled Mouth, 1880-1890, 7 In. 413.00
Healy & Bigelow's Indian Sagwa, Aqua, Tooled Top, 8 1/2 In. ....38.00 to 45.00
Healy & Bigelow's Indian Sagwa, Picture Of Indian Chief, Green Aqua, BIMAL, 8 In. ... 65.00
Healy & Bigelow's Kickapoo Indian Oil, Aqua, BIMAL, 5 1/4 In. 15.00
Healy & Bigelow's Kickapoo Indian Oil, Light Green Aqua, BIMAL, 5 1/2 In. 40.00
Healy & Bigelow's Kickapoo Indian Oil, Olive Yellow, Tooled Lip, 1890-1910, 5 1/2 In. . 123.00
Healy & Bigelow's Kickapoo Oil, Light Aqua, BIMAL, 5 1/4 In. 12.00
Healy & Bigelow's Kickapoo Oil, Shaded Olive Yellow, Tooled Mouth, 5 3/8 In. 125.00
Henry Fees, Jr., Druggist, Milwaukee, Wi., Slug Plate, BIMAL, Oval, 4 1/4 In. 5.00
Henry Waters Druggist, HW, Honey Amber, Square, Embossed, BIMAL, 5 In. 70.00
Henshaw Ward & Co., Druggists, Boston, Olive Yellow Green, OP, 11 In. 6440.00
Herbine Co., St. Louis, Clear, ABM, 6 3/4 In. 83.00
Herbs Of Life, Blood Purifier, Denver, Co., Aqua, 9 In. 225.00
Heyser Druggist, Chambersburg, Pa., Aqua, Rolled Lip, OP, 3 7/8 In. 100.00
Hilmer's Laboratory, San Francisco, Applied Top, 9 In. 33.00
Holister Drug Co Ltd., Fort Street, Honolulu, 2 3/4 In. 99.00
Holman's, Nature's Grand Restorative, Aqua 220.00
Hopkins' Chalybeate, Baltimore, Dark Amber, Slope Collar, Lip Ring, IP, 7 3/8 In. 308.00
Howard's Vegetable, Cancer & Canker Syrup, Orange Amber, Collar, 7 1/8 In. 1456.00
Howland's Ready Remedy, Columba + Roads, P.A., Aqua, Square, Pontil, 5 In. ...190.00 to 235.00
Hunnewell's Tolu Anodyne, Boston, Mass., Aqua, Pontil, 4 In. 146.00
Hunt's Liniment, C.E. Stanton, Sing Sing, NY, Green, c.1860, 4 1/2 In. 715.00
Hunter's Pulmonary Balsam, Bangor, Me., Aqua, Flared Lip, OP, 6 1/4 In. 364.00
Hurd's Cough Balsam, 4 5/8 In. 160.00
Hurlbut & Trythall Druggist, Park City, Utah, 4 3/4 In. 45.00

I. Covert's Balm Of Life, Olive Green, Pontil, 1845-1855, 6 In. 3190.00
I. Covert's Balm Of Life, Olive Green, Sloping Collar Mouth, OP, 6 In. 2585.00
Indian, see also Medicine, Healy & Bigelow
Indian Inhaler, Portrait Of Chief Health Joy, 3 1/2 In. 132.00
Indian Tla-Quillaugh's Balsam, Dr. R. Parker, S.F., Copper Puce, 1864-1867, 8 1/2 In. . . . 5250.00
Indian Tla-Quillaugh's Balsam, Dr. R. Parker, S.F., Light To Dark Copper Puce, 8 1/2 In. . 5880.00
Indian Vegetable Injection, 6 In. 44.00
Indian's Panacea, Green, Yellow Tint, Sloping Double Collar, Pontil, 8 In. 5280.00
Injection Ricord Paris, Blue, Drippy Top, 6 In. 250.00
Inner-Aid Medicine Co., Laxative, Covington, Ky., Box, 8 In. . . . . *Illus* 20.00
Irvine's Horse Liniment, Aqua, OP, Embossed, 7 In. 2310.00
J. & C. Maguire, Chemists & Druggists, St. Louis, Mo., Cobalt, Oval, Pontil, 7 3/4 In. 812.00
J. Duval's Family Antispasmodic, King & Queen, Va., Pale Aqua, OP, 6 In. 168.00
J. Ellwood Lee Co., Conshohocken, Pa., Gauze Jar, Yellow Amber, Clamps, Lid, 3 In. 99.00
J. Henderson & Bro., Pittsburgh, Aqua Blue, Rolled Lip, OP, 5 In. 230.00
J. Starkweather's Hepatic Elixir, Upton, Mass., Green Aqua, 6-Sided, Pontil 143.00
J.B. Irvin, Centralia, Pa., Deep Cobalt, Tooled Mouth, 5 1/4 In. 364.00
J.B. Wheatley Compound Syrup, Dallasburgh, Ky., Aqua, Pontil, 1845-1855, 6 In. . .134.00 to 154.00
J.D. Doughty, Cincinnati, Light Apple Green, OP, 1845-1855, 5 1/8 In. 504.00
J.D. Thompson's Rheumatic & Neuralgic Liniment, Pitts., Pa., Aqua, Pontil, 4 7/8 In. . . . 468.00
J.D. White Pharmacist, Gardner, Me., Honey Amber, Slug Plate, 5 1/8 In. 185.00
J.E. Combault's Caustic Balsam, Aqua, 6 1/2 In. 12.00
J.G. Godding & Co., Apothecary, Cobalt Blue, Tooled Lip, 1890-1910, 6 In. 413.00
J.R. Nichols & Co. Chemists, Boston, Aqua, Long Neck 16.00
J.W. Doran Pharmacist, Juneau, Alaska, 6 1/4 In. 358.00
Jacob Pinkerton Wahoo & Calisaya, Amber, Bubbles 895.00
Jacob's Pharmacy, Atlanta, Medium Amber, 1890-1910, 4 7/8 In. 168.00
Jarvis Blood Renovator, Geo. D. Jarvis & Co., Aqua, Labels, Rectangular, 8 1/8 In. 143.00
John F. Tripp & Co., New York, Blue Aqua, Sloping Double Collar, Pontil, 6 1/8 In. 78.00
John H. Phelps Pharmacist, Phelps Rheumatic Elixir, Scranton, Pa., Aqua, 5 In. 14.00
John Hart & Co., Heart Shape, Amber, Double Collar, 6 7/8 In. 810.00
John J. Smith, Louisville, Ky., Blue Green, OP, 1845-1860, 5 3/4 In. 1980.00
John Lehr Druggist, Cleveland, O., Embossed, 4 1/4 In. . . . . *Illus* 15.00
John Wyeth Bros., Cobalt Blue, Dose Cap, 5 13/16 In. 18.00
Johnson & Johnson, Jar, Cobalt Blue, Square, Glass Lid, Metal Band, 1890s, Qt. 550.00
Johnson & Johnson, New York, Dark Blue, 5 1/4 In. 30.00
Johnson's American Anodyne Liniment, Aqua, Applied Top, 4 1/2 In. 1.50
Jos. Fleming, Pitts Bg, Pa., Aqua Blue, Double Collar, IP, 7 3/4 In. 504.00
Juneau Drug Co., Z.J. Loussack Prop., Juneau, Alaska, Monogram, 7 3/4 In. 121.00
Keasby & Mattison, Chemists, Amber, BIMAL, 3 3/8 In. 6.00
Keasby & Mattison, Cornflower Blue, BIMAL, 6 In. 8.00
Kemp's Balsam, Aqua, BIMAL, Sample, 2 3/4 In. 5.00
Kemp's Balsam For That Cough, ABM, 5 1/2 In. 4.00
Kennedy's Honey & Tar, Chicago, Aqua, Rectangular, Bee On Clover, 5 1/2 In. 31.00
Kickapoo Oil, see Medicine, Healy & Bigelow
Kilmor's Swamp Root, Liver & Bladder Control, Binghamton, N.Y., 7 In. 22.00
Kopp's Cur-A-Cough, Mrs. J.A. Kopp, York, Pa., Clear, 6 1/2 In. 231.00
L.E. Normann, Apothecary, 5th & Green, Phila., Aqua, Pontil, 6 3/4 In. 123.00
L.H. White Homeopathic Pharmacy, Cleveland, Oh., Amber, Square, 4 1/2 In. 35.00
L.P. Dodge Rheumatic Liniment, Newburg, Amber, Applied Tapered Top, Pontil, 6 In. . . . 2860.00
L.P. Dodge Rheumatic Liniment, Newburg, Dark Olive Amber, Pontil, 5 7/8 In. 2912.00
L.P. Dodge Rheumatic Liniment, Newburg, Olive Yellow, Pontil, 6 In. 1568.00
Lacto Phosphate Of Lime & Cod Liver Oil, Wyeth & Bro., Philada., Blue, Applied Top . . 110.00
Lake's New Process Raddish, Denver, Colo., Clear, Horse's Head, 7 1/2 In. 33.00
Laughlin's & Bushfield, Druggists, Wheeling, Va., Blue Aqua, Sloping Collar, 9 1/8 In. . . 179.00
Lediard's Morning Call, Olive Green, Sloping Collar, 1875, 9 3/4 In. 357.00
Lightning Hot Drops No Relief No Pay Herb Medicine Co., Springfield, O., Aqua, 5 In. . 6.00
Lilly, Chlorodyne Tablets, Amber, Label, 4 In. 231.00
Lilly, Elixir, Basham's Mixture, Amber, Label, 7 1/2 In. . . . . *Illus* 25.00
Lilly, Tincture No. 16 Cantharides, N.F., Amber, Screw Cap, 1960s, 1/4 Pt. 44.00
Lincoln Drug Co., Lincoln, Ne., Oil Hemlock, Cork, Contents, 5 1/4 In. 22.00
Lindsey's Blood Searcher, Hollidaysburg, Apple Green, 8 3/4 In. 308.00
Lindsey's Blood Searcher, Hollidaysburg, Aqua Blue, 9 In. 168.00

Lindsey's Blood Searcher, Hollidaysburg, Aqua Blue, Double Collar, IP, 9 1/8 In. 1036.00
Lindsey's Blood Searcher, Hollidaysburg, Blue Aqua, IP, 9 In. 616.00
Lindsey's Blood Searcher, Hollidaysburg, Dark Olive Green, 1865-1875, 9 In. . .4100.00 to 4592.00
Lindsey's Blood Searcher, Hollidaysburg, Ice Blue, 9 In. 420.00
Lindsey's Blood Searcher, Hollidaysburg, Light To Medium Emerald Green, 9 In. 840.00
Lindsey's Blood Searcher, Hollidaysburg, Medium Emerald Green, Olive Tint, 9 In. 1036.00
Lindsey's Blood Searcher, Pittsburgh, Pa., Aqua Green, Double Collar, IP, 8 7/8 In. 1792.00
Lindsey's Blood Searcher, Pittsburgh, Pa., Green Aqua, 1845-1860, 8 7/8 In. 1600.00
Lindsey's Blood Searcher, Pittsburgh, Pa., Ice Blue, Double Collar, 8 7/8 In. 280.00
Lindsey's Blood Searcher, R.E. Sellers & Co., Pittsburgh, Aqua Blue, Variant, 8 7/8 In. . . 146.00
Lindsey's Blood Searcher, R.E. Sellers & Co., Pittsburgh, Pink Amethyst, 8 7/8 In. 112.00
Lindsey's Cholera & Diarrhea, Hollidaysburg, Pa., Aqua Blue, OP, 4 5/8 In. 616.00
Lindsey's Cough Balsam, Hollidaysburg, Pa., Aqua Blue, OP, 5 3/8 In. 868.00
Lindsey's Vermifuge, Aqua Blue, Rolled Lip, OP, 4 3/8 In. 260.00
Liniment, Prairie Weed, Roxbury, Mass., Embossed, Square, 8 In. 75.00
Linonine, Kerr's Flax-Seed Emulsion, Brentwood, Md., Label, Contents . . . . .Illus 30.00
Liquid Opodeldoc, Aqua Blue, Rolled Lip, OP, 5 1/8 In. 84.00
Lloyd Bros., Passiflora Incarnata, Iron Cross Label, Cork, 5 In. 11.00
Log Cabin Cough & Consumption Remedy, Pat. Sept. 6, 1887, Amber, 6 3/4 In. 198.00
Log Cabin Cough & Consumption Remedy, Pat. Sept. 6, 1887, Amber, 9 In. 365.00
Log Cabin Cough & Consumption Remedy, Root Beer Amber, Tooled Mouth, 1895, 9 In. 364.00
Log Cabin Hops & Buchu Remedy, Amber, Label, Seal Cork Top, Corkscrew, Box, 10 In. 2475.00
Log Cabin Scalpine, Rochester, N.Y., Amber, Full Label, Box, 8 3/4 In. 5060.00
Log Cabin Scalpine, Rochester, N.Y., Root Beer Amber, Tooled Mouth, 1895, 9 In. 2576.00
Longley's Panacea, Olive Green, Applied Sloping Double Collar Mouth, 6 5/8 In. 4032.00
Longley's Panacea, Olive Green, Sloping Double Collar, Pontil, 6 3/4 In. 4030.00
Lydia E. Pinkham's Vegetable Compound, Apple Green, 8 1/2 In. 3696.00
Lydia E. Pinkham's Vegetable Compound, Aqua, 14 1/2 Oz., 8 1/8 In. 8.00
Lydia E. Pinkham's Vegetable Compound, Green, Disc Type Mouth, 8 In. 3695.00
Lyman Brown Seven Barks, Box, Round, 3 1/4 In. 72.00
Lynn's Medicines Are Good, Diarrhoea Remedy, Amber, Round, 6 1/2 In. 413.00
Lyon's Kathairon, OP, 4 In. 30.00
Lyon's Powder, B & P, N.Y., Cherry Puce, OP, Rolled Lip, 1855, 4 3/8 In. 363.00
Lyon's Powder, B & P, N.Y., Gold Yellow Amber, OP, 1855, 4 1/4 In. 495.00
Lyon's Powder, B & P, N.Y., Grape Amethyst, Open Pontil, 1860, 4 In. 156.00
Lyon's Powder, B & P, N.Y., Olive Green, OP, Rolled Lip, 1855, 4 1/4 In. 413.00
Lyon's Powder, B & P, N.Y., Pink Amethyst, Rolled Lip, OP, 4 In. 365.00
Lyon's Powder, B & P, N.Y., Purple Amethyst, OP, Rolled Lip, 4 3/8 In. 385.00
M.G. Tielke Druggist, Cleveland, O., Embossed, 5 In. . . . . .Illus 9.00
Mach Lem's Pharmacy, Paloose, Wa., 4 3/8 In. 65.00
Mack & Co Chemist, New York & Newport, Cobalt Blue, Tooled Top, 7 1/2 In. 88.00

Medicine, Lilly,
Elixir, Basham's
Mixture, Label,
7 1/2 In.

Medicine, Linonine,
Kerr's Flax-Seed
Emulsion, Brentwood,
Md., Label, Contents

Medicine, M.G.
Tielke Druggist,
Cleveland, O.,
Embossed, 5 In.

Medicine, Mrs.
Winslow's Soothing
Syrup, Aqua,
Embossed, 4 3/4 In.

Magee's Emulsion, J.A. Magee & Co., Aqua, Cork, Contents, 9 1/4 In. 66.00
Magn. Carb., Lid, Blue, White, 7 In. 144.00
Male Fern Vermifuge, To Treat Worms, Aqua, Complete Label, 5 In. 72.00
Manchester Hospital For Consumption, Cobalt, Embossed, Large 85.00
Manchester Hospital For Consumption, Emerald Green, Embossed, Large 35.00
Manchester Royal Infirmary, Cobalt, Hexagonal, Embossed, Large ....25.00 to 30.00
Manchester Royal Infirmary, Dark Green, Hexagonal, Embossed ....30.00 to 40.00
Manchester Royal Infirmary, Light Green, Hexagonal, Large ....25.00 to 30.00
Mander Weaver & Co., Wolverhampton, Deep Olive, Long Neck, England, 8 7/8 In. 728.00
Manzanita Oil, Sacramento, Light Aqua, 1860s, 4 1/2 In. 440.00
Martin H. Smith, Chemist, New York, Glyco-Heroin, Amber, Tooled Mouth, 7 5/8 In. ... 73.00
Max Samson, New Orleans, La., Amber, 3 5/16 In. 125.00
McLean's Volcanic Oil Liniment, Dark Aqua, OP, 4 In. 75.00
Medicinal Solution Of Purozone, Amber, Applied Top, 5 In. 1.50
Merck, Zinc Metal, Seal Cork, 1910s, 6 1/2 In. 93.00
Minard's Liniment, Boston, Aqua, Round, 5 1/8 In. 6.00
Mitchell's Liniment, Pittsburgh, Pa., Blue Aqua, Pontil, 4 7/8 In. 240.00
Modoc Indian Oil, For Rheumatic Pains, Embossed, Round, 6 1/4 In. 88.00
Moore's Liver-Ax Acts On The Liver, Aqua, Complete Label, 7 In. 66.00
Moore's Revealed, Medium Yellow Amber, 1875-1885, 8 7/8 In. 201.00
Morgan, Russian Cantharides, Amber, Screw Cap, Label, 2 3/4 In. 38.00
Morgan & Sons, Cobalt Blue, Embossed, Stopper, String Tie, Pre-1916, 3 1/2 In. 46.00
Morgan & Sons, Coca-Cola Syrup For Nausea & Vomiting, Label, 7 1/2 In. 44.00
Morgan & Sons, Tablet Of Soda Mint & Pepsin, Green, Label, Screw Cap, 2 1/2 In. 22.00
Morgan's Worm Killer, Philad., Pale Aqua, Rolled Lip, OP, 4 1/2 In. 213.00
Morse's Celebrated, Prov., R.I., Blue Aqua, Applied Sloping Collar, IP, 9 3/8 In. 209.00
Mother's Relief, Aqua, Sloping Collar, Pontil, 8 3/8 In. 392.00
Moxie Nerve Food, Denver, Co., Root Beer Amber, Seed Bubbles 700.00
Moxie Nerve Food, Lowell, Mass., Aqua, Patented, 10 In. 50.00
Mrs. Selzer Dispensing Chemist, Redwood City, Calif., Shield, Letter S, 8 1/8 In. 40.00
Mrs. Winslow's Soothing Syrup, Aqua, Embossed, 4 3/4 In. ....*Illus* 8.00
Mrs. Winslow's Soothing Syrup, Curtis & Perkins Prop., , BIMAL, 5 In. 5.00
Mrs. Winslow's Syrup, Angola American Drug Co., Aqua, ABM, 5 In. 5.00
Muegge, The Druggist, Baker, Ore., Emerald Green, 6 7/16 In. 65.00
Mulford's Digestive Malt Extract, Philadelphia, Amber, BIMAL, 8 1/2 In. 15.00
N. Wood, Portland, Me., Aqua, Rolfe's Pharmacy Label, Pontil, 1840-1860, 7 3/8 In. 198.00
N.B. Danforth, Apothecary, Wilmington, Del., 4 1/4 In. 30.00
N.W. Seat, M.D., Negative Electric Fluid, Aqua, OP, 1845-1855, 4 In. 209.00
National Remedy Co., Aqua, BIMAL, 5 1/2 In. 5.00
New England Cough Syrup, Jos. Spalding, Olive Yellow Amber, Pontil, 9 3/8 In. 330.00
New England Cough Syrup, Oval Rectangular, Stain 245.00
Nichol's Infallible Injection, 7 3/4 In. 110.00
Nixon Remedy Co., Saint Paris, Oh., 2 Men At Top, 6 3/4 In. 61.00
Northrop & Lyman, Newcastle, C.W., Aqua, Rectangular, Recessed Panel, 1860, 5 1/2 In. . 35.00
Norwood's Tinct. V. Viside, Complete Rear Label, 5 1/4 In. 198.00
Nubian Tea For The Liver, Chattanooga, Tenn., Olive Yellow, Tooled Mouth, 8 In. 495.00
O'Rourke & Hurley, Little Falls, N.Y., Dark Blue, 4 1/8 In. 50.00
O'Rourke & Hurley, Little Falls, N.Y., Dark Blue, 5 1/4 In. 50.00
O'Rourke & Hurley Druggists & Pharmacists, N.Y., Cobalt Blue, 1895-1910, 5 In. 235.00
O.Y. Rathburn & Co., Whitenight, Tex., 5 7/8 In. 45.00
Ol. Lini., Amber, Eisenglas White Label, Stopper, 7 In. 20.00
Oleum Morruae, Cobalt Blue, Cylindrical, Ground Stopper, 12 1/2 In. 345.00
Original Balm Of Thousand Flowers, Jules Hauel, Philada, Clear, Pontil, 1845, 5 In. 385.00
Osborne & Shoemaker, Reno, Nev., 1878-1896 .... 66.00
Osgood's Indian Cholacogue, N.Y., Turquoise, Applied Top, OP, 5 In. 77.00
Oswi Catarrh Remedy, Phila., Pa., Aqua, Tooled Lip, Stain, 8 In. 38.00
Otis Clapp & Son's Malt & Cod Liver Oil Compound, Amber, BIMAL, 7 1/4 In. .....6.00 to 8.00
Otto Gramm Druggist, Laramie City, Wyo., 4 In. 75.00
Owbridge's Embrocation Hull, Cobalt Blue, Hexagonal, Large 35.00
Owl Drug Co., 1-Wing Owl, Standard Pharmaceuticals, Emblem, 8 In. 35.00
Owl Drug Co., Amethyst, 5 In. 20.00
P.A. Ryan Druggist, Redwood City, Calif., Mortar & Pestle, 8 In. 40.00
Paine's Celery Compound, Amber, 10 In. 7.00

Palace Pharmacy Drug Co., A.R. Troxell, Cheyenne, Wyo., 4 1/2 In. 15.00
Palace Pharmacy Drug Co., A.R. Troxell, Cheyenne, Wyo., 5 1/2 In. 20.00
Park, Davis & Co., Warburg Tincture, Label Only, Amber, 2 3/4 In. 77.00
Pepsinola, Label Under Glass, 11 In. 187.00
Pepto-Bismol, Indigestion, Sour Stomach, Diarrhea, Norwich, 9 In. 134.00
Pepto-Magnan Gude, Aqua, 6-Sided, ABM, 7 In. 5.00
Perrine's Ginger, Cabin, Gold Amber, Square, 9 3/4 In. 253.00
Peruvian Syrup, Blue Aqua, Cylindrical, OP, 9 1/2 In. 119.00
Peruvian Syrup, Blue, Applied Top, Tubular Pontil, Whittled, 1850s, 10 In. 825.00
Pfeiffer Chemical Co., Philadelphia & St. Louis, Clear, Images Of Kidney, 7 In. 143.00
Phelp's Rheumatic Elixir, Scranton, Pa., Aqua 8.00
Phenique Chemical Co., St. Louis, Mo., ABM, 3 1/2 In. 3.50
Phillip's Milk Of Magnesia, Pat. Aug. 21, 1906, Blue, Strap Sides, 4 1/2 In. 2.00
Phillip's Milk Of Magnesia, Pat. Aug. 21, 1906, Blue, Strap Sides, Cork, 6 1/2 In. 2.50
Phoenix Drug Store, Geo. E. O'Hara, Cairo, Ill., 4 In. 15.00
Phoenix Surgical Dressing Co., Milwaukee, Wi., Amber, Qt. 500.00
Phychine For Consumption & Lung Troubles, Aqua, 9 3/4 In. 19.00
Pinapin, Thomas E. Richards, Phila Pa., Amber, Embossed Pineapple, 6 7/8 In. 78.00
Pine Tree, Diamond, 4-Sided, Cobalt Blue, 1845-1865, 4 1/4 In. 357.00
Pohl's Drug Store, Fremont, Neb., 4 1/2 In. 15.00
Porter's Pain King, Amethyst, ABM, 6 3/4 In. 8.00
Potter Drug & Chemical Corp, Boston, Ginger French Brandy, Aqua, 6 1/2 In. 2.50
Prairie Weed Balsam, Boston, Aqua 127.00
Pratt's Abolition For Abolishing Pain, Backward S, Applied Top, 6 3/4 In. 20.00
Price's Patent Candle Co. Ltd., Cobalt Blue, Diamond, Applied Top, 7 1/4 In. 80.00
Price's Soap Co. Ltd., Cobalt Blue, Sloping Double Collar, England, 7 1/2 In. 336.00
Prof. Dean's King Cactus Oil, Great Barbed Wire Remedy, Cylindrical, 6 1/2 In. . .154.00 to 550.00
Prof. H.K. Flagg's Balm Of Excellence, Star & Bottle, Aqua, OP 160.00
Prof. I. Hubert's Malvina Lotion, Toledo, Ohio, Amber, Tooled Top, 5 In. 44.00
Prof. I. Hubert's Malvina Lotion, Toledo, Ohio, Cobalt Blue, 1880-1900, 5 In. 50.00
Prof. I. Hubert's Malvina Lotion, Toledo, Ohio, Milk Glass, Square, 4 7/8 In. 80.00
Pure Cod Liver Oil, Reed, Carnrick & Andrus, Chemists, N.Y., Cobalt Blue, 10 In. 605.00
Puritana, W.T. & Co., Cobalt Blue, Tooled Mouth, 1890-1910, 6 3/4 In. 110.00
R & C, New York, Cobalt Blue, Embossed, Square, Applied Top, 7 3/4 In. 44.00
R.A. Robinson & Co., Druggists, Louisville, Deep Cobalt Blue, 1885-1895, 7 1/4 In. 523.00
R.E. Sellers Druggist, Pittsburgh, Aqua, Inward Rolled Mouth, 1860, 4 3/4 x 1 5/8 In. ... 77.00
Rawleigh's, ABM, Square, 3 3/4 In. 2.50
Rawleigh's, Amber, Embossed, 8 1/4 In. ....*Illus* 18.00
Rawleigh's, For Colic & Bloat Compound, ABM, 7 1/2 In. 94.00
Rawlin's Drug Co., Osborne Build Rawlin, Wyo., 4 3/8 In. 45.00
Rawlin's Drug Co., Rawlins, Wyo., Clear, 5 In. 110.00
Red Cross Pharmacy, Raton, N.M., 3 3/4 In. 45.00
Rees' Remedy For Piles, Aqua, Oval, Applied Square Collar, 1845-1855, 7 1/8 In.1650.00 to 1848.00
Renne's Pain Killing Magic Oil, Aqua, Labels, Rectangular, 6 In. 25.00
Rheumatic Syrup, 1882, R.S. Co., Rochester, N.Y., Trademark, Tree, 9 3/4 In. 165.00
Rhine Lavender, Disc Shape, Brass Screw Cap, Paper Label, Box, Germany, 4 3/4 In. ... 30.00
Richard's Golden Balsam, San Francisco, Aqua, Applied Top, 6 In. 33.00
Ridgway's Acme Liniment, Samuel Ridgway, Amber, Hydetown, Pa. 10.00
Ridgway's Acme Liniment, Samuel Ridgway, Yellow, Hydetown, Pa., 7 3/4 In. 59.00
Riker's Drug Store, New York, Brooklyn, BIMAL, Oval, 5 1/4 In. 4.00
Rite, Toronto, Tooled Lip, 1 7/8 x 3 x 6 3/8 In., Pt. 9.00
River Swamp Chill & Fever Cure, Augusta, Ga., Dark Amber, Alligator, 6 5/8 In. 176.00
Rolfe's Pharmacy, Brandon, Vt., Aqua, 7 In. 200.00
Rosenoff & Co. Druggists, Ritzville, Wash., 2 3/4 In. 15.00
Rowler's Rheumatism Medicine, Sacramento, Ca., Light Green, Applied Top, 7 In. 1900.00
Roy's Drug Store, 1014 P St., Lincoln, Neb., 4 1/4 In. 15.00
S & Co., Blood Purifier, Light Steel Blue 220.00
S. Brechbill's Worm Medicine, Blue, Aqua, Rolled Lip, 1835-1855, 4 In. 190.00
S.M. Kier Petroleum, Pittsburgh, Pa., Aqua Blue, OP, 6 3/4 In. 84.00
S.M. Kier Petroleum, Pittsburgh, Pa., Light Aqua, Pontil, 6 5/8 In. ....100.00 to 130.00
S.S. Newton's Patent, Dec. 20-76, Green, 5 1/4 In. 33.00
Salvation Oil, Cures Rheumatism, Toothache, Neuralgia, Gout, 5 3/4 In. 132.00
Sanford's Extract Of Hamamelis, Witch Hazel, Cobalt, Rectangular, 8 In. ....260.00 to 358.00

| Medicine, Rawleigh's, Amber, Embossed, 8 1/4 In. | Medicine, Triner's American Elixir, Bitter Wine Laxative, Chicago, Box, 9 1/2 In. | Medicine, Vapo-Cresolene Co., Embossed, Pat. Jul 17, 94, 4 In. | Medicine, Varnum's Drug Store, Dr. Pierce's Payngo, Jonesville, Mich., 4 In. |

Saylor's Cough Remedy, Pensler & Changler, Pottsville, Pa., Aqua, Label 40.00
Schenck's Pulmonic Syrup, Aqua, 8-Sided, Sloping Collar, IP, 7 1/8 In. . . . . .22.00 to 70.00
Schlotterbeck & Foss Co., Portland, Me., BIMAL, 5 In. 3.00
Scovill's Blood & Liver Syrup, Aqua, 9 1/2 In. 30.00
Security Antiseptic Healer, Label, Glass Screw Top, 7 1/2 In. 209.00
Shaker Cherry Pectoral Syrup, Canterbury, N.Y., Aqua, OP, 1855, 5 1/2 In. 145.00
Shaker Fluid Extract Valerian, OP 20.00
Shaker Syrup No. 1, Canterbury, N.H., Aqua, OP, 5 1/2 In. 145.00
Shaker Syrup No. 1, Canterbury, N.H., Aqua, OP, 7 In. 240.00
Shecut's Southern Balm For Coughs, Colds, Consumption & C., Blue, 8-Sided, 6 In. . . .   660.00
Shepherd's Vermifuge, Pittsburgh, Blue Aqua, Rolled Lip, OP, 3 7/8 In. 179.00
Skerrett's Oil, B. Wheeler, W. Henrietta Mon. Co., N.Y., Emerald Green, 6 1/4 In. 2184.00
Skerrett's Oil, B. Wheeler, W. Henrietta Mon. Co., N.Y., Green, 7 In. 2800.00
Skunk Oil, Amber, Paper Label, Contents, Round, 4 1/2 In. 16.50
Smelling Salts, Seahorse Design, Blue & White Stripes, Riggorie, 2 3/4 In. 176.00
Smith & Bates, Leading Druggists, Owensboro, Ky., 5 1/2 In. 25.00
Smith Burch & Co., Fruit Syrup, Montreal, Canada, Pale Blue, Orange, Brown 27.00
Smith Special Elixir, Teal Green, 4 1/4 In. 10.00
Smith's Green Mountain Renovator, East Georgia, Vt., Amber, IP, 7 In. . . . . . . .2700.00 to 3024.00
Smith's Green Mountain Renovator, East Georgia, Vt., Yellow Amber, IP, 7 In. .1155.00 to 2695.00
Smith's Green Mountain Renovator, Olive Yellow Amber, IP, 7 1/8 In. 1210.00
Smith's Green Mountain Renovator, Yellow Amber, IP, 1845-1855, 6 7/8 In. 2800.00
Sparks' Perfect Health For Kidney & Liver Diseases, Man, Yellow Amber, 9 3/8 In. 209.00
Sparks' Perfect Health For Kidney & Liver Diseases, Tobacco Amber, Tooled Lip, 9 In. . .   532.00
Stanley's Celery Malt, P.B. Wait & Co., Le Roy, N.Y., Gold Yellow, 1890, 8 1/4 In. 134.40
Star Drug Co, Market St., Cor. 3rd, San Francisco, Embossed Star, 8 3/4 In. 40.00
Steinhauser & Eaton Prescription Druggist, Green, 8 3/4 In. 90.00
Sterlinie Auld Lang Syne 22.50
Stockton Drug Co., Stockton, Cal., 7 In. 7.00
Stockton Drug Co., Stockton, Cal., Palmer Green, Crown Top, 8 In. 33.00
Swaim's Panacea, Established 1820, St. Louis, Mo., Aqua, BIMAL, 8 In. 60.00
Swaim's Panacea, Philada, Apple Green, Pontil, 8 In. 440.00
Swaim's Panacea, Philada, Green, Vertical Panels, Pontil, 1860, 7 7/8 In. 660.00
Swaim's Panacea, Philada, Medium To Deep Olive Green, 1865, 7 7/8 In. 176.00
Swaim's Panacea, Philada, Olive Green, Pontil, Double Collar, 1845, 7 3/4 In. . . . .700.00 to 756.00
Swaim's Panacea, Philada, Olive Yellow Green, Pontil, 1860, 7 3/4 In. 303.00
Swaim's Panacea, Philada, Rosedown Plantation, Olive Yellow, Applied Top 500.00
Sweet's Black Oil, Rochester, N.Y., Lockport Green, OP, 6 In. 2184.00
Swift's Syphilitic Specific, Cobalt Blue, Applied Disc Mouth, 1885, 9 In. 1344.00
Sylpho Nathol Cabots, USA, Pt., 9 1/2 In. 3.00

Syrup, Pike & Osgood, Boston, Mass., Olive Yellow Amber, 1845-1855, 8 1/2 In. 7560.00
T. Morris Perot & Co., Druggist, Philada, Sapphire Blue, Rolled Lip, Pontil, 5 1/4 In. 1540.00
T.O.D. Co., Owl On Mortar & Pestle, Cobalt Blue, Tooled Mouth, 6 1/4 In. 264.00
T.W. Harper's Cough Remedy, Flared Lip, Round 125.00
Tartar Depurur. Weinstein, Amber, Eisenglas White Label, Stopper, 7 In. 77.00
Tessier Preevost A Paris, Bell, Green, Beveled Corners, Collar Mouth, Pontil, 7 5/8 In. . . 523.00
The Corner Drug Store, Bellows Falls, Vt., Amber, 5 1/8 In. 135.00
Thompson Druggist, Stewart & Market Sts., Aqua, Rainbow Effect, 5 1/8 In. 40.00
Thornton's Blistering Balsam, Cookshire, Quebec, Rectangular, BIMAL, 6 In. 55.00
Tilden & Co., New Lebanon, N.Y., Olive Yellow, Square, Tooled Collar, IP, 6 7/8 In. 1456.00
Tinct. Cinnamomi, Label Under Glass, Flared Lip, Stopper, Pontil, 6 In. 34.00
Tinct. Digitalis, Amber, Eisenglas Red & White Label, Stopper, 7 In. 20.00
Toilet Articles, Translucent Lid, 15 1/2 In. 805.00
Trask's Ointment, D. Ransom Son & Co., Buffalo, N.Y., 13 3/8 In. 209.00
Triner's American Elixir, Bitter Wine Laxative, Chicago, Box, 9 1/2 In. . . . . *Illus* 40.00
Trommer Extract Of Malt Co., Fremont, Ohio, Dark Amber, 8 In. 88.00
True Cephalic Snuff, Turquoise, Rolled Lip, OP, 3 3/4 In. 77.00
Tumenol-Ammon, Amber, Eisenglas White Label, Stopper, 7 In. 20.00
Turlington's Balsam, King's Patent, Aqua, Pontil, 1825-1835, 2 5/8 In. 143.00
Turlington's Balsam, King's Patent, Blue Aqua, OP, 2 3/4 In. 128.80
Turlington's Balsam Of Life, Northrop & Lyman Co., Toronto, BIMAL, Box 55.00
Turner's Ess. Of Jamaica Ginger, N.Y., OP, Turquoise, 5 3/4 In. 66.00
U.S.A. Hosp. Dept., Cobalt Blue, 3-Piece Mold, Tooled Mouth, 7 3/8 In. 605.00
U.S.A. Hosp. Dept., Cobalt Blue, Flared Lip, Oval, 1860-1875, 3 1/4 In. 743.00
U.S.A. Hosp. Dept., Cobalt Blue, Flared Lip, Oval, 1860-1875, 5 3/4 In. 176.00
U.S.A. Hosp. Dept., Copper Amber, Swirls, 5 13/16 In. 1430.00
U.S.A. Hosp. Dept., Medium Cobalt Blue, 1860-1875, 7 1/8 In. 246.00
U.S.A. Hosp. Dept., Medium Olive Yellow Green, Double Collar, 1860-1870, 9 1/2 In. . . . 633.00
U.S.A. Hosp. Dept., Olive Lime Green, Double Collar, 1860-1870, 9 1/2 In. 952.00
U.S.A. Hosp. Dept., Olive Yellow, Applied Top, Round 660.00
U.S.A. Hosp. Dept., Olive Yellow, Double Collar Lip, 9 1/2 In. . . . . 616.00 to 990.00
U.S.A. Hosp. Dept., Olive Yellow, Double Collar, 1860-1870, 8 7/8 In. 578.00
Udolpho Wolfe's Schiedam Schnapps, Amber, Square, Applied Collar Lip, IP, 9 3/4 In. . . 896.00
Umatilla Indian Hogah, Campbell & Lyon, Detroit, Mich., Tooled, 9 In. 100.00
Union Liniment, Aqua, Rolled Lip, Hutchinson, OP, 5 In. 73.00
United States Marine Hospital Service, Clear, BIMAL, Square, 3 1/4 In. 12.00
University Free Medicine, Philadelphia, Blue Aqua, 6-Sided, Pontil, 4 7/8 In. 143.00
University Free Medicine, Philadelphia, Blue Aqua, 6-Sided, Pontil, 5 7/8 In. 88.00
University Pharmacy, F.J. Steinmetz, Palo Alto, Calif., 12-Sided, 4 1/2 In. 40.00
Valentine Hassuc's Lung & Cough Syrup, Dark Amber, 1886 . . . . 400.00
Vapo-Cresolene Co., Embossed, Pat. Jul 17, 94, 4 In. . . . . *Illus* 12.00
Varnum's Drug Store, Dr. Pierce's Payngo, Jonesville, Mich., 4 In. . . . . *Illus* 22.00
Vaughn's Mixture Vegetable Lithontriptic, Medium Aqua, Applied Top, 6 1/4 In. 30.00
Vaughn's Vegetable Lithontriptic Mixture, Buffalo, Aqua, Square, 1860, 8 In. . . . . . 88.00 to 150.00
Vial, Puce Amethyst, 1855-1865, 4 In. 29.00
W. Olmsted & Co. Constitutional Beverage 303.00
W.C. Sweet's, H.C.B. & L., Rochester, Aqua, OP, Applied Mouth, 6 In. 168.00
W.C. Sweet's, King Of Oils, Rochester, N.Y., Emerald Green, 4 3/4 In. 3472.00
W.D. Co., Amber, Yellow, BIMAL, 6 1/2 In. 5.00
W.E. Hagan, Tray, N.Y., Cobalt Blue 358.00
W.E. Schatman, Druggist, N.W. Pittsburgh, With Measure 5.00
W.H. Bone Co., C.C. Liniment, San Francisco Cal., Blue, Tooled Top 55.00
W.H. Hooker & Co., Sole Agents, North & South America, Cobalt Blue, 5 1/2 In. 33.00
W.J. Bartholomew, Druggist, Gothenburg, Neb., 3 1/2 In. 10.00
W.J. Camden Red Cross, Walhalla, N.D., Embossed, 4 1/2 In. 75.00
W.M.C. Wilson Druggist, Laramie City, Amethyst, 6 5/8 In. 75.00
W.S. Merrell & Co., Cincinnati, Light Steel Blue 66.00
W.T.Co., Jar, Cer. Cantharid, Milk Glass, 1880s 55.00
W.W. Turner, Apothecary, Chatham, Ont., Chemist, BIMAL, 4 In. 10.00
Wakelee's Camelline, Cobalt Blue, 4 3/8 In. . . . . 33.00 to 78.00
Wakelee's Camelline, Cobalt Blue, 5 In. 45.00
Wakelee's Camelline, Cobalt Blue, Applied Mouth, 7 1/2 In. 255.00
Wakelee's Camelline, Cobalt Blue, Applied Top, 3 1/4 In. 525.00

Wakelee's Pharmacies, San Francisco, Green Citrate, Tooled Top 385.00
Waldron Drug Store, Dennison, Tex., Mortar & Pestle, Clear, 5 In. 35.00
Warner's Log Cabin Rose Cream, Etc., Rochester, N.Y., Clear, Ground Lip, 2 5/8 In. 532.00
Warner's Log Cabin Sugar Coated Liver Pills, Original Box 179.00
Warner's Safe Compound, Amber, Miniature 375.00
Warner's Safe Cure, London, Olive Green, Rounded Lip, 1/2 Pt. 9.00
Warner's Safe Cure, Rochester, N.Y., Red Amber, 1880-1895, 9 5/8 In. 145.00
Warner's Safe Diabetes Cure, Rochester, N.Y., Amber, Embossed, 9 1/2 In. 1485.00
Warner's Safe Diabetes Remedy, Rochester, N.Y., Amber, Tooled Lip, 9 5/8 In. 364.00
Warner's Safe Kidney & Liver Cure, Rochester, N.Y., Amber, Embossed, 9 1/2 In. 413.00
Warner's Safe Kidney & Liver Remedy, Rochester, N.Y., Amber, Blob Top, 9 1/2 In. 308.00
Warner's Safe Kidney & Liver Remedy, Rochester, N.Y., Olive Green, 5 1/2 In. 605.00
Warner's Safe Nervine, Amber, Tooled Mouth, 1895, 7 1/4 In. 72.00
Warner's Safe Nervine, London, Amber 66.00
Warner's Safe Nervine, London, Yellow, 1/2 Pt. 140.00
Warner's Safe Nervine, Slug Plate, Pt. 70.00
Warner's Safe Remedies Co., Amber, Oversized S, Tooled Top 88.00
Warner's Safe Remedies Co., Rochester, N.Y., Amber, 7 1/4 In. 448.00
Warner's Safe Remedies Co., Rochester, N.Y., Amber, 9 In. ....231.00 to 358.00
Warner's Safe Remedies Co., Rochester, N.Y., Yellow Amber, Tooled Mouth, 7 In. 448.00
Wayne's Diuretic Elixir, F.E. Suir & Co., Cincinnati, Cobalt Blue, 1870-1880, 7 In. 330.00
Weaver's Canker & Salt Rheum Syrup, 9 5/8 In. 170.00
Wetherell's Cream Of Benzoin & Roses, Milk Glass, 1880-1895, 5 In. 246.00
Willes Horne Dule Co., Salt Lake City, Utah, 5 1/2 In. 25.00
Wm. Radam's Microbe Killer, Germ Bacteria, Amber, Label, 10 5/8 In. ....165.00 to 280.00
Wm. Radam's Microbe Killer, Germ Bacteria, Gold Amber, 10 1/2 In. 330.00
Wm. Radam's Microbe Killer, Germ Bacteria, Red Amber, 10 1/4 In. 253.00
Wm. Radam's Microbe Killer, Jug, Stoneware, Handle, 11 In. ....140.00 to 303.00
Wm. S. Merrell & Co., Druggist's, Cincinnati, Blue Aqua, IP, 1855, 8 In. 303.00
Wm. Thebus Drug Co., Denver, Co., Owl, Purple, 7 1/2 In. 125.00
Wolff-Wilson Drug Co., Slug Plate, Swirl Lines, BIMAL, 5 1/2 In. 7.00
Wolff-Wilson Drug Co., St. Louis, Mo., BIMAL, 5 1/4 In. 15.00
Wolff-Wilson Drug Co., St. Louis, Mo., BIMAL, 9 In. 5.00
Womarrin, Park Hill, Aqua, Rectangular, Recessed Panels, BIMAL, Canada, c.1870, 5 In. 25.00
Woodwards Pharmacy, Aberdeen, S.D., 5 1/4 In. 45.00
Wormser Bros., San Francisco, Barrel, Orange Amber, 9 1/2 In. 2420.00
Wormwood, Thomas Hollis, 23 Union St., Boston, Label, Cork, 4 1/2 In. 1.50
Wright's Indian Cough Balsam, Aqua, Rectangular, BIMAL, 7 In. 26.00
Wyeth, Morphine Sulfate Triturates, Amber, Screw Cap, Glassine Wrapper, 4 1/2 In. 25.00
Wyeth & Bro., Phosphate Of Lime & Cod Liver Oil, Blue, 8 3/4 In. 190.00
Wynkoop's Iceland Pectoral, New York, Aqua, Lip Iridescent, 5 1/4 In. 200.00
Zoeller's Kidney, Remedy, Pittsburgh, Pa., Yellow Amber, Tooled Lip, 9 1/2 In. 112.00

─────────────────────── MICHTER'S ───────────────────────

Michter's claims to be America's oldest distillery, established in Schaefferstown, Pennsylvania, in 1753, before it was even the state of Pennsylvania. The building was named a national historic landmark in 1980. Special ceramic jugs were first made in 1955 and figural decanters were made beginning in 1977. One of the most famous series was King Tut (1978-1980). About 3,000 were made of the large size. Miniature bottles were also made. Production ended in 1989.

230th Anniversary, 1983 .... 30.00
Amish Buggy 57.00
Atlantic City Casinos, 1980 ....*Illus* 27.00
Auto, York Pullman, 1977 .... 100.00
Barn, Daniel Boone, 1977 .... 30.00
Canal Boat, 1977 ....22.00 to 26.00
Christmas Bell, 1983 .... 53.00
Christmas Ornament, 1984 .... 25.00
Christmas Tree, 1978 .... 50.00
Christmas Wreath, 1980 ....*Illus* 34.00
Conestoga Wagon, 1976 .... 62.00
Covered Bridge, 1984 .... 47.00
Doughboy, 1979 .... 23.00

Michter's,
Atlantic City
Casinos, 1980

Michter's,
Christmas
Wreath, 1980

Michter's,
Policeman, Los
Angeles, 1980

Easton Peace Candle, 1979	20.00
Fireman, Volunteer Statue, 1979	86.00
Football On Tee, Pennsylvania, 1979	20.00
Goddess Selket, 1980	32.00
Halloween Witch, 1979	55.00
Hershey Trolley, 1980	48.00
Ice Wagon, 1979	19.00
Indian Kneeling	50.00
Jug, 1955	60.00
Jug, 1957, 1/2 Gal.	68.00
Jug, 1957, Qt.	20.00
Jug, Sheridan, 1970, Qt.	20.00 to 22.00
Jug, Sheridan, 1976, Qt.	10.00
Jug, Sheridan, 1978, Qt.	10.00
King Tut, 1978	60.00
King Tut, Miniature	42.00
Knights Of Columbus, 4th Degree	100.00
Liberty Bell, Brown, 1976	43.00
Liberty Bell, With Cradle, 1976	14.00
Liberty Brown, Bisque, 1975	75.00
Packard, Fleetwood, 1979	36.00
Penn State Nittany Lion, 1978	48.00
Pennsylvania, Keystone State, 1980	20.00
Pennsylvania Hex, 1977	12.00
Pitt Panther, 1977	53.00
Policeman, Los Angeles	*Illus* 30.00
Queen Nefertiti, 1979	42.00
Reading, Pagoda, Pa., 1977	24.00
Stagecoach, 1978	17.00
USC Trojan	35.00

MIKE WAYNE

Mike Wayne Distilled Products Company was founded in Bardstown, Kentucky, in 1978. The company was formed to sell original ceramic decanters. A John Wayne bust, a portrait, and two full-figure bottles are among the many decanters made until about 1982.

Grandfather Clock, 1981	55.00
John Wayne, Bust, 1980	50.00
John Wayne, Portrait, 1979	40.00
John Wayne, Statue, White, 1981	87.00
Masonic, Past Master, 1981	35.00
Mercedes Benz, 450 SL, 1980	25.00
Nebraska Cornhuskers, 1982	25.00
Norman Rockwell, Plumber, 1978	23.00
Pheasant, 1981	20.00

Pope John Paul II, 1980	20.00
Razorback Hog, 1982	35.00

─────────────── MILK ───────────────

The first milk bottle we have heard about was an earthenware jar pictured on a Baby-lonian temple stone panel. Evidently, milk was being dipped from the jar while cream was being churned into butter.

Milk came straight from the cow on early farms; but when cities started to grow in America, a new delivery system was needed. The farmer put the milk into large con-tainers. These were taken to the city in horse-drawn carts and delivered to the consumer. The milkman took a slightly dirty dipper and put it into the milk, ladling a quantity into the customer's pitcher.

Flies, dirt, horse hairs, and heat obviously changed the quality of the milk. By the 1860s iceboxes were developed. One type of milk can claimed to keep milk from becoming sour in a thunderstorm. In 1895, pasteurization was invented and another source of dis-ease from milk was stopped. The first milk bottle patent was issued in the 1880s to the Warren Glass Works Company. The most famous milk bottle was designed in 1884 by Dr. Harvey D. Thatcher, a physician and druggist from Potsdam, New York. His glass bottle had a *Lightning* closure and a picture on the side of a cow being milked. In 1889 The Thatcher Company brought out the bottle with a cap that is still used.

The characteristic shape and printed or embossed wording identify milk bottles for col-lectors. The round bottle was the most popular until 1936, when the squat round bottle was invented. In 1940 a square squat bottle became the preferred shape. The paper car-ton was introduced in 1932. Plastic has been used since 1964. A slug plate was used in the manufacture of a special type of round milk bottle. The manufacturer would change the name embossed on the bottle by changing a metal plate in the glass mold. The let-ters *ISP* seen in some publications mean *inserted slug* plate. In the following list of bot-tle prices, the words *slug plate* are used. Amber-colored glass was used for a short time. Makers claimed it resisted spoiling. A green bottle was patented in 1929. *Pyro* is the shortened form of the word *pyroglaze,* an enameled lettering used on milk bottles after the mid-1930s. Before that, the name had been embossed. Some bottle collectors now refer to these as *ACL,* Applied Color Label. In this listing, color refers to the applied color of the label not to the color of the glass.

Cop the top, babyface, toothache, and *cream top* are some of the terms that refer to the shapes of bottle necks popular in the 1930s. Near the top of the bottle there was an indentation so the cream, which separated from the standing milk, could be poured off with little trouble. Today, with homogenized milk, few children realize that the cream on natural milk will rise to the top. The glass bottle was displaced by cartons by the 1960s. There are two newsletters for collectors,The Milk Route, 4 Ox Bow Road, West-port, CT 06880-2602 and The MOOSletter, 240 Wahl Avenue, Evans City, PA 16033.

A Bottle Of Milk Is A Bottle Of Health, 1/3 Pt.	20.00
A.G. Smalley Co., Clear, Qt.	72.00
A.J. Carter Dairy, Frewsburg, N.Y., Babyface, Cop The Cream, ABM, Qt.	121.00
Absolutely Pure Milk, Milk Protector, Potsdam, N.Y., Cylindrical, Wire Bail, Qt.	467.00
Acawam Goat Dairy, Wash, Scald & Return, Embossed, 1/2 Pt.	40.00
Alden Bros., 80 Ruggles St., Boston, Embossed, Qt.	45.00
Aldrich Dairy, Norwich, N.Y., ACL, Round, Qt.	35.00
Aldrich Dairy, Norwich, N.Y., Orange ACL, Stork & Baby, Qt.	24.00
Allegheny Bottling Council, 1763 Pgh., Pa., Stars Around Neck, 1/2 Pt.	5.00
Allenbury's Feeder, England, Turtle Shape, BIMAL, 1885-1895, 7 In.	85.00
Alta Crest Farms, Spencer, Mass., Cows Head, Yellow Green, 1929-1935, Qt.	672.00
Alta Crest Farms, Spencer, Mass., Green ACL, Round, Qt.	1250.00
Alta Crest Farms, Spencer, Mass., Green, Steer's Head, Qt.	1400.00
Alta Crest Dairy, Spencer, Mass., Kelly Green	1500.00
Amador Goat Dairy, Glendale, Ariz., Maroon ACL, Square, Qt.	30.00
American Seal-Kap Corporation, Red, Square, 1/2 Pt.	25.00
Anderson Bros., Worcester, Ma., Embossed, Round, 1929, 1/2 Pt.	20.00
Anderson Bros., Worcester, Ma., Embossed, Round, Qt.	20.00
Angell's Guernsey Milk, Embossed, Qt.	25.00
Annie Oakley Coleman Milk Company, Qt.	1.00
Ashton Dairy, Petersburg, Virginia, Red ACL, Qt.	32.00

Auburn Guernsey Farm Inc., Golden Guernsey, Gold ACL, Qt.	25.00
Avondale Farms Dairy, 1/2 Pt.	20.00
B & W Dairy, Wahpeton, N.D. & Breckenridge, Minn., ACL, Square, Qt.	20.00
B.C.H.D., Dairy Plant, Cop The Cream, Embossed, Round, Qt.	100.00
Baker & Son Dairy, Altanta, Mich., Large Cow, ACL, Qt.	24.00
Barnegat Ranch, Grass Valley, Calif., Green ACL, Cap, Round, Qt.	54.00
Baxter's Dairy, Watkins Glen, N.Y., ACL, Square, Qt.	8.00
Bear Creek Dairy, Jim Thorpe, Pa., 2 Colors, ACL, Square, Qt.	40.00
Becks Milky Way Dairy, Marshfield, Mo., Milky Way Is Healthy Way, Red ACL, Qt.	40.00
Bell Ice Cream, Texas, Dacro Top, ACL, Round, Qt.	15.00
Benson's Dairy, Huntingdon, Pa., Embossed, Tall, Round, Qt.	35.00
Bentley & Renckens Dairy, Dunkirk & Fredonia, N.Y., ACL, Qt.	25.00
Bentley's, Boston, Mass, Embossed, Round, 6 Oz.	8.00
Benware Creamery, Malone, N.Y., Large Barn Scene, Red ACL, Qt.	24.00
Berry Farm, Stratham, N.H., Orange ACL, Long Neck, Square, Qt.	25.00
Beverly Farms, Chocolate Milk, Red ACL, 1/2 Pt. ....*Illus*	12.00
Bieber's Mill Creek Farm Dairy, Woodworth, Ohio, 2 Colors, Tall, Round, Qt.	45.00
Big Elm Dairy Co., One Quart Liquid, Registered, Amber, ABM, Cap, Qt.	180.00
Birch Lawn Dairy, Tarrs, Pa., Farm Scene, ACL, Round, Qt.	55.00
Blanding's, Greenville, Mi., Clear, ACL, 1/2 Pt.	21.00
Blanket Meadow Dairy, Stepney, Ct., Red, Round, Qt.	30.00
Blue Hen Farm, Wilmington, Del., Embossed, Cream Top, 1/2 Pt.	30.00
Bob Vetter Dairies, Moriah Center, N.Y., Cow's Head, ACL, Qt.	24.00
Bonny Brook Farm, Kearny, North Grafton, Mass., Embossed, Round, Pt.	20.00
Bonny Meade Farm Pure Jersey Cream, Mass. Seal, Embossed, 1/2 Pt.	15.00
Booth's, Dunkirk, N.Y., ACL, Qt.	18.00
Borden's, Cream Top, Square, Qt.	5.00
Borden's, Elsie The Cow On 2 Sides, Square, Gal.	80.00
Borden's, Elsie, N.Y., ACL, Square, 1/2 Pt.	35.00
Borden's, Embossed, Disc Cap, Round, c.1925, Pt.	75.00
Borden's, Embossed, Disc Cap, Squat, c.1900, 1/2 Pt.	50.00
Borden's, Embossed, Tin Top, Round, c.1889, Qt.	200.00
Borden's, On 2 Sides, Embossed, Round, Qt.	20.00
Borden's, Red ACL, Tall, Qt.	25.00
Borden's, Sour Cream, Embossed, Round, Pt.	5.00
Borden's Condensed Milk Co., Embossed Eagle, Qt.	88.00
Borden's Dairy, Chicago, Illinois, Embossed, Qt.	5.00
Bowman Dairy Company, Embossed, Pt. ....*Illus*	70.00
Branglebrink Farm, St. James, N.Y., Round, Embossed, 1/2 Pt.	6.00
Briggs, Dunkirk, N.Y., It Whips On Bulb, Cream Top, Round, Qt.	35.00
Broadbrook Preston City Conn., Blue ACL, Qt.	25.00
Brock-Hall, New Haven, Ct., ACL, Embossed, Round, 1/3 Pt.	5.00

Milk, Beverly Farms, Chocolate Milk, Red ACL, 1/2 Pt.

Milk, Bowman Dairy Company, Embossed, Pt.

Milk, C. Durand Cream & Milk, Canton, O., Qt.

Milk, Chickagami Dairy, Charles T. Lathers, Brutus, Mich., Red ACL, Qt.

Brookfield Dairy, Hellertown, Pa., Embossed, Round, 1/2 Pt. 35.00
Brookfield Dairy, Hellertown, Pa., Phone TE 8-3041, Babyface, Paper Cap, 1/2 Pt. 73.00
Brookside Dairies, Waterbury, Ct., Embossed, Round, 1/2 Pt. 10.00
Brookside Dairies, Waterbury, Ct., Embossed, Round, Qt. 10.00
Brookside Farm, Peabody, J.A. Roome, Embossed, Qt. 30.00
Browns Shamokin, Pa., ACL, Qt. 200.00
Burroughs Brothers, Walnut Grove Farm, Knightson, Calif., Red ACL, Round, Qt. 29.00
Butler's Dairy, Keep Fit With Milk, 3 Soldiers, Red ACL, Qt. 450.00
C. Brigham Co., Cambridge, Embossed, Pt. 18.00
C. Durand Cream & Milk, Canton, O., Qt. ....*Illus* 62.00
C.A. Dorr, Watertown, N.Y., ACL, Round, Pt. 50.00
C.D. Wearne Dairy, Bloomfield, Nebr., Phone No. 132, Qt. 30.00
C.N. Baker, Charlotte, N.C., Embossed, Round, Pt. 16.00
C.P. Beers, Russell, Pa., Embossed, 1/2 Pt. 15.00
Capital Dairy Co., Eureka, Calif., Orange ACL, Round, Qt. 39.00
Carnation, Coated Inside, Red ACL, Round, Qt. 50.00
Carnation Fresh Milk, Carnation Co., Amber, Square, Qt. 45.00
Carnation Malted Milk, 8 1/2 In. 375.00
Castonguay Dairy, Sabattus, Maine, Red ACL, Square, Qt. 15.00
Chapman's Dairy, Greenville, S.C., ACL, Round, Qt. 40.00
Charest Dairy, Fall River, Maroon, Qt. 20.00
Charlotte Dale Dairy Farm, Visitors Always Welcome, Brown & Orange ACL, Pt. 33.00
Chautaugua Lake Creamery, Jamestown, N.Y., ACL, Qt. 22.00
Chelko, Plainville, Ct., Embossed, Round, 1/2 Pt. 20.00
Chestnut Farms, Chevy Chase Dairy, Washington, D.C., Short, Round, Qt. .... .22.00 to 30.00
Chickagami Dairy, Charles T. Lathers, Brutus, Mich., Red ACL, Qt. ....*Illus* 30.00
Christiansen Bros. Dairy Co., Chicago, Il., Embossed, Round, Qt. ....10.00 to 25.00
Churchill's Dairy, Bethlehem, N.H., ACL, Round, Qt. 35.00
Citizen's Dairy, Hockey & Baseball Players, Red, Round, Canada, 1/2 Pt. 40.00
City Creamery Milk, Carlsbad, N.M., Red ACL, Cream Separator, Round, Qt. 125.00
City Farm Dairies, Orange, Square, c.1957, 5 1/2 In. 13.00
Clardy's Dairy, Home Of Space Ship Crash, Roswell, N.M., ACL, 1947, Qt. 95.00
Clark Dairy Limited, Canada 1939, King, Queen & Maple Leaf, Red ACL, Qt. 160.00
Clear View Farm, Millbury, Mass., G.D. Allaire, Red ACL, Round, Qt. 20.00
Clearview Farm Dairy, Gouldsboro, Pa., Embossed, Round, Qt. ....25.00 to 35.00
Climax, Patent Nov. 15, '98, Tin Top, Square, 1/2 Pt. 125.00
Cloverland Dairy, New Orleans, La., Embossed, Pt. 30.00
Cloverleaf Dairy, Gary, Indiana, Embossed, Qt. 10.00
Cloverleaf Dairy Inc., BB Mass Seal, Green ACL, Round, Qt. 25.00
Cloverleaf Farms, Stockton, Calif., Cream Top, Ribbed Neck, Orange ACL, Qt. 28.00
Co-Op Golden Crust Bread, ACL, Round, Qt. 50.00
College View Dairy, Norwich, Vt., Maroon, Square, Pt. 30.00
Colonial Dairies, Albany, Georgia, Embossed, Pt. 20.00
Cooperstown Dairy, Cooperstown, N.Y., For Mothers Who Care, Farm Scene, ACL, Qt. . 30.00
Cortez Dairy, Colorado, Embossed, Round, Pt. 45.00
Country Club Dairy, ACL, 1/2 Pt. 24.00
Cow's Head, Red Islamic Writing, Pre-Revolution, Iran, 1/2 Pt. 30.00
Crane, Leominster, Mass., Embossed, Round, Qt. 20.00
Cranson's Golden Rule Dairy, Phone 426, La Junta, Colo., 1/2 Pt. 30.00
Cream Valley Dairy, Woodstown, N.J., ACL, Square, Qt. 10.00
Creamer, Army Medical Center, 2 Oz. 50.00
Creamer, Borden's, If It's Borden's, It's Got To Be Good, ACL, Round 40.00
Creamer, Carricks Dairy Cream 37.50
Creamer, Gnagey's Dairy, Meyesdale, Pa., ACL, Round 40.00
Creamer, Neidig's Dairy, Somerset, Pa., ACL, Square 30.00
Creamer, Rosebud Creamery, ACL, Square 30.00
Creamer, Sunshine Dairy, Paducah, Ky., ACL, Round 40.00
Creamer, Tranquility Farm, Blue, Round 40.00
Creamer, Wigtownshire Creamery Co., Part Dundas, Stoneware, 4 In. 41.00
Creamery Service Inc., Santa Cruz, Calif., Maroon ACL, Round, Qt. 49.00
Creamland, Albuquerque, N.M., Embossed, Round, 1/2 Pt. 25.00
Crescent, Jar, Clear, 1/2 Pt., 5 1/4 In. 44.00
Crystal Dairy, Guelph, Visit Our Modern Dairy Bar, Orange ACL, Qt. 550.00

Crystal Quality Creamed Cottage Cheese, Vancouver, Red ACL, Round, 1920s, Qt. 35.00
Cumberland Dairy, Embossed, Round, Pt. 20.00
Curly's Dairy, Salem, Oregon, Dutch Boy, Green & Brown ACL, Qt. 65.00
D'Arbonne Dairy, Homer, La., ACL, Round, Pt. 20.00
Dairy Cooperative, Torrington, Ct., Embossed, Round, 1/2 Pt. 5.00
Dairy Maid, Squat, Square, 1/2 Pt. 5.00
Dairylea, Double Babyface, Clear 52.00
Dairylea, Eagle, Girl With Hoop & Family, ACL, Round, Qt. 30.00
Dairylee, Red & Orange ACL, Babyface, Square, c.1930, Qt. 100.00
Dairymen's Co-Op Assn., Ma., Embossed, Round, Qt. 10.00
Damascus, Portland, Ore., ACL, Cream Top, Round, Qt. 35.00
Darigold, ACL, Round, Qt. 60.00
David Fiske Warehouse, Point, Conn., Embossed, Round, Qt. 18.00
Dean Morningdale, Boylston, Ma., Embossed, Round, 1927, Pt. 20.00
Deerfoot Farms, Southboro, Ma., Bowling Pin, Embossed, Qt. 150.00
Deerfoot Farms, Southboro, Ma., Embossed, Round, 1/2 Pt. 15.00
Dell Newtown Bucks Co., Pa., ACL, Round, Qt. 125.00
Dellinger Dairy, Jeffersonville, In., ACL, Round, Qt. 55.00
Dellwood Dairy Co., Yonkers, N.Y., Embossed, Round, Pt. 15.00
Deposit Dairylea, United States Patent Office, Qt. 8.00
Detwiler's Dairy, Long Level, Pa., Qt. 120.00
Diamond Milk Dairy Farms, For Mothers Who Care, Orange ACL, Tall, Qt. 20.00
Diamond's Cafeteria, Embossed, Round, Pt. 18.00
Dietrichs, Cream, Milk, Butter, ACL, Square, 1/2 Pt. 25.00
Dixie Dairies, Macon, Ga., Embossed, Short, Round, Qt. 18.00
Dufresne, Shrewsbury, Ma., Embossed, Round, 1918, 1/2 Pt. 15.00
Duncan's Dairy, Catskill, N.Y., Milk-Pioneers The Way To Health, 1965, Qt. 18.00
Dyke's Dairy, Youngsville, Warren, Pa., War Slogan, 1/2 Pt. 40.00
E.C. Earl Dairy Farm, Edward P. Dubricki, Kalamazoo, Mich., Embossed, Qt. 30.00
E.F. Mayer, Hullenbeck St., Amber Glass, Embossed, Round, Qt. 100.00
Earl Lapan's Dairy, South Burlington, Vt., ACL, Round, 1/2 Pt. 12.00
Edwin P. Hartsock Dairy, Duquoin, Il., Embossed, Pt. 18.00
El-Fre Nubian Goat Farm, Ebenezer, N.Y., Blue ACL, Square, Qt. 30.00
Elm Haven Farm, Real Guernsey Milk, Dunstable, Orange ACL, Round, 1/2 Pt. 35.00
Elmhurst Dairy, Shrewsbury, Ma., Embossed, Round, 1928, Qt. 20.00
Elmwood Farm, Hanover, Mass., Guernsey Milk, Orange ACL, Pt. .... 20.00 to 25.00
Embossed, Patent 1898, Tin Lid, Handle, Pt. 150.00
Empire State Dairy Co., Brooklyn, Registered Strictly Pure Milk, 1920, Qt., 9 In. 66.00
English's Dairy, Holbrook, Ma., Embossed, Round, Qt. 20.00
Eureka Cooperative Dairies, Eureka, Calif., Maroon ACL, Round, Qt. 139.00
Eureka Cooperative Dairies, Eureka, Calif., Orange ACL, Round, Qt. 32.00
Evans Amityville Dairy Inc., Amityville, LI, Orange ACL, Cream Top, Qt. 55.00
Eveleth Creamery, Eveleth, Minn., ACL, Cream Top, Qt. 45.00
F.A. Nerogic & Sons Buttermilk, Salamanca, N.Y., Dutch Girl, Orange, Green, White, Qt. 14.00
F.W. Elliott, Petersham, Mass., 2-Color ACL, Round, Qt. 45.00
F.W. Elliott, Petersham, Mass., Twin Farm Dairy, Black & Orange ACL, Qt. 26.00
F.W. White Lone Pine, Red ACL, Round, Qt. 25.00
Fairlea Farms, Red, Square, 1960, Qt. 16.00
Fairview Dairy, Lock Haven, Pa., Babyface, Pt. 125.00
Fairview Dairy, Lock Haven, Pa., Embossed, Babyface, Tall, 1/2 Pt. 175.00
Falkner Dairy, Henderson, N.C., Red ACL, Family Picture, Qt. 26.00
Farmers Dairy, Cumberland, Md., Yellow ACL, Round, Qt. 85.00
Farmers Dairy, Martinsburg, W.V., Embossed, Round, Qt. 35.00
Farmers Dairy, Portland, Oregon, Tall, Qt. 35.00
Farmers' Co-Op Inc., Hartford, Conn., Maroon ACL, Tall, Qt. 15.00
Fitzpatrick, Great Barrington, Embossed, Round, Qt. 20.00
Forest Lake Dairy, Palmer, Ma., Embossed, Cream Top, Pt. 10.00
Forest Lake Dairy, Palmer, Ma., Embossed, Cream Top, Round, Pt. 20.00
Forrest E. Mason, Lynn, Mass., Embossed, Pt. 18.00
Fort Lewis A&M College, Hesperus, Colorado, Red ACL, Round, Pt. 75.00
Franz Dairy Knox Clarion, Emlenton, Pa., ACL, Round, Qt. 45.00
Frasure & Brown Dairy, Logan, Oh., ACL, Square, Qt. 10.00
Frasure & Brown Dairy, Logan, Ohio, Chief Logan 2 Sides, Maroon ACL, Qt. 30.00

French Bros. Dairy Co., Ill., Embossed, Round, Pt. 50.00
Friend's Dairy Farm, Flint, Mich., Green ACL, Round, Qt. 15.00
Friendship Sanitary Dairy, Gloucester, N.J., Pt. 20.00
Frink, Serving Denver, Make America Strong, Eagle, Girl With Hoop, ACL, Round, Qt. .. 60.00
Fruit 'n' Brek, Try It Cold With Milk, Orange ACL, Pt. ....*Illus* 17.00
Fryes Dairy, Leominster, Mass., ACL, Babyface, Square, Qt. 75.00
Furman Bros., Ithaca, N.Y., ACL, Cop The Cream, Qt. 200.00
G. Rico, Cortez, Colo., Etched, Round, 1/2 Pt. 10.00
G.C. Kaufman, Kingston, N.Y., Embossed, Tin Top, Round, 1/2 Pt. 50.00
Gaffney Bros., Worcester, Ma., Clover Design, Embossed, Round, Qt. 20.00
Gaffney Bros., Worcester, Ma., Embossed, Round, 1928, Pt. 20.00
Gagnon's, Huron, S.D., ACL, Round, Qt. 45.00
Gail Borden, Amber Glass, Qt. 20.00
Gail Borden, Pet, Amber Glass, 1/2 Gal. 30.00
Gail Borden 's Eagle Brand, Borden Milk Co., Ltd., Embossed, Ribs, Round, Qt. 100.00
Gamelin's Dairy, Winookie, Vermont, ACL, Square, Qt. 15.00
Garden Farm Dairy, Denver, Colo., Polar Bear Ice Cream, 2 Color ACL, Round, Qt. 85.00
Gaylords Guernsey Farms, Oklahoma City, Okla., Embossed, Round, 1/3 Qt. 10.00
Gayoso Farms, Horn Lake, Miss., ACL, Round, Qt. 55.00
Gefke Dairy, Oregon, Wis., Black ACL, Qt. 26.00
Gendrons Dairy, Bedford, N.H., ACL, Round, 1/2 Pt. 35.00
Generic, Paper Carton, 1.5% Milkfat, 1/2 Gal. ....*Illus* 5.00
Genesee Valley Dairy, Mt. Morris, N.Y., 5 Cent Deposit, Blue ACL, Qt. 21.00
Geo. G. Gillingham, Meadow Brook Farm, Alexandria, Virginia, Embossed, Pt. 25.00
George Godin, Richfort, Vt., ACL, Round, Qt. 60.00
George W. Bryant, Worcester, Ma., Embossed, Round, 1927, Qt. 20.00
George's Dairy, Batavia, N.Y., ACL, Square, Qt. 25.00
Germantown Farms, Geo. M. Hackinson, Quincy, Mass., Embossed, 10 Oz. 15.00
Gesner & MacRorie, Heovelton, N.Y., Blue & Orange ACL, Round, Qt. 25.00
Gibbs Farm Dairy, Rochester, Mass., Embossed, Pt. 18.00
Giles Dairy, Franklin, N.H., Green ACL, Squat, Qt. 20.00
Giles Dairy, Franklin, N.H., Orange, Square, c.1960, Qt. 16.00
Gippy Plantation Dairy, Moncks Corners, S.C., Orange ACL, Round, 1/2 Pt. 20.00
Glemmie's Milk, From The Andovers Mass., Embossed, Seal, Qt. 30.00
Gold Medal Creamery, Medford, Oregon, Qt. 30.00
Golden Royal, Amber, Embossed, 1/2 Gal. 8.50
Goose Acres Hatch Jersey Milk Cream Supreme, Embossed, 1/2 Pt. 12.00
Green Meadow Dairy, Calumet City, Illinois, Embossed, Qt. 15.00
Greenhill Dairy, Wilmington, De., Embossed, Round, Qt. 35.00
Guernsey Dairy, Boise, Idaho, Idaho's Finest, Red & Green ACL, Qt. 316.00
Guernsey Farms, Waynesboro, Pa., ACL, Square, 1/2 Pt. 18.00
H & L Hometown Dairy, Keokuk, Ia., ACL, Round, Qt. 45.00

Milk, Fruit 'n' Brek, Try
It Cold With Milk,
Orange ACL, Pt.

Milk, Generic, Paper
Carton, 1.5% Milkfat,
1/2 Gal.

Milk, Kaste's Dairy, Milk
Is Nature's Most Perfect
Food, Red ACL, Qt.

Milk, Kysilka Dairy,
Red ACL,
Qt.

H.C. Dunn, Grove Cottage, Worcester, Ma., Embossed, Round, 1919, Qt. 25.00
H.E. Johnson, Rutland, Vermont, Amber Glass, White ACL, Qt. 25.00
H.E. Larrimore's Dairy, Seaford, De., ACL, Round, Qt. 50.00
H.P. Hood, Boston, Embossed, Round, 1941, Qt. 10.00
H.P. Hood & Sons, Boston, Sour Cream, Embossed, Round, 1/2 Pt. 10.00
H.P. Hood & Sons Dairy Experts, Red ACL, Round, 1/2 Pt. 45.00
Hall's Dairy, Millerstown, Pa., 5 Cent Deposit, Maroon ACL, Qt. 18.00
Hamden Creamery Co., Registered, ABM, Wire Closure, 1/2 Pt. 90.00
Hammond Dairy, Hammond, In., Embossed, Qt. 10.00
Hancock County Creamery, Ellsworth, Me., Black ACL, Qt. 30.00
Hancock County Creamery, Ellsworth, Me., Red, Black & White, Wax Cone, Qt. 15.00
Hanover Co-Op, Orange ACL, Round, Qt. 20.00
Harm's, Savannah, Ga., Green ACL, Qt. 30.00
Harney's Dairy, Embossed, Round, 1/2 Pt. 5.00
Harris Dairy, St. Joseph, Mo., ACL, Round, Squat, Qt. 30.00
Heiss & Sons Dairy, Rochelle Park, N.J., Barn Scene, Orange ACL, Qt. 20.00
Herlihy's Cream Milk, Orange ACL, Round, Qt. 28.00
Hickerson Dairy, Batesville, Arkansas, ACL, Round, Qt. 100.00
Hickerson Dairy, Batesville, Arkansas, Tall, Qt. ....20.00 to 75.00
Hicks Dairy, Albion, Mich., ACL, Round, 1/2 Pt. 5.00
Hidden Acres, Farming, Md., Orange, Square, Qt. 15.00
High Hill Farm, South Dartmouth, Ma., ACL, Round, 1/2 Pt. 35.00
Highland Farms Dairy, Washington, D.C., Farm Scene, Round, Green ACL, 1/2 Gal. 40.00
Highland Farms Dairy, Washington, D.C., Green ACL, Qt. 35.00
Highland View Farm, D.A. Swift, Blue ACL, Round, Qt. 30.00
Highview Farms Dairy, Norwichtown, Red ACL, Square, Qt. 25.00
Hillsboro Dairy, H.G. Martin, Black ACL, Round, Qt. 25.00
Hillside Farm Dairy, Winterton, Sul. Co., N.Y., Deep Blue Aqua, Gal. 2800.00
Hilo Dairymen's Center, Mickey Mouse On Reverse, 1/2 Pt. 63.00
Hilton Farm Dairy, Catonville, Md., Embossed, Round, Qt. 35.00
Hollywood Dairy, Durango, Colo., Cream Top, Embossed, Round, 1/2 Pt. 35.00
Homart's Riverside Dairy, Anadarko, Okla., Red ACL, Long Neck, Square, Qt. 12.00
Homecroft Dairy, Bessember, Pa., ACL, Round, Qt. 40.00
Homestead, Mill Hall, Pa., Cream Top, Pt. 35.00
Horlicks Trademark Malted Milk, Racine, Wi., 1/2 Pt. 40.00
Hycrest Tri City Farm, Orange ACL, Square, 1957, 1/2 Pt. 13.00
Ideal Dairy, Manistee, Mich., Black ACL, Round, Qt. 22.00
Ideal Farms Guernsey Products, North Haledon, NJ, Red ACL, Qt. 25.00
Independent Creamery, Chicago, Il., Embossed, Pt. 15.00
Independent Riviera Dairy, Santa Barbara, Cal., ACL, Round, Qt. 35.00
Indian Hill Farm, Charlton, Ma., Embossed, Round, Qt. 20.00
Indian Hill Farm Dairy, Greenville, Me., Indian Head, Orange ACL, Qt. 20.00
Isaac W. Rush, Brooklyn, N.Y., Gray Graniteware Lid, Qt. 225.00
J.C. Harbin, US 51 South Memphis, Tenn., ACL, Round, Qt. 20.00
J.H. Brokhoff, Pottsville, Pa., Buy War Bonds For Victory, Cream Top, Red ACL, Qt. 50.00
J.H. Brokhoff, Pottsville, Pa., Cream Top, Round, 1/2 Pt. 40.00
J.H. Brokhoff, Pottsville, Pa., Tumbling Run Park Dairy, Cream Top, Round, Qt. 35.00
J.H. Wilson & Sons, Detroit, Mich., Embossed, Round, Pt. 10.00
J.M. Stone, Bassett, Virginia, Embossed, 1/2 Pt. 36.00
J.M.P. Sanitary Dairy, Coaldale, Pa., Embossed, Round, Qt. 25.00
J.T. Jensen Mountain View Farm, Shrewsbury, Ma., Embossed, Round, 1918, Qt. 25.00
Jackson's Dairy, San Ysidro, Calif., Grade A Milk, Red ACL, Qt. 35.00
Jarosz Milk Co., Chicago, Il., Embossed, Pt. ....18.00 to 20.00
Jensen's Wayside Dairy, Shrewsbury, Ma., Embossed, Round, Pt. 20.00
Jersey Farm Dairy, Fresno, Ca., Embossed, Qt. 40.00
Joel Parson's, Hazleton, Pa., Cream Separator, Embossed, 1/2 Pt. 80.00
John T. Jensen Wayside Dairy, Shrewsbury, Ma., Embossed, Round, Qt. 20.00
John Zukawski's Dairy, East Stroudsburg, Pa., Embossed, Qt. 28.00
Jones Dairy Products, Red ACL, Square, 1/2 Qt. 32.00
Joppe's Dairy, Grand Rapids, Mich., Embossed, 1/2 Pt. 15.00
Julius Heretick Dairy, Hopewell, Va., Embossed, Round, Pt. 10.00
Kaiko Farm Dairy, Jewett City, Conn., Red ACL, Square, Qt. 15.00
Kane Dairy Co-Operative Ass'n., Embossed, Qt. 30.00

Karts Milk, Cheektowaga, N.Y., ACL, Round, 1/2 Pt. 25.00
Kaste's Dairy, Milk Is Nature's Most Perfect Food, Red ACL, Qt. ....*Illus* 18.00
Katahdin Creamery, Patten, Maine, Square, Red ACL, 1/2 Pt. 14.00
Kelowna Creamery Limited, Blue & Red, Shield, Globe, Round, Canada, Pt. 20.00
Kilfasset Farms, Passumpsic, ACL, Square, Qt. 10.00
King Bros. Dairy, Saratoga Springs, N.Y., Dutch Girl, Yellow ACL, Round, Qt. 42.00
Kingdon, Worcester, Ma., Embossed, Round, 1932, Qt. 25.00
Kinlogh Farm Dairy, Waugh Culpeper, Va., Round, Pt. 20.00
Kline Bros., Cumberland, Md., Embossed, Round, Pt. 15.00
Klondike Farm, Elkin, N.C., Green ACL, Qt. 23.00
Kruger Dairy, Carlisle, Pa., ACL, Round, Qt. 15.00
Kruger Dairy, Carlisle, Pa., Green ACL, Tall, Qt. 40.00
Kysilka Dairy, Red ACL, Qt. ....*Illus* 22.00
L.W. Moyle, Dalton, Pa., Square, Long Neck, Green & Maroon ACL, Qt. 28.00
Lackrone Dairy, Salem, Il., ACL, Round, Qt. 45.00
Lakeview Dairy, Davis Lake, North Dakota, Blue ACL, Round, 1/2 Gal. 65.00
Landels Grocery, Williamville, N.Y., Round, 1/2 Pt. 18.00
Landgren's Dairy, Kenosha, Wis., Red ACL, Cop The Top, Qt. 35.00
Landgren's Dairy, Kenosha, Wis., Red ACL, Cream Top, Square, Qt. 40.00
Lanes Dairy, Jackson, Miss., Embossed, Round, Tall, Qt. 45.00
Laneys Dairy, Skowhegan, Maine, Orange ACL, Square, Qt. 15.00
Lantz Bros., Follansbee, W. Va., Cream Separator, Embossed, Round, 1/2 Pt. 150.00
Lantz's Dairy Pasteurized Milk, St. Clairsville, Ohio, Round, Pt. 75.00
Lassig Dairy, Rhinelander, Wisc., ACL, Square, Qt. 15.00
Lawson Milk Co., Akron, O., Embossed, Qt. ....*Illus* 75.00
Leadbelt Dairy, Bonne Terre, Mo., ACL, Round, Qt. 45.00
Leake Bros., Dairy Fountain Inc., ACL, Stork, Round, 1/2 Pt. 18.00
Legg Dairy, Alpena, Mich., Orange ACL, Round, Qt. 22.00
Leiby's, Tamaqua, Pa., Square, Maroon ACL, Qt. 15.00
Lewes Dairy Inc., Red ACL, Square, Pt. 20.00
Lewis Farms, Salem, N.H., Round, 1/2 Pt. 35.00
Liberty Dairy Products, Jar, 1/2 Pt. 33.00
Liberty Milk Co., Inc., Buffalo, N.Y., Statue Of Liberty, Embossed, Round, Qt. 50.00
Lincoln Dairy Co., W Hartford, Conn., Square, Orange ACL, Qt. 18.00
Linder's Muskellunge View Dairy, Fremont, Ohio, Brown ACL, Square, Pt. 25.00
Linkside Dairy, Guelph, Only The Best, Orange ACL, Qt. 650.00
Lippincott's Dairy Products, E. Rochester, O., Maroon ACL, Pt. 75.00
Lippincott's Dairy Products, E. Rochester, O., Red ACL, Round, Pt. 65.00
Litchefield Dairy, Litchfield, Mich., 2-Color ACL, Round, Pt. 20.00
Little Joe's Dairy, J.B. Malowski, Herkimer, N.Y., Red ACL, Round, 1/2 Pt. 15.00
Lobdell's Dairy Inc., Fairfield, Conn., Gold ACL, Square, Qt. 20.00
Lunt's Dairy, Duncan, Arizona, Embossed, Qt. 50.00
M. Wason-MacDonald Co., Haverhill, Mass., ACL, Qt. 24.00
M.H. Williams Ayrshire Dairy, 4 Ayrshire Cows, ACL, Round, Qt. 45.00
M.P. Ararap Farms, Port Deposit, Maryland, Red ACL, Cream Top, Square, Qt. 24.00
M.S. Hakala, Boylston, Ma., Embossed, Etched, Round, 1905, Qt. 35.00
Mackworth Pure Jersey Cream, Mackworth Island, Me., Stoneware, Tin Top, 1/2 Pt. 845.00
Macomber Dairy, Round, Red ACL, 1/2 Pt. 30.00
Madden's Sunnymeade Dairy, ACL, Round, 1/2 Pt. 30.00
Malenfant's Guernsey Milk, Lewiston, Me., Red ACL, Square, Qt. 20.00
Maple Farms Dairy, Boston, Mass., Embossed, Round, Qt. 25.00
Maple Lane Dairy, There'll Always Be An England, Orange ACL, 1/2 Pt. 325.00
Maple Lane Dairy, Waterloo, 3 Men In Boat, Orange ACL, 1/2 Pt. 300.00
Maple Lawn Dairy, Plymouth, Mich., Red ACL, Square, Qt. 20.00
Maplecrest, Maynard, Green ACL, Square, Qt. 15.00
Marland K. Dairy, Cambridge, Orange ACL, Cap, Round, Qt. 60.00
Marland M. Deaett, East Providence, R.I., Orange ACL, Qt. 20.00
Marrotte's Dairy, Willimantic, Conn., Square, Long Neck, Red ACL, Qt. 20.00
Maui-Haleakala Dairy, Qt. 30.00
Maurer's Dairy, Shamokin, Pa., Orange ACL, Babyface, Qt. 150.00
McDonald's White House Dairy, ACL, 1/2 Pt. 21.00
Meadow Dairies, Buy War Bonds, Red ACL, Square, Qt. 34.00
Meadow Valley Stock Farm, Jewett, New Paltz, N.Y., Embossed, Pt. 20.00

Meadowsweet Dairies, Tacoma, Wa., Embossed, Round, Qt. 22.00
Meadowview Dairy, Johnsonville, Ca., Red ACL, Cap, Round, Qt. 130.00
Medlicott Dairy, N. Milford, Ma., Embossed, Round, 1928, 1/3 Qt. 15.00
Melroy Dairy, Stratford, Milk Truck & Drink Milk, Maroon ACL, Qt. 300.00
Melville, Burlington, N.C., Hoppy's Favorite, Hoppy On Topper, Red ACL, 1/2 Pt. 87.00
Meola, W. Boylston, Ma., Embossed, Square, 1/2 Pt. 5.00
Meyer's Blue Ridge, Ohio's Finest, Blue ACL, Qt. . . . .*Illus* 20.00
Miami County Diary Co., They Guard Your Home, We Guard Your Health, Red ACL, Pt. . 50.00
Mid Valley Farm Dairy, ACL, Square, 1/2 Pt. 10.00
Midland Creamery Co., Colorado Springs, Co., ACL, Round, Pt. 40.00
Midwest Dairy, St. Louis, Mo., War Slogan, ACL, Round, Qt. 65.00
Millen's Dairy, Watkins Glen, N.Y., Red ACL, Round, Qt. 35.00
Miller's Dairy, Frank B. Miller, Watkins Glen, N.Y., Red ACL, Round, Qt. 35.00
Minges Dairy, Wellsville, N.Y., Orange ACL, Dimpled Glass, Cap, Square, Qt. 20.00
Model Dairy, Corry, Pa., Green ACL, Qt. 28.00
Model Dairy, Pittsfield, Ma., Embossed, Round, 7 Oz. 15.00
Model Dairy, Pueblo, Colo., Golden Cream, Barn, Orange ACL, Qt. 40.00
Mohawk Farms, Newington, Conn., Amber, Indian, Product, Yellow ACL, Square 15.00
Mohawk Farms, Staten Island, N.Y., Indian, Embossed, Round, Qt. 50.00
Mojonnier Test Bottles, Chicago, Ill., 8 Oz. 10.00
Mortensen's Creamery, Red ACL, Round, Qt. . . . . .28.00 to 30.00
Mountain Home Creamery, Lakeport, Calif., Yellow ACL, Qt. 35.00
Mrs. J.J. Evans, Maxton, N.C., Embossed, Pt. 20.00
Mutual Milk Company, Indianapolis, Embossed, Round, Pt. 10.00
Nagel's Dairy Inc., Buffalo, N.Y., Embossed, Qt. 22.00
Nakoma Farms, Brighton, N.Y., Circle K, Milk Can, Guernsey, Bar, Orange ACL, Qt. . . . 18.00
National Dairy, Honolulu, Hawaii, Red ACL, Qt. 65.00
Natoma Farm, Hinsdale, Ill., Orange ACL, Round, Qt. 24.00
Natuella's, Hazelton, Pa., Cop The Cream, Pt. 55.00
Natuella's, Hazelton, Pa., Embossed, Cop The Cream, Qt. 55.00
Newsom's Pride Dairy, Albany, Georgia, Boxer Figure, Black ACL, Pt. 20.00
Newton Farm Dairy, Ellicott City, Md., Embossed, Round, Qt. 35.00
Niagara District, N.Y., Embossed, Round, 1/2 Pt. 15.00
None Such Goat Milk, Farm Scene, Rt. 114, So. Sutton, N.H., Black ACL, Square, Qt. . . . 25.00
North Yarmouth Dairy, N. Yarmouth, Maine, Orange ACL, Qt. 15.00
Northwestern Dairy, A. Miller, Portland, Or., Embossed, Round, Qt. 38.00
Noyes, H.R, Red ACL, Babyface, Square, Qt. 75.00
Nutgrove Farm Dairy, Paul H. Lengel, Pine Grove, Emblem, Stain, Qt. 250.00
O.K. Dairy, Canon City, Colo., ACL, Round, Qt. 45.00
Oahu-Moanaloa Dairy, 12 Oz. 12.00
Oak Grove Dairy, Windsor, N.C., Embossed, Round, Qt. 30.00
Oak Park Dairy, Eau Claire, Wis., Embossed, 1/2 Pt. 12.00
Oakland Central Creamery, Red ACL, Round, Qt. 34.00
Oakland Dairy Johnston Bros., Embossed Imperial, Pt. 20.00
Oneonta Dairy Company, Oneonta, N.Y., ACL, Qt. 24.00
Oneonta Dairy Company, Oneonta, N.Y., Orange ACL, Cream Top, Square, Qt. 29.00
Orchard Farm Dairy, Ayrshire Milk, Dallas, Pa., Red ACL, Cop The Top, Qt. 75.00
Orchard Farm Dairy, Dallas, Pa., Red ACL, Cop The Top, Square, Qt. 130.00
Orchard Farm Dairy, Orchard Farm, Dallas, Pa., ACL, Cop The Top, Squat, Qt. 100.00
Orofino Creamery Co., Orofino, Idaho, Red ACL, Qt. 89.00
Palen Sani-Pure Dairy, Nowata, OK, Embossed, Round, Qt. 50.00
Palm Dairies Ltd., Cream Of Them All, Palm Tree, Cottage, Red ACL, Round, 1/2 Pt. . . . 95.00
Palm Dairy, Couple Dancing, Canada, Red & Green ACL, Round, 1/2 Pt. 40.00
Parkers, Nichols, Conn., Square, Orange ACL, Rhyme On Back, Qt. 25.00
Parkside Dairy, East Rochester, N.Y., Amber, Yellow ACL, Square 18.00
Peapack Gladstone Dairy, Embossed, Round, Qt. 15.00
Pecora's, Hazleton, Pa., Baby Sitting On World, Red ACL, Babyface, 1/2 Pt. 75.00
Pecora's, Hazleton, Pa., Pecordale Farms, Red ACL, Babyface, 1/2 Pt. 90.00
Penn Acres Dairy, Ainsworth, Neb., ACL, Round, Qt. 45.00
Peoples Milk Co., 7078 E. Ferry St., Buffalo, N.Y., Amber, Bowling Pin, Tin Top, Qt. . . . 175.00
Pet Milk Co., ACL, Round, Qt. 30.00
Petersburg Creamery, Petersburg, Ohio, Embossed, Qt. 22.00
Pine Creek Farm, Barre Plains, Mass., Embossed, Tin Top, Round, 1/2 Pt. 75.00

| Milk, Lawson Milk Co., Akron, O., Embossed, Qt. | Milk, Meyer's Blue Ridge, Ohio's Finest, Blue ACL, Qt. | Milk, Reiter & Harter, All Star Dairies, ACL, 1/2 Gal. | Milk, Schneider, Little Boy Blue Is Healthy & Gay, He Drinks Milk Every Day, ACL, Qt. |

Pine Grove Dairy, Skaneateles, N.Y., Pine Trees, Green, Orange ACL, Round, Qt. . . .22.00 to 25.00
Pine Ridge Farm, Lowell, Mass., Maroon ACL, Qt. 20.00
Pine State Dairy, Bangor, Me., Green & Orange ACL, Square, Qt. 15.00
Pine State Dairy, Bangor, Me., Green ACL, Babyface, Qt. 65.00
Pinewood Dairy, Flagstaff, Ariz., Past. Milk, House, Orange ACL, Qt. 35.00
Pittsfield Milk Exchange, Pittsfield, Ma., Embossed, Cream Top, Round, Qt. 25.00
Plains Dairy, Valley Falls, R.I., Red ACL, Qt. 15.00
Pleasant Dairy, Lewiston, Maine, Red & Yellow ACL, Square, Qt. 22.00
Pleasant View Dairy, A.W. Croscut & Sons, Sherman, N.Y., Red ACL, Pt. 18.00
Pomeroy, Round, Orange ACL, 1/2 Pt. 30.00
Port Hope City Dairy, Steaming Coffee Cup, Canada, Orange ACL, Round, 1/2 Pt. 50.00
Portland Dairy, Portland, Me., Embossed Store, Qt. 25.00
Producer's Dairy, Red ACL, Pt. 10.00
Pure Milk Corporation Limited, Hamilton, Ont., Amber, Slug Plate, Round, Qt. 210.00
Pure Milk Corporation Limited, Red Amber, Embossed, Slug Plate, BIMAL, Qt. 45.00
Putnam's Dairy, Ilion, N.Y., Horse, Wagon, Milkman, Maroon ACL, Qt. 24.00
Putnam's Dairy, Ilion, N.Y., Pirate, Treasure Chest, Buy Bonds Today, Maroon ACL, Qt. . . 42.00
Qualitee, San Diego, Ca., Brown ACL, Round, Qt. 29.00
Quality Coughlin Dairy, Pierre, S.D., ACL, Round, Qt. 60.00
Quality Dairy W. Fudge, El Dorado, Ark., Embossed, Round, Qt. 30.00
Rathgeb's Dairy, Greensburg, Pa., Orange ACL, Pt. 18.00
Raw Goat Milk, Earth-Bound Foods, Sandy Hook, Conn., Orange, Brown ACL, Square, Qt. 25.00
Ray's Crystal Dairy, New York City, Maroon ACL, Round, Qt. 22.00
Redford Farm, D. Cardillo, Stockbridge, Mass., ACL, Round, Qt. 35.00
Reiter & Harter, All Star Dairies, ACL, 1/2 Gal. . . . . *Illus* 17.00
Return To H.B. Day, Grass Green, Embossed, 10 1/4 In. 198.00
Rhoades Dairy, Asheville, N.C., Embossed, Round, Qt. 35.00
Rices Dairy Benzie County, Benzonia, Mi., ACL, Round, Qt. 45.00
Richmond Dairy, Toothache, Embossed, Squat, Qt. 100.00
Rickers Dairy Inc., Milo, Me., Round, 1/2 Pt. 35.00
Rider Dairy, Danbury, Conn., ACL, Cream Top, Square, Qt. 5.00
Ridge Brook Guernsey Farms, Embossed, Round, Qt. 5.00
Riverdale Supreme Dairy, Salamanca, N.Y., ACL, Qt. 22.00
Riverside Dairy, Haverhill, Mass., Scroll & Saying, Maroon ACL, Embossed Seal, Qt. . . . 21.00
Riverside Dairy Inc., Nicoll Bros., N.Y., Embossed, 1/3 Qt. 14.00
Riverview Farms, Frankfort, Ky., ACL, Round, Pt. 18.00
Roberts Dairy, Embossed, Round, Qt. 40.00
Rock Castle Dairy, Lynchbury, Va., Farm Picture, Green ACL, Qt. 22.00
Roger Jessup Farms, Red ACL, Qt. 11.00
Rogers Rogue River Ranch, Cap, 1950, 8 1/2 In. 150.00
Roselawn Dairy, Guelph, Owl On Reverse, Red ACL, Pt. 375.00
Rosendahl Guernsey Farms, Hoosick Falls, N.Y., J.E. Calhoun & Sons, Orange ACL, Qt. . 20.00

Ross Bros., Worcester, Ma., Embossed, Round, 1/2 Pt. 12.00
Ross Bros., Worcester, Ma., Embossed, Round, 1914, Pt. 20.00
Ross Dairy & Ice Cream Co. Safe Milk, Slug Plate, Stained, Qt. 20.00
Rossingaris Dairy, Waterville, Me., Orange ACL, Round, 1/2 Pt. 35.00
Rossley's Dairy, Leicester, Ma., Brown ACL, Round, Qt. 22.00
Rothermel's Dairy, Minersville, Pa., Cream Separator, Embossed, Round, Pt. 125.00
Rothermel's Dairy, Minersville, Pa., Cream Separator, Embossed, Round, Qt. 100.00
Rothermel's Dairy, Minersville, Pa., Embossed, Cream Separator, Indented Side, Qt. 75.00
Round Hill Dairy, Mt. Vernon, Ohio, ACL, Round, Qt. 65.00
Round Hill Dairy, Mt. Vernon, Ohio, Tall, Qt. 35.00
Round Hill Farm, Greenwich, Conn., Orange ACL, Square, Qt. .... .20.00 to 25.00
Royce Blacks Dairy, Matthews, N.C., Embossed, Round, Pt. 15.00
S. Medlinsky Store, Worcester, Ma., Embossed, Round, 1924, Qt. 20.00
Salem Dairy, Shaklefords, Va., Green ACL, Round, 1/2 Pt. 50.00
Salois Sanitary Dairy, Orange ACL, Pt. 60.00
Sanitary Dairy, Chisholm, Maine, Cream Top, Orange ACL, Qt. 45.00
Sanitary Dairy, Fort Dodge, Ia., ACL, Cream Top, Round, Qt. 35.00
Sanitary Dairy, Healdsburg, Calif., Orange ACL, Cap, Round, Qt. 35.00
Sanitary Dairy Company, Muskegon, 1/2 Pt. 5.00
Sawyer Farms, Gilford, N.H., ACL, Babyface, Round, Qt. 125.00
Schneider, Little Boy Blue Is Healthy & Gay, He Drinks Milk Every Day, ACL, Qt. .*Illus* 18.00
Schwenk Dairy, Southampton, L.I., Deposit, Embossed, Maroon ACL, Qt. 18.00
Sealon Hood, Goldsmith, ACL, Square, 1/2 Pt. 10.00
Seward Dairy, Seward, Alaska, Round, Qt. 143.00
Signor's Dairy, Keeseville, N.Y., Blue ACL, Qt. 60.00
Sistersville Dairy, Sistersville, WV, Embossed, Pt. 25.00
Snider's Grade Milk, Medford, Oregon, Black ACL, Qt. 32.00
Souris Valley Creamery, Estevan, Sask., Blue Crest, Banner, Round, Qt. 65.00
Souris Valley Creamery, Estevan, Sask., Red Crest, Banner, Round, Qt. 56.00
Southern Dairy Farm, Tuscaloosa, Ala., ACL, Round, Qt. 70.00
Southern Vermont 50th Anniversary 1945-1995, Dairy Goat Assoc., Green ACL, Qt. ... 30.00
Southside Dairy, Oneonta, N.Y., Large Tree, ACL, Round, Qt. 40.00
Spencer Farms, Hiram, O., Embossed, 1/2 Pt. 10.00
Spurlin, Carlsbad, N.M., Orange ACL, Tall, Square, Pt. 14.00
St. Elizabeth's Hospital, Washington, D.C., Embossed, Round, Qt. 100.00
St. Jacob's Dairy, Good Morning, Black ACL, Qt. 650.00
Stambauch's Dairy, Carlisle, Pa., Embossed, Round, Qt. 15.00
Statton's Dairy, Ellensburg, Wis., Black ACL, Qt. 35.00
Steeds Dairy Products, Logan, Utah, ACL, Round, 1/2 Pt. 25.00
Stephens Bros. Dairy, Carbondale, Pa., Embossed, Round, Pt. 25.00
Stephens Bros. Dairy, Carbondale, Pa., Embossed, Round, Qt. 20.00
Store Bottle, 5¢, Embossed, 1/2 Pt. ....*Illus* 40.00
Strickler's, Huntingdon, Pa., ACL, Qt. 20.00
Suncrest Farms & Mowrer's, Inc., ACL, 1/2 Pt. 26.00
Sunny Acres Farm, Chepachet, R.I., John Mann, Orange ACL, Square, Qt. 25.00
Sunny Brook Farm, Alhambra, Ca., ACL, Round, 1/2 Pt. 15.00
Sunrise Dairy, Gastonia, N.C., Boy Carrying Bottle, Square, 1951, Qt. 16.00

**If you live in an old house and the locks are
old, check the new types. There have been
many improvements, and new locks provide
much better security.**

Milk, Store Bottle, 5¢,
Embossed, 1/2 Pt.

Sunshine Dairy, Men Like These Defend A Nation, Green, Pt. 500.00
Superior Dairy, Martinsburg, W. Va., ACL, Square, 1/2 Pt. 20.00
Supreme, Alliance, Ohio, Embossed, Round, 1/2 Pt. 5.00
Supreme Dairy, La Salla, Peru, Oglesky, Ill, Blue ACL, Tall, Qt. 40.00
Sweet's Dairy, Fredonia, N.Y., ACL, Cop The Top, Qt. 200.00
Swiss Goat Milk Dairy, Large Goat, Garfield 555, Red, White, Blue, Wax Cone, Qt. 20.00
Sykes Farms, Canton, N.Y., Large Baseball Player, Red ACL, Qt. 32.00
T.E. Cromey Dairy, Clymer, N.Y., Baby Reaching For Bottle, Maroon ACL, Qt. 22.00
T.R. Wentzell, Worcester, Ma., Embossed, Big W Logo, Round, 1926, Qt. 20.00
Tampa Stock Farm, Tampa, Fla., Embossed, Pt. 18.00
Tarbells Guernsey Farms, Smithville Flats, N.Y., Embossed, Round, 1/2 Pt. 25.00
Taskett Farms, Watertown, N.Y., Red ACL, Round, Qt. 20.00
Thatcher, Absolutely Pure Milk, Man Milking A Cow, Embossed, Qt. 300.00
The Milk Plant, Brattleboro, Vt., Embossed, Pt. 18.00
Thompson's Double Malted Milk, 9 1/2 In. 210.00
Tideys Home Dairy, Eau Claire, Mich., Red ACL, Round, Qt. 15.00
Tilton Dairy, Asbury Park, N.J., Embossed, Round, Qt. 35.00
Titusville Dairy Products, Pa., First Line Of Health Defense, Red, Black ACL, Round, Qt. 65.00
Townsend's Dairy, Methuen, Mass., Maroon ACL, Tall, Qt. 20.00
Turner Center Creamery, Maine, Embossed, Round, 1/2 Pt. 15.00
Turner Center Creamery, Maine, Embossed, Round, Qt. 20.00
Tyoga Farms Dairy, Bulk Milk Truck, ACL, Square, Qt. 15.00
U.W., University Of Wyoming, Yellow & Brown ACL, 1/2 Pt. 45.00
Ucker Dairy, Logan, Ohio, Green ACL, Tall, Qt. 40.00
Ulsh-Shinket, HDW Co., Calif., Qt. 30.00
United Dairies, Cedar Rapids, Iowa, Embossed, 1/2 Pt. 15.00
United Dairy System, Cream Top, Embossed, Round, 1/2 Pt. 10.00
Univ. Of Fla., ACL, Round, Qt. 350.00
Univ. Of Maryland, Embossed, ACL, Round, 1/2 Pt. 2090.00
Universal Store Bottle, 5 Cent, Embossed, Round, 1/2 Pt. 5.00
Universal Store Bottle, 5 Cent, Embossed, Round, Qt. 5.00
Upton's Farm, Bridgewater, Mass., Embossed, Black ACL, Babyface, Round, Pt. 75.00
Valley Bell Ice Cream, Red ACL, Round, 1/2 Pt. 12.00
Van's Dairy, Hudson, N.Y., Maroon ACL, Cream Top, Square, Qt. 22.00
Vermillion Dairy, Louisiana, Square, Gal. 35.00
Victor Lucas, Grafton, W.V., Embossed, Round, Qt. 25.00
Vincennes Milk & Ice Cream Co., Tip Top Creamery, Vincennes, Ind., Amber Glass, Qt. . 175.00
Vinyl Dairy, Thomaston, Maine, 2 Poems, Yellow & Black ACL, Square, Qt. 30.00
Vita-Rich Goat Milk, Phoenix, Arizona, Amber Glass, White ACL, Square, Qt. 35.00
W. Weckerle & Sons Inc., Dairies, Buffalo, N.Y., Amber Glass, Qt. 90.00
W.H. Chamberlain, Shrewsbury, Ma., Embossed, Round, 1/2 Pt. 20.00
W.H. Chamberlain, Shrewsbury, Ma., Embossed, Round, 1925, Qt. .... 20.00 to 30.00
W.H. Chamberlain, Shrewsbury, Ma., Embossed, Round, 1926, Pt. 20.00
W.M. Stimson, Worcester, Ma., Embossed, Round, Pt. 20.00
Walter Neilly Co., Cream Top, Round, Pt. 35.00
Walthours Dairy, Greensburg, Pa., Multicolored, ACL, Round, Qt. 75.00
Wana Dairy Farms, Turner Wescott, Orange ACL, Square, Qt. 20.00
Wason MacDonald, Haverhill, Mass., Orange ACL, Qt. 25.00
Wauregan Co. Farm, Wauregan, Conn., Emblem, Pt. 20.00
Wauregan Dairy, W.T. Burn's, Red & Black ACL, Cream Top, Round, Qt. 75.00
WAWA Dairy, Flower Embossed, Cap, 1/2 Pt. 10.00
Weaver Quality Blue Ribbon, Carmel, In., Embossed, Short, Round, Qt. 14.00
Welky's Heights Dairy, Hazleton, Pa., Embossed, Pt. 25.00
Wendt's, On Bulb, Deposit, Red ACL, Cream Top, Square, Qt. 25.00
West Branch Reichards, Nilton, Pa., Cop The Cream, Qt. 200.00
White Belt Dairy, Miami, Fl., Embossed, Short, Round, Qt. 18.00
White Farms, Ipswich, Mass., Golden Guernsey, Red ACL, Long Neck, Square, Qt. 12.00
White's Farm Dairy, Babyface, Red & Yellow ACL, Square, Qt. 75.00
Whiting & Sons, Boston, Embossed, Pt. 18.00
Whiting Milk Cos., Boston, Embossed, Round, 1924, Qt. 10.00
Whiting Milk Cos., Boston, Embossed, Round, 1926, 1/2 Pt. 10.00
Whiting Milk Cos., Boston, Embossed, Round, Pt. 10.00
Wildasin Farms Dairy, Hanover, Pa., Embossed, Qt. 25.00

Willow Farms, Maryland, Red ACL, Cream Top, Square, Qt. 25.00
Wilson Creamery, Detroit, Mich., Embossed, Round, Pt. 15.00
Wilson-MacDonald Co., Haverhill, Mass., Orange ACL, Tall, Qt. 15.00
Winchester Creamery, Winchester, Va., ACL, Round, 1/2 Pt. 40.00
Winona, Winona Lake, Ind., ACL, Round, Qt. 95.00
Wm. E. Hemming, Embossed, Whitesboro, N.Y., Tin Lid 45.00
Wm. M. Evans & Son, Brooklyn, N.Y., Embossed, Tall, Round, Qt. 40.00
Wolcott's Dairy, Brocton, N.Y., Baby Sitting On Globe, ACL, Qt. 24.00
Woodrow Wilson Dairy, Palmyria, Wisc., Embossed, Pt. 10.00
Worden's, Waterbury, Ct., Embossed, Round, Pt. 20.00
Worthmore Ice Cream Co., Lakeworth, Fla., Embossed, 5 Cent Deposit, Qt. 30.00
Wykoff Dairy, Vacaville, Calif., Red ACL, Round, Qt. 30.00
Your Dairy New London, Wi., Red ACL, Qt. 10.00

―――――――――――――――― MILK GLASS ――――――――――――――――

It makes perfect sense to think that white milk-colored glass is known as *milk glass* to collectors. But not all milk glass is white, nor is all white glass milk glass, so the name may cause a little confusion.

The first true milk glass was produced in England in the 1700s. It is a semi-opaque glass, often with slight blue tones. The glass reached the height of its popularity in the United States about 1870. Many dishes and bottles were made. Both new versions of old styles and new styles have been made continuously since that time, many by the Westmoreland and the Kemple glass companies. These pieces, many very recent, often appear at antiques sales.

Westmoreland Glass Company worked from 1890 to 1984. In the early years, they made figural milk glass bottles to hold food products, especially mustard. Later they made reproductions of earlier pieces of tableware. Today it is considered correct to talk about blue milk glass or black milk glass. This is glass made by the same formula but with a color added. It is not correct to call a glass that is white only on the surface *milk glass.* Bottles made of milk glass may also be found in this book in the Cologne, Cosmetic, and Figural categories. There is a newsletter for collectors, The Original Westmoreland Glass Collector's Newsletter, P.O. Box 143, North Liberty, IA 52317.

Armour & Company, Chicago, Flattened Ladies Leg, 8 1/2 In. 45.00
Blue Swirls, Square, Chamfered Corners, Tooled Lip, Pewter Screw Cap, Pontil, 6 1/2 In. 1008.00
E.N. Lightner & Co., Detroit, Mich., Cylindrical, Stopper, 7 1/2 In. 60.00
Enamel Flowers, Applied Pewter Collar, c.1850, 5 1/2 In. 415.00
Hagan's Magnolia Balm Milk Glass, BIMAL, 5 In. 25.00
Jar, Ext. Tartar, Green, Gold Label, 7 1/2 In. 253.00
Quilt, Embossed Men & Women Busts, 4 Panels, Pontil, 10 1/4 In. 357.00
Spirits, Opalescent, Flowers, Rectangular, Beveled, 1735, 5 In. 605.00
Trylon & Perisphere, World's Fair, 1939 .... 8.00

―――――――――――――――― MINERAL WATER ――――――――――――――――

Although today it is obvious which is soda water and which is mineral water, the difference was not as clear in the nineteenth and early-twentieth centuries. Mineral water bottles held the fresh natural spring waters favored for health or taste. Even though some had a distinct sulfur or iron taste, the therapeutic values made them seem delicious. Some mineral waters had no carbonation, but many were naturally carbonated. Soda water today is made with artificial carbonation and usually has added flavor.

Mineral water was mentioned by the ancient Greeks, and the Romans wrote about visiting the famous springs of Europe. Mineral springs were often the center of resorts in nineteenth-century America, when it was fashionable to "take the waters." Often the water from the famous springs was bottled to be sold to visitors. Most of the mineral water bottles collected today date from the 1850-1900 period. Many of these bottles have embossed lettering and blob tops. The standard shape was cylindrical with thick walls to withstand the pressure of carbonation. Most were made in a snap case mold although a few can be found with open or iron pontils. Common colors are clear, pale aqua, and light green. More unusual are dark green, black, and amber bottles, while cobalt blue ones are rare. The bottles were sealed with a cork. A few places, like Poland Springs and Ballston Spa, made figural bottles. Related bottles may be found in the Seltzer and Soda categories.

A.P. Almaden Vichy Water, California, Green, Monogram, Pt. 1760.00

A.W. Cudworth & Co., San Francisco, Green, IP, 7 3/8 In. 176.00
A.W. Rapp, New York, Sapphire Blue, Sloping Collar, IP, Pt. 413.00
Adirondack Springs, Westport, N.Y., Emerald Green, Qt. 175.00
Alburgh A Springs, Vt., Olive Yellow, Ring Collar, Qt. 193.00
Alburgh A Springs, Yellow Amber, Qt. 715.00
Artesian Spring Co., AS, Ballston Spa, Lithia, Emerald Green, Pt. 120.00
Artesian Spring Co., AS, Ballston, N.Y., Blue Green, 1865-1875, Pt. 165.00
Artesian Spring Co., AS, Ballston, N.Y., Yellow Green, Pt. 150.00
Artesian Spring Co., Ballston Spa, N.Y., Emerald Green, Pt. 168.00
Artesian Spring Co., Ballston Spa, N.Y., Green, Pt. 170.00
Artesian Spring Co., Olive Yellow, 1865-1875, Pt. 112.00
Avon Spring Water, Amber, Sloping Double Collar, Qt. 1735.00
Avon Spring Water, C.H. Nowlen, Avon, N.Y., Blue Aqua, 1875, Pt. 687.00
Avon Spring Water, C.H. Nowlen, Avon, N.Y., Emerald Green, Pt. 1456.00
B & G Superior, San Francisco, Cobalt Blue, 10-Sided, Applied Top, Graphite Pontil 170.00
B & G Superior, San Francisco, Cobalt Blue, IP, 6 5/8 In. 690.00
B.R. Lippincott & Co., Stockton, Cobalt Blue, IP, 7 1/4 In. 1100.00
Benecia, Aqua, IP 220.00
Benecia, Blue, IP 165.00
Blount Springs, Natural Sulphur Water, Cobalt Blue, Cylindrical, Qt. 209.00
Blue Lick Water, Stanton & Pierce, Ky., Olive Amber, 10 In. 1700.00
Blue Lick Water Co., Ky., Deep Chocolate Amber, IP, 1855, Pt. .... 660.00 to 825.00
Bolen Waack & Co., New York, Emerald Green, 6 3/4 In. 99.00
Boonville Mineral Spring, Boonville, N.Y., Amber, Hutchinson, 7 In. 784.00
Boyd & Beard, Green, 6 3/4 In. 105.00
Brennan & Graham, Steubenville O, Aqua, IP, 7 1/4 In. 200.00
Brockville Mineral Water Co., F.M. Pilgrim, Aqua Green, Blob Top, 1890, Qt. 45.00
Buffalo Lithia, Teal Blue, Applied Mouth, 1880-1890, 1/2 Gal. ....*Illus* 253.00
Byron Acid Spring Water, Emerald Green, IP, Pt. 3472.00
Byron Acid Spring Water, Emerald Green, IP, Qt. 2912.00
C. Cleminshaw, Troy, N.Y., Sapphire Blue, 1845, 7 In. 88.00
C. Johnson Phoenix, South Africa 53.00
C.F. Freeman, Buffalo, N.Y., Chocolate Amber, IP, 6 1/2 In. 1870.00
Caledonia Spring, Wheelock, Vt., Amber, Qt. 550.00
Campbell Mineral Spring Co., Burlington, Vt., Aqua, Qt 935.00
Carl H. Schultz, N.Y., Blue Green, Pt. 743.00
Champion Spouting Spring, Saratoga, N.Y., Amber, Double Collar, Pt. 413.00
Champion Spouting Spring, Saratoga, N.Y., Aqua, 1865-1875, Pt. 221.00
Champion Spouting Spring, Saratoga, N.Y., Aqua, Applied Mouth, Pt. 300.00
Champion Spouting Spring, Saratoga, N.Y., CSS Co. On Reverse, Aqua, Pt. 61.00
Chase & Co., San Francisco, Cal., Dark Green, ISP, IP, 1855 .... 150.00
Chase & Co., San Francisco, Cal., Emerald Green, Cylindrical, 1850s 190.00
Chase & Co., San Francisco, Cal., Emerald Green, IP, 7 1/4 In. 303.00
Chase & Co., San Francisco, Cal., Green, ISP, IP, 7 3/4 In. .... 165.00 to 190.00
Chase & Co., San Francisco, Stockton & Marysville, Cal., Emerald, Case, 1850s 325.00
Chase & Co., San Francisco, Stockton & Marysville, Cal., Green .... 325.00 to 550.00
Chase & Co., San Francisco, Stockton & Marysville, Cal., Green, Pontil 413.00
Chemung Spring Water, Indian At Spring, Rocks, Gold Yellow Amber, 1/2 Gal. 660.00
Chemung Spring Water, Indian At Well, Rocks, Trees, Embossed, 12 1/2 In. 45.00
Chemung Spring Water, Trade Mark, Blue Aqua, 1/2 Gal., 11 3/4 In. 77.00
Chippewa Spring Water, Aqua, Metal Closure, Stopper, 11 In. .... 220.00 to 275.00
Clarke & Co., New York, Blue Green, IP, 1860, Pt. 231.00
Clarke & Co., New York, Emerald Green, Double Collar, 1855-1875, Pontil, Pt. 132.00
Clarke & Co., New York, Emerald Green, Sloping Double Collar, Pontil, Qt. 88.00
Clarke & Co., New York, Olive Amber, Applied Double Collar, Pontil, Pt. 78.00
Clarke & Co., New York, Olive Green, Double Collar, Cylindrical, 1850-1860, Pt. 187.00
Clarke & Co., New York, Olive Yellow, Bubbles 55.00
Clarke & Co., New York, Teal Blue, Applied Mouth, IP, Pt. ....*Illus* 246.00
Clarke & White, C, New York, Emerald, Rosedown 40.00
Clarke & White, C, New York, Olive Green, Rolled Lip 9240.00
Clarke & White, C, New York, Olive Green, Sloping Double Collar, Qt. 83.00
Clarke & White, C, New York, Olive Yellow Amber, Qt. 35.00
Clarke & White, Emerald Green, 1 On Base, Pt. 77.00

Clarke & White, New York, Emerald Green	100.00
Clarke & White, New York, Emerald Green, Sloping Double Collar, Pt.	90.00
Clarke & White, New York, Forest Green, 1860-1870, Cylindrical, Qt.	40.00
Clarke & White, New York, Green	33.00
Clarke & White, New York, Light Green, Pt.	33.00
Clarke & White, New York, Medium To Deep Olive Yellow, Pontil, Qt.	110.00
Clarke & White, New York, Olive Green	55.00
Clarke & White, New York, Olive Green, Applied Mouth, Pontil, Pt.	132.00
Clarke & White, New York, Olive Green, Ball Type Pontil	66.00
Clarke & White, New York, Olive Green, Double Collar, 1875, Cylindrical, Pt.	60.00
Clarke & White, New York, Olive Yellow Green, Pontil, Qt.	121.00
Clarke & White, New York, Olive Yellow, Ring Mouth, Pontil, Pt.	336.00
Clarke & White, New York, Olive, Rosedown, Pt.	60.00
Clarke & White, Olive Amber, Pontil, Qt.	175.00
Clarke & White, Yellow Green, Pt.	77.00
Cleminshaw, Troy, N.Y., Aqua, 8-Sided, Blob Top, 1870, 7 1/4 In.	77.00
Cloverdale Lithia Water, Harrisburg, Pa., Jug, Cobalt Blue, Gal.	160.00
Cold Indian Spring Water Co., Blue Aqua, Stopper, Gal., 12 3/8 In.	55.00
Congress & Empire Spring Co., Amber, Ring Collar, 1860-1880, Qt.	357.00
Congress & Empire Spring Co., C, Saratoga, N.Y., Blue Green, Pt.	633.00
Congress & Empire Spring Co., C, Saratoga, N.Y., Blue Green, Qt.	61.00
Congress & Empire Spring Co., C, Saratoga, N.Y., Emerald Green, Pt.	468.00
Congress & Empire Spring Co., E, Saratoga, N.Y., Olive Green, Pt.	182.00
Congress & Empire Spring Co., E, Saratoga, N.Y., Red Amber, Ring, Qt.	303.00
Congress & Empire Spring Co., Emerald Green, 1865-1875, Qt.	112.00
Congress & Empire Spring Co., Emerald Green, Applied Double Collar, 1870	55.00
Congress & Empire Spring Co., Forest Green, Pt.	44.00
Congress & Empire Spring Co., Hotchkiss' Sons, C, Emerald Green, Pt.	90.00
Congress & Empire Spring Co., Hotchkiss' Sons, C, Emerald Green, Qt.	224.00
Congress & Empire Spring Co., Hotchkiss' Sons, C, New York, Amber, Pt.	385.00
Congress & Empire Spring Co., Hotchkiss' Sons, C, New York, Emerald Green, Qt.	83.00
Congress & Empire Spring Co., Hotchkiss' Sons, C.W., Olive Green, 1/2 Pt.	330.00
Congress & Empire Spring Co., Hotchkiss' Sons, E, New York, Gold Amber, Pt.	165.00
Congress & Empire Spring Co., Hotchkiss' Sons, E, New York, Olive Yellow, Pt.	633.00
Congress & Empire Spring Co., Hotchkiss' Sons, E, New York, Red Amber, Pt.	413.00
Congress & Empire Spring Co., Hotchkiss' Sons, Emerald Green, 1870, Pt.	242.00
Congress & Empire Spring Co., Hotchkiss' Sons, Light Olive, Pt.	170.00
Congress & Empire Spring Co., Hotchkiss' Sons, Olive Green, 1870, 1/2 Pt.	209.00
Congress & Empire Spring Co., Olive Yellow, Pt.	616.00

Mineral Water, Buffalo Lithia, Teal Blue, Applied Mouth, 1880-1890, 1/2 Gal.

Mineral Water, Clarke & Co., New York, Teal Blue, Applied Mouth, IP, Pt.

Mineral Water, Highrock Congress Spring, C&W, Saratoga, N.Y., Yellow Amber, Pt.

Mineral Water, John Clarke, New York, Olive Amber, Sloping Double Collar, Pontil, Qt.

Congress & Empire Spring Co., Saratoga, N.Y., Blue Green, Qt. 84.00
Congress & Empire Spring Co., Saratoga, N.Y., Green, Pt. ....688.00 to 908.00
Congress & Empire Spring Co., Saratoga, N.Y., Olive Green, Pt. 375.00
Congress & Empire Spring Co., Saratoga, N.Y., Olive Green, Qt. 72.00
Congress & Empire Spring Co., Saratoga, N.Y., Olive Yellow Green, Qt. 290.00
Congress & Empire Spring Co., Saratoga, N.Y., Olive Yellow, Qt. 476.00
Congress & Empire Spring Co., Saratoga, N.Y., Yellow Green 200.00
Congress Spring Co., Saratoga, N.Y., Emerald Green, Pt. ....33.00 to 55.00
Congress Water, Saratoga, N.Y., Emerald Green, Qt. 1760.00
Crystal Spring Co., Saratoga Springs, N.Y., Blue Green, Cylindrical, 1870, Pt. 743.00
Crystal Spring Co., Saratoga Springs, N.Y., Emerald Green, Pt. 1100.00
D.A. Knowlton, Saratoga, N.Y., Olive Green, Embossed, Pt. 160.00
Darien Mineral Springs, Tifft & Perry, Darien Centre, N.Y., Aqua, Pt. ....303.00 to 400.00
Deep Rock Spring, Oswego, N.Y., Orange Amber, 1865-1875, Qt. 908.00
Deep Rock Spring, Oswego, N.Y., Teal, Double Collar, Cylindrical, Pt. 413.00
Dr. Cronk Gibbons & Co., Superior Ale, Buffalo, N.Y., Emerald Green, IP, 6 In. 448.00
E. Bigelow & Co., Springfield, Mass., Sapphire Blue, Blob Top, IP, 7 1/4 In. 303.00
E. Harley, Light Blue Green, Blob Mouth, IP, 1845-1855, 7 1/8 In. 132.00
E. Jenckes, Emerald Green, IP, 1845-1855, 7 1/8 In. 235.00
E. McIntire, Emerald Green, Applied Sloping Double Collar, IP, 6 3/4 In. 980.00
E.E. Race, Boothbay Medicinal Spring Water, Peacock Blue, Blob Top, 11 3/4 In. 90.00
Empire Spring Co., Emerald Green, Qt. 50.00
Empire Spring Co., Saratoga, N.Y., Emerald Green, Qt. 65.00
Excelsior Spring, Saratoga, N.Y., Amber, Pt. 120.00
Excelsior Spring, Saratoga, N.Y., Emerald Green, Sloping Double Collar, Qt. 99.00
Excelsior Spring, Saratoga, N.Y., Lime Green, Qt. 165.00
Excelsior Spring, Saratoga, N.Y., Red Amber, 1865-1875, Pt. 106.00
Excelsior Spring, Saratoga, N.Y., Teal, Double Collar, Cylindrical, Pt. 215.00
Excelsior Spring, Saratoga, N.Y., Yellow 165.00
Excelsior Spring, Saratoga, N.Y., Yellow Green, Embossed, Qt. 220.00
F & B, Blue Green, 1865, 7 In. 70.00
F. Gleason, Rochester, N.Y., Cobalt Blue, 10-Sided, 1855, 7 7/8 In. 385.00
F. Gleason, Rochester, N.Y., Cobalt Blue, Blob Top, IP, 7 5/8 In. 1176.00
F. Schrader, Dunmore, Pa., Emerald Green, 1875, 7 In. 112.00
Franklin Spring, Ballston Spa, Saratoga Co., N.Y., Emerald Green, Pt. ....176.00 to 523.00
Franklin Spring, Saratoga Co., N.Y., Emerald Green, 7 3/4 In. 275.00
G.A. Kohl, Lambertville, N.J., Blue Green, IP, 1855, 7 1/4 In. 168.00
G.W. Weston & Co., Saratoga N.Y., Olive Green, Pt. 143.00
G.W. Weston & Co., Saratoga, N.Y., Olive Amber, Qt. 2128.00
G.W. Weston & Co., Saratoga, N.Y., Olive Green, Qt. ....66.00 to 88.00
G.W. Weston & Co., Saratoga, N.Y., Olive Green, Sloping Double Collar, Qt. 72.00
G.W. Weston & Co., Saratoga, N.Y., Olive Yellow, Pontil, Pt. ....220.00 to 269.00
Gettysburg Katalysine Water, Emerald Green, Bubble, Qt. 55.00
Geyser Spring, Saratoga Springs, Aqua, Double Collar, 1875, 7 3/4 In. 130.00
Geyser Spring, Saratoga Springs, Spouting Spring, Blue Aqua, Qt. 77.00
Geyser Spring, Saratoga Springs, State Of New York, Blue Aqua, Pt. 1904.00
Great Radium Spring Water Co., Inc., Pittsfield, Mass., Aqua, Pt. 8.00
Guilford Mineral Spring Water, Guilford, Vt., Blue Green, 1880, Qt. 90.00
Guilford Mineral Spring Water, Guilford, Vt., Emerald Green, 1865-1875, Qt. .....72.00 to 83.00
Guilford Mineral Spring Water, Guilford, Vt., Olive Yellow, Ring Collar, Qt. 275.00
H. & C. Overdick, Cincinnati, Deep Cobalt Blue, 12-Sided, 1860, 8 5/8 In. 2300.00
H. Knebel's, N.Y., Blue Green, Blob Top, IP, 1855, 7 In. 72.00
H. Knebel's, N.Y., Cobalt Blue, 8-Sided, IP, 7 1/2 In. 364.00
H.L. & J.W. Brown, Hartford, Ct., Emerald Green, 1845-1855, 7 In. 201.00
Haas Bros. Natural, Napa, Cobalt Blue, Applied Lip, 1877 .... 100.00
Hanbury Smith, Vichy Water, Blue Green, Applied Lip, 7 In. 77.00
Hanbury Smith, Vichy Water, Citron, Pt. 66.00
Hanbury Smith, Vichy Water, Dark Citron, 1/2 Pt. 77.00
Hanbury Smith, Vichy Water, Gold Yellow Amber, Double Collar, 1885, Pt. 143.00
Hansard Genuine Aerated Waters Merthyr, Aqua, Bullet Stopper, Small 20.00
Harris, Albany, Blue Green, IP, 1845-1860, 1/2 Pt. 264.00
Hathorn Spring, Amber, Qt. 70.00

Hathorn Spring, Saratoga, N.Y., Emerald Green, Pt. . . . . .44.00 to 100.00
Highrock Congress Spring, 1767, C & W, Saratoga, N.Y., Amber, Pt. . . . . .358.00 to 392.00
Highrock Congress Spring, 1767, C & W, Saratoga, N.Y., Amber, Qt. . . . . .358.00 to 385.00
Highrock Congress Spring, 1767, C & W, Saratoga, N.Y., Olive Yellow, Qt. 330.00
Highrock Congress Spring, 1767, C & W, Saratoga, N.Y., Root Beer Amber, Pt. 165.00
Highrock Congress Spring, 1767, C & W, Saratoga, N.Y., Teal Blue, Qt. 231.00
Highrock Congress Spring, 1767, C & W, Saratoga, N.Y., Yellow Amber, Pt. 231.00
Highrock Congress Spring, C & W, Saratoga, N.Y., Dark Green 210.00
Highrock Congress Spring, C & W, Saratoga, N.Y., Emerald Green, Pt. . . . . .231.00 to 468.00
Highrock Congress Spring, C & W, Saratoga, N.Y., Lime Green, Pt. 275.00
Highrock Congress Spring, C & W, Saratoga, N.Y., Olive Yellow, Pt. . . . . .100.00 to 358.00
Highrock Congress Spring, C & W, Saratoga, N.Y., Teal Blue, Pt. . . . . .357.00 to 523.00
Highrock Congress Spring, C & W, Saratoga, N.Y., Yellow Amber, Pt. . . . .*Illus*   193.00
Highrock Congress Spring, C & W, Saratoga, N.Y., Yellow Green, Pt. 310.00
Highrock Congress Spring, Saratoga, N.Y., Amber, Qt. 2750.00
Hopkin's Chalybeate, Baltimore, Ice Blue, 7 1/2 In. 179.00
Hopkin's Chalybeate, Baltimore, Olive Yellow Green, IP, Pt. 350.00
Humboldt Artisan, Eureka, Cal., Aqua, 7 3/4 In. 55.00
I. Sutton & Co., Covington, Ky., Blue, Applied Lip, 8 1/2 In. 1045.00
Independent, Philadelphia, Teal Blue, Hutchinson, 7 3/4 In. 246.00
Iodine Spring Water, South Hero, Vt., Yellow Amber, 1880, Qt. 1320.00
J. Boardman, New York, Cobalt Blue, 8-Sided, IP, 7 3/4 In. 616.00
J. Esposito, Philada., Olive Yellow, Hutchinson, Tooled Lip, 1905, 7 5/8 In. 825.00
J. Marbacher, Easton, Pa., Blue Green, IP, 1845-1855, 7 In. 176.00
J. Ramroth, Troy, N.Y., Light Green, Hutchinson, 1882 . . . .   30.00
J. Simonds, Boston, Green, IP, 7 1/4 In. 145.00
J. Wise, Allentown, Pa., Cobalt Blue, Blob Top, Milky Interior, 7 In. 72.00
J.G. Byars, Hoosick, N.Y., Light Green 60.00
John Clarke, New York, Olive Amber, Sloping Double Collar, Pontil, Qt. . . . .*Illus*   213.00
John Clarke, New York, Olive Green, Pontil, Applied Double Collar, Pt. 440.00
John Clarke, New York, Olive Yellow Amber, Pontil, Qt. . . . . .110.00 to 154.00
John H. Gardner & Son, Sharon Springs, N.Y., Blue Green, Double Collar, Pt. 231.00
John H. Gardner & Son, Sharon Springs, N.Y., Teal Blue, Pt. 336.00
John H. Gardner & Son, Sulphur Water, Blue Green, 1860-1870, Pt. 330.00
John Ryan, Excelsior, Savannah, Ga., Blue, IP, 1800 . . . .   187.00
John Ryan, Excelsior, Savannah, Ga., Sapphire Blue, Blob Top, IP, 1/2 Pt. 341.00
John S. Baker, Blue Aqua, 8-Sided, IP, 1845-1860, 7 1/2 In. 420.00
Kissingen Water, Raised Lettering, Olive Green, 8 In. 75.00
Knickerbocker, Blue, Blob Top, IP 700.00
L. Gahre, Bridgeton, N.J., Yellow Green, 1860-1870, 6 3/4 In. 89.00
Lancaster Glass Works, Cobalt Blue, IP, 7 3/8 In. 99.00
Lancaster XXX Glassworks, Light Green, Blob Top, IP, 6 5/8 In. 420.00
Latterne, Cincinnati, Aqua, 10-Sided, Sloping Collar Mouth, 1855, 7 1/2 In. 110.00
Luke Beard, Blue Green, Applied Sloping Collar, IP, 7 In. . . . . .504.00 to 560.00
Luke Beard, Boston, Aqua, Blob Top, 1855-1865, 7 In. 75.00
Luke Beard, Boston, Aqua, Blob Top, 6 7/8 In. 70.00
Lynch & Clarke, N.Y., Deep Olive Amber, 1840-1855, Pt. 2016.00
Lynch & Clarke, New York, Olive Amber, Sloping Double Collar, Pontil, Pt. . . . . .358.00 to 420.00
Lynch & Clarke, New York, Olive Yellow Amber, Pontil, 1830-1840, Pt. . . . . .358.00 to 468.00
Lynch & Clarke, New York, Olive Yellow Amber, Pontil, Qt. 330.00
Lynch & Clarke, New York, Olive Yellow, Double Collar, Pontil, Pt. 392.00
Lynde & Putman, San Francisco, Cal., Teal Blue, IP, 7 1/2 In. 355.00
Lynde & Putnam, San Francisco, Cal., Cobalt 550.00
Lynde & Putnam, San Francisco, Cal., Cobalt Blue, Blob Top, IP, 7 3/8 In. 235.00
Lynde & Putnam, San Francisco, Cal., Cobalt Blue, Hutchinson, Pontil 275.00
Lynde & Putnam, San Francisco, Cal., Emerald Green, Hutchinson, Stopper 220.00
Lynde & Putnam, San Francisco, Cal., Teal Blue 450.00
Lynde & Putnam, San Francisco, Cal., Teal Blue, Blob Top, IP, 7 3/8 In. 308.00
Lynde & Putnam, San Francisco, Cal., Union Glass Works, Blue Green, IP 275.00
Lynde & Putnam, Union Glassworks, Cobalt Blue 275.00
M.M. Battelle, Brooklyn, N.Y., Teal, Blob Top, Cylindrical, 1845-1855, 7 3/8 In. 65.00
M.M. Battelle, N.Y., Blue Green, IP, 1845-1855, 7 3/8 In. 145.00

M.T. Crawford, Hartford, Ct., Teal Blue, IP, 1855, 7 1/8 In. 78.00
Massena Spring, Blue Green, Sloping Collar, Ring, 1880, Pt. 265.00
Merriam's, Cobalt Blue, Blob Top, IP, 1852-1856, 7 1/2 In. 715.00
Middletown Healing Springs, Grays & Clark, Middletown, Vt., Amber, Qt. 660.00
Middletown Healing Springs, Grays & Clark, Vt., Yellow Amber, Qt. ....28.00 to 94.00
Middletown Healing Springs, Vt., Olive Amber, Qt. ....55.00 to 72.00
Middletown Mineral Spring Co., Emerald Green, Qt. 660.00
Mineral Waters, Cobalt Blue, Applied Mouth, Cylindrical, 1855, 7 1/4 In. 121.00
Minnehaha Natural Spring, Blue Aqua, Wire Closure, Stopper, 11 3/4 In. 121.00
Minnequa, Bradford Co., Pa., Ring Collar, 1860-1890, Pt. 330.00
Missisquoi A Springs, Blue Green, Sloping Double Collar, Qt. 77.00
Missisquoi A Springs, Emerald Green, Sloping Collar, Qt. 112.00
Missisquoi A Springs, Emerald Green, Sloping Double Collar, Qt. 39.00
Missisquoi A Springs, Olive Yellow, Qt. ....105.00 to 303.00
Missisquoi A Springs, Squaw & Papoose, Olive, Qt. 330.00
Missisquoi A Springs, Squaw, Blue Green, Sloping Double Collar, Qt. 1018.00
Missisquoi A Springs, Squaw, Olive Yellow, Sloping Double Collar, Qt. 450.00
Napa Soda, Natural Mineral Water, Sapphire Blue, 7 5/8 In. 185.00
Neyman & Drake, Mok Hill, Dark Teal, Blob Top, Cylindrical, IP, 1850s 1500.00
Oak Orchard Acid Springs, G.W. Merchant, Lockport, N.Y., Blue Green, Qt. ......83.00 to 110.00
Oak Orchard Acid Springs, G.W. Merchant, Lockport, N.Y., Green, Qt. 95.00
Oak Orchard Acid Springs, Genesee Co., N.Y., Green, Ring Mouth, Qt. 213.00
Oak Orchard Acid Springs, H.W. Bostwick, Blue Green, 1865-1875, Qt. 187.00
Oak Orchard Acid Springs, H.W. Bostwick, Yellow Amber, Qt. ....50.00 to 89.00
Oak Orchard Acid Springs, Yellow Green, Sloping Double Collar, Qt. 420.00
Ogemawa Spring Water, Aqua, Tooled Lip, 1880-1895, 1/2 Gal. 176.00
Olden Hill, Toledo, Ohio, Jug, White, 4 3/4 In. 75.00
P. Conway, Bottler, Philad.A, Cobalt Blue, IP, 1855, 7 In. 280.00
Pacific Congress Water, Aqua, Embossed Deer 66.00
Pacific Congress Water, P. Caduc, Green Aqua, Big Lip, 7 1/2 In. 33.00
Pacific Congress Water, Sage's Pacific, Saratoga, Ca., Lime Green, 8 In. 825.00
Pacific Congress Water, Saratoga, Ca., Green 330.00
Pacific Congress Water, Saratoga, Ca., Running Deer, Aqua 125.00
Pacific Congress Water, Saratoga, Ca., Running Deer, Green, 7 In. 1760.00
Pacific Congress Water, Saratoga, Ca., Yellow Green 999.00
Patterson & Brazeau, N.Y., Vichy Water, Forest Green, Pt. 200.00
Pavilion & United States Spring Co., P, Saratoga, N.Y., Tobacco Amber, Pt. 495.00
Pavilion & United States Spring Co., Saratoga, N.Y., Blue Green, Pt. 149.00
Pavilion & United States Spring Co., Saratoga, N.Y., Emerald, Pt. 275.00
Pavilion & United States Spring Co., Saratoga, N.Y., Olive Yellow, Pt. ....66.00 to 190.00
Philadelphia XXX Porter & Ale, Teal Blue, IP, 1855, 6 1/2 In. 78.00
Poland Water, H. Ricker & Sons, Aqua, 11 In. 220.00
Quaker Springs, I.W. Meader & Co., Saratoga Co., N.Y., Emerald Green, Pt. 2090.00
Robinson, Wilson & Legallee, 102 Sudbury St., Boston, Blue 110.00
Roussel's, Manufactured In Silver, Dyottville, Emerald Green, IP, 1/2 Pt. 165.00
Rutherfords Premium, Cincinnati, Cobalt Blue, 10-Sided, 7 3/8 In. 672.00
S. Smith, Auburn, N.Y., Cobalt Blue, 10-Sided, 1855, 7 3/8 In. 420.00
S. Smith, Auburn, N.Y., Cobalt Blue, Applied Sloped Blob Top, 1860, 8 In. 523.00
S. Smith, Auburn, N.Y., Green, IP, 1/2 Pt. 264.00
S.B. Winn, Salem, Mass., Light Blue Green, Blob Top, 1875, 7 1/8 In. 179.00
S.H. Boughton, Rochester, N.Y., Cobalt Blue, Blob Top, IP, 7 1/4 In. 476.00
Santa Barbara, A Natural Medicinal Water, Amber, 8-Sided, Tooled Lip 165.00
Saratoga A Hathorn, Carl H. Schultz, N.Y., Blue Green, 1875-1885, Pt. 578.00
Saratoga A Spring Co., N.Y., Dark Olive Amber, Double Collar, 1865, Pt. 121.00
Saratoga A Spring Co., N.Y., Emerald Green, Double Collar, 1889, Qt. 60.00
Saratoga A Spring Co., N.Y., Emerald Green, Pt. ....121.00 to 154.00
Saratoga A Spring Co., N.Y., Olive Yellow, 1860-1880, Qt. 121.00
Saratoga A Spring Co., N.Y., Olive Yellow, Pt. 605.00
Saratoga High Rock Spring, Saratoga, N.Y., Emerald Green, Pt. 1320.00
Saratoga Red Spring, Blue Green, 1865-1875, Pt. ....123.00 to 134.00
Saratoga Red Spring, Emerald Green, Cork, Wire Closure, Contents, Pt. 105.00
Saratoga Red Spring, Teal Blue, 1865-1875, Qt. 134.00

Saratoga Star Spring, Amber, Applied Double Collar, Qt. 99.00
Saratoga Star Spring, Blood Red, Applied Mouth, Qt. 121.00
Saratoga Star Spring, Emerald Green, Cylindrical, Tall Neck, 1875, Pt. 495.00
Saratoga Star Spring, Gold Amber, Ring Collar, 1860-1880, Qt. 99.00
Saratoga Star Spring, Olive Green, 1865-1875, Qt. . . . . .88.00 to 132.00
Saratoga Star Spring, Olive Green, Applied Mouth, Qt. 179.00
Saratoga Star Spring, Olive Green, Bubbles, 1865-1875, Qt. 132.00
Saratoga Star Spring, Olive Green, Double Collar, 1875, Qt. 143.00
Saratoga Star Spring, Olive Green, Sloping Double Collar, Pt. 110.00
Saratoga Star Spring, Olive Yellow Green, Qt. 132.00
Saratoga Star Spring, Red Amber, Applied Sloping Double Collar, Qt. 94.00
Saratoga Star Spring, Red Amber, Bubbles, Qt. 155.00
Saratoga Star Spring, Root Beer Amber, Double Collar, Qt. 110.00
Saratoga Star Spring, Tobacco Amber, 1865-1875, Pt. 140.00
Saratoga Star Spring, Yellow Amber, 1865-1875, Pt. 168.00
Saratoga Star Spring, Yellow Amber, Double Collar, Cylindrical, 1875, Pt. 231.00
Saratoga Star Spring, Yellow Amber, Double Collar, Qt. 132.00
Saratoga Vichy Spouting Spring, V, Saratoga, N.Y., Amber, 1875, Pt. 495.00
Saratoga Vichy Spouting Spring, V, Saratoga, N.Y., Aqua, 1875, 1/2 Pt. 66.00
Saratoga Vichy Water, Saratoga, N.Y., Amber, Double Collar, 1880, Qt. 121.00
Seymour & Co., Buffalo, N.Y., Cobalt Blue, Blob Top, IP, 7 1/8 In. 420.00
Simpson Spring Co., South Easton, Aqua, 1920s, 1/2 Pt. 1.50
Smith & Kelly's, Green, IP 230.00
Southern Mineral Water Co., Atlanta, Ga., Aqua, 1885-1895, 1/2 Gal. . . . . .88.00 to 132.00
Southwick & Tupper, New York, Cobalt Blue, 10-Sided, IP, 7 1/2 In. 303.00
Star Spring Co., Saratoga, N.Y, Amber, 1 On Base, Pt. 154.00
Star Spring Co., Saratoga, N.Y., Olive Amber, Sloping Double Collar, Pt. 187.00
Star Spring Co., Saratoga, N.Y., Red Amber, 1865-1875, Pt. 209.00
Star Spring Co., Saratoga, N.Y., Red Amber, Double Collar, 1875, Pt. 143.00
Star Spring Co., Saratoga, N.Y., Star, Red Amber, Pt. 134.00
Star Spring Co., Saratoga, N.Y., Star, Tobacco Amber, Pt. 134.00
Star Spring Co., Saratoga, N.Y., Yellow Amber, 1875, Pt. 165.00
Stirlings Magnetic, Eaton Rapieds, Mich., Red Amber, 1860-1880, Qt. 165.00
Syracuse Springs, D, Excelsior, Gold Amber, Pt. 420.00
Syracuse Springs, D, Excelsior, New York, Amber, Pt. 672.00
Syracuse Springs, D, Excelsior, Yellow Amber, Sloping Double Collar, 1/2 Pt. 743.00
T. Monroe, Herkimer, N.Y., Blue Green, 1860s, 5 1/2 In. 35.00
Tahoe Soda Springs, Aqua, Tooled Lip, 7 In. 185.00
Thompsons, Union Soda Works, San Francisco, Aqua, 10 In. 110.00
Tolenas Soda Springs, Natural, Light Turquoise, 1885-1906 . . . .   44.00
Triton Spouting Spring, Saratoga, N.Y., Blue Aqua, Cylindrical, 1880, Pt. 853.00
Tweddle's Celebrated, Light Emerald Green, Sloping Collar, OP, 7 In. 1176.00
Tweddle's Celebrated, New York, Blue Green, Bubbles, 7 1/2 In.   1600.00
Tweddle's Celebrated, New York, Cobalt Blue, IP, 7 3/8 In. 303.00
Twin Peaks, San Francisco, Aqua, Embossed Mountains, Crown Top 154.00
Twitchell, Philada, Teal, Squat, IP, 7 In. . . . . .90.00 to 100.00
Union Glass Works, Phila., Emerald Green, IP, Blob Top, 7 1/2 In. 84.00
Vermont Spring, Saxe & Co., Bright Olive, Qt. 220.00
Vermont Spring, Saxe & Co., Sheldon, Vt., Emerald Green, Qt. . . . . .84.00 to 165.00
Vermont Spring, Saxe & Co., Sheldon, Vt., Yellow Green, 1860-1880, Qt. 154.00
Vermont Spring, Saxe & Co., Sheldon, Vt., Yellow Olive Green, Qt. 78.00
W. Eagle, Teal Blue, Blob Top, ISP, IP, 7 1/8 In. 336.00
Washington Lithia Well, Ballston Spa, N.Y., Aqua, Double Collar, 1860, Pt. 330.00
Washington Lithia Well, Ballston Spa, N.Y., Aqua, Double Collar, 1880, Pt. 303.00
Washington Spring, Ballston Spa, N.Y., Emerald Green, Cylindrical, Pt. . . . . . .1073.00 to 1650.00
Washington Spring, Bust Of Washington, Blue Green, Pt. 1232.00
Washington Spring, Saratoga, N.Y., Emerald Green, Pt. . . . . .230.00 to 253.00
Washington Spring, Saratoga, N.Y., Grass Green, Double Collar, Cylindrical, Pt. 220.00
Wm. Eagle, Premium Soda Water, New York, Cobalt Blue, 10-Sided, 7 In. 253.00
Wm. W. Lappeus, Premium, Albany, Cobalt Blue, 10-Sided, Blob Top, IP, 8 In. 1120.00
York Springs, Aqua, Torpedo, Blob Top, Canada, 1880, 7 In. 70.00
Young's Natural, Napa Co., Cal., Blue Aqua, 6 1/2 In. 35.00

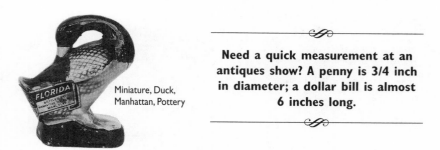

Miniature, Duck,
Manhattan, Pottery

Need a quick measurement at an antiques show? A penny is 3/4 inch in diameter; a dollar bill is almost 6 inches long.

MINIATURE

Most of the major modern liquor companies that make full-sized decanters and bottles quickly learned that miniature versions sell well too. Some modern miniatures are listed in this book by brand name. There are also many older miniature bottles that were made as give-aways. Most interesting of these are the small motto jugs that name a liquor or bar, and the comic figural bottles. Collectors sometimes specialize in glass animal miniatures, beer bottles, whiskey bottles, or other types. Interested collectors can join the Lilliputian Bottle Club, 54 Village Circle, Manhattan Beach, CA 90266-7222; or subscribe to Miniature Bottle Collector, P.O. Box 2161, Palos Verdes, CA 90274.

A. Lancaster's Indian Vegetable, Jaundice Bitters, 1852, Purple, Taiwan, 3 1/4 In. 5.00
Arkansas Corn Straight, Uncle Sam Distilling, Jug, Stoneware, 3 3/8 In. 120.00
Bells, Jug, England 12.00
Benton, Myers & Co., Cleveland, Oh., Jug, Whiskey, Stoneware ....*Illus* 150.00
Black & White, Jug, England 12.00
Blockhouse Rye, Walther Robertson Co., Pittsburg, Pa., Stoneware, 5 1/4 In. 140.00
Blown, Globular, Olive Yellow, Applied Lip, Pontil, FB, 3 1/4 In. 1344.00
Blown, Jar, Pale Green, Wide Flared Mouth, Pontil, 1800-1850, 2 7/8 In. 715.00
C.W. Butcher & Son, Neodesha, Kansas, Jug, Pottery, 3 1/8 In. 100.00
Canadian Club Whiskey, Jefferson, Peoria, Barrel, Stoneware, Nip, 2 1/8 In. 132.00
Compliments Of G.J. Keene, Elkhart, Ind., Jug, Stoneware, Dark Brown, Incised, 5 In. ... 88.00
Compliments Of Short & McGuire, Celeste, Tex., Jug, Dark Brown Albany Slip, 3 In. ... 303.00
Corona Light Beer, 3 In., 6 Piece 12.00
Duck, Manhattan, Pottery ....*Illus* 15.00
Duroy Wine Co., Tokay, Cleveland, Ohio, Jug, Stoneware ....*Illus* 120.00
Elk's Pride Whiskey, Jn. S. Low, Carlisle, Pa., Jug, Pottery, 2 1/2 In. 176.00
Fred Roush, Frankfurt, Ind., Jug, 1900, 3 In. 110.00
Gin, Case, Dark Olive Green, Tapered Lip, 5 1/2 In. 24.00
Glenlivet, Jug, England, 3 In. 12.00

Miniature, Benton, Myers & Co.,
Cleveland, Ohio, Jug,
Whiskey, Stoneware

Miniature, J. Fries, Cleveland,
Ohio, Jug, Whiskey,
Stoneware

Miniature, Duroy Wine Co.,
Tokay, Cleveland, Ohio, Jug,
Stoneware

Hoffman House Blended Whiskey, H.P. Corbin & Co., Cincinnati, Jug, 2 3/4 In. 66.00
J. Fries, Cleveland, Oh., Jug, Whiskey, Stoneware . . . .*Illus*   130.00
John McColl Family Grocer & Wine Merchant, Glasgow, Jug, Stoneware, 3 1/2 In. 55.00
Medicine Hat Pottery Co., Ft. Bathhurst St., Toronto, Jug, Stoneware, 4 In. 310.00
Night Cap, Sleeping Man's Face, Milk Glass, Red, Blue, Cream, 4 In. 179.00
Real West Country Cream British Sherry, 3 1/2 In. 8.50
Sandeman, Decanter, Royal Doulton, 4 1/2 In. 78.00
Take An Eye Opener Whiskey, Examine Buggies Bred In Old Kentucky, Cream, 3 In. . . .   143.00
Tullamore, Jug, England 12.00
Vulcanizing Solution, Akron, O., Stoneware, Bristol Glaze, 4 3/4 In. 33.00
MR. BOSTON, see Old Mr. Boston

─────────────────── **NAILSEA TYPE** ───────────────────

The intricate glass called *Nailsea* was made in the Bristol district of England from 1788 to 1873. The glass included loopings of white or colored glass worked in patterns. The characteristic look of Nailsea was copied and what is called Nailsea today is really Nailsea type made in England or even America. Nailsea gemel bottles are of particular interest to collectors.

Bellows, Clear, Opalescent Looping, Neck Rings, Rigaree, Handles, 13 1/4 In. 145.00
Bellows, Clear, White Looping, Rigaree 185.00
Bellows, Whimsy, Cranberry, White Looping, Knopped Stem, 1840-1870, 8 3/4 In. 413.00
Bellows, White, Red & Blue Looping, Quilled Neck, Prunt, Rigaree, Handles, 11 3/4 In. . .   460.00
Flask, Clear, Allover White Looping, Pontil, 1840-1865, 7 1/2 In. 110.00
Flask, Clear, White Looping, Pontil, 1870, 7 3/8 In. 93.00
Flask, Cobalt Blue, White Speckle, 19th Century, 10 3/4 In. 258.00
Flask, Olive, White Loops, 5 1/4 In., 1/2 Pt. 300.00
Flask, Opaque White On Clear, 7 3/8 In. 192.00
Flask, Pocket, Flattened, Black, White Loops, c.1850, 4 3/4 In.   220.00
Flask, Red, White & Blue Looping, 7 3/4 In. 275.00
Flask, Red, White Looping, Outward Rolled Lip, Pontil, 6 5/8 In. 355.00
Flask, Ruby, White Looping, Pontil, Rolled Lip, 1860-1880, 6 5/8 In. 357.00
Flask, Teardrop, Clear, Cranberry & White Swirls, Tooled Lip, Pontil, 8 3/4 In. 213.00
Flask, White, Red Loops, 7 1/4 In. 160.00
Gemel, Opaque White, Cobalt Blue Lips, 9 3/4 In. 165.00
Nurser, Elongated, Flattened, Blue, Pink, White Loops, c.1870, 5 1/2 In. 110.00
Onion, Black Glass, 1800 . . . .   660.00
Pink, White Loops, 5 3/4 In. 160.00

─────────────────── **NURSING** ───────────────────

Pottery nursing bottles were used by 1500 B.C. If a bottle was needed, one was improvised, and stone, metal, wood, and pottery, as well as glass bottles were made through the centuries. A glass bottle was patented by Charles Windship of Roxbury, Massachusetts, in 1841. Its novel design suggested that the bottle be placed over the breast to try to fool the baby into thinking the milk came from the mother. By 1864 the most common nursing bottle was a nipple attached to a glass tube in a cork that was put into a glass bottle. Unfortunately, it was impossible to clean and was very unsanitary. The nursing bottle in use today was made possible by the development of an early 1900s rubber nipple.

Nursing bottles are easily identified by the unique shape and the measuring units that are often marked on the sides. Some early examples had engraved designs and silver nipples but most are made of clear glass and rubber. There is a collectors club, The American Collectors of Infant Feeders, 1849 Ebony Drive, York, PA 17402-4706, and a publication called *Keeping Abreast*. A reference book, *A Guide to American Nursing Bottles* by Diane Rouse Ostrander, is also available.

Allenbury Feeder, Banana Boat Shape, Clear, 1890 . . . .   50.00
Blown, Applied Ring Around Filler Hole On Side, Polished Pontil, 1860, 5 3/4 In. 88.00
Burr's Patent, M.S. Burr & Co. Prop., Boston, Mass., Blue, Baby, 1870s, 5 1/2 In. 176.00
Clear, c.1800, 6 1/2 In. 68.00
Cow & Gate Milk Food, Blue, White Tin, Baby, Laughing, Wearing A Crown 25.00
Crown Feeder, Turtle Shape, Embossed, 1870-1880, Large 45.00
Dorselia Milk Food, Blue, Cream Tin, Baby, Smiling, Large 35.00
H.G. Paris, Scroll Design With Logo, Clear, 3 In. 135.00

If you have a small-neck decanter or bottle that doesn't seem to dry after it is washed, try putting a small amount of rubbing alcohol in the bottle. Shake, pour out, and wait for the remaining drops to evaporate.

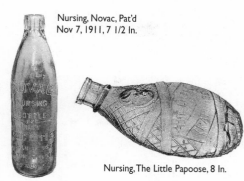

Nursing, Novac, Pat'd Nov 7, 1911, 7 1/2 In.

Nursing, The Little Papoose, 8 In.

Hughes Chemist Altrincham, Turtle Shape, Aqua, Non Screw Necks 45.00
Hygienic Feeder, Clear, Banana Boat Shape . . . . .30.00 to 35.00
Kuwa In U Ausl, Made In Germany, Graduations, Thermometer, 1930, 7 3/8 In. 56.00
Manchester Feeding, Boat Shape, Tablespoon Markings, 9 In. 70.00
Morgan, Turtle Shape, Horn Nipple Shell, Pre 1916, 3 1/2 In. 82.00
Novac, Pat'd Nov 7, 1911, 7 1/2 In. . . . .*Illus*   65.00
Savars Feeder, Embossed 45.00
Star, St. Of David, Mo., Clear, 2 5/8 In. 55.00
Submarine Shape Infant Feeder, England, 1850-1860, 8 1/2 In.   90.00
T. Eggington, Manchester, Perfect Feeding, Turtle Shape, Aqua, BIMAL, 1885, 6 In. 60.00
The Little Papoose, 8 In. . . . .*Illus*   70.00

OBR

Old Blue Ribbon, or OBR, bottles were made from 1969 to about 1974.

Balloon, 1969 . . . . .10.00 to 17.00
Bus, 5th Avenue, 1971 . . . .   18.00
Caboose, 1973 . . . .   25.00
Engine, General, 1974 . . . . .15.00 to 20.00
Football Player, 1972 . . . .   28.00
Pierce-Arrow, 1969 . . . .   42.00
Prairie Wagon, 1969 . . . .   8.00
River Queen, 1967 . . . .   10.00
Titanic, 1970 . . . . .45.00 to 55.00
W.C. Fields, Top Hat, 1976 . . . . .45.00 to 55.00

OIL

Motor oil, battery oil, and sewing machine and lubricating oils were all sold in bottles. Any bottle that has the word *oil* either embossed in the glass or on the paper label falls in this category. A battery jar has straight sides and an open top. It was filled with a chemical solution. The jars were usually made with a zinc plate or a copper plate plus a suspended carbon plate. With the proper connections the chemicals and metals generated an electric current. Many companies made batteries that included glass jars, and the jars are now appearing at bottle shows. In the Edison battery, the solution was covered with a special protective layer of oil which kept it from evaporating. Edison battery oil jars, dating from about 1889, were specially made to hold the protective oil and can still be found.

Elk-O-Lene Motor Oil, Qt. 110.00
Extra Refined Machine Oil, Grover & Baker Co., Clear, Tooled Mouth, 1885, 5 3/8 In. . .   55.00
Fill To Line One Liquid, Mater Mfg. Co., Litchfield, Il., Clear, Patd Sept 14 1926, Qt. . . .   65.00
Hemlock Oil Co., Derry, N.H., USA, 1 x 1 x 6 In. 25.00
Mobiloil, Arctic, Aqua, Spout, Tin, Qt., 14 3/4 In. 110.00
Penn-Bee Motor Oil, Qt. 120.00
Polaris Snowmobile Oil, Plastic, Qt. 40.00
Salvation Oil, A.C. Meyer Co., Baltimore, Md., Light Apple Green, 6 3/4 In. 25.00

OLD BARDSTOWN

Old Bardstown was made and bottled by the Willit Distilling Company in Bardstown, Kentucky. Figural bottles were made from about 1977 to 1980. One unusual bottle pictured Foster Brooks, the actor who is best known for his portrayal of drunks.

Affirm & Alydar	300.00
Christmas Card, 1977	16.00
Clemson Tiger, 1979	70.00
Delta Queen, 1980	38.00
Fiddle, Miniature	15.00
Fighting Gamecock	200.00
Football Player	37.00
Foster Brooks, 1978 ....20.00 to 28.00
Georgia Bulldog, 1980 ....275.00 to 310.00
Horse, Citation, 1979	175.00
Iron Worker, 1978 ....28.00 to 35.00
Keg With Stand, 1977, 1/2 Gal.	14.00
Keg With Stand, 1977, Gal.	27.00
Kentucky Colonel, No. 1, 1978	18.00
Kentucky Colonel, No. 2, 1979	55.00
Kentucky Derby, 1977 ....11.00 to 15.00
Surface Miner, 1978	20.00
Tiger, 1979	30.00
Trucker, 1978 ....20.00 to 25.00
Wildcat, No. 2, 1979 ....31.00 to 40.00

OLD COMMONWEALTH

Old Commonwealth bottles have been made since 1975 by J.P. Van Winkle and Sons, Louisville, Kentucky. They also put out bottles under the Old Rip Van Winkle label. An apothecary series with university names and other designs such as firemen, coal miners, fishermen, Indians, dogs, horses, or leprechauns was made from 1978 to the present. As few as 1,600 were made of some of these designs. Some of the decanters were made with music box inserts.

Alabama Apothecary, 1980	27.00
Alabama Crimson Tide, 1981	17.00
Auburn Tigers, 1979	38.00
Castles Of Ireland, 1990	30.00
Chief Illini, No. 1, 1979 ....100.00 to 125.00
Chief Illini, No. 2, 1981 ....*Illus* 125.00
Clemson Tigers, 1979	45.00
Coal Miner, Coal Shooter, 1983 ....28.00 to 35.00
Coal Miner, Lump Of Coal, 1977 ....33.00 to 40.00
Coal Miner, Lump Of Coal, 1981 ....33.00 to 40.00
Coal Miner, Lunch Time, 1980	40.00
Coal Miner, Lunch Time, 1983, Miniature	40.00
Coal Miner, Pick, 1976	45.00

Old Commonwealth,
Chief Illini,
No. 2, 1981

Old Commonwealth,
Coal Miner, Pick, 1982

Old Commonwealth,
Fireman, No. 4, Heroic
Volunteer, 1981

Coal Miner, Pick, 1982	Illus	45.00
Coal Miner, Shovel, 1975	85.00 to	95.00
Coal Miner, Shovel, 1980	85.00 to	95.00
Coins Of Ireland, 1979		30.00
Cottontail Rabbit, 1981		35.00
Dogs Of Ireland, 1980	25.00 to	30.00
Fireman, Modern Hero, 1982		62.00
Fireman, Modern No. 2, Nozzle Man, 1983	62.00 to	75.00
Fireman, Modern No. 3, On Call, Boots, Yellow Hat, 1983	75.00 to	85.00
Fireman, Modern No. 4, Fallen Comrade, 1982		70.00
Fireman, No. 1, Cumberland Valley, 75th Anniversary, 1976		115.00
Fireman, No. 2, Volunteer, 1978		74.00
Fireman, No. 3, Valiant Volunteer, 1979		76.00
Fireman, No. 4, Heroic Volunteer, 1981	Illus	85.00
Fireman, No. 5, Lifesaver, 1983	60.00 to	70.00
Fisherman, Keeper, 1980		46.00
Flowers Of Ireland, 1983		23.00
Happy Green, 1986		25.00
Horses Of Ireland, 1981	30.00 to	35.00
Irish At The Sea, 1989		25.00
Irish Idyll, 1982	20.00 to	25.00
Irish Lore, 1988		25.00
Kansas State Wildcats, 1982		34.00
Kentucky Peach Bowl, 1977		30.00
Leprechaun, No. 1, Elusive, 1982	34.00 to	40.00
Leprechaun, No. 2, Irish Minstrel, 1982	40.00 to	45.00
Leprechaun, No. 3, Lucky, 1983		25.00
Louisville Champs, 1980		38.00
LSU Tiger, 1979	43.00 to	50.00
Lumberjack, Old Time, 1979		45.00
Maryland Terps, 1977		25.00
Missouri Tigers, 1979		40.00
Princeton University, 1976		23.00
Sons Of Erin, No. 2, 1978		25.00
Sports Of Ireland, 1987		24.00
St. Patrick's Day Parade, 1984		23.00
Statue Of Liberty, Miniature		25.00
Symbols Of Ireland, 1985		25.00
Thoroughbreds, Kentucky, 1977		40.00
Waterfowler, No. 1, Hunter, 1978		62.00
Waterfowler, No. 2, Here They Come, 1980		62.00
Waterfowler, No. 3, Good Boy, 1981		55.00
Western Logger, 1980		44.00
Yankee Doodle, 1982		24.00

—————————————— OLD CROW ——————————————

Dr. James Crow of Kentucky was a surgeon and chemist from Edinburgh, Scotland. He started practicing medicine but decided to improve the quality of life by distilling corn whiskey instead. In those days, about 1835, whiskey was made by a family recipe with a bit of that and a handful of the other. The results were uneven. Dr. Crow was a scientist and used corn and limestone water to make a whiskey that he put into kegs and jugs. He used charred oak kegs, and the liquid became reddish instead of the clear white of corn liquor. More experiments led to his development of the first bourbon, named after northeastern Kentucky's Bourbon County, which had been named for the French royal family.

Old Crow became a popular product in all parts of the country and was sold to saloons. Salesmen for competing brands would sometimes try to ruin the liquor by putting a snake or nail into the barrel. In 1870, for the first time, bourbon was bottled and sealed at the distillery. The distillery was closed during Prohibition, and when it reopened in 1933, Old Crow was purchased by National Distilleries. That Old Crow would be packaged in a crow-shaped decanter was inevitable, and in 1954 National Distillers Products Corporation of Frankfort, Kentucky, put Old Crow bourbon into a ceramic crow. Again in 1974 a crow decanter was used; this time 16,800 Royal Doulton bottles were made. The bourbon was sold in the 1970s in a series of bottles shaped like light or dark green chess pieces. Jim Beam Brands bought National Distillers in 1987. Old Crow is still made, but not in figural bottles.

Chess Set, Pawns	22.00
Chess Set, Queen, Light Green	16.00
Chess Set, Rook, Light Green	16.00
Chess Set, With Rug, 32 Piece	315.00
Crow, Red Vest, 1974	25.00
Crow, Royal Doulton	90.00

─────────────────── **OLD FITZGERALD** ───────────────────

In 1908, Julian P. Van Winkle, Sr., and another salesman for W.L. Weller & Sons, liquor wholesaler, bought the Weller company. Later they bought A. Ph. Stitzel Distillery, of Louisville, Kentucky, which had supplied sour-mash whiskey to W.L. Weller & Sons. The Stitzel Weller firm became known as The Old Fitzgerald Distillery. President Van Winkle, Sr., created the Old Rip Van Winkle series just before Prohibition. Van Winkle remained an active distiller until his death in 1965. His son, Julian, Jr., had become president of Stitzel-Weller in 1947. In 1968 the Old Fitzgerald decanter, "Leprechaun Bottle" carried the words *plase God.* The use of "God" was ruled objectionable under Federal law and the decanters were changed to read *prase be.* In 1972, the distillery was sold to Somerset Importers, Ltd., a division of Norton Simon Company, Inc. Somerset Importers continued to market the Old Rip Van Winkle series until 1978, when they sold to J.P. Van Winkle & Son, a distillery created by Julian Van Winkle, Jr., with his son, Julian, III, after the sale of Stitzel-Weller.

J.P. Van Winkle & Son sold whiskey under the new label, Old Commonwealth, and also the Old Rip Van Winkle series. The Van Winkle series of bottles for both brands included only 20 different bottles through 1986.

Esmark purchased Norton Simon in 1984, then sold the Old Fitzgerald label to Distillers of England in 1985, who sold it to Guinness Stout of Ireland in 1986. The last Old Fitzgerald decanter was made in 1989. Guinness Stout has since become Guinness Distillers Worldwide in Edinburgh, and its Louisville distillery is called United Distillers Mfg., Inc.

An out-of-print pamphlet, *Decanter Collector's Guide,* pictures Old Fitzgerald decanters offered between 1951 and 1971. Most are glass in classic shapes. Besides Old Fitzgerald, the distillery made Cabin Still, W.L. Weller, and Rebel Yell bourbons.

America's Cup, 1970	22.00
American Sons, 1976	15.00
Around We Go, 1983	20.00
Birmingham, 1972	47.00
Birmingham, 2nd Edition	40.00
Blarney, Irish Toast, 1970	10.00
Cabin Still, Early American, 1970	4.00
Cabin Still, Hillbilly, 1954, Gal.	80.00
Cabin Still, Hillbilly, 1954, Pt.	20.00
Cabin Still, Hillbilly, 1954, Qt.	18.00
Cabin Still, Hillbilly, 1969	15.00
Candlestick, 1955	20.00
Candlestick, 1961	10.00
Classic, 1972	6.00
Colonial, 1969	5.00
Crown, 1957	7.00
Davidson, N.C., 1972	30.00
Diamond, 1959	12.00
Diamond, 1961	12.00
Double Candlelite, 1956	8.00
Eagle, 1973	8.00
Early American, 1970	5.00
Executive, 1960	7.00
Flagship, 1967	8.00
Fleur-De-Lis, 1962	*Illus* 10.00
Florentine, 1961	9.00

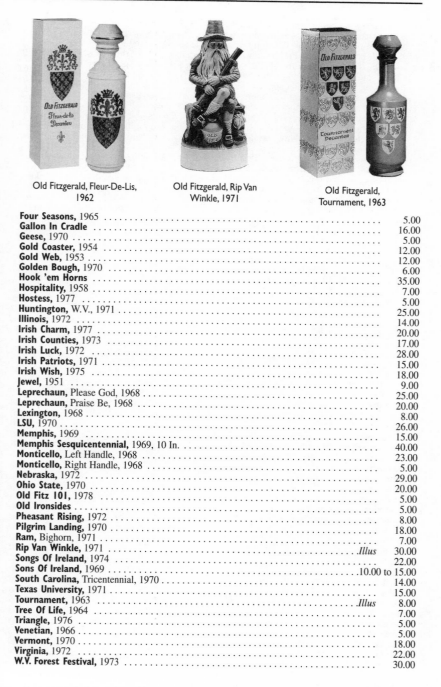

Old Fitzgerald, Fleur-De-Lis, 1962

Old Fitzgerald, Rip Van Winkle, 1971

Old Fitzgerald, Tournament, 1963

Four Seasons, 1965	5.00
Gallon In Cradle	16.00
Geese, 1970	5.00
Gold Coaster, 1954	12.00
Gold Web, 1953	12.00
Golden Bough, 1970	6.00
Hook 'em Horns	35.00
Hospitality, 1958	7.00
Hostess, 1977	5.00
Huntington, W.V., 1971	25.00
Illinois, 1972	14.00
Irish Charm, 1977	20.00
Irish Counties, 1973	17.00
Irish Luck, 1972	28.00
Irish Patriots, 1971	15.00
Irish Wish, 1975	18.00
Jewel, 1951	9.00
Leprechaun, Please God, 1968	25.00
Leprechaun, Praise Be, 1968	20.00
Lexington, 1968	8.00
LSU, 1970	26.00
Memphis, 1969	15.00
Memphis Sesquicentennial, 1969, 10 In.	40.00
Monticello, Left Handle, 1968	23.00
Monticello, Right Handle, 1968	5.00
Nebraska, 1972	29.00
Ohio State, 1970	20.00
Old Fitz 101, 1978	5.00
Old Ironsides	5.00
Pheasant Rising, 1972	8.00
Pilgrim Landing, 1970	18.00
Ram, Bighorn, 1971	7.00
Rip Van Winkle, 1971 ....*Illus*	30.00
Songs Of Ireland, 1974	22.00
Sons Of Ireland, 1969 ....10.00 to 15.00	
South Carolina, Tricentennial, 1970	14.00
Texas University, 1971	15.00
Tournament, 1963 ....*Illus*	8.00
Tree Of Life, 1964	7.00
Triangle, 1976	5.00
Venetian, 1966	5.00
Vermont, 1970	18.00
Virginia, 1972	22.00
W.V. Forest Festival, 1973	30.00

OLD MR. BOSTON

It seems strange that a liquor company began as a candy factory, but that is part of the history of Old Mr. Boston. The Ben Burk Candy Company started in 1927 making non-alcoholic cordials during Prohibition. After Repeal, they became the first Massachusetts company to get a license for distilled spirits. They built a still and started making gin. One of the first brand names used was Old Mr. Boston. There was even a live Mr. Boston, an actor who made appearances for the company. In the early 1940s the company was sold to American Distilleries, but four years later Samuel Burk and Hyman Burkowitz, brothers, bought the company back. They expanded the Old Mr. Boston brand to include other beverages, such as flavored cordials and homogenized eggnog. They claim to be the first to introduce the quarter-pint size. In the mid-1960s the company began putting the liquor in decanters. No decanters were made after the early 1970s. They also made Rocking Chair Whiskey in a bottle that actually rocked. Traditionally, whiskey barrels were rolled back and forth on ships to improve the taste. Ships' captains liked the improved flavor and when they retired they would tie barrels of whiskey to their rocking chairs. A series of liquors in glass cigar-like tubes called *The Thin Man* were made in the mid-1960s. Glenmore Distillers Company acquired Old Mr. Boston in 1969. The brand name was changed to Mr. Boston about 1975. Barton Brands bought the Mr. Boston name about 1994. Mr. Boston products are still made.

The Mr. Boston trademark was redesigned in the 1950s and again in the 1970s. Each time he became thinner, younger, and more dapper. The slogan *An innkeepers tradition since 1868* was used in the 1980s. It refers to the year the Old Mr. Boston mark was first registered.

AMVETS, Iowa Convention, 1975	10.00
Anthony Wayne, 1970	10.00
Assyrian Convention, 1975	21.00
Bart Starr, No. 15	40.00
Berkley, W.V.	24.00
Bingo In Illinois, 1974	13.00
Black Hills Motor Club, 1976	25.00
Clown Head, 1973	16.00
Clown Head, Signature, 1974	16.00
Cog Railway, 1978	30.00
Concord Coach, 1976	26.00
Dan Patch, 1970	15.00
Dan Patch, 1973	15.00
Daniel Webster Cabin, 1977	19.00
Deadwood, South Dakota, 1975	16.00
Eagle Convention, 1976	8.00
Eagle Convention, 75th Anniversary, 1973	14.00
Eagle Convention, 78th Anniversary, 1973	13.00
Eagle Convention, Atlanta, 1972	14.00
Eagle Convention, Boston, 1971	8.00
Elkins, W.V., Stump, 1975	20.00
Fire Engine, 1974	30.00
Green Bay, No. 87	30.00
Greensboro Open, Golf Bag, 1976	34.00
Greensboro Open, Golf Shoe, 1978	37.00
Guitar, 1968	10.00
Illinois Capitol, 1970	16.00
Lincoln, Rider, 1972	12.00
Lion, Sitting, 1974	14.00
Miss Madison Boat, 1973	36.00
Miss Nebraska	16.00
Mississippi Bicentennial, 1976	16.00
Molly Pitcher, 1975	8.00
Monticello, 1974	12.00
Mooseheart, 1972	12.00
Nathan Hale, 1975	14.00
Nebraska, No. 1, Gold, 1970	45.00
Nebraska Czechs, 1970	8.00

New Hampshire, 1976	17.00
Paul Bunyan, 1971	10.00
Paul Revere, 1975	10.00
Polish American Legion, 1976	15.00
Presidential Inauguration, 1953	18.00
Prestige Bookend, 1970	9.00
Race Car, Mario Andretti, No. 9, Yellow	45.00
Red Dog Dan, 1974	12.00
Sherry Pitcher	4.00
Ship Lantern, 1974	18.00
Shriner, AAONMA, Camel, 1975	14.00
Shriner, Bektash Temple, 1976	25.00
Steelhead Trout, 1976	14.00
Tennessee Centennial	10.00
Town Crier, 1976	12.00
Venus	15.00
W.V. Forest Festival, 1975	50.00
W.V. National Guard, 1973	35.00
Wisconsin Football	25.00
York, Nebraska, 1970	13.00

--------------------------- **OLD RIP VAN WINKLE** ---------------------------

Old Rip Van Winkle apothecary jars and figurals shaped like Rip Van Winkle were made from 1968 to 1977. J.P. Van Winkle and Son, Louisville, Kentucky, made these bottles and others under the Old Commonwealth and Old Fitzgerald labels. Old Rip Van Winkle bourbon is still sold.

Bay Colony, 1975	13.00
Cardinal, 1974	15.00 to 17.00
Colonial Virginia, 1974	12.00
Kentucky Sportsman, 1973	25.00
Kentucky Wildcat, 1974	27.00 to 33.00
New Jersey Bicentennial, 1975	15.00
New York Bicentennial, 1975	16.00
No. 1, Rip Van Winkle, Green, 1975	24.00
No. 2, Rip Van Winkle, Reclining, 1975	30.00
No. 3, Rip Van Winkle, Standing, 1977	30.00
Sanford, N.C., Centennial, 1974	12.00

------------------------------- **PACESETTER** -------------------------------

Bottles shaped like cars and trucks were made under the Pacesetter label from 1974 to about 1983.

Ahrens Fox Pumper, 1983	190.00
Camero Z-28, Gold, 1982	46.00 to 48.00
Camero Z-28, Platinum, 1982	53.00
Corvette, 1975	27.00
Corvette, 1975, Moving Wheels	69.00
Corvette, 1978, Black, 375 Milliliter	39.00 to 42.00
Corvette, 1978, Brown, 375 Milliliter	39.00
Corvette, 1978, White, 375 Milliliter	39.00
Corvette, 1978, Yellow, 375 Milliliter	39.00
Corvette, 1980, White, 1 Liter	57.00
Corvette, 1980, Yellow, 1 Liter	57.00
Fire Truck, LaFrance, White, 1982	68.00
Fire Truck, Snorkle, Red, 1982	64.00
Mack Pumper	190.00
Olsonite Eagle, No. 8, 1974	70.00
Pirsch Pumper, Red, 1983	69.00
Pirsch Pumper, White, 1983	60.00
Pontiac Firebird, 1980	40.00
Tractor, Massey Ferguson, 1943	95.00
Tractor, No. 1, John Deere, 1982	140.00 to 155.00
Tractor, No. 3, International Harvester, 1983	105.00

Tractor, No. 3, International Harvester, 1983, Miniature 122.00
Tractor, No. 4, 4-Wheel Drive, Big Red, 1983 .... 120.00
Tractor, No. 4, 4-Wheel Drive, Ford, 1983 .... 100.00
Tractor, No. 4, 4-Wheel Drive, Green Machine, 1983 .... 90.00
Tractor, No. 5, Allis Chalmers, 1984 .... 100.00
Tractor, Steiger, 4-Wheel Drive, 1959 .... 180.00
Truck, Coca-Cola 245.00
Truck, Distillery, Barrel, Mack 125.00
Truck, Distillery, Mack ....115.00 to 125.00
Truck, Elizabethtown 255.00
Vukovich, 1974 .... 90.00

PEPPER SAUCE

There was little refrigeration and poor storage facilities for fresh meat in the nineteenth century. Slightly spoiled food was often cooked and eaten with the help of strong spices or sauces. Small hot chili peppers were put into a bottle of vinegar. After a few weeks the spicy mixture was called *pepper sauce.* A distinctive bottle, now known as a pepper sauce bottle, was favored for this mixture. It was a small bottle, 6 to 12 inches high, with a long slim neck. The bottle could be square or cylindrical or decorated with arches or rings. Most were made of common bottle glass in shades of aqua or green. A few were made of cobalt or milk glass. Very early examples may have a pontil mark. More information on pepper sauce can be found in the book *Ketchup, Pickles, Sauces* by Betty Zumwalt.

Aqua, 4-Sided, Applied Top, 8 1/2 In. 22.00
Cathedral, 1 Panel, Ribs, Square 15.00
Cathedral, 4-Sided, Aqua, Applied Top, Smooth Base 110.00
Cathedral, 4-Sided, Aqua, Olive Green, Applied Top 358.00
Cathedral, 4-Sided, Blue Aqua, Applied Top, Smooth Base 66.00
Cathedral, 4-Sided, Green 55.00
Cathedral, 6-Sided, Aqua, Applied Top, OP, 10 1/2 In. 209.00
Cathedral, 6-Sided, Aqua, Double Collar, 10 3/4 In. 165.00
Cathedral, Applied Top, OP, 10 3/4 In. 300.00
Cathedral, Aqua, Applied Double Collar, OP, 8 1/2 In. 88.00
Cathedral, Aqua, Applied Top, 8 3/4 In. 55.00
Cathedral, Blue Aqua, Applied Top, 11 In. 176.00
Cathedral, Blue Green, Double Collar, OP, 8 5/8 In. ....230.00 to 231.00
Cathedral, Dark Green, Applied Top 110.00
Cathedral, Gothic, Aqua, Applied Double Collar, 8 1/2 In. 45.00
Diamond Packing Co., Bridgeton, N.J., Aqua, Diamond Logo, Bulbous 20.00
Gothic Style, 6-Sided, Aqua 44.00
Knickerbocker, Blue Aqua, 8-Sided, Sloping Double Collar, Pontil, 6 1/2 In. .... *Illus* 392.00
L & B, Cathedral, Aqua, Double Collar, 9 1/8 In. .... *Illus* 525.00
L & B, Gothic Style, 4-Sided, Aqua, Embossed, OP 358.00
Light Green, 10-Sided, Applied Ring, IP, 9 1/4 In. 44.00
Medium Green Aqua, Flowers Around Neck, Applied Top, 8 3/4 In. 50.00

Pepper Sauce,
Knickerbocker, Blue
Aqua, 8-Sided, Sloping
Double Collar, Pontil,
6 1/2 In.

Pepper Sauce,
L & B, Cathedral,
Aqua, Double
Collar, 9 1/8 In.

Never run an ad that says "Call after 6 P.M." It is an announcement that you are away from the house during the day.

Teal Green, Ribs 15.00
W.K. Lewis & Co., Amethyst, Applied Top, OP, 8 1/4 In. 143.00
Wells Miller & Provost, No. 217 Front Street, New York, Aqua, 8 1/4 In. ....77.00 to 121.00

———————————— **PEPSI-COLA** ————————————

Caleb Davis Bradham, a New Bern, North Carolina, druggist, invented and named Pepsi-Cola. Although he registered the trademark, the word *Pepsi-Cola* in calligraphy script, in 1903, he claimed that it had been used since 1898. A simpler version was registered in 1906. The bottle is marked with the name. The name in a hexagonal frame with the words *A Sparkling Beverage* was registered in 1937. This logo was printed on the bottle. The bottle cap colors were changed to red, white, and blue in 1941 as a patriotic gesture. Until 1951, the words Pepsi and Cola were separated by 2 dashes. These bottles are called *double dash* or *double dot* by collectors. In 1951 the modern logo with a single hyphen was introduced. The simulated cap logo was used at the same time. The name *Pepsi* was started in 1911, but it was not until 1966 that the block-lettered logo was registered. Both names are still used. A few very early Pepsi bottles were made of amber glass. Many other Pepsi bottles with local bottlers' names were made in the early 1900s. Modern bottles made for special events are also collected. There is a club, Pepsi-Cola Collectors Club, P.O. Box 817, Claremont, CA 91711. The company has archives at One Pepsi Way, Somers, NY 10589.

2-Color, Large Logo, ACL, 1960s, 26 Oz. 10.00
2-Color Label Challenge, 25 Cents, 1980s, 26 Oz. 10.00
3-Color Paper Label Challange, 25 Cents, ACL, 1980s 10.00
Aqua, BIM, Crown Top, c.1908 .... 50.00
Buffalo Sabers, Long Neck, 1970-1990, 20 Years, ACL 10.00
Canada, Swirl, Contents, ACL, 10 Oz. 20.00
Cincinnati Reds, 1975 World Baseball Champions, 1976, 16 Oz. ....7.00 to 12.00
Clemson University, Undefeated Season, Schedule & Scores, 1974, 12 Oz. 10.00
Commemorative, Richard Petty, Long Neck, ACL 10.00
Dallas Cowboys, 1971 NFL World Champs, January 16, 1972, 16 Oz. 35.00
Danville, Va, Aqua, Embossed, Registered, Not To Be Sold, 6 1/2 Oz. 76.00
Diet, 3-Color, ACL, 1980s 10.00
Diet, Less Then One Calorie Per Bottle, 11 In. 4.00
Double Dot, Green, 544 B On Bottom, Augusta, Ga., 7 3/4 In. 45.00
Double Dot, Red & White ACL, Embossed Vertical Logos, Sedalia, 1942 .... 154.00
Double Dot, Red, White & Blue Label & Cap, Lincoln, Neb., 1947 .... 20.00
Fountain Syrup, Double Dot, Cap Pictures Palm Tree, Fairview, Mont. 40.00
Fountain Syrup, Double Dot, Long Island, Ny., 1942, 12 Oz. 35.00
Fountain Syrup, Double Dot, Neodesha, Kan., Contents, 1943, 12 Oz. 59.00
Green, Double Dot, 1950s, 12 Oz. 36.00
Green, Throw-A-Way, Crown Cap, 1960s, 10 Oz. 20.00
Greenville, N.C., Double Dot, P.C.B., Embossed, Early 1900s 48.00
Jar, Porcelain, Syrup, Meadow Scene, Handle Lid, Signed RSP, Reproduction, 1970 ..... 2860.00
Lima-Wapakoneta, Ohio, Red & White ACL, 8 Oz. 11.50
N.Y. 5 Cent Refund, Red, White & Blue Label, Cap, Contents, 7 Oz. 17.00
Nebraska Cornhuskers Bottle, Original Cap, Contents, 1976 .... 10.00
New York, N.Y., Clear, Crown Top, ABM, 8 3/4 In. 8.00
North Carolina, The Tarheel State, 1976, 10 Oz. ....7.00 to 12.00
Paper Label, No Deposit, 1980s, 40 Oz. 10.00
Pepsi Light, Cap, Twisted Base, Blue, White & Yellow ACL, 1975, 32 Oz. 26.00
Pepsi-Cola Of Charlotte 75th Anniversary, 1905-1980, 1980, 10 Oz. ....10.00 to 15.00
Quincy Ill., 1946, 12 Oz. 15.00
Raleigh, N.C., Double Dot, Embossed, C.G. Co., Green, Crown Top, c.1908 .... 70.00
Red, White & Blue Label, ACL, Cap, 1957, 10 Oz. 13.00
Red, White & Blue Paper Label, No Return, Cap, 1960s, 28 Oz. 10.40
Red Lodge, Mont., Double Dot, Red, White & Blue Label, 9 3/4 In. 20.00
St. Louis Blues, 6 Years In The NHL, 6 Years In The Playoffs, Contents, 1973, 16 Oz. ... 16.50
Straight Sides, Middlesboro, Kentucky, c.1920 .... 204.00
Straight Sides, Ribs, Embossed Quality Beverages, Roanoke, Ala., c.1930, 9 Oz. 46.00
Swirl, 1960s, 6 1/2 Oz. 20.00
Swirl, 1972 .... 10.00
Swirl, Script One Side, Block Letters Other Side, No Return, 1970s, 12 Oz. 16.00
Woodland Ice & Bottling Works, Woodland, Calif., Double Dot, Amber, Label, 12 Oz. ... 32.50

—————————————————————— PERFUME ——————————————————————

Perfume is a liquid mixture of aromatic spirits and alcohol. Cologne is similar but has more alcohol in the mixture so it is not as strong. Perfume bottles are smaller than colognes and usually more decorative. Most perfume bottles today are from the twentieth century. Some were made by famous glass makers such as Lalique or Webb, and some held expensive perfumes such as Schiaparelli, Nina Ricci's Coeur de Joie, or D'Orsay's Le Lys D'Orsay. DeVilbiss is a manufacturer of the spray tops used on perfume bottles and the name sometimes appears in a description. The word *factice*, which often appears in ads, refers to store display bottles. The International Perfume Bottle Association publishes a newsletter (3314 Shamrock Rd., Tampa, FL 33629). Related bottles may be found in the Cologne and Scent categories.

2 Cherubim, Clear & Frosted, Dancing Couple Stopper, Czechoslovakia, 7 1/4 In.	660.00
3 Orange Enameled Floral Panels, Black Glass, Signed, DeVilbiss Atomizer, 7 In.	187.00
A. Bourjois & Cie, Ideal Oeillet, Decanter Shape, Clear Glass Stopper, 1915, 5 In.	88.00
A.A. Vantine, Jafleur, Turk Wearing A Fez Shape, 1915, 2 3/4 In.	431.00
Adrian, Saint, White Cap, Sinner, Black Cap, Celluloid Box, 2 1/4 In., 2 Piece	66.00
Ahmed Soliman, Egyptian Design, Plastic Case, 4 1/2 In.	201.00
Ahmed Soliman, Egyptian Figure, Rectangular, Gilt, Jewel Stopper, c.1919, 3 1/2 In.	488.00
Amber, Acorn Finial, Pedestal, DeVilbiss Atomizer, 10 1/4 In.	550.00
Amber, Tassel, DeVilbiss Atomizer, 6 3/8 In.	110.00
Amber Glass, Deep Opaque Yellow Enamel, Metal Atomizer, 5 In.	132.00
Amber Glass, DeVilbiss Atomizer, Curvilinear Metal Stand, 2 In.	220.00
Amber Iridescent, Pedestal Base, Metal, Signed, DeVilbiss Atomizer, 7 In.	253.00
Aqua Gazelle Enamel, Wheel Cut Leaves, Blue Glass, Signed, DeVilbiss Atomizer, 4 In.	440.00
Art Deco, Black Base, Floral Relief Stopper, 5 3/4 In.	2300.00
Art Deco, Blue Grape Stopper, 12 In.	633.00
Art Deco, Blue, Stylized Foliate Sides, Black Leaves, Orange, 2 1/2 In.	403.00
Art Deco, Cloisonne, Geometric Design, Black, White, 9 1/2 In.	4313.00
Art Deco, Cupid, Piping, Silver, Gold, Black, Red Stopper, 5 1/2 In.	345.00
Art Deco, Frosted Glass, Black Base, Stopper, 4 In.	2013.00
Art Deco, Malachite Elephant Stopper, 5 In.	2300.00 to 5463.00
Art Deco, Molded, Hemispherical Shape, Cupid Stopper, 4 In.	748.00
Art Deco, Nude Figures, Blue Mottled, 1935, 8 In.	4313.00
Art Deco, Nude Figures, Red, 5 1/2 In.	748.00
Art Deco, Nude Figures, Red, 6 In.	4888.00
Art Deco, Red Flowers, 7 In.	4025.00
Art Deco, Stylized Flowers, Blue Mottled, 8 In.	173.00
Art Deco, Stylized Flowers, Gilt, Orange, Stopper, 5 1/4 In.	8050.00
Atkinson, Chef D'Oeuvre, Faceted 8-Sided Stopper, Red Satin Lined Box, 4 In.	605.00
Aurene, Atomic Cloud, Gold, Stopper, Ruffled Neck, Signed, 2 In.	1980.00
Babani, Ambre De Delhi, Vertical Panels On Side, Molded Roses Stopper, 3 1/8 In.	550.00
Babani, Secret Princess Nefertiti, Gold Egyptian Figure, Stopper, 4 1/8 In.	1980.00
Babs Creations, Yesteryear, Woman With Long Dress, Red Velvet Bow, 2 In.	77.00
Baccarat, Bichara, Myrbaha, Pyramid, Head Stopper, Label, c.1913, 4 In.	632.50
Baccarat, Clear With Red Overlay, Metal Atomizer Pump, MV Emblem, 4 3/8 In.	286.00
Baccarat, Coty L'Or, Eardrop Shape & Stopper, Presentation Box, 1959, 6 3/8 In.	5500.00
Baccarat, D'Orsay, Porte-Bonheur, Elephant Stopper, On Ball, Box, 3 1/2 In.	1840.00
Baccarat, D'Orsay, Toujours Fidele, 3 1/2 In.	690.00
Baccarat, Elizabeth Arden, It's You, Hand Form, Stand, Glass Stopper, 1937, 8 1/2 In.	460.00
Baccarat, Empire, Flute, 7 In.	285.00
Baccarat, Forest, Ming Toy, Figural, Chinese Woman, Fan, 1923, 4 3/8 In.	2760.00
Baccarat, Guerlain, Coque D'Or, Cobalt Blue, Gold Enameled, Bowtie Shape, 3 In.	467.00
Baccarat, Guerlain, Jicky, Quadrilobe Stopper, Unopened, Brown Box, 3 7/8 In.	143.00
Baccarat, Houbigant, Subtilite, Sitting Buddha Shape, Brass Ring Stopper, 3 3/8 In.	495.00
Baccarat, Jovoy, Gardez-Moi, Figural, Black Panther, 1926, 6 In.	2530.00
Baccarat, Lubin, Kismet, Elephant Form, Seated Man Stopper, 1921, 4 1/4 In.	2990.00
Baccarat, Maunday, Muquet, Gilt Foliate Panels, 2 In.	575.00
Baccarat, Pois De Senteur, Decanter Shape, Label, Box, 3 7/8 In.	412.00
Baccarat, Ramses, Ramses IV, 1919, 5 In.	3450.00
Baccarat, Schiaparelli, Le Roy Soleil, Sea, Sun Stopper, Salvador Dali, Box, 1946, 7 In.	3450.00
Balenciaga, Quadrille, Atomizer, Box, France	20.00
Ball Shape, Intaglio Cut Thistles, Leaves, DeVilbiss Atomizer, 1908, 5 In.	88.00

Band Of Grapes & Leaves, Gold Metal Neck, Metal Atomizer, Ball, Tassel, 4 In. 154.00
Bell Shape, Band Of Flowers & Leaf, Gold Stopper, 6 In. 55.00
Bell Shape, Daisy & Leaf Design, Wheel Cut With Daisy Stopper, 5 In. 44.00
Bell Shape, Pleated, Faceted Ball Stopper, Cut Crystal, 5 In. 22.00
Benoit, Merry Christmas, Madonna & Child Stopper, Maurice Depinoix, 1927, 4 3/4 In. . 2760.00
Bernard Lalande, La Tour Eiffel Shape, Crystal Stopper, Signed, 2 In. 440.00
Bichara, Syriana, Pyramid Shape, Pharaoh's Head Crystal Stopper, 1913, 4 In. 4125.00
Bienaime, Caravane, Molded Facets Bottle & Stopper, Gold Box, 4 In. 308.00
Bigny, Beau Catcher, Molded Large Squares, Stopper, Box, 2 1/2 In. 66.00
Black, Gold Enamel, Ball, Signed, DeVilbiss Atomizer, 5 In. ....187.00 to 253.00
Black, Gold, Gilt Vertical Stripes, Pedestal, DeVilbiss Atomizer, c.1920, 9 In. 300.00
Black Bakelite Finial, Black Glass, DeVilbiss Atomizer, Original Box, Signed, 5 In., Pair . 825.00
Black Enamel, Gold, Light Amber Glass, Metal Atomizer, 3 In. 132.00
Black Enamel, Pedestal Base, Signed, DeVilbiss Atomizer, 6 In., Pair 275.00
Black Enamel, Silver Design, Metal Atomizer, 5 In. 110.00
Black Enameled Interior, Gold Scroll Exterior, DeVilbiss Atomizer, 5 In., Pair 715.00
Black Enameled Internal, Gold Exterior, Metal Neck, DeVilbiss Atomizer, 2 In. 308.00
Black Flowers, DeVilbiss Atomizer, 2 In. 99.00
Black Glass, Pyramid, Etched Flowers Band, Long Glass Dabber, 6 3/8 In. 297.00
Black Glass, Signed, DeVilbiss Atomizer, 5 In. 143.00
Black Glass Medallion, Amber Glass, Gold Enamel, Signed, DeVilbiss Atomizer, 6 In. ... 176.00
Black Glass Medallion, Chrome Metal Pedestal Base, DeVilbiss Atomizer, 6 In. 385.00
Blue, Dancer & Flowers Metal, Clear Dancer Stopper, Czechoslovakia, 5 1/2 In. 935.00
Blue, Metal Filigree, Blue Stones, Filigree Cap, Czechoslovakia, 4 5/8 In. 231.00
Blue, Polished Facets, Molded Nude, Floral Garlands Stopper, Czechoslovakia, 7 7/8 In. . 1650.00
Blue, Triangular, Pink Molded Nude, Flowers Stopper, Czechoslovakia, 7 1/8 In. 2970.00
Blue Enamel, Crochet Cover, DeVilbiss Atomizer, 7 In. 99.00
Boucheron, Boucheron Parfum, Blue Glass, Ring Shape, Blue Glass Stopper, 3 In. 110.00
Bourjois, Ashes Of Roses, Black Glass Stopper, Red Box, 2 In. 220.00
Bourjois, Blue Glass, Cork Lined Stopper, Box, 8 In. 77.00
Bourjois, Courage, Enamel, Blue Glass Stopper, Enamel, Oval, 1940, 7 In. 88.00
Bourjois, Evening In Paris, Blue Glass, Frosted Glass Stopper, 5 In. 231.00
Bourjois, Evening In Paris, Blue, Clear Fan Stopper, Silver Label, 4 1/8 In. 176.00
Bourjois, Evening In Paris, Blue, Frosted Glass Stopper, Silver Label, Box, 4 In. 220.00
Bourjois, Evening In Paris, Clear, Blue Speckled Cap, 4 Oz. 15.00
Bourjois, Evening In Paris, Dark Blue, Black Cap, Clam Shell Holder, 2 In. 176.00
Bourjois, Evening In Paris, Soir De Paris, Cobalt Blue, Blue Bakelite Owl, 2 In. 209.00
Bourjois, Evening In Paris, Urn Shape, Blue Glass, Clear Stopper, 2 In. 154.00
Bourjois, Glamour, Scalloped Shape, Gold Cap, Green, White Box, 1950, 2 1/2 In. 44.00
Bourjois, Jasmin, Molded Open Blossom, Floral Bouquet, Brass Cap, 3 In. 143.00
Bourjois, Kobako, Chrysanthemum Design On Box, Glass Stopper, 7 In. 319.00
Bourjois, Kobako, Oriental Snuff Shape, Leafy Design, Red & Black Box, 3 1/2 In. 357.00
Bourjois, Ramage, Lovebird, Gold Ribbed Cap, White Satin, Signed, 1950, 5 In. 66.00
Brilliantine, Amber, Stopper, 1885-1925, 4 In. 110.00
Brilliantine, Barrel Shape, Gilt, Enamel, Rose Shape Stopper, 1885-1925, 4 In. 468.00
Brilliantine, Green, Gilt, Enamel, Ferns, Poppy Shape Stopper, 1885-1925, 3 In. 990.00
Brilliantine, Strawberry, Satin, Gilt, Enamel, 8-Sided Cut Shoulders, Stopper, 3 In. 770.00
Bryenne, Chu Chin Chow, Oriental Fat Man, Gold, Dark Blue, Inner Stopper, 2 3/8 In. ... 2310.00
Bullet Shape, Brass Scroll Frame, Black Glass, DeVilbiss Atomizer, 6 In. 365.00
Bunker Hill Monument, Milk Glass, 12 In. 165.00
C'Est Le Moment, Square Pillar Shape, Ball Stopper, Box, 4 1/2 In. 88.00
Calliste Mon Studio, Round Overcap, Black Glass, Black Glass Inner Stopper, 3 In. 110.00
Cameo Glass, Seascape, Sailboat, Olive Green To Ocher Ground, Atomizer, 9 In. 127.00
Capucci, Graffiti, Triangular Shape, Yellow Box, Clear Glass Stopper, 1960, 5 In. 22.00
Carle, Beau K, Black, Oval, Black Round Stopper, Tassel, Box, 3 1/8 In. 154.00
Carnelian Glass, Gold Metal Neck & Hinged Cap, Stopper, Leather Box, 2 1/8 In. 880.00
Caron, Bellodgia, Gold Lions' Heads Sides, Black Silk Lined Box, 6 1/2 In. 1100.00
Caron, Fleurs De Rocaille, Urn Shape, Flowers Under Glass Stopper, Box, 3 1/2 In. 176.00
Caron, Le Tabac Blond, Flat Oval Shape, Modeled Stopper, Label, Box, 3 1/3 In. 165.00
Caron, Mimosa, Rectangular, Gold Medal, Faceted Stopper, 4 3/8 In. 297.00
Caron, Nocturnes, Gold Metal Pendant, Black Sack & Box, 1 In. 66.00
Caron, Or Et Noir, 2 Bees Molded Either Side Gold Stopper, Box, 4 1/4 In. 467.00
Caron, Royal Bain De Champagne, Champagne Shape, Screw Cap, Box, 6 1/2 In. 77.00

Caron, Voeu De Noel, Christmas Wish, White Glass, Open Flowers, Stopper, 6 In. 495.00
Chabrawichi, It's You, My Life, Nothing But You, Gold Caps, Box, 3 In. 121.00
Chanel, No. 5, 2 Flacons 58.00
Charcoal, Jeweled Base, Stepped Sides, Prism Stopper, Czechoslovakia, 5 1/2 In. 770.00
Charles Of The Ritz, Directoire, Urn Shape, Original Box, 1946, 3 1/2 In. 173.00
Chevalier De La Nuit, Black Crystal, Box 190.00
Chevalier Garde, Fleur De Perse, Ball Shape, Amber Patina, Stopper, 6 In. 165.00
Chinaman, Cobalt Blue, Atomizer Head, Ground Lip, 5 5/8 In. 700.00
Christian Dior, Diorissimo, Atomizer, Box, 7/16 Oz., 3 1/2 In. 24.00
Christian Dior, J'Appartiens A Miss Dior, 7 In. 6325.00
Christian Dior, Miss Dior, Amphora Shape, Stopper, Unopened, 3 3/4 In. 55.00
Christian Dior, Miss Dior, Amphora, Crystal Windows, Gold Enamel, Stopper, 7 In. 302.00
Cigar Shape, Black Glass, Band Of Swirling Roses, Orange, Gold Enamel, 4 In. 1045.00
Cigogne, Stork Club, Wooden Stork Holding Vial, 1930, 8 In. 144.00
Ciro, Bouquet Antique, Blue, Gold Enameled Stopper, 9 In. 121.00
Ciro, Danger, Inner Stopper, Black Art Deco Overcap, Box, 4 1/8 In. 1650.00
Ciro, Le Chevalier De La Nuit, Stylized Knight Shape, Stopper, Black, Box, 4 3/4 In. 440.00
Ciro, Le Chevalier, Knight's Armor, Frosted, Julien Viard, 1923, 7 3/4 In. 345.00
Ciro, Oh La La, Torso Shape, Gold Cap, 5 x 7 In. 33.00
Ciro, Oh La La, Torso Shape, Leather Skirt, Gold Top, Box, Contents, 2 1/8 In. 440.00
Ciro, Parfum Maskee, Pierrot Shape, White Opaque, Black Glass Stopper, 2 In. 412.50
Ciro, Surrender, Faceted Gemstone Shape, Beige, Gold Box, Stopper, 6 In. 22.00
Clear, Cut, Elaborate Facets, DeVilbiss Atomizer, 10 In. 220.00
Clear, Frosted, Diamond Shape, Clear & Red Stopper, Czechoslovakia, 3 7/8 In. 220.00
Cobalt Blue, Ground Lip, Rectangular, Glass Stopper 35.00
Coeur Joie Store Display, Box 260.00
Colgate & Co., Caprice, Apothecary Shape, Clear Stopper, 1890, 7 In. 22.00
Conde, Seville, Label, Amber Glass Stopper, Box, 1920s, 3 7/8 In. 99.00
Corday, Circular Box, Stopper, 1/4 Oz. 110.00
Corday, Jet Parfume, Fountain Shape, Frosted & Aqua Stopper, 1924, 5 7/8 In. 2310.00
Corday, Nude Figure, Rose Patina, Glass Atomizer, Marked, 3 In. 220.00
Corday, Tambour Frenzy, Egg Shape, Gold Stopper, Contents, Box, 3 7/8 In. 198.00
Corday, Toujours Moi, Flat Round Shape, Brown Patina, Design, Stopper, Box, 3 In. 154.00
Corday, Zigane, Violin Shape, Gold Enamel, Pink Box, Pink Satin Lining, 3 In. 187.00
Corday, Zigane, Violin Shape, Stopper, Pink Violin Box, 3 7/8 In. 231.00
Corinne, Damier Damao, Nude Male Torch Runner On Gold Metal Stopper, 3 In. 412.50
Cornucopia, Flacon, Necklace Attached To Bottle, Silver Sterling Cap, 4 In. 133.00
Coty, L'Or, Crystal, Teardrop, Oval Facets, Yellow, White Fabric Box, 1959, 6 1/3 In. 5500.00
Coty, L'Origan, 8-Sided, Frosted Molded Berries Stopper, Box, 5 1/8 In. 522.00
Coty, Meteor, Flask Shape, Gold Cap, Clear Plastic Case, 1 7/8 In. 99.00
Coty, Muse, Inner Stopper, Frosted Overcap, Contents, Box, 3 1/4 In. 275.00

Perfume, Cut Glass, Blue, Swirled Facets, Intaglio Floral Stopper, Czechoslovakia, 4 1/2 In.

Perfume, Cut Glass, Fan-Shaped Facets, Intaglio Grape, Leaf Stopper, Czechoslovakia, 5 1/2 In.

Perfume, Cut Glass, Green, Intaglio, Cutout Scarf Dancer Stopper, 4 7/8 In.

Perfume, Cut Glass, Intaglio, Ribbons & Roses, Dabber, Czechoslovakia, 6 In.

Cranberry, Acid Textured Finish, Gilt, Signed, Bohemia, DeVilbiss Atomizer, 6 1/4 In. ... 123.00
Cranberry Swirl, Metal Neck & Stopper, Long Dabber, DeVilbiss Atomizer, 6 1/4 In. 495.00
Cri D'Amour, Purse Shape, Gold Label, Stopper, France, Box, 2 3/8 In. 44.00
Crown Perfumery Company, London, Dark Emerald Green, Stopper 25.00
Crusellas, Lucresia Bordi, Bird Holding Branch, Green, Brown, Stopper, 4 In. 1100.00
Crystal, Etched, Trumpet Form, Chrome Mounts, Atomizer, Black Bulb, 4 In. 165.00
Crystal, Red Overlay, Grapes & Leaves Middle, Prism Stopper, Bohemia, 7 In. 176.00
Cut Glass, Black, Hemisphere Shape, Fan Shape Floral Stopper, Czechoslovakia, 5 In. ... 412.00
Cut Glass, Blue, 6 Oval Panel Sides, Oval Lovers Stopper, Czechoslovakia, 8 7/8 In. 2420.00
Cut Glass, Blue, Diamonds, Adam & Eve Stopper, 7 3/8 In. 1430.00
Cut Glass, Blue, Intaglio Flowers, Spire Stopper, Czechoslovakia, 5 1/2 In. 275.00
Cut Glass, Blue, Pleats & Rays, Arrow Intaglio Roses Stopper, Czechoslovakia, 9 1/2 In. . 550.00
Cut Glass, Blue, Sleigh Shape, Intaglio Stopper, Czechoslovakia, 5 1/2 x 8 1/4 In. 605.00
Cut Glass, Blue, Swirled Facets, Intaglio Floral Stopper, Czechoslovakia, 4 1/2 In. ...*Illus* 319.00
Cut Glass, Diamonds, Intaglio Daisy & Butterfly Dabber, Czechoslovakia, 5 1/2 In. 297.00
Cut Glass, Fan Facets, Intaglio Grape, Leaf Stopper, Czechoslovakia, 5 1/2 In. ......*Illus* 220.00
Cut Glass, Geometric Facets, Blue Stones, Molded Flowers, Czechoslovakia, 7 In. 253.00
Cut Glass, Green, Intaglio, Cutout Scarf Dancer Stopper, 4 7/8 In. ....*Illus* 275.00
Cut Glass, Green, Leaf Facets, Cutout Hearts Stopper, Czechoslovakia, 4 3/8 In. 209.00
Cut Glass, Inner Stopper, Silver Hinged Flowers Cap, 2 In. 110.00
Cut Glass, Intaglio, Amber, Frosted, Czechoslovakia, 4 1/2 In. 286.00
Cut Glass, Intaglio, Ribbons & Roses, Dabber, Czechoslovakia, 6 In. ....*Illus* 297.00
Cut Glass, Oblong Shape, Star Shape Stopper, Czechoslovakia, 6 In. 357.00
Cut Glass, Panels, Royal Blue To Clear, Steeple Stopper, 5 1/4 In. 135.00
Cut Glass, Peach, Diagonal Band, Frosted Floral Stopper, Czechoslovakia, 8 1/2 In. 357.00
Cut Glass, Pink, Asymmetric Shape, Spire Stopper, Czechoslovakia, 4 7/8 In. 220.00
Cut Glass, Stepped Pyramid, Art Deco Dancer Stopper, Czechoslovakia, 5 7/8 In. 495.00
Cut Glass, Upward Star Shaped, 6 Points, Mushroom Stopper, 5 1/8 In. 330.00
Cut Glass, Violet, Molded Flowers Sides, Oval Roses Stopper, Czechoslovakia, 5 In. 550.00
Cut Glass, Yellow, Abstract Vertical Design, Stopper, 6 7/8 In. 385.00
Cut Glass, Yellow, Hearts, Ball Shape, Cut Flowers Stopper, Paris, 8 In. ....*Illus* 297.00
Czechoslovakia, Baccarat Type, Gem Stone Shape, Red & Crystal Stopper, 2 3/8 In. 120.00
D'Orsay, Chypre, Stopper, 1913, 3 3/4 In. 374.00
D'Orsay, Duo, Coat Of Arms Molded On Top Of Stopper, Oval, 3 In. 154.00
D'Orsay, Duo, Rectangular Shape Box, Crystal Stopper, 7 In., Pair 88.00
D'Orsay, Fantastique, Pyramid Shape, Pointed Stopper, 1952, 5 In. 99.00
D'Orsay, Intoxication, Petals Of Skirt Shape, Gold Lame Bag, Gold Metal Cap, 2 In. 33.00
D'Orsay, Intoxication, Pleated Star-Like Shape, Hanging Label, Stopper, Box, 5 In. 176.00
D'Orsay, Le Succes, Snail's Shell Shape, Frosted, Nude Maiden Stopper, 3 7/8 In. 1870.00
D'Orsay, Mystere, Intoxication, Clear Glass Stopper, White Box, 5 x 3 In., Pair 66.00
D'Orsay, Toujours Fidele, Pillow Shape, Black Enamel, Stopper, 1912, 5 In. 330.00
Dana, Emir, Square, Vertical Panels, Contents, Black Cap, 7 1/8 In. 88.00
Dancer, Wearing Yellow Dress, Holding Urn, Metal Crown Stopper, 2 In. 330.00
Darnay, Du Monde, Clear & Frosted, Panels, Molded Leaves Stopper, 4 1/4 In. 165.00
De Raymond, Mimzy For Romance, Maroon Box, Lucite Cap, 6 In., 1.4 Oz. 77.00
Deep Orange Frosted, Gold Flowers, DeVilbiss Atomizer, 6 7/8 In. 522.00
Delettrez, Amaryllis Du Japon, Apothecary Shape, 4 1/8 In. 66.00
Depinoix, Balbani, Ambre De Delhi, Rectangular, Gold, 6 In. 460.00
Depinoix, Balbani, Chypre Egyptian, 3 3/4 In. 805.00
Depinoix, Pelissier Aragon, Les Fontaines Parfumees Grasse, 1924, 5 1/2 In. 460.00
Des Courtisanes, Salambo, Rectangular, Frosted Stopper, Box, 1925, 3 3/8 In. 440.00
Devon, Violets, Poodle Shape, Black, White Plastic Base, Black Box, 3 1/8 In. 110.00
Dorothy Gray, Indigo, Winged Cupid Stopper, 3 1/2 In. 546.00
Dralle, Veilchen, Bird Carrying A Flower Stopper, Wood Case, 4 In. 44.00
Dubarry, Blue Lagoon, Seated Woman Stopper, J. Viard, 1919, 4 In. 7475.00
Dubarry, Bouchon Pierrot En Pied, Frosted, White Dots, J. Viard, c.1916, 5 In. 1725.00
Dubarry, Bouchon Pierrot En Pied, Frosted, White Dots, J. Viard, c.1916, 6 In. 2760.00
Dubarry, Garden Of Kama, Seated Woman Stopper, 1919, 3 1/4 In. 1840.00
Dubarry, Heart's Delight, White Cap, Box With Green Glass Pierrot Top, 2 1/8 In. 308.00
Dubarry, Old English Lavender, Label, Pierrot Shape Stopper, 5 3/8 In. 2090.00
Dutch Girl Holding Barrel, Metal Atomizer, 3 In. 165.00
E.M. Hessler's Triple Extract Edelweiss, Enameled Label, Stopper, 7 1/2 In. 121.00
E.N. Lightner & Co., Detroit, Mich., Milk Glass, Label Under Glass, Stopper, 6 3/8 In. 963.00

Eisenberg, Lady In Formal Gown Holding Bouquet Of Flowers, Stopper, 5 In. 467.50
Electric Blue, Abstract Leaf Design, DeVilbiss Atomizer, 1 In., Pair 220.00
Elizabeth Arden, Blue Grass, Oval Shape, Large Round Stopper, Box, 7 1/2 In. 412.00
Elizabeth Arden, Memoire Cherie, Woman, Arms Around Bosom, Stopper, 4 In. 357.50
Elizabeth Arden, My Love, Brosse, 1948, 4 In. 201.00
Elizabeth Arden, My Love, Frosted, Inkwell Shape, Feather Stopper, Box, 2 5/8 In. 5220.00
Ellipse Pattern, Apple Green, Gilt Trim, 6-Sided, Stopper, 1870, 8 In. 275.00
Enameled, Gold Swirl Exterior, Black Interior, Signed, DeVilbiss Atomizer, 3 In. 2750.00
Ene, The Duke, Gentleman In Formal Attire, With A Cane, Red Enamel, 1930, 8 In. 88.00
Eroy, Adoree, Kneeling Nude Woman, Frosted Glass Stopper, 4 In. 176.00
Estee Lauder, Cinnabar, Faux Ivory Cat Scratching His Neck, 4 In. 357.50
Evyan, Golden Shadows, Bell Shape, Vertical Lines, Golden Silk Box, 9 In. 88.00
Evyan, Most Precious, Faceted Indentations, White Lace Case, Stopper, 4 In. 55.00
F. Wolff & Sohn, Divinia, Decanter, Mushroom Stopper, Label, Box, 3 5/8 In. 143.00
F. Wolff & Sohn, Violette Rococo, Gold Enamel, Green Satin Lining, 1908, 5 In. 187.00
Faberge, Straw Hat, Glass, Goldtone Case, Purse Size, 3 In. 10.00
Flapjack, Table Sprayer, Bakelite Atomizer, On Stand, 5 1/4 In. 633.00
Fleurettes, Flowers, Vertical Ribs, Brown, 1919, 8 In. 550.00
Floret, Les Jardins De Floret, Crystal Inner Stopper, 1924, 2 In. 55.00
Forest, Ming Toy, Oriental Lady Shape, Purple, Enamel, Stopper, 4 1/4 In. 2750.00
Forget-Me-Nots, Floral Border, Gold Metal Cap, DeVilbiss Atomizer, Signed, 2 In. 143.00
Formia Murano, Burgundy, Green Inside, Suspended Bubbles, 9 1/2 In. 90.00
Forvil, Cinq Fleurs, Clear & Frosted, Molded Rope Design, Stopper, 2 7/8 In. 770.00
Fragonard, Belle De Nuit, Gold Cap, Label, White & Gold Box, Contents, 2 In. 154.00
Fragonard, Orchidee, Black, Fruit Branches Gold Stopper, Tortoiseshell Box, 3 In. 330.00
Frances Denney, Night Life, Stage & Curtain Shape, Faceted Stopper, Box, 3 1/2 In. 165.00
Francis Whittemore, Crimped Red Rose, Stopper, W On Yellow Cane .... .400.00 to 460.00
G. Lemoine, Oeillet, Vertical Facets, Stopper, Contents, Box, 1920s, 3 In. 35.00
G.K. Benda, Bryenne, Chu Chin Chow, Seated Chinese Man, c.1918, 2 1/2 In. 460.00
Gabilla, Gardenia, Brown Box, Signed, Gabilla, 4 In. 121.00
Galle, Burgundy On Peach, Atomizer, Signed, 7 1/4 In. 1500.00
Galle, Deep Burgundy Berries & Leaves, Green, Cameo, 4 1/4 In. 1725.00
Galle, Purple Bleeding Hearts, Satin, Atomizer, Signed, 7 3/4 In. 920.00
Garden Scene With Figures, Gilt Metal Putti, 5 1/4 In. 980.00
Germaine Monteil, Laughter, Oval, Clear & Frosted Stopper, Box, 2 7/8 In. 99.00
Germaine Monteil, Nostalgia, Deep Indentation Shape, Stopper, Signed, 1940, 5 In. 22.00
Glass, Red & Gold Flowers & Leaves Enameled, Metal Hinged Cap, 2 1/8 In. 143.00
Godet, Chypre, Shield Shape, Pyramid Stopper, Label, Seal, 3 3/4 In. 143.00
Gold, Black Floral Trellis, Gold Acorn Finial, Amber Glass, DeVilbiss Atomizer, 9 In. ... 440.00
Gold Aurene, Steuben, New Ball & Tassel, DeVilbiss Atomizer, 9 1/2 In. 660.00
Gold Enameled, Black Flowers, Egg Shape, Pedestal, DeVilbiss Atomizer, 6 In. 495.00
Gold Enameled, Black Trim, Baluster, Metal Neck, Glass Dabber, 7 1/4 In. 330.00
Gold Enameled, Lady Shape, Peach Glass, Signed, DeVilbiss Atomizer, 4 In. 1650.00
Gold Enameled, Metal Neck, Glass Dabber, DeVilbiss Atomizer, 6 1/8 In. 605.00
Gold Enameled, Scroll Design, Acorn Finial, DeVilbiss Atomizer, Amber, 3 In. 357.50
Gold Enameled, Yellow Opalescent, Embossed Pansies, 6 In. 220.00
Gold Flowers, White Enamel, Turquoise Glass, 7 In. 99.00
Gold Triangular Windows, Light Amber Glass, DeVilbiss Atomizer, 8 In. 286.00
Gourielli, Five O'Clock, Cocktail Shaker Shape, Coat Of Arms Overcap, Box, 1947, 3 In. .. 143.00
Gourielli, Something Blue, Scalloped, Winged Cupid Head, 1943, 3 In. 1840.00
Green, Art Deco Gold Circles, Black Lines, Glass Dabber, DeVilbiss Atomizer, 7 In. 357.00
Green, Geometric Cut, Faceted Spire Stopper & Dabber, Czechoslovakia, 2 1/2 In. 154.00
Green Cut To Clear, Stopper, Flowers, Leaves, Bohemian, 6 1/2 In. 374.00
Green Enameled, Pedestal, DeVilbiss Atomizer, 6 7/8 In. 88.00
Green Enameled Interior, Floral Black Exterior, Signed, DeVilbiss Atomizer, 5 In. 357.00
Green Enameled Interior, Ring, Chevron Gold Exterior, DeVilbiss Atomizer, 7 In. 264.00
Grenoville, Casanova, Rooster Crowing Shape, Gilded Stopper, Original Box, 4 In. 330.00
Gueldy, Alcee, Molded Roses, Rectangular, 1920s, 4 1/8 In. 412.00
Gueldy, La Feuilleraie, Metallic Label, Flower Stopper, 1913, 3 7/8 In. 231.00
Gueldy, Le Prestige, Kneeling Winged Nymph Stopper, Julien Viard, 4 In. 460.00
Guerlain, Baccarat Urn, Fan Form Light Blue Glass Stopper, 5 5/8 In. 86.00
Guerlain, Fleur De Feu, Ribs, Square Pedestal, Stopper, Contents, Box, 1948, 5 1/2 In. ... 357.00
Guerlain, Jasmin, Frosted, Urn Shape, Women's Faces, Stopper, Box, 3 7/8 In. 1980.00

Perfume, Cut Glass, Yellow, Hearts, Ball Shape, Cut Flowers Stopper, Paris, 8 In.

Perfume, Ingrid, Opaque Aqua, Classical Nudes Around, Firebird Stopper, 7 7/8 In.

Perfume, Lalique, Claire, Oree I Side, Claire Paris Other, Flacon Center, Stopper, 3 1/8 In.

Guerlain, Mouchoir De Monsieur, Swirls, Triangular, Stopper, c.1904, 4 1/2 In. 110.00
Guerlain, Nahema, Teardrop Shape, Hemispherical Base, Circular, Stopper, 1992, 4 In. .. 77.00
Guerlain, Parure, Green Plastic Top, 1957, Miniature 220.00
Guerlain, Vol De Nuit, Olive Green, Rays From Center, Stopper, Contents, Box, 2 7/8 In. . 77.00
Guyla, Divin Narcisse, Champagne Flute Shape, Hand Painted, Box, 1926, 5 3/4 In. 460.00
H.F. Sorel, Mademoiselle Pigalle, Kneeling Nude Shape, 1930, 4 3/4 In. 575.00
Happy Oriental, Wearing Gold Gown, Metal Crown Stopper, 1 In. 77.00
Harriet Hubbard Ayer, Tuliptime, Frosted, Wisteria Blossoms, Stopper, 2 1/8 In. 1430.00
Hattie Carnegie, Hattie Carnegie, Black, Pyramid Shape, Gold Stopper, 3 In. 495.00
Hattie Carnegie, No. 7, Woman's Bust, Head Stopper, Box, 3 3/8 In. 905.00
Helen Of Troy, Black Glass, Flower Bud Stopper, Box Base, France, 3 1/4 In. 220.00
Helena Rubenstein, Apple Blossom Time, Pillow, Rhinestone Metal Cap, 2 1/3 In. 55.00
Helena Rubenstein, Apple Blossom, Pink Cap, Gold Box, Celluloid Window, 1 2/3 In. .. 99.00
Helena Rubenstein, Gala Performance, Female Dancer, 1940, 5 1/2 In. 2300.00
Helena Rubenstein, Heaven Sent, Curved Ribs, Blue Cap, Harlequin Doll, Box, 2 7/8 In. . 121.00
Hermes, Eue De Hermes, Mushroom Stopper, Leatherette Box, 5 1/2 In. 110.00
Hoffman, Black, Venus & Cupid Frieze, Pan & Flute Stopper, Butterfly Mark, 5 3/8 In. .. 715.00
Hoffman, Crystal & Amber, Nude Woman Dabber, Roses Stopper, 5 5/8 In. 4400.00
Hoffman, Green, Oval, Intaglio Goddess, Child Stopper, Czechoslovakia, 4 7/8 In. 385.00
Houbigant, Chantilly, Decanter Shape, Gold Enamel, Crystal Stopper, 9 In. 330.00
Houbigant, Chantilly, Eau De Toilette, 2 Oz., Pink Ribbon, Plastic Cap, 4 3/4 In. 10.00
Houbigant, Chantilly, White Plastic Cap, Lable, On Lace Handkerchief, Round Box, 2 In. 99.00
Houbigant, Essence Rare, Gold Ball Stopper, 2 In. 209.00
Houbigant, La Belle Saison, Frosted Woman Portrait, Shadowed Box, 3 7/8 In. 1980.00
Houbigant, Le Parfum Ideal, Decanter Shape, Crystal Stopper, 1923, 2 In. 77.00
Houbigant, Presence, Zigzag Pleated Design, Stopper, Moire Box, 1930s, 4 1/8 In. 143.00
Houbigant, Quelques Fleurs, Gold Cap, Straw Basket Presentation, 1 1/2 In. 77.00
Houbigant, Violette, Flask Shape, Gold Enameled Stopper, Box, 3 In. 22.00
House Of Tre-Jur, Abstract Design, Dark Blue Patina, Torso Stopper, 5 In. 467.50
I. Rice & Co., Inc., Pink Crackle, Flower Top Plunger, Label, Japan, 3 1/2 In. 45.00
Imonetta, Incanto, Black Glass, Clear Stopper, Gold Label, White & Gold Box, 2 In. 154.00
Ingrid, Elephant, Malachite, Jade Green Stone Stopper, Silver Label, 2 In. 330.00
Ingrid, Malachite, Square Flat Shape, Reclining Nude Stopper, 7 1/2 In. 1870.00
Ingrid, Opaque Aqua, Classical Nudes Around, Firebird Stopper, 7 7/8 In. ....*Illus* 3080.00
Ingrid, Opaque Aqua, Stylized Flowers & Leaves Cluster, Stopper, 6 5/8 In. 1430.00
Ingrid, Red, Molded Scrolls & Roses, Clear Scrolls & Roses Stopper, 6 In. 825.00
Iridescent, Gold Metal Holder, 3-Footed, DeVilbiss Atomizer, 2 In. 357.50
Isabey, Jasmin, Pearl Shape, Pearlized Enameled Stopper, Box, 2 1/2 In. 220.00
J. Giraud, Fils Parfum Cassins, Triangular, Faceted Shoulders, Stopper, Box, 2 1/4 In. 485.00
Jacques Fath, Fath De Fath, 8-Pointed Star, Stopper, Flocked Box, 4 In. 99.00
Jacques Fath, Fath's Love, Inverted Cone Shape, Pedestal, Stopper, Box, 3 1/8 In. 44.00
Jacques Fath, Iris Gris, Pleated Shape, Pointed Stopper, Signed, 1952, 5 In. 44.00

Jacques Heim, Alambic, Wire Holder, Box, 6 In. 632.50
Jacques Heim, J'Aime, Molded Ribs, Clear Glass Stopper, Box, 9 In. 44.00
Je Suis L'Amo, Floral Stopper, 3 1/2 In. 288.00
Jean DeParys, Sous Le Gui, 1919, 4 1/2 In. 4600.00
Jean Desprez, Bal A Versailles, 18th Century Courtesans, Lyre Stopper, 4 In. ....66.00 to 77.00
Jean Desprez, Escarmouche, Sword Shape, Gold Tip, Gold Cap, Gold Tassel, 8 In. 110.00
Jean Desprez, Jardanel, Heart Shape, Light Green Box, White Silk Interior, 4 In. 77.00
Jean Desses, Celui, Ribs, Gold, Metal Cap, Satin Lined Box, Signed, 2 In. 110.00
Jean Patou, Amour Amour, Stopper, Signed, 2 In. 77.00
Jean Patou, Caline, Gold Cap, Contents, Blue & White Box, 2 1/4 In. 44.00
Jean Patou, Gold Enameled Label, Crystal Stopper, Signed, 4 In. 99.00
Jergens, Ben Hur, Molded Flowers, Flower In Center, Orange Silk Box, Stopper, 4 In. ... 143.00
Jergens, Ben Hur, Oval Shape, Metallic Label, Stopper, Presentation Box, 2 1/2 In. 110.00
Jergens, Jockey Club, Frosted, Rectangular, Ionic Capital Stopper, Holly Box, 4 In. 121.00
Jodelle, Parfum D, Barrel Shape, Green Enamel, Green Enameled Stopper, 2 In. 209.00
John Fredericks, Golden Arrow, Arrow Shaped Stopper, 1935, 4 In. 460.00
John M. Rice Co., Sweet Marie, Cork Stopper, 1880, 3 In. 66.00
Jovan, Sculptura, Black Plastic Stand, Original Box, 1981, 4 In. 44.00
Karoff, Castanettes, 3 Senoritas With Scrapes & Hats, 1937, 8 In. 115.00
Karoff, Floral Quintuplets, Wood Stoppers, Original Box, 5 1/2 In. 115.00
Karoff, Picanette, Black Child Shape, 1938, 4 In. 98.00
Karoff, Set, Floral Jackettes, Racing Silk Jacket, Wood Face Cap, Box, 3 In., 5 Piece 275.00
Kathryn, Forever Amber, Woman's Torso Shape, Abstract Vegetable Stopper, 5 In. 132.00
L.T. Piver, Floramye Concentre, Gold Lettering In Front, Crystal Stopper, 4 In. 154.00
L.T. Piver, Floramye, Decanter Shape, Faceted Stopper, 6 In. 660.00
L.T. Piver, Mascarade, Red Glass, Swirled Line Design, Stopper, 2 In. ....633.00 to 1760.00
Lady Wearing Blue Luster Dress, Yellow Rose, Brown Hair, Cork Stopper, 5 In. 132.00
Lalique, Bouchon Fleurs De Pommiers, Scalloped, Cascade Stopper, 1919, 5 1/2 In. 8625.00
Lalique, Claire, Oree 1 Side, Claire Paris Other, Flacon Center, Stopper, 3 1/8 In. .... Illus 2090.00
Lalique, D'Orsay, Mystere, Black, Molded, Bears, Red Leather Case, 3 3/4 In. 3360.00
Lalique, D'Orsay, Poesie, Frosted, Classical Maiden, Cone, 5 7/8 In. 3190.00
Lalique, D'Orsay, Renommee, 5 Pots, Floral Stoppers, Box, Signed, 1922, 9 In. 2530.00
Lalique, Deux Figurines, Bouchon Figurines, Inset Oval, Nudes Stopper, 1912, 5 In. 6325.00
Lalique, Deux Fleurs, Clear & Frosted, 2 Overlapping Flowers, Stopper, 1935, 3 1/2 In. .. 176.00
Lalique, Forvil, La Perle Noire, Molded, Frosted, Glass Box, Paper, 1925, 4 1/4 In. 4500.00
Lalique, Guerlain, Bouquet De Faunes, Urn Form, Frosted, Gray Stain, 1925, 3 3/4 In. ... 490.00
Lalique, Hirondelles, Rectangular, Frosted, Molded Birds, Signed, 1920, 3 1/2 In. 1725.00
Lalique, Houbigant, La Belle Salson, Molded, Frosted, Box, 1925, 4 In. 4600.00
Lalique, Lancome, Marrakech, Oval Base, 2 Wings Side, Stopper, 5 1/8 In. 990.00
Lalique, Lucien Lelong, Parfum A, Skyscraper, Frosted, Enamel, Box, 1929, 4 3/4 In. ... 8400.00
Lalique, Maison, Frosted, Lily Of The Valley, Cylindrical, Atomizer, 3 3/8 In. 495.00
Lalique, Molinard, Habanita, Frosted, Brown Stain, Molded Nudes, Box, 1929, 4 In. 1610.00
Lalique, Molinard, Le Baiser Du Faune, Molded, 1928, 5 3/4 In. 10800.00
Lalique, Nina Ricci, L'Air Du Temps, Swirl Shape, Gold Cap, Box, 2 1/2 In. 412.00
Lalique, Nina Ricci, Urn, 8-Sided Stopper, 2 3/8 In. 46.00
Lalique, Pan, Frosted, Green Stain, Satyr Masks, Signed, 1920, 5 In. 1610.00
Lalique, Roger & Gallet, Flausa, Maiden In Flowers, Flower Stopper, 4 7/8 In. 2310.00
Lalique, Roger & Gallet, Paquerettes, Frosted, Cascade Stopper, 1919, 3 In. ....2530.00 to 7200.00
Lalique, Worth, Requete, Scalloped Sides, Box, 1946, 6 1/2 In. 1380.00
Lancome, Fleches, Frosted, Molded Swirls, Swirl Stopper, Box, 1944, 4 7/8 In. 1320.00
Lander, Jasmin, Woman In Full Evening Gown, Cork Tip Stopper, Amber, 1 In. 198.00
Langlois, Coeur D'Or, Clear & Frosted, 6-Sided, Stopper, Contents, Box, 5 1/8 In. 522.00
Langlois, Duska, Skyscraper Shape, Red, Black Stopper, Label, 2 3/4 In. 231.00
Langlois, Narcisse, Cube Form, Cube Impressed Diamond Stopper, Box, 2 7/8 In. 176.00
Lanvin, Arpege, Black, Ball Shape, Gold Raspberry Stopper, Box, 2 1/8 In. 198.00
Lanvin, Stopper, Gilded Raspberry Finial, Signed, Lanvin, 4 In. 77.00
Le Galion, Gardenia, Ship, Sailing, Black Glass Stopper, Signed, 4 In. 55.00
Le Galion, Sortilege, 12-Sided, Stopper, Green & White Box, Some Contents, 2 In. 33.00
Le Prestige, Black Crystal, Box 195.00
Leaf & Berry Design, Ball, Tassel, DeVilbiss Atomizer, 5 In. 422.50
Leaf & Scroll Design, Ball, Tassel, DeVilbiss Atomizer, 5 In. 110.00
Leaves, Triangular Stopper, Metal Neck, Blue Flash, Signed, DeVilbiss Atomizer, 5 In. ... 385.00
Leaves & Scrollwork, Sterling Silver, Long Dabber & Stopper, Hinged Box, 2 In. 121.00

Legrain, Promenade A Paris, 19th Century Woman Shape, Frosted, 6 1/2 In. 440.00
Leigh, Dulcinea, Oval, Star Lines Stopper, Contents, Lucite Base Box, 3 In. 22.00
Lentheric, Tweed, Black Enamel, Gold Cap, 7 In. 33.00
Leon Applebaum, Purple, Bubble Twists & Ring, Clear Stopper, 3 x 3 3/4 In. 55.00
Lerys, Happy Days, Flacon De Sac, Stopper, 1920s, 3 In. 33.00
Light Amber Iridescent, DeVilbiss Atomizer, 7 In., Pair 121.00
Light Amber Iridescent, Metal Neck, Signed, DeVilbiss Atomizer, 4 In. 77.00
Light Green Glass, Gold Rings, Signed, DeVilbiss Atomizer, 4 In., Pair 357.00
Lightner, Lily Of The Valley, Milk Glass 55.00
Lilly Dache, Dashing, Figural, Poodle, Bow On Head, 1941, 7 In. 1150.00
Lilly Dache, Drifting, Woman's Bust Shape, 1941, 3 1/2 In. 805.00
Lily, Blue Ground, Gold Flecks, Stopper, Signed With Gold K, Charles Kaziun 690.00
Lily, Gold Flecks, Stopper, Signed With Gold K, Charles Kaziun 748.00
Lincourt, Pour Toi Seule, Vertical Strands Of Beads, Clear Glass Stopper, 4 In. 66.00
Linetti, Profumi Seimitar, Original Box, 9 1/2 In. 518.00
Linetti, Profumi, Vial, Dagger Shape, 18thk Gold Plated Handle, Box, 1935, 9 5/8 In. ... 1100.00
Lionceau, Le Fleuve Noir, Black, Swirls Around, Oval, Stopper, 3 1/8 In. 440.00
Lionceau, Parfum Pour Blondes, Green Glass, Beige Patina, Signed, 5 In. 935.00
Lionceau, Place De La Opera, Flask, Clear & Frosted, Stopper, Contents, Box, 3 3/8 In. .. 296.00
Louis D'Or, Joey, Mold Mark, France, Full, Miniature 8.00
Lubin, Au Soleil, Frosted Crystal, Lizard Relief, Maurice Depinoix, c.1910, 5 3/4 In. 1092.00
Lubin, Au Soleil, Frosted Crystal, Lizard Relief, Maurice Depinoix, c.1910, 8 3/4 In. 632.00
Lubin, Au Soleil, Trumpet Shape, Molded Salamander Side, Enameled, 5 5/8 In. 2310.00
Lubin, Eva, Frosted, Flat Round , 4 Side Garlands, Eve & Snake Stopper, 3 7/8 In. 2090.00
Lubin, Magda, Crystal, Frosted Head Stopper, Julien Viard, 1921, 5 1/4 In. 2070.00
Lucien Lelong, Castel, Box, Small 290.00
Lucien Lelong, Jabot, Large Bow, Frosted, Inner Stopper, Overcap, 3 In. 440.00
Lucien Lelong, Parfum L, Square, Lelong Logo, Mushroom Stopper, Box, 3 1/2 In. 715.00
Lucien Lelong, Taglio, Rectangular, Rectangular Stopper, Lucite Box, 1/4 Oz., 1 1/2 In. .. 132.00
Lucien Lelong, Tailspin, Molded Concave Ribs, Clear Glass Stopper, 4 In. 121.00
Lucretia Vanderbilt, Blue Metal Oval Box, Frosted Stopper, 6 In. 154.00
Lucretia Vanderbilt, Blue, Fitted Case, 4 In. 345.00
Marc Fael, My Jerry Can, Stopper, 1940, 9 In. 242.00
Marcel Franck, Escale, Vertical Facets, Rectangular, Stopper, Signed, 5 In., Pair 66.00
Marcel Guerlain, Mai Wang, Metal Cap, Original Box, 9 In. 231.00
Marcel Rochas, Femme, Opaque White, Gold Metal Stopper, 6 In. 77.00
Marly, Adagio, Box 275.00
Marquay, Prince Douka, Seated Figure Shape, 1951, 6 1/2 In. 173.00
Mary Chess, Souvenir D'Un Soir, Frosted Crystal, Pulitzer Fountain Form, 4 3/4 In. 5175.00
Mary Dunhill, Escape, Round Cruet Shape, Ball Stopper, Box, 4 1/8 In. 132.00
Mary Dunhill, Frou-Frou De Gardenia, Concentric Ribs, Contents, Box, 2 1/2 In. 143.00
Mary Quant, P.M. Perfume, Gray Enameled In Front, Column Stopper, 1960, 4 In. 33.00
Massenet, Altesse, Frosted Molded Floral Stopper, Box, 4 1/2 In. 88.00
Mercoeur, Coeur De France, Square, Facets, Stopper, Glass Overcap, 1955, 4 1/2 In. 209.00
Merle Norman, Impact, White Enamel, Box, Frosted Glass Stopper, 1950, 2 In. 99.00
Merle Norman, Jolly Sin, Black, Gold Box, Clear Glass Stopper, Oval, 4 In. 143.00
Metal, Urn Shape, Vertical Floral Band, Pedestal, Atomizer, Tassel, 6 7/8 In. 743.00
Miahati, Four Moods, Plastic Cap, Gold Box, 1 1/2 In., 4 Piece 55.00
Milk Glass, Hand Painted Flowers, Gilt Stopper, 5 3/8 In. 55.00
Millot, Crepe De Chine, Trapezoidal Panels, Disk Stopper, Peach Gold Box, 2 In. 44.00
Millot, Crepe De Chine, Variegated Stone, France, 1925, 3 In. 209.00
Moiret, Pois De Senteur, Sweet Pea, Royal Blue Glass Stopper, 5 In. 88.00
Molded As Bird Perched On Branch, Frosted Glass Stopper, 5 In. 990.00
Molded Band Of Leaves & Berries, Black Glass, Signed, DeVilbiss Atomizer, 4 In. 187.00
Molinard, Christmas Bells, Cobalt Blue, Bell Shape, Stopper, 2 1/2 In. 165.00
Molinard, Habanita, Cubes, Square Facet Stopper, Foil Box, 2 1/2 In. 231.00
Molinard, Habanita, Rectangular, Molinard Emblem Stopper, Box, 3 7/8 In. 66.00
Molinard, Orval, Round, Scalloped Edges, Stopper, Box, 2 In. 77.00
Molinard, Sketch, Amber & Frosted, Nude Frieze Top, Stopper, Box, 4 7/8 In. 1980.00
Molinard, Soir D'Italie, Evening In Italy, Napoleon's Hat Stopper, 1938, 4 In. 231.00
Molinari, Coax Me, Clear & Frosted, Flat Top Stopper, Velvet Box, 1940s, 2 7/8 In. 44.00
Molyneux, Rue Royale, Elegant Apothecary Shape, Crystal Disc Stopper, 1930, 3 In. 154.00
Moser, Amber, Centaurs & Warriors Frieze, Stopper, Czechoslovakia, 6 5/8 In. 275.00

Moser, Cobalt Blue, Gilt Leaves, Atomizer, 6 1/2 In. 196.00
Mury, Le Narcisse Bleu, Blue Narcissus, Stylized Flower On Front, Blue Stopper, 4 In. .. 275.00
Mushroom Shape, Black Enamel, Gold Enameled Exterior, Pyramid, 6 In. 165.00
Myrurgia, Embrujo De Sevilla, Gold Enameled Stopper, 4 In. 357.50
Myrurgia, Liria, Glass Bottle, Orange, Blue Velvet, Silk Lined Box, Stopper, 4 In. 522.00
Myrurgia, Nueva Maja, Rectangular Panels, Gold Label, Stopper, 3 In. 132.00
Myrurgia, Suspiro De Granada, Black, Bell Shape, Molded Floral Stopper, Gilt, 3 In. 357.00
Myrurgia, Suspiro De Granada, Pompoms, Julien Viard, Bakelite Box, 1922, 3 1/2 In. ... 920.00
Neos-Nice, Frosted Child Stopper, Amber Patina, Silk Lined Box, 1924, 3 7/8 In. 2640.00
Nina Ricci, Coeur Joie, Frosted, Flowers On Heart, Butterfly Stopper, Box, 5 7/8 In. 770.00
Nina Ricci, Fille D'Eve, Apple Shape, Woven Wicker Basket, 1952, 2 1/2 In. 978.00
Nina Ricci, L'Air Du Temps, Round Bottle, Ball Stopper, Box, 3 1/8 In. 286.00
Nina Ricci, L'Air Du Temps, Swirl Shape, Green Stopper, Birdcage Box, 3 7/8 In. 164.00
Nitchevo, Onion Dome Shape, Frosted Glass Bottle, 3 In. 187.00
Norelle, Glass, Gold Screw Top, Purse Size, Box 28.00
Norman, Adoration, Seated Goddess Shape, 7 1/2 In. 546.00
Novelty Guild, Vanidon, 2 Flacons In Dressing Table Box, 4 1/2 In. 58.00
Opalescent, Wing Like Shape, Petal Stopper, Signed France, 7 1/2 In. 715.00
Opaque Light Peach Interior, Gold Band Exterior, DeVilbiss Atomizer, 5 In. 121.00
Orange, Black & Gold Enameled, New Ball & Tassel, DeVilbiss Atomizer, 7 3/8 In. 522.00
Orange Enameled Interior, Gold Roses Exterior, Signed, DeVilbiss Atomizer, 2 In. 385.00
Orange Fold Heart & Vine, Gilt DeVilbiss Atomizer, 10 In. 1495.00
Orange Interior, Gold Enameled Exterior, Signed, DeVilbiss Atomizer, 5 In. 3080.00
Oriza-L. Legrand, Deja Le Printemps, Petals Pointing Down, Signed, 7 In. 2860.00
Ota, Lilas, 3 Pearls, Box, 3 1/2 In. 920.00
Palmer, India Bouquet, Ground Stopper, 9 In. 374.00
Palmer, Jockey Club, Bulbous Stopper, 9 In. 316.00
Pansy Design, Black, Gold, Green, White Enamel, 2 In., Pair 275.00
Park Avenue Perfumer, Gardenia Corsage, Molded With Berries, Stopper, 2 In. 55.00
Patanwalla, Salim, Ocean Liner Form, S.S. Patanwalla, 4 In. 770.00
Paul Rieger, Flower Drops, Arabian Nights, Stopper, Original Box, 3 In. 77.00
Pauline Trigere, Trigere, Cube Shape & Stopper, Metal Hanging Turtle, Box, 1 1/2 In. ... 88.00
Perfums De Marcy, Le Collier Miraculeux, String Of Pearls, Box, 1927, 11 1/2 In. 2300.00
Petit Point, Rose, Leaves, Buds, Frame, 2 1/2 In. 15.00
Pierre Baquere, Seashell Shape, Red Glass, Black Glass Stopper, Signed, 5 In. 66.00
Pierre Dune, Pres Du Coeur, 1945, 4 3/4 In. 2875.00
Pin Type, Clear Glass, Allover Metal Filigree, Blue Stone, Dabber Stopper, 1 5/8 In. 33.00
Pink, Metal Filigree & Stones Cover, Intaglio Cut Woman Stopper, 6 In. 825.00
Pink, Orange, Black Abstract Enameled Design, DeVilbiss Atomizer, 9 In. 286.00
Pink, Pink Enameled Inside, Silver Design, Atomizer, 6 1/4 In. 412.00
Pink Enameled Middle Band, Gold Metal Atomizer, Tassel, 6 1/2 In. .. 110.00
Pink Glass Wheel Cut Leaves, Gold Pheasants, Signed, DeVilbiss Atomizer, 3 In., Pair .. 1980.00
Pink Satin Glass, Brass Mounts, Glass Applicator, Signed, DeVilbiss Atomizer, 6 In. 138.00
Plein Coeur, Heart Shape, Lay Down, Mini, Silver, Red Box, White Cap, 1 5/8 In. 18.00
Potter & Moore, Mitcham, Gondola Shape, Original Box, 5 1/2 In. 58.00
Pressed Glass, Hemisphere Shape, Bird With Long Tail Stopper, 5 In. 99.00
Prince George Of Russia, Pierre Tappe, Black Glass, 3 In. 99.00
Prince Matchabelli, Ave Maria, Crown Shape, Blue Box, Satin Lining, Stopper, 2 In. 66.00
Prince Matchabelli, Stradivari, Gold Enamel, Black Patina, Cruciform Stopper, 1 In. 121.00
Prince Matchabelli, Wind Song, Enameled Green Crown, Gold Metal Cap, Box, 1 2/3 In. 121.00
Pyramid, Black Glass, Gold Flowers, Metal Atomizer, Label, 7 1/4 In. 357.00
Raffy, Petals Of Brittany, Butterfly Wing Shape, Stopper, 3 In. 242.00
Raised Gold, Yellow Enameled Design, Violet Iridescent, Metal Atomizer, 5 In. 154.00
Raphael, Replique, Clear, Stopper, Signed, 3 In. 44.00
Raphael, Replique, Ribbon, Box 125.00
Renaud, Sweet Pea Ambre, Opaque Green Glass, Gold Label, Stopper, 4 In. 319.00
Renaud, Violette, Chartreuse Glass Stopper, 4 In. 660.00
Revillon, Carnet De Bal, Inverted Brandy Snifter Shape, Label Stopper, Box, 2 In. 55.00
Richard Hudnut, Deauville, Bottle By Depinoix, Julien Viard, 4 In. 1610.00
Richard Hudnut, La Soiree, Blue Overlay, Diamonds, Blue Crystal Stopper, 6 In. 935.00
Richard Hudnut, Le Debut Noir, Black, 8-Sided, Gold Stopper, 2 1/2 In. 286.00
Richard Hudnut, Le Debut Vert, Green Glass, Stopper, 2 In. 176.00
Richard Hudnut, Les Cascades, The Waterfall, Gold Enamel, Stopper, 2 In. 412.50

Rieger, Crabapple, Flask Shape, Frosted Glass Stopper, 3 In. 177.00
Rieger, Parfum, Opaque Green Glass, Rectangular Form, Button Stopper, 1937, 3 In. 231.00
Ring Mold, Green Glass, Metal Atomizer, Opaque White, 6 In. 132.00
Roger & Gallet, Bouquet Nouveau, Pierced Brass Sides, Signed L. Chalon, 1900, 4 In. ... 1093.00
Roger & Gallet, Fleurs D'Amour, Faceted Stopper, 1902 .... 575.00
Roger & Gallet, Fleurs D'Amour, Stopper, 3 In. 132.00
Roger & Gallet, Iris Blanc, Decanter Shape, Blue, Gold Label, Stopper, 3 In. 467.00
Roger & Gallet, Night Of Delight, Nuit D'Extase, Lotus Blossoms, Box, 4 In. 143.00
Roger & Gallet, Oeillet Bleu, Blue Carnation, Stopper, 2 In. 242.00
Roger & Gallet, Violette De Prame, Stopper, 2 In. 77.00
Rolex, Perpetually Yours, Gold Metal, Stopper, Lined Green Satin Box, 2 In. 605.00
Rose & Leaf Enamel Design, Metal Shaker Top, DeVilbiss Atomizer, 4 In. 66.00
Rose Valois, Aigrette, White Cap Has Black & White Hat, Plastic Case, 2 1/4 In. 253.00
Rosemelon, Green, Yellow, Egg Shape, Yellow Coil, Orange Stopper, 5 3/4 In. 242.00
Roses, Gold Leaves, Clear Glass Stopper, 4 In. 55.00
Rosine, Nuit De Chine, Chinese Snuff Shape, Bakelite Ring Sides, Stopper, 4 1/2 In. 2420.00
Round Flat Shape, Molded Black Cat Stopper, France, 3 In. 1045.00
Saint-Cyr, Fleches D'Amour, Love Arrows, Gold Enameled Stars, Inner Stopper, 4 In. ... 253.00
Salvador Dali, Display Bottle, 12 In. 345.00
Schiaparelli, Radiance Face Powder, Heart Shaped Box, 5 In. 4025.00
Schiaparelli, S, Frosted, Pink Metallic Ball Cap, Signed, 3 In. 143.00
Schiaparelli, Sleeping, Candlestick Shape, 1938, 7 In. 173.00
Schiaparelli, Sleeping, Red Glass Stopper, Gold Enamel, 4 In. 231.00
Schiaparelli, Zut, Woman's Torso Shape, Gold Enamel Stopper, 5 In. 715.00
Scroll & Leaf Design, Cranberry Glass, DeVilbiss Atomizer, 7 In., Pair 550.00
Shalimar, Clear Base, Amber Body, Ground Stopper, Factice, 18 In. 825.00
Silka, Narcisse, Long Dabber, Green Stopper, Label, Box, 2 1/8 In. 44.00
Silver Deposit, Flowers & Leaf Design, 2 In. 77.00
Silver Floral Overlay, Pinched Glass, 4 1/2 In. 135.00
Silver Overlay On Clear Glass, Pear Shape, Ball Stopper, 3 In. 86.00
Solon Palmer, Brocade, Triangular Shape, Faceted Spire Stopper, 3 In. 55.00
Solon Palmer, Glenecho, Circle Design Radiating Outward, Stopper, 4 In. 55.00
Solon Palmer, Perfumer, SP, N.Y., Label Under Glass, Stopper, 7 7/8 In. 635.00
Steuben, Aurene Atomic Cloud, Blue Aurene, Ruffled Neck, Stopper, 6 In. 2420.00
Steuben, Aurene, Blue Iridescent, Ground Pontil, Stopper, 6 In. 504.00
Steuben, Green Jade & Alabaster, Baluster, Pedestal, Teardrop Stopper, 7 1/2 In. 605.00
Steuben, Melon Shape, Jade Green Opalescent, Jade Green Stopper, 5 In. 495.00
Steuben, Opalescent, Melon Shape, 8 Lobes, Long Neck, Teardrop Stopper, 5 In. 330.00
Stork Club, Logo, Glass With Metal Encased, Metal Cap, Miniature 110.00
Suzy, Ecarlate De Suzy, Stopper, Round Celluloid Box, 1 7/8 In. 55.00
Suzy, Ecarlate De Suzy, Woman's Head & Chapeau, Red Enamel, Stopper, 4 In. 990.00
Suzy, Ecarlate De Suzy, Woman's Head Shape, Red Enamel, Inner Stopper, 5 In. 880.00
Swank, Flora Danica, Beveled, Beveled, Silk Painted Flowers, Stopper, 2 In. 66.00
Swirl Design, Gold Inclusions, Stopper, 5 In. 44.00
Teardrop Shape, Brass, Pink Glass, DeVilbiss Atomizer, 6 In. 385.00
Tokalon, Narcisse, Amber Patina, Fostoria, Reclining Woman Stopper, 3 1/2 In. 7150.00
Tosca, Square, Gold & Turquoise Label, Molded Roses Stopper, Box, 3 1/8 In. 121.00
Translucent, Iridescent Inclusions, Long Dabber, Signed Erik Holt, 1982, 6 In. 231.00
Translucent Violet Glass, Violet Moonstone Finial, Signed, DeVilbiss Atomizer, 5 In. 44.00
Traveler's Set, Inner Glass Stopper, Metal Cap, Leather Case, 3 1/8 In., 3 Piece 23.00
Triangle Shape, Circle Medallions, Elevated Pedestal Black Glass, Stopper, 7 In. 77.00
Triangular Windows, Gold Etched Metal, Pedestal, DeVilbiss Atomizer, 8 1/8 In. 209.00
Trumpet Shape, Flowers, Leaf Design, Amber Glass, DeVilbiss Atomizer, 5 In. 357.50
Trumpet Shape, Nude Figure, Black Enamel, Yellow Glass, Metal Atomizer, 4 In. 176.00
Turquoise, Dragonflies, Flowers, Faceted Stopper, Metal Carrier, Crystal Windows, 3 In. . 550.00
Turquoise, Gold Speckles, DeVilbiss Atomizer, Silk Interior Box, 6 1/8 In. 412.00
Turquoise Enamel On Copper, New Metal Atomizer, 5 1/2 In. 154.00
Vantine's, Sandalwood, Red Lacquer Box With Bird, Flowers, Stopper, 2 In. 77.00
Vaseline, Opalescent Glass Jewels, Black Stopper, Austria, 5 In. 2860.00
Vaseline Glass, Green Enamel, Greek Goddess, Musicians, Hoffman, 5 In. 2200.00
Verre De Soie, Melon Ribs, Celeste Blue Stopper, 4 3/4 In. 425.00
Vert Vert, Balmain, Square, Brown Label, Screw Cap, Miniature, 1 5/16 In. 19.00
Victorian King Edward, Jasmine Perfumes, Ground Stopper, 9 1/2 In. 374.00

Victorian King Edward, Rose Perfumes, Ground Stopper, 9 1/2 In. 170.00
Vigny, Golliwogg, Signed, M. DeBrunhoff, 6 In. 460.00
Violet, Pourpre D'Automne, Molded, Enameled Flowers, L. Guillard, Box, 1922, 3 1/2 In. 460.00
Violet, Quintessence De Violettes, Decanter Shape, Faceted Ball Stopper, 5 In. 220.00
Violet, Tanagra, Greek Key Design Top & Base, Maiden Shape Stopper, 5 1/2 In. 2530.00
Violet Design, Gold Diamond Windows, Metal Atomizer, Metal Pedestal, 9 In. 220.00
Violet Enameled Interior, Black, Gold Square Design, DeVilbiss Atomizer, 7 In., Pair ... 880.00
Vivaudou, Narcisse De Chine, Vertical Ribs, Cork, Unopened, Box, 2 1/3 In. 66.00
Volupte, Gold Plate Metal Stand, Atomizer, Signed, 9 In. 231.00
Volupte, Orange, Gold Enameled, Ball & Cord, Atomizer, 7 3/8 In. 495.00
W. & H. Walker Perfumers, Lavender Salts, Pittsburg, USA, Teal, 3 1/4 In. 78.00
Weil, Cobra, Stylized Flower Form Stopper, Blue Velvet Plinth, 4 In. 132.00
Weil, Noir, Black Square Glass, Quilted Blue Silk Interior Box, Stopper, 2 In. 440.00
Weil, Noir, Rectangle, Black, Ribbon, Gold Stamp, 3 3/4 In. 345.00
Wheel Cut, Crystal, Red Overlay, Etched Diamond Pattern, Stopper, 8 3/4 In. 165.00
Wheel Cut, Crystal, Red Overlay, Grapevine Design, 8-Sided, Stopper, 6 In. 155.00
White, Green Opalescent Glass, Violet Stones, DeVilbiss Atomizer, 8 In. 3080.00
White Flower, Pink Lavender Colored Perfume, Goldtone Cap, Belgium, 3 1/4 In. 10.00
White Swirls, Blue, White Glass, DeVilbiss Atomizer, 6 In. 275.00
Wine Glass Shape, Long Stem, Circular Base, Atomizer Ball, 5 In. 165.00
Woman Medallion, Goddess Diana Medallion Stopper, Czechoslovakia, 7 1/2 In. 2200.00
Woodworth, Viegay, Oval Shape, Fish Scale Design, Red Glass Stopper, 3 In. 495.00
Worth, Je Reviens, Diamond Shape Label, Screw Cap, Box, 1/20 Fl. Oz., 1 5/16 In. 22.00
Worth, Je Reviens, Round Silver Label, Red Lettering, Gold Cap, Box, Mini 22.00
Worth, Lilas, Allover Flower Blossoms, Stopper, Label, Box, 2 7/8 In. 885.00
Yardley, Flair, Freeform, Frosted Stopper, Gold Label, Molded Dancers, Box, 1 5/8 In. ... 264.00
Yardley, Snowman Shape, Brass Cap, Red Enamel Lips, 3 1/2 In. 275.00
Yardley & Co., London, Flared Lip, Clear 20.00
Yellow Enamel, Gold Ring Exterior, Yellow Satin Glass, DeVilbiss Atomizer, 9 In. 154.00
Yellow Glass, Rose In Bloom Shape, Molded Roses Stopper, Czechoslovakia, 5 1/2 In. ... 1540.00
Yellow Opalescent, Gold Enamel, Metal Atomizer, Ball, Tassel, 2 In. 220.00
Young Quinlan Co., YQ, Decanter Shape, Crystal Stopper, 7 In. 176.00
Zofaly, Passion, Scroll Stopper, Box, c.1946, 3 1/2 In. 172.50

--------------------------------- **PICKLE** ---------------------------------

Pickles were packed in special jars from about 1880 to 1920. The pickle jar was usually large, from one quart to one gallon size. They were made with four to eight sides.
The mouth was wide because you had to reach inside to take out the pickle. The top was
usually sealed with a cork or tin cover. Many pickle jars were designed with raised
gothic arches as panels. These jars are clear examples of the Victorian gothic revival
designs, so they are often included in museum exhibitions of the period. Their large size
and attractive green to blue coloring make them good accessories in a room. Bottle collectors realize that pickle jars are examples of good bottle design, that they are rare, and
that a collection can be formed showing the works of many glasshouses. Elaborate
molded clear glass pickle jars were popular after 1900. They were decorated with gold,
red, and other colors of cold-painted enamel to make a type known as *goofus glass.*
Pickle bottles are so popular that they are being reproduced. For more information on
pickle jars, see *Ketchup, Pickles, Sauces* by Betty Zumwalt.

6-Sided, Applied Tooled Round Lip, 1880, 13 1/2 In. 150.00
6-Sided, Applied Top, M.G. Co., 3 Stripes, Flowers 220.00
Amber, Stoddard Type, Applied Lip, 3-Piece Mold, Western 121.00
Aqua, 6-Sided, Flowers 160.00
Barrel, Yellow Green, Rings On Top & Bottom, Square Collar, Pontil, 9 1/2 In. 55.00
Bunker Hill, Lime Citron, Cylindrical, 7 1/2 In. 185.00
Cathedral, Applied, Folded Top, Graphite Pontil, 1877, 9 In. 1320.00
Cathedral, Aqua, 11 3/4 In. 176.00
Cathedral, Aqua, 4-Sided, 1855-1865, 7 1/4 In. 209.00
Cathedral, Aqua, 4-Sided, Graphite Pontil, 8 1/4 In. 358.00
Cathedral, Aqua, 6-Sided, 13 In. 198.00
Cathedral, Aqua, 6-Sided, Rolled Lip, OP, 1/2 Pt., 6 5/8 In. 160.00
Cathedral, Aqua, Applied Top, Rounded Shoulder, IP, 11 In. 303.00
Cathedral, Aqua, Double Arch Windows, Pt. 119.00
Cathedral, Aqua, OP, 9 In. 231.00

Pickle, Cathedral, Emerald Green, 8 7/8 In.

Pickle, Frank Vogel Co., Gherkins, Allegheny, Pa., Label, 7 In.

Pickle, G.P. Sanborn & Son, Union Brands, Amber, Shield, Sunburst, Tooled Mouth, 5 1/8 In.

Cathedral, Blue Aqua, 4-Sided, Diamond-Lattice, 7 3/8 In. 193.00
Cathedral, Blue Aqua, Applied Mouth, 1855-1865, 11 7/8 In. 357.00
Cathedral, Blue Aqua, Applied Top, 9 In. 220.00
Cathedral, Blue Aqua, Applied Top, 11 1/2 In. 190.00
Cathedral, Blue Aqua, Crosshatching, Drippy Applied Top, 7 1/2 In. 170.00
Cathedral, Blue Aqua, Rolled Lip, Pontil, 8 7/8 In. 355.00
Cathedral, Blue Green, 1855-1865, 11 3/4 In. 1045.00
Cathedral, Blue Green, 4-Sided, 1855-1865, 11 3/8 In. 468.00
Cathedral, Blue Green, 4-Sided, IP, 13 5/8 In. 1850.00
Cathedral, Blue Green, Applied Mouth, 1855-1865, 7 3/8 In. 440.00
Cathedral, Dark Green, Applied Top, 11 1/2 In. 198.00
Cathedral, Emerald Green, 8 7/8 In. ....*Illus* 467.00
Cathedral, Emerald Green, Applied Mouth, 1855-1870, 11 5/8 In. 336.00
Cathedral, Emerald Green, Applied Top, 11 1/2 In. 715.00
Cathedral, Green Aqua, 4-Sided, 11 1/2 In. 220.00
Cathedral, Green Aqua, 4-Sided, Star & Diamond Design In Windows, 1870, 11 In. 242.00
Cathedral, Green Aqua, 6-Sided, Rolled Lip, Pontil, 1718-1830, 13 In. 385.00
Cathedral, Green Aqua, 8-Sided, Tulip Design, Applied Top, Graphite Pontil, 10 1/2 In. .. 300.00
Cathedral, Green Aqua, Applied Top, 7 1/4 In. 300.00
Cathedral, Green Aqua, Applied Top, 11 1/2 In. 300.00
Cathedral, Green Aqua, Applied Top, OP, 8 3/4 In. 325.00
Cathedral, Green Aqua, Rolled Lip, 11 5/8 In. 175.00
Cathedral, Green, Clock Faces, Arches, Shells, 11 1/8 In. 3920.00
Cathedral, Ice Blue, Crosshatch On 3 Panels, 13 1/4 In. 1400.00
Cathedral, Light Apple Green, Applied Mouth, 1855-1870, 11 3/4 In. 385.00
Cathedral, Light Blue Green, Rolled Lip, 1855-1870, 14 In. 688.00
Cathedral, Light Green, 6-Sided, 5 Panels, 6th Is Plain For Label, 14 1/4 In. 2100.00
Cathedral, Light To Medium Blue Green, Rolled Lip, 1865, 13 5/8 In. 550.00
Cathedral, Pale Blue, 6-Sided, Embossed, 13 In. 165.00
Cathedral, San Francisco, 12 1/4 In. 523.00
Cathedral, Square, Blue Green, Tooled Collar, 11 5/8 In. 728.00
Cathedral, Square, Green, Tooled Collar, 10 7/8 In. 364.00
Cathedral, Teal Blue Green, 1855-1870, 11 7/8 In. 616.00
Cathedral, Teal, 1880s, 8 3/4 In. 293.00
Cathedral, Turquoise, 6-Sided, Applied Top, 13 In. 231.00
Cloverleaf, Gold Amber, 8-Sided, Applied Collar Lip, 8 In. 616.00
Cloverleaf, Gold Amber, Tooled Collar, 1860-1870, 8 In. 330.00
Deep Purple, 4-Sided, 7 In. 77.00
Frank Vogel Co., Gherkins, Allegheny, Pa., Label, 7 In. ....*Illus* 160.00
G.P. Sanborn & Son, Boston, Gold Yellow Amber, Cylindrical, 5 1/8 In. 143.00
G.P. Sanborn & Son, Union Brands, Amber, Shield, Sunburst, 5 1/8 In. ....*Illus* 123.00
G.R. & Co., Cathedral, Blue Aqua, IP, 1850-1860, 11 3/4 In. 770.00
Gold Amber, 4-Sided, 8 In. 121.00
Green, Ground Lip, Early 20th Century, 4 1/2 In. 25.00
Green, Heart & Anchor, Tooled Top, 8 In. 330.00
Green, Paneled, Rounded Shoulder, IP, 1855-1865, 12 1/4 In. 1705.00

Pickle, Milwaukee Pickle
Co., Wauwatosa, Wis.,
Amber, 1/2 Gal., 9 5/8 In.

Pickle, T.B. Smith &
Co., Philada.,
Cathedral, Blue Aqua,
Pontil, 9 1/4 In.

Pickle, Puritan Brand,
Boston Packing Co.,
Amber, Applied Mouth,
Label, 13 5/8 In.

Jar, Goofus Glass, Aqua, Ground Lip, Embossed Flowers, 13 In. ....88.00 to 175.00
Jar, Goofus Glass, Cobalt Blue, Rose Design, Ground Lip, 1880-1910, 15 1/4 In. 3360.00
Jar, Goofus Glass, Embossed Flowers, Aqua, 15 In., Pair 350.00
Jar, Goofus Glass, Flowers, American Eagle, Early 20th Century, 9 1/2 In. 65.00
Jar, Goofus Glass, Statue Of Liberty, Eagle, Early 20th Century, 12 1/2 In. 175.00
Jar, Green, Large IP, 1855-1865, 12 1/2 In. 437.00
Milwaukee Pickle Co., Wauwatosa, Wis., Amber, 1/2 Gal., 9 5/8 In. ....*Illus* 145.00
Olive Green, Applied Top, 11 In. 110.00
Puritan Brand, Boston Packing Co., Amber, Applied Mouth, Label, 13 5/8 In. ......*Illus* 260.00
Red Amber, Outside Columnar Corners, Applied Top, 1860-1875, 8 1/4 In. 358.00
Sanborn Parker & Co., Boston, Amber, Conical, Ground Top, 8 In. 165.00
Shaker Society Home Made Ripe Cucumber Pickles, Yellow Olive, 1890, 7 In. 448.00
Skilton Foote & Co's, Bunker Hill, Figural, Lighthouse, Yellow Green, 11 1/4 In. 825.00
Skilton Foote & Co's, Bunker Hill, Yellow Amber, 7 In. 78.00
Skilton Foote & Co's, Bunker Hill, Yellow, Tooled Top, 7 1/2 In. 66.00
Spanish Onions, Beige, Yellow Green, Black, 2 1/8 x 6 3/4 In. 6.00
Standard Packing Company Gherkins, Applied Top, Star On Base, Label, 9 In. 358.00
T.B. Smith & Co., Philada., Cathedral, Blue Aqua, Pontil, 9 1/4 In. ....*Illus* 330.00
T.B. Smith & Co., Philada., Cathedral, Blue Green, Panels, 9 In. 1540.00
T.B. Smith & Co., Philada., Cathedral, Blue Green, Square, OP, 9 In. 1540.00
W.D. Smith, N.Y., Cathedral, Light To Medium Teal, OP, 8 1/2 In. 660.00
W.K. Lewis & Co., Cathedral, Green, Cylindrical, IP, 10 3/4 In. 855.00
West India Pickle, Crosse & Blackwell, Aqua, ABM, 3 x 8 In. 6.00

──────────────────── **POISON** ────────────────────

Everyone knows you must be careful about how you store poisonous substances. Our
ancestors had the same problem. Nineteenth-century poison bottles were usually made
with raised designs so the user could feel the danger. The skull and crossbones symbol
was sometimes shown, but usually the bottle had ridges or raised embossing. The most
interesting poison bottles were made from the 1870s to the 1930s. Cobalt blue and
bright green glass were often used. The bottle was designed to look different from any
type of food container. One strange British poison bottle made in 1871 was shaped like
a coffin and was often decorated with a death's head. Another bottle was shaped like a
skull. Poison collectors search for any bottle that held poison or that is labeled poison.
Included are animal and plant poisons as well as dangerous medicines. A helpful reference book is *Poison Bottle Workbook* by Rudy Kuhn. See also Household, Ammonia.

A. Jacob Hulle, Strychnine, 8-Sided, Cobalt Blue, Label, BIMAL, England, 3 1/2 In. 90.00
A.M. Bickford & Sons, Ltd, Not To Be Taken, Yellow Amber, 1915, 8 3/4 In. 112.00
Boot's The Chemist, Toxol., Square, Emerald Green, England, 4 In. 110.00
Boots Cash Chemists, Brown, 4 3/4 In. 15.00
Boots Cash Chemists, Brown, Oval, 5 3/4 In. 20.00
Boots Cash Chemists, Embossed, Brown, Square, 5 3/4 In. 20.00
Boots The Chemist, Coffin, Brown, Monster, 6 5/8 In. 40.00
Boots The Chemist, Green, Oval, 7 In. 20.00
Bowman's Drug Store, Cobalt Blue, 1890-1910, 4 1/2 In. 134.00
Bowman's Drug Store, Cobalt Blue, 1890-1910, 6 1/4 In. 140.00

Bowman's Drug Stores, Cobalt, Embossed, 4 7/8 In. 325.00
Burgons Limited Manchester, Cobalt Blue, Rectangular, 5 1/8 In. 20.00
Chemists, C2H5OH, Stoneware, Painted Devil & Skull, Crossbones . . . . *Illus* 65.00
Cobalt Blue, 6-Sided, 4 1/2 In. 40.00
Cobalt Blue, 6-Sided, 4 7/8 In. 50.00
Cobalt Blue, 6-Sided, Horizontal Ribs, 3 1/2 In. 33.00
Cobalt Blue, Embossed Skull, Tooled Lip, 1880-1890, 3 3/8 In. 1980.00
Cobalt Blue, Hobnail, BDH In Diamond Base, 1930, 4 In. 20.00
Cobalt Blue, Quilted, 4 In., Pair 55.00
Coffin, Amber, Pointed Diamond Rows, 1890-1910, 3 1/2 In. 303.00
Coffin, Cobalt Blue, Tooled Lip, 1/2 In. 77.00
Coffin, Cobalt Blue, Tooled Lip, 3 1/4 In. 143.00
Coffin, Cobalt Blue, Tooled Mouth, 1890-1910, 3 5/8 In. 77.00
Coffin, Embossed N, Not To Be Taken, Green, 5 1/4 In. . . . . *Illus* 8.50
Cuming, Smith & Co., Formalin, Amber, Cylindrical, ABM, Shield, Australia, 8 1/2 In. . . 95.00
Cyllin Medical, Honey Amber, Cylindrical, Ribs, BIMAL, Australia, 4 1/2 In. 85.00
Dark Green, 6-Sided, Ribs, 5 In. 88.00
Davis & Geck, Inc., Brooklyn, N.Y., Cobalt Blue, Monogram, 1890-1910, 3 1/8 In. 1265.00
Davis & Geck, Inc., Brooklyn, N.Y., U.S.A., Cobalt Blue, 1890-1910, 3 1/8 In. 1270.00
De-Dro, Giftflasche Des Deutschen, Green, 3-Sided, ABM, Germany, 4 1/2 In. . . . .358.00 to 377.00
Dead Stuck For Bugs, Cottlieb Marshall & Co., Phila., Pa., Aqua, Oval, 6 1/2 In. 15.00
Embossed Not To Be Taken, 6-Sided, 5 1/2 In. 15.00
Embossed Not To Be Taken, Blue, 6 1/2 In. 15.00
Embossed Not To Be Taken, Cobalt Blue, 5 3/4 In. 23.00
Embossed Not To Be Taken, Cobalt Blue, 6 In. 10.00
Embossed Not To Be Taken, Cobalt Blue, 6-Sided, 2 Oz., 4 1/2 In. 12.00
Embossed Not To Be Taken, Cornflower Blue, Crescent, Slash Lines, BIMAL, 4 1/2 In. . . 130.00
Embossed Not To Be Taken, Emerald Green, 8-Sided, ABM, Paper Label, 4 3/4 In. 55.00
Embossed Not To Be Taken, Green, Flat Back, 1899, 2 Oz., 4 1/4 In. 4.00
Embossed Not To Be Taken, Green, Flat Back, 1899, 3 Oz., 5 In. 4.25
Embossed Not To Be Taken, Hastings, Worcester, Mass., Yellow Green, 6 1/2 In. 775.00
Embossed Not To Be Taken, Lime Green, 8-Sided, BIMAL, England, 6 Oz. 40.00
Embossed Not To Be Taken, Sapphire Blue, Crescent, Slash Lines, England, 3 1/2 In. . . . 130.00
Embossed Poison, Amber, 6-Sided, Rows Of X's, Tooled Top, 3 In. 44.00
Embossed Poison, Aqua, Cylindrical, 6 1/2 In. 25.00
Embossed Poison, Cobalt Blue, 1890-1910, 2 3/4 In. 100.00
Embossed Poison, Cobalt Blue, 2 Oz. 30.00
Embossed Poison, Cobalt Blue, 4 Oz. 35.00
Embossed Poison, Cobalt Blue, 6-Sided, 4 1/2 In. 25.00
Embossed Poison, Cobalt Blue, 8 Oz. 45.00
Embossed Poison, Not To Be Taken, Cobalt Blue, 6 1/2 In. 25.00
Embossed Poison, Not To Be Taken, Cobalt Blue, Oval, Ribs, 7 In. 30.00
Embossed Poison, Sawtooth Ribs, BIMAL, 3-Sided, 1890-1910, 3 In. 168.00
Embossed Poison, Tinct Iodine, Cobalt Blue, Skull & Crossbones, 3 1/8 In. 77.00
Embossed Poison, Wide Mouth, Vertical Lines, Cobalt Blue, 6-Sided, 2 3/4 In. 25.00
Embossed Poison Be Careful, 6-Sided, Toronto, Rows Of X's, 4 1/4 In. 94.00
Embossed Poison On 2 Sides, Green, 6-Sided, Embossed, Horizontal Ribs, Tooled Top, 5 1/2 In. . . . 66.00

Poison, Chemists, C2H5OH,
Stoneware, Painted Devil & Skull,
Crossbones

Poison, Coffin, Embossed
N, Not To Be Taken,
Green, 5 1/4 In.

Poison, Marshall's
Lysol, Amber,
Embossed Fishnet,
3 3/4 In.

Embossed Poison Tinct Lobelia Simp., Aqua 25.00
Embossed Poisonous, Phenyl, Green, Diamond Shape, BIMAL, Australia, 6 1/2 In. 75.00
Embossed Poisonous Not To Be Taken, Aqua, Oval, 6 1/2 In. 30.00
Embossed Poisonous Not To Be Taken, Cobalt Blue, 6 1/2 In. 25.00
Embossed Poisonous Not To Be Taken, Cobalt Blue, 6 In. 6.00
Embossed Poisonous Not To Be Taken, Cobalt Blue, 6-Sided, 6 3/4 In. ....25.00 to 30.00
Embossed Poisonous Not To Be Taken, Cobalt Blue, 8 Oz. 40.00
Embossed Poisonous Not To Be Taken, Cobalt Blue, Embossed, 10 Oz. 40.00
Embossed Poisonous Not To Be Taken, Cobalt Blue, Oval, 6 1/2 In. ....25.00 to 30.00
Embossed Poisonous Not To Be Taken, Cobalt Blue, Oval, Monster, 8 1/4 In. 45.00
Embossed Poisonous Not To Be Taken, Cobalt Blue, Raised Diamond Points, 12 Oz. ... 55.00
Embossed Poisonous Not To Be Taken, Cobalt Blue, Rectangular, 8 1/4 In. 30.00
Embossed Poisonous Not To Be Taken, Coffin, Amber, 6 Oz. 35.00
Embossed Poisonous Not To Be Taken, Cornflower Blue, ABM, 6 1/2 In. 35.00
Embossed Poisonous Not To Be Taken, Dark Green, 6 Oz. 45.00
Embossed Poisonous Not To Be Taken, Emerald Green, Stopper, 6 In. 35.00
Embossed Poisonous Not To Be Taken, Green, 10 Oz. ....40.00 to 45.00
Embossed Poisonous Not To Be Taken, Green, 6-Sided 25.00
Embossed Poisonous Not To Be Taken, Green, Rectangular, 3 3/4 In. 40.00
Embossed Poisonous Not To Be Taken, Green, Rectangular, Monster, 7 3/4 In. 65.00
Embossed Poisonous Not To Be Taken, Medium Blue, Rectangular, 10 Oz. 40.00
Embossed Poisonous Not To Be Taken, Moss Green, 5 1/2 In. 60.00
Embossed Poisonous Not To Be Taken, Wide Mouth, Green, 5 1/2 In. 25.00
Embossed Poisonous Not To Be Taken, Wide Mouth, Green, 6-Sided, 3 In. 25.00
Embossed Skull & Crossbones, 8-Sided, ABM Lip, 1920-1930, 6 5/8 In. 231.00
Embossed Skull & Crossbones, Amber, 6-Sided, Tooled Lip, 1900-1920, 9 1/2 In. ...*Illus* 132.00
Embossed Skull & Crossbones, Clear, 6-Sided, Tooled Lip, 1920-1930, 10 In. 220.00
Embossed Skull & Crossbones, Green Aqua, 8-Sided, ABM, 1925-1935, 2 In. 60.00
Embossed Skull & Crossbones, Green, 6-Sided, Tooled Lip, 1900-1910, 7 1/2 In. 303.00
Embossed Skull & Crossbones, Pale Aqua, 6-Sided, ABM, 1920-1930, 5 In. 198.00
Embossed Skull & Crossbones, Tooled Lip, 1900-1920, 7 1/2 In. 220.00
Embossed Skull & Crossbones, Yellow Green, 6-Sided, 1900-1920, 9 1/2 In. 154.00
Embossed Skull & Crossbones, Yellow Green, Tooled Lip, 1915-1925, 4 3/8 In. ....*Illus* 121.00
F.A. Thompson & Co., Detroit, Coffin, Yellow Amber, Tooled Top, 3 1/8 In. 935.00
Federation Francaise Droguistes, Olive Yellow, 6-Sided, France, 10 3/4 In. 330.00
Fergusson's Arsenate Of Lead, Stoneware, Brown, Wide Mouth, England, 5 1/2 In. 114.00
Figural, Skull, Cobalt Blue, Pat. June 26th, 1894, Tooled Mouth, 1894-1910, 4 1/4 In. ... 3300.00
Figural, Skull, Embossed Poison, Crossbones, Cobalt Blue, 3 3/4 In. 2860.00
Flask, Allover Hobnail, Medium Sapphire Blue, Sheared Lip, Pontil, 4 1/4 In. 1092.00
Flask, Diamond, Clear, Pontil, Rolled Lip, 1810-1830, 4 3/4 In. 99.00
Giftflasche, Skull & Crossbones, Olive Green, 6-Sided, Germany, 1900, 6 1/2 In. 83.00
Giftflasche, Skull & Crossbones, Olive Green, 6-Sided, Germany, 5 1/2 In. 88.00
Giftflasche, Skull & Crossbones, Yellow Green, 6-Sided, Germany, 1920, 6 1/2 In. 72.00
Giftflasche, Skull & Crossbones, Yellow Green, 6-Sided, Germany, 1920, 6 5/8 In. 220.00
Giftflasche, Skull & Crossbones, Yellow Green, 6-Sided, Germany, 5 In. 38.00
Godstone & Haslemere, Surrey Flagon 38.00
Green, 6-Sided, Horizontal Ribs, 5 In. 66.00
Izal Disinfectant, Square, Emerald Green, Recessed Panels, Sample, BIMAL, 4 In. 140.00
J.F. Hartz Co. Limited, Toronto, Cobalt Blue, Embossed Hearts, 5 In. 825.00
J.F. Hartz Co. Limited, Toronto, Cobalt Blue, Embossed Hearts, BIMAL, 7 1/2 In. 36.00
J.T.M. Co., Amber, BIMAL, 1890-1910, 5 In. 532.00
Jacobs' Bed Bug Killer, W.T. & Co., Amber, Skull & Crossbones, 1890, 5 3/8 In. 1245.00
Jacobs' Bed Bug Killer, W.T. & Co., Amber, Tooled Mouth, 1910, 5 3/8 In. 2150.00
James Woolley & Sons & Co., Manchester, Cobalt Blue, 6-Sided, Cork, Small 30.00
Jeyes Lysol, Property Of Ockelford's, Brisbane, Not To Be Taken, Amber, Jug, BIMAL .. 180.00
Jitter Bug Insect Repellent, Dark Amber, ABM, 3 In. 7.00
Kilner Bros., Cornflower Blue, Cylindrical, 9 1/2 In. 45.00
Kirwan-Porter Drug Co., Carbolic Acid, Label, Lattice & Diamond, 4 1/2 In. 77.00
Lattice & Diamond, Cobalt Blue, Poison Stopper, 1890-1910, 4 3/4 In. 115.00
Lattice & Diamond, Cobalt Blue, Tooled Lip, 1890-1910, 4 In. 94.00
Lattice & Diamond, Cobalt Blue, Tooled Lip, Clear Glass Stopper, 10 7/8 In. 868.00
Lattice & Diamond, Cobalt Blue, Tooled Lip, Poison Stopper, 1890-1910, 3 3/4 In. 134.00
Lattice & Diamond, Cobalt Blue, Tooled Lip, Poison Stopper, 1890-1910, 3 3/8 In. 179.00

Poison, Embossed
Skull & Crossbones,
Amber, 6-Sided,
Tooled Lip, 1900-
1920, 9 1/2 In.

Poison, Embossed Skull
& Crossbones, Yellow
Green, Tooled Lip,
1915-1925, 4 3/8 In.

Poison, Owl Drug Co.,
Owl on Mortar &
Pestle, Cobalt Blue,
3-Sided, 9 5/8 In.

Poison, Pat. Amtl.,
Gesch, Orange Amber,
ABM, Glass Stopper,
1915-1930, 6 1/4 In.

Lattice & Diamond, Cobalt Blue, Tooled Lip, Poison Stopper, 1890-1910, 3 5/8 In. 146.00
Lattice & Diamond, Cobalt Blue, Tooled Lip, Poison Stopper, 1890-1910, 4 3/4 In. 134.00
Lattice & Diamond, Cobalt Blue, Tooled Lip, Poison Stopper, 1890-1910, 5 1/2 In. 155.00
Lattice & Diamond, Cobalt Blue, Tooled Lip, Poison Stopper, 1890-1910, 7 In. 280.00
Lattice & Diamond, Cobalt Blue, Tooled Lip, Poison Stopper, 1890-1910, 7 1/4 In. 308.00
Lattice & Diamond, Cobalt Blue, Tooled Lip, Poison Stopper, 1890-1910, 9 In. 364.00
Lattice & Diamond, Cobalt Blue, Tooled Lip, Poison Stopper, 5 1/2 In. 143.00
Lattice & Diamond, Cobalt Blue, Tooled Lip, Stopper, 1890-1910, 10 3/4 In. 588.00
Lattice & Diamond, Cobalt Blue, Tooled Lip, Stopper, 9 1/8 In. 420.00
Light Cornflower Blue, Cylindrical, Embossed, 8 1/4 In. 25.00
Lilly, Tincture No. 63 Opium, Red Poison Label, Glassine Wrapper, 1/4 Pt., 5 1/4 In 66.00
Little Giant, Sure Death To All Kinds Of Bugs, Aqua, Tooled Lip, 8 1/2 In. 40.00
Lloyd Bros, Cantharis, Skull & Crossbones, Square, Iron Cross Label Border, 5 In. 28.00
Lyon's Powder, B & P, N.Y., Grape Puce, Rolled Lip, OP, 4 1/2 In. 165.00
Lyon's Powder, B & P, N.Y., Purple Amethyst, Rolled Lip, OP, 4 3/8 In. 179.00
Manchester & Salford Hospital For Skin Disease, Cobalt Blue, Monster, 6 3/4 In. 65.00
Manchester & Salford Hospital For Skin Disease, Cobalt Blue, Monster, 8 3/4 In. 100.00
Marshall's Lysol, Amber, Embossed Fishnet, 3 3/4 In. ....*Illus* 29.00
Melvin & Badger Apothecaries, Boston, Mass., Cobalt Blue, 6 In. 132.00
Mercury Bichloride, Cobalt Blue, 3-Sided, Label, Skull & Crossbones, ABM, 3 1/8 In. .. 88.00
Norwich, Coffin, Amber, Tooled Lip, 1890, 5 In. 935.00
Norwich, Coffin, Cobalt Blue, Tooled Lip, 1890-1910, 7 1/2 In. 1018.00
Owl Drug Co., 1-Wing Owl, Cobalt Blue, 3-Sided, Label, 6 In. 209.00
Owl Drug Co., 1-Wing Owl, Cobalt Blue, 3-Sided, Tooled Top, 2 7/8 In. 90.00
Owl Drug Co., 2-Wing Owl On Mortar & Pestle, Tinct Iodine, Deep Cobalt Blue, 4 In. ... 110.00
Owl Drug Co., 2-Wing Owl, Cobalt Blue, 3 1/4 In. 125.00
Owl Drug Co., 2-Wing Owl, Cobalt Blue, 4 1/2 In. 175.00
Owl Drug Co., 2-Wing Owl, Cobalt Blue, 5 In. 200.00
Owl Drug Co., 2-Wing Owl, Cobalt Blue, 6 1/2 In. 350.00
Owl Drug Co., Owl On Mortar & Pestle, Cobalt Blue, 1890-1910, 9 3/4 In. 560.00
Owl Drug Co., Owl On Mortar & Pestle, Cobalt Blue, 3-Sided, 8 In. 440.00
Owl Drug Co., Owl On Mortar & Pestle, Cobalt Blue, 3-Sided, 9 1/2 In. 448.00
Owl Drug Co., Owl On Mortar & Pestle, Cobalt Blue, 3-Sided, 9 5/8 In. ....*Illus* 1073.00
Owl Drug Co., Owl On Mortar & Pestle, Cobalt Blue, Flared Mouth, 9 1/2 In. 715.00
Pat. Amtl., Gesch, Orange Amber, ABM, Glass Stopper, 1915-1930, 6 1/4 In. ......*Illus* 60.00
Permal Solution Poisonous, Not To Be Taken, Blue, 6 1/4 In. 50.00
Polusterine Products Co., Toronto, Gold Amber, Embossed, Tooled Lip, 3 x 6 In. 9.00
Polusterine Products Co., Toronto, Honey Amber, 2 1/4 x 3 1/2 In. 3.00
Santonin, Skull & Crossbones, Amber, White Lettering, 1930, 6 In. 840.00
Schieffelin, Arsenic Trioxide, Amber, Ribs, Red Paper Label, 3 1/4 In. 49.00
Sercsol, Elliot, Not To Be Taken, Amber, 5-Sided, 1890-1920, 5 1/4 In. 578.00

Sharp & Dohme, Baltimore, Amber, Cork Stopper, 1910, 5 In. 235.00
Sharpe & Dohme, Amber, 2-Sided, Label, Embossed, Crisscross, 2 3/4 In. 132.00
Star, Green, 8 Oz. 187.00
Strychnia, Rolled Lip, BIMAL, Oval, 1890-1925, 2 3/8 In. 123.00
Submarine, Cobalt Blue, Tooled Lip, 1890-1910, 2 1/2 In. 231.00
Submarine, Deep Cobalt Blue, Embossed Registry Numbers, BIMAL, England, 2 In. 130.00
Submarine, Embossed Poison, Cobalt Blue, England, 1890-1910, 2 1/2 In. 231.00
Sulpholine, Cobalt Blue, Rectangular, Embossed 25.00
Sulpholine, Cobalt Blue, Rectangular, Embossed, Large 30.00
Sulpholine, Cobalt Blue, Rectangular, Ribs, Embossed, England, 1890, 4 1/2 In. 45.00
Sun Drug Co., 7-Up Green, 2 Oz., 4 In. 465.00
Tinct. Iodine, Skull & Crossbones, Amber, Reverse Mortar & Pestle, ABM, 3 In. 110.00
Tinct. Iodine, Skull & Crossbones, Cobalt Blue, 1910, 3 1/8 In. 77.00
Tinct. Iodine, Skull & Crossbones, Cobalt Blue, 2 1/8 In. 95.00
Tinct. Iodine, Skull & Crossbones, Cobalt Blue, 3 In. 88.00
United Drug Co., Mercury Bichloride, 3-Sided, Sapphire Blue, 8 1/4 In. 1210.00
Upjohn Co., Kalamazoo, Mich., Mercury Bichloride, Amber, 1910, 3 3/8 In. 94.00
Vorsicht, Gift, Skull & Crossbones, Olive Green, 6-Sided, Germany, 6 7/8 In. 121.00
Wide Mouth, Dark Green, 6-Sided, Embossed, 4 1/4 In. 15.00
Wide Mouth, Green, 6-Sided, Vertical Warning Lines, 3 3/4 In. 20.00
Wide Mouth, Green, 6-Sided, Vertical Warning Lines, 4 1/2 In. 20.00
Woodward Chemist Nottingham, Light Blue, Oval, 5 7/8 In. 15.00
Yellow Amber, Vertical Ribs, 2 1/2 x 4 5/8 In. 6.00

————————————————— PURPLE POWER —————————————————

Purple power is the Kansas State University slogan. A series of bottles was made from 1970 to 1972 picturing the wildcat at a sporting event. They were distributed by Jon-Sol.

Football Player, 1972 .... 15.00
Wildcat, On Basketball, 1971 .... 15.00
Wildcat, Walking, 1970 .... 17.00
SANDWICH GLASS, see Cologne; Scent

————————————————————— SARSAPARILLA —————————————————————

The most widely distributed syphilis cure used in the nineteenth century was sarsaparilla. The roots of the smilax vine were harvested, cleaned, dried, and sold to apothecaries and drug manufacturers. They added alcohol and other flavorings, such as the roots of yellow dock, dandelion, or burdock or the bark from prickly ash, sassafras, or birch trees. A few makers also added fruit or vegetable juice and clover blossoms. All of this was mixed to make the medicine called *sarsaparilla.* It was claimed to cure many diseases, including skin diseases, boils, pimples, piles, tumors, scrofulous conditions including king's evil (a swelling of the neck), and rheumatism. It could cleanse and purify the blood, a process doctors thought should take place regularly for good health.

The first labeled sarsaparilla was made in the early 1800s. Some bottled products called sarsaparilla are still made today. The bottles were usually rectangular with embossed letters, or soda-bottle shaped. Most were light green or aqua but some amber and cobalt bottles were made. Later bottles had paper labels.

Bristol's Genuine, New York, Aqua, Rectangular, Sunken Panels, 10 1/2 In. 44.00
Brown's Sarsaparilla For The Kidneys, 9 1/4 In. ....*Illus* 85.00
Chas. Langley & Co., Compound Extract, San Francisco, Applied Top, 9 3/4 In. 176.00
Cook's, Black Amethyst, Applied Sloping Collar, IP, 7 7/8 In. 6944.00
Dana's, Belfast, Maine, Aqua, Rectangular, BIMAL, 9 In. 22.00
Dr. Cronk's, 12-Sided, Stoneware, Red Brown, 9 7/8 In. 60.00
Dr. De Andries, E.M. Rusha, New Orleans, Amber, Applied Top 1430.00
Dr. E.R. Palmer's Compound Extract, Wild Cherry, Blue Aqua, 9 3/8 In. 812.00
Dr. Guysott's Compound Extract, Emerald Green, IP, 9 1/2 In. 165.00
Dr. Guysott's Yellow Dock, Cincinnati, O., Blue Aqua, Oval, IP, 9 3/4 In. 420.00
Dr. J.S. Rose's, Philadelphia, Blue Aqua, IP, 9 1/4 In. 687.00
Dr. King's Compound Extract Of Sarsaparilla, Label, Box, 9 In. ....*Illus* 125.00
Dr. Schartze's Compound, Washington, D.C., Blue Aqua, OP, 7 3/4 In. 448.00
Dr. Townsend's, Albany, N.Y., 7-Up Green, Applied Top, 9 In. 88.00

Dr. Townsend's, Albany, N.Y., Blue Aqua, Sloping Collar, Pontil, 9 1/8 In. 1456.00
Dr. Townsend's, Albany, N.Y., Dark Green, Applied Top, IP 358.00
Dr. Townsend's, Albany, N.Y., Dark Green, Square, Pontil, 9 1/4 In. 500.00
Dr. Townsend's, Albany, N.Y., Dark Olive, Applied Top, Pontil 303.00
Dr. Townsend's, Albany, N.Y., Dark Olive, Pontil 55.00
Dr. Townsend's, Albany, N.Y., Emerald Green, Square, Applied Collar, IP, 9 3/4 In. 336.00
Dr. Townsend's, Albany, N.Y., Green, Applied Top, 9 In. 330.00
Dr. Townsend's, Albany, N.Y., Green, Applied Top, 9 1/2 In. .... 120.00 to 185.00
Dr. Townsend's, Albany, N.Y., Light To Medium Green, Graphite Pontil, 9 In. 385.00
Dr. Townsend's, Albany, N.Y., Moss Green, Applied Top, 9 In. 132.00
Dr. Townsend's, Albany, N.Y., Olive Amber, Pontil, 9 1/2 In. 468.00
Dr. Townsend's, Albany, N.Y., Olive Yellow Green, Square, 1855, 9 7/8 In. 198.00
Dr. Townsend's, Albany, N.Y., Olive Yellow Green, Square, Pontil, 9 1/2 In. 357.00
Dr. Townsend's, Albany, N.Y., Olive Yellow, Square, Applied Collar, Pontil, 9 3/4 In. 392.00
Dr. Townsend's, Albany, N.Y., Peacock Teal, Applied Top, 9 1/2 In. 154.00
Dr. Townsend's, Albany, N.Y., Teal Blue, 9 In. .... 176.00 to 209.00
Dr. Townsend's, Albany, N.Y., Teal, Square, Pontil, 9 1/4 In. 700.00
Dr. Townsend's, Albany, N.Y., Yellow Green, Square, IP, 9 5/8 In. 176.00
Dr. Townsend's, Blood Purifier, Aqua, 4-Sided, Embossed, 7 1/2 In. 95.00
Dr. Townsend's, New York, Teal, IP, 9 3/4 In. 325.00
Dr. Wilcox's Compound Extract Of Sarsaparilla, Square, Emerald Green, 9 1/4 In. 132.00
Gold Medal, Amber, 9 In. 79.00
Gooch's Extract, Cincinnati, O., Light Cobalt, Tooled Mouth, 9 3/8 In. 476.00
Hood's Compound Extract, C.I. Hood & Co., Lowell, Mass., Aqua, 8 In. 2.00
John Bull Extract, Louisville, Aqua, BIMAL, 9 1/2 In. 35.00
John Bull Extract, Louisville, Ky., Blue Aqua, 1860, 9 In. 275.00
Log Cabin, Rochester, N.Y., Pat. Sept. 6, 1887, Chocolate Amber, 9 In. .... 187.00 to 235.00
McLean's, St. Louis, Mo., Aqua, 9 1/8 In. 578.00
Mineral Water, Buffum & Co., Pittsburg, Sapphire Blue, 1860, 8 In. 1904.00
Myer's Rock Rose, New Haven, Green, IP, 1850, 9 In. 2860.00
Old Dr. Jacob Townsend's, Blood Purifier, Clear, 7 1/2 In. 88.00
Old Dr. Townsend's, N.Y., Green, IP, Applied Mouth, 1855, 9 1/2 In. 700.00
Old Dr. Townsend's, N.Y., Green, IP, Applied Mouth, 1855, 9 3/4 In. 756.00
Old Dr. Townsend's, N.Y., Green, Sloping Collar, IP, 9 1/2 In. 700.00
Old Dr. Townsend's, N.Y., Light Blue Green, 1855-1865, 9 1/2 In. 149.00
Old Dr. Townsend's, N.Y., Light Green, 1855-1870, 9 1/2 In. 143.00
Old Dr. Townsend's, N.Y., Light Green, Square, Beveled Corners, 10 In. 180.00
Old Dr. Townsend's, N.Y., Teal Blue Green, IP 330.00
Old Dr. Townsend's, Yellow Blue, Pontil, Square, 1845-1860, 9 3/4 In. 88.00
Smith's True Fruit Concentrated Syrup, Stoneware, Jug, 1890, 12 In. 330.00
W. Bidwell, 12-Sided, Stoneware, Tan, 9 3/4 In. 325.00
Wetherall's, Exeter, N.H., Aqua, 9 3/8 In. 150.00
Wynkoop's Katharismic, Honduras, Cobalt Blue, OP, 10 1/8 In. 5500.00
Wynkoop's Katharismic, New York, Cobalt Blue, IP, 9 5/8 In. 9800.00
Yager's, Aqua 60.00

Sarsaparilla, Brown's
Sarsaparilla For The
Kidneys, 9 1/4 In.

Sarsaparilla, Dr.
King's Compound
Extract Of
Sarsaparilla,
Label, Box, 9 In.

Scent, Sunburst, Pink
Amethyst, Pontil,
1870, 2 7/8 In.

Scent, Swirled Right,
Cobalt Blue,
Pontil, 3 In.

SCENT

Perfume and cologne are not the same as scent. Scent is smelling salts, a perfume with ammonia salts added for a sharp vapor that could revive a person who was feeling faint. Because our female ancestors wore tightly laced corsets and high starched collars, the problem of feeling faint was common. Scent bottles were sometimes small mold-blown bottles in the full spectrum of glass colors. Sometimes the bottles were free blown and made in elaborate shapes to resemble, perhaps, a seahorse. By the mid-nineteenth century molded scents were made, usually of dark green, cobalt, or yellow glass. These were rather squat bottles, often with unusual stoppers. There is much confusion about the difference between cologne and scent bottles because manufacturers usually made both kinds. Related bottles may be found in the Cologne and Perfume categories.

Cat, Frosted, Flared Lip, France, 1890-1915, 1 7/8 In.	176.00
Cat, Playing Violin, Ceramic, Green, Metal Crown Stopper, Germany, 2 1/2 In.	165.00
Cut Yellow Glass, White Pompeiian Swirl, Flat Side, Sterling Silver, 3 3/4 In.	115.00
Diamond Shape, Embossed Star, Cobalt Blue, 1810-1830, 2 5/8 In.	672.00
Diamond Shape, Embossed Sunburst, Cobalt Blue, 18 Beads On Each Side, 2 In.	588.00
Diamond Shape, Embossed Sunburst, Cobalt Blue, 30 Beads On Each Side, 3 In.	560.00
Dog, Brown, Googly-Eye, Ceramic, Metal Crown Stopper, Germany	99.00
Old Man, In Stuffed Chair, Ceramic, Metal Crown Stopper, Germany, 2 3/8 In.	242.00
Pink Amethyst, Tooled Mouth, Pontil, 3 1/2 In.	154.00
Porcelain, Enamel Heart With Flowers, Cork Lined Stopper, France, 3 In.	99.00
Porcelain, Hand Painted Flowers, Blue Ground, Metal Cap & Necklace Chain, 1 1/2 In.	187.00
Red, Faceted, 2 Ended, 1 Silver Screw Cap & Other Hinged, 4 3/4 In.	220.00
Round, Embossed Sunburst, Amethyst, 1810-1830, 1 3/4 In.	364.00
Round, Embossed Sunburst, Medium Teal Green, 1810-1830, 2 In.	3080.00
Scallop Shape, Black Amethyst, 1810-1830, 2 1/2 In.	336.00
Scallop Shape, Cobalt Blue, 1850-1870, 2 1/4 In.	156.00
Scallop Shape, Medium Sapphire Blue, 1850-1870, 1 3/4 In.	308.00
Seahorse, Blue & White Stripes, 2 3/4 In.	175.00
Soccer Player Kicking Ball, Metal Crown Stopper, 6 In.	286.00
Sunburst, Cobalt Blue, Pontil, 1865, 3 1/4 In.	3410.00
Sunburst, Pink Amethyst, Pontil, 1870, 2 7/8 In. ....*Illus*	1075.00
Swirled Right, Cobalt Blue, Pontil, 3 In. ....*Illus*	175.00
Vertical Ribs, Teal Green, Pontil, 3 In.	155.00
Vertical Ribs, Emerald Green, Pinched Waist, Ornate Handle, Tooled Lip, Ring, Pontil, 3 In.	1232.00

SEAL

Seal or sealed bottles are named for the glass seal that was applied to the body of the bottle. While still hot, this small pad of glass was impressed with an identification mark. Seal bottles are known from the second century but the earliest examples collectors can find today date from the eighteenth century. Because the seal bottle was the most popular container for wine and other liquids shipped to North America, broken bottles, seals alone, or whole bottles are often found in old dumps and excavations. Dutch gin, French wine, and English liquors were all shipped in large seal bottles. Seal bottles also held rum, olive oil, mineral water, and even vinegar. It is possible to date the bottle from the insignia on the seal and from the shape of the bottle.

A.H., Amber, White, Orange, Cobalt Blue, Green Loops, Ribs, England, 1800s, 3 5/8 In. . . .   201.00

Seal, A.S.C.R., Olive
Green, Pontil, England,
1780, 8 3/4 In.

Seal, Jas. Oakes
Bury, Black Glass,
Olive Green,
Applied Mouth,
Pontil, 1793,
10 In.

If you have unopened
bottles of drugs or other
pharmaceuticals, be sure to
check for ether or picric
acid. These can explode
spontaneously and are
dangerous to keep.

A.S.C.R., Olive Green, Pontil, England, 1780, 8 3/4 In. . . . .*Illus*   308.00
Black Glass, Bladder, Blue Green, OP, Continental, 1739, 7 1/4 In. 5780.00
Black Glass, Olive Yellow Amber, 3-Piece Mold, England, 1835-1838, 9 3/4 In. 410.00
Braddon, Black Glass, Shoulder Star, England 540.00
Christopher & Co., Black Glass, 118 Pall Mall, London, Olive Green, 11 In. 360.00
Daniel Visser & Zonen Scheidam, Dark Amber, Cobalt Shoulder Seal, 11 In. 415.00
Dyottville Glass Works, Phila, Olive Green, Amber Tone, 11 In. 415.00
EG 1769, Black Glass, Medium Yellow Olive Green, String Collar, 9 1/8 In. 1455.00
Ellwood Cooper Pure Olive Oil, Santa Barbara Cal., Aqua, 11 In. 44.00
Eman Coll., Black Glass, Olive Green, Double Collar, Pontil, England, 11 1/2 In. 88.00
Emmanual College, Black Glass, 3-Piece Mold, England, c.1840 . . . .   256.00
F. Peters, Amber, Applied Top, Germany 66.00
Fox Beneath Coronet, Black Glass, Olive Green, Pontil, England, c.1705, 5 1/8 In. 2310.00
Gordon Of Gordonstown, Sans Criante, Black Glass, 3-Piece Mold, 1860 . . . .   360.00
H. Rickett's & Co.Black Glass, English, Ca., 1831, Olive Amber, 12 1/2 x 4 1/2 In. 260.00
H.C., Human Hand, Olive Yellow Green, Applied Collar, Pontil, 1800-1850, 10 1/4 In. . . .   467.00
I. Smith, Black Glass, Olive Amber Onion, Applied String Lip, England, 1706, 6 5/8 In. . .   7700.00
I.L.M. Smith Wine Merch. Baltimore, Black Glass, Pontil, 1800-1850, 10 In. 1210.00
Inner Temple, Black Glass, Olive Amber, Pontil, England, 11 5/8 In. . . . . .60.00 to 70.00
J & C McG 1820, Spirits, Dark Olive Amber, Decanter Shape, 10 5/8 In. 3740.00
J.N., Cylindrical, Olive Amber, Applied String Collar, Pontil, 1790, 10 1/4 In. 200.00
J.V.H. In Circle, Forest Lawn, Green, IP, 7 In. 715.00
Jas. Oakes Bury, Black Glass, Olive Green, Applied Mouth, Pontil, 1793, 10 In. . . . . .*Illus*   625.00
Jn. Furse 1823, H. Rickett's Co. Glass Works, Bristol, Deep Olive, Cylindrical, 10 3/4 In.   440.00
John Tabor 1767, Black Glass, English, Ca., Olive Amber, String Collar, 10 1/8 In. 2690.00
John Winn Jr., H. Ricketts, Glassworks, Bristol, Patent, Mid 1850s, 8 1/2 x 3 3/4 In. 220.00
John. Wills, Black Glass, Deep Olive Amber, Applied Mouth, England, 1818, 9 5/8 In. . . .   580.00
L. Thorndike, Green, Applied Top, Pontil, 10 1/4 In. 440.00
L.E. 1772, Star In Center, Onion, Olive, Applied String, Pontil, England, 11 In. 1100.00
Mallet, R.I. Olborne 1735, Black Glass, Olive Amber, English, 7 In. 3360.00
Manufacture De Tabac De Natchitoches, Blue Green, Sloping Double Collar, 10 1/4 In. .   413.00
Manufacture De Tabac De Natchitoches, Olive Amber, Bubbles, 9 1/8 In. 633.00
Marken Schutz Gesetz V. Bolen 1876, 6-Sided, Olive Amber, 9 1/4 In. 415.00
Michael's Lindeman, New York, Orange Amber, 3-Piece Mold, 11 In. 88.00
Middle Temple, Black Glass, Olive Green, Double Collar, England, 1800, 11 1/8 In. 130.00
Middle Temple, Black Glass, Olive Green, Pontil, England, 1780-1800, 9 In. 275.00
Mist. Gonnorr, Cobalt Blue, 3-Piece Mold, 1880, 12 1/2 In. 575.00
OH Von Pet, Amber, Applied Collar 66.00
R.P., Crown, Spirits, Foil Around Mouth, Continental, 1860-1880, 10 In. 209.00
Redges & Butler, Tobacco Amber, 3-Piece Mold, Pontil, 8 1/2 In. 255.00
S.B. Rothenberg, Sole Agent, U.S., Case, Gin, Milk Glass, Applied String Collar 100.00
Shaft & Globe, Black Glass, England 2850.00
Skene 1742, Mallet, Black Glass, Olive Yellow Amber, Kick-Up, Pontil, 9 In. 1490.00
Stiffel Brothers Ale, Black Glass, Olive Green, 3-Piece Mold, Australia, Pontil, 9 1/8 In. .   300.00

Tabac De A. Delpit, Nouvelle Orleans, Black Glass, Amber, 1880, 10 3/4 In. 880.00
Tabac De A. Delpit, Nouvelle Orleans, Black Glass, Olive Yellow, 1850-1880, 10 1/8 In. .   825.00
Tabac De A. Delpit, Nouvelle Orleans, Olive Yellow, 1850-1880, 10 1/8 In. 825.00
Trelaske, Deep Olive Green, Applied Collar, Pontil, England, 1820-1840, 10 7/8 In. 154.00
Victoria Inn, Powell & Co., Bristol On Base, Black Glass 650.00
Vieille Cure De Cenon, Olive Green, 3-Piece Mold, 1865, 11 3/4 In. 240.00
W. Oakley, Black Glass, Olive Amber, Applied String Collar, Pontil, England, 1789, 11 In.   2063.00

━━━━━━━━━━━━━━━━━━━━━━━━━ **SELTZER** ━━━━━━━━━━━━━━━━━━━━━━━━━

The word *seltzer* was first used for mineral water with medicinal properties at Selters, Germany. Seltzer was thought to be good for intestinal disorders. The word soon was used for any of the artificially carbonated waters that became popular in the nineteenth century. Seltzer bottles were advertised in Philadelphia by 1816. *Soda* and *seltzer* mean the same thing. Some collectors want the bottles that say *seltzer* and the special pump bottles that dispensed it. These pump bottles were usually covered with a metal mesh to keep glass from flying in case of an explosion. The top of the bottle was a spigot and carbonation was added to the water when the spigot was pressed. Related bottles may be found in the Coca-Cola, Mineral Water, Pepsi-Cola, and Soda categories.

Alfonz Dewitte Gent, Blue, Bird & Fern, 9 1/2 In. 70.00
Calistoga Mineral Water & Bottling Works, Calistoga, Calif., Green, Panels 180.00
Coca-Cola Bottling Co., Superior, Wis., Etched 1045.00
E. Bunting, Mansfield, Olive Green, Pontil, Rolled Lip, Hamilton, England, 1830s 2556.00
Green, Vertical Ribs 60.00
New York Seltzer Water Co., Detroit, Mich., Deep Turquoise Blue, 11 In. 95.00
Orange Crush, 12-Sided, Blue, Etched, 12 1/2 In. 88.00
Orange Crush, Rock Island, Ill. 83.00
Pilgrim Bros., Hamilton, Ont., Blue, Etched, Eagle On Rock, 12 In. 150.00
Saratoga Seltzer Co., Saratoga, N.Y., S.S.S., Emerald Green, Double Collar, 1870, Pt. . . .   2640.00
Saratoga Seltzer Water, Teal Blue, Applied Mouth, Pt. 78.00
Shamrock Saloon, Pat. Patrick Gallagher, Replaced Pewter Top 1430.00
Siphon, Pilgrim, Blue, Etched Eagle, On Rock, Raised, Wings, c.1890, 12 In. 150.00
Sniderman Bros., Soda Water Man, West Toronto, Ont., Etched, DJ, 12 In. 30.00
Sparkling Soda, Orange Crush Bottling Co., Silhouette Scottie Dog & Clown, 11 In. 65.00
Steinike & Weinlig Shultz Marke, Green, Applied Top, Embossed, 9 3/4 In. 33.00
Susanville Bottling Company, 11 3/4 In. 325.00
Upper Blue Lick Water, Maysville, Ky., Olive Yellow Amber, Oval, 10 1/8 In. 1904.00

━━━━━━━━━━━━━━━━━━━━━━━━━ **SKI COUNTRY** ━━━━━━━━━━━━━━━━━━━━━━━━━

Ski Country bottles are issued by The Foss Company of Golden, Colorado. These decanters are sold empty and filled by various distillers. The first bottles were made in 1973. By 1975 the company was making about 24 different decanter designs in each size each year, plus one decanter in the gallon size. They made 3 designs in 1995. The firm has marketed many series of decanters.

Animal, Antelope, Pronghorn, 1979 . . . .   60.00
Animal, Badger Family, 1981 . . . .   60.00
Animal, Basset Hound, 1978 . . . .   50.00
Animal, Bear, Brown, 1974 . . . .   36.00
Animal, Bobcat, 1981 . . . .   62.00
Animal, Buffalo, Stampede, 1982 . . . .   65.00
Animal, Buffalo, Stampede, 1982, Miniature 16.00
Animal, Bull Rider, 1980 . . . .   80.00
Animal, Bull, Charolais, 1974 . . . .   50.00
Animal, Circus, Tiger, On Ball, 1975 . . . .   45.00
Animal, Cow, Holstein, 1973 . . . .   65.00
Animal, Coyote, Family, 1978 . . . .   50.00
Animal, Deer, White-Tailed, 1982 . . . .   160.00
Animal, Dog, Basset Hound, 1978 . . . .   67.00
Animal, Dog, Basset Hound, 1978, Miniature 47.00
Animal, Dog, Labrador With Mallard, 1978 . . . .   135.00
Animal, Dog, Labrador With Mallard, 1978, Miniature 39.00
Animal, Dog, Labrador With Pheasant, 1978 . . . .   90.00
Animal, Dog, Labrador With Pheasant, 1978, Miniature 40.00
Animal, Elk, American, 1979 . . . .   200.00

Animal, Ferret, Blackfooted, 1976, Miniature 55.00
Animal, Fox, Family, 1979 .... 62.00
Animal, Fox, Family, 1979, Miniature 35.00
Animal, Fox, On Log, 1974 .... 85.00
Animal, Fox, On Log, 1981, 1.75 Liter 275.00
Animal, Fox, With Butterfly, 1983 .... 75.00
Animal, Fox, With Butterfly, 1983, Miniature 41.00
Animal, Giraffe, Circus Wagon, 1977 .... 47.00
Animal, Goat, Mountain, 1975 .... 80.00
Animal, Jaguar, 1983 .... 160.00
Animal, Jaguar, 1983, Miniature 59.00
Animal, Kangaroo, 1974 .... 37.00
Animal, Koala, 1973 .... 35.00
Animal, Leopard, Snow, 1979 .... 50.00
Animal, Lion, Mountain, 1973 .... 55.00
Animal, Lion, Mountain, 1975, Miniature 37.00
Animal, Lions, African, Safari 50.00
Animal, Lions, African, Safari, Miniature 30.00
Animal, Moose, Bull, 1982 ....100.00 to 104.00
Animal, Mountain Goat, Gal. 650.00
Animal, Otter, River, 1979 .... 70.00
Animal, Raccoon, 1975 .... 55.00
Animal, Ram, Big Horn, 1973 .... 70.00
Animal, Ram, Big Horn, 1973, Miniature 45.00
Animal, Sheep, Dall, Grand Slam, 1980 .... 180.00
Animal, Sheep, Desert, Grand Slam, 1990 .... 115.00
Animal, Sheep, Rocky Mountain, 1981 .... 70.00
Animal, Skunk, Family, 1978, Miniature ....45.00 to 48.00
Animal, Squirrels, 1983, Club Decanter 135.00
Animal, Squirrels, 1983, Miniature, Club Decanter 105.00
Animal, Walrus, Alaskan, 1985 ....50.00 to 60.00
Bird, Blackbird, Red Wing, 1977 ....40.00 to 42.00
Bird, Blue Jay, 1978 .... 82.00
Bird, Cardinal, 1977, Miniature 35.00
Bird, Cardinal, 1979 .... 75.00
Bird, Cardinal, Holiday, 1991 .... 65.00
Bird, Chickadee, 1981 .... 70.00
Bird, Condor, California, 1973 .... 55.00
Bird, Dove, Peace, 1973 .... 60.00
Bird, Duck, Blue Wing Teal, 1976 .... 250.00
Bird, Duck, Canvasback, 1981 ....58.00 to 60.00
Bird, Duck, Green Wing Teal, 1983 .... 180.00
Bird, Duck, King Eider, 1977 .... 60.00
Bird, Duck, King Eider, 1977, Miniature 45.00
Bird, Duck, Mallard Drake, 1973 .... 60.00
Bird, Duck, Mallard Family, 1977 .... 75.00
Bird, Duck, Mallard, Banded, 1980 .... 60.00
Bird, Duck, Merganzer, Female Hooded, 1981 .... 50.00
Bird, Duck, Merganzer, Male Hooded, 1983 ....76.00 to 80.00
Bird, Duck, Pintail, 1978 .... 100.00
Bird, Duck, Pintail, 1979, 1/2 Gal. 200.00
Bird, Duck, Red Head, 1974 .... 70.00
Bird, Duck, Widgeon, 1979 ....58.00 to 60.00
Bird, Duck, Wood Duck, Banded, 1982 .... 95.00
Bird, Duck, Wood, 1974 .... 170.00
Bird, Eagle, Bald, On Water, 1981 .... 140.00
Bird, Eagle, Birth Of Freedom, 1976 .... 105.00
Bird, Eagle, Birth Of Freedom, 1976, Miniature 70.00
Bird, Eagle, Birth Of Freedom, 1977, Gal. ....1600.00 to 1800.00
Bird, Eagle, Easter Seals, 1980 .... 82.00
Bird, Eagle, Easter Seals, 1980, Miniature 35.00
Bird, Eagle, Harpy, 1973 .... 125.00
Bird, Eagle, Majestic, 1971 .... 225.00

Bird, Eagle, Majestic, 1971, Miniature 75.00
Bird, Eagle, Majestic, 1973, Gal. 1650.00
Bird, Eagle, Mountain, 1973 . . . . 165.00
Bird, Eagle, On Drum, 1976 . . . . 130.00
Bird, Falcon, Gyrfalcon, 1983 . . . .   80.00
Bird, Falcon, Gyrfalcon, 1983, Miniature 39.00
Bird, Falcon, Peregrine, 1979 . . . .   95.00
Bird, Falcon, Peregrine, 1979, Gal. 300.00
Bird, Falcon, Peregrine, 1979, Miniature 35.00
Bird, Falcon, Prairie, 1981 . . . . 100.00
Bird, Falcon, Prairie, 1981, Miniature 65.00
Bird, Falcon, White, 1977 . . . .   80.00
Bird, Falcon, White, 1977, Miniature 55.00
Bird, Flycatcher, 1979 . . . . 120.00
Bird, Flycatcher, 1979, Miniature 25.00
Bird, Gamecock, Survivor 90.00
Bird, Gamecock, Survivor, Miniature 40.00
Bird, Gamecocks, Fighting, 1980 . . . . 150.00
Bird, Gamecocks, Fighting, 1982, Miniature 60.00
Bird, Goose, Canada, 1973 . . . . 100.00
Bird, Goose, Canada, Banded, 1986 . . . . 125.00
Bird, Goose, Canada, Banded, 1986, Miniature . . . . .49.00 to 50.00
Bird, Goose, Canada, Family, 1980 . . . .   65.00
Bird, Goose, Canada, Family, 1980, Miniature 40.00
Bird, Goose, Canada, Single, 1973 . . . . 135.00
Bird, Goose, Canada, Single, 1973, Miniature 99.00
Bird, Goose, Snow, 1988 . . . .   76.00
Bird, Goose, Snow, 1988, Miniature 33.00
Bird, Grouse, Ruffed, 1981 . . . . .55.00 to 65.00
Bird, Grouse, Ruffed, 1981, Miniature . . . . .33.00 to 35.00
Bird, Grouse, Sage, 1974 . . . .   75.00
Bird, Hawk, Red-Tailed, 1977 . . . . .68.00 to 70.00
Bird, Hawk, Red-Tailed, 1977, Miniature 60.00
Bird, Kestrel, Plaque, 1986 . . . .   75.00
Bird, Mallard, Banded, 1980 . . . .   75.00
Bird, Mallard, Banded, 1980, Miniature 43.00
Bird, Mallard, Drake, 1973 . . . .   85.00
Bird, Mallard, Drake, 1973, Miniature 50.00
Bird, Mallard, Family, 1977 . . . .   85.00
Bird, Mallard, Family, 1977, Miniature 59.00
Bird, Meadowlark, 1980 . . . .   55.00
Bird, Oriole, Baltimore, 1977 . . . . .55.00 to 60.00
Bird, Oriole, Baltimore, 1977, Miniature 40.00
Bird, Owl, Barn, 1979 . . . . .80.00 to 85.00
Bird, Owl, Barred, 1981 . . . . 130.00
Bird, Owl, Great Gray, 1985 . . . .   65.00
Bird, Owl, Great Horned, 1974 . . . .   85.00
Bird, Owl, Great Horned, 1974, Gal. 1400.00
Bird, Owl, Saw Whet, 1977, Miniature 60.00
Bird, Owl, Screech, Family, 1977 . . . . .105.00 to 145.00
Bird, Owl, Screech, Family, 1977, Miniature 110.00
Bird, Owl, Screech, Family, 1979, Gal. 340.00
Bird, Owl, Spectacled, 1975 . . . . 110.00
Bird, Owl, Spectacled, 1976, Miniature 105.00
Bird, Owls, Barred, 1981, Club Decanter 130.00
Bird, Owls, Barred, 1981, Miniature, Club Decanter 49.00
Bird, Owls, Burrowing 60.00
Bird, Owls, Burrowing, Miniature 30.00
Bird, Partridge, Chukar, 1979 . . . .   45.00
Bird, Partridge, Chukar, 1979, Miniature 29.00
Bird, Peacock, 1973 . . . . 105.00
Bird, Pelican, Brown, 1976 . . . .   55.00
Bird, Pelican, Brown, 1976, Miniature 35.00

Ski Country, Bird,
Swan, Black, 1974

Ski Country, Christmas,
Bob Cratchit & Tiny
Tim, 1977

Ski Country, Lady,
Blue Dress, 1973

Bird, Penguin, Family, 1978	60.00
Bird, Penguin, Family, 1978, Miniature	40.00
Bird, Pheasant, Golden	54.00
Bird, Pheasant, In Corn, 1982	70.00
Bird, Pheasant, In Corn, 1982, Miniature	22.00
Bird, Pheasants, Fighting, 1977	115.00
Bird, Pheasants, Fighting, 1977, Miniature	65.00
Bird, Pheasants, Fighting, 1979, 1/2 Gal.	180.00
Bird, Pigeons, Passenger, 1983	135.00
Bird, Pigeons, Passenger, 1983, Miniature	69.00
Bird, Prairie Chicken, 1976	63.00 to 65.00
Bird, Robin, 1975, Miniature	80.00
Bird, Seagull, Plaque, 1985	50.00
Bird, Swallows, Barn, 1977	46.00
Bird, Swan, Black, 1974	*Illus* 50.00
Bird, Turkey, 1976	80.00 to 100.00
Bird, Whooping Crane, 1983	50.00
Bird, Woodpecker, Gila, 1972	70.00
Bird, Woodpecker, Ivory Billed, 1976	50.00
Bluebirds, 1984, Club Decanter	75.00
Bluebirds, 1984, Miniature, Club Decanter	40.00
Bonnie, Customer Specialty, 1974	35.00
C.S.M. Burro, Customer Specialty, 1973, Miniature	70.00
Caveman, Customer Specialty, 1974	20.00
Christmas, Bob Cratchit & Tiny Tim, 1977	*Illus* 54.00
Christmas, Cardinal, 1990	67.00
Christmas, Cardinals, Special Edition, 750 Milliliter	95.00
Christmas, Cedar Waxwing, 1985	55.00
Christmas, Chichadees, 1981	70.00
Christmas, Chichadees, 1981, Miniature	45.00
Christmas, Mrs. Cratchit, 1978	61.00
Christmas, Mrs. Cratchit, 1978, Miniature	35.00
Christmas, Scrooge, 1979	55.00
Christmas, Scrooge, 1979, Miniature	24.00
Christmas, Woodland Trio, 1980	70.00
Circus, Clown, 1974	55.00
Circus, Elephant, 1974	37.00 to 44.00
Circus, Horse, Lippizaner, 1976	60.00
Circus, Horse, Palomino, 1976	52.00
Circus, Jenny Lind, Blue, 1976	70.00
Circus, Jenny Lind, Yellow, 1976	130.00
Circus, Jenny Lind, Yellow, 1976, Miniature	70.00
Circus, Lion, 1975, Miniature	33.00
Circus, Lion, 1976	49.00
Circus, P.T. Barnum, 1976	50.00

Circus, Ringmaster, 1974	35.00
Circus, Ringmaster, 1974, Miniature	29.00
Circus, Tiger, 1975	45.00
Circus, Tiger, 1975, Miniature	37.00
Circus, Tom Thumb, 1974	32.00
Clyde, Customer Specialty, 1974	37.00
Cowboy Joe, Customer Speciality, 1980	75.00
Fire Engine, 1923 Ahrens-Fox, 1981	185.00
Fish, Salmon, 1977	42.00
Fish, Trout, Brown, 1976, Miniature	40.00
Fish, Trout, Rainbow, 1976	65.00
Indian, Ceremonial Dancer, Olla Maiden	75.00
Indian, Ceremonial Dancer, Basket	80.00
Indian, Ceremonial Dancer, Basket, Miniature	39.00
Indian, Ceremonial Dancer, Butterfly	88.00 to 90.00
Indian, Ceremonial Dancer, Butterfly, 1975, Miniature	18.00 to 40.00
Indian, Ceremonial Dancer, Eagle, 1979, Miniature	50.00
Indian, Ceremonial Dancer, Falcon, 1983	145.00
Indian, Ceremonial Dancer, Falcon, 1983, Miniature	75.00
Indian, Ceremonial Dancer, No. 1, Eagle, 1979	150.00
Indian, Ceremonial Dancer, No. 2, Buffalo, 1980	165.00
Indian, Ceremonial Dancer, No. 3, Deer, 1980	125.00
Indian, Ceremonial Dancer, No. 4, Wolf, 1981	85.00
Indian, Ceremonial Dancer, No. 5, Antelope, 1982	80.00
Indian, Ceremonial Dancer, No. 6, Falcon, 1983	135.00
Indian, Ceremonial Dancer, Olla Maiden, Miniature	41.00
Indian, Ceremonial Dancer, Rainbow, 1984	80.00
Indian, Cigar Store, 1974	40.00 to 45.00
Indian, End Of Trail, 1976	240.00
Indian, Great Spirit, 1976	105.00
Indian, Lookout, 1977	55.00
Indian, North American Tribes, 1977, 6 Piece	225.00
Indian, North American Tribes, 1977, 6 Piece, Miniature	120.00
Indian, South West Dancers, 1975	350.00
Indian, Warrior, Hatchet, Chief, No. 1, 1975	140.00
Indian, Warrior, Lance, Chief, No. 2, 1975	140.00
Lady, Blue Dress, 1973 *Illus*	27.00
Phoenix Bird, Customer Specialty, 1981	60.00
Political, Donkey, Customer Specialty, 1976	45.00
Political, Elephant, Customer Specialty, 1981	42.00
Rodeo, Barrel Racer, 1982	80.00
Rodeo, Bull Rider, 1980	75.00
Rodeo, Bull Rider, 1980, Miniature	45.00
Rodeo, Snake River Stampede, 1980	85.00
Rodeo, Wyoming Bronco, 1978	75.00
Rodeo, Wyoming Bronco, 1979, Miniature	44.00
Skier, Blue, Customer Specialty, 1972	40.00
Skier, Gold, Customer Specialty, 1972	70.00 to 90.00
Skier, Olympic, Customer Speciality, 1980	62.00
Skier, Olympic, Customer Speciality, 1980, Miniature	30.00
Skier, Red, Customer Specialty, 1972	25.00 to 40.00
Submarine, Customer Specialty, 1976, Miniature	30.00
U.S. Ski Team, Olympic, 1980	40.00

SNUFF

Snuff has been used in European countries since the fifteenth century, when the first tobacco was brought back from America by Christopher Columbus. The powdered tobacco was inhaled through long tubes. The French ambassador to Portugal, Jean Nicot, unknowingly made his name a household word when he sent some of the powdered tobacco to his queen, Catherine de Medici. The stuff became known as *nicotine.* Tobacco was at first considered a remedy and was used in many types of medicines. In the sixteenth and seventeenth centuries, royalty enjoyed snuff and kept it in elaborate gold and silver snuffboxes. Snuff was enjoyed by both royalty and laboring classes by the eighteenth century. The nineteenth-century gentleman no longer used snuff by the 1850s, although poor Southern women used snuff by dipping, not sniffing, and putting it in the mouth, not the nose. Snuff bottles have been made since the eighteenth century. Glass, metal, ceramic, ivory, and precious stones were all used to make plain or fancy snuff holders. Commercial bottles for snuff are made of dark glass, usually shaped more like a box or a jar than a bottle. Snuff was also packaged in stoneware crocks. Most oriental snuff bottles have a small stick with a spoon end as part of the closure. The International Chinese Snuff Bottle Society, 2601 North Charles Street, Baltimore, MD 21218, has a colorful, informative publication.

Agate, Carp With Carved Fins, Glass Stopper, 3 In.	375.00
Agate, Flowers, Chinese	460.00
Agate, Horses & Monkeys, 1 1/2 x 6 1/2 In.	260.00
Agate, Moss, Cafe Au Lait & Chocolate Inclusions, Shield Shape	258.00
Agate, Moss, Fu Dog Mask, Mother-Of-Pearl Inlay, Flattened Rectangular Shape	201.00
Agate, Red, Brown Glaze, Tiger's-Eye Stopper, 1900, 1 1/2 In.	80.00
Agate, Rotund Bearded Man, Red Stopper, Oriental, 2 3/4 In.	230.00
Agate, Shield Shape, Carved Foo Lion Mask, Ring Handles, Chinese	185.00
Agate, Silver Stopper, Boy On Ox	750.00
Amber, Birds In Tree, Dragon Head, Faux Handles, Brass Stopper, 3 In.	250.00
Baltic Amber, Coral Stopper, 18th Century, 2 1/2 In.	1150.00
Bamboo, Carved Jadeite Stopper, 2 In.	196.00
Carnelian, Heart Shape, Silver-Mounted Jade Stopper	1035.00
Carnelian, Insect & Flowering Branch, 19th Century, Chinese	805.00
Chalcedony Agate, Flowers & Vine Design, No Stopper, 2 5/8 In.	105.00
Cinnabar, Carved, Horse Design, 3 In.	150.00
Coral, White, Raised Leaf & Vine, Melon Shape, Green Serpentine Top, 2 1/4 In.	300.00
Enamel, Woman Musician, Mother & Child, 6 Floral Reserves, 2 1/2 In.	259.00
Glass, 2 Elephants, Carved, White, Brown Overlay, Metal Stopper	340.00
Glass, A. Delpit No 16 St. Louis St., New Orleans, Gold Yellow, 184-1860, 4 1/4 In.	2016.00
Glass, A. Delpit No 16 St. Louis St., New Orleans, Gold Yellow, IP, 1860, 4 3/4 In.	1570.00
Glass, A. Delpit No 16 St. Louis St., New Orleans, Yellow Olive Amber, IP, 4 3/4 In.	1345.00
Glass, Agate, 2 Male Figures In Relief, Chinese	400.00
Glass, Bird Perched On Rookery, Flowering Prunus Tree, White, Blue Overlay	115.00
Glass, Black, Gray Striations, Simulated Coral Stopper, 20th Century, 2 In.	50.00
Glass, Black, Iron Red Warrior Decoration, Chinese, 4 In.	160.00
Glass, Boys On Raft, Amber, Purple Overlay, Tortoise & Metal Stopper, 1 In.	250.00
Glass, Brilliant Yellow Green, Tooled Mouth, New England, 1840, 4 5/8 x 2 3/8 In.	880.00
Glass, Cameo, Black Hair, Lotus On 1 Face, Rose Quartz Stopper, 2 1/4 In.	805.00
Glass, Carved Dragon, Wave, Ivory Stopper, Early 19th Century, 2 1/4 In.	978.00
Glass, Carved Fish, Sea Green Design, Rose Quartz Stopper, 19th Century, 2 In.	115.00
Glass, Children Planting Blossom Tree, Carved Foot, 20th Century, 3 1/4 In.	230.00
Glass, Dark Green, Pontil, Flared Lip	66.00
Glass, Dark Green, Rough Lip	44.00
Glass, Doct. Marshall's, Aqua, 3 1/4 In.	30.00
Glass, Ducks & Flowering Lotus Plants, Green Overlay, Turquoise Stopper, Chinese, 3 In.	173.00
Glass, E. Roome, Troy, N.Y., Medium Olive Yellow Green, Pontil, 1820-1830, 4 In. . .*Illus*	1550.00
Glass, E. Roome, Troy, N.Y., Olive Amber, Square, Sheared Lip, Pontil, 4 3/8 In.	308.00
Glass, E. Roome, Troy, N.Y., Smoky Olive Green, Tooled Mouth, Pontil, 4 3/8 In.	330.00

Snuff, Glass,
E. Roome,
Troy, N.Y.,
Medium Olive
Yellow Green,
Pontil,
1820-1830,
4 In.

Glass, E. Roome, Troy, N.Y., Yellow Amber, Tooled Lip, 4 3/8 In. 392.00
Glass, Landscape Design, Green Stone Stopper, Early 20th Century, 2 5/8 In. 230.00
Glass, Lavender, Green, 2 Glass Cicada, Stopper, 20th Century, 2 In. 980.00
Glass, Medium Emerald Green, Square, Tooled Mouth, Pontil, 4 1/8 In. 504.00
Glass, Military Scene, Red Overlay, Green Jade & Brass Stopper, 1 1/2 In. 240.00
Glass, Olive Amber, Beveled Corner Panels, Tooled Flared Lip, 6 1/8 In. 259.00
Glass, Olive Amber, Tooled Mouth, 1815-1834, 4 1/4 In. 198.00
Glass, Olive Green, Square, Tooled Lip, 4 5/8 In. 198.00
Glass, Olive Yellow Green, Rectangular, Tooled Lip, Pontil, 1790-1810, 4 1/2 In. 209.00
Glass, Olive Yellow, Square, Pontil, 6 1/8 In. 728.00
Glass, Pale Olive Green, Champhered Corner, Pontil, 1770-1800, 5 1/2 In. 440.00
Glass, Reverse Painted, Green Glass Top, Cork, Square, 3 In. 23.00
Glass, Ruby Cut To White, Scrolling Archaic Dragon, Tourmaline Glass Stopper 630.00
Glass, Yellow Green, Square, FB, Tooled Flared Lip, Pontil, 5 1/2 In. 308.00
Hornbill, 1 Side Figures, Birds, Calligraphy On Other, Chinese 1610.00
Hornbill, Boys Among Lotus Flowers, Leafy Tree, Birds, Chinese 230.00
Hornbill, Cicada Design, Chinese 2300.00
Hornbill, Figural Design, Shaped Cartouches, Flattened Oval, Chinese 635.00
Ivory, Bearded Man Holding A Fan, Stopper, 1900, 3 1/2 In. 90.00
Ivory, Cafe Au Lait Tone, Melon Shape, Chinese 160.00
Ivory, Carp In The Water, 19th Century, 2 In. 489.00
Ivory, Cicada Design, Chinese 460.00
Ivory, En Grisaille, Figures, Mountain Landscape, Calligraphy, Japan 175.00
Ivory, Exotic Fruit Design, Chinese 460.00
Ivory, Figural Medallions, Bat & Cloud Design, Chinese 161.00
Ivory, Figural, Floral, Bird, Brocade Design, Lozenge Shape 258.00
Ivory, Grisaille Riverscape, Calligraphy, Shield Shape, Chinese 173.00
Ivory, Leaping Carp, Frog, Lotus, Patina & Ivory Stopper, Stand, c.1800, 3 1/4 In. 850.00
Ivory, Man & Woman Figures Seated On Elephants, Late 19th Century, Pair 373.00
Jade, Buddha's Hand, Green 200.00
Jade, Double Fish, Brass & Red Porcelain Stopper, 4 1/4 x 2 In. 300.00
Jade, Ivory, Lapis Lazuli, Flattened Vase Shape, Seed Pearl Stopper, 3 In. 400.00
Jade, Scroll Designs, Vase Shape, Seed Pearl Lid, 3 1/2 In. 402.00
Jade, White Crane Standing On Rock Under A Pine Tree, Children At Play 1090.00
Jade, White To Light Gray Tones, Russet, Pebble Form, Chinese 230.00
Jade, White, 4 Mask Ring Handles, Rose Quartz Stopper, 2 1/4 In. 290.00
Jade, White, Mountain Landscape Scene, Black, Coral Stopper, 2 1/8 In. 1840.00
Jade, White, Yellow Inclusion, Green Stone Stopper, 19th Century, 2 1/4 In. 345.00
Malachite, Carved Musician, Flowers, Stopper, Chinese, c.1950, 3 In. 316.00
Milk Glass, 5 Color Overlay, Fish & Flowers, Mock Mask Ring Handles, China, 2 1/4 In. . 173.00
Mother-Of-Pearl, European Subjects, Chinese 115.00
Nephrite, Lotus Pond, Green Glass Cabochon, Brass Stopper, 1 x 3/4 x 2 1/4 In. 260.00
Onyx, Black, Flowers, Calligraphy, Pear Shape, Chinese 172.00
Porcelain, Actor With A Boat Paddle, No Stopper, 19th Century, 3 In. 29.00
Porcelain, Allover Magpies Perched On A Flowering Prunus Tree, 1850 .... 488.00
Porcelain, Bats, Tortoises, Carp Scene, Chinese, 19th Century 460.00
Porcelain, Butterfly, Flowers, Ceramic Stopper, 19th Century, 2 1/4 In. 69.00
Porcelain, Celadon, Apple Green, Cabbage Design 160.00
Porcelain, Celadon, Figural, Fruit & Butterfly Design, Angular, Chinese 230.00
Porcelain, Celadon, Jade, Iris On 1 Side, No Stopper, 2 3/4 In. 115.00
Porcelain, Children At Play, Blue, White 288.00
Porcelain, Children, Blue Border, Red Glass Stopper, Marked, 1800s, 2 x 3/4 In. 475.00
Porcelain, Erotic Graphics, Yellow, Faux Gilt, Stopper, 1800s, 1 3/4 x 2 3/4 In. 575.00
Porcelain, Famille Rose, Boat With Figures, Chinese 290.00
Porcelain, Famille Rose, Johan Design, 19th Century, Chinese 402.00
Porcelain, Famille Rose, Mountainous Riverscape Scene 115.00
Porcelain, Ivory, Bird, Flowers, Stopper, Early 20th Century, 2 1/2 In. 127.00
Porcelain, Raised Basketry Design, Handles, 2 In. 127.00
Porcelain, Rounded Shoulder, Concave Foot, Coral Stopper, 19th Century, 3 In. 200.00
Porcelain, Sage Asleep Under Pine Tree, Red, Blue Underglaze, Stopper, 3 In. 80.00
Rock Crystal, Animal & Nut, Flattened Oval, Chinese 170.00
Rose Quartz, Birds & Flowering Branches, Rose Quartz Stopper 145.00
Silver, Dragons On 2 Sides, 3 x 2 In. 130.00

Silver, Repousse Foo Lion Design, Stopper, Late 19th Century, 2 1/4 In. 290.00
Smoky Quartz, Square Shoulder, Carnelian Agate Stopper, 19th Century, 2 In. 259.00
Stone, Celadon, Carved, Leaves, Fruit, Asymmetrical, Blue Stopper, 3 In. 403.00
Tortoiseshell, Faceted, Calligraphy, Green Hardstone Knob Finial, 2 1/2 In. 518.00
Wood, Carved Burl, Foo Dog Shoulders, No Stopper, 2 1/8 In. 50.00

SODA

All forms of carbonated drink—naturally carbonated mineral water, artificially carbonated and flavored pops, and seltzer—are forms of soda. The words are often interchanged. Soda bottles held some form of soda pop or carbonated drink. The early soda bottle had a characteristic thick blob top and heavy glass sides to avoid breakage from the pressure of the carbonation. Tops were cleverly secured; the Hutchinson stopper and Coddball stopper were used on many early bottles. The crown cap was not developed and used until 1891. The cork liner inside the crown cap was outlawed in 1969. Some bottles have embossed lettering made with a slug plate, an extra piece inserted into the mold. The first soda was artificially carbonated in the 1830s by John Matthews. He used marble chips and acid for carbonation. It is said he took all the scrap marble from St. Patrick's Cathedral in New York City to use at his plant, which made, so they say, 25 million gallons of soda water. In 1839 a Philadelphia perfume dealer, Eugene Roussel, had the clever idea of adding flavor to the soda. Soon colors were added and the soft drink industry had begun. The late 1800s saw the beginning of Coca-Cola (1886), Pepsi-Cola (1898), Moxie (1876), Dr Pepper (1885), and others. The English brand Schweppes was already established, but they added artificially carbonated sodas as well. Collectors search for the heavy blob top bottles and the newer crown top sodas with embossed lettering or silk-screened labels. Collectors refer to *painted label bottles* as *ACL* or *Applied Color Label*. Recent commemorative bottles are also in demand. In this book, the soda bottle listing includes modern carbonated beverage bottles as well as the older blob tops, Hutchinsons, and other collectible soda bottles. Coca-Cola, Pepsi-Cola, mineral water, sarsaparilla, and seltzer bottles are listed in their own sections. Collector clubs with newsletters include Painted Soda Bottle Collectors Association, 9418 Hilmer Drive, LaMesa, CA 91942; Dr Pepper Collectors Club, 3100 Monticello, Suite 890, Dallas, TX 75205; and the clubs listed in this book in the Coca-Cola and Pepsi-Cola sections. Related bottles may be found in the Coca-Cola, Mineral Water, Pepsi-Cola, Sarsaparilla, and Seltzer categories.

7-Up, Carbondale, Il., You Like It As It Likes You, Green, ABM, 8 In. 2.00
7-Up, Indianapolis 500, 1978, Green, ACL, 16 Oz. . . . .*Illus*   4.00
7-Up, Kansas City, Mo., Green, ABM, 8 In. 2.00
7-Up, Moberly, Cape Girardeau, Mo., Carbondale, Il., Green, ABM, 8 In. . . . . .1.50 to 2.00
7-Up, Quincy, Il., Girl In Swimsuit, Green, 1951, 8 In. 5.00
7-Up, Salutes The Bicentennial, Green, Red, White, Blue Printing, 1976, 16 Oz. 6.00
7-Up, St. Louis, Girl In Swimsuit, Green, ABM, 1947, 8 In. 5.00
A Craven Hulme Manchester, Codd, 10 Oz. 25.00
A. Blonwoll Beverage, Castleton, N.Y., Green, Painted Label, 7 Oz. 1.50
A. Eichler, Roundout, N.Y., Aqua, BIMAL, Blob Top, 6 1/2 In.   9.00
A. Mette & Bros., Chicago, Aqua, Pre-Hutchinson, Blob Top, 7 In. 10.00
A. Schabel, Meridan, Conn., Aqua 10.00
A.F. Dietz, Altamont, N.Y., Light Aqua, Hutchinson, Qt., 9 In.   45.00
A.O. Bright Webb City, Mo., Aqua, Oval Slug Plate, Hutchinson, 6 In. 40.00
A.W. Cudworth & Co., San Francisco, Cal., Emerald Green, Pontil, Hutchinson 160.00
A.W. Cudworth & Co., San Francisco, Cal., Green, Blob Top, IP 242.00
A.W. Cudworth & Co., San Francisco, Cal., Green, Graphite 160.00
A.W. Cudworth & Co., San Francisco, Cal., Green, Slug Plate 130.00
Acme Soda Water Co., Pittsburgh, Monogram, Hutchinson 12.00
Aiken & Walker, Orangeville, Ont., Aqua Blue, Stags Head, BIMAL, Qt., 11 In. 65.00
Alexandria Bottling Works, Alexandria, Ont., SCA, BIMAL, Slug Plate, Crown Top, Qt. .   20.00
America Dry, Green, ACL, 8 Oz. . . . .*Illus*   9.50
American Ginger Ale, J.S. Hazard & Co., Norwich, Conn., Aqua, Torpedo, 1870, 8 In. . . .   65.00
American Soda Works, S.F., Aqua, Hutchinson, Embossed Flag 44.00
American Steam Bottling Works, O.R. Perry, Kingston, Ont., Lime Green, Label, Qt. . . .   160.00
Angel's Brewery & Soda Works, E.F. Hugler, Amber, Tooled Top, Qt. 165.00
Aqua, Original Bail, Stopper, Blob Top, Marked, LSC, 9 1/2 In.   8.00
Aqua, Tooled Blob Top, 9 1/2 x 2 3/4 In. 2.50
Arctic Beverages, Keen Bottling Works, Conroe, Tex., Crown Top, 1948, 9 1/2 In. . . .10.00 to 20.00

Soda, 7-Up,
Indianapolis 500, 1978,
Green, ACL, 16 Oz.

Soda, America Dry,
Green, ACL,
8 Oz.

Soda, Arctic
Beverages, Polar
Bears, ACL, 10 Oz.

Soda, Bayer's
Beverages, ACL,
7 Oz.

Arctic Beverages, Polar Bears, ACL, 10 Oz. . . . . *Illus*	8.50
Arctic Soda Works, Honolulu, Aqua, 8-Sided, Tooled Lip, Pt.	110.00
Arctic Soda Works, Honolulu, H.T., Aqua, Hutchinson, Tooled Lip	132.00
Arose Tansan Ginger Ale, Cobalt Blue, 1890-1920, 4 1/4 In.	49.00
Arthur Cooper, Montreal, Green Aqua, Round Bottom, Blob Top, 1880, 9 In.	85.00
Atkinson Spring Water Co., Indians Taking Water From Stream, Crown Top, ABM, 8 In. .	10.00
August Hohl, Catasauqua, Pa., Pale Ginger Ale, Mug Base, Hutchinson	40.00
B & Co., Aqua, Hutchinson, Applied Lip	77.00
B.C.M. Co., Memphis, Tenn., Amber, Crown Top, BIMAL	80.00
B.R. Lippincott & Co, Stockton, Blue, 10-Sided Base, Graphite Pontil, 1852-1858	880.00
Babb & Co., San Francisco, Cal., Blue Green, IP, 1852-1854	358.00
Babb & Co., San Francisco, Cal., Dark Green, 1852-1854	150.00
Babb & Co., San Francisco, Cal., Green, Graphite Pontil, 1852-1854	160.00
Babb & Co., San Francisco, Cal., Light Green, Hutchinson, Closure, 1850s	160.00
Baltimore, Green, Blob Top, BIMAL, 9 3/4 In.	2.00
Bardwell's Root Beer, Canteen, Stoneware, Tan & White Glaze, Bail Handle, 10 In.	468.00
Bardwell's Root Beer, Stags On Rear, Wire Handle, 10 In.	546.00
Barr's Soda, Hardwick Bottling Works, Hardwick, Vermont, 8 Oz.	9.00
Barret & Co., Manchester, Aqua, Stopper, Embossed, 1860	40.00
Bathgate & Co., Calcutta, Torpedo, Stoneware, India, 1880, 8 In.	625.00
Bay City Soda Water Co., S.F., Cal., Green, Cylindrical, Stopper Type, 1870s	160.00
Bay City Soda Water Co., S.F., Cobalt Blue, 1871-1880	100.00
Bay City Soda Water Co., S.F., Green, Gravitating Stopper, Applied Lip, 1870s	160.00
Bay City Soda Water Co., S.F., Sapphire Blue, Star	121.00
Bay City Sodaworks Co., Medium Cobalt Blue, 7 1/4 In.	121.00
Bayer's Beverages, ACL, 7 Oz. . . . . *Illus*	7.50
Bel & Co., St. Louis, Mo., Aqua, Hutchinson, Pontil	70.00
Belcher & Co., Dubuque, Excelsior, Cobalt Blue, Blob Top, IP, 7 1/2 In.	1430.00
Belfast Ginger Ale, San Francisco, Cal., Aqua, Hutchinson, Applied Lip, 1880	70.00
Berkie, Coca-Cola Bottling Co., Rutland, Vt., Painted Label, 1950s, 6 Oz.	2.50
Biederbeck Bottling Co. Limited, Philada., Aqua, Monogram On Back	25.00
Big Chief, Chief In Headdress, White Paint	20.00
Big Shot, Jefferson Bottling Co., New Orleans, Picture Of Man With Cigar	42.00
Bolen & Byrne, Light Green, Tooled Lip	90.00
Boley & Co., Sac City Cal., Cobalt Blue, Blob Top, IP, 7 1/4 In.	413.00
Boley & Co., Sac City Cal., Cobalt Blue, Graphite Pontil, 7 1/4 In.	242.00
Boley & Co., Sac City Cal., Union Glass Works, Philada., Blue, IP, 7 1/4 In.	450.00
Boonville Mineral Spring, N.Y., Amber, Tooled Lip, Hutchinson, 7 In.	785.00
Brandon & Kirrmeyer, Leavenworth, Kansas, Aqua, Hutchinson, 6 1/2 In	40.00
Brecheisen Bottling Co., Kenton, O., Aqua, Slug Plate, BIMAL, Hutchinson, 6 3/4 In. . . .	16.00
Bremenkampf & Regli, Eureka, Nev., Blue Aqua, Blob Top	132.00
Bremenkampf & Regli, Eureka, Nev., Light Turquoise, 1878-1885	150.00

Bremenkampf & Regli, Eureka, Nev., Lime Green, Blob Top 231.00
Brennan & Graham, Steubenville, Aqua, Applied Lip, IP, 7 1/4 In. 198.00
Bridgeton, N.J., Emerald, IP 120.00
Burl W.H., San Francisco, Emerald Green, Blob Top, IP, 1852 .... 150.00
C & K Eagle Works, Sac City, Cobalt Blue, Western, 1858-1866 .... 176.00
C. Abel, St. Louis, Mo., Light Blue Green, IP, 1857-1859 .... 165.00
C. Abel & Co., St. Louis. Mo, Aqua, 10-Sided, Applied Lip, Graphite Pontil 70.00
C. Burkhardt, Philada, Peacock Blue, Squat 200.00
C. Cleminshaw, Soda & Mineral Water, Troy, N.Y., Light Sapphire Blue, IP, 7 In. 88.00
C. Cleminshaw, Troy, N.Y., Cobalt Blue, Cylindrical, 1860-1870, 1/2 Pt. 154.00
C. Damhorst, St. Louis, Aqua, BIMAL, Crown Top, 1899, 7 1/2 In. 6.00
C.A. Dorman, Hamilton, SCA, Cylindrical, Blob Top, Canada, 1870, 8 In. 55.00
C.A. Hargan, Memphis, Tenn., Aqua, Blob Top, 7 1/4 In. 25.00
C.A. Reiners & Co., S.F., Moon & Stars On Reverse, Aqua, 1882 .... 40.00
C.A. Reiners & Co., San Francisco, Light Turquoise, 1875 .... 143.00
C.W. Fries, St. Louis, Mo., Aqua, Hutchinson, 6 1/2 In. 6.00
Cal Lemonade & Seltzer Water Co., S.F., Cal., Hutchinson, Aqua, Stopper, 1900 .... 550.00
California Natural Seltzer Water, Bear, Aqua 99.00
California Soda Works, Eagle, Aqua, Olive Streaks, Hutchinson 77.00
California Soda Works, Eagle, Blue Aqua, Hutchinson, 12 Oz. 33.00
California Soda Works, Eagle, Light Blue, Hutchinson, 7 In. 55.00
California Soda Works, H. Ficken, S.F., Embossed Eagle, Turquoise, 1878-1879 .... 121.00
Campbell & Co., Philada., Aqua, Squat 25.00
Canada Dry, Quinine Water, Painted Label, 12 Oz. 1.50
Cape Argo, Soda Works, Marshfield, Ore., Blue, Hutchinson 44.00
Carter & Wilson, Boston, Emerald Green 550.00
Casey & Cronan, Eagle Soda Works, Green, Gravitating Stopper, Hutchinson 264.00
Casey Eagle Soda Works, Sac City, Cobalt Blue, Cylindrical, 1870 .... 90.00
Cassin's English Aerated Waters, Green, Applied Lip, Round Bottom 600.00
Caswell Hazard & Co., N.Y., Ginger Ale, Light Blue Green, Blob 35.00
Challand & Jenks, Hamilton, Ont., Monogram, Aqua, Blob Top, 8 In. 35.00
Champlin Bottling Works, Laconia, N.H., This Bottle Not To Be Sold, 8 Oz. 2.00
Chas Wilson, Toronto, Squirrel, c.1890, 11 In. 95.00
Chauvin & Ferland, Toronto, Aqua, Round Bottom, Blob Top, 1875, 8 In. 30.00
Chero Cola, Hattiesburg, Miss., Aqua, Straight Side 25.00
Cherry Smash, 5 Cents, Reverse Glass Label, 12 In. 176.00
Cherry Smash, Backbar, Label Under Glass, Original Cap, c.1915-1920 .... 154.00
Cherry Smash, Syrup, Reverse Label, 12 In. 1045.00
Choctaw Bottling Works, Mobile, Ala., Aqua, Slug Plate, Crown Top, 8 In. 5.00
Christ Gross, St. Louis, Mo., Aqua, Slug Plate, Blob Top, 7 In. 32.00
City Bottling Works, Chicago Hts., Il., Hutchinson, 6 3/4 In. 14.00
City Consumers Seltzer & Mineral Water Co., Aqua, BIMAL, Hutchinson 25.00
City Soda Works, Eureka, Amber, Qt. 176.00
Classen & Co., San Francisco, Pacific Soda Works, Green, Blob Top ....59.00 to 198.00
Clinton Bottling Works, Augusta, Ga., Gold Amber, Tooled Collar, 7 In. 110.00
Collins & Latham Barton, Aqua, Embossed, Codd, 1877-1881, 10 Oz. 25.00
Columbia Mineral Water Co., St. Louis, Mo., Aqua, ISP, Crown Top, ABM, 7 1/2 In. 6.00
Columbia Soda Works, S.F., Seated Liberty, Aqua, Applied Lip 99.00
Connecticut Ginger Ale, J.S. Hazard & Co., Norwich, Conn., Aqua, 8 1/2 In. 65.00
Consolidated Soda Co, Limited, Honolul, HI CSWW Co., Aqua, Crown Top 44.00
Corvallis Soda Works, Blue, Hutchinson 55.00
Coventry Cathedral, Picture, Codd, England 53.00
Cozadd & Ray, Sharon, Pa., Aqua, Squat 10.00
Cross & Co., Vancouver, Canada, SCA, Blob Top, 1890s, 9 In. 75.00
Crown Bottling & Mfg. Co., Ardmore, Aqua, Hutchinson, Cleaned, 6 1/2 In. 385.00
Crush, Rochester, Minn., 8 In. 2.00
Crystal Soda Water Co., Patented Nov. 12 1872, Taylor's U.S., Cobalt Blue, 7 5/8 In. 61.00
Crystal Soda Water Co., Patented Nov. 12 1872, Ten Pin, Sapphire Blue, Pt. 110.00
Crystal Soda Works, Honolulu, Hi., Trademark J.A.P., Aqua, Hutchinson, Bubbles 88.00
Cub Beverages, Lock Haven, Bear Cub, ACL, Crown 12.00
D. Ferguson, London, Canada, Aqua, Squat, Arrow Neck, 7 1/2 In. 80.00
D. O'Kane, Philada, Blue Green, Double Collar, Squat 45.00
D. Palliser's Sons, Mobile, Ala., Crown Top, 8 In. 6.00

Dawson, Green, Codd, 10 Oz. 112.50
Deamer, Grass Valley, Aqua, Blob Top 77.00
Dean Foster & Co., Aqua, Original Bail, Stopper, Blob Top, 9 1/2 In. 5.00
Denwood Carlisle, Queen Victoria's Head, Codd, England 9.00
Diamond Soda Water Co., Honolulu, Aqua, Hutchinson, Tooled Lip 55.00
Dr Pepper, ABM, Crown Top, 9 1/2 In. 4.00
Dr Pepper, Birmingham, Ala., Light Green, Debossed, Crown Top, 8 In. 7.00
Dr Pepper, Bloomington, Ind., Light Green, Debossed, Crown Top, ABM, 8 In. 5.00
Dr Pepper, Good For Life, Chillicothe, Ohio, Clock On Back 20.00
Dr Pepper, Good For Life, Debossed, Crown Top, 1947, 8 1/2 In. 8.00
Dr Pepper, Light Green, ABM, Crown Top, 1968, 9 3/4 In. 5.00
Dr Pepper, Light Green, Debossed, Crown Top, 1952, 8 In. 7.50
Dr Pepper, Light Green, Debossed, Crown Top, 1954, 6 Oz. 6.50
Dr Pepper, Salem, Ore., Light Green, Crown Top, ABM, 9 3/4 In. 4.00
Dr. Brown's Root Beer, Gray, Cobalt Slip Over Mouth, Pottery, 9 1/4 In. 246.00
Dr. Cronk & Gibbons, Cobalt Blue, Blob Top, 1865-1880, 7 In. 200.00
Dr. Cronk Gibbons & Co., Superior Ale, Buffalo, N.Y., Green, Blob Top, 6 5/8 In. .440.00 to 495.00
Drink Ice Cold, Shows 76 Colonial Children Marching With Drums, 8 In. 6.00
Dugald Brown, Gravenhurst, Aqua, Hutchinson, 1890 .... 85.00
E. Bigelow & Co., Springfield, Mass., Green, Metal Closure, 1860-1870, 7 1/4 In. 66.00
E. Ottenville, Nashville, Tenn., Cobalt Blue, Hutchinson 295.00
E. Wagner, Manchester, N.H., Olive Yellow, Blob Top, Lightning Stopper 70.00
E.L. Billing's, Sacramento, Cal., Dark Aqua, Gravitating Stopper, Burst Bubble, 7 1/2 In. .. 15.00
E.L. Billing's Sac City, Geyser Soda, Aqua, 1872-1879 ....70.00 to 99.00
E.M. Gatchell & Co., Charleston, S.C., Green, IP, 1845-1860, 7 7/8 In. 550.00
E.S. & H. Hart, Superior, Union Glass Works, Teal Blue, 8 In. 201.00
E.S. Bilton, London, Canada, C.W., Aqua, Squat, Blob Top, 1863, 7 1/2 In. 150.00
E.W. & Co. Works, Blue Aqua, Flying Eagle, Squat, 1860-1865 .... 180.00
Eagle, Dark Green, IP 160.00
Eagle, Green Teal, Embossed Eagle, Slug Plate, White Graphite Pontil 231.00
Eagle, Green, Applied Lip, IP 120.00
Eagle & Flags, On Banner, Cobalt Blue, Blob Top, IP, 7 3/8 In. 532.00
Eagle In Slug Plate, Emerald Green, Blob Top, IP, 6 7/8 In. 364.00
Eagle Soda Water & Bottling Co., Santa Cruz, Cal., Light Green, Embossed Eagle 77.00
Eamer & Cameron, Cornwall, Ont., Bird Holding Rod, Flint, BIMAL, Crown Top, Qt. ... 35.00
Eastern Cider Co., Amber, Blob Top 132.00
Eckersleys Bolton, Blue, Codd, 6 Oz. 75.00
Eckersleys Bolton, Blue, Codd, 10 Oz. 60.00
Eclipse Carbonations Co., St. Louis, Amber, Horseshoe Plate Mold, Hutchinson, 6 In. ... 195.00
Eclipse Patent, Bulb Neck, Codd 52.50
Eel River Valley Soda Works, Springville, Cal., Aqua ....*Illus* 253.00
Elmer's Medicated Soda, Sapphire Blue, 8-Sided, Applied Lip, IP, 1850, 7 In. ......*Illus* 7560.00
Empire Soda Works, D & M, San Francisco, Medium To Deep Cobalt Blue 242.00
Empire Soda Works, San Francisco, Blue, Bubbles, 1861-1871 .... 110.00
Empire Soda Works, San Francisco, Frank S. Waldo, Aqua, 1880-1882 .... 90.00
Empire Soda Works, Vallejo, Turquoise, 1874-1890 .... 130.00
Eureka-California Soda Water Co., S.F., Aqua, Eagle 55.00
Eurkea-California Soda Water Co., S.F., Blue Eagle 44.00
EWA Bottling Works, H.T., Aqua, Tooled Lip, 7 1/2 In. 77.00
Excelsior Bottling Works, Jersey City, Aqua, Panels, Hutchinson 20.00
Excelsior Water, Blue Green, 8-Sided, Blob Top, IP, 7 1/8 In. 168.00
F. Mathews, Brampton, Canada, Bunch Of Grapes, Hutchinson, 1890 .... 60.00
F. Seitz, Easton, Pa., Blue Green, Blob Top, IP, 1845-1855, 7 In. 308.00
F.C. Lang Bottling Co., Chicago, Il., Stopper, BIMAL, Hutchinson, 6 1/2 In. 10.00
Fortier & Co., Quebec, Aqua Green, Hutchinson, Applied Lip, 7 3/4 In. 6.00
Francis Bros., Doylestown, Pa., Aqua, Block Top, Pony 17.00
Frank Bros. Co., Reno, Nevada, Aqua, Tooled Crown Lip, 7 7/8 In. 73.00
Frank Matejka, Chicago, Il., BIMAL, Hutchinson, 7 In. 15.00
Frederick Meincke, Savannah, Geo., Gold Amber, Cylindrical, Cleaned, 1882, 8 1/4 In. .. 99.00
Fruit Bowl Beverage 5.00
G. Eland's Potass, Cobalt, Torpedo Shape, 1837 .... 264.00
G. Sudhoff, St. Louis, Mo., Aqua, Blob Top, 7 In. 8.00

G.A. Kohl, Lambertville, N.J., Teal Blue Green, Sloping Double Collar, IP, 7 1/2 In. 246.00
G.P. Morrill, Blue Teal, 7 1/2 In. 440.00
G.P. Morrill, Light Green, 1863-1873 .... 1045.00
G.S., Green, Debossed, 1852-1854 .... 523.00
G.W. Hubbard, Middletown, Conn., Aqua, Collar Lip, Slope Shoulders, IP, 1/2 Pt. 179.00
G.W. Weston & Co., Saratoga, N.Y., Olive Green, Double Collar, 1860, Pt. 154.00
Gay Ola, Memphis, Tenn., Orange Amber, Crown Top, Script, BIMAL 80.00
Geo. Burrill, Gold Amber 385.00
Geo. Muehlenbach Brewing Co., Kansas City, Mo., Aqua, Crown Top 2.00
Geo. N. Hembdt, Monticello, N.Y., Aqua, Tombstone Plate Mold, Hutchinson, 6 1/2 In. .. 18.00
Geo. Schmuck, Cleveland, O., Aqua, Hutchinson ....15.00 to 25.00
Geo. Schmuck's Ginger Ale, Cleveland, O., Gold Amber, 12-Sided, Blob Top, 8 In. 110.00
Gimmie World Bottling Company Ltd., New Orleans, Embossed, Large 40.00
Golden Gate, Dark Teal, Blob Top, Graphite Pontil, Not Cleaned, 1855 .... 275.00
Golden West, S. & E. Soda Works, San Jose, Cal., Aqua, Crown Top, 1893-1920 .... 33.00
Grape-Julep, Backbar, Foil Label, No Cap 412.50
Graven-Hurst, Aqua, Hutchinson, Stopper Inside, 1890 .... 85.00
Grone & Whelan, St. Louis, Aqua, Blob Top, 7 In. 8.00
Groves & Whitnall, Globe Works, Amber, Codd, England 17.00
Groves & Whitnall, Salford, Amber, Codd, Small ....25.00 to 40.00
Groves & Whitnall, Salford, Amber, Embossed, Codd, 10 Oz. ....35.00 to 40.00
Groves & Whitnall, Salford, Globe With Rays Picture, Peach Yellow, Blob Top, England . 40.00
Groves & Whitnall, Salford, Globe, Olive 50.00
Groves & Whitnall, Salford, Gold Amber, Tooled Crown Cap, Small 25.00
H. & C. Overdick, Cincinnati, Cobalt Blue, 12-Sided, Applied Lip, IP, 8 5/8 In. 2576.00
H. Ackerman, St. Louis, Aqua, Blob Top, BIMAL, 7 In. 17.00
H. Ackerman, St. Louis, Mo., Blob Top, 7 In. 10.00
H. Durholt & Co., Quincy, Ill., Aqua, Blob Top ....5.00 to 12.00
H. Mau & Co., Eureka, Nevada, Aqua, Original Wire Bail, 1882-1886 .... 99.00
H. Mau & Co., Eureka, Nevada, Blue Aqua, Tooled Lip, Wire Bail, 6 3/4 In. 100.00
H. Mau & Co., Eureka, Nevada, Blue, 1880s 77.00
H. Nash & Co., Root Beer, Cincinnati, 12-Sided, Forest Green, Applied Lip, 8 1/2 In. 3190.00
H. Nash & Co., Root Beer, Cincinnati, Cobalt Blue, Paneled Sides, IP, Cylindrical 1000.00
H.C. Briemeyer, St. Louis, Mo., Blob Top, 7 1/4 In. 12.00
Haas Bro's. Natural, Napa Soda, Aqua 88.00
Haas Bros. Natural, Napa Soda, Blue ....132.00 to 154.00
Hagerty's Glass Works, Aqua, Blob Top, 1855-1865, 6 1/4 In. 50.00
Hassinger & Petterson, 15th Street, St. Louis, Aqua, 8-Sided, Hutchinson, Pontil 100.00
Hawaiian Soda Works, Honolulu, Hawaii, Aqua, Crown Top, 8 3/4 In. 77.00
Hawaiian Soda Works, Honolulu, Hawaii, Blob Top, 9 1/2 In. 55.00
Hayward's, S.J. Simons, Soda Works, Aqua, 1890-1920 .... 22.00

| Soda, Eel River Valley Soda Works, Springville, Cal., Aqua | Soda, Elmer's Medicated Soda, Sapphire Blue, 8-Sided, Applied Lip, IP, 1850, 7 In. | Soda, Husky Beverages, Dog, ACL, Embossed Allover Texture, 7 Oz. | Soda, M.B. & Co., 145 West 35th St., N.Y., Green, Blob Top, 7 1/4 In. |

Hennessy & Nolan, Ginger Ale, Albany, N.Y., Applied Lip, Light Aqua, 1876 .... 30.00
Henry Winkle, Sa. City-XX, Green, Blob Top, OP, 1852-1854 .... 1650.00
Highland Ginger Ale, San Mateo, Cal., Aqua, Crown Top 11.00
Highlander Ginger Ale, Redwood City, Cal., Aqua, Crown Top, Cylindrical 30.00
Highlander Ginger Ale, Redwood City, Calif., Blue 30.00
Hindlea & Co., Blackpool, Codd, England 21.00
Hires, Old Homemade Root Beer From Hires Extract, 7 1/2 In. 144.00
Hires, Root Beer Concentrate, Original Seal, 10 In. 29.00
Holloway Bottling Co., Lock Haven, Pa., Hutchinson 25.00
Howell & Smith, Buffalo, Cobalt Blue, IP, Applied Lip, 1845-1855, 7 1/2 In. 253.00
Hubbell, Philada., Blue Green, Donut Top, Squat, 7 3/4 In. 45.00
Hugh McFadden, S. Bethlehem, Pa., Green Aqua, Hutchinson 59.00
Husky Beverages, Dog, ACL, Embossed Allover Texture, 7 Oz. ....*Illus* 10.00
I. Sutton & Co., Covington, Ky., Cobalt Blue, 12-Sided, IP, Applied Lip, 8 In. . .1045.00 to 1760.00
I. Sutton & Co., Covington, Ky., Cobalt Blue, Paneled Sides, IP, Cleaned 500.00
Iola Steam Bottling Works, Iola, Kan., Slug Plate, Crown Top, BIMAL, 8 In. 8.00
Italian Soda Water Manufactory, San Francisco, Dark Green, IP, 1856-1863 .... 160.00
Italian Soda Water Manufactory, San Francisco, Green, IP, 7 1/8 In. 465.00
Italian Soda Water Manufactory, San Francisco, Light Cobalt Blue, Blob Top 303.00
Italian Soda Water Manufactory, San Francisco, Teal Green, Blob Top 385.00
Italian Soda Water Manufactory, Union Glass Work, Philad., 1863 .... 110.00
J. Esposito, 812 & 814, Kokanola, Washington Ave., Yellow, Hutchinson, 7 5/8 In. 1288.00
J. Kennedy, Pittsburg, Blue Green, Blob Top, IP, 1845-1855, 7 1/4 In. 95.00
J. Monier & Co, Cal., Blue, IP, 1856-1858 .... 1400.00
J. Mullins, Buffalo, N.Y., Aqua, BIMAL, Embossed Base, Hutchinson, 6 3/4 In. 20.00
J. Zagelbaum, Bronx, N.Y., Spritzer, Light Blue, 26 Oz. 69.00
J.A. Aitken, Alliston, Canada, Hutchinson, 1885 .... 50.00
J.A. Lomax, 14 & 16, Charles Place, Chicago, A. & D.H. Co., Blue, 7 In. 110.00
J.B. Seegers, St. Louis, Mo., Lindell Glass Co., Aqua, Blob Top, 7 In. ....7.00 to 10.00
J.D. Ludwick, Pottstown, Pa., Tombstone, Crown Top, Bright Green, Slug Plate, 1889 .... 45.00
J.J. McLaughlin, Toronto, Amber, Mortar & Pestle, Squat, Blob Top, 6 1/4 In. 1275.00
J.M. Roseberry & Co., Alexandria, Va, Green, Slope Shoulders, Lip Ring, IP, 1/2 Pt. 2464.00
J.T. Brown, Chemist, Boston, Blue Green, Torpedo, 8 5/8 In. 165.00
J.W. Harris, New Haven, Conn., Cobalt Blue, 8-Sided, Blob Top, IP, 7 1/4 In. 560.00
Jackson's, Napa Soda, Cobalt Blue, Blob Top 299.00
Jackson's, Napa Soda, Natural, Aqua, Blob Top 18.00
Jackson's, Napa, Natural Mineral Water, Aqua, 7 In. 15.00
James Crozier, Orangeville, Ont., Aqua, Stag's Head, BIMAL, Crown Top, Qt., 11 In. ... 70.00
James Crozier, Orangeville, Ont., Stag's Head, Hutchinson, 7 1/2 In. 30.00
James Lingard, S Lingard, Salford, Aqua, Codd, 6 Oz. 25.00
James Lingard & Co., Codd, 10 Oz. 25.00
Jas. Scherrer, Moline, Il., Aqua, Slug Plate, BIMAL, Hutchinson, 6 3/4 In. 18.00
Jesse Yoakum, Clifton, Ariz., Blue, Crown Top 80.00
John Brown Klienburg, Canada, JB, Aqua, Squat, Arrow Neck, Blob Top, 7 In. 80.00
John Clancy, New Haven, Conn., Aqua, Hutchinson 18.00
John Graf, Milwaukee, Wi., Dark Amber, Original Wire Bail, Stopper, BIMAL, Blob Top . 45.00
John J. Smith, Louisville, Ky., Hand Applied Top, Aqua, 6 1/2 In. 15.00
John J. Smith, Louisville, Ky., S.C. Co., Aqua, 6 1/2 In. 8.00
John Ryan, 1866-Excelsior Soda Works, Savannah, Geo., Blue, Blob Top, IP, 1/2 Pt. 83.00
John S. Baker Soda Water, Peacock Blue, 8-Sided, Applied Lip, IP, 7 1/4 In. 420.00
John Yusek, Cleveland, O., Aqua, ISP, Hutchinson, 7 In. 15.00
Jordan & Pawley, Green Top 87.00
Kelliam Bottling Works, Ft. Smith, Ark, Aqua, Slug Plate, Hutchinson, 6 1/2 In. 30.00
Kiefer's City Bottling Works, Indianapolis, Aqua, 20-Sided, Hutchinson, Stopper 70.00
Kimball & Co., Cobalt Blue, IP, 7 In. 200.00
Kimball & Co., Dark Cobalt Blue, Graphite Pontil, Hutchinson, 1850s 190.00
Knicker-Bocker, Soda Water, Cobalt Blue, 8-Sided, Blob Top, IP, 7 1/2 In. 448.00
Koch & Reyber, So. Chicago, Il., Aqua, Hutchinson, 7 In. 15.00
Koenan Mfg. Co., Butte, Montana, Light Green, Slug Plate, ABM, Crown Top, 8 In. 6.00
L & B, Green, Blob Top, Graphite Pontil, 7 3/8 In. 121.00
L & V, Dark Emerald Green, Applied, Pontil, 1852-1857 .... 110.00
L. & H. Rinninsland, Cincinnati, O., Aqua, Blob Top 35.00

Lamont, Honey Amber, Bullet Stopper, Large 35.00
Lamont, Light Amber, Bullet Stopper, Small 35.00
Lancaster Glass Works, Cobalt Blue, IP, 1845-1855, 7 1/2 In. 242.00
Lancaster XXX Glassworks, Light Green, Blob Top, IP, 6 5/8 In. 420.00
Lawrence Baldico, Laconia, N.H., Slug Plate, Crown Top, 8 3/4 In. 5.00
Leigh & Co., Salford, Amber, Blob Top, Large 20.00
Leigh & Co., Salford, Amber, Codd, 6 Oz. 25.00
Leigh & Co., Salford, Amber, Codd, 10 Oz. 25.00
Leigh & Co., Salford, England, Globe On Front, Yellow Amber, Codd, 1890, 7 1/2 In. 75.00
Lihue Ice Co., Aqua, 4-Piece Mold, Hutchinson 495.00
Luke Beard, Blue Green, Sloping Collar Mouth, Tenpin, IP, 7 In. 505.00
M Pomfret Albion Works, Aqua, Codd, 1877, 6 Oz. 25.00
M.B. & Co., 145 West 35th St., N.Y., Green, Blob Top, 7 1/4 In. ....*Illus* 33.00
M.B. & Co., 145 West 35th Street, New York, Philadelphia, XXX Porter & Ale, 1861 .... 110.00
M.M. Battelle, Brooklyn, N.Y., Teal Blue Green, IP, 1855, 7 1/2 In. 198.00
M.R., Sacramento, Cobalt Blue, Blob Top, Graphite, 1851-1863 .... 660.00
M.R., Sacramento, Cobalt Blue, IP, 1851-1863, 7 1/4 In. 1045.00
M.R., Sacramento, Dark Cobalt Blue, IP, Blob Top, 1850-1855, 7 1/2 In. 660.00
M.R., Sacramento, Union Glass Works, Philada., Blue Green, IP, 1863, 7 In. 1760.00
M.R., Sacramento, Union Glass Works, Philada., Cobalt Blue, Blob Top, IP, 7 1/2 In. 2090.00
M.T. Crawford, Hartford, Ct., Teal, Collar Lip, IP, 1/2 Pt. 308.00
Manchester Coffee Tavern Co., Aqua, 1870 .... 25.00
Martinelli's Soda Works, M.S., Aqua, Applied Lip, Hutchinson, 1875-1885 .... 40.00
Maui Soda Works, Aqua, Tooled Lip, Hutchinson 55.00
Mayfield Soda Works, Aqua, Crown Top, Cylindrical 50.00
Mayfield Soda Works, Blue, Crown Top 80.00
McGovern Bros., Albany, N.Y. In Circle, Blue Green, Hutchinson 18.00
McGrudden & Campbell, Philada., Aqua 25.00
Meriam's, Cobalt Blue, IP, Applied Lip, 1852-1856, 7 3/8 In. 4840.00
Missouri Drink, St. Louis, Mo., 10 Large Panels, Crown Top, ABM, 9 1/4 In. 6.00
Mokelumne Hill Soda Works, Amber, Crown Top, Qt. 99.00
Monterey Works, Cal., Green, Hutchinson 100.00
Mooney, Visalla, Aqua, Short Neck, 1872-1881, Hutchinson 70.00
Morrell's, Dark Green, Codd 142.50
Mountain Dew, Hillbilly, Green, ACL, 8 Oz. ....*Illus* 12.00
Moxie Nerve Food, Lowell, Mass., Pre-1900, 10 In. 35.00
Mt. Madison Beverages, Mt. Madison Spring Water Co., Gorham, N.H., Green, 7 Oz. ... 5.00
N.C. Peterson, Laramie, Wyo., Blue, Applied Lip, Hutchinson, 6 In. 110.00
N.C.W. Flanage, Green, ... 110.00
Napa, Blue, 1861-1873 .... 176.00
Napa, Phil Caduc Cobalt Blue, 1873-1881 .... 190.00
Napa, Phil Caduc, Aqua, 1873-1881 .... 240.00

Never display a
bottle with labels
in a sunny window.
The labels will
fade.

Soda, Mountain
Dew, Hillbilly,
Green, ACL, 8 Oz.

Soda, Ontario, Dry
Ginger Ale, Green,
ACL, 7 Oz.

Soda, Owen Casey,
Eagle Soda Works, Sac
City, Blue, Blob Top

Napa, Phil Caduc, Natural Mineral Water, Green Aqua, Blob Top, 1870s 110.00
Napa, Phil Caduc, Natural Mineral Water, Cobalt Blue, Blob Top 110.00
Napa Natural, Cobalt Blue, 1870-1872 .... 350.00
Napa Woods, Cobalt Blue, 1870-1872 .... 209.00
Napa Woods, T.W.F.-A.G.T., Purple Cobalt, Embossed Stars 275.00
National Dope Co., Birmingham, Al., Aqua, Hutchinson 225.00
Nesbitt's, California, Painted Black Label, 28 Oz. 1.50
Nesbitt's, California, Ribs, Black Print, 1938 .... 5.00
New Tacoma Soda Works, Washington, Aqua, Olive Streak, Hutchinson 33.00
Neyman & Drake, Mok Hill, Philada., Union Glass Works, Aqua, IP, 1850s 1600.00
Nezinscot Beverages, Picture Of Indian Maiden, 20 Vertical Panels, 1973, 9 In. 5.00
Norland & Co. Limited, Aqua Green, Torpedo Shape, 2 1/4 x 7 1/2 In. 6.00
Norris, Titusville, Pa., Aqua, Applied Lip 110.00
Northop & Sturgis Company, Portland, Oregon, Aqua, Hutchinson 60.00
Northwestern Bottling Co., Kremmling, Colo, Hutchinson, 6 1/2 In. 175.00
NuGrape, L.G.W., Light Green, ABM, Embossed Base, Crown Top, 8 In. 5.00
O. & E.M. Fremont Factory, Blue, Blob Top 110.00
Oceanview Bottling Works, N. & B. Props, Mendocino, Cal., Aqua 33.00
Ontario, Dry Ginger Ale, Green, ACL, 7 Oz. ....*Illus* 6.50
Orange Crush, Figural, Peeled Orange, Upside Down, Green, 16 1/2 In. 88.00
Orange Crush, Pat'd July 20, 1920, Stained, 6 Oz............................... 6.00
Orange Crush, Picture 2 Sides 10.00
Orange Crush, Rock Island, Illinois, Small Chip 83.00
Owen Casey, Eagle Soda Works, Aqua, 1867-1871 ....55.00 to 90.00
Owen Casey, Eagle Soda Works, Blue, 1867-1871 ....70.00 to 160.00
Owen Casey, Eagle Soda Works, Cobalt Blue, Sloping Collar, 7 In. 145.00
Owen Casey, Eagle Soda Works, Green, 1867-1871 .... 385.00
Owen Casey, Eagle Soda Works, Light Green, 1867-1871 .... 40.00
Owen Casey, Eagle Soda Works, Sac City, Blue, Blob Top ....*Illus* 77.00
Owen Casey, Eagle Soda Works, Sac City, Cobalt Blue, 1871, 7 1/4 In. ....90.00 to 100.00
Owen Casey, Eagle Soda Works, Sac City, Green, Blob Top 132.00
Owen Casey, Eagle Soda Works, Sac City, Steel Blue, Blob Top ....*Illus* 176.00
P. Horan, 75 West 27th St., N.Y., Aqua....................................... 77.00
P. Seasholtz, Pottstown, Pa., Blue Aqua, Double Collar 45.00
P.A. Green, West Brom, Green, Codd, 10 Oz.................................... 135.00
P.W. Perkins, Tannersville, N.Y., ISP, Hutchinson, 6 1/2 In. 16.00
Pacific & Puget Sound Soda Works, Seattle, Wa., Light Aqua, Tooled Lip 220.00
Pacific & Puget Sound Soda Works, Seattle, Wa., Lime Green, Tooled Lip 150.00
Pacific & Puget Sound Soda Works, Seattle, Wa., Wire Bail, Light Aqua, 1880s 325.00
Pacific Soda Works, Klausen & Co, San Francisco, Aqua, Blob Top, 1868-1870 .... 77.00
Paul Jeenicke, San Jose, P.J., Amber, Applied Lip, Western, Hutchinson, 1890 .... 4180.00
Paul Vanderberg, Roseland, Il., Aqua, Slug Plate, Hutchinson, Embossed 15.00
Pearson Bros., Placerville, Aqua, Wide Mouth, Cylindrical, Hutchinson, 1890-1900 ..... 70.00
Pearson's Soda Works, Aqua, Short Neck, Cylindrical, Hutchinson 50.00
Pearson's Soda Works, Blue, Tooled Lip, Hutchinson, Squat..................... 50.00
Pelican Beverages, 2 Pelican Pictures 20.00
Pic-A-Pop, ACL, 10 Oz. ....*Illus* 3.00
Pink Poodle, La Junta, White, Gray & Black, Co. 95.00
Pioneer Brown & Co., Blue Aqua, Blob Top, 1880s 523.00
Pioneer Brown & Co., Blue, 1860 .... 1000.00
Pioneer Soda Water Co., S.F., Aqua, Bear & Crown Top 33.00
Queen City Soda Works, Seattle, Wa., Turquoise 303.00
R. Stothert & Son, Atherton, Embossed Mr. Stothert, Codd, England 14.00
R. Taylor, Strathroy, Blue Aqua, Horse Leaping, BIMAL, Crown Top, Qt. 130.00
R.M. Mills & Co., Bourne, England, Amber, Monogram, Barrel, 5 In. 30.00
Regent Supreme Beverages, Pittsburg, Pa., ACL, 7 Oz. 3.00
Robertson & Brooks From Mount Forest Ont., Rabbit, Crossed Guns, Hutchinson, 1890 65.00
Ross's Belfast, Lime Green To Honey Amber, Round Bottom, Blob Top, 7 In. 40.00
S Lingard & Co, Salford, Codd, 10 Oz. 254.00
S. Charlton Soda Water, Toronto, Aqua, Blob Top, Torpedo, c.1865, 9 1/2 In. 500.00
S. Hoyle Keighley, Blue 67.50
S.J. Estern, Emerald Green, Applied Blob Top, 1855-1865, 7 1/4 In. 99.00
Sacramento Eagle Soda, Blue, Pontil 143.00

| Soda, Owen Casey, Eagle Soda Works, Sac City, Steel Blue, Blob Top | Soda, Pic-A-Pop, ACL, 10 Oz. | Soda, Tops Sparkling Beverages, Bottle Cap Logo, Mansfield, Oh., ACL, 10 Oz. | Soda, Vess, Party Things, ACL, 8 Oz. |

San Francisco Glass Works, Cornflower Blue 330.00
Scarborough, Green, Codd, 6 Oz. 82.50
Schick & Fett, Reading, Pa., Aqua, Squat 35.00
Schweppes Ltd., Stoneware, Chocolate Brown Treacle Glaze, 1915 .... 10.00
Seymour & Co., Buffalo, N.Y., Cobalt Blue, Blob Top, IP, 7 In. 420.00
Sheffield Miners, Lion Holding Bottle, Codd, England 7.00
Smart's, Green, Codd, 10 Oz. 165.00
Smile, Orange Smile, St. Louis, ABM, Crown Top, 1922, 7 3/4 In. 6.00
Smith & Kelly's Soda & Mineral Waters, Green, Applied Lip, IP 230.00
Snowdrop, Lyon & Co., Manchester, Aqua, Fluted Base, Codd, 6 Oz. 20.00
Squeeze, Cushing, Ok., Ribs, Crown Top, 8 1/2 In. 5.00
Squeeze, Oklahoma City, 8 Panels, Crown Top, 1920, 8 In. 10.00
Stegmaier Brewing Co., Wilkes Barre, Pa., Olive Yellow, Crown Top 30.00
Sullivan, 36 Vertical Ribs, Crown Top, ABM, 8 In. 8.00
Sun Crest, Blue Label, 8 1/2 In. 4.00
Sun-Drop, As You Like It! Green, ABM, 9 3/4 In. 1.50
Sun-Drop, Edw. Hebbler & Son, New Haven, Mo., As You Like It! ABM, 1960, 9 1/2 In. . 2.00
Sun-Drop, Golden Cola, Special Dietary Beverage, Amber, ABM, 1964, 9 3/4 In. 3.00
Swan Beverages, London, Blue 67.50
T. Pepper, Ashland, Pa., Aqua, Squat, Blob Top, Metal Closure 80.00
T.W. Gillett, New Haven, Aqua, Applied Collar Lip, IP, 1/2 Pt. 476.00
T.W. Gillett, New Haven, Peacock Blue, 8-Sided, Blob Top, IP, 7 1/2 In. 756.00
Taplin & Co., New Port, I.W., Codd, 9 In. 35.00
Taylor & Co., San Francisco, Eureka, Sapphire Blue, Blob Top, Hutchinson, 1850s .220.00 to 440.00
Taylor & Co., Valparaiso, Chili, Green, Graphite, Blob Top, IP, 1850s ....200.00 to 231.00
Taylor & Co., Valparaiso, Chili, Light Blue, IP, 1850 .... 650.00
Taylor & Co., Valpariso, Chili, Blue, Bubbles, White Graphite Pontil 275.00
Taylor Never Surrenders, Union Glass Works, Philad.A., Cobalt Blue, IP, 7 1/2 In. 1905.00
Texas Soda, Crown Top, Fayetteville, Tex., Rows Of X's Around Bottle 27.00
Thacker & Christmas, Warwick, England, Christmas Pudding, Codd 14.00
Thos. McGovern, Albany, N.Y., Aqua, BIMAL, Hutchinson, 7 In. 10.00
Tolle Bottling Works, Litchfield, Ill., Aqua, ISP, Embossed, Hutchinson 12.00
Tolle Bottling Works, Litchfield, Ill., Light Amethyst, Hutchinson, 7 In. 12.00
Tops Sparkling Beverages, Bottle Cap Logo, Mansfield, Oh., ACL, 10 Oz. ....*Illus* 8.50
Tossell & Son, Niagara Falls, Aqua, Hutchinson, Embossed 35.00
Tune & Robertson, Stratford, Canada, Lime Green, Fox Head & Whips, Hutchinson, 7 In. 80.00
Tune Co., London, Ont., Honey Orange Amber, Red, Yellow & Navy Paper Label 30.00
Tweddle's, Celebrated Soda Or Mineral Water, New York, Green, Applied Lip, OP 1600.00
Tweddle's, Celebrated Soda Or Mineral Waters, Courtland Street 38, Aqua, OP, 7 1/2 In. . 330.00
Tweddle's, Celebrated Soda Or Mineral Waters, New York, Applied Lip, Graphite Pontil .. 240.00
Tweddle's, Celebrated Soda Or Mineral Waters, New York, Blue, IP 110.00
Underwood Carlisle Brewery, Picture, Codd, England 11.00

Union Lava Works, Conshohocken, Patented 1852, Sapphire Blue, IP, 1855, 7 In. 578.00
Union Spring, Saratoga, N.Y., Emerald Green, Double Collar, 1870, Pt. 3190.00
Vallets Patent Liverpool, Aqua, Bullet Stopper, Embossed 20.00
Vess, Party Things, ACL, 8 Oz. ....*Illus* 5.50
Vess Billion Bubble Beverage, St. Louis, ABM, 9 3/4 In. 3.00
W. Eagle, Union Glass Works, Phila., Blue Green, IP, 1855, 7 3/8 In. 209.00
W. Eagle's Superior Soda Or Mineral Waters, W.E., Cobalt Blue, IP, 7 In. 231.00
W. Richardson, Strathroy, Canada, Aqua Green, Hutchinson, c.1890 .... 80.00
W.B. Co. Limited, Buffalo N.Y., Aqua, Panels, Hutchinson 20.00
W.H. Burt, San Francisco, Green, Graphite Pontil, 1852 .... 165.00
W.H. Burt, San Francisco, Green, IP, 7 1/4 In. ....120.00 to 190.00
W.H. Cawley Co., Somerville Dover, Flemington, N.J., Citron, Blob Top 45.00
W.H.H., Chicago, Ill., Cobalt Blue, H On Base, Applied Lip 70.00
W.H.H., Chicago, Ill., Cobalt Blue, Stopper, Hutchinson 70.00
W.H.H., Chicago, Ill., Ice Blue, Short Neck, Mug Base, Tooled Lip, Hutchinson 1210.00
W.H.H., Chicago, Ill., W.M.C. & Co., Ice Blue, Mug Base, Applied Lip 120.00
W.H.H., Pittsburgh, Pa., Cobalt Blue, Blob Top, 1855-1865, 7 1/4 In. 336.00
W.I. Hay, DuBois, Pa., Blob Top 10.00
W.S. Wright, Pacific Glass Works, Blue Aqua, Blob Top 550.00
W.S. Wright, Pacific Glass Works, Blue, 1860 .... 1000.00
W.S. Wright, Pacific Glass Works, Nevada, Aqua, Early 1860s 660.00
Waimea, Soda & Ice Works, Aqua, Tooled Lip 121.00
Walker & Homfray Limited, Salford, Aqua, Embossed, Codd, 6 Oz. 20.00
Walter's Napa County, Blue, Horseshoe, Applied Lip, 1899 .... 50.00
Watertown Bottling Establishment, N.Y., Green Aqua, Blob Top, IP, 7 3/8 In. 146.00
West Side Bottling Works, Massillon, O., Case, Hutchinson 6.50
Wetter & Co., South, St. Louis, Mo., Aqua, Blob Top, 7 1/2 In. 50.00
Whistle, Blue & White, 8 In. 4.00
White Pine Soda Co., Ely, Nevada, Etched 143.00
Wielands Bottling Works, Reno, Nev., Aqua, Tooled Crown Lip, 8 In. 56.00
Williams & Severance, San Francisco, Blue, Graphite Pontil, 1852-1854 .... 303.00
Williams & Severance, San Francisco, Cal., Green, Tapered Top 170.00
Williams & Severance, San Francisco, Graphite Pontil, Drip, 1854 .... 200.00
Williams Bros., San Jose, Cal., Aqua, Etched, Gravitating Stopper, 7 1/2 In. 8.00
Wilson Mf'g Co., Sacramento, Cal., Aqua, Crown Top, 1910, 9 1/2 In. 8.00
Wm. Currie, Leith, England, Crowing Cock, Green Marble, Codd 40.00
Wm. Pipe, Kingston, Light To Medium Lime Green, Blob Top, 7 1/2 In. 390.00
Yosemite Soda Works, Redwood City, Aqua, Crown Top 176.00
SPIRIT, see Flask; Gin; Seal

———————————————————— **STIEGEL TYPE** ————————————————————

Henry William Stiegel, an immigrant to the colonies, started his first factory in Pennsylvania in 1763. He remained in business until 1774. Glassware was made in a style
popular in Europe at that time and was similar to the glass of many other makers. It was
made of clear or colored glass that was decorated with enamel colors, mold blown
designs, or etchings. He produced window glass, bottles, and useful wares. It is almost
impossible to be sure a piece is a genuine Stiegel, so the knowing collector now refers
to this glass as Stiegel type. Almost all of the enamel-decorated bottles of this type that
are found today were made in Europe.

Amethyst, 12 Diamond, Pocket, Sheared Mouth, Pontil 1650.00
Amethyst, 20 Pointed Arches Over Flutes, Pontil, 1780, 6 In. 1320.00
Amethyst, 20th Century, 6 1/4 In. 420.00
Amethyst, 21 Diamond, Fluted, Chestnut, Pontil, 1790-1800, 6 1/2 In. 743.00
Amethyst, Daisy In Diamond, 4 3/4 In. 4730.00
Amethyst, Diamond Daisy, Pocket, Sheared Mouth, Pontil 3575.00
Enameled, 6-Sided, Flowers, Red, Blue, Yellow White, 5 7/8 In. 165.00
Enameled, 8-Sided, White Doves, Yellow, White, Blue, Red, 7 In. 110.00
Enameled, White Dove On Red Rose, Flowers, 5 7/8 In. 165.00
Mustard, Green, Blue & Red, Bride's Cologne, 6 1/2 In. 375.00
Peacock Green, Flask, 15 Diamond, 1972, 5 3/8 In. 440.00
Red, Yellow, White, Blue, Pale Green, 8-Sided, Flowers, 5 5/8 In. 300.00
White Doves, Yellow Circles, Flowers, Yellow, White, Blue, Red, 7 In. 110.00

──────────────────────── STONEWARE ────────────────────────

Stoneware is a type of pottery, not as soft as earthenware and not translucent like porcelain. It is fired at such a high temperature it is impervious to liquid and so makes an
excellent bottle. Although glazes are not needed, they were often added to stoneware to
enhance its appearance. Most stoneware bottles also have the name of a store or brand
name as part of their decoration.

Bottle, Brush Blue Flowers, 1820, 6 1/2 In.	1595.00
Bottle, Clay Mottled, 9 1/2 In.	11.00
Bottle, Cobalt Highlights, Marked, G.F. Hewett, 10 1/4 In.	27.00
Bottle, Dr. Cronk At Shoulder, 10 In.	44.00 to 88.00
Bottle, Marked, H. Fuller, Cinnamon Clay Glaze, 8 1/2 In.	44.00
Bottle, Marked, John Howell, 10 In.	11.00
Canteen, Robert F. Falkner, Gray Tan Glaze, Ocher 1860, 10 3/8 In.	253.00
Flagon, J. Waite, Eyres Hill, Leather Lane, Holborn, England, Salt Glaze, 1/2 Gal.	40.00
Flagon, J.C. Smith, Brandy Merchant, Dog Inn, Norton, Salt Glaze, England	64.00
Flagon, W.M. Dale & Co., York, T.S.R., Castleford Stone Pottery, England, 1830s, 6 Gal.	92.00
Flask, Jug, Tan, Green, England, 8 In.	85.00
Goodyear Tire & Rubber Co., Toronto, Light Gray Cream, 3 1/8 x 8 In.	12.00
Jar, 2-Tone Brown, Gray Salt Glaze, Applied Shoulder Handles, 12 1/2 In.	385.00
Jar, A.P. Donaghho, Parkersburgh, W. Va., Gray, Cobalt Blue Stenciled Letters	132.00
Jar, Blue Clover Leaf Design, Brushed , 1860, 6 1/2 In.	275.00
Jar, Blue Leaf Design, Brushed, 1860, 6 1/2 In.	330.00
Jar, C. Hart & Son, Flowers, 1860, 12 In.	198.00
Jar, Canning, 4 Brushed Cobalt Stripes, Cone Shape, 12 In.	440.00
Jar, Canning, 5 Blue Stripes, 1850, 1/2 Gal., 8 In.	209.00
Jar, Canning, 7 Alternating Cobalt Blue Stripes, 1850, 1/2 Gal., 8 In.	330.00
Jar, Canning, A.P. Cook, Brooklyn, Mich., Cobalt Blue, 9 In.	248.00
Jar, Canning, A.P. Donaghho, Parkersburg, W. Va., 1860, 7 1/2 In.	55.00
Jar, Canning, Blue Horizontal Flowers, Plume Design, 1850, 13 In.	154.00
Jar, Canning, Brushed Plume Design, 1860, 6 1/2 In.	198.00
Jar, Canning, Cobalt Blue Brushed Flowers, 10 1/2 In.	192.50 to 248.00
Jar, Canning, Cortland, Double Dot Flowers, 1860, 10 1/2 In.	176.00
Jar, Canning, G. Apley & Co., Ithaca, N.Y., Double Tulip Design, 1860, 10 1/2 In.	660.00
Jar, Canning, Hamilton & Jones, Greensboro, Pa., Cobalt Blue Design, 8 1/2 In.	132.00
Jar, Canning, Harrington & Burger, Triple Oak Leaf, Blue, 1853, 11 1/2 In.	660.00
Jar, Canning, Haxstun & Co., Fort Edward, N.Y., Lid, Bird On Tree Stump, 13 In.	495.00
Jar, Canning, James Hamilton & Co., Greensboro, Pa., Cobalt Blue Brushed Rim, 8 1/4 In.	110.00
Jar, Canning, James Hamilton, Greensboro, Pa., Cobalt Blue Design, 9 3/4 In.	220.00
Jar, Canning, Jas. Hamilton & Co., Greensboro, Pa., Blue Accent Stripes, 1870, 9 1/2 In.	248.00
Jar, Canning, John Burger, Rochester, Large Blue Poppy, 1865, 10 In.	1017.00
Jar, Canning, Lyons, Brush Flowers, Blue Accents, Handles, 1860, 11 In.	300.00
Jar, Canning, Lyons, Brushed Leaf Design, Blue Accents, Handles, 1860, 9 1/2 In.	209.00
Jar, Canning, Lyons, Double Flowers, Blue Accents, Handles, 1860, 10 In.	198.00
Jar, Canning, N.A. White & Son, Utica, N.Y., Flowers, Cobalt Leaves, 1870, 13 In.	715.00
Jar, Canning, Red Glaze, Black Sponge Accents, 1830, Gal.,10 1/2 In.	187.00
Jar, Canning, S. Bell & Son, Strasburg, Brush Swag Design, 1850, 7 3/4 In.	275.00
Jar, Canning, Satterlee & Morey, Stylized Leaf Design, 1870, 2 Gal., 11 1/2 In.	143.00
Jar, Canning, Stylized Cobalt Wreath, Dot In Center, Applied Ear Handles, 9 In.	193.00
Jar, Canning, W. Hart, Ogdensburg, N.Y., Double Dot Flowers, 1860, 11 In.	275.00
Jar, Canning, White's, Utica, Bird On Branch, 1865, 10 1/2 In.	495.00
Jar, Canning, Wm. A. MacQuoid & Co., N.Y., Triple Flowers, 1870, 12 In.	248.00
Jar, Cobalt Blue Brushed Design, Freehand Flowers, Greensboro, Pa., 15 In.	1980.00
Jar, Cobalt Blue Brushed Flowers, 12 In.	165.00
Jar, Cobalt Blue Brushed Flowers, Applied Shoulder Handles, 17 1/4 In.	1045.00
Jar, Cobalt Blue Brushed Flowers, Double Handles, Swags, 12 3/4 In.	300.00
Jar, Cobalt Blue Crane With Fish, Blue Handles, 11 1/2 In.	4400.00
Jar, Cobalt Blue Design, Marked, E.H. Merrill, Ohio, 10 In.	110.00
Jar, Cobalt Blue Design, Signed, Hamilton & Jones, Greensboro, Pa., 8 In.	165.00
Jar, Cobalt Blue Tulip, Strap Handle, Marked, I.M. Mead, Mogadore, Ohio, 14 In.	247.00
Jar, Cobalt Blue, Applied Shoulder Handles, 13 3/4 In.	523.00
Jar, Cover, McDonald & Benjamin, Cin. O, Light Brown, Was Seal Ring, 10 1/2 In.	413.00
Jar, Cream, Dark Tan, Brantford Stoneware Mfg. Co., Canada, c.1890, Qt.	150.00

Jar, Dark Blue Tulip Design, Marked, T.A. Packer, Tuscarawas Co., Ohio, 13 In. 1100.00
Jar, E. & L.P. Norton, Bennington, Vt., Lid, Ribbed Leaf Design, 2 Gal. 1870.00
Jar, Fine MacCoboy, Dark Glaze, 1880, 9 1/2 In. 66.00
Jar, Francis Dingle Wine Merchant, Worcester, Gal. 30.00
Jar, Goodwin & Webster, Gal. 165.00
Jar, J. & E. Norton, Bennington, Vt., 2 Gal. 358.00
Jar, J. & G. Hart, Sherburne, Slip Blue, Lug Handle, N.Y., 1840, 10 In. 132.00
Jar, Julius Norton, Bennington, Vt., Brush Slip Blue Design, 1848, 3 Gal., 13 In. 165.00
Jar, Lid, Blue Flowers, Double Handles, 9 In. 192.00
Jar, Lid, Blue Slip Elephant Head Design, 1870, 7 1/2 In. 275.00
Jar, N. Clark & Co., Mt. Morris, Brushed Leaf Design, 1835, 11 1/2 In. 357.00
Jar, O.L. & A.K. Ballard, Burlington, Vt., Lid, Blue Long-Tailed Bird, 1860, 11 In. 825.00
Jar, Pottery Works Little West, N.Y., Lid, Blue Accents, 1870, 9 1/2 In. 209.00
Jar, Pottery Works Little West, N.Y., Lid, Triple Flowers, 1870, 11 1/2 In. 440.00
Jar, R. Lawrence, Albany, N.Y., Gal. 182.00
Jar, Tulip Design, Double Handles, Allentown, Pa., 7 In. 248.00
Jar, W.A. MacQuoid & Co., N.Y., Cluster Of Cherries On Front, 1870, 10 1/2 In. 248.00
Jar, W.H. Farrar & Co., Geddes, N.Y., Brushed Blue Tulip Design, 1850, 11 In. 385.00
Jar, West Troy Pottery, N.Y., Lid, Blue Slip Bird, Plume Design, 1880, 11 1/2 In. 633.00
Jar, William & Reppert, Greensboro, Pa., Brush Blue Accent Lines, 1880, 12 In. 220.00
Jug, A. & C.W. Underwood, Fort Edward New York, Gray, Cobalt Blue Flowers, 3 Gal. ... 165.00
Jug, A.J. Buttler Manufacturing, New Brunswick, N.J., Beehive, Flowers, 1865, 10 In. ... 578.00
Jug, A.K. Ballard, Burlington, Vt., Syrup, Cluster Of Grapes, 1870, 12 1/2 In. 605.00
Jug, A.O. Whittemore, Havana, N.Y., Beehive, Drooping Flowers, Blue, 1870 .... 605.00
Jug, Acker Edgar & Co., N.Y., Beehive Shape, American Flag Flying, Gal. 5500.00
Jug, Adolph Moesch, Buffalo, N.Y., Blue Script, 1880, 13 1/2 In. 412.00
Jug, Aug. Baetzhold, Wines & Liquors, Buffalo, N.Y., Black Stencil, 1890, 11 In. 33.00
Jug, Ballard & Bros., Burlington, Vt., 2 Gal. 275.00
Jug, Barnhardt Bros., Buffalo, N.Y., Blue Accents, c.1870, 2 Gal. 248.00
Jug, Batter, Blue Flowers, Bail Handle, Pour Spout, 10 1/4 In. 82.00
Jug, Batter, Cobalt Blue Flowers, Applied Handle, 11 1/2 In. 300.00
Jug, Blue Pecking Chicken, Tan Glaze, Albany, N.Y., 14 1/4 In. 1045.00
Jug, Blue, Gray Ground, 1860-1870, 2 Gal. 250.00
Jug, Brush Plum Design, Carved Wooden Stopper, N.Y., c.1870, Gal. 143.00
Jug, Brushed Cobalt Blue Flowers, Leaves, 3 In. 5225.00
Jug, Brushed Cobalt Blue Highlights, Handle, 1802, 7 1/4 In. 8690.00
Jug, Brushed Cobalt Blue Peacock, Applied Handle, 4 3/4 In. 550.00
Jug, Bullard & Scott, Cambridgeport, Mass., Cobalt Blue Leaves, 16 In. 165.00
Jug, Bullard & Scott, Cambridgeport, Mass., Gray, Blue Flower Design, 5 Gal. 358.00
Jug, Burger & Lang, Rochester, N.Y., Flowers, 1870, 17 In., 3 Gal. 66.00
Jug, C. Crolius, Brown Glaze, Cobalt Blue, Applied Handle, N.Y., 11 1/2 In. 330.00
Jug, C.W. Weaver, Cobalt Blue Design, Cincinnati, O., Strap Handle, 13 1/2 In. 110.00
Jug, Campbell, Penn Yan, Double Flower Design, Blue, 1850, 10 1/2 In. 495.00
Jug, Cobalt Bird Design, Handle, 11 1/2 In. 440.00
Jug, Cobalt Blue Brushed Design, Handle, Akron, Ohio, 14 In. 220.00
Jug, Cobalt Blue Brushed Flowers, 3-Part Design, Strap Handle, 13 3/4 In. 357.00
Jug, Cobalt Blue Chicken Pecking, Applied Strap Handle, West Troy, N.Y., 11 In. 1650.00
Jug, Cobalt Blue Design, Gray Salt Glaze, Brown Highlights, 11 In. 220.00
Jug, Cobalt Blue Design, Strap Handle, 14 In. 55.00
Jug, Cobalt Blue Design, Strap Handle, Fort Edward, N.Y., 13 1/2 In. 302.00
Jug, Cobalt Blue Flowers, Gray Salt Glaze, Strap Handle, 15 3/4 In. 72.00
Jug, Cobalt Blue Flowers, Strap Handle, 12 In. 137.00
Jug, Cobalt Blue Flowers, Strap Handle, 14 In. 264.00
Jug, Cobalt Blue Flowers, Strap Handle, 15 In. 137.00
Jug, Cobalt Blue Leaves, Flowers, Strap Handle, 11 1/4 In. 248.00
Jug, Cobalt Blue Slip Branch, Bird, Tails Feathers On Branch, Strap Handle, 14 In. 3330.00
Jug, Cobalt Blue Slip Design, Bust Of Man With Mustache, Strap Handle, 14 In. 4290.00
Jug, Cobalt Blue Slip Design, Strap Handle, 14 1/4 In. 495.00
Jug, Cobalt Blue Swan, Strap Handle, 11 1/2 In. 110.00
Jug, Cobalt Blue, Applied Strap Handle, 14 1/2 In. 165.00
Jug, Cortland, Long-Stemmed Flowers, Handle, 1870, 11 In. 154.00
Jug, Cowden & Wilcox, Harrisburg, Brushed Triple Iris, Handle, 1870, 14 In. 330.00
Jug, Cowden & Wilcox, Harrisburg, Pa., Gray, Cobalt Blue Slip Flower, 2 Gal. 231.00

If you want to clean a bottle that has a paper label, try to protect the label. Wrap the bottle tightly in thin plastic wrap. Seal the wrap with tape and rubber bands. Clean the inside carefully, using a mixture of water, automatic dishwasher detergent and slightly abrasive kitty litter. Fill bottle part way and shake.

Stoneware, Jug, Fine Prepared Mustard, James Marden & Co., Rochester, Label, 6 In.

Jug, D.W. Graves, Westmoreland, Blue Brush Tree Design, 1860, 11 In.	248.00
Jug, Deehan, 2 Gal.	215.00
Jug, E. & L.P. Norton, Bennington, Vt., Dotted Floral Spray, 1880, 14 In.	247.00
Jug, E.A. Buck & Co., Boston, Mass., Cobalt Blue Foliage, Gal.	192.00
Jug, E.A. Buck & Co., Large Plume Dot Design, 1860, 14 In., 2 Gal.	187.00
Jug, Edmunds & Co., Blue Slip Design, 1870, 15 In.	165.00
Jug, F. Laufersweiler Empire City Pottery, N.Y., Blue Slip Triple Leaf, 1880, 2 Gal.	495.00
Jug, F. Stetzenmeyer & G. Goetzman, N.Y., Large Sunflower, 1857, 14 1/2 In.	688.00
Jug, F.B. Norton & Co., Worcester, Mass., Bird Design, 1870, 13 1/2 In.	1265.00
Jug, F.B. Norton & Co., Worcester, Mass., Bird On Branch Design, 1870, 13 In.	770.00
Jug, F.J. Gribbin, Orilla, Ont., Cream, 1/2 Gal.	90.00
Jug, F.P. Goold & Co., Brantford C.W., Cobalt Blue Flower, Incised 2, c.1860, 2 Gal.	350.00
Jug, Fine Prepared Mustard, James Marden & Co., Rochester, Label, 6 In. ....*Illus*	55.00
Jug, Finley Acker & Co, Acker's High Grade Groceries, Phila., Pa., Brown, Tan, Qt.	140.00
Jug, G.I. Lazier, Picton C.W., 2 IMP, Cream, Incised Cobalt Blue Lettering, 2 Gal.	65.00
Jug, Geddes, N.Y., Large Dotted Geometric, Floral Spray Designs, 1870, 13 In.	303.00
Jug, Gray Salt Glaze, Ovoid, Cobalt Flowers, 3 Gal.	660.00
Jug, Hamilton & Jones, Cobalt Blue Leaves, Greensboro, Pa., 14 1/2 In.	137.00
Jug, Handle, Herman Bernhardt Wines & Liquors, Buffalo, N.Y., c.1890, 1/2 Gal.	66.00
Jug, Haxstun & Co., Fort Edward, N.Y., Bird Design, 1870, 12 In.	742.00
Jug, Haxstun & Co., Fort Edward, N.Y., Blue Slip Tornado Design, 1870, 11 In.	413.00
Jug, Haxstun Ottman & Co., N.Y., Stylized Plume Design, 1870, 10 1/2 In.	198.00
Jug, Henry K. Wampole & Co., Manufg. Pharmacists, Phila., Cream, Gal.	90.00
Jug, Henry Miller, Attica, N.Y., Bristol Glaze, c.1890, 1/2 Gal.	99.00
Jug, Hudsons Bay Co., HB Co., Cream, Brown, 1880-1910, 3 Gal., 16 In.	120.00
Jug, J. & E. Norton, Bennington, 2 Gal.	275.00
Jug, J. & E. Norton, Bennington, Vt., Bird On Branch Design, Blue, 1855, 11 1/2 In.	522.00
Jug, J. & E. Norton, Bennington, Vt., Bull's-Eye Geometric, Blue Cobalt, 11 In.	495.00
Jug, J. & E. Norton, Bennington, Vt., Bull's-Eye, Plume Design, 1855, 13 In.	176.00
Jug, J. Burger, Jr., Rochester, N.Y., Blue Slip Sunflower Design, Handle, 1885, 14 In.	198.00
Jug, J. Clark & Co., Troy, Blue Accents, Double Plume Design, 1824, Gal.	330.00
Jug, J. Fisher Lyons, N.Y., Geometric Slip Design, Handle, 1880, 13 1/2 In.	165.00
Jug, J. Norton & Co., Bennington, Vt., Benny Blue Bird, Handle, 1861, 11 In.	798.00
Jug, J.J. Lawlor, Albany, N.Y., 2, Tan Gray Glaze, Flowers, Cylindrical, 2 Gal.	193.00
Jug, J.J. Lawlor, Albany, N.Y., Blue Flowers, Tan Glaze, Cylindrical, 14 3/4 In.	88.00
Jug, J.P. Ames Wholesale Liquor Dealer, Ogdensburgh, N.Y., Blue Stencil, 14 In.	77.00
Jug, John J. Fake, Lansingburgh, Brush Flower Design, Blue Accents, 1825, 11 In.	605.00
Jug, John K. Malone, Blue Design, Marked, Buffalo, N.Y., 14 In.	192.00
Jug, John L. Smith Co., Wheeling, W. Va., Blue Flower, Handle, 1860, 16 In., 3 Gal.	1072.00
Jug, Julius Norton, Bennington, Vt., Brush Blue Butterfly Design, 1848, 13 In.	908.00
Jug, L. & B.G. Chace, Gray Salt Glaze, Ovoid, Blue Flower, Gal.	231.00
Jug, L. B.G. Chace, Somerset, Bird Design, Handle, 1850, 11 1/2 In.	935.00
Jug, L. Norton & Co., Bennington, Blue Flowers, Gray Tan Glaze, Oval, 15 In.	495.00
Jug, L. Young, Dark Green, Oval, Pine Tree With Cones, 3 Gal., 16 In.	88.00

Jug, Lewis & Cady, 3 Gal. 413.00
Jug, M. Callahan & Co., Buffalo, N.Y., Blue Script, 1870, 11 In. 187.00
Jug, Morrison & More Druggist, Lowville, N.Y., Blue Accents, Handle, c.1870, Qt. 522.00
Jug, N. Clark & Co., Mt. Morris, Blue Brushed Design, Handle, 1820, 11 1/2 In. 176.00
Jug, New York Stoneware Co., Fort Edward, N.Y., Bird Design, Handle, 16 In. 165.00
Jug, New York Stoneware Co., Fort Edward, N.Y., Bull's-Eye Flowers, 1870, 14 In. 187.00
Jug, Nicholas & Boynton, Burlington, Vt., Blue Slip Flowers, 1855, 4 Gal., 17 In. 440.00
Jug, Nicholas & Boynton, Burlington, Vt., Stylized Plume Design, 1856, 11 In. 330.00
Jug, O.L. & A.K. Ballard, Burlington, Vt., Pinwheel Flower Design, 1870, 14 In. 330.00
Jug, Orcutt Humestone, 2 Gal. 275.00
Jug, Ottman Bros. & Co., Fort Edward, N.Y., Blue Bird, 1870, 11 In. 220.00
Jug, Ottman Bros. & Co., Fort Edward, N.Y., Gray Salt Glaze, Blue Flower, Gal. 121.00
Jug, Ottman Bros. & Co., Fort Edward, N.Y., Stylized Bull's-Eye Flowers, 1870, 2 Gal. .. 176.00
Jug, Phil G. Kelly Co., Straight K Whiskies, Richmond, Va., Tan, 7 1/8 In. 105.00
Jug, Philip Miller, Brush Blue Dotted Flowers, 1854, 3 Gal., 15 In. 798.00
Jug, Redware, 10 Accent Lines, Yellow, Red Clay, 1820, 8 1/2 In. 275.00
Jug, Redware, Dark Specks, 1/2 Gal. 95.00
Jug, Redware, Yellow Spots, Canada, 1/2 Gal. 80.00
Jug, Riedeinger & Caire, N.Y., Cobalt Singing Bird Design, 1870, 2 Gal. 633.00
Jug, S. Hart & Son, Arrows Shooting In Geometric Design, 1870, 11 In. 440.00
Jug, S. Hart, Brush Plume Design, Blue Highlights, 1875, 9 3/4 In. 143.00
Jug, S. Risley, 2 Gal. 330.00
Jug, Slip Blue Heart Design, 1871, 2 Gal. 660.00
Jug, Spirits, Blue Accents, 6 x 2 In., 3 Gal. 198.00
Jug, Stephen Stevenson Grocer, Brooklyn, Gray Salt Glaze, Blue Letters, 2 Gal. 99.00
Jug, Stylized Blue Snowflake Design, Gray, Lug Handles, 10 1/2 In. 525.00
Jug, W. Hart, Ogdensburg, Triple Blue Flowers, Cobalt Blue, 1860, 15 In. 495.00
Jug, W.H. Farrar, Geddes, N.Y., Blue Dotted Tornado, Cobalt Blue, 1860, 16 In. 1815.00
Jug, W.M. Moyer, Harrisburg, Pa., Spitting Flowers, Blue, Handle, 1860, 14 In. 688.00
Jug, Welding & Belding, Brantford, Ont., Gray, Cobalt Blue Flower & Letters, Gal. 300.00
Jug, West Troy Pottery, Stylized Bull's-Eye Flowers, 1880, 2 Gal., 14 In. 165.00
Jug, White's Binghamton, Dotted Flowers, 1860, 11 In. 121.00
Jug, White's, Utica, Blue Vine Design, Wooden Stopper, 1865, 14 In. 440.00
Jug, White's, Utica, Floral Slip Design, 1865, 10 1/2 In. 132.00
Jug, White's, Utica, Long Tailed Bird On Twig, Handle, 1865, 11 In. 798.00
Jug, White's, Utica, Orchid Leaf In Center, Handle, 1865, 11 1/2 In. 88.00
Jug, White's, Utica, Pine Tree Design, Blue Accents, 1865, 11 In. 176.00
Jug, White's, Utica, Squiggles, Dots, Blue Slip Center, 1873, 11 In. 330.00
Jug, Wme. Warner West Troy, Thick Blue Line Of Flowers, Curls, Dots, 1850, 15 In. 962.00
Jug, Woodman, Gillett & Co Grocers, Philadelphia, Pa., 1870, 11 In. 632.00
Marie Brizard & Roger Liqueur, Bordeaux, Brown, Handle, Tooled Lip, 3 x 10 In. 12.00
Moeriein Old Jug Lager Bier, Cherubs, Black Transfer, Nashville, Tenn., Pt. 130.00
Warner & Kline, Philadelphia, Jug, Wreath Painted Design, 1/2 Gal. 500.00
Water Cooler, Blue Bands, Airplane, Love Field Potteries, 1900, 2 Gal. 85.00
Water Cooler, Geometric Design, Large Red Bands, Red Wing, 5 Gal. 169.00
Water Cooler, Satterlee & Morry, Fort Edward, N.Y., Tan Glaze, Flowers, Handles, 19 In. 275.00
Water Cooler, Vertical Bands, Cobalt Blue Flowers, Fort Edward, N.Y., 15 1/2 In. 165.00

TARGET BALL

Target balls were first used in England in the early 1830s. Trapshooting was a popular sport. Live birds were released from a trap and then shot as they tried to fly away. The target balls, thrown into the air, replaced the live birds. The first American use was by Charles Portlock of Boston, Massachusetts, about 1850. A mechanical thrower was invented by Captain Adam Bogardus and with this improvement, trap shooting spread to all parts of the country. Early balls were round globes but by the 1860s they were made with ornamental patterns in the glass. Light green, aqua, dark green, cobalt blue, amber, amethyst, and other colors were used. Target balls went out of fashion by 1880 when the *clay pigeon* was invented.

A. Bogardus, Patd Apr. 10th 1877, Yellow, Amber Tint, Diamond Pattern, 2 5/8 In. 715.00
Allover Diamond, Amber, Irregular Sheared Mouth, Germany, 1895, 2 5/8 In. 495.00
Amber, 3-Piece Mold, Diamond Mark 155.00
Blue, 5-Piece Mold 180.00
BMP, London, Cobalt Blue, Sheared Mouth, Tall Neck, 1900, 2 1/8 In. 185.00

Target Ball, Charlottenburg
Glashutten, Yellow, Diamond,
1895, 2 5/8 In.

Target Ball, L. Jones Gunmaker,
Blackburn, Diamond, Cobalt
Blue, Sheared Mouth, 2 5/8 In.

Target Ball, N.B. Glass Works,
Perth, Pale Green Aqua,
Sheared Lip, 1880-1890, 2 5/8 In.

BMP, London, Cobalt Blue, Sheared Mouth, Tall Neck, 1900, 2 In. 220.00
Bogardus, Pat'd Apr 10 1877, Amber, 1 3/4 In. 385.00
Bogardus, Pat'd Apr 10 1877, Diamond, Yellow Amber, 1895, 3 In. 500.00
Bogardus, Pat'd Apr 10 1877, Fishnet, Amber 540.00
Bogardus, Pat'd Apr 10 1877, Hobnail, Golden Yellow, Sheared Lip, 2 3/4 In. 385.00
Bogardus, Pat'd Apr 10 1877, Hobnail, Medium Amber, 1895, 3 In. 3920.00
Bogardus, Pat'd Apr 10 1877, Moss Green, Diamond, 2 3/4 In. 1760.00
C.T.H., Composite Pitch, Sept. 19, 1879, 1880, Round, 2 3/4 In. 415.00
Charlottenburg Glashutten, Dr. A. Frank, Diamond, Olive Yellow, 2 1/2 In. 588.00
Charlottenburg Glashutten, Olive Yellow, Diamond, Sheared Mouth, 2 5/8 In. 616.00
Charlottenburg Glashutten, Yellow, Diamond, 1895, 2 5/8 In. ....*Illus* 745.00
Cobalt Blue, 3-Piece Mold, 1890, 2 5/8 In. 120.00
Cobalt Blue, 7 Horizontal Bands, 2-Piece Mold, 1890, 2 5/8 In. 240.00
Cobalt Blue, 7 Horizontal Bands, Sheared Lip, 1880-1890, 2 5/8 In. 303.00
Cobalt Blue, Square Pattern, Black Center Band, Sheared Lip, 2 5/8 In. 77.00
Deep Purple, Man, Shooting, 2 5/8 In. 375.00
Diamond, Cobalt Blue, 1880-1900, 2 5/8 In. 784.00
Diamond, Cobalt Blue, Amber, 1880-1895, 2 3/4 In. 616.00
Diamond, Copper Puce, Sheared, 1890, 2 5/8 In. 165.00
Diamond, Gold Yellow Amber, 1880-1890, 2 5/8 In. 195.00
Diamond, Man, Shooting, Pink Amethyst, 1880-1895, 2 5/8 In. 672.00
Dot, Gold Yellow Amber, Sheared Mouth, 2 5/8 In. 1372.00
E.E. Eaton Guns & C., Chicago, Yellow Amber, 1880-1895, 2 5/8 In. 4480.00
Embossed Horizontal Bands Around Ball, Tobacco Amber, 1880-1895, 2 5/8 In. 392.00
For Hockey's Patent Trap, Green Aqua, England, 1880-1895, 2 3/8 In. 1008.00
Ira Paine's, Pat. Oct. 23, 1877, Cobalt Blue, Sheared Mouth, 2 5/8 In. 5376.00
Ira Paine's, Pat. Oct. 23, 1877, Gold Yellow Amber, Sheared Lip, 2 5/8 In. ....240.00 to 448.00
Ira Paine's Filled Ball, Pat. Oct. 23, 1877, Yellow Amber, 1880-1895, 2 5/8 In. 476.00
J.H. Johnston, Gold Yellow Amber, Sheared Mouth, 2 5/8 In. 4256.00
J.H. Johnston, Great Western Gun Works, Pittsburgh, Root Beer Amber, 2 5/8 In. 4884.00
L. Jones Gunmaker, Blackburn, Diamond, Cobalt Blue, Sheared Mouth, 2 5/8 In. ...*Illus* 440.00
Man, Shooting, Diamond, Clear, Sheared Lip, 1880-1890, 2 5/8 In. 413.00
Man, Shooting, Diamond, Moss Green, Sheared Mouth, England, 2 5/8 In. 420.00
Man, Shooting, Diamond, Pink Amethyst, Sheared Mouth, England, 2 5/8 In. 560.00
Man, Shooting, Diamond, Purple Amethyst, Sheared Mouth, 2 In. 395.00
Mauritz, Wid'fors, Medium Honey Amber, Sweden, 1880-1895, 2 5/8 In. ....672.00 to 1064.00
Mauritz-Wid'fors, Yellow Amber, Sweden, c.1890, 2 5/8 In. 1485.00
Medium Cobalt Blue, 5-Piece Mold, Sheared Lip, 1890, 2 5/8 In. 198.00
Medium Yellow Amber, 3-Piece Mold, Sheared Lip, 1880-1890, 2 5/8 In. 99.00
N.B. Glass Works, Perth, Blue Aqua, Inside Feathers, 1 5/8 In. 165.00
N.B. Glass Works, Perth, Diamond, Green Aqua, Sheared Mouth, 2 3/4 In. 143.00
N.B. Glass Works, Perth, Diamond, Sapphire Blue, 2 5/8 In. 130.00
N.B. Glass Works, Perth, Pale Green Aqua, Sheared Lip, 1880-1890, 2 5/8 In. ......*Illus* 154.00

Olive Yellow, Blown, 3-Piece Mold, Sheared Mouth, 2 5/8 In. 420.00
Prussian Blue, Embossed 5-Pointed Star On Both Sides, England, 2 1/4 In. 550.00
Purple Amethyst, 3-Piece Mold, Sheared Mouth, 1890, 2 5/8 In. 275.00
Smoky Yellow Olive, Embossed, 1880-1895, 2 5/8 In. 560.00
Square Pattern, Blank Center Band, Cobalt Blue, England, 1900, 2 5/8 In. 105.00
Square Pattern, Blank Center Band, Cobalt Blue, Seed Bubbles, 1900, 2 3/4 In. 132.00
Square Pattern, Blank Center Band, Cobalt Blue, Sheared Lip, 2 1/8 In. 187.00
Square Pattern, Medium Sapphire Blue, Blue, 1880-1890, 2 5/8 In. 121.00
Square Pattern, Sapphire Blue, 1890, 2 5/8 In. 275.00
Sunburst On Both Sides, Sapphire Blue, Embossed, England, 1880-1900, 1 5/8 In. 358.00
Teal Green, Rough Sheared Lip, England, 1880-1895, 2 1/4 In. 523.00
Tobacco Amber, 2-Piece Mold, Sheared Lip, 1880-1890, 2 5/8 In. 193.00
Van Gutsem A St. Quentin, Diamond, Blue, Sheared Mouth, France, 2 5/8 In.55.00 to 120.00
Van Gutsem A St. Quentin, Web Design, Blue 110.00
W.W. Greeners, St. Mary's Works, Diamond, Cobalt Blue, 2 5/8 In. ....143.00 to 255.00
Yellow, Amber Tint, 5-Piece Mold, 1880-1895, 2 5/8 In. 187.00
Yellow Amber, 7 Horizontal Bands, Sheared Lip, 1890, 2 3/4 In. 253.00
Yellow Amber, Dot Design, Horizontal Lines, 3-Piece Mold, 2 In. 1370.00
TOILET WATER, see Cologne

─────────────────────────────── **TONIC** ───────────────────────────────
Tonic is a word with several meanings. Listed here are medicine bottles that have the word *tonic* either on a paper label or embossed on the glass. In this book *hair tonic* is listed with cosmetics or cure. There may be related bottles listed in the Cure and Medicine categories.

Baume Tranquille, Opium Wine Tonic, Cork, Paper Label, France, 11 In. 11.00
Blud-Life, The Great Anti-Toxic, ABM 6.50
Clemen's Indian, Aqua, Oval, Tooled Lip, Pontil, Label, 1840-1860, 5 5/8 In. 896.00
Clemen's Indian, Geo. W. House, Blue Aqua, OP, 1855, 5 5/8 In. 616.00
Doctor I.T. Henderson's Eureka, Deep Blue Aqua, OP, 6 1/2 In. 952.00
Dr. D. Jayne's Vermifuge, 242 Chest. St., Phila., Aqua 6.50
Dr. J. Speed's Fever, New Orleans, Blue Aqua, 6-Sided, Flared Lip, Pontil, 3 1/4 In. 280.00
Dr. Townsend's Aromatic Hollands, Amber, 9 In. 220.00
Elmer & Amend, New York, Phosphorcin, Organic Preparations, Green, 1920s, Contents . 2.00
Golden's Liquid Beef, G.N. Grittenton, Prop'r, N.Y., Peacock Blue, 9 3/4 In. 45.00
Hawkers Nerve & Stomach, St. John, N.B., Aqua, Rectangular, Label, 8 In. 45.00
Kloor Kool Beverages, Manchester Tonic Co., Neck Green, 32 Oz. 1.00
Primley's Iron & Wahoo, Elkhart, Ind., Medium Gold Amber, 1895, 9 1/2 In. 123.00
Primley's Iron & Wahoo, Elkhart, Ind., Root Beer Amber, 1875-1885, 8 3/4 In. 132.00
Primley's Iron & Wahoo, Elkhart, Ind., Straw Yellow, 1895, 9 1/2 In. ....257.00 to 440.00
Primley's Iron & Wahoo, Elkhart, Ind., Tobacco Amber, 8 3/4 In. 375.00
Primley's Iron & Wahoo, Jones & Primley Co., Elkhart, Ind., Tobacco Amber, 8 5/8 In. .. 110.00
Reed & Cornick, Roboline, Amber, 1 Flattened Side, Cork, 8 1/2 In. 104.00
Reed's Gilt 1878 Edge, Amber, Applied Mouth, 1870-1880, 8 5/8 In. 94.00
Rohrer's Expectoral Wild Cherry, Lancaster, Pa., Amber, IP, 10 1/2 In. ....308.00 to 357.00
Rohrer's Expectoral Wild Cherry, Lancaster, Pa., Gold Amber, 1865-1875, 10 In. 100.00
Rohrer's Expectoral Wild Cherry, Lancaster, Pa., Gold Amber, Pyramidal, 10 1/2 In. 220.00
Smith Sex O-Tine The Great Tonic For Men, Mobile, Ala., 6 3/4 In. 66.00
Spillman's Alterative Ague, Blue Aqua, Double Collar, IP, 7 3/4 In. 728.00
Stewart D. Howe's Arabian, Blood Purifier, New York, Blue, 10 1/2 In. 265.00
W.F. Smith, M.D.'s Tonic & Nervous Regenerator, Philada., Aqua, Pontil, 7 1/4 In. 532.00
Warner's Safe, Rochester, N.Y., A. & D.H.C., Amber, 7 1/2 In. 870.00
Warner's Safe, Rochester, N.Y., Amber, Applied Mouth, 1895, 7 1/2 In. 868.00
Wynkoop & Co's Mixture, New York, Cobalt Blue, OP, 6 5/8 In. ....5750.00 to 6440.00

─────────────────────────────── **VINEGAR** ───────────────────────────────
Vinegar was and is sold in glass bottles. Most vinegar packers prefer a large glass jug-shaped bottle with a small handle, the shape used today even for modern plastic vinegar bottles. The collector wants any bottle with the name *vinegar* on a paper label or embossed on the glass. The most famous vinegar bottles were made by National Fruit Product Company for their White House Brand vinegar. Bottles with the embossed brand name and a picture of a house, the trademark, were made in the early 1900s. Jugs

Vinegar, Decanter, Embossed Star Design, Qt.

Vinegar, Buy Leo Vinegar, O.J. Gregory Vinegar Co., Rogers, Ark., Pottery, 4 1/2 In.

in three or four sizes, apple-shaped jars, canning jars, fancy decanters, cruets, a New York World's Fair bottle, rolling pins, vases, a refrigerator water jar, and other fanciful reusable shapes were used until the 1940s. The company is still in business.

Buy Leo Vinegar, O.J. Gregory Vinegar Co., Rogers, Ark., Pottery, 4 1/2 In. . . . .*Illus*	80.00
C.I. Co., L.T.D., East Rindge, N.H., Cobalt Blue, Ring Lip, Fluted, 11 3/8 In.	1008.00
Decanter, Embossed Star Design, Qt. . . . .*Illus*	15.00
Heinz's Pure Malt, Stopper, Contents, Sample, 4 5/8 In.	143.00
Jones Bros. & Co., Blue Glass Belle Vinegar, Jug, Tan, Blue Letters, 4 3/4 In.	90.00
Maple Sap & Boiled Cider, Blue, Tooled Top, Qt.	495.00
Maple Sap & Boiled Cider, Cobalt Blue, Cylindrical, Scalloped Shoulder, Qt.	825.00
Maple Sap & Boiled Cider, East Rindge, N.H., Cobalt Blue, 1890, 11 3/8 In.	840.00
Pacific & Pickle Vinegar Works, San Francisco, Amethyst, 11 In.	130.00
White House, Apple, Jug, Qt.	30.00
White House, Embossed Building, 1/2 Pt.	50.00
White House, Panels, Spout, 1909, Qt.	25.00

W.A. LACEY, see Lacey
WATER, MINERAL, see Mineral Water

WHEATON

Wheaton Glass Co. produced machine-made reproductions of old American bottles and commemorative bottles from 1967 to 1975 and sold them through their Nuline division. From 1975 to 1982 some Wheaton commemorative limited editions bottles were made on semiautomatic bottling machines. In 1982 the rights to make the bottles were sold to Millville Art Glass Co. The company is now out of business. Reproductions of Wheaton bottles have been made by Viking Glass Co. and others.

Abraham Lincoln, 7 1/2 In.	35.00
Andrew Jackson, 7 1/2 In.	20.00
Andrew Johnson, 7 1/2 In.	15.00
Benjamin Harrison, 7 1/2 In.	25.00
Calvin Coolidge, 7 1/2 In.	25.00
Chester A. Arthur, 7 1/2 In.	30.00
Dwight D. Eisenhower, Peace With Justice, Amethyst, Iridescent, 7 1/2 In. . . . .*Illus*	25.00
Franklin Pierce, 7 1/2 In.	35.00
Franklin Roosevelt, Nothing To Fear, Emerald, Iridescent, 7 1/2 In. . . . .*Illus*	25.00
George Bush, 7 1/2 In.	15.00
George Washington, 7 1/2 In.	35.00
Gerald R. Ford, 7 1/2 In.	15.00
Grover Cleveland, 7 1/2 In.	25.00
Harry S. Truman, 7 1/2 In.	40.00
Herbert C. Hoover, 7 1/2 In.	15.00
James A. Garfield, 7 1/2 In.	30.00
James Buchanan, 7 1/2 In.	15.00
James K. Polk, 7 1/2 In.	35.00
James Madison, 7 1/2 In.	35.00

Wheaton, Dwight D. Eisenhower, Peace With Justice, Amethyst, Iridescent, 7 1/2 In.	Wheaton, Franklin Roosevelt, Nothing To Fear, Emerald, Iridescent, 7 1/2 In.	Wheaton, Martin Luther King, Jr., Non-Violence, Light Amber, Iridescent, 8 1/4 In.

James Monroe, 7 1/2 In. 60.00
Jimmy Carter, 7 1/2 In. 12.00
John Adams, 7 1/2 In. 25.00
John F. Kennedy, 7 1/2 In. 75.00
John Quincy Adams, 7 1/2 In. 40.00
John Tyler, 7 1/2 In. 25.00
Lyndon B. Johnson, 7 1/2 In. 20.00
Martin Luther King, Jr., Non-Violence, Light Amber, Iridescent, 8 1/4 In. .... *Illus* 14.00
Martin Van Buren, 7 1/2 In. 35.00
Millard Fillmore, 7 1/2 In. 35.00
Paul Revere, American Patriot, Cobalt Blue, Iridescent, 8 1/4 In. .... *Illus* 18.00
Richard M. Nixon, 7 1/2 In. 30.00
Robert E. Lee, Gray Fox, Teal, Iridescent, 8 1/4 In. .... *Illus* 14.00
Ronald Reagan, 7 1/2 In. 15.00
Rutherford B. Hayes, 7 1/2 In. 40.00
Theodore Roosevelt, 7 1/2 In. 20.00
Thomas Jefferson, 7 1/2 In. 25.00
Ulysses S. Grant, Warrior Statesman, Light Amber, Iridescent, 7 3/4 In. .... *Illus* 22.00
Warren G. Harding, 7 1/2 In. 25.00
William H. Harrison, 7 1/2 In. 15.00
William Howard Taft, 7 1/2 In. 25.00
William McKinley, 7 1/2 In. 35.00
Woodrow Wilson, 7 1/2 In. 25.00
Zachary Taylor, 7 1/2 In. 35.00

——— WHISKEY ———

Whiskey bottles came in assorted sizes and shapes through the years. Any container for whiskey is included in this category. Although purists spell the word *whisky* for Scotch and Canadian and whiskey for bourbon and other types, we have found it simpler in this book to use only the spelling *whiskey*. There is also blended whiskey, which includes blended bourbon, Scotch, Irish, or Canadian. Although blends were made in Scotland and Ireland for many years, it was not a process popular in the United States until 1933. One way to spot very new whiskey bottles is by the size. The 1 3/4-liter bottle is slightly less than a half gallon, the 1-liter bottle slightly more than a quart, and the 3/4-liter bottle almost the same size as a fifth. These bottles were introduced in 1976. Several years ago there was a contest to find the oldest bourbon bottle made in America. It was thought to be one dated 1882. The contest turned up an even older bottle, a Bininger made in 1848. Bourbon was first made in 1789 in Kentucky. Rum was made in America by the mid-seventeenth century; whiskey made of corn, rye, or barley by the early 1700s. It was the tax on this whiskey that caused the so-called Whiskey Rebellion of 1794. See also modern manufacturers categories by brand name, and the Figural category.

2-Piece Mold, Bulbous, Strawberry Puce, Applied Sloping Collar, Handle, IP, 6 1/2 In. 235.00

Wheaton, Paul Revere,
American Patriot, Cobalt Blue,
Iridescent, 8 1/4 In.

Wheaton, Robert E. Lee,
Gray Fox, Teal,
Iridescent, 8 1/4 In.

Wheaton, Ulysses S. Grant,
Warrior Statesman, Light
Amber, Iridescent, 7 3/4 In.

8-Sided, Olive Yellow, Amethyst Striations, Paneled, 5 1/4 In. 495.00
A.A.A. Lexington Club, Backbar, Gold Lettering, Qt. 110.00
A.K. Clark, Denver, Col., Qt. 1200.00
A.P. Hotaling & Co.'s Old Kirk, Kiselbar, Bakersfield, Cal., Label, ABM 88.00
A.P. Hotaling's Private Stock Bourbon, Amber, 12 In. 2970.00
A.S. Gigliani, San Francisco, Cal., 8-Sided Base, Tooled Top, c.1890, 17 1/2 In. 110.00
AAA Old Valley, Amber, Cross, Rolled Lip, 1880 . . . . 1540.00
AAA Old Valley, Red Amber, Single Roll Flask, 1870-1880 . . . . 715.00
Acorn Distillery Tipperary Co., Jug, Ripe & Mellow, Cream, Brown, Ireland, 7 5/8 In. . . . 385.00
Adams-Booth Co., Sacramento, Cal., Dark Amethyst, Anchor, c.1900, Fifth, 12 In. 150.00
Adams-Booth Co., Sacramento, Cal., Dark Amethyst, Cylindrical, 12 In. 120.00
Adler Company, Cleveland, Ohio, Root Beer Amber, Tooled Mouth, 7 3/8 In. 110.00
Adolph Harris & Co., San Francisco, Amber, Deer Head, c.1900, Fifth, 12 In. . . . .440.00 to 523.00
Altschul Distilling Co., Springfield, Ohio, Amber, Barrel & Monogram 12.00
Amber, Bell Shape, 24 Vertical Ribs, Swirl To Right, Handle, Double Collar, 8 1/8 In. . . . 756.00
Amber, Bell Shape, Applied Mouth & Handle, 1870, 8 1/2 In. 360.00
Amber, Conical, Swirled Vertical To Right, Applied Handle, c.1860, 8 In. 358.00
Argonaut, Shield, Medium To Dark Amber, 1900-1906, Fifth, 11 In. 40.00
Argonaut Rye, Famosa, Calif., Light Amethyst, Pumpkinseed, Label, Pt. 99.00
Argonaut Rye, Famosa, Calif., Light Amethyst, Pumpkinseed, Paper Label, 1/2 Pt. 77.00
Aromatic Schnaps, J.J., Melcher's, Schiedam, Green 110.00
Atlas Bourbon, Mohns & Kaltenbach, S.F., Cylindrical, Fifth, 11 5/8 In. . . . . .210.00 to 300.00
Auld Lang Syne, Pure Old Barley Malt Rye, Weideman Co., Jug, Tan, 7 3/4 In. 154.00
B.E. Borrowe, Cluster Of Grapes, Double Collar Mouth, 10 5/8 In. 1680.00
B.M. & E.A. Whitlock & Co., Barrel, Aqua, Pontil, 1840-1860, 7 7/8 In. 825.00
Backbar, Always Pure Old Elk, Ear Of Corn, Bright Green, Stopper, 8 In. 385.00
Backbar, Bitters, Clear, Gold & Black Label Under Glass, Tooled Mouth, 11 7/8 In. 134.00
Backbar, Catawba, Clear, Black & Gold Label Under Glass, Tooled Mouth, 11 7/8 In. . . . 134.00
Backbar, Chicken Cock Bourbon, Rooster, Enamel, Glass Stopper, 7 In. 1155.00
Backbar, Decanter, Rib, Ruby Red, Sterling Silver Overlay, 1910-1920, 7 1/4 In. 224.00
Backbar, G.R. Sharpe, Fluted Shoulder, White On Blue Enamel, Incised Frame, 11 In. . . . 106.00
Backbar, Gold Eagle Rye, Union Club, White & Gold Enameled Letters, Pontil, 9 3/4 In. . 231.00
Backbar, Molded, Pillar, Sapphire Blue, Pinched Waist, Pittsburgh District, 10 7/8 In. 825.00
Backbar, Old Green Bottle, Tooled Mouth Pontil, Glass Stopper, 1890-1910, 11 In. 440.00
Backbar, Old Overholt Pure Rye, Clear, Black & White Bust Of Man, Gold Letters, 11 In. 336.00
Backbar, Paul Jones, Multicolor, Man Pouring Whiskey, Tooled Mouth, 6 3/8 In. 88.00
Backbar, Peacock Blue, 8-Sided, Floral Wreath, Stopper, Pontil, 11 In. 200.00
Backbar, Ruby Red, Silver Overlay, Stopper, Scotch & Rye, 10 1/2 In., Pair 143.00
Backbar, Scotch, Deep Ruby Red, Silver Overlay, 1900-1925, 10 3/4 In. 308.00
Backbar, That Weaver Whiskey Pure All Rye, Clear, White Enamel Letters, 11 In. 364.00
Backbar, W.N. Walton's, Cobalt Blue, Shield, Applied Mouth, 12 1/8 In. 190.00
Batholomay's, Gold Band At Top, P.H. Zang Brewing Co., 4 In. 29.00

Bear Grass Bourbon S.F., Embossed, Bear In Triangle, Tooled Top, 12 In. . . . . . . .143.00 to 350.00
Bear Grass Kentucky Bourbon, Amber, Applied Top, 1881-1885, 11 7/8 In. 3960.00
Beiser & Fisher, N.Y., Amber, Pig Shape, Double Collar, 9 1/2 In. 812.00
Belle Of Anderson, Old Fashion Hand Made Sour Mash, Milk Glass, 6 7/8 In. 72.00
Bennet & Carroll, 120 Wood St. Pitts, Pa., Chestnut, Gold Amber, IP, 8 1/2 In. 1100.00
Bertin & Leperi, S.F., Red Amber, Rectangular, Flask, Qt., 9 1/2 In. 90.00
Bininger, see the Bininger category
Black Horse, Dark Olive Green, Embossed Horse, Diamond Mark, Australia, Large 178.00
Blended Highland Whisky, Bulloch Lade & Co., Label, Aqua, 3-Piece Mold, Qt. 9.00
Bonanza Bourbon, Amber, Applied Top, Bubbles, Slug Plate, 1880s, 11 3/4 In. 2700.00
Booth & Co., Sacramento, Embossed Anchor, Amethyst, Tooled Top, Fifth, 12 In. 300.00
Booth's Distillery, London, 6-Sided, Embossed, Tooled Lip, Qt. 3.00
Bottled By Goldberg Bowen & Lebenbaum, S.F., Applied Top, Fifth, 11 1/2 In. 110.00
Boulevard Bourbon Buneman Mercantile Co., San Francisco, Ca., Amber 88.00
Boulevard O.K. Bourbon, Buneman & Martinoni, Smoky, Applied Top, Fifth 440.00
Boulevard O.K. Bourbon, Buneman, S.F. Cal., Amber, Belt, Buckle, Tooled Top 253.00
Braunschwager & Co., S.F., Slug Plate Askew, 1/2 Pt. 110.00
Buchanan's Black & White, Jug, Ask For It, 2 Scotty Dogs, White, 5 In. 281.00
Buchanan's Black & White, Jug, White, Checkerboard Design, 5 In. . . . . .93.00 to 187.00
Buchanan's Extract Of Sugar Corn, Cannon, Amber, 8 3/4 In. 1850.00
Buffalo Old Bourbon, Geo. Dierssen & Co., Sacramento, Ca., Amber, Tooled Top 1000.00
Burke's Fine Old Irish, Dublin, Ireland, Aqua, 3-Piece Mold, Cylindrical, Qt. 4.80
C.A. Richards & Co., 99 Washington St., Boston, Mass., Blue Aqua, Pt. 75.00
C.A. Richards & Co., 99 Washington St., Boston, Mass., Olive Yellow Green, 9 3/4 In. . . . 260.00
C.A. Richards & Co., Boston, Mass., Orange Amber, Square, Labels, 9 1/2 In. 392.00
C.J. Stubling, The Dalles, Ore., Amber, Tooled Top, Fifth, 11 In. 330.00
Campus, Gossler Bros., Columbus Ave. & 104th St., N.Y., Amber, Handle, 3 1/4 In. 660.00
Carnegie Brae Aberdeen Finest Scotch Malt, Jug, Pottery, Cream, Brown, 6 7/8 In. 55.00
Casey & Kavanaugh, Sacramento, Cal., Amber, Cylindrical, Fifth, 11 1/4 In. . . . . . .45.00 to 60.00
Casper Co., Winston Salem, N.C., Jug, Cream, Blue Lettering, Gal. 70.00
Casper's, Made By Honest N.C. People, Cobalt Blue, Fluted, Ring Lip, 12 In. . . . .523.00 to 616.00
Casper's, Made By Honest North Carolina People, Cobalt Blue, 1900, 11 In. 605.00
Catto's Extra Special, Jug, Cream Base, Brown Top, Stopper, 1920, 9 In. 75.00
Catto's Highland, Aberdeen, Jug, Cream, Brown Glaze, 8 3/8 In. 303.00
Chapin & Gore, Amber, Cylindrical, Sloping Double Collar, 11 1/8 In. 28.00
Chapin & Gore, Gold Amber, 8-Sided, Round, Inside Screw Applied Top, Fifth 121.00
Chapin & Gore Sour Mash 1867, Barrel, Amber, Pat. Aug 6 '72, Stopper, 8 1/2 In. 224.00
Chenery Souther & Co., S.F., Amber, Fifth, 11 1/2 In. . . . . .95.00 to 143.00
Chestnut Grove, C. Wharton, Amber, Applied Handle, OP 209.00
Chestnut Grove, C. Wharton, Amber, Seal, Vertical Ribs, Double Collar, 9 In. 1065.00
Chestnut Grove, C. Wharton, Red Variant, Handle, Pontil 210.00
Chestnut Grove, Flattened Chestnut Shape, Gold Amber, Handle, Pontil, Qt. 99.00
Chestnut Grove, Jug, Seal, Gold Amber, Pontil, 1840-1860, 9 In. 242.00
Chevalier's Old Castle Whiskey, San Francisco, Pale Aqua, Spiral Neck, Fifth 9900.00
Chicken Cock, Pure Rye Whiskey, Embossed, Tin Cap, 7 1/2 x 4 1/2 In. 20.00
Chivas Regal, Jug, Wade 22.50
Choice Old, Cabinet, Ky., Bourbon, Medium Amber, Glob Top 2400.00
Choice Old, Cabinet, Ky., Bourbon, San Francisco, Yellow Amber, 1878-1883 . . . . 935.00
Clinch & Co., Dealers In Wines & Liquors, Grass Valley, Cal., Fifth, 11 In. . . . . .65.00 to 90.00
Clinch Mercantile Co., Grass Valley, Cal., Clear, Fifth, 11 1/8 In. 55.00
Cobalt Blue, Applied Top, Half Post, Germany, 10 1/2 In. 413.00
Cognac, Dark Amber, OP, 9 In. 143.00
Collins & Wheeland, San Francisco, Dark Amber, Slug Plate, Applied Top, 1897 . . . . 375.00
Coming Thru The Rye, Cobalt Glaze, Stoneware, 5 In. 448.00
Commodores, Royal, O.K., Old Bourbon, 4-Piece Mold, Tooled Mouth 700.00
Compliments Of Kentucky Liquor Co., Jug, Silver Plate, 1890-1915, 7 1/4 In. 364.00
Continental Jug, 2-Tone, 3 In. 44.00
Cordial, see the Cordial category
Cottage Brand, Cabin, Aqua, Shingled Roof, 1860-1890, 6 1/2 In. 154.00
Crigler & Crigler Company, Square, Label, Qt. 8.50
Croff & Collins Wines & Liquors, Denver & Salida, Coffin, Qt. . . . . .900.00 to 1400.00
Crown Cocktails, Ready To Drink, Dark Amber, Tooled Top, Fifth 100.00
Crown Distilleries Co., Crown & Shield, Amber, Inside Screw Threads . . . . .25.00 to 35.00

Cruiskeen Lawn Old Irish Whiskey, Belfast 39.00
D & J McCallum's Perfection Whisky, Cream, Green Neck, Handle, 5 1/2 x 6 In. 45.00
D.J. O'Donnell Fine Liquors, Washington D.C., Label, Dated 1906, Qt. 40.00
Davy Crockett Pure Old Bourbon, Amber, Tooled Top, Fifth, 11 3/4 In. 50.00
DBW, Embossed Tower With Flag, Shield, Amber, Double Collar, 10 1/2 In. 17.00
Detrick Distilling Co., Dayton, O., Jug, Dark Brown, Eat, Drink & Be Merry, 4 1/2 In. ... 60.00
Dewar's Perth Whisky, Jug, Pottery, Brown, 9 3/4 In. ....*Illus* 210.00
Dewey's American Brandy, Broadway, N.Y., Amber, 3-Piece Mold, Label, Qt. 15.00
Duffy Malt Whiskey, Amber, 4 In. 72.80
Duffy Malt Whiskey, Amber, 10 1/4 In. 9.00
Duffy Malt Whiskey, D.M.W. Co., Olive Yellow, Patd. Aug. 24, 10 In. 179.20
Duffy Malt Whiskey, Olive Amber, 10 1/4 In. 15.00
Duffy Malt Whiskey, Rochester, N.Y., U.S.A., Amber, Labels, Pt. 45.00
E.A. Fargo & Co., Wholesale Liquors, San Francisco, Cal., Cylindrical, 11 5/8 In. ....38.00 to 50.00
E.A. Fargo & Co., Wholesale Liquors, San Francisco, Cal., Dark Amber, 12 In. ......35.00 to 40.00
E.G. Booz's Old Cabin, Amber, Chamfered Corners, Qt. 3080.00
E.G. Booz's Old Cabin, Amber, Qt. 3550.00
E.G. Booz's Old Cabin, Amber, Sloping Collar, 7 3/4 In. 4255.00
E.G. Booz's Old Cabin, Federal Law Prohibits Sale, Wood Stopper, Reproduction, 8 1/2 In. 45.00
E.G. Booz's Old Cabin, Philadelphia, Cabin, Amber, 1875, 7 7/8 In. 2600.00
E.G. Booz's Old Cabin, Philadelphia, Cabin, Amber, Sloping Collar, 7 7/8 In. 2912.00
E.G. Booz's Old Cabin, Robin's-Egg Blue, 1840, Reproduction, 7 1/2 In. 65.00
E.G. Booz's Old Cabin, Yellow Green, Late 20th Century, Reproduction, 7 1/2 In. 45.00
E.G. Booze's Old Cabin, Yellow Amber, 8-Sided, Blown, 1840, Reproduction, 8 1/4 In. .. 55.00
Eagle Bottling Co., Cleveland, O., Aqua, Eagle Emblem, Tall 8.50
Eagle Liqueur Distillers, Cincinnati, Eagle With Shield, Embossed, 7 7/8 x 3 5/8 In. 79.00
Ear Of Corn, Ceramic, Yellow & Green Glazes, 7 7/8 In. 100.00
Evans & O'Brien, No. 22 Main Street, Stockton, Amber, Applied Top 5500.00
F. Chevalier & Co., San Francisco, Green, Ringed Top 165.00
F. Kuppelwieser, Bozen, Weingut, St. Magdalena-Hortenberg, Olive, 6 1/8 In. 72.00
F. Zimmerman, Full Measure, Light To Medium Amber 25.00
F. Zimmerman & Co., Portland, Ore., Amber, Bubbles, 32 Oz., 12 1/4 In. 18.00
Family French Liquor Store, S.F., Amber, Flask, Pt. 66.00
Famous Queen Of Nelson, Clear, Blue Leather Cover, 1/2 Pt. 44.00
Flask, see the Flask category
Fly Fishing Whisky, Ceramic, Fly Fishing Scenes, British Isles, 10 In. 43.00
Forest Lawn, J.V.H., Olive Amber, Onion Shape, Long Neck, IP, 7 1/4 In. 364.00
Forest Lawn, J.V.H., Olive Green, Onion Shape, Long Neck, IP, 7 1/2 In. 420.00
Forest Lawn, J.V.H., Olive Green, Onion Shape, Long Neck, Sloping Collar, IP, 7 1/8 In. . 476.00
Forest Lawn, J.V.H., Olive Yellow, Bulbous, Molded Seal, Pontil, 7 1/4 In. 385.00
Four Roses Whiskey, Jug, Cream Body, Red & Green Roses, Black Print, England 36.00
Fraser Perth, Flask, England 45.00
Freeblown, Amethyst, Beveled Corners, Applied Pewter Collar, Screw Cap, 6 3/8 In. 440.00
G.O. Blake's, Bourbon Co., Ky., Golden Amber, Embossed Barrels, Fifth 468.00
G.O. Blake's, Bourbon Co., Ky., Miller, Stewart & Co., Barrels, Amber, 11 3/8 In. .224.00 to 280.00
G.O. Blake's, Bourbon Co., Ky., More, Reynolds & Co., Amber, 11 7/8 In. 990.00
G.O. Taylor, Registered Trademark, Orange Amber, 3-Piece Mold, Cork, 11 1/2 In. 66.00
G.W. Matthews, Terrell, Tex., Stoneware, Canteen Shape, Gray, Blue Glaze, 9 1/4 In. 550.00
Galway Bay, Jug, Sailing Boat, Cream, Black Outline, 1885-1910, 6 7/8 In. 364.00
Geo. H. Bennett & Bros., Pittsburg, Pa., Cone, 13 1/4 In. 20.00
Geo. S. Ladd & Co., Wholesale Liquors, Stockton, Cal., Amber, Cylindrical, 11 In. ...40.00 to 60.00
Gilmour Thompson, Stag, Stoneware 113.00
Gin, see the Gin category
Glen Garry, Very Old Scotch Whisky, Tan & Brown 35.00
Glenfiddich Pure Malt, Jug, Black Body, Gold & Black Print, England 36.00
Glenfiddich Whiskey, Green, White, Black 37.50
Gold Crown, Felterson & Co., Sacramento, Cal., Bubbles, 11 5/8 In. 300.00
Gold Dust, Barkhouse Bros., John Van Bergen, Amber, 11 3/4 In. 2090.00
Gold Dust, Barkhouse Bros., N. Van Bergen, Amber, 11 5/8 In. 1760.00
Gold Dust, Kentucky Bourbon, N. Van Bergen, Amethyst, Tooled Top 2200.00
Gold Dust, Kentucky Bourbon, N. Van Bergen, Applied Top, 11 3/4 In. 440.00
Gold Dust, Kentucky Bourbon, N. Van Bergen, Tooled Top, 11 7/8 In. 330.00
Golden & Co., Mail Order House, San Francisco., Cal., Amber, Qt., 12 In. ....60.00 to 75.00

Whiskey, Dewar's Perth Whisky, Jug, Pottery, Brown, 9 3/4 In.

Whiskey, Gottschalk Co., Baltimore, Md., Jug, Pottery, Cream, Black Transfer, 7 3/8 In.

Golden Eagle, Sacramento, Pumpkinseed, Paper Label, Eagle, 1/2 Pt. 121.00
Golden Harvest Old Bourbon Whiskey, F.W. Hunt, 3-Piece Mold, Qt. 5.00
Golden Rule XXXX, Braunschweiger & Co., S.F., Cal., Amber, Tooled Top, Fifth . . .80.00 to 220.00
Golden Rule XXXX, San Francisco, Ca., 1895-1905 .... 400.00
Golden Wedding Rye, Amber, Embossed, Paper Label, Metal Cap, 4 1/2 In. 8.00
Gottschalk Co., Baltimore, Md., Jug, Pottery, Cream, Black Transfer, 7 3/8 In. ......*Illus* 685.00
Grannymede 76, White Enameled Letters, Silver, Cork Stopper, 11 1/2 In. 63.00
Grant DeLuxe Scotch, White China, Multicolored Thistle, England 12.00
Gray Thur, Erin-Go-Brach, Dew Thom & Cameron, Glasgow, Jug, Cream, 7 3/4 In. 49.00
Greybeard Heather Dew, Jug 112.00
Griffith Hyatt & Co., Baltimore, Jug, Olive, Pontil, 7 1/4 In. 1073.00
Griffith Hyatt & Co., Baltimore, Olive Green, Applied Mouth, Handle, OP, 7 1/4 In. 812.00
Griffith Hyatt & Co., Baltimore, Yellow Amber, Applied Mouth, Handle, OP, 7 1/4 In. ... 560.00
Griffith Hyatt & Co., Baltimore, Yellow Amber, OP, 7 1/4 In. 308.00
Gundlach-Bundschu Wine Co., Sonoma, Bacchus Brand, Amber, Fifth, 11 1/4 In. . . .75.00 to 100.00
H. Brikwedel & Co., Wholesale Liquor Dealers, Flask, Amber, Applied Top, 1/2 Pt. 1870.00
H. Pharazyn, Phila., Right Secured, Amber Indian Queen, 12 3/8 In. 1456.00
H.L. Nye Bourbon, Amber, Cylindrical, Fifth, 1900, 11 In. 22.00
Haig, Jug, Red, Black Print, Carltonware, England 43.00
Haig Carltonware, Jug, Brown 52.00
Hall Luhrs & Co., Sacramento, Clear, Blob Top 90.00
Hall Luhrs & Co., Sacramento, Blob Top, Fifth 75.00
Handled Chestnut, Chestnut Grove, Amber, OP, Handle, 8 In. 207.00
Handled Chestnut, Chestnut Grove, C.W., Yellow, Amber, Handle, 8 In. 1176.00
Hanley Bros. Wines & Liquors, Harrisburg, Pa., Label Under Glass, Flask, 5 1/8 In. 440.00
Happy Days Famous Old Rye, Jug, Cream, Brown Glaze Neck, 7 5/8 In. 94.00
Haynors Whisky Distillery, Troy, Ohio, 1897, Qt. 3.00
Hazel Valley Whiskey, Warren F. Witherell Co., Boston, Mass., Cylindrical, Label 12.00
Heather Euroceramics, White 92.00
Heinric Kamp, Polar Bear, South Africa 50.00
Henry Chapman & Co., Montreal, Flask, Amber, Straw Yellow, Teardrop, 5 7/8 In. 330.00
Herman Burnhardt Wines & Liquors, Buffalo, N.Y., Jug, Applied Handle, Blue Stencil .. 55.00
Hollywood, One Quart, Honey Amber, Embossed, Qt. 6.00
Honolulu, Hawaii, Amber, Tooled Top, 11 1/2 In. 120.00
Hot Tamale, Tied & Gathered Ends, Figural, Cream, Brown Letters, Nip 44.00
House Of Peers Deluxe, White China, Gold Print, England 36.00
Imperial, Dark Emerald Green, Flat, Applied Double Lip, Qt. 12.00
Imperial, Sea Green, Flat, Applied Double Lip, Qt. 12.00
It's A Long Time Between Drinks, Clock Label Under Glass, Flask, 1890, Pocket 253.00
J & R Dunster, London, Yellow Amber, Label, Square 24.00
J. Aronson, Full Measure, Seattle, Wash., Amber, Bubbles, Cylindrical, 12 In. . . . . . . .18.00 to 25.00
J. Gundlach & Co., California Wines, Brandies, San Francisco, Amber, 1880-1885 ...... 1800.00
J. Lewit Boston, Amber, Applied Top, 8 1/2 In. 165.00
J. Schneidemeyer, Swirl Design, Blue, Pink Enameled Lettering, Cork Stopper, 12 In. ... 115.00
J.A. Gilka Berlin, Ruby Red, Applied Top, 9 1/2 In. 33.00

J.F. Cutter, Extra Old Bourbon, Amber, Single Roll Collar, Flask, Fifth 1650.00
J.F. Cutter, Extra Old Bourbon, Star & Shield, Amber, Applied Top, 12 In. 303.00
J.F. Cutter, Extra Old Bourbon, Star & Shield, Light Amber, Fifth 90.00
J.F. Cutter, Trade Mark, E. Martin & Co., San Francisco, Cal., Amber, Fifth 81.00
J.H Cutter, Old Bourbon, Honey Amber, Applied Mouth, Fifth 143.00
J.H. Cutter, Old Bourbon, A.H. Hotaling & Co., Amber, Blob Top, 11 7/8 In. ....50.00 to 66.00
J.H. Cutter, Old Bourbon, A.P. Hotaling & Co., A No. 1, Amber, 11 7/8 In. 40.00
J.H. Cutter, Old Bourbon, A.P. Hotaling & Co., A No. 1, Yellow Olive 120.00
J.H. Cutter, Old Bourbon, A.P. Hotaling & Co., Amber, Blob Top, Bubbles, 11 7/8 In. 40.00
J.H. Cutter, Old Bourbon, A.P. Hotaling & Co., Amber, Whittled, Blob Top, 11 7/8 In. ... 40.00
J.H. Cutter, Old Bourbon, A.P. Hotaling & Co., Chocolate Amber, Fifth 468.00
J.H. Cutter, Old Bourbon, A.P. Hotaling, Amber, Crown & Shield, Fifth, 12 In. ...935.00 to 990.00
J.H. Cutter, Old Bourbon, C.P. Moorman, Amber, Applied Top, 11 1/2 In. 413.00
J.H. Cutter, Old Bourbon, C.P. Moorman, Amber, Tooled Top, 11 1/2 In. 132.00
J.H. Cutter, Old Bourbon, Clear, Purple Tint, Pt. 605.00
J.H. Cutter, Old Bourbon, E. Martin & Co., Green, 1874-1879, Fifth 1045.00
J.H. Cutter, Old Bourbon, Golden Amber, Crown, Barrel, Fifth 99.00
J.H. Cutter Old Bourbon, Cutter O.K. Whiskey, Amber, Glob Top, 11 7/8 In. 75.00
J.H. Cutter Old Bourbon, Cutter O.K. Whiskey, Amber, Tooled Top, 11 7/8 In. 50.00
J.H. Fisher, New Albany, Jug, Holiday Special, Corn Whisky, Stoneware, 3 In. 99.00
J.H. Hanks Sinera Aromatica Azulejo, Olive Green, Applied Top, Mexico 110.00
J.J. Hanifin & Co., Oakland, Clear, 4-Piece Mold, 12 In. 100.00
J.M. Rosey, Wholesale Liquors, Santa Rosa, Pumpkinseed, Bubbles, 1/2 Pt. 154.00
J.T. Gayen, Altoona, Cannon, Yellow Amber, 14 1/8 In. 2016.00
Jeroboam, Royal Blend, A.G. Thomson & Co., Glasgow, Jug, Cream, 7 7/8 In. 176.00
Jeroboam, Royal Blend, Glasgow, Jug, Pottery, Cream, Cobalt Letters, Stag, 8 In. 90.00
Jesse Moore & Co., Louisville, Ky., Amber, Embossed Antlers, Applied Top 143.00
Jesse Moore & Co., Louisville, Ky., Gold Amber, Embossed Antlers, 6 In. 210.00
Jesse Moore & Co., Louisville, Ky., Light Gold Amber, Fifth 132.00
Jesse Moore & Co., Louisville, Ky., Red, Amber Tone, 11 3/4 In. ....500.00 to 550.00
Jesse Moore-Hunt Co., San Francisco, Cal., Antlers, Tooled Top, 11 1/4 In. 154.00
Jesse Moore-Hunt Co., San Francisco, Cal., Red Amber, Crown Top, Fifth 303.00
John Dewar & Sons, Jug, Dark Brown, Handle, 5 3/4 x 5 In. 45.00
John Dewar & Sons, Perth, N.B., Jug, Robert Burns, Countryside Scenes, 6 In. 120.00
John Gibsons & Co., Pure Old Rye, Gold Yellow Amber, 1855-1870, 8 In. 560.00
John Hudspeth, Merchants Bar, El Reno, O.T., Flask, Strap Side, 1/2 Pt., 6 In. 330.00
Johnnie Walker Red Label, Jug, Gray, Johnnie Striding Picture, 7 1/2 In. 54.00
Jos. Melczer & Co., San Francisco, Ca., Clear, Applied Top 150.00
Joseph Fleming & Son, Pittsburg, Pa., Tall 12.00
Judges Favorite Whiskey, Chester Groves & Sons, Amber, Label, Qt. 9.00
Jug, Cream, Brown Glaze Neck, 7 5/8 In. 94.00
Jug, Here's Health To The Handyman, England, 1914-1918 .... 121.00
Julius Berendsen Groceries & Saloon, Devisadero & Fulton Sts., S.F., Amethyst 330.00
Kane O'Leary & Co., 223 Bush Street, S.F., Light Amber, 12 In. 1320.00
Kellogg's Nelson County, W & Co., Amber, Tooled Top, Fifth, 11 3/4 In. 125.00
Kellogg's Nelson County Extra Kentucky Bourbon, Amber, Fifth, 11 3/4 In. ....132.00 to 200.00
Kellogg's Nelson County Extra Kentucky Bourbon, Dark Amber, Red, 11 3/4 In. 660.00
Kennel Club Co., San Francisco., Cal., Amber, 1900, Fifth, 11 1/2 In. ....45.00 to 60.00
Kentucky, Embossed, Brown, 12 In. 115.00
Kentucky Club Sour Mash, Davies County Distilling Co., Owensboro, Ky., Amber, Qt. .. 18.00
Kentucky Club Whiskey, Clear, No Stopper, Bulbous Base, 9 In. 29.00
Kentucky Dew, Backbar, Enamel Letters 145.00
Kentucky Gentleman, Man With Walking Stick, 11 1/2 In. 9.00
Kentucky Nectar, Amber Label, Applied Top, Fifth, 11 1/4 In. ....75.00 to 80.00
Kern's, 110 La Salle, Amber, Flask, 1870-1885, Pt. 202.00
King George IV, Old Scotch, Jug, Light Brown, Cobalt Glaze Neck, 7 3/4 In. 159.00
King William IV, Amber, Cylindrical, ABM, Qt. 3.00
Label Under Glass, Soldier & Sailor Shaking Hands, Shot Glass Lid, Flask, 5 1/4 In. 560.00
Lancaster Glass Works, Lancaster, N.Y., Barrel, Olive Yellow Green, 9 1/2 In. 1175.00
Landsberg's Pure Blackberry Brandy, A. Heller & Bro., N.Y., Aqua, 11 In. 4510.00
Lebenbaum Bros., S.F., Amber, Applied Top 99.00
Lilienthal & Co., Amber, Blob Top, Cylindrical, 12 In. 80.00
Lilienthal & Co., Cincinnati, San Francisco & N.Y., Golden Amber, Double Collar 660.00

Lindsay's Liqueur, Perth Scotland, Olive Green, 3-Piece Mold, Label, Qt. 9.00
Liqueur, Bernardin, Bernard Jean & Cie Distillateurs, Dark Green, Label, Qt. 12.00
Livingston & Co., Amber, Tooled Top 60.00
Livingston's Pure Black Berry Brandy, Dark Amber, 1877-1884 . . . . 1800.00
Lock Leven, Province Of Quebec, Montreal, Jug, Cream, Brown Glaze, 6 7/8 In. 204.00
Louis Hunter, Pure Rye, Amber, Jaffe & Co., Cylindrical, 1900s, 11 In. . . . . .18.00 to 25.00
Louis Taussig, Wholesale, San Francisco, Cal., Tooled Top, 12 In. 35.00
Louis Taussig & Co., San Francisco, Cal., Light Amethyst, Fifth, 11 In. . . . . .20.00 to 30.00
Louis Taussig & Co., San Francisco, Cal., Tooled Top, Fifth, 12 In. 25.00
Lovejoy & Co., Honolulu, T.H., Amber, Tooled Top, 11 In. 275.00
M. Gruenberg, Old Judge, Light To Medium Amber, 4-Piece Mold, Blob Top, 11 3/8 In. . . 900.00
M. Rothenberg, Gamecock Whiskey, Embossed Chicken, 1/2 Pt. 165.00
Macfarlane, Medium To Dark Amber, Tooled Top, 11 1/2 In. 200.00
Manhattan Club Pure Rye, Santa Barbara, Ca., Amber, Tooled Top, 1905 . . . . 80.00
Mayaofu Dim'aolila Trademark, Sitting Cat, Green, Applied Top, 8 1/2 In. 121.00
Mayfield Hotel, Charles Mayer, Mayfield, Cal., 1/2 Pt., 6 1/2 In. 66.00
McDonald & Conn, San Francisco, Amber, Gutta-Percha Stopper With Monogram 24.00
McGinnis Pure Rye, Gilt Highlights, Bulbous, 11 1/2 In. . . . . .69.00 to 86.00
McKenna's Nelson County, Amber, Applied Top, 12 In. 715.00
Meredith's Diamond Club Pure Rye, East Liverpool, Oh., Jug, White, 4 3/4 In. 99.00
Meredith's Diamond Club Pure Rye, East Liverpool, Oh., Jug, White, 7 3/8 In. 83.00
Meredith's Diamond Club Pure Rye, Jug, White China, Blue, Green, 8 In. 145.00
Meredith's Rye, Blue Green Lettering, Barley Sprigs, Serpent Handle, 5 In. 55.00
Milk Glass, Opalescent, Enamel Flowers, Inscribed 1735, Pontil, 5 1/8 In. 605.00
Miller's Extra, E. Martin & Co., Old Bourbon, Olive, Flask, Pt. 1045.00
Miller's Extra, Medium To Light Amber, Single Ring, Blob Top, Flask, Pt. 1100.00
Miller's Extra Old Bourbon, Olive Green Variant, Flask, 7 1/2 In. 3080.00
Miller's Gamecock, Sun Colored 25.00
Miniature, see the Miniature category
Mohawk Pure Rye, Feb 11, 1868, Figural, Indian Queen, Yellow Amber, 12 In. . . . . .*Illus* 2630.00
Monk's Old Bourbon, Medicinal Purposes, Olive Yellow, 7 In. 1736.00
Monogram, Dark Amber, Squat, Tooled Mouth, 9 1/2 In. 30.00
Monogram, Pure Rye Whiskey, Rosskam, Gerstley & Co., Amber, Cylindrical, Qt. 22.00
Munro Dalwhinnie, Scotland, Dark Green, Square, Labels 6.00
Munro's King Of King's Old Whisky, Scotland, Jug, Cream, Handle, 4 5/8 x 7 In. 36.00
N. Grange Sole Agent Pacific Coast, Amber 800.00
N. Van Bergen & Co., Gold Dust Kentucky Bourbon, Aqua, Applied Top 1000.00
Nathans Brothers, Phila., Amber, Applied Top, 9 1/2 In. 110.00
Nathans Brothers, Phila., Blob Seal, Glob Top, 1863 . . . . 80.00
National League, White Enamel, Cork Stopper, 11 1/2 In. 115.00
New Louvre, W.J. Ferguson, San Jose, 1904-1912, 1/2 Pt. 66.00
Newmark Gruenberg Old Judge Bourbon, San Francisco, Amber, Yellow, 1881 . . . . 600.00
Night Cap, Milk Glass, Sleeping Man's Face, Painted, Metal Screw Cap, 4 In. 180.00
O.K., Samuel Bros., Amber, Square, Long Neck, Blob Top, 11 1/8 In. 300.00
O.K. Old Bourbon Castle, Amber, Applied Top, 12 In. . . . . .193.00 to 231.00
O.P.S. Bourbon, A.P. Hotaling Old Private Stock, Amber, Tooled Top 550.00
O.P.S. Bourbon, Medium Amber, Curved R's, Blob Top, 11 3/4 In. 2400.00
Oak Valley Distilling Co., Griffin In Triangle, Clear, Tooled Mouth, 9 1/2 In. 100.00
Oak Valley Distilling Co., Tooled Top, Qt. 70.00
Old Beaver Dam Bourbon, Detroit, Mich., Amber, Wicker, Label, Handle, 11 3/8 In. 616.00
Old Bourbon, Mike Sea, Blue Grass Exchange, Jug, Fifth 90.00
Old Bourbon, Shea, Bocqueraz & McKee, Amber, Glob Top, Cylindrical, Fifth, 12 In. . . . 650.00
Old Bushmill's, Jug, Pottery, Gray, White Print, Giants Causeway Picture, 4 1/2 In. 54.00
Old Club House, Macy & Jenkins, New York, Jug, Amber, Handles, Label, 1986 . . . . 12.00
Old Gilt Edge OK Bourbon, Wichman & Lutgen & Co., Applied Top, Fifth, Variant 231.00
Old Gilt Edge OK Bourbon, Wichman & Lutgen, San Francisco, Green, 12 In. 275.00
Old Gilt Edge OK Bourbon, Wichman & Lutgen, San Francisco, Amber, Glob Top 990.00
Old Kentucky Bourbon, N.Y., Amber, Qt. 132.00
Old Man, With Robe, Figural, Here's The Poison, Bisque, Germany, 8 7/8 In. 355.00
Old Maryland 1881 Pure Rye, G. Riesmeyer, St. Louis, Jug, White, 7 3/4 In. 303.00
Old Metropolitan, Aluminum Thimble Slide Over Cap, Cork Stopper, 12 In. 58.00
Old Plantation Distilling Co., Los Angeles, Amber, Cylindrical, Qt., 11 1/4 In. . . . . .38.00 to 45.00
Old Quaker Rye, Labels 10.00

Old Rye, Label Under Glass, Dark Amber, Shield, Gold Letters 176.00
Old Tom Parker, Kolb & Denhard, San Francisco, Red Amber, Deer Head, Fifth 468.00
Olive Amber, Pontil, Slag Blue, Early 19th Century, 9 1/4 In. 175.00
Olive Green, Applied String Lip, Pontil, 9 In. 95.00
Oud Haalem Holland, Schnapps, Olive, Square 250.00
Our Choice Old Bourbon, Hencken & Schroder, Amber, Tooled Top, Fifth ......220.00 to 358.00
P. Tiernan & Son, Baltimore, Olive Yellow, Applied Sloping Collar, 11 1/4 In. 121.00
P.J. Kelly Pure Whiskey, 138 Bleeker, N.Y., Golden Amber, Tooled Lip, 1/2 Pt. 66.00
Palm Cafe, Talmadge & Loftus, Dunsmuir, Cal., Square, Tooled Mouth, 11 In. 300.00
Park & Tilford, New York, Golden Amber, Cylindrical, Label, Double Collar, 11 3/8 In. .. 78.00
Parker Rye, Jug, Stoneware, Gray Salt Glaze, Cobalt Decoration, Stopper, 8 1/4 In. 176.00
Parole Pure Rye, Horse, Amber, Blob Top, Dug, 9 3/4 In. 320.00
Pattern Molded Handle, Amber, Applied Mouth, 8 1/4 In. 495.00
Paul Jones Pure Rye, Amber, Blob Seal, 10 In. 20.00
Pennsylvania Club Pure Rye, Jug, White, Maroon Transfer, 7 3/4 In. ....151.00 to 275.00
Pepper Distillery, Hand Made Sour Mash, Amber, Tooled Top, 11 3/4 In. ....160.00 to 198.00
Phoenix, Naber, Alfs & Brune, Amber, Bird Facing Right, 11 3/4 In. 125.00
Phoenix Bourbon, Naber, Alfs & Brune, S.F., Bird Facing Left, Amber, 11 3/4 In. .. 176.00 to 185.00
Phoenix Bourbon, Naber, Alfs & Brune, S.F., Bird Facing Right, Gold Amber, 11 3/4 In. . 176.00
Phoenix Old Bourbon, Naber, Alfs & Brune, S.F., Bird Facing Left, Amber, 11 3/4 In. ... 935.00
Phoenix Old Bourbon, Naber, Alfs & Brune, S.F., Bird Facing Left, Amber, Flask, Pt. ... 275.00
Phoenix Old Bourbon, Naber, Alfs & Brune, S.F., Bird, Gold Amber, Fifth 770.00
Phoenix Old Bourbon, Naber, Alfs & Brune, S.F., Bird, Olive Yellow, 1/2 Pt. 413.00
Pig, Corn Cob In Mouth, c.1890, 6 1/4 In. 522.00
Pioneer Bourbon, Braunschweiger & Co., San Francisco, Amethyst, Fifth ....110.00 to 140.00
Pipe Major Scotch Whisky, Jug, Blue Top, Handle, 5 In. 97.00
Pointer Maryland Rye, Baltimore, Md., Jug, Cream, Brown Glaze, Handle, 1915, 8 In. .. 89.00
Pride Of Kentucky, Old Bourbon, Livingston, Ca., Amber, Tooled Top, Fifth, 11 5/8 In. .. 660.00
Pure Cognac, Amber, Applied Double Collar, Handle, Seal, Pontil, 8 7/8 In. 853.00
Pure Malt Bourbon Co., Kentucky, Amber, Applied Mouth, Handle, 9 In. 308.00
Queens Club Scotch, Jug, James Munro & Son 237.00
R. Gerret & Sons Leven, Sash Shape, Dark Green, Large 55.00
R.B. Cutter, Louisville, Ky., Jug, Cherry Puce, Applied Handle, Pontil, 8 1/2 In. 495.00
R.B. Cutter, Louisville, Ky., Jug, Gold Amber, Applied Mouth, Handle, Pontil, 8 5/8 In. .. 440.00
R.B. Cutter, Louisville, Ky., Jug, Pear Shape, Gold Amber, Blob Top, Pontil, 8 3/4 In. ... 220.00
R.B. Cutter, Louisville, Ky., Jug, Root Beer Amber, Handle, Pontil, 8 1/2 In. 358.00
R.B. Cutter, Louisville, Ky., Jug, Yellow, Amber Tint, Applied Handle, 8 5/8 In. 798.00
R.B. Cutter, Louisville, Ky., Yellow Amber, Applied Lip, Handle, 8 1/2 In. 420.00
R.B. Cutter Pure Bourbon, Burgundy, Applied Mouth, Handle, 8 In. 1850.00
Rex Distilling, Boston, 1900, Pt. 4.00
Rock & Rye, Label Under Glass, Late 19th Century, 9 1/2 In. 175.00
Rosenberg & Jackson, N.Y., Cylindrical, Orange Amber, 12 In. 69.00
Rosskam Gerstley & Co., Old Saratoga, Philadelphia, Aqua, Flat, Cylindrical, Qt. 15.00
Roth & Co., San Francisco, Amber, Bubbles, Monogram, 11 3/4 In. 24.00
Roth & Co., San Francisco, Emblem, Tooled Top, Fifth 66.00
Roth & Co., San Francisco, Red Amber, Monogram, Applied Mouth, 12 In. .... *Illus* 202.00
Rothenberg Co., Old Judge Kentucky Bourbon, Amber, 11 1/4 In. ....230.00 to 250.00
Rum, Black Glass, Olive Green, Pontil, Late 18th Century, 9 1/4 In. 165.00
Rum, Deep Olive Green, Applied Lip, Pontil, Late 18th Century, 9 In. 95.00
S.H.M. Superior Old Bourbon Trademark, Amber, Fleur-De-Lis, Fifth 2060.00
Samuel Bros. & Co., O Monogram, Amber, Glob Top, Square, Fifth, 11 1/8 In. 300.00
Sanderson's Liqueur Special Scotch, Jug, Red Brown Neck, Handle 36.00
Sandy Macdonald Scotch, Emerald Green, Label, Cylindrical, Qt. 9.00
Saxlehners Hunyadi Janos Bitterquelle, Olive Green, 9 1/4 In. 10.00
Schiedam, Schnapps, Bright Olive Green 83.00
Scotch, Vieux Paris, Floral Bouquets, Gilt Palmettes, 11 In., Pair 228.00
Siebe Bros. & Plagemann, Rosedale Ok Whiskey, Dark Amber, 1882-1885 .... 1500.00
Simmond's Nabob, Red Amber, 4-Piece Mold, Variant, 10 3/4 In. 800.00
Sociedad Vinicoi, Hamburg, Trade Mark, Rooster On Bicycle, Amber, Oval, 8 3/8 In. 364.00
Special Froehlich & Sons, Pinched Sides, Gilt Highlights, Clear, Stopper, 9 1/2 In. 29.00
Spring Lake Handmade Sour Mash Bourbon, Cincinnati, O., Jug, White China, 7 In. ... 112.00
Spruance Stanley & Co., Horseshoe, Amber, Tooled Top, 11 3/4 In. 45.00
Spruance Stanley & Co., S.F., Cal., Horseshoe, Amber, Star Base, Tooled Top, Fifth 38.00

Whiskey, Mohawk Pure
Rye, Feb 11, 1868,
Figural, Indian Queen,
Yellow Amber, 12 In.

Whiskey, Roth & Co.,
San Francisco, Red
Amber, Monogram,
Applied Mouth, 12 In.

Whiskey, Wilmerding &
Co., S.F., Cal., United
We Stand, Red Shaded
To Yellow Amber, 12 In.

Spruance Stanley & Co., S.F., Cal., Horseshoe, Gold Amber, Star Base, Tooled Top	110.00
Spruance Stanley & Co., San Francisco, Cal., Horseshoe & Sunrays, Amber	320.00
Spruance Stanley & Co., San Francisco, Cal., Horseshoe, Amber, Applied Top	330.00
Spruance Stanley & Co., San Francisco, Cal., Horseshoe, Red Amber, Fifth	275.00
Spruance Stanley & Co., San Francisco, Cal., Horseshoe, Tooled Top	176.00
St. George Vineyard, San Francisco, Cal., Yellow Amber, 11 1/2 In. . . . . .100.00 to 125.00
Standard Old Bourbon, Weil Bros., Light To Medium Amber, Glob Top, 12 In. . . .468.00 to 900.00
Standard Perf'w'ks, N.Y., Light Yellow Amber, Tooled Top, 8 3/4 In.	22.00
Star, New York, W.B. Crowell Jr., Amber, Vertical Ribs, 8 In.	2128.00
Star Wine Co., Los Angeles, Calif., Amber, Megaphone Shape, Tooled Top, 1/2 Gal.	450.00
Stoddard Patent, Amber	77.00
Strawberry Puce, Handle, Sloping Collar, Pontil, 1855-1870, 6 1/4 In.	198.00
Sunflower, Pennsylvania Rye, Spruance Stanley & Co., Amber, Brandy Top, 10 In. . .40.00 to 50.00
Superior Old Rye, Wertz, Philadelphia, Amber, Glob Top	90.00
Tabard Inn, Aluminum Cap Cork, White Enamel Letters, 11 3/4 In.	173.00
Teachers, Jug, Pottery, White, Black Print, 3 1/4 In.	42.00
Teakettle Old Bourbon, Bocqueraz & McKee Agents, Amber, 12 In. . . . . .700.00 to 880.00
Teakettle Old Bourbon, Bocqueraz & McKee Agents, Yellow Green, Blob Top, 12 In. . . .	3000.00
That's The Stuff, Barrel, Gold Yellow, Amber, Applied Mouth, 9 7/8 In.	2800.00
Thistle Dew, Light Amber, 10 5/8 In.	798.00
Thistle Dew, Medium Amber, 4-Piece Mold, Blob Top, 10 5/8 In.	200.00
Tiffany Club, Embossed Animal Over Monogram, Fluted Neck & Base, 12 In.	75.00
Treadwell, San Francisco, Amber, Tooled Top, Western, Squat, Fifth	30.00
Try The Famous Box Whiskey, Jug, Emerald Green, White Lettering, 1950, 6 1/4 In.	156.00
Turkey, Figural, Amber, 4 1/2 In.	77.00
Turner Brothers, New York, Barrel, Olive Yellow Green, 9 7/8 In.	4480.00
Turner Brothers, New York, Barrel, Olive Yellow, Disc Mouth, 9 In.	2352.00
Turtle, Figural, Pewter Top, Ground Lip, Nip	55.00
Udolpho Wolfe's Aromatic Schnapps, Amber, 8 In.	44.00
Udolpho Wolfe's Aromatic Schnapps, Apricot Puce, Applied Top, 8 In.	180.00
Udolpho Wolfe's Aromatic Schnapps, Citron, 8 In. . . . . .44.00 to 66.00
Udolpho Wolfe's Aromatic Schnapps, Gold	121.00
Udolpho Wolfe's Aromatic Schnapps, Schiedam, Amber, Applied Top	22.00
Udolpho Wolfe's Aromatic Schnapps, Schiedam, Apricot Puce, Rectangular, 8 1/4 In. . . .	143.00
Udolpho Wolfe's Aromatic Schnapps, Schiedam, Dark Amber, Graphite Pontil	110.00
Udolpho Wolfe's Aromatic Schnapps, Schiedam, Green Amber, Applied Top	88.00
Udolpho Wolfe's Aromatic Schnapps, Schiedam, Light Green, Applied Top	44.00
Udolpho Wolfe's Aromatic Schnapps, Schiedam, Yellow	385.00
Udolpho Wolfe's Aromatic Schnapps, Schiedam, Yellow, Applied Top	165.00
Udolpho Wolfe's Aromatic Schnapps, Schiedam, Yellow Green, Applied Top, 9 3/4 In. . .	66.00
Udolpho Wolfe's Schiedam Aromatic Schnapps, Gold Amber, 8 In.	45.00
Udolpho Wolfe's Schiedam Aromatic Schnapps, Olive Green, 8 In.	179.00
Udolpho Wolfe's Schiedam Aromatic Schnapps, Olive Green, Label, 8 1/8 In.	180.00
Udolpho Wolfe's Schiedam Aromatic Schnapps, Yellow Green, Bubbles, IP, 8 In.	140.00
United We Stand, Charles Kohn & Co., Portland, Or., Dark Amber, 1884-1888	1400.00

United We Stand, Old Bourbon Whiskey, S.F., Ca., Red Amber, 1871-1883, 12 In. 3100.00
Van Der Zee & Co., Aromatic Schnapps, Schiedam, Medium Olive Green, 9 In. 112.00
Vivard & Sheehan, Yellow Green, Applied Mouth, 9 7/8 In. 2420.00
Voldner's Aromatic Schnapps, Schiedam, Lime Green, Applied Top 198.00
Voldner's Aromatic Schnapps, Schiedam, Medium Olive Lime, Applied Top 99.00
Voldner's Aromatic Schnapps, Schiedam, Olive Amber, Pontil, 9 7/8 In. 165.00
Voldner's Aromatic Schnapps, Schiedam, Olive, Applied Top 77.00
Vonthofen's Aromatic Schiedam Schnapps, Blue-Green, Graphite Pontil, Pt., 8 In. 210.00
Vonthofen's Aromatic Schiedam Schnapps, Green, IP, 8 1/8 In. 185.00
W & A Gilbey, Silver Stream Schnapps, SCA, Square, BIMAL, 9 In. 35.00
W. McCully & Co., Pittsburgh, Olive Yellow Green, Cylindrical, 9 3/4 In. 67.00
W.A. Gaines & Co's, Old Crow, Flask, Screw Lid, Cleaned, 1/2 Pt. ....143.00 to 231.00
W.B. Quigley Col, Clay St., Oakland, Cal., Light Amethyst, Pocket Flask, 6 1/4 In. 66.00
W.C. Peacock, Honolulu, Amber, Tooled Top, Fifth, 11 In. 140.00
W.C. Peacock, Light Amber, Tooled Top 150.00
W.C. Peacock & Co., Honolulu, Hi., Dark Amber, Applied Top, 1880 .... 300.00
W.C. Peacock & Co., Honolulu, Wine & Liquor Merchants, Red Amber, 11 In. 415.00
W.H. Johnson & Co., Boston, Bear Emblem, Pewter Cover, Ground Lip, Flask, 1851 ..... 15.00
W.J. Van Schuyver, Dark Red Amber, Inside Threads 40.00
W.J. Van Schuyver & Co., Portland, Red Amber, Bubbles, Fifth, 11 1/2 In. 30.00
W.N. Walton's, Pat. Sept. 12, 1862, Cognac, Chocolate Amber, 12 1/8 In. 143.00
W.N. Walton's, Pat. Sept. 23, 1862, Cobalt Blue, Backbar, 12 1/8 In. 121.00
West India Bay Rum, Imported, Tin Screw Cap, North Shore Dist., 9 In. 12.00
Wharton's, 1850, Chestnut Grove, Amber, Teardrop, Flask, 5 3/8 In. 205.00
Wharton's, 1850, Chestnut Grove, Teardrop, Amber, Bubbles, Flask, 5 1/4 In. 200.00
Wharton's, 1850, Chestnut Grove, Whitney Glass Works, Amber, 10 In. 935.00
Wharton's, Chestnut Grove, Amber, Applied Handle, Tooled Spout, Flask, 10 In. 550.00
Wharton's, Chestnut Grove, Yellow Amber, Applied Handle, Tooled Spout, Flask, 10 In. . 935.00
White Horse, Jug, Pottery, Blue Crocodile Skin, White Print, 5 3/4 In. 64.00
White Horse Scotch, Jug, Pottery, Blue, White Print, Kirkham Pottery, 6 In. 46.00
White Oak Rye, Cincinnati, O., Petal Pattern, Label, Tooled Lip, Qt. 6.00
Whitney Glass Works, Jug, Golden Amber, Tooled Rim, Spout, 10 1/8 In. 235.00
Wichman Lutgen, San Francisco, Ca., Gold Amber, Tombstone, Tooled Lip 70.00
Wilmerding & Co., S.F., Cal., United We Stand, Red To Yellow Amber, 12 In. ......*Illus* 3472.00
Wilson & Carlson, Bakersfield-Kern, Monogram, Pt. 154.00
Wise's Old Irish, Jug, Clover Leaf, Cream, Brown Glaze, Handle, 7 1/2 In. 123.00
Wm. H. Spears & Co., S.F., Light Golden Amber, Slug Plate, Walking Bears, Fifth 1430.00
Wm. Provis Fine Liquors, Grass Valley, Red Amber, Tooled Top, 10 7/8 In. 440.00
Wolf, Wreden & Co., San Francisco, Ca., Amber ....264.00 to 275.00
Wolfe's Aromatic Schiedam Schnapps, Gold Honey Amber, Square, Paper Wrap 33.00
Wolter's Bros. & Co., San Francisco, Amber, 1886-1895 .... 660.00
Wolter's Bros. & Co., San Francisco, Amber, Applied Top, 11 7/8 In. 220.00
Wolter's Bros. & Co., San Francisco, Red Amber 550.00
Woodcock, Eagle Distillery, T E O'Keefe, 3-Piece Mold, Label, Tooled Lip, Qt. 12.00
Wreden, Kohlmoos Co. Sole Agents, San Francisco, Amber, 11 7/8 In. 99.00
Xlint, Pittsburg, Pa., Jug, Cream, 2 Ear Handles, 3 3/4 x 10 1/2 In. 33.00
Young's Y.P.M., Gold Highlights, Glass Stopper, 8 1/2 In. 29.00

————————————— **WILD TURKEY** —————————————

Wild Turkey is a brand of bourbon made by Austin Nichols Distillery. The company says the bourbon was originally made as a gift for some hunting companions and so was named for their favorite gamebird. A crystal bottle with an etched flying turkey design was made in 1951. The company made turkey-shaped ceramic bottles from 1971 to 1989. The first bottle, filled with bourbon, sold for $20. In 1981 the company added miniature bottles. For a short time during the 1980s, the company marketed a line of *go-withs* such as plates and plaques. After 1989, Wild Turkey sold two limited-edition bottles: a Rare Breed Whiskey bottle in a teardrop shape, which is still made, and a Kentucky Legend decanter shaped like a violin, which is no longer in production. Since mid-1994, under the Rare Breed label, Austin Nichols & Co. Distillery has issued a Kentucky Spirit, single barrel bourbon in a distinctive bottle with a pewter-style top, available year-round in a gift box. Wild Turkey figural decanters are no longer being made.

Crystal Anniversary, Purple Ribbon, Foil Label, 1955 , Box 1550.00
Decanter, Baccarat, Crystal, 1979 .... 226.00

Wild Turkey, Series 1,   Wild Turkey, Series 1,   Wild Turkey, Series 3,   Wild Turkey, Series 4,
No. 4, With Poult,   No. 5, With Flags,   No. 9, With Bear   No. 1, Habitat,
1974   1975   Cubs, 1985   Female, 1988

Decanter, Series 1, No. 2, Perched On Log, 1972	45.00
Decanter, Wedgwood, 1 Liter	215.00
Series 1, No. 1, Standing, Male, 1971	180.00
Series 1, No. 2, On Log, Female, 1972	125.00
Series 1, No. 2, On Log, Female, 1981, Miniature	125.00
Series 1, No. 3, On Wing, 1973	60.00
Series 1, No. 3, On Wing, 1982, Miniature	60.00
Series 1, No. 4, With Poult, 1974	*Illus* 45.00
Series 1, No. 4, With Poult, 1982, Miniature	45.00
Series 1, No. 5, With Flags, 1975	*Illus* 32.00
Series 1, No. 5, With Flags, 1983, Miniature	30.00
Series 1, No. 6, Striding, 1976	24.00
Series 1, No. 6, Striding, 1983, Miniature	24.00
Series 1, No. 7, Taking Off, 1977	32.00
Series 1, No. 7, Taking Off, 1983, Miniature	25.00
Series 1, No. 8, Strutting, 1978	40.00
Series 1, No. 8, Strutting, 1983, Miniature	40.00
Series 2, No. 1, Lore, 1979	30.00
Series 2, No. 2, Lore, 1980	32.00 to 40.00
Series 2, No. 3, Lore, 1981	40.00
Series 2, No. 4, Lore, 1982	48.00
Series 3, No. 1, In Flight, 1983	92.00 to 100.00
Series 3, No. 1, In Flight, 1984, Miniature	25.00
Series 3, No. 2, With Bobcat, 1983	100.00 to 140.00
Series 3, No. 2, With Bobcat, 1985, Miniature	25.00
Series 3, No. 3, Turkeys Fighting, 1983	140.00
Series 3, No. 3, Turkeys Fighting, 1983, Miniature	25.00
Series 3, No. 4, With Eagle, 1984	90.00
Series 3, No. 4, With Eagle, 1984, Miniature	35.00
Series 3, No. 5, With Raccoon, 1984	85.00 to 100.00
Series 3, No. 5, With Raccoon, 1984, Miniature	25.00
Series 3, No. 6, With Poult, 1984	70.00 to 80.00
Series 3, No. 6, With Poult, 1984, Miniature	20.00
Series 3, No. 7, With Fox, 1984, Miniature	25.00
Series 3, No. 7, With Fox, 1985	85.00 to 95.00
Series 3, No. 8, With Owl, 1985	80.00 to 90.00
Series 3, No. 8, With Owl, 1985, Miniature	25.00
Series 3, No. 9, With Bear Cubs, 1985	*Illus* 90.00
Series 3, No. 9, With Bear Cubs, 1985, Miniature	30.00
Series 3, No. 10, With Coyote, 1986	90.00
Series 3, No. 10, With Coyote, 1986, Miniature	25.00
Series 3, No. 11, With Falcon, 1986	90.00

Series 3, No. 11, With Falcon, 1986, Miniature 35.00
Series 3, No. 12, With Skunk, 1986 . . . . 110.00 to 125.00
Series 3, No. 12, With Skunk, 1986, Miniature 35.00
Series 4, No. 1, Habitat, Female, 1988 . . . . *Illus* 110.00
Series 4, No. 1, Habitat, Female, 1988, Miniature 50.00
Series 4, No. 2, Habitat, 1989 . . . . 115.00 to 125.00
Series 4, No. 2, Habitat, 1989, Miniature 50.00

WINE

Wine has been bottled since the days of the ancient Greeks. Wine bottles have been made in a variety of sizes and shapes. Seal bottles were used from the second century and are listed in their own section in this book. Most wines found today are in the standard shapes that have been used for the past 125 years. The Bordeaux shape has square shoulders and straight sides while the Burgundy shape is broader with sloping shoulders. The German or Rhine wine flute bottle is tall and thin. Other wines, such as champagne, are bottled in slightly different bottles.

8-Sided, Opalescent Olive Green, Applied String Lip, Pontil, England, c.1750, 9 1/4 In. . . 2860.00
Black Glass, String Rim, Pontil, England, 24 In. 639.00
Blue, Bubbles, Spout Top, Curved Base, 9 1/2 In. 75.00
Dutch, Blue Green, Horse Hoof Shape, Applied Collar, Pontil, 6 1/2 In. 170.00
Dutch, Light To Medium Olive, Applied String Top, OP, 11 In. 176.00
Dutch, Olive Green, Applied Collar, Pontil, 7 1/2 In. 88.00
Dutch, Olive Yellow, Applied Collar, Pontil, 18th Century, 7 1/2 In. 130.00
Dutch Onion, Black, Applied String Collar, OP, 7 3/4 In. 165.00
Dutch Onion, Dark Olive Green, Applied Ring, Pontil 99.00
Dutch Onion, Emerald Green, Olive Tone, String Rim, Pontil, 1750, 7 In. 77.00
Dutch Onion, Olive, String Top, Pontil, 6 In. 176.00
Golden Gate Wine Co., Baltimore, Md., Amber, Spiral Fluting, Ring Lip, 1 1/2 In. 560.00
H.J. Woolacott Pure Wines, Los Angeles, Ca., Amber, 11 3/4 In. 176.00
Helen Carmichael, 1875, Bulbous, Olive Green, Stippled, Bird, Ship, Heart, 7 In. 420.00
John Routledge Wine & Spirit Merchant, Waterloo Road Blyth, 1900, 8 In. 18.00
Jug, Virginia Seal Wild Cherry Wine Co., Winchester, Va., Pottery, Applied Ears, 2 Gal. . . 400.00
London, White Dinner, Ship Shape, Woven Basket, Screw Cap, 1965, 11 1/2 In. . . . . 14.00 to 19.00
Longworth, Chocolate, Embossed, Applied Top, Improved Pontil 2600.00
Mallet, Light To Medium Olive Yellow, String Rim, 1760, Pontil, 7 5/8 In. 242.00
Medium Honey Amber, Pontil, Footed, 6 x 2 3/8 In. 151.51
Miniature, see the Miniature category
Mount Diablo Wine Co., San Francisco & Clayton, Cal., Amber, 10 1/4 In. 330.00
Olive Green, Applied String Top, OP, 11 In. 176.00
Olive Green, Shaft & Globe Shape, Applied Disk Lip, Pontil, England, c.1660, 8 3/4 In. . . 2970.00
Poire Williams, Amber, Seal Label, 19 x 13 In. 225.00
Port, Embossed, Brown, Backbar, 12 In. 178.00
Port, Green, Metal Top, Cork Stopper, Backbar, 13 In. 144.00
S Rosenthall & Co., Wines & Liquors, Canal St., N.Y., Medium Gold Amber 12.00
Salzmann & Singelman, Brooklyn, N.Y., Port Wine, Jug, 2-Tone Tan, 7 In. 44.00
Speers Samburg, Port Wine, New York, Vintage 1860, Sea Green, Cylindrical, Qt. 24.00

ZANESVILLE

The Zanesville Manufacturing Company started making glass in Zanesville, Ohio, in 1815. This glassworks closed in 1838 but reopened from 1842 to 1851. The company made many types of blown and mold blown pieces. At least one other glassworks operated in Zanesville from 1816 to the 1840s. The products of all the Zanesville factories are sometimes identified as *Midwestern* glass and are grouped with pieces made in Mantua, Kent, Ravenna, and other Ohio towns. The blown glass pieces include diamond patterned and ribbed pieces in clear, blue, amethyst, aquamarine, and amber colored glass. Collectors prize the Zanesville swirl pieces and identify them as *right* or *left* swirl.

10 Diamonds, Yellow Green, Pocket, 1815-1835, 1/2 Pt., 5 1/2 In. 5940.00
12 Swirled Ribs, Aqua, Globular, 7 3/4 In. 5940.00
16 Swirled Ribs, Green Aqua, Globular, Applied Lip, Pontil, 8 In. 235.00
24 Broken Swirl Ribs, Globular, Aqua, 7 3/4 In. 5940.00
24 Melon Ribs, Globular, Aqua, 7 5/8 In. 275.00
24 Swirled Ribs, Amber, Globular, 8 1/2 In. 495.00

24 Swirled Ribs, Amber, Globular, OP 715.00
24 Vertical Ribs, Amber, Globular, Rolled Lip, 1820-1830, 7 7/8 In. 1815.00
24 Vertical Ribs, Amber, Globular, Rolled Lip, Pontil, 8 In. 2408.00
24 Swirled Ribs, Blue Aqua, Rolled Lip, Pontil, 8 5/8 In. 123.00
24 Swirled Ribs, Citron, 7 1/2 In. 4510.00
24 Swirled Ribs, Globular, Amber, 8 In. 770.00
24 Swirled Ribs, Globular, Aqua, 7 1/2 In. 330.00
24 Swirled Ribs, Globular, Citron, 7 1/2 In. 4510.00
24 Swirled Ribs, Globular, Dark Amber, 8 In. 770.00
24 Swirled Ribs, Globular, Gold Amber, Blown, 7 1/2 In. 2200.00
24 Swirled Ribs, Gold Amber, Olive Tint, Globular, Rolled Lip, 7 5/8 In. 1925.00
24 Swirled Ribs, Orange Amber, Globular, Rolled Lip, 7 3/4 In. 660.00
24 Swirled Ribs, Red Amber, Globular, Rolled Lip, 7 1/8 In. 495.00
24 Vertical Ribs, Globular, Dark Amber, 5 7/8 In. 798.00
Clear, Globular, 6 1/2 In. 100.00
Flask, Chestnut, 10 Diamonds, Amber, 5 1/4 In. 3960.00
Globular, Aqua, 8 1/2 In. 165.00
Globular, Dark Amber, 3 1/8 In. 1320.00
Globular, Light Aqua, 3 1/8 In. 302.50
Globular, Olive Green, 7 3/8 In. 385.00
Globular, Olive Green, 8 1/2 In. 825.00
Globular, Olive Green, Applied Lip, 7 3/8 In. 385.00

─── GO-WITHS ───

There are many items that interest the bottle collector even though they are not bottles: all types of advertising that picture bottles or endorse bottled products like whiskey or beer, many small items like bottle openers or bottle caps, and related products by well-known companies like trays and plaques. Collectors call all of these *go-withs*. A variety of the items are listed here. Many others can be found under company names in other price lists such as *Kovels' Antiques & Collectibles Price List*. Clubs and publications that will help collectors are listed in the bibliography and club list in this book.

Bank, Pepsi-Cola, Ford Model T, Cast Metal, Box, 1912 .... 25.00
Bank Check, Coca-Cola, Art Deco Design, 1940s 2.00
Banner, A & W Root Beer, Dennis The Menace, Canvas, 36 1/2 x 91 1/2 In. 220.00
Banner, Coca-Cola, Edgar Bergen & Charlie McCarthy, Canvas, 42 x 60 In., 1950s 1210.00
Banner, Drink Moxie, Man On Horse, Horseless Carriage, Cloth, 27 x 36 In. 1850.00
Barometer, Ushers Whiskies, Round, 8-Sided Wood Frame, England 170.00
Beer Pull, Brut Super Premium 13.00
Beer Pull, Cee Bee, 1960s 550.00
Beer Pull, Colorado Imperial, 1960s 10.00
Beer Pull, Great Lakes Beer, Lacrosse Version, 1970s 20.00
Beer Pull, Lime Lager, 12 Oz. 11.00
Blotter, Coca-Cola, 1953, 4 x 8 In. 6.60
Blotter, Coca-Cola, 58 Million Bottles Produced A Day, 1957, 4 x 8 In. 6.60
Blotter, Coca-Cola, Drink Coca-Cola, I Think It's Swell, Lithograph, 1942 .... 18.00
Blotter, Coca-Cola, Elf Digging Bottle From Snowbank, 1952, 3 1/2 x 7 1/2 In. 15.00
Blotter, Silver Top, Pale Export Beer, 1910s 26.00
Booklet, Hood Dairy, Magic Booklet 14.00
Bookmark, Coca-Cola, Fishtail Logo, Plastic, In Package, 1950s, 3 In. 6.50
Bookmark, Coca-Cola, Opera Singer Hilda Clark, c.1904, 6 1/4 In. 522.00
Bottle Caddy, H.P. Hood & Sons 35.00
Bottle Cap, 7-Up, Service Award, 9/16 In. 75.00
Bottle Cap, Coca-Cola, 1950s 2.00
Bottle Cap, Coca-Cola, Cork, 1920s 7.00
Bottle Cap, Hires Root Beer, Orange, White Lettering 8.00
Bottle Opener, Alligator, Black Boy, Cast Iron, 2 3/4 In. 145.00
Bottle Opener, Black Face, Cast Iron, 1940s, 4 1/4 x 3 1/2 In. ....125.00 to 155.00
Bottle Opener, Boot, Corkscrew Inside, Sterling Silver, 4 In. 175.00
Bottle Opener, Calvert Gin, Bottle Shape 10.50
Bottle Opener, Clown's Head, Cast Iron, 4 1/4 x 3 3/4 In. 97.00
Bottle Opener, Cowboy With Guitar, Cast Iron, 4 3/4 In. 95.00
Bottle Opener, Dog, Black, Metal, Scott Products, 4 x 5 In. 85.00
Bottle Opener, Elephant, Gray, Cast Iron, 3 1/2 In. 58.00

Bottle Opener, Fish, Largemouth Bass, Metal, Scott Products, 6 1/4 x 2 1/4 In. 110.00
Bottle Opener, Fisherman, Cast Iron, Painted, 4 1/4 In. .... *Illus* 75.00
Bottle Opener, Four Eyes Man, Cast Iron, 1940s, 3 3/4 In. ....65.00 to 125.00
Bottle Opener, Horse Head, Aluminum, Brass Tone 45.00
Bottle Opener, Horse Head, Black Mane, White Streak On Face, Rubal, 1960s, 4 1/2 In. . 110.00
Bottle Opener, Horse, Hindquarters, Cast Iron, 5 1/4 In. 47.00
Bottle Opener, Ice Pick, Coca-Cola, Wooden Handle, Metal Pick, 10 1/2 In. 25.00
Bottle Opener, Lady's Leg, Big Boys Saloon, Royalton, Ill., Skate Key, Steel, 3 In. 85.00
Bottle Opener, Lobster, Red & Black, Cast Iron, 3 1/2 In. 36.00
Bottle Opener, Mallard Duck, Metal, 2 1/4 x 5 1/2 In. 75.00
Bottle Opener, Paddy The Pledgemaster, Blue Shirt, Phi Kappa Psi On Paddle, 4 In. 225.00
Bottle Opener, Parrot, On Stand, Cast Iron, 5 1/4 In. 95.00
Bottle Opener, Pelican, On Ashtray, Orange Beak & Feet, Cast Iron, 3 1/4 In. 75.00
Bottle Opener, Pelican, On Ashtray, Orange Beak & Feet, Cast Iron, 4 3/4 In. 175.00
Bottle Opener, Pepsi-Cola, Church Key 6.00
Bottle Opener, Pepsi-Cola, Starr X, 2 3/4 x 23 1/2 In. 22.00
Bottle Opener, Pretzel, Brown, White Dots, Cast Iron, 3 1/2 In. 88.00
Bottle Opener, Ram's Head, Chromium Alloy, 4 1/4 In. 95.00
Bottle Opener, Rooster, Orange, Yellow, Brown & Black, Cast Iron, 3 1/4 In. 75.00
Bottle Opener, Signpost Drunk, Black Tuxedo, Plymouth, Mass. On Post, 4 1/4 In. 20.00
Bottle Opener, Squirrel, Gray & White, Cast Iron, 3 In. 125.00
Bowl, Coca-Cola, Pretzel, Aluminum, 3 Coke Bottle Legs, 1930s 100.00
Box, Clicquot Club Beverages, Eskimo, Wooden, Holds 48 Bottles, 20 x 13 In. 45.00
Box, Dovetail, Horlick's 70.00
Box, Government Standard Ink, Dovetail 50.00
Box, Home Beverage Co., Leominster, Mass., Beer, Wood, 1930s, Holds 12 Quarts 8.00
Box, Turtle Ink & Moore's Excelsior, Wood, Stenciled, 8 x 10 In. 70.00
Brace, Screen Door, Pepsi-Cola, 1940s 88.00
Bridge Tally, Compliments Of Coca-Cola Bottling Company, La Grange, Georgia 3.00
Bucket, Drink Coca-Cola In Bottles, Steel, 12 In. 154.00
Calendar, Coca-Cola, 1915, Elaine, With Hat & Parasol, Frame, 12 1/2 x 31 1/2 In. 1100.00
Calendar, Coca-Cola, 1917, Constance, Sitting At Table, Frame, 11 1/2 x 30 1/2 In. 1650.00
Calendar, Coca-Cola, 1919, Knitting Girl, Holding Bottle Of Coke, 27 1/2 x 13 In. 635.00
Calendar, Coca-Cola, 1924, Flapper Girl, Holding Bottle, 12 x 24 In. 201.00
Calendar, Coca-Cola, 1925, Girl At Party, White Fur Stole, Frame, History Page 3520.00
Calendar, Coca-Cola, 1933, Village Blacksmith, Cover Page, Metal Strip 715.00
Calendar, Coca-Cola, 1935, Out Fishin', Boy & His Dog, Norman Rockwell, 12 x 25 In. . 172.00
Calendar, Coca-Cola, 1937, Boy Walking, Fishing Pole, Dog, N.C. Wyeth, Frame, 25 In. . 550.00
Calendar, Coca-Cola, 1947, Girl Holding Skis, Frame, 8 In. 190.00
Calendar, Coca-Cola, 1950, Girl With Serving Tray & 4 Bottles 110.00
Calendar, Dr Pepper, 1951 .... 82.00
Calendar, Hood's Sarsaparilla, Frame, 1894 .... 143.00
Calendar, Pepsi-Cola, 1911, Girl, I Love Its Flavor, Frame, Under Glass, 10 x 20 In. 3520.00
Calendar, Squirt, 1949 .... 66.00
Carrier, 7-Up, Cardboard, 6 Bottles, 1930-1940 .... 88.00
Carrier, 12-Pack, Marked Property Of Coca-Cola, Vicksburg, 11 1/2 x 9 x 3 In. 300.00
Carrier, Coca-Cola, 4-Pack, New Coke Classic Crowns 55.00
Carrier, Coca-Cola, 6-Pack, Light Aqua, Embossed, 8 1/4 x 8 x 5 1/2 In. 52.00
Carrier, Coca-Cola, Aluminum, 12 Pack, 1950s 125.00
Carrier, Pepsi-Cola, 6-Bottle, Aluminum 62.00
Carrier, Pepsi-Cola, 6-Bottle, Red Lettering, 1940, 11 x 6 x 9 In. 155.00
Carrier, Pepsi-Cola, Cardboard, 12-Bottle, 1940s 22.00
Carton, Hoppy Milk, 1/2 Gal. 12.00
Carton, Hoppy Milk, Qt. 7.00
Carton, Pepsi-Cola, Your Personal Carton For Pepsi-Cola, Wood, 9 1/4 x 8 1/2 In. 175.00
Case, Pepsi-Cola, Wood, Varnished, 1950s 40.00
Case, Toronto Stone Ginger Beer Co., Elgin 2968, Wood, 24-Bottle, Canada 20.00
Catalog, Duraglas Milk Bottle, 1952 .... 380.00
Chalkboard, Coca-Cola, Embossed, Tin, 27 1/4 x 19 1/4 In. 135.00
Chest, El Dorado Brewing Co., Stockton, Ca., Wood, Brass Closure, 24 x 17 x 14 In. 66.00
Clock, Clicquot Club, Light-Up, Time To Serve Clicquot Club, Square, 1959, 15 In. 195.00
Clock, Coca-Cola, Betty, 1970s 55.00
Clock, Coca-Cola, Bottle Shape, Green, 1948 .... 950.00

Clock, Coca-Cola, Delicious Drink 5 Cents Refreshing, Regulator, Ornate, 38 In. 517.00
Clock, Coca-Cola, Plastic, Metal, Light-Up, 37 1/4 x 24 x 3 1/2 In. 300.00
Clock, Coca-Cola, Select-O-Clock, Wood Frame, Selected Devices Co., 1939, 16 x 16 In. . 258.00
Clock, Dr Pepper, Neon, Square, 1940s, 16 In. 853.00
Clock, Drink Coca-Cola, In Bottles, Please Pay When Served, Countertop, 1950s 650.00
Clock, Drink Coca-Cola, Walnut, Sidney, 69 x 28 x 10 In. 4200.00
Clock, Drink Dad's Root Beer, Light-Up, Glass, Metal, Square, 1950s, 15 3/4 In. 231.00
Clock, Pepsi-Cola, Electric, Double Bubble, 1950s, Round, 16 In. 687.00
Coaster, Bub's Pilsen, 1940s, 4 1/4 In. 34.00
Coaster, Daeufer's Beer, 1930s, 4 1/4 In. 13.00
Coaster, Haberle's Light Ale, Square, 1940s, 4 1/4 In. 17.00
Coaster, Hoosier Beer, 1930s, 4 1/8 In. 39.00
Coaster, Nickle Plate Beer, 1930s, 3 1/2 In. 28.00
Coaster, Schaefor Braulager On Tap, Beer .... .75
Coaster, Schmidt's Beer & Ale, Original Wrapper, 2-Sided, 4 1/4 In. 7.00
Coaster, Tivoli Beer, 1930s, 4 In. 17.00
Cooler, Coca-Cola, 4 Tin Embossed Signs, English & French Letters, Wood Lids, 35 In. ... 495.00
Cooler, Coca-Cola, Picnic, Cavalier, Inner Tray, 1950s 303.00
Crate, Coca-Cola, 24 Full Bottles, Wooden, Masonite, 1940s 413.00
Crate, Coca-Cola, Drink Coca-Cola, Refresh Yourself, Red Ground, 7 x 9 3/4 x 5 In. 275.00
Crate, M. Morrison Bottling Works, Ingersoll, Ontario, Wood, Black On Gray, 1910 ..... 23.00
Crate, Mortimer & Mowbray, Hampton's Vegetable Tincture, 19 1/2 x 11 1/2 In. 67.00
Crate, Pepsi-Cola, Wood, Vintage, 18 x 5 x 12 In. 48.00
Crock, Old Creamery, Delavan, Minn., 1926 .... 10.00
Cup, Pepsi-Cola, Red, White, Blue Lily Tulip, 4 Piece 10.00
Dart Board, Drink Coca-Cola, 4 Red Circles, Milton Bradley, 1950s 75.00
Dispenser, Always Drink Cherry Smash, 5 Cents, Porcelain, Pump, c.1920 .... 2970.00
Dispenser, Buckeye Root Beer, Dark Brown Ground, Original Pump, 1930, 9 In. 1200.00
Dispenser, Buckeye Root Beer, Jovial Elves, Ceramic, 8 x 15 In. 2200.00
Dispenser, Cardinal Cherry Syrup, Gilt Lettering On Base, c.1910, 9 In. 4600.00
Dispenser, Cherry Smash, Red Glass, Faucet, 1930s 325.00
Dispenser, Dr. Swett's Root Beer, Bottle Form, 22 x 7 In. 1760.00
Dispenser, Dr. Swett's Root Beer, Boy Drinking, Grass Around Bottom, 13 In. 6600.00
Dispenser, Drink Hires, It's Pure, Ceramic, Hourglass Style, c.1920s, 14 In. ......523.00 to 805.00
Dispenser, Meredith's Club Pure Rye Whiskey, 4 1/2 & 6 & 7 1/4 In., 3 Piece 230.00
Dispenser, Mission Orange, Black Porcelain Top, Orange Wrinkle Finish, 26 In. 200.00
Dispenser, Mission Real Fruit Juice, Chrome, Vaseline Glass, Logo, Lid, Stirrer 660.00
Dispenser, Old French Brandy, Blown Base, Bung Hole, Pontil, 19 In. 132.00
Dispenser, Orange Crush, Metal Base, Glass Jar, 14 In. 360.00
Dispenser, Robertson's Dundee Whiskey, 12 1/2 In. 58.00
Dispenser, Rochester Syrup, Barrel On Stump, 12 1/4 x 7 In. 357.00
Dispenser, Ward's Lemon Crush Syrup, Ceramic Lemon, Floral Base, 13 In. 1380.00
Dispenser, Ward's Orange Crush Syrup, Orange, 14 In. 975.00
Display, Coca-Cola, Girl At Fountain, The Pause That Refreshes, 3-D, 1929 .... 12100.00
Display, Coca-Cola, No After-Lunch Drowsiness, Easel, Die Cut, 1933 .... 3740.00
Display, Coca-Cola, Sign Of Good Taste, Cardboard, 1956, 16 x 27 In. 500.00
Display, Falls City Beer, Balloon, Vinyl, 1970s, 24 In. 26.00
Display, Pepsi-Cola, Monkey, Electric, Plastic, Metal, 37 x 26 In. 1100.00
Display, Rieger's Perfumes, 8 Beveled Bottles, Lazy Susan Base, 9 In. 1725.00
Display, Smile Soda, Waffled Bottle, Embossed, July 11, 1922, Gal., 18 In. 575.00
Display, Whistle, Thirsty? Just Whistle, Cardboard, Die Cut, 1939, 13 x 27 In. 525.00
Doll, Bud Man, Rubber, Flesh Color, Red Outfit, 1960s, 18 In. 175.00
Doll, Pepsi-Cola, Elf, Plush, 34 In. ....155.00 to 167.00
Door Pull, Coca-Cola, Bottle Form, Aluminum, 1940s 358.00
Door Pull, Coca-Cola, Delicious, Refreshing, Bakelite, Tin, Box, 1930s-1940s, 3 x 12 In. . 605.00
Door Pull, Coca-Cola, Metal & Bakelite, Bottle, 1930-1940, 13 In. 523.00
Door Push, 7-Up, Aluminum, Yellow Ground, Black Lettering, 1940s, 8 1/2 x 8 3/4 In. .. 165.00
Door Push, Bireley's, 1940, 9 1/2 In. 150.00
Door Push, Coca-Cola, Thanks Call Again, Porcelain, Canada, 1950s, 4 x 11 1/2 In. 660.00
Door Push, Drink Coca-Cola, Be Really Refreshed, 2 Piece, Tin, 1950s, 4 x 8 In. 825.00
Door Push, Golden Bridge Root Beer, Tin, Embossed, 11 3/4 x 3 3/4 In. 95.00
Door Push, Hires Root Beer, Tin, 1940s-1950s, 3 3/4 x 14 In. 110.00
Door Push, Hires, Bottle Cap Picture, 4 x 29 1/2 In. 55.00

Go-Withs, Bottle Opener, Fisherman, Cast Iron, Painted, 4 1/4 In.

Go-Withs, Figurine, Portly Man, Big Bill Best Bitters, Plaster, 1910, 15

A dating tip for bottle collectors: The words "Federal Law forbids sale or re-use of this bottle" were used on liquor bottles from 1933 to 1964.

Door Push, Orange Crush, Porcelain, 1930s-1940s, 3 1/2 x 9 1/2 In.	415.00
Door Push, Pepsi-Cola, Bigger-Better, 12 x 2 3/4 In.	550.00
Door Push, Refresh Yourself, Drink Coca-Cola, 2 Piece, Porcelain, 1950s, 4 x 8 In.	1375.00
Door Push, Refreshing Coca-Cola, Tin, Embossed, Bakelite Handle, 1930s, 3 x 12 In.	605.00
Door Push, Vicks For Colds, Bottle Pictures, Porcelain, 7 7/8 x 3 3/4 In.	385.00
Door Push, Vicks, Come In To Help Prevent Many Colds, Red Ground, 1940, 8 In.	488.00
Doorknob, Ballantine Beer, Bakelite, Enameled Insert Logo, Newark, N.J., 1940s	30.00
Dose Cup, Beans Drug Store, Gardner, Me., Embossed Around Base, Pedestal, 3 In.	28.00
Dose Cup, Our Native Herbs, Alonzo O. Bills Com., Washington, D.C.	12.00
Dose Cup, Rigo Medicine Measure, Canada, 8 Teaspoons	10.00
Dose Glass, Blair's Where Quality Counts, Round Up, Mont., Graduations, 2 3/4 In.	66.00
Dose Glass, Dr. Petzold's German Bitters, SCA, Goblet Style, Pedestal, 3 1/4 In.	60.00
Drink Stirrers, Zulu Lulu, Card, Nos. 15, 20, 25, 30, 35, 40, On Card, Plastic, 1940s	25.00
Earrings, Coca-Cola, Classic Formula, Pierced	8.00
Fan, Pepsi-Cola, Rattan, 2-Sided, 9 x 14 In., 1910-1915	1210.00
Figurine, Fashion, Avon, 1971, 4 Oz.	12.00
Figurine, Fashion, Roaring '20s, Avon, 1972, 3 Oz.	10.00
Figurine, Portly Man, Big Bill Best Bitters, Plaster, 1910, 15 1/4 In. *Illus*	1650.00
Foam Scraper, Berghoff Beer, Celluloid, 2-Sided, Curved, 1930s	50.00
Foam Scraper, Valley Forge, Rams, 2-Sided, 1940s	25.00
Foam Scraper Holder, Pabst, The Original Is Here, Bottle, 4 Patrons, Metal, 11 In.	45.00
Foam Scraper Holder, Schmidt's Of Philadelphia, Bartender, Metal, 13 In.	60.00
Funnel, Brantford, Green Glaze, Vertical Ribs, Handle, 3 1/4 In.	120.00
Funnel, Compliments Of Lash's Bitters Co., Brass, Soldered Handle, 1920, 8 1/4 In.	100.00
Glass, Beer, Carpet & Rug Store, J.A. Stern, Slater, Mo., Etched, 3 3/4 In.	33.00
Glass, Beer, Merry Christmas, Wilson & Evans Bros., Pipestone, Minn., 3 3/4 In.	33.00
Glass, Braumeister Fine Beer, Red & Blue Print, 1950s, 5 1/2 In.	4.00
Glass, Brewery's Own Bottle, Gold Rim, Frosted	45.00
Glass, Carnation Malted Milk, Milk Glass, Tin Lid, 8 In.	270.00
Glass, Chief Oshkosh Beer, Red & White Logo, 1950s, 5 1/2 In.	4.00
Glass, Coca-Cola, 5 Cents, Flared, 1912-1913	187.00
Glass, Dr Pepper, 2-Color Applied Logo, White Ground, 1960s, 9 1/2 In.	90.00
Glass, Dubois Budweiser, Red Print, 1950s, 3 In.	29.00
Glass, Grace Brothers Brewing Co., Santa Rosa, Cal., Etched Barrel & Fern, 3 3/4 In.	132.00
Glass, Grand Rapids Brewing Co., Grand Rapids, Mich., White Lettering, 2 1/4 In.	29.00
Glass, Gunther Beer, Red Print, 1960s, 6 3/8 In.	3.00
Glass, Holihan's Ale & Beer, Red, Blue Print, 1950s, 4 1/2 In.	4.00
Glass, Los Angeles Brewing Co., White Enamel, Gold Band At Top, 2 3/4 In.	17.00
Glass, Magnolia Old Bourbon, Portland, Oregon, 2 1/4 In.	29.00
Glass, Miller High Life, Red Print, 1950s, 4 1/4 In.	4.00
Glass, Milwaukee Brewing Co., Milwaukee, Wisc., 3 1/2 In.	58.00
Glass, National Bohemian Beer, Red Print, 1950s, 4 1/2 In.	13.00
Glass, Old German Lager, Independent Brewing Co., Seattle, Keg Shape, Frosted	45.00
Glass, Old Kentucky Liquor, CC Cripple Creek, Colo., Etched Badger, 2 1/2 In.	231.00
Glass, Old Reading Beer, Red, Black, Yellow Logo, 1930s, 7 3/4 In.	165.00

Glass, Pepsi-Cola, Hits The Spot, Syrup & Fill Lines, Anchor Hocking, 1930s, 4 1/4 In. ...   40.00
Glass, Pepsi-Cola, Raised Lettering, Tapered, 4 1/2 In. 30.00
Glass, Pepsi-Cola, Sylvester & Friends 5.00
Glass, Pepsi-Cola, Tweety Bird 5.00
Glass, Rainier Beer, Etched Graphics, 1890s, 3 1/2 In. 175.00
Glass, Valley Brew Lager, El Dorado Brewing Co., Stockton, Cal., Etched, 3 3/4 In. 66.00
Golf Club, Pepsi-Cola, Putter, 35 In. 236.00
Grill Plate, Truck, Coca-Cola In Bottles, Aluminum, 1920-1930, 17 In. 330.00
Hat, Pepsi-Cola, Driver's, One Size Fits All 25.00
Ice Bowl, Coca-Cola, Vernonware, Green, c.1930s, 10 In. 715.00
Ice Chopper, Lash's Bitters, Metal 78.00
Ice Pick, Drink Coca-Cola, Delicious & Refreshing, Wooden Handle, 1960s, 8 In. 19.50
Ink Pourer, Copper, Soldered, 1880-1910, 5 In. 303.00
Jar, Coca-Cola Chewing Gum, Glass, 1903-1905 . . . .   1430.00
Jar, Coca-Cola, Pepsin Gum, Embossed, Lid, c.1905-1911 . . . .   1760.00
Jar, National Beer, Glass, Red Print, 1960s, 1/2 Gal. 25.00
Kaleidoscope, Pepsi-Cola, Catch The Spirit, Soda Can Shape, Steven, 1981, 5 In. 60.00
Key Chain, Pepsi-Cola, Bottle Cap Logo, Gold, 1950s 45.00
Key Fob, Duquesne, Good Luck Penny, Plated, 1940s 4.00
Kick Plate, Coca-Cola, Bottle, Arrow, 1950s 93.00
Kick Plate, Dr Pepper, 1970s 44.00
Kick Plate, Dr Pepper, Tin, Embossed, 1970s 44.00
Kick Plate, Drink Nehi, Red Lettering, Embossed, 1940s, 11 1/2 x 29 In. 200.00
Kick Plate, NuGrape Soda, Flavor You Can't Forget, 1930, 12 x 30 In. 207.00
Label, Beer, Haehnle's Temperance, Early Prohibition 22.00
Label, Beer, K & S Special Bock Brew, Prohibition 17.00
Label, Beer, Pabst Hofbrau, Pre-Prohibition, N.Y. 94.00
Label, Beer, Tivoli Brewing Co., Denver, 1950s, 3 x 3 3/4 In. 3.00
Label, El Rey California Burgundy, Elk Grove Winery Inc., 1950s 30.00
Label, Ginger Ale, Caddy, Prohibition Label, Neck 33.00
Label, Grape Vines, El Rey California Sherry, Cutler, California, Amber, Gal. 40.00
Label, Whiskey, Cap'n Jack, Cincinnati Distillers, 1930s, 3 1/2 x 4 1/2 In. 6.00
Label, Whiskey, Old Anvil Brand, Louisville, Ken., 1940s, 3 1/2 x 5 In. 5.00
License Plate Tag, Buckeye Beer, Drive Safely, Metal, Embossed, 1930s 45.00
Lid, Columbia, Amber 15.00
Lid, Gem, Aqua, Midget 16.00
Lid, Glassboro Improved, Aqua 3.00
Lid, Jollwood Lee Co., Conshohockon, Pa., Amber 5.00
Lid, Leader Fruit 5.00
Lid, Rudds 5.00
Lighter, Coca-Cola, Bottle Shape, Plastic, Metal Cap, 1953, 2 1/2 x 3/4 In. 25.00
Mask, Mr. Peanut, Cardboard, Attached Hat, 15 1/2 x 11 1/2 In. 413.00
Menu, Coca-Cola, Tin, 1950s, 14 x 60 In. 2530.00
Menu Board, Bireley's, Orange Pop, 20 1/8 x 14 1/8 In. 235.00
Menu Board, Coca-Cola, Cap & Wings Each End, Tin, 1950s, 14 x 60 In. 2530.00
Menu Board, Coca-Cola, Sport Characters On Sides, 34 1/2 x 31 In. 25.00
Menu Board, Ehret's Extra Beer, 1940s 10.00
Menu Board, Fitzgerald's Beer & Ale, 1930s 13.00
Menu Board, Hires Root Beer, Tin, Embossed, 29 1/4 In. 187.00
Menu Board, Hires, Cardboard, 24 x 12 In. 225.00
Menu Board, Pepsi-Cola, Say Pepsi Please, Black, 19 1/2 x 30 In. 30.00
Menu Board, Pepsi-Cola, Self-Framed Tin, Bottle Cap Logo, 30 x 19 1/2 In. 120.00
Milk Bottle Cap, Abbeville Pasteurizing Plant, Abbeville, South Carolina, Plug Type 1.50
Milk Bottle Cap, Ayshire Dairy, Great Falls, Mont., Plug Type 2.00
Milk Bottle Cap, Bolger Farm's Milk, Light Green Lettering 66.00
Milk Bottle Cap, Clover Leaf Dairy, Helena, Mont., Plug Type 2.00
Milk Bottle Cap, Coggshall Dairy, Norwich, Conn., Cardboard 25
Milk Bottle Cap, Creamer, Lincoln Dairy Co., Better Dairy Products, Pull Tab 1.00
Milk Bottle Cap, Cunningham's Dairy, Bentonville, Ark., Pure Jersey, Blue Lettering 1.00
Milk Bottle Cap, Indian Valley Creamery, Pull Tab 3.00
Milk Bottle Cap, Jenkins Dairy, Gastonia, N.C., Plug Type, Dust Cap 1.50
Milk Bottle Cap, Maple Island Farm, Stillwater, Minn, Pull Tab, 56 mm 2.00
Milk Bottle Cap, Moove's Goat Dairy, Moovingsport, La., Plug Type, Dust Cap 6.00

Milk Bottle Cap, Pearman's Dairy, Anderson, South Carolina, Plug Type 1.50
Milk Bottle Cap, Prats Dairy, Abita Springs, La., Plug Type, Pull Tab 8.00
Milk Bottle Cap, Rainbow Dairy, Butte, Mont., Plug Type 1.00
Milk Bottle Cap, Seward Dairy, Seward, Alaska, Plug Type 4.00
Milk Bottle Cap, Silver Leaf Dairy, Greer, South Carolina 2.50
Milk Bottle Cap, Table Cream, Pull Tab 3.00
Milk Bottle Cap, Thacher's Dairy, N.Y. ....4.00 to 5.00
Milk Bottle Cap, W.T. Rawleigh Co. Grade A Milk, Red & Black Printing 7.00
Milk Bottle Cap, Weltner's Fairy Dairy, Perrysville, Ohio, Plug Type, Pull Tab .... .75
Milk Bottle Cap, Western Milk & Cream Co., Butte, Mont., Plug Type 2.00
Mirror, Coca-Cola, 1916, Pocket 495.00
Mirror, Coca-Cola, Celluloid, Hamilton King Calendar Girl, 1910, 2 3/4 x 1 3/4 In. 303.00
Mirror, Coca-Cola, Green, Women On Beach, Atlanta, Purse, 1918 .... 10.00
Mirror, Coca-Cola, Woman In Flowery Hat, 1911, Pocket, 2 x 3 In. 330.00
Mirror, Coca-Cola, Woman, With Bottle, 1908, Pocket 359.00
Mirror, Hamm's Beer, Colors, 1980s, 17 1/2 x 13 1/2 In. 24.00
Mirror, Royal Crown Cola, With Thermometer 110.00
Mirror, Stoney's Beer, Reverse Glass, 1970s, 12 x 10 In. 8.00
Mug, Beer, Cafe Bistro, Bateman, Dohrmann & Co., Stoneware, Pewter Top, 6 In. 143.00
Mug, Dr. Swett's Original Root Beer, Man's Head, Embossed, Stoneware 330.00
Mug, Drink Hires Root Beer, Hires Boy, Potbelly, Germany, 4 1/4 In. 110.00
Mug, Feel-Ter-Hum, Bartholomay Brewing Co., Rochester, Tan Glaze, c.1911, 2 1/4 In. .. 165.00
Mug, Gluek Brewing Co., Red Wing Stoneware, Barrel Shape, 6-Pointed Star 180.00
Mug, Hartman's Bitters, The Appetizer, Milk Glass, Handle, Monk Picture 100.00
Mug, Hires Root Beer, Boy With Bib, Ceramic, Mettlach, 5 In. 300.00
Mug, Lowenbrau, Rebers Motel, Barryville, N.Y., Ceramarte, 1970s, 5 3/4 In. 3.00
Mug, M.K. Goetz Brewing Co., St. Joseph, Mo., Cream, Brown, 1915, 6 In. ....*Illus* 176.00
Mug, Schlitz Beer, University Of Iowa, Reunion, 1960s, 16 Oz. 9.00
Napkin Holder, RC Cola, 1940s 385.00
Paperweight, Taylor's Stomachic Mixture, Cures Indigestion, Heartburn, Wind, 1890 .... 75.00
Pie Plate, Glennon's Beer, Liberty Brewing Co., Pittston, Pa., 1930s, 13 In. 140.00
Pie Plate, St. Louis ABC Beers, American Brewing Co., 1900s, 12 In. 400.00
Pie Plate, Stegmaier Gold Medal Beer, Wilkes-Barre, Pa., 1930s, 13 In. 190.00
Pillow, Dr Pepper, Heart Shape, To Try It Is To Like It, Love, 1960s 30.00
Pin, Compliments Of Hiram Walker & Sons, Walkerville, Canada, Maple Leaf, 1 1/4 In. .. 90.00
Pin, Pabst Brewing, Ribbon, 1950s, 1 3/4 x 3 In. 8.00
Pin, Pepsi-Cola, Bottle Cap Type, Red, White & Blue, Celluloid, 1 In. 40.00
Pin, Thirsty? Just Whistle, Bottle Cap, 1950s, 2 In. 413.00
Pin, You'll Love Dad's, Tastes Like Root Beer Should, Bottle Cap, 1950s, 2 In. 385.00
Pitcher & Mugs, Leisy Brewing Co., Desert Oasis, 5 Piece 115.00
Plate, Coca-Cola, Bottle & Glass, Knowles China, 1930s, 7 1/4 In. 275.00
Poster, Coca-Cola Ice Cold As Always, 5 Cents, Masonite, 1839, 12 x 18 In. 100.00
Poster, Coca-Cola, Bottle, Food, Die Cut, 4 Hanging 2-Sided Cards, 1954, 36 x 42 In. ... 193.00
Poster, Coca-Cola, Circus, 49 x 32 In. 9350.00
Poster, Coca-Cola, So Good With Food, Vertical, 1952 .... 908.00
Poster, Coca-Cola, The Best Of Taste, Vertical, 30 x 50 In. 935.00
Poster, Have A Coke, Bottle In Iceberg, Cardboard, 20 x 36 In. 575.00
Poster, Hires, Delicious Healthful, So Good With Food, 34 x 57 1/2 In. 288.00
Pot Lid, Bears Grease, H.P. Wakelee Druggist, San Francisco, Multicolored Transfer 18.00
Pot Lid, Breidenbach's Toothpaste, Base 24.00
Pot Lid, C.E. Monell, Compound Extract Of Copaiba, Cubebs & Iron, 2 7/8 In. 532.00
Pot Lid, Cherry Tooth Paste, Patronized By The Queen, Gold Paint, 3 1/4 In. 55.00
Pot Lid, Cherry Toothpaste, Inmans 33.00
Pot Lid, Cherry Toothpaste, S. Maw 33.00
Pot Lid, Cold Cream Of Roses, A. Davison, Chemist, Kimberley, Rectangular 742.00
Pot Lid, Compound Extract Of Cubebs & Copaiba, Tarrant & Co., Druggist, 2 3/4 In. ... 165.00
Pot Lid, David S. Brown's Superior Pearl Shaving Paste, N.Y., Blue Transfer, 3 5/8 In. ... 440.00
Pot Lid, Dyer's Orange Flower & Orris Tooth Paste, Black Transfer, Prov. R.I., 2 5/8 In. . 715.00
Pot Lid, Eugene Roussel, Rose Tooth Paste, Philada., Black Transfer, 2 3/4 In. 179.00
Pot Lid, H.P. & W.C. Taylor, Buffalo Hunt, Multicolored Transfer, 5 1/8 In. 6875.00
Pot Lid, Harp & Hops Carlton Ware, Stilton 68.00
Pot Lid, Hazard, Hazard & Co., Cucumber Cream, N.Y., Black Transfer, 2 7/8 In. 146.00
Pot Lid, Improved Cold Cream Of Roses, X. Bazin, Philadelphia, 2 1/4 In. 264.00

Go-Withs, Mug, M.K.
Goetz Brewing Co., St.
Joseph, Mo., Cream,
Brown, 1915, 6 In.

Go-Withs, Salt &
Pepper, Fort Pitt
Beer, Glass, Label

Pot Lid, Jules Hauel Saponaceous Shaving Compound, Phila., Purple Transfer, 4 In. 280.00
Pot Lid, Jules Hauel, Genuine Lion Pomade, Black Transfer, 2 7/8 In. 963.00
Pot Lid, Jules Hauel, World's Fair, Premium Perfumery 845.00
Pot Lid, Kirchen Zahn-Pasta, Cherry Tooth Paste, Pale Yellow Rim, Germany 445.00
Pot Lid, Man Shaving In Mirror, Purple Transfer, Philadelphia, 1820 .... 259.00
Pot Lid, Parisian Toothpaste, D. Atkinson, Oval, White, Black Transfer, 3 In. 30.00
Pot Lid, R. & G.A. Wright, Amandine, Philadelphia, Black Transfer, 3 3/8 In. 660.00
Pot Lid, Sanoline Tooth Paste, For Whiteness & Purity, 2 Women Under Parasol 1038.00
Pot Lid, T.H. Peters, Purified Pine Wood Charcoal Tooth Paste, Square, 2 3/4 In. 176.00
Pot Lid, Taylor's Saponaceous Compound, White, Purple Transfer, 3 3/8 In. 308.00
Pot Lid, Wright's Shaving Cream, Man Shaving In Front Of Mirror, Gray 920.00
Pot Lid, Wright's Wild Cherry Dentifrice 2818.00
Pot Lid, X. Bazin, Highly Perfumed Bear's Grease, 2 Standing Bears, Black Transfer 1210.00
Punchboard, Coca-Cola, Win A 6 Bottle Carton, 1940s, 4 x 5 In. 4.50
Rack, Bottle, Coca-Cola, Wire & Metal, 3 Tiers, c.1950 .... 320.00
Rack, Sunoco Motor Oil, Mercury Made, 28 x 29 x 19 In. 2200.00
Radio, Coca-Cola, Bottle Shape, 1930s 2640.00
Radio, Coca-Cola, Cooler Shape, Red, White Lettering, 1950s, 12 1/2 x 8 x 9 In. . .506.00 to 600.00
Salt & Pepper, Drink Pepsi-Cola, 4 1/4 In. 22.00
Salt & Pepper, Falstaff Beer, Red & White Label, 1950s, 3 1/2 In. 6.00
Salt & Pepper, Fort Pitt Beer, Glass, Label ....*Illus* 12.00
Saltshaker, Acme Beer, Partial Label 7.00
Saltshaker, Blatz Beer 10.00
Sheet Music, Coca-Cola Girl, 1927 .... 200.00
Shot Glass, Ramsey's Trinidad Aromatic Bitters, Clear, Red & White ACL, 2 3/4 In. 106.00
Sign, 7-Up Likes You, Flange, 10 x 12 In. 110.00
Sign, 7-Up, Bottle Shape, Tin, Die Cut, 1962, 13 x 45 In. 99.00
Sign, 7-Up, Bottle, Flange, 1954, 18 x 20 In. 1430.00
Sign, 7-Up, Fresh Up With 7-Up, Bottle & Hand, Embossed, 1949, 20 x 28 In. 550.00
Sign, 7-Up, Fresh Up With 7-Up, It Likes You, 8-Sided, 1940s, 14 x 14 In. 330.00
Sign, 7-Up, Fresh Up With 7-Up, Light-Up, Revolving, 1950s, 12 x 14 In. 495.00
Sign, 7-Up, Glass With Ice & Straw, 3 Colors, Neon, Box, 13 x 28 In. 220.00
Sign, 7-Up, Revolving, Light-Up, 1950s, 14 x 12 In. 495.00
Sign, 7-Up, Tin, Flange, 16 x 16 In. 176.00
Sign, 7-Up, Tis Uncola Season, Santa Claus & Holly, 2-Sided, String Hanger, 10 In. 39.00
Sign, 7-Up, You Like It, It Likes You, Bottle Center, Dispenser, 1950s, 17 x 6 1/2 In. 468.00
Sign, A & W Root Beer, My Root Beer's Here! Dennis The Menace, 36 x 91 1/2 In. 200.00
Sign, A & W Root Beer, Plastic, Wood Frame, Cutout Barrel, 1960s, 52 x 21 In. 121.00
Sign, Acme Beer, On Tap, Reverse On Glass, Back Lighted, 5 x 13 In. 230.00
Sign, Arden Protected Milk, 27 Protections, Red Ground, 41 1/2 x 15 In. 525.00
Sign, Ask For A Crush, Tin, 3 1/4 x 26 1/2 In. 60.00
Sign, Barq's Root Beer, Bottle Image, Paper Lithograph, Frame, 12 1/2 x 30 In. 90.00
Sign, Berkeley Club Ginger Ale, Bottle Cap, Tin Face, Yellow Lettering, Black, 1950 .... 94.00
Sign, Bireley's, Natural Thing To Drink, 3 13/16 x 9 1/2 In. 135.00
Sign, Borden's Elsie, Frame, Tin, 17 1/2 In. 303.00

Sign, Buffalo Brewing Company, Tin, Self-Framed, 28 x 22 1/2 In. 460.00
Sign, Carnation Fresh Milk, Bottle Picture, Porcelain, 15 x 14 1/4 In. 660.00
Sign, Cerva, A Soft Drink, St. Louis, Mo., 6 5/8 x 4 5/8 In. 170.00
Sign, Chamberlain's Cough Remedy, Cardboard, 1882, 10 In. 144.00
Sign, Chief Oshkosh Beer, Indian Chief In Middle, Red Lettering, 18 x 13 1/2 In. 750.00
Sign, Clicquot Club Beverages, Red Ground, 47 3/4 x 17 3/4 In. 210.00
Sign, Clicquot Club Ginger Ale, Woman With Little Boy, 7 1/4 x 9 5/8 In. 110.00
Sign, Clicquot Club, Enjoy Clicquot Club Kola, Cardboard, 23 1/2 x 9 5/8 In. 30.00
Sign, Clicquot Club, Enjoy Clicquot Club Kola, Tin, Embossed, 30 x 12 In. 55.00
Sign, Cliquot Club Kola, Boy & Bottle Left Side, Tin, 30 x 12 In. 60.00
Sign, Coca-Cola, 2 Glasses, Metal Trim, Wood, 1930, 11 x 9 In. 518.00
Sign, Coca-Cola, 5 Cents, Drink Coca-Cola, 24 1/2 x 11 In. 285.00
Sign, Coca-Cola, 6-Pack, Tin, Embossed, 6 Bottles, Die Cut, 1960s, 36 In. 798.00
Sign, Coca-Cola, Bottle Cap, Ice Cold Coca-Cola Sold Here, 19 5/8 In. 400.00
Sign, Coca-Cola, Bottle Cap, Sign Of Good Taste, 36 In. 600.00
Sign, Coca-Cola, Bottle Shape, Die Cut, Embossed, 1933, 39 In. 605.00
Sign, Coca-Cola, Bottle Shape, Embossed, 30 x 108 In. 1150.00
Sign, Coca-Cola, Bottle Shape, Tin, Die Cut, 1960, 20 x 72 In. 518.00
Sign, Coca-Cola, Bottle, Ice Cold, Die Cut Arrow, Hanging Bracket, 2-Sided, 1936, 23 In. 2640.00
Sign, Coca-Cola, Bottle, Tin, Embossed, Die Cut, December 25, 1923, 39 In. 467.00
Sign, Coca-Cola, Bottle, Trademark, Cutout, Tin, 1950, 36 In. 440.00
Sign, Coca-Cola, Cap Shape, Tin, Silkscreen, Red Background, 24 In. 374.00
Sign, Coca-Cola, Coca-Cola Belongs, Military Couple, Cardboard, 1943, 20 x 36 In. 1210.00
Sign, Coca-Cola, Coke Bottle, Tin, Die Cut, 1952, 72 In. 550.00
Sign, Coca-Cola, Countertop, Glass, Wood, Silver Reverse Paint, 1948, 18 x 12 In. 715.00
Sign, Coca-Cola, Drink Coca-Cola, 4 1/2 x 12 1/2 In. 575.00
Sign, Coca-Cola, Drink Coca-Cola, Red Ground, 17 3/4 x 5 3/4 In. 325.00
Sign, Coca-Cola, Drink Coca-Cola, Silver Ground, 18 1/2 x 5 1/2 In. 675.00
Sign, Coca-Cola, Drink Coca-Cola, Things Go Better, Bottle Picture, 1963, 12 x 32 In. ... 300.00
Sign, Coca-Cola, Enjoy Coke, Tin, 1960s, 18 x 54 In. 231.00
Sign, Coca-Cola, Enjoy That Refreshing, Bottle At Bottom, 1960s, 54 x 18 In. 330.00
Sign, Coca-Cola, For Sparkling Holidays, Bring Home The Coke, Santa Claus, 20 x 11 In. 180.00
Sign, Coca-Cola, Fountain Service, Drink Coca-Cola, 22 3/4 x 25 1/2 In. 500.00
Sign, Coca-Cola, Fountain Service, Drink Coca-Cola, Delicious & Refreshing, 60 x 42 In. 2300.00
Sign, Coca-Cola, Gas Today, Tin, 20 x 28 In. 4950.00
Sign, Coca-Cola, Ice Cold Coca-Cola In Bottles, Red Ground, 41 3/4 x 4 1/4 In. 525.00
Sign, Coca-Cola, Ice Cold Coca-Cola Sold Here, Red Ground, 1933, 20 In. 1155.00
Sign, Coca-Cola, Ice Cold Coca-Cola, Sign Of Good Taste, 27 3/4 x 19 3/4 In. 225.00
Sign, Coca-Cola, In Bottles, Drink Coca-Cola 5 Cents, Red Ground, 1922, 6 x 23 In. 1155.00
Sign, Coca-Cola, Let Us Put A Case In Your Car, Woman & Deliveryman, 12 x 15 1/4 In. . 750.00
Sign, Coca-Cola, Lunch, Porcelain, 1950s, 28 x 26 In. 2200.00
Sign, Coca-Cola, Marilyn Monroe In Center, 35 1/2 x 34 In. 600.00
Sign, Coca-Cola, Pause That Refreshes, Cardboard, Cutout, 1937, 14 x 34 In. 220.00
Sign, Coca-Cola, Plastic Fishtail Background, Neon, Box, 28 x 15 In. 330.00
Sign, Coca-Cola, Season's Greetings, Boy Dreaming Of Santa & Coke, 31 1/2 x 49 In. 400.00
Sign, Coca-Cola, Things Go Better With Coke, Bottle, Tin, 1960s, 54 x 18 In. 385.00
Sign, Coca-Cola, Things Go Better, Tin, Square, 1960s, 24 In. 319.00
Sign, Coca-Cola, Woman Preparing Buffet On 1 Side, Picnic On Other, 50 x 29 In. 172.00
Sign, Cool Soda 5 Cent Fruit Syrups, Wood, 19 x 30 x 2 In. 3800.00
Sign, Copenhagen Castle Beer, Tin Over Cardboard, Embossed, 1940s, 9 x 11 In. 35.00
Sign, Cremo Old Stock Ale, Cardboard, Die Cut, 1930s, 11 x 15 1/2 In. 45.00
Sign, Dad's Black Cow Root Beer, Die Cut Cardboard, Cow Image, 21 x 33 In. 190.00
Sign, Dad's Root Beer, Bottle Cap Form, 28 x 20 In. 375.00
Sign, Dad's, Bottle Cap, Deliciously Yours, The Old Fashioned Root Beer, 20 x 28 In. ... 275.00
Sign, Demuth Golden Lion Cigars, Tin, Raised Letters, Red & Green Paint, 13 x 9 1/2 In. 84.00
Sign, Dr Pepper Bottling Company, Triangular, Porcelain, 22 x 14 In., 1940s 330.00
Sign, Dr Pepper, Good For Life, Flange, 2-Sided, Sidewalk, 24 x 36 In. 1045.00
Sign, Dr Pepper, Please Pay When Served, Tin, 1940, 9 x 12 In. 110.00
Sign, Dr Pepper, Tin, Embossed Bottle Cap, 1963, 36 In. 330.00
Sign, Dr. Pepper, Drink Dr Pepper, Good For Life, Porcelain, Embossed, 10 1/2 x 26 In. .. 250.00
Sign, Dr. Pepper, Drink Dr. Pepper, Beveled Edge, 1940s, 10 1/2 x 26 In. 385.00
Sign, Dr. Pepper, Drink Dr. Pepper, Clock, Tin, 2-Sided, Metal Bracket, 1940s, 24 x 36 In. 1045.00
Sign, Dr. Pepper, Thermometer, Tin, 1940s, 10 x 26 In. 770.00

Sign, Dr. Swett's Root Beer, Tin On Cardboard, Red, Blue, Gold, 9 1/4 x 6 1/4 In. 1725.00
Sign, Emmerling's Beer, Tin, 19 1/2 x 28 In. 400.00
Sign, Enterprise Brewery, Tin, 24 x 17 In. 410.00
Sign, F & S Beer & Ale, Football Players, Flocked Foil, Cardstock, 1940s, 14 x 22 In. 359.00
Sign, F & S Beer & Ale, Ice Skater, Foil, Cardstock, 1940s, 14 x 22 In. 560.00
Sign, Fresh Milk, Green Lettering, White Field, Porcelain, 30 x 6 In. 165.00
Sign, Frostie Old Fashioned Root Beer, Tin, 1930s, 19 1/2 x 3 In. 80.00
Sign, Golden Bridge Root Beer, Remember, 3 3/4 x 11 3/4 In. 85.00
Sign, Hamm's Beer, Cardboard, Die Cut, 1960s, 10 x 14 In. 9.00
Sign, High Ball Ginger Ale, Crown Cork & Seal, Baltimore, Tin Lithograph, 9 x 9 In. 160.00
Sign, Hires R-J Root Beer, Flower Basket, 3-Dimensional, Die Cut, 1940s, 10 x 12 In. ... 121.00
Sign, Hires Root Bear, Enjoy Hires, It's Always Pure, Tin, c.1920s, 10 x 28 In. 578.00
Sign, Hires Root Beer, Bottle Shape, Embossed, Painted, 57 In. 385.00
Sign, Hires Root Beer, Bottle Shape, Tin, Die Cut, 1950s, 16 x 57 1/2 In. 315.00
Sign, Hires Root Beer, Bottle, Tin, Die Cut, Embossed, c.1940s, 16 x 58 In. 440.00
Sign, Hires Root Beer, Celluloid Over Tin, c.1917, 10 x 7 In. 345.00
Sign, Hires Root Beer, Drink Hires, Embossed, 1950, 18 x 54 In. 220.00
Sign, Hires Root Beer, Finer Flavor Because Of Real Root Juices, Ice Cold, 3 x 11 In. ... 170.00
Sign, Hires Root Beer, Girl About To Take A Drink, Tin, Embossed, 11 x 29 In. 415.00
Sign, Hires Root Beer, R-J, Girl Holding Tray, Standup, Cardboard, Die Cut, 11 In. 110.00
Sign, Hires Root Beer, Tin Over Cardboard, Easel Back, 9 3/4 x 8 In. 303.00
Sign, Hood's Ice Cream, Cow, Tin, Flange, 1930s, 19 x 22 In. 3410.00
Sign, Howell's Root Beer, Bottle, Tin, Die Cut, c.1940s, 16 x 58 In. 385.00
Sign, Kemp's Balsam, Best Cough Cure, Cardboard, 11 1/2 x 7 1/2 In. 40.00
Sign, Kist Beverages, She's Happy Drinking A Bottle Of Kist, 18 1/2 x 13 In. 275.00
Sign, Kops Ale & Stout, Enamel, England, 20 x 30 In. 483.00
Sign, Korbel Champagne, Young Woman Holding Cluster Of Grapes, Tin, 19 In. 189.00
Sign, Ma's Root Beer, The Kind That Mother Used To Make, Tin, 1930s, 12 x 28 In. 154.00
Sign, Moxie, Drink Moxie, Distinctly Different, Tin, Frame, 1930s-1940s, 20 x 28 In. 330.00
Sign, Moxie, Drink Moxie, Factory At Bottom, Cardboard, 39 x 28 In. 120.00
Sign, Moxie, Drink Moxie, Man, Wearing White Coat, Pointing Finger, 1920, 6 1/4 In. ... 330.00
Sign, Moxie, Drink Moxie, Moxiemobile, Motorcycle, Horse, Lithograph, 7 x 10 In. 250.00
Sign, Moxie, Wake Up! Send A Case Of Moxie, Couple, Cardboard, Frame, 22 x 37 In. .. 1430.00
Sign, National Bohemian, Oh Boy, What A Beer, Glass, Metal, Light-Up, 1940s, 14 In. 375.00
Sign, Nesbitt's Orange Soda, Metal, Weigard Mfg. Co., St. Louis, 17 1/2 x 22 1/2 In. 75.00
Sign, NuGrape Soda, Tin, 32 x 14 In. 160.00
Sign, NuGrape, Drink NuGrape, Hand With Bottle, Tin, Embossed, 1930s, 5 x 14 In. 385.00
Sign, NuIcy, Drink Nu Icy, Embossed, Paper Traces, 1930s, 9 x 20 In. 330.00
Sign, OFC Whiskey, Cardboard Lithograph, Stecher Litho Co., 15 x 26 In. 220.00
Sign, Old Dutch Beer, Tin Over Cardboard, 1950s, 13 x 9 In. 55.00
Sign, Old Overholt Rye Whiskey, Lithograph On Canvas, Gilt Frame, 30 x 19 In. 585.00
Sign, Orange Crush Carbonated Beverage, Tin, 1940s, 17 x 47 In. 303.00
Sign, Orange Crush Soda, There's Only One, Tin, Painted, 2-Sided, 13 1/2 x 18 In. 300.00
Sign, Orange Crush, Drink Orange Crush, Carbonated Beverage, 9 1/8 x 11 1/8 In. 250.00
Sign, Orange Crush, Reverse Painted Mirror, Logo, Frame, 9 1/8 x 11 1/8 In. 275.00
Sign, Orange Crush, Rush! Rush! To Orange Crush, 1942, 18 x 48 In. 863.00
Sign, Orange Crush, Schoolgirl, 3-D Hand Holding Bottle, Die Cut, 1930s, 18 x 20 In. ... 500.00
Sign, Pabst Ale, Glass, Reverse, 1940s, 14 x 8 3/4 In. 230.00
Sign, Park Brewing, Pheasant, Mallard, Park Malt Extract, 1910, 24 In. 825.00
Sign, Pepsi-Cola, Bottle Cap, Celluloid, 1940s, 9 In. 247.00
Sign, Pepsi-Cola, Bottle Cap, Drink Pepsi-Cola, 1950s 110.00
Sign, Pepsi-Cola, Bottle Cap, Green, White Lettering, 1910 .... 50.00
Sign, Pepsi-Cola, Bottle Cap, Metal, Die Cut, Double Dot, Embossed, 1940s-1950s, 13 In. 249.00
Sign, Pepsi-Cola, Bottle Cap, More Bounce To The Ounce, Tin, 11 3/4 In. 10.00
Sign, Pepsi-Cola, Bottle Cap, Neon, Aqua, 17 x 6 In. 100.00
Sign, Pepsi-Cola, Bottle Cap, Tin, Embossed, 1960s, 28 In. 288.00
Sign, Pepsi-Cola, Bottle Cap, Tin, Embossed, 27 x 7 In. 40.00
Sign, Pepsi-Cola, Bottle Form, Tin, 13 1/4 In. 160.00
Sign, Pepsi-Cola, Bottle, Die Cut, Tin, 1930s, 30 In. 264.00
Sign, Pepsi-Cola, Bottle, Tin, Die Cut, Embossed, Painted, 44 1/2 In. 200.00
Sign, Pepsi-Cola, Come In For That Big, Big Bottle, Buy It By The Carton, 10 In. 500.00
Sign, Pepsi-Cola, Drink Pepsi-Cola, 12 Ounce Bottle, 5 Cents, Handle, 7 3/4 x 12 In. 95.00

Sign, Pepsi-Cola, Embossed Script, Dark Green, White, Red, Tin, 1910, 10 In. 595.00
Sign, Pepsi-Cola, Have A Pepsi, 2-Sided, 1950s 578.00
Sign, Pepsi-Cola, Ice Cold, Sold Here, Flange Type, 1930s, 16 x 17 In. 880.00
Sign, Pepsi-Cola, Marker, Metal, 36 x 4 1/2 In. 32.00
Sign, Pepsi-Cola, More Bounce To The Ounce, Tin, 1950s, 48 x 18 In. 577.00
Sign, Pepsi-Cola, Pepsi Presents Evervess Sparkling Water, Celluloid, Round, 9 In. 715.00
Sign, Pepsi-Cola, Pub Clock, Wood, 22 x 16 In. 149.00
Sign, Pepsi-Cola, Refresh Without Filling, Woman On Phone With Pepsi, 8 x 12 In. 200.00
Sign, Pepsi-Cola, Refreshing & Enjoyable, A Sparking Beverage, 12 Oz., 12 x 44 In. 900.00
Sign, Pepsi-Cola, Sold Here, Flange, 13 1/2 x 18 In. 30.00
Sign, Pepsi-Cola, Tin, Bottle Shape, Cutout, 1920-1940, 30 In. 264.00
Sign, Pepsi-Cola, Tin, Cardboard, 1970s, 8 x 12 In. 66.00
Sign, Pepsi-Cola, Tin, Embossed, 8 x 29 1/2 In. 210.00
Sign, Pilsener Brewing, Cleveland, Ohio, P.O.C., Plastic, 1950s, 11 1/2 In. 175.00
Sign, Pop Kola, Drink Pop Kola, White Lettering, 1940s, 10 x 27 In. 135.00
Sign, Pschitt, Bottle Cap, With Thermometer, 2 Bottles, Tin, 1970s 308.00
Sign, Rainier, For Good Cheer! Girl With Horse, Wearing Orange Shirt, 15 x 23 In. 30.00
Sign, Rheingold Beer, Wood, Composition, Paper Logo, 1950s, 12 x 15 In. 30.00
Sign, Royal Crown Cola, Figural Bottle, Tin, Die Cut, 1951, 58 1/2 x 16 In. 288.00
Sign, Royal Crown Cola, Relax & Enjoy, 2-Sided, 1940, 24 x 16 In. 1210.00
Sign, Royal Crown Cola, We Serve Ice Cold, 19 1/2 x 3 1/2 In. 220.00
Sign, Royal Crown, Best Of Taste Test, Red Ground, 1951, 18 x 54 In. 303.00
Sign, Ruppert's Beer, New York, Reverse Glass, Silver Letters, 20 x 28 In. 385.00
Sign, S.B. Goff's Valuable Medicines Herb Bitters, Cardboard, 1880, 11 x 16 In. 200.00
Sign, Schell's Bock Beer, Flat, Frame, 1970s, 12 x 9 1/2 In. 21.00
Sign, Schlitz Beer, Chas. Shonk Lithograph, 13 1/2 x 19 In. 2233.00
Sign, Schmidt & Sons Brewing Co., Cherubs, Woman, Stone Lithograph, 16 x 22 In. 385.00
Sign, Schwarz Weiss Beer, Drink Schwarz Weiss Beer, Metal, Cardboard, 9 1/4 x 6 3/4 In. .. 44.00
Sign, Spiffy, Stop, Here's Spiffy, A Swell Cola Drink, 2-Sided, Tin, c.1940s, 10 x 13 In. .. 385.00
Sign, Student Prince Beer, Heidelberg Brg. Co., Covington, Ky., 16 In. 150.00
Sign, Sunshine Beer, Cardboard, Frame, 1960s, 34 1/4 x 27 1/4 In. 300.00
Sign, Teem, A Lemon-Lime Drink, Pepsi-Cola Co., Tin, Embossed, 12 x 32 In. 11.00
Sign, Triple 16 Cola, It's Bigger, It's Better, 11 1/2 x 31 1/2 In. 44.00
Sign, Triple XXX, Drinkk Triple XXX Root Beer, Curved, Porcelain, 13 1/2 x 17 1/2 In. . 240.00
Sign, Welch's, Drink A Bunch Of Grapes From Welch Juniors, 10 Cents, 6 x 9 In. 99.00
Sign, Welch's, Drink A Bunch Of Grapes From Welch Juniors, 1930, 13 x 20 In. 400.00
Sign, Welch's, For Quick Energy, Refreshing Welch's Grape Juice, 6 x 9 In. 77.00
Sign, Whistle Soda, Bottle Image, Cardboard, Frame, 9 x 31 In. 155.00
Sign, Whistle Soda, Thirsty? Just Whistle, 4 Elves, Tin, Embossed, 1946, 32 x 57 In. 743.00
Sign, Whistle Soda, Thirsty? Just Whistle, Arrow, Self-Framed, 1930s, 7 x 27 In. 242.00
Sign, Whistle Soda, Thirsty? Just Whistle, Boy Holding Bottle, Die Cut, 1939, 13 x 27 In. . 523.00
Sign, Wilke's, Drink Wilke's Better Buttermilk, Sample Nicolene Sign No. 6, 11 x 6 In. .. 70.00
Straws, Coca-Cola, Graphics On 4 Sides, 1930s, 8 1/2 In. 638.00
String Dispenser, SSS For The Blood, Cast Iron Cauldron, 4 3/4 In. 168.00
Tap Knob, Beverwyck Irish Brand Cream Ale, Bakelite, Enameled Insert, 1940s 52.00
Tap Knob, Chief Oshkosh Beer, Polyester, Enameled Insert, 1940s 45.00
Tap Knob, Evans Ale, Bakelite, Enameled Insert, 1930s 358.00
Tap Knob, Hamm's Beer, Chrome, Enameled Insert, 1950s 139.00
Tap Knob, India Pale Ale, Bakelite, Painted Metal Insert, 1930s 108.00
Tap Knob, Stroh's Pilsener, Plastic, Enameled Insert, 2-Sided, 1940s 143.00
Tape Measure, Orange Crush, Celluloid, 1930s, 1 1/4 In. 132.00
Thermometer, Bireley's, Got A Minute? It's Different, 4 x 15 In. 200.00
Thermometer, Bireley's, Grapette, Plastic, 11 In. 95.00
Thermometer, Coca-Cola, 1950s, 3 x 9 In. 860.00
Thermometer, Coca-Cola, Bottle Shape, c.1953, 16 3/4 In. 55.00
Thermometer, Coca-Cola, Bottle Shape, Tin, Late 1950s, 17 In. 80.00
Thermometer, Coca-Cola, Cap Top, Tin, 1950s, 9 In. 413.00
Thermometer, Coca-Cola, Celluloid, 2 1/2 x 6 In. 88.00
Thermometer, Coca-Cola, Cigar, Tin, 8 1/4 x 30 In. 575.00
Thermometer, Coca-Cola, Coke Bottle, Tin, 5 1/4 x 17 In. 44.00
Thermometer, Coca-Cola, Coke Bottle, Tin, 8 1/2 x 29 1/4 In. 77.00
Thermometer, Coca-Cola, Donasco, Tin, Original Box, 1970s, 16 In. 55.00

Thermometer, Coca-Cola, Drink Coca-Cola, 2 Bottles, Tin, 1941, 7 x 16 In. 110.00
Thermometer, Coca-Cola, Red Ground, Tin, 16 x 6 3/4 In. 120.00
Thermometer, Coca-Cola, Silhouette Girl, Drinking Coke, Tin, 6 3/4 x 16 In. 440.00
Thermometer, Coca-Cola, Tin, 1972, 8 x 19 1/4 In. 72.00
Thermometer, Dr Pepper Hot Or Cold, 12 In. 140.00
Thermometer, Dr Pepper, Red Bottle Thermometer In Center, 1940, 5 x 17 In. 748.00
Thermometer, Drink Coca-Cola In Bottles, Red Ground, 1950, 12 In. 330.00
Thermometer, Hires Root Beer, Drink Hires, 8 x 27 In. 140.00
Thermometer, Hills Brothers Coffee, Porcelain, 8 3/4 x 21 In. 1200.00
Thermometer, Koca Nola, Wooden, 1905-1915, 7 x 24 In. 468.00
Thermometer, Mail Pouch Tobacco, Treat Yourself To The Best, 8 x 39 In. 330.00
Thermometer, Mail Pouch Tobacco, Wood Frame, 1930s, 19 x 74 In. 660.00
Thermometer, Nature's Remedy, Black Ground, 1930s, 7 x 27 In. 430.00
Thermometer, NuGrape Soda, Have Fun With NuGrape, Tin, 5 3/4 x 13 1/2 In. 245.00
Thermometer, Orange Crush, Turquoise Ground, 5 3/4 x 16 In. 110.00
Thermometer, Pepsi-Cola, Any Weather's Pepsi Weather! 8 x 27 In. 175.00
Thermometer, Pepsi-Cola, Bottle Shape, 1940s, 15 1/2 In. 120.00
Thermometer, Pepsi-Cola, Bottle, Bigger, Better, 1930s, 15 3/8 x 6 1/4 In. 577.00
Thermometer, Pepsi-Cola, Double Dash, 27 x 7 1/8 In. 365.00
Thermometer, Pepsi-Cola, Gibson Girl Holding Pepsi In Glass, Wood, 22 In. 29.00
Thermometer, Pepsi-Cola, Tin, 7 1/4 x 27 In. 165.00
Thermometer, Pepsi-Cola, Wood, 24 x 9 1/2 In. 100.00
Thimble, Drink Pepsi-Cola, 5 Cents, Gold Band Base 9.00
Tip Tray, Coca-Cola, 1901, Hilda Clark, With Roses, Coke Glass On Table, 4 1/2 x 6 In. . . 1980.00
Tip Tray, Coca-Cola, 1909, Exhibition Girl, St. Louis World's Fair, 4 1/2 x 6 In. .1208.00 to 1322.00
Tip Tray, Coca-Cola, 1910, Coca-Cola Girl, 4 1/2 x 6 In. 345.00
Tip Tray, Coca-Cola, 1913, Hamilton King Girl, 4 1/2 x 6 In. 248.00
Tip Tray, Coca-Cola, 1914, Betty, 4 1/2 x 6 In. 132.00
Tip Tray, Detroit Brewing Co., Eagle Design, 4 1/4 In. 95.00
Tip Tray, Goebel Brewing, 1910s, 4 3/8 In. 72.00
Tip Tray, Indianapolis Brewing, World's Standard Of Perfection, 5 1/4 In. 60.00
Tip Tray, King's Pure Malt, Vintage Nurse Carrying Tray, 6 x 4 1/4 In. 80.00
Tip Tray, Lemon Kola, Kaufmann Strauss Lithograph, 4 1/4 In. 198.00
Tip Tray, Los Angeles Brewing Co., Home Of East Side Beer, Factory Scene, 5 In. 90.00
Tip Tray, Lulu Soda Co., Betty Boop On Moon, Space Dog, Mexico, c.1970, 6 In. 125.00
Tip Tray, Monticello Whiskey, Scene In Front Of Monticello, 4 1/2 x 6 1/4 In. 60.00
Tip Tray, Moxie, I Just Love Moxie, Don't You? Young Lady Drinking, 6 In. 145.00
Tip Tray, National Beer, Head Shot Of Thoroughbred Race Horse, 1908, 4 1/4 In. 115.00
Tip Tray, Tennessee Cola, Dog, Wearing Glasses, Cigar, 4 In. 450.00
Token, J. Klein, Liquor Dealer, Omaha, Hard Rubber, Yellow, Uniface 125.00
Token, Key Chain Fob, Harvard Beer, Good Luck, 1930s 24.00
Token, Potosi Brewing Co., Good For 50 Cents With Return Of Empty Keg 17.00
Token, Prima Beer, Picture Of FDR, 1930s 14.00
Token, Stern Brau Beer, Good For Free Bottle Of Beer, 1930s 10.00
Toy, Truck, Coca-Cola, Bottles, Plastic, Marx, Box, 10 In. 500.00
Toy, Truck, Coca-Cola, Sprite Boy On Sides, Yellow, Box, 1950s, 20 In. 1430.00
Toy, Truck, Coca-Cola, Yellow Plastic, Gull Wing Doors, 6 Cases, Marx, 10 3/4 In. 238.00
Toy, Truck, Pepsi-Cola, No. 4 . . . . 69.00
Toy, Whistle, Pepsi-Cola, 2 Bottles 150.00
Toy, Yo-Yo, Coca-Cola, Kooky Kap, Crimped Like Bottle Cap, 1950s-Early 1960s 32.00
Toy, Yo-Yo, Fanta, Laughing Man Logo, Transparent Orange, Russell, Mexico 30.00
Toy, Yo-Yo, Pepsi-Cola, Wood, White, Red Double Dash Logo, Late 1930s 250.00
Tray, Anheuser-Busch Brewing Co., St. Louis, Mo., 10 x 13 In. 30.00
Tray, Anheuser-Busch, Eagle, Cherubs Holding Beer, Tin, 13 1/2 x 16 1/2 In. 300.00
Tray, Ballantine's Ale & Beer, 1950s, 12 In. 28.00
Tray, Barmann Beer, P. Barmann Brewing Co., Round, 1930s, 12 In. 100.00
Tray, Batholomay Brewery, Rochester, N.Y., Tin, Round, Pre-Prohibition, 12 In. 500.00
Tray, Beer Driver's Union 132, Independent Union Beer Workers, 16 x 13 In. 265.00
Tray, Berghoff Dortmunder Style Beer, 1930s, 10 x 13 In. 105.00
Tray, Beverwyck Brewing Co., Albany, N.Y., c.1910, 17 1/4 x 12 1/4 In. 555.00
Tray, Bevo, Duquesne Brewing, Prohibition Era, 10 x 13 In. 30.00
Tray, Black Horse Ale, Pictures Handler, Pint Bottle 192.00
Tray, Blatz, Round, 1960s, 13 In. 30.00

Tray, Boswell Ale & Porter, Canada, Pre-Prohibition, Round, 12 In. 70.00
Tray, Braumeister Beer, Independent, Milwaukee, Round, 1950s, 12 In. . . . . .35.00 to 50.00
Tray, Brilliant Ale, Porter & India Pale, Syracuse, N.Y., Round, 1930s, 12 In. 250.00
Tray, Canadian Ace Brewing, Round, 1950s, 13 In. 17.00
Tray, Cincinnati Cream, Waiter With Bottle On Tray, Canada, Round, 13 In. 40.00
Tray, Coca-Cola, 1916, Elaine, Yellow Dress, Glass Of Coke, 19 x 8 1/2 In. . . . . . .230.00 to 522.00
Tray, Coca-Cola, 1923, Flapper Girl, Drinking Coca-Cola 237.00
Tray, Coca-Cola, 1927, Soda Jerk, American Art Works, 13 1/4 x 10 1/2 In. 345.00
Tray, Coca-Cola, 1933, Frances Dee, 13 1/4 x 10 1/2 In. 180.00
Tray, Coca-Cola, 1938, Girl In Yellow Hat, 13 1/4 x 10 1/2 In. . . . . .121.00 to 225.00
Tray, Coca-Cola, 1939, Springboard Girl, 13 1/4 x 10 1/2 In. 175.00
Tray, Coca-Cola, 1940, Sailor Girl, 10 1/2 x 13 1/4 In. 100.00
Tray, Coca-Cola, 1941, Skater Girl, 13 1/4 x 10 1/2 In. 175.00
Tray, Coca-Cola, 1942, 2 Girls At Car, 13 1/4 x 10 1/2 In. 605.00
Tray, Coca-Cola, 1950, Menu Girl, 13 1/4 x 10 1/2 In. 75.00
Tray, Cream Beer, John F. Oertel Co., Inc., Louisville, Ky., Kaufmann & Strauss Co. 165.00
Tray, Dawson's Ale & Beer, New Bedford, Mass., Round, 1930s, 12 In. 76.00
Tray, Derby Cream Ale, National Brewing Co., Horse Picture, Round, 1930s, 12 In. 325.00
Tray, Dow Old Stock Ale, Black, White & Red Enamel, Round, 13 In. 35.00
Tray, Edelbrew Beer, Round, 1940s, 12 In. 46.00
Tray, Ehret's Extra Beer, Round, 1930s, 13 In. 66.00
Tray, Eichler Beer, New York, N.Y., Woman Picture, Pre-Prohibition, Round, 12 In. 115.00
Tray, Esslinger's Ale, Esslinger Brewing Co., Philadelphia, Round, 1940s, 12 In. 80.00
Tray, Fort Pitt Special Beer, Round, 1950s, 13 In. 28.00
Tray, Frank's Ginger Ale, 1920s, 10 1/2 x 13 1/4 In. 45.00
Tray, George Ehret's Extra, New York, N.Y., Round, 1910s, 12 In. 46.00
Tray, Goldenrod Beer, Hittleman Goldenrod, Brooklyn, N.Y., 1930s, 15 x 12 In. 75.00
Tray, Grain Belt Beer, Schlitz Brewing, Round, 1950s, 13 In. 90.00
Tray, Harvard Beer, Tin, Round, 12 In. 190.00
Tray, Hires, Josh Slinger, Things Is Getting Higher, But Hires Are Still A Nickel, 1920s . . 143.00
Tray, Horse Head Beer & Ale, Lang Brewery, Round, 1940s, 12 In. 160.00
Tray, Kuntz's Beverages, First For Thirst, Yellow, Black, Star, 1900s, Round, 13 In. 130.00
Tray, Monarch, Eagle Brewing Co., Utica, N.Y., Bottle Picture, Round, 12 In. 255.00
Tray, Muchener, Pilsener White Seal, St. Louis, Mo., 1900, 13 3/4 x 10 In. 330.00
Tray, Oertel's Brew, Cream Beer, Marked Bottled By John F. Oertel Co., Louisville, Ky. . . 165.00
Tray, Old Timer's Lager, West Bend, Wisc., Round, 1940s, 12 In. 55.00
Tray, Pepsi-Cola, Enjoy Pepsi-Cola, Hits The Spot, 13 3/4 x 10 3/8 x 1/2 In. 175.00
Tray, Phoenix Beer, Moffats Ale, Round, 1930s, 13 In. 78.00
Tray, Pickwick Ale, Haffenreffer Brewing, Round, 1940s, 12 In. 22.00
Tray, Rheingold Beer, Round, 1950s, 12 In. 33.00
Tray, Ruhstaller's Brewing Co., Sacramento, Calif., Pre-Prohibition, Round, 12 In. 100.00
Tray, Schlitz Brewing Co., Milwaukee, Wisc., Pre-Prohibition, Round, 12 In. 125.00
Tray, Seipp's Extra Pale Beer, Chicago, Ill., Pre-Prohibition, Round, 12 In. 195.00
Tray, Sunrise Beer, Field, Sunrise Brewing Co., Cleveland, Round, 1930s, 12 In. 185.00
Tray, Trommer's Malt Beers, Brooklyn, N.Y., 1910, 15 1/2 x 12 1/2 In. 200.00
Tray, Zipp's Cherri-O, Bird, Soda, H. D. Beach Co., Coshocton, Ohio, Round, 12 In. 748.00
Wrench Set, For Lugged Mason Jar Lids, 3 Piece 54.00
Yard Stick, Stroh's Beer, Folding, Wooden, 1960s 18.00

K O V E L S

SEND ORDERS & INQUIRIES TO:
CROWN PUBLISHERS
c/o RANDOM HOUSE, 400 HAHN ROAD,
WESTMINSTER, MD 21157
ATTN: ORDER DEPARTMENT

SALES & TITLE INFORMATION:
1-800-733-3000
FOR ORDER ENTRY:
FAX# 1-800-659-2436
WEBSITE: WWW.RANDOMHOUSE.COM

NAME _____

ADDRESS _____

CITY & STATE_____ ZIP_____

Please send me the following books:

ITEM NO.	QTY.	TITLE	PRICE	TOTAL
0-609-80841-9	___	Kovels' Antiques & Collectibles Price List —*current edition*	PAPER $16.95	___
0-517-70137-5	___	Dictionary of Marks—Pottery and Porcelain	HARDCOVER $17.00	___
0-517-55914-5	___	Kovels' New Dictionary of Marks	HARDCOVER $19.00	___
0-517-56882-9	___	Kovels' American Silver Marks	HARDCOVER $40.00	___
0-609-80757-9	___	Kovels' Bid, Buy, and Sell Online	PAPER $14.00	___
0-609-80623-8	___	Kovels' Bottles Price List—*current edition*	PAPER $16.00	___
0-609-80640-8	___	Kovels' Depression Glass & Dinnerware Price List —*current edition*	PAPER $16.00	___
0-517-57806-9	___	Kovels' Know Your Antiques, Revised and Updated	PAPER $17.00	___
0-517-58840-4	___	Kovels' Know Your Collectibles Updated	PAPER $16.00	___
0-517-88381-3	___	Kovels' Quick Tips: 799 Helpful Hints on How to Care for Your Collectibles	PAPER $12.00	___
0-609-80417-0	___	Kovels' Yellow Pages: A Collector's Directory of Names, Addresses, Telephone and Fax Numbers, E-Mail, and Internet Addresses to Make Selling, Fixing, and Pricing Your Antiques and Collectibles Easy	PAPER $18.00	___

_____ TOTAL ITEMS

TOTAL RETAIL VALUE _____

CHECK OR MONEY ORDER ENCLOSED
MADE PAYABLE TO CROWN PUBLISHERS
or telephone 1-800-733-3000   (No cash or stamps, please)

CHARGE: ☐ Master Card ☐ Visa ☐ American Express
Account Number (include all digits) Expires: MO.___ YR.___

Shipping & Handling
Charge (per order)   **$5.50**

Please add applicable
sales tax.   _____

TOTAL AMOUNT DUE   _____

PRICES SUBJECT TO CHANGE
WITHOUT NOTICE.

If a more recent edition of a price li
has been published at the same pric
it will be sent instead of the old editio

Thank you for your order

....

Signature